The
Feminine Influence
in Business

Lady In Black

Mike Lehr

Llumina Press

Credits:
Cover Design: Mike Lehr, Omega Z Advisors
Photo: Don Weimer, Gemini Photographics & Productions

ISBN: 1-59526-319-5
        1-59526-318-7
Printed in the United States of America by Llumina Press

Library of Congress Cataloging-in-Publication Data

Lehr, Mike.
  The feminine influence in business : "lady in black" / by Mike Lehr.
      p. cm.
  ISBN 1-59526-319-5 (hardcover : alk. paper) -- ISBN 1-59526-318-7 (pbk. : alk. paper)
  1. Businesswomen 2. Women executives. 3. Women employees. 4. Women--Employment. 5. Businesswomen--Conduct of life. 6. Women executives--Conduct of life. 7. Feminist economics. I. Title.
  HD6053.L354 2004
  650.1'082--dc22   2004012705

Dedication

To Kathy, the feminine influence in my life.

To Max and Rebecca, my creative influences.

To the participants in my seminars, my inspiration
(and they have a plane to show for it).

To the introvert in all of us, the source of all our talents
and known informally as our soul.

To our talents, without which everything would be valueless
no matter what the price.

To Ken Hensley, the author of the song, "Lady In Black",
who demonstrates the immense power in art.

Contents

Prelude

You know you have something when you innocently present a concept that gets you fired. What you have before you is my second book related to the feminine influence in business. What role does this influence play, and why might she interest us?

The feminine influence is a major force in the identification and development of business talent, ours and others. As in life, man and woman form the most potent relationship we know. Similarly, when we integrate the feminine influence with its masculine counterpart in business, nothing is more potent in unleashing our talents.

Since ultimately a business' success is dependent upon its employees' talents, the feminine influence greatly impacts the life of a business. While you don't need to appreciate this influence to run a business, to develop your talents or to help others discover and grow theirs, you will be more effective at all three if you do which will extend your influence throughout the organization. Moreover, you will have a decided advantage because many ignore her – she is difficult to grasp and apply. Many just don't want to put forth the effort or simply can't. Just as you need certain physical attributes to do well at athletic endeavors and certain mental attributes to do well at cognitive pursuits, you also need certain emotional attributes to do well at intuitive pursuits. Life integrates all three and laughs at our cerebrally derived classifications which attempt to atomize it. It ignores them as a bird does a stop sign. Thus, to integrate the feminine influence with the masculine requires a holistic, unscientific approach.

My first book dealt with this subject more superficially and specifically because it was intended to help a particular person and company by presenting a strategy and its introductory, underlying principles. It was to serve later as the basis for a deeper discussion on this topic.

As you may know or will come to know in this book, the individual is the basis of any human endeavor and relationship. Business is no exception. The most dynamic ideas originate with the individual and resonate outward. Thus, if we are to help an entire company, we must first find an individual to help. The plan in my first book aimed at helping my boss become the next CEO of our company. After initially exploring the idea with her and gaining her approval to proceed, I began the documentation of some broad ideas that we initially discussed.

In high school, I had a calculus teacher who stressed an appreciation for the concepts behind equations. The day before a test he gave us some studying advice. On the left hand side of the board he wrote five mathematical expressions that encompassed the major concepts for the test. On the right hand side he wrote the twenty-two equations that would be used on it. He then offered us a choice: learn the five concepts or memorize the twenty-two equations. Those who had taken one of his tests knew they were better off learning the concepts rather than memorizing the formulas because his tests always seemed to exploit the gaps between appreciating a concept and memorizing equations. No series of equations can adequately encompass all that a concept has to offer, including ourselves.

Even though the concepts were only five, memorization is far easier than appreciation. The latter requires more qualitatively. Relatedly, with any plan there are the steps in it and the concept around it. No number of steps can encompass the entire concept around a plan. An appreciation for the concept is far better than knowledge of the steps; however, expressing concepts, especially ones not routinely espoused, requires more effort than the mere recitation of steps. What my high school teacher taught me was this: appreciation for the concepts around a plan will most likely allow you to be more effective in its implementation.

As I began to document the concepts around the plan in my first book, I soon discovered they were difficult to explain in a way that not only was understandable but also persuasive and inspirational. Understanding and agreement don't automatically generate positive action; inspiration is a far better partner but certainly a more difficult one too. People are more motivated by what they like than what they understand. Too often when someone understands us we assume they also agree and will take action accordingly. How many times have we heard, "Do you understand?" Symbolically, this exposes our love affair with logic and other cognitive pursuits without consideration for the declaration, "just because we're reasonable doesn't mean we're right." Life has a tendency to expose the canyon between the two when we think it's only a crack.

Such an approach yielded a book just under a couple hundred pages that was to serve as the basis to explore these concepts and steps more deeply. I presented it to my boss and asked her to keep it between the two of us until we had a chance to talk about it. My only other request was for her to return it to me when she was done reading it. If she found it particularly helpful, we could talk about its future if at all. Her only request was to give her some time to read it.

An exploration of these concepts with my boss never occurred because one day I was given short notice to attend a meeting late in the afternoon at which I was told it was my last day. At the meeting unattended by my boss, there were two other people, one I knew well, one I did not know at all. They pulled out the book I had given my boss and told me that writing it was unprofessional and was the basis for letting me go. I asked why it was unprofessional and received the response that my inability to see why only served to prove the correctness of their decision. Suddenly, a circular reference in Excel flashed before my eyes, so I attempted to clarify my understanding of what was happening by asking, "Let me understand this. I'm basically being let go because I was trying to help my boss and this company?" They responded, "That's the problem. You thought you were helping." A canyon appeared before my eyes so I left, and six months later my boss submitted her resignation to join another company.

A friend once said to me when I was perturbed over something that the moon doesn't care if the wolf howls at it. If what you have isn't important to someone, he won't pay any attention to it. If what you have prompts someone to take the most hostile action against you he can, then you know there must be something in it because usually this type of action is reserved for when we feel threatened. The real confusion occurs when it happens to be something you've always found very positive. Nevertheless, I'm thankful to my boss for having something that inspired me to write the first book. I'm appreciative because life is about finding people who inspire you to tackle great things. Fortunately, they do not need to realize they're doing that.

I've always enjoyed helping people and have been fortunate to have had opportunities to do that. The most important thing I found when helping others is that I usually ended up learning something that helped me. Even though they would leave appreciatively I couldn't help wondering if perhaps the help they gave me was better than that which I gave them. From this I've concluded that you're effectively helping others when you find they are helping you too. I suspect this has something to do with the inability to really help others unless you learn something about them and how they interpret the situation for which they want help. Since every person and situation is different, this gives you many opportunities to learn things that can help you in the future. It's not important that they realize how they're doing this, but it's good to let them know. Conversely, if they didn't help you much, then you may want to question how helpful you were to them.

The advantage of this mutual help culminated in the book you now hold. As a result of what I've given and received, I know what lies in these pages works. The most noticeable difference between my first and second book is size. While this one is substantially longer, the more important differences to you are its expansiveness and depth. Much is missing in this book from the first because it referred to a specific person, company, situation and group of people. The new material falls into three categories. First, there is that which would have come out in a follow up discussion that never took place. Second, there is the content of our preliminary discussion that laid the foundation for the first book but needed documentation here. Third, there is the new material which either elaborates on existing concepts or presents new ones which were not applicable to the purpose behind the first book. I've also changed the style and tone slightly from one of addressing another specific, known individual to one of addressing myself. A friend who initially read this paragraph asked, "Aren't you addressing the reader too?"

To answer this question, I'm going to take a step back by first saying that, ideally, I would love to be able to write a version of this book for each person attracted to this concept in a way that is conducive that person's personality. Unfortunately, I don't believe I've been granted the necessary lifespan to carry this out. Even with the exhaustive changes and additions I've made to create this book, I have not come close to exhausting the implications of this topic.

As for addressing the reader, the problem rests in determining who that reader is unless I'm specifically addressing someone that I know. No matter how thoroughly I contemplate and visualize a reader to represent a group of readers who may appreciate this book, that person does not exist. This is akin to saying that averages don't exist which is something we will discuss later. Furthermore, no representative reader I've created in my head will come close to acknowledging all the aspects of you, the reader's personality. In essence then if I follow a path of trying to address some fictitious person I've designated to be you, I am writing a book for a reader that does not exist. What's the difference between writing a book for someone who doesn't exist and for no particular person at all?

If I'm not addressing the reader, whom am I addressing? I've learned that people often like to observe and listen to a conversation between two people, and this is supported by the numerous programs in the media where one person interviews another. As I've said, I wrote this as though I were addressing myself, so the interview to which the reader is observing and listening is one where I'm running through this concept with myself. The various questions I ask myself and the answers I find to those questions manifest themselves as the text in this book. Some of the questions appear as questions in the book. Others have played a role in directing the path this book took. The overall text in the book is the culmination of trying to answer why the identification and development of talent in business tend to cause certain responses and events.

People special to me who have had a chance to either read or discuss parts of this book often inquired about the title. A first read of the title often leads people to initially think this book is related to women in business, but when they realize it's about talent's identification, development, and impact in business the title seems to disconnect from the subject so the questions begin to follow that attempt to make a reconnection.

The short answer, that seeks to connect talent and the feminine influence, finds its basis in the heavy correlation between emotional capabilities and talent. Since woman are more associated with the feeling aspects of life and men more with the cognitive aspects, connecting women to talent via emotions emerges as the next step and culminates in its refinement as the "feminine influence." Essentially, we're talking about the impact emotions can have in business which we often consider an unemotional, "bottom-line" affair.

Of course, this begs the question as to why I didn't simply incorporate emotions or talents in the title to make it more gender neutral as my explanation suggests. The problem is that those words don't form immediate, relatively focused pictures in our mind. Both tend to create fairly nebulous pictures if they create any at all. So, if my plan is to use a fairly allegorical approach, the task becomes very difficult if I don't have a picture or symbol upon which to build an allegory. Moreover, anything I would create would run the risk of not penetrating deeply enough with you. Consequently, by using the term feminine influence, I can use a woman in a symbolic sense to carry the approach more effectively because many of us can at least picture a woman of some kind in our head while some even have the attributes and capacity to visualize a woman simply by looking in the mirror.

Using a woman to symbolize the approach also allows me to use her opposite, a man, to symbolize opposing aspects. Ultimately, such a pairing allows me to play off the interactions between men and women, something that is not only extremely pertinent on a personal level but fun. In this way, I believe I can create pictures that help me communicate an understanding and appreciation of the concepts in a way that will allow us to enjoy ourselves. Of course, the risk I run is that some people interpret fun as unprofessional.

The main impetus for expanding upon the first book was the realization that practicality necessitated a strong conceptual framework as my story about my high school calculus teacher illustrated. Without this framework, the practicality was too shallow, too narrow, and too inflexible especially since the original audience for the book was very narrow, one person. Essentially, even though there are concrete action steps that appear pragmatic on the surface, they are useless, impractical, without the right feel that only a conceptual framework can deliver. Analogously, I was outlining the steps to swing a baseball bat without communicating how it should feel when you've done it effectively. The deep nature of feelings do not allow for their appreciation through short, sparse bullet points. If this were the case, we could transfer the feeling we get from a movie to another person in a few lines and have him feel as though he saw the movie.

In considering how to present the strategy, I realized the need for a more allegorical approach rather than an analytical one. The later approach would constrict and suffocate the fundamentals behind the strategy too much for them to deliver their dynamism.

While the analytical approach favors conveying information quickly and directly, and behaves more as a sieve by only keeping the information necessary for communicating the message; it lacks the emotional impact and energy necessary to plant the right feel that might inspire action. As with hitting a baseball, having the right feel is more important than the right thoughts. By the time you are able to think about how to hit the baseball that approaches, it will have already spent plenty of time in the catcher's mitt. To get the right feel requires more than receiving the right information. No one can hit a baseball simply by reading how to hit one. Thus, an analytically dominated approach would be no more effective than attempting to carry water in our sieve. An allegorical approach allows one to more deeply and comprehensively communicate the right feel necessary to effectively employ the strategy in this book.

In addition to using the allegorical approach to effectively convey the strategy in a pragmatic, persuasive, and inspirational manner, since the current flowing through the strategy springs from the inherent power in the feminine influence, it's only natural to request her to present the strategy. Presenting the feminine influence using a direct, analytical methodology creates the contradiction, "If she's so effective, why did I not call upon her to deliver the message?" Essentially, an analytical approach would subvert her efforts.

On the other hand, allegories don't deliver the clean, structured, direct messages that analysis does. Their indirectness requires a contemplation that eventually leads to appreciation, but this work is not for everyone. This is the nature of the feminine influence. Messages without contemplation are just words that become rules or programs for us to follow blindly. No woman seeks to surrender her essence to the hordes, yet her beauty attracts and soothes them. This is the paradox she lives. Through subtleties she wards herself by exhausting the patience of the impatient until they voluntarily cease their pursuit of her without having to raise a finger; only those willing to appreciate her will remain.

From this theme evolved the title of this book but did not crystallize it until I came across a song titled "Lady In Black" by the rock group Uriah Heep:

Lady In Black
Uriah Heep

She came to me one morning, one lonely Sunday morning
Her long hair flowing in the mid-winter's wind
I know not how she found me, for in darkness I was walking
And destruction lay around me, from a fight I could not win.

She asked me name my foe then, I said the need within some men
To fight and kill their brothers, without thought of love or God
And I begged her give me horses to trample down my enemy
So eager was my passion to devour this waste of life

But she wouldn't think of battle that, reduces men to animals
So easy to begin and yet impossible to end
For she the mother of all men, had counseled me so wisely that
I feared to walk alone again and asked if she would stay
Oh lady lend your hand I cried, oh let me rest here by your side
Have faith and trust in me she said, and filled my heart with life
There's no strength in numbers, have no such misconception
But when you need me be assured I won't be far away

Thus having spoke she turned away, and 'though I found no words to say
I stood and watched until I saw her black cloak disappear
My labor is no easier but now I know I'm not alone
I find new heart each time I think upon that windy day
And if one day she comes to you, drink deeply from her words so wise
Take courage from her as your prize and say hello from me

"Lady In Black" personifies the feminine influence in a way that inspires an insight into how she can impact business powerfully when we "drink deeply from her words so wise." Unlike her aggressive counterpart, the masculine influence, she does not thrust herself upon us but rather only visits when extreme despair is about to consume us or when we have joined with sincerity and have striven to seek her out. As with any woman, she does not bare her soul to us until her heart grants permission. Ostensibly this book conveys information about the feminine influence and a strategy for her employment in business. On a much deeper level, it will feel like a contemplative search for answers to questions we eventually ask ourselves.

Part of that contemplation is the eventual discovery of a secret that this book holds about talent. I did not intend for it to have a secret, but I came across it as I approached the end of my writing. Of course, whether it's a secret is debatable because it's in the open for all to see but cloaked in implications. Unfortunately, whereas most secrets encourage us to share them with others, this one would just make talent identification and development more difficult if many knew it. Fortunately, even without knowing this secret, you can use this book to help you identify and develop talent in you and others. Conversely, even if everyone knew the secret, this book would help because it contains sentries that will ensure it remains of great help.

One day in the past my wife suggested a short walk around the neighborhood. As we headed out, I told her about a trail that might be fun to hike. On the map it didn't seem very long, but a two dimensional paper conceals three dimensional undulations and ravines. Three hours later, with my wife lamenting how I can turn even a simple walk around the block into a marathon, we completed our walk. We've taken many walks around the block since then but don't remember any of them, but we always remember this hike, quite humorously now. That hike symbolizes this book; a walk around the block that turned into something much more and more likely to be remembered.

Such is the background behind this book.

Introduction

I magine Sherlock Holmes' arrival upon a crime scene in a mansion. Automatically, everything associated with the scene tells him something about the crime. In essence, everything becomes evidence.

For instance, a fallen lamp means one thing while its upright position means another. Whereas the first could indicate a struggle; the second might indicate the lack of one. Furthermore, the location and condition of the lamp can even enhance what its fallen state says. Conversely, an upright lamp could say several things too. The variations are many.

In general, what the lamp says as evidence can help us address four things about the crime:

- Its nature.
- Its flow relative to events happening before and after.
- The people involved.
- The likelihood the crime will be solved.

Before Sherlock Holmes can determine what the evidence says about these four points, he must realize that the evidence can say something. Initially, this may seem obvious because we've assumed that the crime scene introduced to Holmes is complete; however, let's add doubt with this question: How does he know for sure that he is dealing with the entire crime scene?

Another way to look at this is to imagine a military engagement where a reconnaissance officer approaches you and declares there are no enemy troops in the area. How do we define "area"? If we define area as an enclosed territory within which enemy troops could reasonably strike us, then the question becomes "What if the enemy does something unreasonable, unexpected?"

Relating this to Holmes' predicament, the crime scene itself is in question and is typically bounded by where we reasonably expect to find important evidence. However, as with the military scenario, we're making assumptions and predictions about what we can expect. The enemy and crime may fall outside of our expectations for each.

Now, if we return to the conclusion that Holmes must first realize the evidence says something, we can more easily see how this isn't necessarily obvious if Holmes is wandering in an area he does not consider part of the crime scene. If a neighbor sees a flickering light on in your house while you're away, he's more likely to think nothing of it if break-ins rarely occur than if there has been a recent rash of them. Your neighbor doesn't realize this flickering light could be something unusual in your house.

Thus, the first step for Holmes is to realize that everything could tell him something about the crime. The next step is to realize that every piece of evidence may not tell him right away what it says. In other words, he must not jump to conclusions about the evidence because of the issue of context. To do so is like trying to get a handle on a song by listening to only a single note. That note, like every note, has a role that becomes clear as the whole song plays out. Similarly, the evidence in a crime scene does not present a clear picture until all evidence is heard.

For Holmes, it's not a matter of looking at one piece of evidence, determining what it means, and moving on to the next piece. It's taking each in as it is, looking at all together, and figuring what they say holistically. In this way, the whole process is more similar to a jigsaw puzzle than a regimented process where one step logically follows another.

How this connects to the discussion upon which we are about to embark is that we will be working a puzzle rather a process. Why we intend to do this is simple to explain: life presents itself as a puzzle not a process. Unfortunately, we are often taught to organize our thoughts in a logical, ordered pattern so we take our listener from point "A" to point "B". We're even told to tell our listener we're taking them from A to B. What's important in our discussion is not so much that you get from A to B but rather how you get there. If this second point isn't successful, the first really doesn't matter.

Initially, this seems more contrary to our thinking than it really is until we look at an example. In Italy there are five towns collectively called Cinque Terra. A train ride from the first town to the last takes eight minutes; however, hiking the trail connecting the five takes about five hours, including a half hour for lunch.

Using both methods one can get from A to B, but this is secondary to the experience of getting from one to the other. Since the terrain is mountainous, the train, except for the station stops, carries one through one tunnel after another; the entire ride is shrouded in blackness. Contrastingly, the hike weaves us in and out, up and down along the coast to the relentless serenade of the ocean waves breaking upon the rocks below.

Even from this brief description of the two ways to get from the first town to the last, one can easily see the appreciation for the experience the hike gave us versus the train's. From the hike we had an appreciation for what it took for these ancient Roman towns to communicate and interact with one another before trains.

Likewise, the purpose of this discussion about the feminine influence in business is not to get you from A to B but rather to enhance your appreciation for her to such a degree that you are more inclined to integrate her in your daily business practices. In the end, she will help you and those with whom you interact.

Two diagrams in Figure 1.1 will help me demonstrate how this will happen:

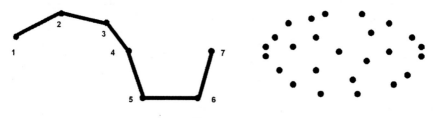

Figure 1.1

The left-handed diagram represents a logically ordered argument from one through seven. The right-handed one represents an oval.

Figure 1.2

If we connected the dots in the left-handed diagram of Figure 1.1 in a different way such as in Figure 1.2, we would get something totally different; however, with the oval it doesn't matter what order we introduce each point because after all the points are placed we still have an oval. This illustrates the presentation method I'm about to use versus one that is more regularly taught and shown. A jigsaw puzzle is no different. We can put the pieces together in any order and still arrive at a completed puzzle.

Earlier, I said this was important because that's the way life is. Life does not present itself at any particular moment as a series of segmented, connected steps but rather as a synergistic, integrated fusion of infinite points bombarding us with such intensity that our consciousness is overwhelmed and unable to recall it all at a later time. Who can walk through a forest and later account for every leaf on every tree? Yet, we definitely recall the feeling we derived from the walk. Many things in life are going on at one time. Collectively, at that particular moment they represent the oval called "Life." Life's points are not delivered to us in a series of steps so we can see how one point relates to another but rather all at one time so we can see the total picture immediately.

Ideally, I'd like to be able to deliver all the points we're about to discuss at once – such as life does every moment of every day in every millennium. However, I cannot. For this reason, I'm asking you to play the role of Sherlock Holmes and gather the evidence you're about to read without trying to evaluate, judge, or interpret it as you go. Once you're done, I suggest sitting back and reflecting upon the vision all the points create for you. In this way, I believe you're more apt to gain the appreciation for the feminine influence that I'm trying to convey.

The reasons for using this approach opposed to the more traditional, sequential one extend beyond similarities to life and appreciation for experiences. This approach is the best one to achieve our purposes around the feminine influence. As we will see, a connect-the-dots type of an approach is incongruent to gaining appreciation for this influence. Analogously, it's like trying to describe the life of a fish by demonstrating how it functions on land. In order to effectively convey the feminine influence one must use a methodology that allows her to be in her element. A scientific, clinical, logical approach alone cannot convey her essence in a way that will allow practical application.

What we are trying to do is convey the beauty of the feminine influence in business. As with the beauty of any woman, we cannot capture this through a collection of sophisticated measurements and analysis. There is no formula for beauty.

Hopefully, in the end, you will have a better feel for beauty in business and her dynamism. Yet, this should not be confused with having a complete understanding because we cannot completely understand a woman's beauty. What is true with Holmes and the crime scene will be true with us. After everything is said and done, while Holmes may have a good feel for the crime that occurred at the crime scene, he will never be able to tell exactly what happened for what reasons. Everyone can feel what beauty is but no one can definitely describe what it is.

In conjunction with the jigsaw metaphor as a way to address this topic, I'd like to introduce a long distance running one as well. This analogy comes into play when we consider the implications of various facts.

Often, just welcoming a fact into one's understanding is only the first step. With any fact there are implications. Consider a chess game. Every move changes the realm of viable future moves. What may be a viable move in the near future can become impotent depending upon the move made in the present.

Facts live in the same world; they affect how we think about things beyond the fact itself. For instance, something as simple as saying, "The sun rises everyday," carries some profound implications. One is that there are things in life that are unalterable by us. No matter what we do and how we do it, the sun will rise. The implication here is that there are some universal truths in our lives; truths that are irrelevant to whatever we may accept. In Stalinist Russia a law was passed that said the sun was highest at 1 p.m. rather than at noon. Regardless of our laws, nature ignores us. In putting together our jigsaw, we will run with the implications of various ideas to the limits of our emotional endurance.

Let's enter our discussion by taking a short run. Consider this statement:

A. Every person is different.

And, along with this statement consider this:

B. Every person has a personality.

Despite what we may think about some people, have you really met anyone who didn't have a personality? Of course, we're looking at live people. The demonstration here is that if "A" is true and "B" is true, then this statement must also be true:

C. Every personality is different.

Now, for some, this may seem a little frivolous, but this frivolity is important because through small, barely significant changes grow huge transformations. We cannot see a tree move, but if it truly does not move then how does it grow? Thus, our move from one statement to another is in the same manner. We may not detect movement but one day we wake up to find that a fact's implications have delivered us to another place. In this way, we can view the implications of a fact as a tree's growth. Figure 1.3 demonstrates such growth through a connotative journey via small, incremental changes in words. By extending the flow beyond the immediacy of the next word on either side of the word at which we entered, we find ourselves on a journey that takes us to the polar opposite of that word and back again. In a similar way, by extending the flow beyond the immediacy of the next implication of the fact under consideration, we can find ourselves on a journey that will move us along an implicational path that possibly delivers us to a place we did not originally anticipate.

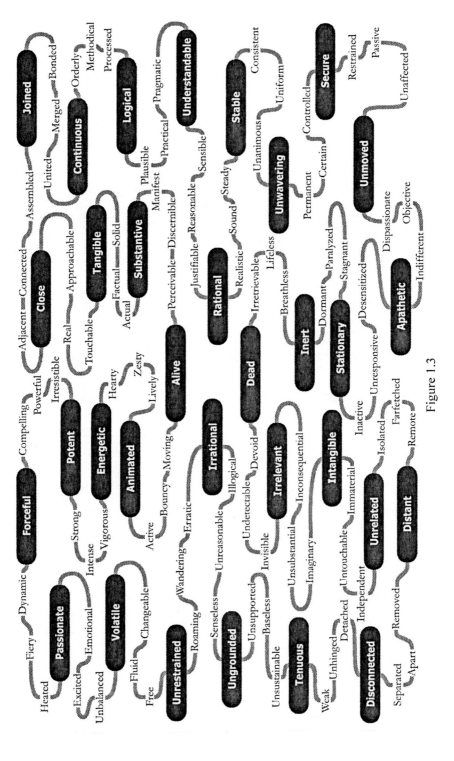

Figure 1.3

Continuing our short run with this theme in mind, from these three statements we can also say:

D.   A personality tells us something about the person.

At this point, let's cover our flank. Imagine a sun that doesn't shine; is it still a sun? Furthermore, let's ask, "If it doesn't shine, is it because it doesn't or because we're blind?" Try this:

E.   Every personality manifests itself.

Is it possible to have a personality that doesn't express itself in some way? Now, granted a blind man can't see the sun, so if we're emotionally blind we won't see someone's personality but does this mean he doesn't have one? If ninety-nine blind people vote in opposition to one sighted person that the sun doesn't shine, are they right? Are they professing truth?

Consider the things and people we have around us; they are there based upon our likes and dislikes. Can you tell something about someone's personality by the things he owns and by the people with whom he associates? What good is a personality that doesn't express itself? Can we even call it a personality? Is a person who doesn't exist still a person? What's the difference between a personality that doesn't exist and one that doesn't express itself? Regardless of whether a sun doesn't shine or does not exist, darkness prevails. When a personality doesn't shine or does not exist, emotionlessness prevails.

From C and E, we can now claim:

F.   Each personality manifests itself differently.

This statement allows us to carry D further by saying:

G.   The manifestation created by a personality tells us something about the personality.

With this we've returned to our Holmes analogy by having a crime scene symbolize personality and evidence symbolize manifestations of that personality. Of course, by going back through D to G we can also claim:

H.   The manifestation created by a personality tells us something about the person.

To this point we've followed an implicational stream that began with a person, moved onto to personality and now rests with manifestations:

Person > Personality > Manifestation

Let's continue further by expanding upon manifestations:

I.   There are many different means by which a personality manifests itself.

Returning to Holmes this is no different than saying there are many pieces of evidence that create a picture of a crime, but it also means there are many different types of evidence including furniture, food, and utensils. This point allows us to begin entering into the business theme of this book by stating the following:

J.   Business is a collection of such means.

Our implicational stream now takes on this appearance:

Person > Personality > Manifestation > Means > Business

From this stream we can state three final statements that will close our short run. They make the connection between business with manifestation, personality, and person:

K. Business is a means by which personality manifests itself.
L. Business can tell us something about personality.
M. Business can tell us something about the person.

All of this appears rather mundane but it exemplifies exactly the kind of insignificant increments from which great journeys are spawned. For instance, a large number of small strides comprise a hike, many of which slip under the radar of our consciousness and fall into mental oblivion. Yet, without those steps the hike would not be possible.

Before we move on though, let's solidify the business connection to personality and ultimately the person. If, as F states, each personality manifests itself differently, we can conclude that if this manifestation shows up in our likes and dislikes for certain things such as homes, cars, and lamps, then it can easily show up in the careers we pursue. If this applies to careers we pursue it can also apply to the business ventures we pursue.

Manifestations extend beyond physical things to behaviors. Personality projects itself through behaviors and words. Words not only mean the thoughts and feelings they convey as a group but also individually. An example of the latter is when folks describe any ethnic group with a derogatory descriptive rather than the accepted one. Business is filled with thoughts, feelings, words, behaviors, and things. Collectively they represent business as a means to manifest a person's personality.

We need to talk about four things before we can dive into the feminine influence's affect in business. The first is relationships with a focus on business relationships. Second is the exploration of the conclusions we made in the implicational series above and in the one we are about to review as to why they are not as obvious as they may appear. Third is the introduction of the preliminary groundwork as to how the feminine influence can exist in business so that we can enter into a more thorough discussion of it in this book. Fourth and last is the outline of how I'll present the "evidence" for your contemplation afterwards.

First, let's summarize the implicational stream regarding a person and his personality as it relates to business:

A. Every person is different.
B. Every person has a personality.
C. Every personality is different.
D. A personality tells us something about the person.
E. Every personality manifests itself.
F. Each personality manifests itself differently.
G. The manifestation created by a personality tells us something about the personality.
H. The manifestation created by a personality tells us something about the person.
I. There are many different means by which a personality manifests itself.
J. Business is a collection of such means.
K. Business is a means by which personality manifests itself.
L. Business can tell us something about personality.
M. Business can tell us something about the person.

Now, let's take this relationship between the person and business and use it as our base to enter a discussion about relationships with a focus on business relationships. When we talk about relationships and their connection to business, the implicational stream is similar to that of personality to business. The primary differences are the first two statements that connect persons to a relationship:

A. A relationship is interplay between two persons.
B. A relationship between two persons is a relationship between two personalities.

The emphasis is on two, for even if a person has a relationship with a group, that relationship is a culmination of all his relationships with each individual in the group. This difference is illustrated by Figure 1.4.

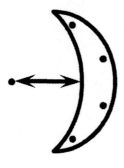 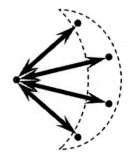

Figure 1.4

The left diagram shows a group comprising of four individuals. Any group is comprised of individuals, so the relationship of a person to the group is with the individuals as the right diagram shows. The person's relationship to the group will be determined by the relationships he has with each individual. To some degree this helps explain why two people can have a relationship with the same group but have different experiences; the individuals with whom they interact are different.

With the focus of "two" implied in the term relationship behind us, we can now follow through with an implicational stream that is very similar to the one above that ends with the connection of person and personality to business:

C.   Every relationship is different.
D.   A relationship tells us something about the personalities of the persons.
E.   A relationship tells us something about the persons.
F.   Every relationship manifests itself.
G.   Each relationship manifests itself differently.
H.   The manifestation created by the relationship tells us something about the personalities.
I.   The manifestation created by the relationship tells us something about the persons.
J.   There are many different means by which a relationship manifests itself.
K.   Business is a collection of such means.
L.   Business is a means by which a relationship manifests itself.
M.   Business can tell us something about the relationship.
N.   Business can tell us something about the personalities.
O.   Business can tell us something about the person.

We can take both of these streams and summarize them in a single conclusion that will serve as an operating statement for us as we move forward:

Business is an extension of personality by other means.

Unfortunately, the methodology by which we arrived at this conclusion makes its acceptance seem far easier than truth suggests. Now that we've fused the person, relationships, and business to show their interrelationship, I'll elaborate to show why the interrelationship these implicational streams established are not as obvious as they suggest. In fact, frequently, they are ignored.

For instance, we often hear people making distinctions between how they feel personally about someone and how they plan to do business with that same person. Sometimes these appear in the form of statements, "This isn't personal. It's business." Essentially, this statement seeks to sever the connection between the two. How many times have we attempted to sever our business lives from our personal ones? The way we dress for each is often different and reinforces segregation of the two. However, the implication of our conclusion is that there is no difference between our personal and business lives in what they say about us as individuals and our personalities. Consider this rewording of our conclusion:

Business relationships are extensions of personal relationships by other means.

If business and its relationships truly say something about us and our personalities, can we really say, "It's not personal?" Since the conflict between our conclusions and our everyday operating assumptions about business are greater than the ease at which we arrived at our conclusions, let's spend some time exploring and addressing this conflict.

Contrary to our inclinations to segment personal from business, we also often hear how business is about relationships. In this way, business is just another form of human interaction and no different than friendship or intimacy. All of it is associated. Any human interaction is going to create a relationship to some degree. All our terms only serve to define the nuances of that relationship. How that relationship develops is heavily influenced by personality for the person initiating the interaction as well as the one receiving. Relationships are difficult because people are not as malleable as land forms. Digging a hole in the ground alters the landscape but how do you alter a personality?

Business usually comes in the form of a monetary exchange. Considering this, how do we view a personal relationship that involves money? Furthermore, even if we assume that a monetary exchange typically denotes a business relationship, some kind of relationship is going on before money exchanges. Many factors influence the purchase of a product or service and extending our time frame even further into the past, we find much that influences a business relationship even before the consideration of a monetary exchange occurs.

With the birth of a child, defining when a child is born is less important than appreciating the many factors influencing his birth. While we may consider the birth of a child to occur when he leaves a mother's womb, nature doesn't care. She will influence the birth of that child regardless of how we define her influence. Our definitions and parameters do not alter nature's influence. They exist only to provide us with an orderly, segmented, executable understanding that has the dangerous potential of locking us into preconditioned responses causing us to ignore the unique, integrated aspects of situations that always exist. While this ignorance may not, and usually does not, create immediate harm; it can, and usually does, sometime in the future.

Likewise, in a business relationship, we can claim one to exist with the exchange of money; however, nature tells us that much goes into that exchange before it even takes place. All of that is included in a personal relationship. The Soviets may claim the sun to be at its highest point at 1pm, but the sun doesn't care. Nature doesn't care how we define things because it will act of its own accord regardless of what we do. Thus, the exchange of money is just a manifestation of that relationship such as a wedding ring is a manifestation of a marriage. The wedding ring does not by itself consummate a marriage but rather the natural intimacy between man and woman does. Similarly, money does not by itself consummate a business relationship.

Returning to our statement, "Business relationships are an extension of personal relationships by other means," money from this perspective seeks to define and quantify a personal relationship, interplay between two persons, two personalities.

The propensity for a relationship is a function of personality. How one conducts business is related to how one conducts his personal life. For both are extensions of his personality. Money is important because it affects our existence and survival in this world. As a result it can really challenge that person and his relationships when events threaten his existence and survival. This is why we are able to gain insight into a person's personality by the way he conducts his business. Looked upon in this way, products, services, marketing, advertising, finances, income, and expenses are all impacted by relationships. Relationships are the axel around which all of these revolve and reflect more traditional aspects of business manifesting the relationships and the personalities behind them. They do not drive business; personalities do.

In business, differentiation is important. How are you different from others? Differentiation is also important in our personal lives. People prefer to not be one of the masses indistinguishable from another person. We reflect this in our need to feel special and unique and in our need to find someone who would regard you as such. Everyone seeks to some degree a way to stand out and to be who they are. The counterbalance is acceptance. Human nature tends to draw us to the hero who does something well in the face of great odds. If one person is just like the rest, then it doesn't matter who we like because they're all the same.

Mastering business is mastering relationships. Typical success in business is reflected by the income brought in by the business as determined by revenues and expenses. Little thought is given to the quality of that revenue except when looking at margins – the ratio of income to total revenue. How much does a company make on each dollar of revenue?

Qualitatively, let's extend this concept further to show how there is indeed little thought given to other aspects of quality around revenue. For the moment, regardless of your religious views, let's assume God and Satan exist. In business, selling deodorant to God is no different than selling it to Satan. No where on the income statement does this materialize. For Satan this is an advantage. He would like things to be this way. This is how business can take place with threatening regimes and peoples. In the world of the financial statement there is no difference between good and evil. In fact, the difference becomes what generates profits (good) and what erodes them (evil). Satan would like to make sure there is no difference.

The conflict between the two is illustrated by a business owner my wife and I met who owns a seafood restaurant and fish store. While seeking some fresh fish to cook on vacation, we stumbled upon him and developed an instant, mutual affinity. He was giving one of his employees a reprieve from watching the store when we entered. In addition to helping us with our selection of fish, he gave us a tour and demonstrated his filleting techniques. His experience and age quickly gave the impression that his business was more his pastime, but his filleting technique also communicated that it was anything but a pastime earlier on in his life.

During his lesson to us, a couple walked in and asked for a particular kind of fish. There was some small talk; however, the owner quickly declared he didn't have any of that kind. After the couple left, he quickly returned his attention to us, but my wife declared she saw some of the fish they wanted in one of the refrigerators he had opened for us while conducting his tour. The man smiled and replied, "Honey, I didn't like those folks. When you get to where I'm at, you don't have to do business with people you don't like."

Not only does this story illustrate the tension we sometimes feel between those with whom we would interact because of a business activity and because of a personal preference, but it also illustrates the influence and manifestation of personality in business. The emotional aspects of personality collide with the rational ones of business, as symbolized by the refusal to make a sale. To some degree we can empathize and feel a certain anxiousness because of this business owner's declination of a sale; his actions are contrary to the nature of business – profit making. To him, there is a qualitative aspect of his profits that extend beyond what his financial statements show. Despite not being able to distinguish this on those statements, he is guided by what he knows rather than by what numbers say.

Nevertheless, while the difference between a dollar from God and a dollar from Satan does not appear on the financial statement, we cannot say there is no effect of these dollars on doing business from a public relations perspective or a legalistic perspective. We see this most clearly when we look at the celebrities who sponsor businesses. The more regarded is the celebrity the more likely his dollar would translate into more value than another. Conversely, a celebrity with a negative image would damage business.

Taking God and Satan as the two extremes, as we move inward toward, we find various degrees of quality in the clients. As the drive for more clients increases, the likelihood of attracting poorer quality clients increases too. Typically, we're taught to look for eroding margins, but even this statistical measure doesn't capture quality in its many forms. Again, no where on the financial statement does someone closer to God appear any differently than someone closer to Satan. As a result, good and evil prosper equally. At some point, our laws enter the picture; however, legislating morality is difficult at best and impossible generally.

However, this does not mean we do not consciously restrict doing business with specific people although this occurs with more sophisticated products and services rather than commodities. Examples are high priced items such as luxury items or professional services with high fees. Sometimes price is maintained at the expense of doing more volume in order to preserve the status or image of the product or service. We also see this more clearly in the membership acceptance process for various groups such as country clubs or in the encouragement to only do business with certain businesses. Whereas the first qualitative measurement is based more on price; the second is more on affinity. Whether these are right or wrong is not the question. The point is two-fold. First, there is some qualitative assessment of clients going on beyond what they contribute directly in profits. Second, one is unable to distinguish on a financial statement a dollar from a good client and a bad client.

In the vein of this second point let's expand the simple distinction of "good" and "bad." We often hear, "Your money is green just like anybody else's." This statement eradicates the differences within the human spirit and is truly the important distinction. A business perspective along this line reduces a relationship to something closer to communism because it looks at everyone collectively and part of the masses. In effect, the difference between capitalism and communism in terms of the relationships between employee and customer erodes; we treat clients differently not because of their inherent personality differences but because of their quantifiable ability to purchase our product or service. In this manner, we objectify personalities; a dollar from someone we like is no different in a financial statement's world than a dollar from someone we dislike. A greater tension arises when the one we don't like gives us more dollars. As we move down this perspective further and further, it becomes increasingly difficult to distinguish business from prostitution. In the later, we remove affection from love making while in the former, we remove emotions from relationships. Our personal preferences submit to the quantifiable aspects of business.

The point of exploring the difficulties in assessing qualitative aspects of business relationships and personalities is to show that despite our conclusion, "Business is an extension of personality by other means," the inability to see this readily in the numbers assaults our conclusion. The assault carries weight because the financial statement characterizes all relationships, regardless of personalities, as the same – a dollar from one is accounted the same as a dollar from another. Thus, it's important that we do not underestimate the weight attacking our conclusion because it's difficult to quantify.

For this reason, more indirect methods of capturing its impact are necessary. While we may not be able to extend a tape measure to measure directly the height of a tree or may not be able to place a ship on a scale to determine its tonnage, indirect ways exist to measure both. The other related consideration is whether we need to quantify something in order to know it has an effect on outcomes. Do we need to know the height of a tree to know it shades us from the sun? Do we need to know the tonnage of a ship to know it can carry the cargo we have? Does the mere fact we don't have those measurements mean their capabilities don't exist? Just because we cannot measure the qualitative aspects of relationships and their personalities on financial statements does not mean they don't impact it. Additionally, just because we don't have those measurements doesn't mean we can't gauge how they affect business. If I can walk comfortably in the hull of a cargo ship whose tonnage I don't know, I can conclude it can carry the packages I carried by hand to the dock in a couple trips despite not knowing the weight or size of those packages.

Thus, while it may be easy for us to see little difference in the relational fundamentals between what we consider business and personal and to see business as an extension of personality by other means, there is constant, objective and quantifiable pressure attempting to dislodge us from these insights. In this way, we return to Holmes and his crime scene for he finds himself under the same pressures; the immediate, clear message of the evidence creates pressure to overlook its interpretive message that is derived from its contextual relationship with all the evidence in the crime scene.

The situation we're facing is similar to our flying in a plane. Typically, we look at the plane as simply a means of getting from a point of origin to a destination. Our trips become defined by the nature of that trip such as business, pleasure, or personal. Yet, the nature of the trip has no impact on the fundamentals of flying. The aerodynamics is the same regardless of the trip's nature. Likewise, the "aerodynamics" of relationships is the same whether we are talking business, personal, or social. Thus, the fundamentals of one apply to the other.

From the perspective of this book, after considering the influence of personalities and their relationships on business and the constant assaults on this position by indiscriminant metrics, the task remains to lay the preliminary groundwork that allows us to enter into a discussion on the feminine influence in business. How do we begin to integrate her into it?

We enter into a discussion about the feminine influence in business by delving deeper into relationships. Since a business relationship is an extension of a personal relationship by other means, the aspects creating a personal relationship extend to a business one.

When we explore the basis of relationships, picturing a particular relationship helps. Culturally, relationships take on various formalities so it's important to strip these away and examine them in their raw, natural form. Essentially, this means going in the opposite direction to the one that we just went. Whereas we showed business relationships to be an extension of personal relationships by other means, it will help if we try to see the fundamentals underlying a personal relationship.

When we think of a relationship between two persons, there is no relationship more prominent in mankind's history than the one between a man and a woman. Even if we looked no further than the content of our entertainment, aspects of this relationship dominate. No relationship is stronger or more complete than this one. By appreciating the dynamism this union creates, we can gain insights into how to transfer this dynamism to other relationships, including business ones. This is how I'm connecting the feminine influence to business, by looking at the fundamental nature of the most significant of all personal relationships.

In order to do this, we will transcend the physicality of this relationship that says a man and a woman comprise it and look deeper into their masculine and feminine aspects. We'll not only try to gain an appreciation for what they are but also for how they interplay. How they will help us appreciate our business relationships and translate this into pragmatics is a question that is a challenge for this book. For the moment, just accept that the fundamentals of all relationships find their roots in the interplay of the masculine and feminine. Appreciation for those roots can translate into actions enhancing effectiveness. To some degree, acceptance of this premise for now may not be that difficult when we consider all the ways gender impact our daily emotions, thoughts, and actions. Consciously, we may want to keep business and personal separate, but nature does not recognize our demarcations.

With this I've introduced another challenge for this book beyond demonstrating how the masculine-feminine interplay affects business activities and that is transforming an appreciation for this into practicality. How do we take an appreciation for this and apply it?

From this perspective this book outlines a strategy by which you can assume a leadership position in a business organization. Much of that involves the enhancement of your ability to identify and develop talent in yourself and others. A longer term strategy is to make your leadership a successful one. Similarly, the act of becoming President of the United States is quite different from the act of being President. A leadership role in business is no different. Obtaining influence is one thing but wielding it successfully is another. Thus, a strategy that aims at securing a leadership position and sowing the seeds for a successful tenure is comprehensive and complete. Few enjoy commanding over the demise of their organization or their own future.

As we will discuss in this book, "leadership position" has meanings beyond a strict hierarchical one. The implication of this statement is that even though you may not be striving to be the CEO of a major corporation or striving for a higher position within an organization, this book can help you extend your influence throughout an organization or group. I call this concept *de facto* power versus hierarchical power which we will explore in more detail in the Strategy chapter. It means greater business effectiveness for you.

I am not intending this to be a comprehensive strategy for there are many ways to expand one's influence. Some are pretty standard and routinely used by everyone, so my focus will be on the more dynamic aspects that can clearly differentiate you because few in business are currently employing them. The obviousness and the reasons behind that will become apparent as we proceed on our way.

There are many reasons why few are implementing the theme I present in this strategy, but they all come down to the difficulty in employing it. To some degree we can associate this difficulty to education, training, and experience but to a larger extent personality and gender. Additionally, appreciation for the true impact that this strategy can have requires severe effort while its effective employment requires relentlessness. All of this winnows down the field of those who not only employ this strategy but also who even have an affinity to investigate it.

Much of the appreciation is gender driven, primarily female. For this reason, I call the fundamental influence powering this strategy the feminine influence. Consequently, people leaving this book would most likely do so thinking it primarily applies to women in business; however, if they were to follow the deeper implications they would find that the feminine influence has application to both men and women.

Employing the feminine influence in business is not about her replacement of the masculine but rather about how to integrate her with current, masculine practices. Effective employment of the strategy and of the feminine influence requires persistent, relentless application, an attribute more associated with the masculine than the feminine. Symbolically, we are drawing the picture that just as the human race cannot continue on without men and women, businesses can't either. The integration of both genders will not only increase survival rates but make life better.

In the business world, however, politically and pragmatically it's easier for a woman to employ masculine attributes than it is for a man to employ feminine ones. While it's true that a woman is more likely to appreciate and employ the themes in this book, a man is still able to do the same and not only preserve his personality and masculinity but enhance both.

Fortunately, this difficulty, while deterring others, will only make the application by others rarer and thereby further enhance the appeal of those who can. Unlike many other strategies, this one does not require the buy-in of other people typically seen in most plans. Even if others around you do not believe in the power of the feminine influence or the practicality of this strategy, you can still employ it without their consent. It's only important that you believe in it and employ it relentlessly; there's no need to share with others.

Historically, business has been a masculine-dominated endeavor. Representatively, we see this in the ratio of men to women in business and its hierarchy as well as in business's gender mix through the centuries. Beyond the mere physical presence of men we can feel the masculine orientation in more tangible things such as statistics, objectives, results, and timing as well as in communication styles through the use of various words and analogies. Together we see the use of militaristic and sporting analogies attempting to explain the extensive numbers and aggressive actions necessary to run a business and to establish a competitive masculine feel. This eventually leads to pictures of a "dog-eat-dog world" truly associated with an aggressively masculine world rather than an attractively feminine one.

Essentially, the eventual outcome of this book is one that seeks to infuse the feminine influence into business. If we believe business is a predominantly masculine affair, then what we are really doing is creating a marriage of the masculine and feminine influences in business. This marriage is inherently stronger than a life resting solely on the masculine. If this were not the case, our nature to seek out such a relationship would actually be an instinct seeking to make us weaker, a counterintuitive concept to the one of growth in nature. Thus, if the relationship between the masculine and feminine is one that delivers each to a better place, then there must be some inherent fundamentals about this relationship that apply to all aspects of our lives because nature has no regard for the definitions, rules, policies, and laws we seek to enforce upon ourselves. The sun, the moon, and the stars live and breathe without concern for us. If we are also part of the same nature that guides them, then we must contain natural aspects that also ignore man's commandments. Two of those aspects, man and woman, masculine and feminine, existed long before such commandments. They are guided by nature and not by our rationale. Therefore, the strength and completeness provided by their relationship transcends all aspects of our lives because as with nature, they ignore our self-imposed boundaries.

Symbolically, we see this effect in all our manmade creations; no building can remain standing without maintenance. We must enter into a constant vigilance to ensure the preservation of our structures. As time passes, the cost of this vigilance increases to such a point that the cost to maintain our original structure becomes greater than tearing it down and building anew. The asphalt and concrete we lay for our roads and driveways eventually crack. Initial patchwork makes temporary repairs, but at some point the whole foundation must be ripped from the bed and reset once again. This course of nature applies not only to the tangible components encompassing our various structures such as buildings but also to the intangible parameters encompassing our various endeavors such as business. The sun's rising and setting influences the rhythm of our behavior in a business endeavor, so this implies that other natural forces such as the masculine and feminine influences within us will influence it as well. Nature's strength surpasses our will and requires us to make regenerative efforts part of any strategy.

In fusing this to our discussion at hand, we arrive at two conclusions:

- First, no matter in what logical frame of mind we choose to live or work, nature's strength to influence that framework far exceeds our will and ability to retard it. We can no more do this than enforce our will upon a god. Thus, the natural influence of the masculine and feminine will influence our business frame of mind regardless of our attempts to prevent it.

- Second, eventually our efforts to enforce our will against nature will show cracks necessitating repair or rebuilding. If we do not respect the regenerative efforts this requires, our structures, tangible and intangible, will fall into disrepair and become useless to all involved. In business we typically see this as research and development, but for our discussion we are applying this concept to the emotional state of those with whom we work.

With nature's full force behind the love between a man and a woman, this relationship is the most celebrated and strongest among people, enduring tremendous hardships and achieving dynamic accomplishments through a solid completeness of the two. This book seeks to take the symbolism of a male-female relationship and overlay it onto business in such a way that pictures the feminine influence as a vital partner to the long-term success of any endeavor within the masculine realm of business.

Even though by the nature of this symbolism gender strongly drives this book, personality plays a significant role in it as reflected by the title, "Lady In Black," because it came from a song eliciting a strong personal response from the one who inspired this book. While no book ever knows who will read it, somehow we need to incorporate personality because we arrived at this point by linking gender to business through personality:

Gender > Person > Personality > Manifestation > Means > Business

Beyond this we also looked at the duality of this implicational stream by looking at relationships, the interplay of two personalities:

Personal Relationships > Business Relationships

This duality not only has a physical aspect as expressed by "two persons," but it also has a personal aspect impacting personality. In this sense, we're talking about duality within a single person as expressed by the action of "talking to oneself." This concept takes duality beyond physicality and delivers us to a place where we can look at it from an emotional perspective. Essentially, this becomes another relationship, the one with one-self:

Self-image > Personal Relationships > Business Relationships

Through the term "self-image" we express the difference between "who we are" versus "who we think we are" as expressed by some idea, concept, or role that we have attributed to ourselves. The hyphenated nature of this word symbolizes the duality of this emotional state by illustrating a connection between self and the image the self generates. What we have now is interplay between two. A more visual representation of this is the act of looking into a mirror. The one gazing into the mirror is the self while the reflection is the image. Again, duality is at work. More importantly, this symbolism demonstrates the vast inferiority of the image to the self.

We originally began this relational journey with, "A relationship is interplay between two persons," and "A relationship between two persons is a relationship between two personalities." Implicatively, we have arrived at the conclusion that the fundamentals of personality and relationship are the same because personality is nothing more than a relationship between self and image. This connection reinforces the need to fuse personality into any discussion of relationships.

The problem we face is integrating personality to an extent beyond a mere clinical, scientific perspective. Just as we drain passion from a woman's beauty by attempting to describe it in a rational sense, we do the same to personality by using the same method. Thus, infusing personality in a generic sense, by attempting to appeal to some form of average, will not work well because when we make our appeal to the average personality we are making an appeal to a personality that does not exist; averages don't exist except on paper. Stripping the emotionalism from a human leaves a carcass. Illustratively, this is the difference between a man touching a woman as her gynecologist and another as her lover. To appreciate the impact the feminine influence has in business, there is a necessity to look at her and to look at personality as something more than a carcass.

In order to avoid this nihilistic approach to the human spirit, this book needs to have its own relationship to personality. Ideally, as mentioned earlier, this would entail a rewrite for every potential reader to match his or her personality. Unfortunately, I've not been granted a lifetime in which I could accomplish this; thus, I have chosen to write this with a particular personality in mind and the song, "Lady In Black", symbolizes it.

Despite this secondary emphasis on personality, superficially, there is a strong gender orientation that will easily reinforce the interpretation that this book is only helpful to businesswomen. Cosmetically, I could have written this strategy by choosing an approach and words that would have made it more appealing to men; however, conceptually we slip back into the rut of trying to talk about something feminine in a masculine way. Of course, I didn't even need to use the terms "masculine" and "feminine" to describe the respective influences; however, after contemplating what I wanted to say and reading other materials touching upon this subject, a strong image emerged supporting their use. As people, we're men and women far more than we are clients, employees, or managers. The gender orientation given to us by nature dominates us to a far superior degree than any role orientation given to us in any business setting by any person or group of persons.

Thus, since man and woman are derived from nature rather than from artificial conditions established by man, as influences they are more powerful, enduring, and comprehensive. In essence, since everything in nature is integrated into what we commonly call an ecosystem and a man and a woman are parts of that same nature, we can explain and associate any natural phenomena in terms of one, the other, or in their interplay. With this we extend our narrow, physically oriented view of man and woman into something more conceptual, almost divine. Various cultures throughout history have associated different names to them such as, *yin* and *yang, creative* and *receptive, heaven* and *earth*, and *light* and *dark*.

I've chosen *masculine* and *feminine* to describe these influences for exactly the reasons that their risks entail. Even though they are more likely to be confused with man and woman in a physical sense, this confusion is exactly what makes them strong advocates. Since gender dominates our personalities, we observe its evidence frequently. From a tangible perspective the images of masculine and feminine are far more impactive than *yin* and *yang* or *heaven* and *earth*. When was the last time someone realized he touched *yin* or *yang*? *Heaven* or *earth*? Conversely, who has realized they touched a man or a woman? Consequently, the challenge becomes for us to take all that we associate to men and women in a tangible sense and extrapolate them into general, natural concepts that impact business. What works in the relationship between a man and woman, will work in the relationship between client and employee and employee and manager.

For the moment, we don't need to concern ourselves with how to do this because that is a challenge left to this book; however, let's just assume that it can be done. Nevertheless, we do need to acknowledge the difficulties in doing this because as we mentioned there are risks involved in using masculine and feminine. The major one is that the reader will never be able to transcend the physicality of the masculine and feminine influences to their more conceptual aspects. This can manifest itself in comments such as, "I'm a man so this feminine stuff won't work for me," or it's converse, "I'm a woman so this masculine stuff won't work for me."

As we will see, the feminine influence carries a power all her own. If this were not the case, then she would not be able to survive; however, her impact does not come about without her integration with the masculine. This book is not about implementing the feminine at the expense of the masculine; it's about integrating the feminine with the masculine that already dominates the business arena. By doing so, a business entity can minimize the natural destruction inherent in economic development, or any masculine dominated field. Without the feminine, this destruction will eventually deliver finality for she provides the capacity for rebirth and regeneration as symbolized by the birth of a child upon the union of man and woman. Without a woman, the fate of a man's generational line is death.

Despite this brief reassurance that there is a connection between our physical interpretation of gender and our conceptional one, the risks of becoming stranded in a mindset that locks in on a man and woman rather than their essences are still great. Emotionally, for a man to adopt something he considers feminine stirs fears of emasculation. For a woman, fears of defloration rise as she tries to adopt something she considers masculine. The domination of masculinity in business eradicates the distinction between masculine and feminine by simply resorting to the excuse "that's the way business is." This manifests itself in a negative sense when fears arise of "looking soft." As a result, women, who by nature are more possessed by the feminine influence, find the business realm more challenging than men; however, those that have reconciled the masculine aspects of business with their feminine inclinations are in the best position to tap into the power of the feminine influence.

A woman's success and position in business say much about her ability to handle the masculine aspects of business. Many men have the same or perhaps stronger abilities simply based upon their masculine orientation. It's quite likely that there is a rival male in an organization possessing a better grasp on the masculine aspects of business than any woman in that organization, but for him and the other men to truly succeed they would need to incorporate important aspects of the feminine influence. However, this is an extremely difficult accomplishment for a man in a masculine field because conditions and personality create the difficulty.

As a result of a woman's natural orientation to the feminine influence and a man's emotional difficulty in incorporating her, a woman in business is more likely to integrate aspects of the feminine influence into her regular working discipline. Despite this we cannot underestimate the struggle of women with business' masculinity that manifests itself in two basic ways.

First, it arises as a woman tries to maintain a woman's perspective in a masculine field. Everyone does better with a "home field" advantage; however, a woman in business is playing "away" by being compelled to compete on a masculine field. Second, we see this in the tendency for woman to struggle more with the more objective and statistical parts of business than a man does.

With this part of our discussion, we automatically begin to introduce the variety of personalities inherent in women. These two points alone show that while this book may have a strong gender overtone, there is still much room for personality to play its natural role. Some women will naturally be able to integrate the feminine influence better than others, especially those who already have a strong handle on business' masculine aspects. This is important because while we will see that the feminine influence is more powerful than the masculine, she is more dependent upon the masculine than the masculine is on her. Likewise, albeit with more challenges, men's personalities will weigh in on the integration of the feminine influence. Some men will be better suited than others to integrate her into their business lives. Thus, personality and circumstances are integrated throughout this book with the question being one of how do the male-female influences and personality translate into a pragmatic strategy.

As we had discussed earlier, the problem of talking about more feminine aspects of business or any situation is how to present those because we cannot convey them with the same tools as the masculine in the hope to be effective. Tactically, from a persuasive perspective, masculine themes follow a purely cognitive path beginning and concluding at clear points with intermediary, supportive points reinforced by easily quantifiable evidence. The goal is to communicate and persuade through the power of rationale.

By contrast, in order to present the feminine influence, an approach that fits this influence will be more effective. Trying to present a woman as a man or vice versa is a recipe for disaster, so it will also not work well conceptually if I try to present the feminine influence in the attire of the masculine. This is why I constantly make the relationship between the feminine influence and the beauty of a woman because beauty, especially a woman's beauty, does not conform to any quantifiable rational that declares to any extent possible the beauty contained in a woman's essence. An essence that isn't so much understood as she is appreciated.

Beauty is not understood so easily that we could program a computer to recognize her; however, she is the kind of force that a person, especially a man, can appreciate. Additionally, beauty is hard to appreciate without experiencing her. Thus, the beauty of the feminine influence in business is not necessarily something that becomes effective through understanding but rather through appreciation. With the feminine influence the goal is to communicate and persuade through the power of emotion because appreciation is a feeling not a thought.

This makes the feminine influence difficult for a lot of men because the essence of beauty is far more than what appears on the surface or in measurements. An easy way to transition into this is to use the analogy of a hike through the woods in a park.

If I were to describe such a hike to you, it may only take me a few minutes to give you an understanding of it; however, if I were to convey to you the feeling that hike gave me, that would be more difficult and take longer. If you were to develop your own feelings for the hike, you would need to make the hike yourself. This would take longer still. Similarly, a scenic picture on a postcard is nothing like you experiencing the scene yourself.

What I attempt to do in this book is to encourage you to take a journey through the feminine influence from a business perspective in the hope you come away with your own feeling for her. In effect, you're making the hike yourself. In this way, the strategy for integrating her will be more successful for you. As it is with beauty where no one can tell you how to appreciate her, it is the same for this integration. While I outline steps and examples for doing this, their full impact will not be conveyed and felt unless there is an appreciation for their power – there is power in beauty.

Thus, while the final aim of this book is to outline a strategy for business leadership, it will also create a backdrop by exploring the "feminine influence" concept and your company's current environment. This will allow you to place the Lady In Black Strategy in a proper context so you can develop your own feel for how it may work for you.

Everything we've already discussed and everything in this book centers around two fundamental business implications of the feminine influence:

- When we can finally quantify, rationalize, or objectify a business event in a logical expression, the optimal time to seize the opportunity or prevent the crisis it manifests has generally already passed.

- The essence of any successful business is relationships, the relationships between the clients and employees and between employees and managers.

The first does not mean we cannot address the event. It just means waiting to see something quantifiable will most likely require additional effort, time, or expense to address the situation. This is the preventative aspect of addressing any disease before it shows up in test results or buying into any business opportunity before it shows up in print for everyone.

The second implies that without these two strong relationships running a business successfully is very difficult. Products, services, marketing, cash flow, and all other more traditional aspects of business are secondary.

Organizationally, this book flows from the abstract to the practical in five sections:

- Feminine Influence
- The Company
- You
- Strategy
- Masculine Influence

A thorough discussion of the abstract will help create the right feel for the plan as a whole so the presentation of the pragmatic steps is clearer.

As with any plan, we are trying to draft a strategy now for future events. Since no human can consistently predict future events and can capture all the detail life contains, any plan is but a superficial speculation of the future. The implications are that while we need some practical steps that allow us to visualize how to implement this strategy they by no means are all the steps we need or necessarily the right steps.

For these reasons, having the right feel for this plan is far more important than having the right understanding since there will be the need to seize unexpected opportunities that only intuition can maximize. We cannot rely upon facts and figures to guide us because they are only a delayed, shallow manifestation of what has already occurred. Organizing this book around making sure we present the right feel will ensure the ideas remain practical but yet flexible to accommodate the events and actions we neither can predict nor document.

Feminine Influence

The purpose of this section is twofold. First, it will introduce the fundamentals of the feminine influence, and second, extend beyond them to make her applicability to the business world firmer. The dual purpose will present the feminine influence as being present in every aspect of life so her basic elements apply to everything.

Consequently, looking at her fundamentals and expanding upon them will take us on a journey that will meld the existence of the feminine influence in our personal lives to that in our business ones. Since the feminine influence is nature's creation, she has no regard for the distinction between personal and business, similar to the sun having no regard for whether we think it's a weekday or a weekend. As a result, despite the most intense application of our conscious will or manufactured rationale, we will not be able to deter her influence anymore than we can deter the influence of the sun; the forces of nature far surpass the forces of man.

Fundamentals

The fundamental force behind the feminine influence is beauty. What is beauty though? How does one go about describing it? Beauty is one of those things difficult to describe but of which everyone feels they know. Beauty is also something about which no two people can feel exactly the same. More importantly for our discussion there is an aspect to beauty that compels an action by another. One such action is attraction in the form of acquisition or closeness.

Many things have a beauty to them that attracts us. This includes artwork, landscapes, scenery, clothing, jewelry, cars, homes, ideas, and people. To symbolize the beauty in all things I will use a woman. By understanding and appreciating the beauty in women, we can understand and appreciate better the effect beauty has on us when she arrives in the form of the other things I just mentioned.

Regardless of how we describe beauty, she influences us. For this reason, we can claim her to be a power or force. The basic nature of this influence is attraction. Beauty draws others to her; she does not need to seek them out because they find her. Imagine a strawberry field and the work it would require for you to pick it. How different would your effort be if the strawberries came to you?

While the imagery seems preposterous, it has a business corollary: imagine clients coming to you versus you having to find them. Compare the effort of a sales force searching for prospects versus one having prospects coming to them. At a rudimentary level, advertising represents the later; however, there are more intricate aspects of beauty at work that other marketing techniques seek to tap. Branding is such an example.

Marketing is one business application of beauty because it seeks to make a business' products or services more attractive to the client. Conversely, sales is the pursuit of clients. Marketing is to sales as feminine is to masculine:

Marketing – Sales : Feminine – Masculine

The manifestation of this relationship shows up in the higher ratio of women to men in marketing (advertising) versus sales. Women attract; men pursue.

The problem becomes the identification of beauty in all her many business forms. While it may not seem readily apparent, beauty has an infinite number of business variations that become subject matters onto themselves in numerous publications. Trying to understand beauty's application in all her detail is daunting. Symbolizing her influence through the beauty in a woman, will give us a frequent, tangible picture by which we can more effectively superimpose her onto business and seek her help in injecting dynamism into our business. Since beauty associates itself more with the female than the male, beauty's tangibility is most effectively seen in a woman. Thus, rather than focusing on the "influence of beauty," a more effective picture crystallizes when we refer to her as the "feminine influence."

In this respect, our discussion becomes more of understanding and appreciating concepts as opposed to memorizing the voluminous situations and conditions which make applying feminine influence effective. This returns us to my high school teacher mentioned earlier who wrote on a chalk board five formulas representing the major mathematical concepts covered by the test and to the right of these, he then listed the twenty-two formulas derived from these concepts. He then suggested two methodologies by which we could study in order to have a good chance at passing the test. The first entailed working to understand the five concepts while the second entailed memorizing the twenty-two formulas within these five concepts. Our discussion is the same except I'm offering the appreciation of one concept versus the memorization of how to handle an infinite number of situations with an infinite number of conditions. The only limitation to the business situations to which we can apply the feminine influence is our awareness.

Making one aware of the feminine influence in business is easier than showing the degree of her influence. Any man who has come in contact with a woman can feel the degree to which he is attracted to her. Likewise for a woman, she can feel an attraction for a man. As we will see, the fundamentals of these two attractions are the same. A more neutral manifestation of the degree to which the feminine influence attracts us is the acquisition of any object such as a car. The beauty of that object is so intense that our attraction to it can approach obsessiveness. Naturally, we don't always call it beauty but for now simply calling it an attraction will suffice.

The power behind the feminine influence is symbolized in Greek mythology by Helen's abduction that launched the Trojan War. She was the most beautiful woman in the ancient world whose rescue became the mission of the entire Greek army. Helen's story underscores beauty's power to encourage men to fight and die for her. Similarly, a man designed and built a mosque possessing the largest stone dome ever created. His passion for constructing this was to demonstrate the love for a woman he could not have. She was the queen and married to the king. More contemporarily anyone can recall a case of two men fighting over a woman that resulted in death for one or both. In our movies, we find men falling in love with women who subsequently fall into danger. The heroes rescue the heroines only after death-defying adventures and challenges. These movies not only illustrate the power behind the feminine influence in the energy the heroes expend to overcome these dangers, but the story lines themselves emit an attractive influence. The unrelenting *beauty* of this story line has *attracted* audiences throughout the ages. People have flocked to these stories in much the same way Greek men flocked to gaze upon Helen: the beauty of anything is an influence limited only by the qualitative aspect of that beauty, as beauty increases so does her power.

Uriah Heep's "Lady In Black" symbolizes another aspect of beauty, the rescuing force that makes men's toil easier in a life filled with struggles. Basically, the feminine influence makes life worthwhile because without her the masculine influence would dominate life and transform it into an endless struggle with no positive end in sight. The same survival instinct that encourages man to assert himself can also send him on an eternal campaign to bring all that he surveys within his control, including his fellow man. The empathic influence of the feminine is the counterbalance to this aspect of the masculine, "Do unto others as you would have others do onto you."

Empathy in its ultimate form would have no man able to kill another because he would also kill himself. A person committing suicide after killing others, especially loved ones, is often a manifestation of this theme in our daily lives. As with the man in the song, endless conquest results in a reprieve where there are no more conquests, only the resulting destruction. It's at this point the "Lady In Black" arrives on the scene to open empathy's floodgates that have to this point remained locked. Exclaiming, "What have _____ (I, we, you, they) done?" illustrates this. For some, the flood is too much, and for others an internal ark allows them to ride out the storm and regenerate with a new appreciation for life.

The feminine influence not only delivers this empathy but she also gives birth to this new appreciation, insight, or wisdom. Symbolically we've seen this throughout history in our stories when the hero is nursed back to health by a caring woman. In this form, beauty heals the wounds incurred from savage struggles for not only physical survival, but mental and emotional ones as well. When a person looks upon the vastness of the world and what it takes to create a life, the realization strikes him that he won't be able to do this without enduring severe wounds. The feminine influence, "Lady In Black", gives birth to a regeneration and empathy that encourages one to avoid despair and move forward. Rather than giving in to the destructive methods of others, beauty makes life worthwhile so one desires to seek creative alternatives.

As with any power, there is the aspect of its application. How does one apply the attractive force behind the feminine influence? In many ways, one cannot attract without some awareness of what it is she is trying to attract. For instance, a magnet can attract a metal object but not a wooden one. Likewise, the application of the feminine influence is ineffective without an appreciation for what one is attempting to attract.

In the business world, marketing runs into this frequently via market research. Researching the preferences of a target market will hopefully result in the creation of products and services attractive to that market. While this is a reactive application of the feminine influence, there are proactive applications that arise when one seeks to anticipate preferences. Many new products and services such as radio and television did not meet with initial approval of the consumer but rather developed as various applications and acceptance of those applications grew – as *appreciation* for their applications grew. The internet originated as the domain of governmental and educational institutions heavily involved in technology. Few considered application to a technologically illiterate consumer; however, as the technology became simpler with various operating systems and software integrated with the internet, the expansion of the internet's application to the consumer increased.

In many ways these experiences are similar to a woman attracting a man. A woman can enhance her attractiveness if she is aware of the man's preferences and enhances those attributes that would be most appealing to him. However, all of this is for naught if she never has the occasion to meet the man. The same holds true for the marketing of a product or service; if it never comes in contact with its target market, it will remain unsold. This gets into business concepts such as availability and awareness within the target market.

The problem with market research is the delay between the receipt of that knowledge and the emergence of those preferences it documents. The preferences existed long before their documentation. This is far more obvious than it may initially sound, but it demonstrates the fragility of any objectified information about a market.

For instance, imagine we're looking down a straight road running to the horizon when suddenly from that horizon we see a set of lights. At that moment we have no idea as to the type of vehicle, but as it comes closer we begin to accumulate information from our observations so that at some point we are able to correctly identify the vehicle. Even though we were able to finally identify the vehicle, that vehicle was approaching long before we made the identification. In fact, it was approaching long before we even saw its headlights.

Market research, or any information we receive about the market, works in the same way. By the time we are able to identify and quantify the preferences in a market, they've been in existence even prior to our thought about investigating them. This holds true for any opportunity or problem, not just market research.

Using the vehicular analogy as shown in Figure 2.1, we can visualize this discovery process by using a solid circle to identify the point at which we identify the vehicle along its drive on the road from the horizon.

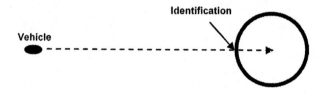

Figure 2.1

We can enhance this diagram into Figure 2.2 by showing our sighting of the lights and our ongoing accumulation of information about the vehicle. We designate this accumulation by the increasing shadiness from the sighting of the lights to the identification of the vehicle.

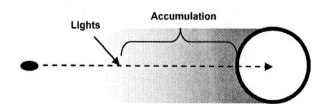

Figure 2.2

This analogy also illustrates the segregation of sales figures and other business metrics from truth. Essentially, the sales identified today are the result of actions taken much earlier. Typically, we identify a sale when money exchanges hands, but the vehicle carrying that sale had its beginnings beyond the horizon of our vision. Thus, responding to today's numbers is responding to actions long since completed. In effect, it's akin to constantly living in the past.

Let's superimpose the vehicular analogy onto business through an example such as a person entering a store. If we run the store, our initial sighting of the person occurs upon his entrance while the identification of the sale occurs when he purchases something as shown in Figure 2.3.

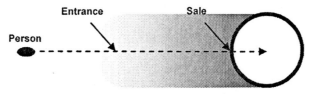

Figure 2.3

At any point between these two points the sale may not occur for any number of reasons such as product availability, price, assistance, or ambiance. Conversely, a sale does occur for many other reasons such as the positive attributes of the same things we just mentioned for a sale not occurring. How we determine the nature of those reasons is multi-faceted and includes market research and client surveys.

Beyond this though we must consider the question of what caused this person to enter the store in the first place. Likewise, we would benefit by considering the converse of this condition by asking what causes another person to avoid the store. The reasons for both are as variable as personalities. We can associate this analogy to any business and not just ones using a store setting. Virtual stores utilizing the web and service providers supplying tangible or intangible products also benefit from this analogy. Figure 2.4 shows these situations. We have the identification of an opportunity and then the sale.

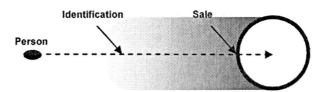

Figure 2.4

In order to work this analogy to fit more transactional businesses such as some online purchases, we need to adjust the distance between identification and the transaction such as Figure 2.5 shows us. In some cases this could be one and the same.

Figure 2.5

However, what this analogy implies is that while we shorten the distance between identification and sale we cannot automatically conclude we've also shorten the distance of the entire evolution of the sale. All we've done is accepted a larger "blind spot." By adjusting these elements, our analogy has greater application to various aspects of business.

One of those applications is to other business metrics besides sales such as expenses. When any expense is finally documented on the books as such, extensive processes were run before someone at the business did that. Figure 2.6 shows to some degree that expenses and sales are the same with only a directional difference; someone's sale is another's expense and vice versa.

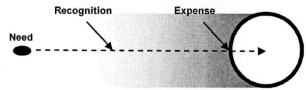

Figure 2.6

Essentially, the need for any expense exists before our recognition of it. Illustratively, by looking at an unexpected home or car expense, we find that expense and the conditions creating it existed prior to our knowledge of them. Sometimes, we see this as an oversight while other times we see it as the result of the growth, maintenance, or decline of the business. Thus, actual expenditures rarely match budget projections.

In effect, what we're saying from an extremely tactical perspective is that we cannot predict the future; however, as the future approaches the present from the horizon, its impact in the form of a new present becomes clearer. For instance, what may happen two days from now will tend to be clearer than two years hence. Figure 2.7 shows our recognition of the future's arrival as manifesting itself in business plans with their many contingencies across various time frames.

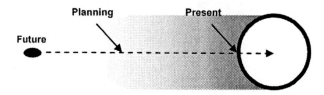

Figure 2.7

Today's events impact tomorrow's outcomes; yesterday's events impacted today's outcomes. Again, this may seem rather obvious but that's exactly why the implications of this statement are so powerful especially if we link it to another obvious statement, "Things are always changing." Combining these two concepts we can arrive at the conclusion that the events and conditions impacting today's outcomes have already changed.

Analogously, we can say the yards a running back in football records on any play are the result of events and situations that arose at various times in the past. We can include practicing and conditioning among such events. The same holds true for the music our ears document from a musician. Many *past* events, including those affecting our attendance at the concert, impact that outcome *today*.

Additionally, the impact of some events in the past is so great that no matter what we do now there is highly unlikely that we'll see results immediately in the direction we want. If a football player or a musician suffers from insufficient practice or conditioning, very little today will alter the next day's performance. Many business events and actions have impacts that make them almost impossible to alter immediately once their potential outcomes become clear. By the time we receive numbers, the events impacting those numbers have already occurred.

More importantly, those events and their effects have changed. They are by no means static, singular, or isolated but rather fluid, rhythmic, and integrated. A severe storm generates high waves, but its intensity varies with its duration. The eye of the storm is quite different from the prelude of high winds and darkening skies, and between the two yet, there are many different intensity levels as well. The waves from this storm will have an intensity that varies directly with their duration as well; however, peak waves arrive slightly after the storm's peak. By the time the waves peak, the storm has begun to subside. These waves have a cascading effect on beach erosion; however, the erosion's peak occurs after the waves' peak which in turn has occurred after the storm's peak. One event triggers another and as the storm's intensity increases the waves become higher and beach erosion increases; however the various peaks of each event – storm, waves, and erosion – do not coincide.

Four "morals of the story" applicable to our discussion are:

- Nothing you do during the storm will substantially deter the erosion.
- By the time you are able to measure the erosion the storm has passed.
- The peak of one event does not coincide with that of another it is affecting.
- The difference between an event's ebb and peak is one of gradation.

Two other analogies will reinforce our discussion. One is the journey of the sun through the daytime sky. The sun reaches its highest point at noon, but typically, the warmest part of the day is around four in the afternoon. The other is the finding that coastal environs are cooler than inland ones on hot days and warmer on cold days especially if the winds arrive from offshore.

The first analogy shows the delay between the event and the outcome, warmer weather as a result of the sun. Similarly, hearing the boom from a malfunctioning firework is often heard after the flash is gone. The second analogy demonstrates the enduring effect an event can have. In this case, water's slower adaptation to temperature changes versus land's, heats winter winds and cools summer ones. Thus, by way of water, summer's heat affects winter's weather and winter's cold affects summer's warmth. An outgrowth of the delaying and enduring effects of an event is its rhythmic nature, waxing and waning. The heating of the land or water grows to a peak and then diminishes to ebb.

All of these analogies imply a cascading, or domino, effect upon other events. We typically see these as residual effects or side-effects. While this may initially seem disconnected to business, we frequently refer to this phenomenon as momentum. What these analogies seek to do is help us begin to get a handle on what momentum actually is in a business context. Essentially, it's the flow of all events, under our control and not, that produce the outcomes impacting a business.

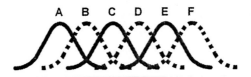

Figure 2.8

Figure 2.8 shows this domino or accordion effect among a group of events, A – F, where the peak of each event occurs somewhat later than the peak of the event influencing it. Thus, if "F" were our measurable event that generated the numbers to indicate a problem, we would have events A – D pretty much over by the time "F" identified the problem for us. In effect, whereas "F" is indicating an opportunity or problem, the other events impacting it are already in remission so the prime time to seize "F", when forces would be on our side, has already passed. Relating this back to our storm analogy, "A" could be the storm, "B" the waves, and "C" the erosion with D, E, and F representing subsequent events caused by the erosion such as damage to our home.

Still, what further increases the complexity of Figure 2.8 is that there are many events influencing each event A – F, a singular chain reaction never really occurs as shown above. Nevertheless, it illustrates the delayed reaction our initial actions can have and the reactions unseen or immeasurable events can have on our future actions. Relying upon only what we can measure to make a decision increases the likelihood of error.

Some business examples include technological investments and lay-offs. In the first, there is a delay between when the investment is made and when the benefits begin to arrive; while in the second, there is a delay between when the expenses are eliminated and the impact to service may be felt. In both, the impact grows to a peak and then wanes as adjustments occur. When and how we measure these impacts do not affect the impact itself. It has a nature exclusive of our ability to measure it.

At this point we can modify our vehicular analogy to encompass these themes by making it more multilateral through the integration of many events (multiple lines) melding to influence us in a way that shows up as an outcome. The appearance of the vehicle's lights now becomes when we are aware that an event may influence an outcome. The identification of the vehicle now becomes our ability to visualize the impact an event will likely have on the outcome. We now have Figure 2.9.

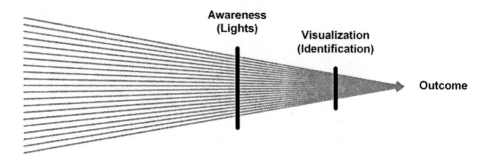

Figure 2.9

At some point we become aware of the various events potentially affecting an outcome; however, as we saw in the one-dimensional vehicular analogies of Figures 2.1 and 2.2, the evolution of an event was going on long before our awareness of it or our identification of its influence's nature. Expanding this analogy to incorporate the many events that usually converge upon us in the form of an outcome as opposed to one, it is unlikely that we will become aware of all these events or will be able to visualize their impact all at the same time. Consequently, Figure 2.10 allows us to incorporate this in our model.

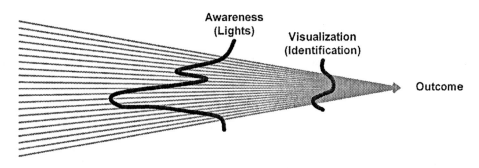

Figure 2.10

What we now reflect with serpentine lines is that our awareness and visualization of the many events impacting an outcome are not likely to be simultaneous for all events. We can even extend this further with the realization that we may never have full awareness of or have full ability to visualize all events affecting an outcome, so our solid lines should really be broken ones like the ones in Figure 2.11 to reflect the uncertainty in identifying some events influencing the outcome.

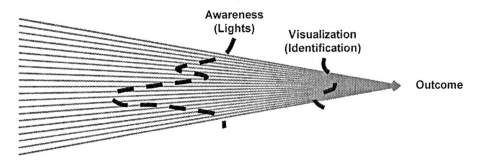

Figure 2.11

Thus, the implication here is that simply because we cannot prove conclusively through tangible evidence or rationale that an event influences an outcome doesn't mean that it does not influence. There is no correlation between our ability to have awareness for an event and its influence on an outcome; the events we notice are not necessarily more influential than those we do not. Our natural tendency is to attribute more influence to those events of which we are aware than those of which we are not. How can we attribute any importance to something of which we are unaware?

Going back to the statistics we gather everyday in business, these analogies further disrupt the apparent clarity we receive from them when we point out that we've only been talking about whether an event influences an outcome and whether we're aware of it. We've only hinted on the question of the *degree* in both of these cases, adding still many more dimensions to the discussion. Even if we were able to accurately measure the influence, the actual measurement will come well after the event's development. The statistics, and most importantly the score, of any game arrive after the various events have played themselves out. To fully base any decision on the metrics manufactured by outcomes is akin to living in the past, to acknowledging events and conditions do not change, and to stating that an influence does not influence unless it's measurable. Nevertheless, the tendency is to await such information so as to have more comfort that we're making an appropriate decision, and when we do receive those numbers, we tend to overemphasize the influence of that event on results simply because we are able to quantify it. Unfortunately, this hesitation will more than likely cause us to miss the most opportune time to act. A snowball rolling down a hill is easier to stop when we first become aware of it as opposed to when we can measure the impact of it striking us.

We can summarize the discussion in the last two paragraphs as the graph in Figure 2.12 with the degree of awareness as one axis and the degree of influence as another. Anyone who has worked with numbers knows the power they have to change our interpretation of the particular event's influence they're measuring, irrespective of the methodology used to derive them. Thus, our tendency is to attribute greater influence, positive or negative, to that event when we've quantified it than when we've merely visualized its influence.

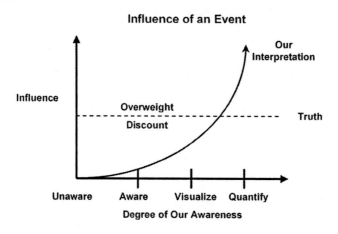

Figure 2.12

It helps if we look at the influence of an event as its proportionate share out of all events influencing the outcome. With this we can more easily see how we can overweight the events we can measure because there are some events of which we are unaware so they don't even factor into the calculation. Consequently, the proportionate share of influence for the events that show up on our radar will tend to occupy a greater proportionate share of the influence in our minds than in truth. This is no more than extending the implication of the commonly expressed statement, "You don't know what you don't know."

At this time, let's step back from this discussion and approach it from another perspective shown in Figure 2.13 which moves away from visualization to awareness.

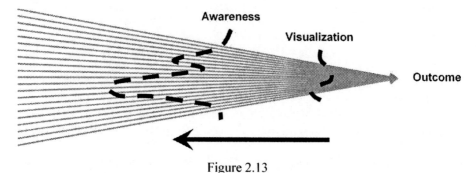

Figure 2.13

Events do not develop as distinct lines but as a melded picture. By blurring the distinction among the various events affecting an outcome, we can further enhance our diagram and refer to the outcome as some impact on us in Figure 2.14.

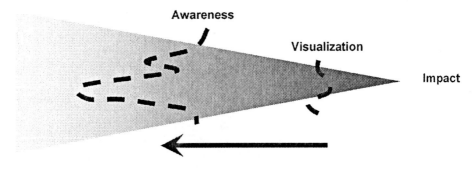

Figure 2.14

Embellishing our snowball analogy into an avalanche, awareness is the feeling that conditions are ripe for an avalanche, visualization is the hearing or seeing of the avalanche, and impact is the avalanche striking us. We can also relate this to radar where the appearance of an object on the radar is the awareness of something approaching, the sighting of the object is the visualization along with further evaluation, and the landing of the object is the impact to us. Thus, as we move away from the point of impact that assumes the form of the present we confront today, the confluence of events becomes vaguer, similar to the movement from the mouth of a large river to the numerous springs that initiate water's confluence in the form of tributaries, streams, and smaller rivers.

Since the vehicle approaching us can do so from any direction, we can modify our diagram further to incorporate the feeling demonstrated by radar. The solid circle in Figure 2.15 represents visualization, the shaded portion awareness, and the center, impact.

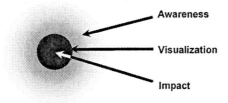

Figure 2.15

Again, the point is that by the time the impact of melded events strikes us, we will already have gone through a process by which our awareness grows and our visualization of potential outcomes and actions crystallize. Naturally, as Figures 2.11, 2.13, & 2.14 showed with the broken serpentine lines, our awareness and visualization can be sieves that allow events to impact us totally by surprise through a stealthy fashion beneath our radar and line of sight.

Using this diagram we can better take our journey to the fringes of awareness where we first detect potential opportunities and problems. Since visualization occurs after our awareness develops, tackling situations only when we can visualize them increases the likelihood of missing prime opportunities for action. For instance, if we consider a military analogy where unidentified objects appeared on our radar, we would be inclined to take some precautionary action to thwart them in case our visuals determined they were a foe. Without such precautions, we would be in greater harm.

The implications of this analogy crystallize when we remember humans are born with different abilities. This not only includes physical and mental but also emotional. In chess, some players are blessed with greater insight into the combinations of moves and the po-tentialities in various situations. Typically, we try to quantify this as the number of moves a player can see into the future; however, it also includes the ability to see and evaluate the opportunities available to a piece positioned on one square as opposed to another.

Translating this to everyday life, we arrive at the conclusion that awareness and visu-alization vary by person. An opportunity that reaches one person's awareness could likely not be detected by another. Furthermore, two people could be aware of an opportunity, but one may be able to formulize it better than the other. While it's hard to quantify this dif-ference in abilities, the difference exists nonetheless. Again, as we saw previously in Figure 2.12, we have to avoid the tendency to discount attributes we cannot measure and overweight those we can.

At this juncture, we finally return to the main path of our journey to the feminine in-fluence. First, we need to broaden our concepts of awareness and visualization by associating them with intuition and cognition respectively as we see in Figure 2.16.

Figure 2.16

Intuition is the feeling for something while cognition is the rationalization of it. The first is the domain of emotions while second is the domain of mental processes developed by sensing and knowledge. For instance, feeling danger for something without prior ex-perience or knowledge of it is an intuition. Often, people will read the writings of another and claim, "He put into words what I've been feeling." This statement exemplifies the difference between the two: cognition is the construct by which we form a feeling. Often our mental processes cannot capture a feeling in such a construct so it remains intuited.

Gender factors heavily into a person's ability to intuit and cognize, to feel and think. If we take Figure 2.16 and use it to represent a man's intuition and cognition, we can place a woman's right along side him to get Figure 2.17.

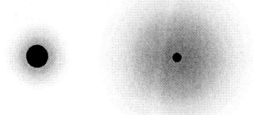

Figure 2.17

With these two representations, we can see the enhanced cognitive abilities of the man over a woman but the enhanced intuitive abilities of the woman over the man. Whereas men tend to have better objective, logical, and reasoning functions allowing them to more easily express ideas, women possess better subjective, emotional, and intuitive functions allowing them to receive an earlier and better feel for things. There's a reason why "woman's intuition" is not called "man's intuition." Thus, while a man may be better able to put his feelings into thoughts, he is less able to have feelings for things further removed from his immediacy. A woman is more likely to receive an indication that something is an opportunity or threat before a man even realizes something is happening; however, once a man realizes something is going on, he is more apt to be able to formulate it into a documented thought. This is why a woman can have a feeling for something but have her male companion think she's hallucinating; he cannot "see" what she does. Furthermore, she also has difficulty explaining her feelings in a rational format conducive to his mental processes. For her, she is trying to explain how the sun looks to a blind man while he is trying to understand it in a context with which he has little experience.

Of course, we are addressing these in an abstract sense meaning the specific picture applicable to each man and woman varies, but our original purpose for this tangential journey was to address the question, "How does one apply the attractive force behind the feminine influence?"

By showing the intuitive power behind her, we can now infer some answers to this question with the primary one being that attraction requires empathy. It's very difficult to attract anything if we cannot empathize with what we're trying to attract. Sometimes, this can relate to a pure understanding for something, but other times it's through having a feeling for what may work by being able to place yourself emotionally in another's life. Simply relying upon more cognitive avenues doesn't maximize one's ability to attract.

The shortfall in a cognitive approach is acute with anything involving another person. As we've shown and experienced in business, we cannot easily assess or measure something such as morale and have a lot of confidence in the assessment or measurement. In these situations an ability to emotionally relate to other people becomes necessary. Since cognition fails to capture all that we need to accomplish this, intuition becomes a valuable ally to assess what we cannot assess and measure what we cannot measure. Relationships fall truly in this realm.

Since business has as its roots two major groups of relationships, client-employee and employee-manager, sensitivity to these relationships increases one's access to this world beyond the fringes of our ability to visualize, verbalize, and quantify. Sensitivity to these relationships increases with one's emotional abilities. People are born with varying emotional abilities just as they are born with varying physical and mental abilities. While women may not have the physical or rational abilities of men, they have a counterbalance in the realm of emotions in the form of intuition.

The more one displays sensitivity to others, the more likely he has the empathy necessary to assess the intangibles of relationships. Additionally, since empathy is grounded in feelings for another's life, these same feelings power one's intuition so he can better grasp the intangibles in life in general. Emotions allow one to intuit, and emotions thrive in the realm of the feminine influence.

<u>Extension</u>

With this introduction of some fundamentals of the feminine influence, we can now extend ourselves by delving deeper into some implications by covering:

- Background documenting the feminine influence.
- Explanation of how this influence works.
- Examples showing her at work in traditionally masculine environments.
- Flash Points this influence creates with the masculine influence.

Background

The feminine influence is not new. She has been around ever since the first woman and probably earlier. While this seems obvious in the abstract, what is less so is that this influence has been a documented part of practical government, philosophy, war, and economics since 500 – 1000 BC. In fact, Sun Tzu's *The Art of War*, written sometime around 500 BC, and a guide for many business consultants and leaders, incorporates many aspects of the feminine influence.

What is extremely challenging about this influence is that she requires intelligence and courage to understand, appreciate, and apply her because she's subtle and requires time. As a result, rather than admit ignorance or cowardliness, people would rather argue that she's insignificant, inapplicable, impractical, or loony. It's much easier to humiliate a woman than to admit inadequacy in connecting emotionally to her. Some men fear the latter so much that they won't hesitate to do the former. This condition translates into important implications.

A humorous story about Adam & Eve will highlight this point:

After God created the universe, the earth, and everything in and on both, he sat down to create the first man, Adam. Realizing that He had created quite a daunting masterpiece, he wanted to make sure Adam was blessed with the confidence to tackle the task of living and not be overwhelmed by the vastness of His creation.

After Adam had been around for a few days, he called to God. "Hey God!"

"Yes Adam," He responded.

"I just wanted to let you know that I think you have a real neat place here."

"Why thank you, Adam."

"Yes God, I've got it all figured out too and I'll be able to have some fun now. I've identified all the animals, plants, and rocks in the place. I understand the heavens and the earth and all that run through it."

"I see," said God quite perturbed at Adam's brashness at simplifying so quickly His creation.

"Yeah God, it's really great. This Life stuff is going to be a snap."

"Yes, I guess it will," God said holding back his anger. So, that night He went back to creating.

The next morning Adam was out wandering the earth admiring how he knew so much in such a short time. Suddenly, he heard a soft voice that said, "Hi Adam." Just from the melodic, soprano tone he knew it wasn't God, so he turned around to see Eve waving to him and walking into a nearby forest. Before Adam could get over his surprise, Eve disappeared into the forest.

When Adam recovered, he ran to the nearest mountain and yelled, "Hey God! Come here for a minute."

God being everywhere at all times arrived quickly and replied, "Yes, Adam."

"God, I just saw something wandering about that said 'hi' to me."

"Oh, that must be Eve," said God.

"What's an Eve?"

"Well Adam, Eve is a woman. She is my latest creation. What do you think?"

"What do I think? I think you've outdone yourself God! Eve's fantastic! I can't stop thinking about her!"

"Thank you, Adam."

"You're welcome God, but tell me. I'm having problems here. What's her story?"

Pausing a moment, God responded "I'm not really sure Adam. I was daydreaming for a brief moment while creating her, and I forgot what I did. Do me a favor though?"

"Sure God. You name it."

"Well, when you figure her out, get back to me."

People chuckle at this story because they can relate to its conceptual truth. Whereas the masculine influence relies upon the tangibility of sight, sound, smell, taste, and touch, the feminine influence relies upon the mysterious intangibles of feelings – intuition. The later is much harder, if not impossible, to quantify. While the first is direct, the second is indirect. "Woman's intuition" is the common term for this influence.

Explanation

Even though there are several lifetime's worth of reading on this topic and experts who have devoted their lives to it in many different fields, we will need to attempt a general explanation that will enable us to begin talking about the application of the feminine influence. We'll do this by visualizing her, by addressing her impact and by exploring the roles intelligence and courage play with her. Again, the fundamental force behind the feminine influence is beauty; that's what powers her attractive qualities.

Visual

In order to better visualize the feminine influence we will incorporate the masculine influence as well in both our discussion and picture. We can do that with these simple expressions in Figure 2.18.

Masculine Influence:	$O \Rightarrow X$	Pursue	Direct
Feminine Influence:	$O \Leftarrow X$	Attract	Indirect

Figure 2.18

These are pure expressions of these influences. The "O" represents the person pursuing or attracting whereas "X" represents the person being pursued or attracted. The first is called the "subject" while the second the "object." We'll stay focused on people, but these expressions also work for things, places, and ideas.

They're pure expressions because neither influence can exist by itself. We can see this if we first view each as being clearly the opposite of the other. Second, by extending this line of thought, we can conclude that one cannot have pursuit without attraction and cannot have attraction without pursuit. We can see this by looking at each from "X's" perspective. When we do, each influence becomes its opposite. In the masculine influence, we say "X" is attracting "O," and in the feminine influence that "X" is pursuing "O." This perspective transforms each influence into the other. Again, neither influence can exist without the other.

To complete the relationship between these two influences, we must address the retort: "Just because I'm attracted to something doesn't mean I pursue it." The perspective around this retort is purely masculine because it's focused on tangible actions – something that can be seen, heard, tasted, smelled, or touched. It does not consider more intangible actions involving thoughts and emotions. These show up as "distractions." The most comical example is the man who drives into an obstruction because an attractive woman distracts him while she walks. True, he did not physically pursue the woman but mentally and emotionally he did, thus the reason for his crash. There is no denying that he was attracted to her, and such situations are common. We'll call this invisible pursuit a "distraction."

This example is a good introduction to other examples because it begins to touch the nebulous, mysterious nature of the feminine influence. That is why we can also call it "indirect" and the masculine influence "direct." These words are important because they will help us visualize and identify the influences in the examples to come.

Before we explore these examples we still need to address the impact of the feminine influence and the roles intelligence and courage play – first, impact.

Impact

As we had already discussed, the force behind the feminine influence is beauty – the healer of daily wounds caused by life's struggles. She is inherently far more powerful than the masculine influence; however, the compensation for this is that she's far more dependent on the masculine influence than the masculine is on the feminine.

The easiest way to picture this is to say the feminine influence makes the masculine far better, almost super human. If the masculine influence makes the house, the feminine influence makes the house a home. We take this analogy further to express the dependent nature of the feminine influence by saying it's hard to have a home without a house but it's easier to have a house without a home. This analogy also expresses the tremendous warmth of the feminine influence when you ask: Would you rather live in a house or a home?

This analogy also shows the independent, but lifeless, nature of the masculine influence. As a result, we can employ him more easily but all the coldness that objectivity, logic, and reason deliver retards effectiveness far below what the feminine influence can inspire. This is why the masculine approach alone tends to deliver mediocre results; people are more inspired by homes than houses.

We can further express the interplay between these two influences in Figure 2.19.

Masculine Influence:	Independent	Practical	Cold
Feminine Influence:	Dependent	Inspirational	Warm

Figure 2.19

Consequently, this makes the application of the feminine influence more involved because the masculine serves as the foundation for the feminine. From a business perspective the masculine becomes the "positioning" element. It's the setting of the stage so an attraction will occur.

Despite the foresight required for the feminine influence, the "return on investment" exceeds a purely masculine approach. Yes, the masculine approach can achieve his stated goals and objectives, but the question becomes "Were the goals and objectives mediocre because they only considered masculine approaches?" This is hard to see until we realize that many times the setting of mediocre goals and objectives are done under the guise of "making sure they're realistic" or "making sure they're simple."

This is why the feminine influence cannot be explained without understanding the intelligence required in order to employ her – our third topic in explaining this influence.

Intelligence

Intelligence goes beyond who knows the most facts and figures and who can arrange them most logically. A five-year old girl next door knows the names to all the dinosaurs and something about them. Is she an expert? Hardly. Intelligence includes intuition, imagination, and creativity. If the feminine influence is subjectivity, emotion, and intuition; one cannot apply her without these.

In fact, when it comes to a hierarchy within intelligence, information and logic are at the bottom while intuition, imagination, and creativity are at the top. A computer can hold information and run programs logically, but it misses something and is best expressed by the statement, "It's far better to have a feel for the business than an understanding of the business."

Consequently, in a marketplace where there is a rush to sell millions of copies of a book, it's hard to justify the publication of involved ideas. Unless a fairly rigorous education is taking place, it inherently follows that an intelligence-oriented product can only increase market share by appealing to a lesser intelligence level. Since creative ways of increasing market share are difficult and rare, the inclination is to reach out to new markets by watering down the content for easier understanding. This is no different than upper end car manufacturers coming out with "economy" vehicles to sell more. They could not find a creative way to increase revenues without "watering down" the affluent status associated with their vehicles.

This is why the vast amount of business material on the shelves today emphasizes, recycles, and tweaks the solely masculine approach to business. Very few incorporate the feminine influence that has been around for a couple thousand years and documented in rarer, more difficult-to-read works. The rareness of this information in modern business literature also gives us insights as to why it requires courage to employ the feminine influence, the fourth point extending us beyond the fundamentals.

Courage

There are external and internal factors regarding the need for courage. External ones are cultural while internal ones are personal.

Externally, the prevalence of the masculine influence in business can exert the feeling that one who applies the feminine approach is out of touch or alone. While many business publications touch on the feminine influence by addressing the positioning and preparation side of business, they don't address much the irrational, chaotic, sensitive, and intuitive elements. Scripts are preferred to spontaneity, the planned over "seizing the moment", and why "Lady Liberty" personifies freedom. A woman, not a man, holds the torch of freedom.

Lying upon the same path is Adam's inability to understand Eve – she escapes the slavery of his rationale. Yet, in most business publications the push is to understand and control business events as much as possible at the expense of learning how to thrive on the opportunities life's chaotic nature generates. No one can comprehensively predict the future; yet, achieving the objective becomes more important than seizing the opportunity. We often chain ourselves to the original objective by assessing people based upon their success in achieving those objectives through a process some call "management by objectives." Someone can seize every opportunity that comes along and still not achieve objectives. In this way, we live in the past by following an incomplete rationale – the objectives reinforcing the plan.

Are people more attracted to freedom or slavery? Who is more likely to lead them to freedom: one who is scripted or spontaneous? Who's more likely to "chain them to their desks?" Essentially, "peer pressure" forces one to conform to the easily understood and direct approach of looking for tangible facts and reasons for business decisions. The most intelligent, as is the case with the qualitative aspect of any attribute, is in the minority. Those who can only handle the simple and easy outnumber those who can also handle the involved and difficult. Confronting the collective power of a group, especially a majority, requires courage. Symbolically, we see this courage possessing appeal throughout our entertainment in movies such as *Star Wars*, *Lord of the Rings*, *The Last Starfighter*, and many others where the qualitative aspects of a minority challenge the oppressive uniformity of a majority.

Internally, the makeup of men and women creates personal struggles that require courage. For a man, it's the fear of coming across feminine or gay. For a woman, it's the fear of being humiliated as unattractive when she feels no one is attracted to her.

The feminine influence exists in us all, but she's stronger in women. Men must find her in their feelings but it is difficult when they often can't even use the word "feelings." This is why in athletics men often talk about "instincts" as opposed to feelings. While they are very similar, instincts are more appealing to men. As a result, it seems more macho to compel someone to accept their point of view than it is to have someone attracted to their point of view. Thus, aggressiveness is vastly preferred to patience.

For women, the fear is whether someone will find them attractive. Are they beautiful? How can the feminine influence work without attraction? This is further compounded when our culture through its media manufactures extremely superficial, standards of "beauty". As a result, the masculine influence prevails here as well. What is visible, rational, and tangible drives our actions rather than what is invisible, emotional, and intangible. Here too logic rules over feeling, the difference between sex and love.

For both men and women, there are severe internal struggles going on that require courage to overcome and to allow the feminine influence work her mysterious, synergistic magic. Now, that we've created a way to visualize the feminine influence, explored her impact, and saw the need for intelligence and courage, we can now take a look at some examples where the feminine influence has some powerful, practical implications in some very masculine domains.

Examples

Before we run through some examples, Figure 2.20 consolidates some key words we've associated with the masculine and feminine influences. There are two aspects to a word, its definition and connotation. The first is the meaning of the word while the second is the impression it gives. My favorite joke illustrating the difference is,

> Opening Line: "What's the difference between escargot and snails?"
> Punch Line: "No one eats snails."

Two words may be synonyms but differ in connotation. We saw this previously with "house" and "home." Connotation is more encompassing because it allows us to explore the many tangential aspects of a word. For instance, explaining the connotative difference between the two words in this joke might allow us to explore French cooking's connection to snails. More importantly, to the listener, even though the words are synonyms they create different pictures in our minds. For me, thinking of snails causes me to picture the ones I saw crawling along the ground in my parents' gardens as a child whereas escargot creates one of my first eating them in restaurant at which I worked. For you different pictures may enter your mind. This is how connotation can vary by individual depending upon the personal experience a person has with that word.

Masculine	Feminine
Pursue	Attract
Direct	Indirect
Independent	Dependent
Practical	Inspirational
Cold	Warm
Reason	Feeling
Objective	Subjective
Logic	Intuition
Tangible	Intangible
Scripted	Spontaneous
Chained	Free
Focus	Distract
Simple	Involved
Mediocre	Intelligent
Easy	Courage
Quantity	Quality

Figure 2.20

Demonstrating this we'll take the sentence:

A.   The boy ran to the store to avoid getting wet by the rainstorm.

Now, let's change it into two other versions:

B.   The brat fled to the mart to weasel out of getting dunked by the cloudburst.
C.   The lad sprinted to the market to evade getting engulfed by the downpour.

Definitively, all three sentences say the same thing, but connotatively their impressions are different. In fact, some may feel that the impressions are so different that even the events these sentences describe are now different so they are now definitively different. If you were the subject of these sentences, which one would you prefer? In effect, it doesn't matter which one you would choose, including deciding you had no preference, because the point is that not everyone would make the same decision.

For the moment, we'll stop here since we will dive deeper into this concept later; however, the point is to show how the above table of words is very similar to a picture without a caption. Through word association we are creating an impression without necessarily describing what that impression is. Impressions are more comprehensive than any words for they are pictures generated by the feelings these impressions stir; "one picture is worth a thousand words."

Seeing how I associate the words in Figure 2.20 to the masculine or feminine influence is not always easy, but it helps if we address the question "Is this word more closely associated with a man or a woman?" As you will see throughout this book, I try to show how these words are associated with their respective influence; the effort is very similar to using a thesaurus to find synonyms except that we are going beyond the immediate family of words surrounding masculine or feminine and tapping into their more distant relatives. If you happen to have a thesaurus around that does not use alphabetization as its main organizational theme but rather, groups and categories, you'll be able to see a more extensive example of this process.

The implication of this categorization of words is that word choice is important beyond the construction of the actual message and into the actual impression it gives. Using words becomes very similar to writing a song; their impression has a rhythm. No song has a consistent tone, pitch, volume, rhythm, or harmony; yet, there is something about it that elevates it above mere noise. Take the notes from any song and scramble them randomly, and you could easily come up with noise. Likewise, words from a connotative perspective can create their own song. We would no sooner speak monotonically or randomly but often this is what happens impressionistically with our words. Consequently, our message may be clear but its impression is scattered or flat. Unfortunately, the pictures we create with our words are not as easily discerned as the definitions in a dictionary. This book's theme, integrating the feminine influence, manifests itself in word choice by implying that neither masculine or feminine words are inherently good or bad but rather integrating them in conversation will more likely yield dynamic results. Thus, what is editorial correct may not be impressionistically.

People will quickly see a business application in marketing and advertising, but there is also one where striving for consistent communication is not necessarily effective communication. Connotations create problems because they can be highly individualistic encouraging the interpretation of impressions different from what we believe we're communicating. Thus, communicating a consistent message tends to take on such a priority that its effectiveness drastically diminishes. The simple and commonly applied solution is to use a communication methodology utilizing "vanilla" words, words whose frequent and common use has watered down their connotations almost to the point that alone they do not create much of an impression, positive or negative.

Analogously, we can illustrate this by a well-worn path that is eventually expanded into a road and subsequently asphalted. Their only purpose is to communicate thoughts without impressions, to build a house without making it a home. Scientific terminology is a prime example of vocabularies designed for a specific purpose along with many sports' terms, but the need extends to all professions. While this "vanilla" methodology seems efficient and simple, severe downsides exist.

One is that it actually increases the need for communication because the words lack any pictures. Imagine trying to convey the message in a picture without showing the picture. Thus, we create an increasing number of words designed to communicate an extremely specific action, thought, or picture. Consider the quantitative definitional differences between "run" and "electroplate." Depending upon the dictionary, one could find dozens of definitions for the first and only a couple for the second. In business, we often take common words or phrases, reduce them to a specific meaning, and produce "buzz" words and phrases such as "branding" or "best practice."

No language is more specified than that of computers. The code required for computers to perform even simple functions is lengthy. Contrast the challenges of teaching a human to run to the store and programming a robot to do it. Whereas a human can accommodate the many variable variables life can throw into such a simple command, the specificity of computer language makes this a programming monstrosity.

An additional downside of resorting to "vanilla" words is the removal of emotion from communication. One cannot inspire without emotion, but the fear of instilling the wrong emotion becomes so overwhelming that "vanilla" becomes a safety blanket. Thus, eliminating words with any kind of connotative ability for fear of being vague or inconsistent increases the challenges of communicating and inspiring.

Possessing a feel for the deeper connotations behind masculine and feminine influences will help in appreciating the examples we're about to review. We'll explore examples in five categories:

- Warfare
- Hunting
- Business
- Sales
- Public Speaking

Warfare

Two military examples will help us see the feminine influence from a practical perspective in warfare. In most battles one army attacks another, so we'll see how an attacker and a defender apply a feminine approach. Of course, in military publications this approach is called by other names, one of the more common and comprehensive is the "indirect approach." Emphasis here is on "indirect." Liddell Hart wrote *Strategy,* a detail classic on this approach which greatly influenced my life.

- Background -

The irony about warfare is that with all other things being equal, the attacker, or aggressor loses. Typically, most view aggressiveness as a strength and not a weakness especially in warfare; however, many of the most resounding military defeats have occurred because of aggressiveness. We're going to examine one of them.

Before we look at it we need to state a fundamental military axiom: with all other things being equal it takes an attacker about three times larger than the defender to ensure a favorable chance of victory. That is why if you're outnumbered it is better to entice the aggressor to attack you rather than attack him yourself. We can substitute the word "attract" for "entice." Automatically, we see that a military encounter naturally favors a feminine approach.

Other factors can compound this effect such as terrain. High ground can increase the strength of the defending force by two to three times especially if the defender entrenches himself. Thus, if we're outnumbered four or five to one, it's best to entice our opponent into attacking us on favorable terrain to equalize the odds.

The hardest aspect of this to fathom is why any army would attack another if it meant equalizing the odds? There are many complex reasons but they all boil down to two: first, man is not a rational creature, and life does not conform to simple, rational calculations.

- Gettysburg -

One of the most famous examples of defense's inherent strengths is the battle of Gettysburg during the American Civil War. In this battle, Federal forces soundly defeated the Confederates by not launching a single assault on the confederate line. By fighting totally on the defensive they enticed the Confederate army to exhaust itself to such a degree that it never regained its previous effectiveness for rest of the war. Not only were the Federals on the defensive but were also on generally high ground often protected by stone walls, ditches, and fences.

Why the Confederates attacked under such unfavorable circumstances, may never be fully known but a few reasons will help us appreciate the attractiveness they saw in this opportunity and apply to our discussion.

One such reason is aggressiveness fueled by a string of victories over the Federals including their victory in Chancellorsville two months before this battle. On that occasion, the Confederates were able to defeat a Federal army almost twice their size. It's easy to simply call this overconfidence without exploring its deeper implications. The important point for elaboration is that aggressiveness is an emotion that can cause us to rationally distort the advantages in a situation and the likelihood of a favorable outcome. Positively, aggressiveness allows us to muster courage, but negatively it encourages us to see advantages where there are none. Overconfidence is but one implication of many around aggressiveness' weaknesses.

Figure 2.21 will allow us to understand a second reason, emotional momentum:

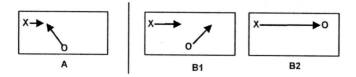

Figure 2.21

In all diagrams we're "O" and the opposing force is "X." Diagram "A" shows the immediate inclination of attacking "X" once we see him; however, this allows "X" to defend. If, however, we could determine the direction of "X's" momentum and place ourselves in his way, he would be inclined to attack us. Diagrams "B1" and "B2" illustrate this. "B1" has us moving directly in the line of "X's" path so in "B2" "X" would attack us. From the standpoint of "O", this illustrates "positioning." From a purely rational, masculine perspective this almost seems absurd because it's very difficult to understand why "X" would continue along its line and attack us. This is the danger of ignoring the emotional elements in any situation.

We can see this effect more tangibly with a speeding car attempting a sharp turn. The faster the car is going the less sharp it's able to turn. The same is true with emotions heavily invested in a particular outcome, and aggressiveness accentuates these emotions. Emotionally, what we're doing as "O" is to establish an emotional roadblock "X" cannot avoid. He will become so committed in his direction that he will be unable to avoid us.

An interesting way to get a feel for the extensiveness of the emotional possibilities is to not look at these diagrams as military maneuvers but as the relational maneuvers of a woman "O" around a man "X." In "A" if the woman sees a man she likes, approaches him, and asks him out, this is less likely to work than if she attractively positions herself in his life's path as shown in "B1" and "B2." Imagine the many subtleties at play that make "O" attractive to "X". The extensiveness of that list is no less than the list for the many subtleties at work in the military version of these diagrams.

What makes the "B" diagrams work lies in what the arrow represents. It can represent many things including the flow of events, the aggressiveness of "X", the attraction of "O", and the momentum behind the current action at work. By applying the many subtleties involved in a gender encounter to a military one, we can see how army "X" would attack "O." From a military perspective we would call these deceptions.

Various subtleties played at Gettysburg. Some were the series of communications, marches, and deployments that had all the confederate forces converge at this town. The emotion of, "Well, we did all this work to get here, so we might as well attack something" was an immense driver behind the decision to attack the Federals then and there. To suddenly command the troops to pack up and disperse in the face of an opposing force that may attack at any time would have been a difficult order to give.

Still, to consciously see and utilize these subtle phenomena in a military engagement are difficult to do. Even at Gettysburg, many of these were there without the combatants' thoughts. On the other hand, there are many examples of generals from other battles that did. More importantly, conditions allowing the employment of these subtle phenomena from the feminine influence exist at all times.

Gettysburg highlights five major concepts involving the feminine influence:

1. There is an inherent advantage in having someone approach you over you approaching him.
2. Positioning allows the flow of events or personalities to encourage someone to approach you.
3. Aggressiveness is an emotion, a compulsion, causing one to approach another.
4. Attractiveness is an emotion that encourages another to approach.
5. Phenomena allowing the feminine influence to blossom exist at all times.

1. Inherent Advantage

We've already talked a lot about the first point when we discussed the inherent advantage of defense and introduced the Gettysburg example, but it would help if we could relate this to a business situation. A business example showing the tremendous strength in "defense" involves inertia in the face of adopting a new idea or promoting an initiative, commonly expressed as "but we've always done it this way." Anyone in business knows the tremendous effort required to overcome this attitude and is akin to the much greater amount of gasoline a car requires in "stop-n-go" traffic than on the expressway; it takes more fuel to go from zero to ten mph than it does to go from fifty to sixty mph.

The implication of this helps us relate to the approaching aspect of the first point – it's better to have someone approach you than to approach him. An example is where there is a need to discuss with an employee a plan for his improvement. It's far more effective for the employee to approach the manager asking for her advice on improvement than it is for the manager to initiate the discussion. Whereas the first assumes the appearance of a quest for advice, the second can easily take on the form of a command.

In the second situation, the employee is very likely to take a "defensive" position respective to the manager, whereas the first situation has him coming out of his "defenses" seeking guidance. The likelihood of this second event increases as the manager's attractiveness exerts an influence on the employee. Of course, the chance exists that the employee may never seek advice.

Positioning is the second of the five attributes of the feminine influence that the Gettysburg example will highlight for us.

As with the inherent advantage of having someone approach you as opposed to having to approach him, we've talked a lot about positioning when we covered the influence of terrain on a battle and the momentum behind events. Again, we're going to spend some more time on it with the help of another business example.

We can extend the above example by having the manager visit more frequently with the employee on a casual "how's it going" basis. The objective here is to create situations that would encourage the employee to open up and discuss possible professional growth strategies. Naturally, depending upon the employee and the manager, and the employee's perception of the relationship between his manager and him, this may not occur at the initial meeting but may require time incorporating many such interactions. A manager would also need to have some talent in listening for and taking advantage of openings that occur in the conversation. Figure 2.22 illustrates the challenge here:

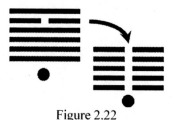

Figure 2.22

Each line, solid or broken, represents a point about a topic in a conversation. A group of such lines represents an entire conversation around a topic punctuated at the end by a dot signifying the end of conversation on that topic. Solid lines represent topics the employee wishes to discuss while the broken ones represent ones the manager wishes. The concept is that while the employee talks about a topic, the manager is listening for an opening for which to use as a bridge to discuss her point. In this example, it's a professional growth issue. The broken line in the first conversational group represents not only a point the employee wanted to discuss about a topic, but also a point that has relevancy to a topic the manager would like to discuss. The bridge represented by the arrow can take the form of a question or introductory statement that will encourage the employee to discuss the other topic.

2. Positioning

Understanding personalities and sound techniques are only a couple aspects of using positioning effectively; on a larger scale, one must also understand events. As with people, events have a natural life too; they follow a life cycle very similar to a human. They also suffer from negative influences and thrive from positive ones as well. Possessing a feel for this flow or rhythm allows us to position ourselves more effectively so we are going with it rather than fighting it or being left out altogether. In nature, seasonal change best symbolizes this cyclical flow:

- Spring is the best time to introduce a new idea and nurture its growth.
- Summer is the best time to push your idea to its limits.
- Fall is the best time to harvest the fruit of your labors by securing seeds for the future.
- Winter is the best time to contemplate new ways to rejuvenate your idea or create others.

I'm using the seasons symbolically here and do not refer to specific time frames, but we should not ignore the emotional influence seasons have on us. From a business sense is it just a coincident we begin the budget process in late fall by examining the results of what we've done during the current year? That we formulize, receive, localize, and personalize the final global plan in the winter? That we begin to implement the strategies in spring? That we begin to see the tendencies, maximization, and fruition of those strategies in summer? No, it's not.

This also doesn't suggest we only discuss ideas in winter, but what it does suggest is that there is an opportune time to discuss ideas for any event. A good analogy is a tree and its branches. The tree represents a central idea while each branch represents an enhancement of that idea. We can restate the seasonal analogy and personalize it to the tree:

- Spring is the best time for the tree to sprout leaves and begin new growth.
- Summer is the best time for the tree to push its new branches to their limits.
- Fall is the best time for the tree to drop its fruit and leaves in preparation for further growth.
- Winter is the best time for the tree to examine what branches offer future growth.

We'll have a more detailed discussion of this in the next chapter. For the moment, it's just important to realize that events have a certain rhythm to them that allows us to anticipate outcomes. If this were not true, then life from one minute to the next would be purely random. Appreciating momentum around an idea allows us to position ourselves. Practically, anyone with any experience in business can recall a time when an idea or plan could not be stopped even when it was determined it would only have a mediocre impact; the plan took on a life of its own. Changing or stopping it once all the pieces were moving in a particular direction was difficult. Such an idea was approaching its summer stage.

We can also understand the unstoppable momentum behind an idea or event by better understanding the force preventing momentum in the first place, inertia. In business we typically call this "resistance to change" or "lack of initiative." If it's hard to get an idea going, to change inertia into movement, it also makes sense that it's hard to change movement by either bringing it to a halt or altering its direction. It's easier to halt a car rolling at one mph than one at sixty. On a political level, war becomes such an event.

We see the emotional aspects of this when someone publicly expresses his opposition to an idea. It's much more difficult to change his direction once he makes this public declaration than if he hadn't made such a declaration. Usually, it's irrelevant how strong the arguments are in adopting the idea – the individual will have difficulty adopting it. We often call this "saving face," but we see it on a grander field when leaders continue to push an idea that is failing such as Vietnam.

Returning to our rolling car, we find that the best time to halt it is before it has started. By the time its movement has begun, the best time to halt it has past. Taking the necessary precautions while parking a car on a steep hill is much easier than trying to stop the car once it has even begun to move. Reading the landscape and understanding the nature of how things interrelate with one another, will allow us to discover the opportune times.

Many times though expediency doesn't encourage the time for such preparatory steps. Very pragmatically, it means the email we send to someone today could be the base of energy behind a positive interaction with that person a year from now.

All of this is showing but a few aspects of how events or ideas gain momentum and we cannot stop or change them. More importantly, this shows us that conditions exist that will allow us to employ positioning effectively so we can create and seize opportunities. Positioning could not take place if events and actions were purely random – had no connection to previous events or actions. This is not the case; they have a life of their own and flow from what has gone before.

3. Aggressiveness

Aggressiveness is the third of the five concepts related to the feminine influence that the Gettysburg example will highlight for us.

Understanding this emotion is important when trying to get a good feel for the inherent advantages that come with not only defense in battle but also with the feminine influence in business. The tendency, especially in a masculine environment like business, is to look at aggressiveness more as a strength than a weakness. I once had a manager tell me, "Aggressiveness is not a weakness." His comment came as a result of an employment candidate who listed "too aggressive" as his main weakness. The manager's tone indicated that he thought the job applicant dodged the question.

The world is a large, intimidating place when viewed rationally against the picture of a solitary individual. In its positive form, aggressiveness allows one to overcome this fearful intimidation and to feel an inspirational achievement; however, in its negative form, aggressiveness becomes the compulsion to taste victory and the self-delusion to see success as imminent.

Aggressiveness' positive form can be a series of stepping-stones to positive growth. It can inspire one to learn and take on bigger obstacles to growth. We often hear this expressed as "confidence builders" or "success breeds success," but it's much deeper than these statements suggest. When the achievements have substance themselves and are not simply shallow victories, aggressiveness can help one achieve something great. Nevertheless, it's a powerful emotion that is often and easily discounted in any rational calculation.

Its negative form is equally powerful but in the other direction. Rather than inspirational, it's shallow destructiveness. It's victory for victory's sake. The desire to taste victory clouds one's understanding and intuition about a situation; it will encourage one to see success as something easier or more likely than it is. Victory becomes more important than what is won; sometimes what is won is absolutely nothing but will assume an illusionary importance because it's a victory.

Rationally, if we calculate obstacles as being too great, we won't make our attempt. Emotionally, aggressiveness minimizes our rational assessment and encourages the attempt despite the facts being against us. This emotion helps us achieve some extraordinary things. However, on a shallow level when this emotion becomes more of an impulse, we find ourselves doing things that can severely weaken us. These become avenues by which others can take advantage of us.

With Gettysburg, we'll focus on the negative aspect of aggressiveness. We often term this overconfidence or arrogance, but again its implications run deeper than this. We often see it when two men informally compete in something as simple as a round of golf. Nothing is at stake except their pride. We've all seen where insignificant events such as these suddenly take on the emotions of a life or death struggle and change the course of a relationship. Even when one man declines a challenge, the challenger and others will goad him into competing. What's important about the goading is that it doesn't have to be vocal – peer pressure alone, playing upon fears of being goaded, can compel the man to accept the challenge. Again, understanding the powerful influence this form of aggressiveness has that is difficult to quantify and to formulate into any logic for a plan is important.

The essence of aggressiveness encourages certain behaviors. The most obvious one is the predisposition to action over inaction. Aggressiveness will encourage us to view the first as inherently better than the second. We see acute examples of this in difficult times when pressure mounts "to do something."

When this emotion pervades and the masculine influence dominates, there is also a predisposition to the easy, simple, and immediate. While these are not inherently bad, they often times become ends in themselves at the expense of effectiveness. When there is pressure "to do something" it's very hard to argue for an effective plan that is difficult, involved, and long-term while requiring a series of small, subtle, preparatory steps. All of this has a tendency to be viewed by others as inaction. As Gettysburg will show, this assumption that action cloaked in ease, simplicity, and immediacy is good is not automatic. In fact, as with any event, it's at the mercy of the situation, the flow, and the people. Action can be a prelude to disaster especially in the face of unfavorable events.

It's easy to look at the difference between positive and negative aggressiveness as simply the difference between making a good and bad decision, but this ignores the emotional element of aggressiveness that is unquantifiable but very influential. Two people can have the same facts but arrive at different conclusions because of interpretation; interpretations come from emotions. Since having all the facts about anything is impossible, interpretation will always come into play, and thus, emotions such as aggressiveness will always influence interpretation. In its positive form aggressiveness will help us to exceed expectations, but in its negative form it will lay the foundation for disaster.

4. Attractiveness

Another emotion that disrupts a rational calculation about a situation is attractiveness and is the fourth of the five concepts related to the feminine influence that the Gettysburg example will highlight for us.

Again, the force behind it is beauty, but here beauty takes on something more comprehensive and deep than what we see on the surface. In conjunction with aggressiveness, the two can create powerful emotional outcomes that defy reason such as what happened at Gettysburg.

We've already covered much about attraction when we positioned Gettysburg as an example. What we need to cover are the positive and negative forms of attraction and how they relate to the positive and negative forms of aggression. By doing so, we can better spot attractiveness at work in our daily experience.

The reason for extensive time on these examples is to gather the various aspects of attracting so we can more easily see it as an activity or an action, more of a verb than an adjective such as "attractive". Contrastingly, we see pursuit more easily as an activity than we see attraction. When a boy runs after a girl on a playground, we are more likely to view this as an activity on the boy's part than the girl's. The lyrics from two songs help convey the active nature of attraction. Here is the symbolic stanza from "Spider Woman" by Uriah Heep:

I had a Spider Woman and she was so good
She chained me in her web so tight
I lost the freedom of release that night
So I stayed right by her

And two from "Black Magic Woman" by Santana:

I Got a Black Magic Woman
I Got a Black Magic Woman
Yes, I Got a Black Magic Woman
She's got me so blind I can't see
But she's a Black Magic Woman
She's tryin' to make a devil out of me

You got your spell on me baby
You got your spell on me baby
Yes, you got your spell on me baby
Turnin' my heart into stone
I need you so bad
Magic Woman I can't leave you alone

In both of these songs, there is no mention of love but some kind of attraction that causes one to lose control, an attraction we can't easily see. The first song relates this attraction to a spider's web while the second to a spell. The difficulty in seeing a spider web helps make it effective. The connection to a spell is a more direct link to invisibility. Contrast this invisibility with the visible pursuit of the boy in the above example. From the standpoint of making attraction an activity, we would need to consider the girl as having cast some sort of spell over the boy that makes his pursuit of her almost impossible to resist. We could visualize this as pulling the boy along.

Seeing attraction as an activity in this way is very difficult if we are encouraged to see ourselves as having the ability to consciously control our emotions or at least being consciously aware of all our emotions. Under this assumption, the boy chasing the girl is doing so because he consciously decided to do so. Moreover, even though the girl may be attracting the boy, she did not consciously intend to attract the boy.

However, if for the moment we allow ourselves to view this scene through different assumptions, one where our emotions control our thoughts and where we may not necessarily be aware of the emotions driving us, we can more easily see attraction as an activity. For instance, whether we stumble on purpose or by accident, the act of stumbling remains an activity. Likewise, whether we attract intentionally or unintentionally the act of attracting still exists.

Essentially, we're positioning attraction as something irresistible, something beyond our control. We're more commonly aware of these irresistible forces when people suffer from hunger or thirst. Fortunately, many of us have not experienced such extreme feelings, but they can cause any person to do things that he would not normally do. While extreme examples, such irresistibility occurs with other feelings at lower intensities. Conceptually, we are more aware of this than we may know. A common refrain in sales is that people buy emotionally and rationalize their decision. All we're doing is extending the implication behind this refrain to all decisions not just purchasing ones.

Along with emotions controlling our thoughts, goes a question as to whether we're aware of this happening. How can we be aware of something of which we're unaware? What is essentially an emotional decision on our part could only be realized as a conscious decision by us that is unrelated to the aspects of the emotions driving the decision; we may be unaware of them.

Just because we can't feel or sense something doesn't mean it doesn't affect us. We often see this in diseases that go undiagnosed for a long time. If fact, there are sounds and light that can affect us without our knowledge. Infrasound, sounds below the frequency range of our ears, can create nausea in our stomachs. So, what we may consider the flu or bad food may actually be exposure to low frequency sounds that hit us as vibrations that some we can't feel. Typically, these sounds are emitted from construction sites where large equipment is being used. Some animals such as elephants and whales use infrasound for communication. Radiation is a light form that we cannot detect until the damage shows up in the form of various diseases. Everyday, the muscles in our bodies suffer spasms below our sensitivity levels; however, they weaken the muscles nevertheless. Generally, we don't notice them until they grow into bigger knots causing aches, cramps or pulled muscles.

Nature does not have us feel and sense everything consciously. Imagine what would happen if we did! The light our eyes see only covers about two percent of the known spectrum. What would happen if we could see it all? What would happen if we could feel every cell that died in our bodies? Most likely we would suffer from sensory overload. Yet, all these things affect us. If this holds true for our bodies, could it hold true for our minds? Could emotions exist below our sensitivity levels and affect our decisions? While the answer is "yes," it's not necessary for you to believe this now.

The two songs above share this view albeit in a relational sense with a woman. The men's attractions for these women are beyond their control and even defy rationale, since the women do not seem to be returning positive affections for the men. Yet, some kind of attraction exists of which the men are barely aware – a web and a spell. Invisible attractions exist to stir all our emotions. We will look at these more thoroughly when we discuss our business examples of the feminine influence by looking at our needs for long-term security, novelty of experience, and emotional recognition.

At this point, it helps to review Figure 2.17 illustrating the cognitive and intuitive differences between a man and a woman. Intuition and emotions are more associated with women than men; thus, emotional sensitivity to one's self and others falls under the domain of the feminine influence. What we want to do is combine the concepts that Figure 2.17 expresses and the ones we just expressed here with the help of "Spider Woman" and "Black Magic Woman." If emotions exist beneath the radar of our sensitivity and if people are born with varying sensitivity levels, then emotions that reach the awareness level, intuitive level, of one person may not necessarily reach the level of another.

Furthermore, if we look at this empathically, we could have one person who is aware of an emotion affecting a second person but of which the second person is unaware. Anyone who has gone to a massotherapist has experienced this with muscles. The massotherapist is more able to sense damaged muscles in the patient than the patient himself. Looked upon in this light, we could easily see where a woman could have a greater awareness for the emotions stirring a particular man than the man himself.

From this perspective, we can more easily see attraction not only as an activity but also as a consciously applied activity and undetected by the one being attracted. Applying this to our example of the boy chasing the girl, if the girl had a liking for the boy, she may have unintentionally or intentionally dressed to attract his attention. Unintentionally, she could have rationalized this as simply wanting to look nice without being aware of her own emotions of wanting to attract the boy's attention. Intentionally, she may have purposely worn something on which the boy had complimented her earlier.

If we accept the premise of a "woman's intuition" as expressed by Figure 2.17, then at some point we need to consider the implications of this from a practical perspective. What I'm trying to show here with the boy-chasing-girl analogy is a practical implication of that premise; however, there are many other implications more applicable to a business setting that we will explore in the future pages. At this juncture, it's simply important to be open to the possibility of two points:

1. Emotions can affect us without our awareness of them.
2. Others can be aware of an emotion affecting us without us being aware of that emotion or aware that others are aware.

As anyone can feel from these two points, there can be positive and negative consequences. We'll now review the forms these consequences take so that we can begin to crystallize a picture of attractiveness as an active quality rather than an inert one and as a quality with negative aspects as well as positive ones. With the development of this picture, we can begin to focus on expanding beauty, the fundamental force behind attractiveness, beyond a woman to something more along the lines of the spirit expressed in the statement, "The beauty of this situation is . . ." We'll find that the deeper and more sincere the beauty, the more positive she becomes. Conversely, the less she is the more negative she becomes. The difference is analogous to the difference between love and prostitution – deep versus shallow.

To make this analogy work for us it's important to expand beyond lovemaking and sex. In a business setting it's the difference between loving your work and working for money. The first is love while the second is prostitution. Essentially, attractiveness' positive form is qualitative; there is a richness that makes the attraction capable of adding something to the one who is attracted. Its negative form lacks a qualitative aspect or richness that results in an unworthy attraction; yet, an attraction still occurs. It helps to think of this negative form as a distraction – the attraction of a beauty that's only "skin deep" or whose life span is only the moment at hand. In this light, beauty begins to take on the counter role to negative aggression: victory for victory's sake with little regard for what has been won. In their negative form, beauty and aggression are shallow.

We've already talked about the positive forms when we talked about Helen of Greece and the Lady In Black. Their beauty added something to the men's lives in those stories that helped them live and move forward. Again, it helps to think of the vicious nature of life and the world by considering that if a human did nothing he would die. He can only live by doing something such as growing crops, hunting for food, and building shelter or having someone do those things for him. Most likely he will need to do something to earn money or help others. Doing something requires effort, not effortless action. Since a human must apply effort, this implies the existence of a natural resistance blocking his way. Depending upon the resistance's strength, it may require effort on the level of walking through a park or of a Herculean task.

Regardless of the effort needed in the task, there are many tasks requiring effort that cumulatively and relentlessly wear emotionally upon a person. Beauty is what makes all this worthwhile and in nature nothing compares to the beauty in a woman; this is the inspirational aspect of the feminine influence.

From a negative perspective, beauty becomes a distraction because there is no substance – it's a mirage. It's the man who struggles on the desert and is led astray because he sees water nearby only to find it's an illusion. In the movie, *Basic Instinct*, it's Sharon Stone distracting Michael Douglas to the point where he kills his girlfriend. In the battle of Little Big Horn, it's the Indians luring General George Custer into a trap that resulted in the annihilation of an entire union army and the worst military defeat of the Indian Wars. In the movie, *The Sting*, it's Paul Newman and Robert Redford conning a con-man. All of these represent an attraction by something shallow – something that does not help and possibly hurts.

As with aggressiveness, what's important to remember about attraction is that it too is a powerful emotional influence that defies calculation. Any plan or action that does not take these influences into account is sentenced to fantasia.

Emotions are a fact of life; ignoring them is ignoring the facts. Since no one can feel emotions without having the capacity to feel, emotionlessness is impractical because all humans are emotional creatures and empathy is required in order to have access to all the facts. No one can put his feelings aside any more than he can halt the sun's rise. Even if this were possible, empathy would fail to occur because it cannot occur without feelings. If empathy fails to occur, then we are blind to important aspects of others and our world. For these reasons, objectivity is a fantasy. As a result, those who profess objectivity end up operating in the very fantasy world they fear because they attempt to shut down what they perceive as emotional influences.

They fail on two accounts. First, they each make a judgment on what is objective, and second, they all agree to ignore facts that exist.

What is an objective fact? Give this question to a variety of people, and you would receive a variety of answers. Now, there is an argument that would say that even though the answers may not be the same, they may be similar. Let's extend this further and say we have a variety of people evaluate the similarity of answers to this question. How likely would it be that all people would evaluate the answers similarly?

Suppose we go further with this example and have the evaluators determine by a majority, a consensus, or whatever method they choose, what is an object fact. In the whole scheme of life for which we will call this "truth," will this decision matter? Will the universe suddenly conform to our definition of objective? Does it matter whether only one of us or all of us agrees? Will truth suddenly conform to our determinations? In essence, if we answer "yes", then we're all agreeing that the only reason why the sun rises each morning is because we want it to.

Despite this let's say we can determine an objectivity that holds up to truth. Is it the whole truth and nothing but the truth? This is the question underlying our second account for failure. For instance, consider as an objective fact that continuously walking along a path that is obstructed by a tree would eventually cause one to run into the tree. A tree is a tree is a tree. Objectively speaking we could say, "One who does not alter his path that is obstructed by a tree will run into the tree." So what? What does this mean?

If objectivity is the removal of subjectivity and subjectivity is the emphasis of an individual's perspective, then objectivity exists only as an abstraction – a fantasy. In our example, subjective circumstances will make the experience described by this statement different for every occurrence. The meaning of this event will vary according to the person, path, tree, and many other nuances that make up the complete nature of the situation, some covered by the statement and some not. Our objective fact becomes no more than a subset of what actually happens, a subset of the life engulfing the entire event. Suppose the "one" is a squirrel or the "tree" a seedling?

Therefore, we can no more call objectivity true than we can call an arm a person. Without a person an arm has no life; without subjectivity objectivity is dead. Yet, the minute subjectivity invades objectivity, objectivity is no longer objective. In other words, objective facts live in the abstract until they are subjectively interpreted and applied; however, once they are subjectively applied they are no longer objective facts because their individual manifestations will vary each time – no two situations and interpretations are exactly the same.

More importantly, those witnessing an individual event will have different interpretations of the event. For example, the sun rising every morning is a fact, but so what? The *meaning* of the sun rising varies by the individual. Those enduring a drought or a heat wave, will be more inclined to look upon this event negatively while those recovering from extensive rain or cold will look forward to it. In fact, endless blue skies with constant sunshine would mean death. How would we live without rain?

Thus, how can anyone claim objectivity when no two events in the history of life are the same and no two people interpret one event exactly the same. This is why the United States' legal system relies upon a judge to infuse a subjective perspective, an interpretation, upon the blind application of objective law; and why the United States' Constitution preserves this same subjectivity through the protection of individual rights. No one can cling to objectivity without blinding himself to life's truths.

Subjectivity cannot impose itself without the emotions behind it. By its very nature, subjectivity implies emotions. Since feelings thrive under the dominion of the feminine influence, one cannot address the truth of any situation without consideration and appreciation for her. Without her insights, achieving something great will be extremely difficult, and greatness depends upon the interrelationship between aggression and attraction, between masculine and feminine. The strength of these interrelationships depends upon the richness of the beauty in the attracting, similar to what I said earlier about the relationship between the masculine and feminine influence:

> The easiest way to picture this is to say the feminine influence makes the masculine far better, almost super human. If the masculine influence makes the house, the feminine influence makes the house a home.

The other element to add here is the strength or intensity of the aggression or attraction. It's one thing to say something is positive or negative but quite another to gauge the strength or intensity of the positivity or negativity. For instance, what happens when an intensely positive influence comes in contact with a weaker negative influence and vice versa?

We can summarize these interactions in the table of Figure 2.23 that cross-references the positive and negative aspects of both the masculine and feminine influences depending upon which one is more intense. The table speaks of the relationship between the two influences by speaking of the intensity of the masculine compared to that of the feminine. It uses the ">" to identify relationships where the aggressiveness of the masculine, either positive or negative, is stronger than the corresponding attraction of the feminine and uses "<" to describe where it's less than.

	Relationship Balance	Feminine	
		+	-
Masculine +	M > F	Synergy (Rocky)	Discovery (Cinderella)
	M < F	Synergy (Lady In Black)	Ignorance – Distraction (Basic Instinct)
Masculine -	M > F	Conquest – Violation (Hitler)	Conquest – Submission (1984)
	M < F	Discovery (Pretty Woman)	Trap – Distraction (Prostitution)

Figure 2.23

While this table is not comprehensive, it does help us begin to picture the many relationships that occur between the masculine and feminine influence. In this way, it serves as a starting point not only with this journey but in looking at situations we face everyday.

Let's review each of the eight scenarios.

The two in the positive quadrant both picture synergy, but one is greater influenced by the masculine and the other the feminine. The movie *Rocky* helps picture the first while the song "Lady In Black" the second. The first is where the stronger, positive masculine force drives on supported and encouraged by a positive, albeit weaker, feminine influence. The second is where a worn out, positive masculine influence on the brink of desperation is regenerated by a stronger, positive, feminine force. We also see this in Greek mythology where various goddesses assist the efforts of mortal heroes such as Hercules and Achilles.

In the opposite quadrant we have the relationship between the negative aspects of these influences. Where the masculine negativity is greater than the feminine negativity, we get a situation similar to the book and movie *1984* where a big brother rules over a docile population in constant fear of aggression from its enemies. More personally we see individuals with poor self-esteem submitting themselves to someone who can protect them because they cannot, or believe they cannot, provide their own protection.

The movie, *The Burning Bed*, starring Farrah Fawcett demonstrates how the negative form of the masculine seeks to reinforce a negative self-image or compel one on its victim by creating the thought that, "I'm lousy and deserve this abuse; I'm lucky he still wants me around." Where the feminine is weak and ugly in an absolute sense, she will submit to any masculine influence that will have her, no matter how oppressive it may be. In this movie, Farrah did not buy into this and killed her husband, but many times people do not realize as Farrah did that the negative comments delivered by others are nothing more than a way for them to gain our acceptance of their dominance over us or, in other another word, "compliance."

Prostitution describes an intensely negative, feminine influence that overwhelms a weaker, negative, masculine influence. In this picture, beauty is superficial and illusionary so it's a distraction to the point where it becomes a trap, in the case of prostitution it's a legal trap. In movies such as a *Fool for Love* or *Body Heat*, questionable men are lured into undesirable situations because of a woman's attraction. In the first, the man finds himself led astray by a woman who never returns his affection while in the second the man is encouraged by a woman to kill her husband so they could be together.

In the quadrant where the masculine is positive and the feminine negative, there is the opportunity for discovery as symbolized by "Cinderella" when the positive aspect of the masculine is stronger than the negative, feminine aspect. Here the woman discovers a beauty in herself that a man sees. It's the King of England giving up the throne for a common woman. On the other side is a weaker, positive male being distracted through his ignorance of the stronger, negative, feminine influence. We've already discussed this when we talked about the movie, *Basic Instinct*. This is also symbolized by the KGB's attempts to use beautiful women to seduce American diplomats stationed in the Soviet Union in order to blackmail them.

In the quadrant where the feminine is positive and the masculine is negative, we also see discovery but from the masculine perspective. The movie *Pretty Woman*, starring Richard Gere and Julia Roberts, demonstrates how a weaker, negative man can discover his compassionate side through a stronger, positive, feminine influence and achieve growth in his life. It's also represented by the concept of "The Beauty and the Beast" such as the effect a woman has on a giant ape in the story of King Kong.

When the situation is reversed, we have a stronger, negative masculine overwhelming a weaker, positive feminine as symbolized by Hitler. He conjures up visions of taking others by force against their will. Against this kind of masculine force, whereas a weaker, negative feminine influence will show herself in submission, a weaker, positive one will come across as violated – some act she did not want. Any kind of horror movie containing a negative, male stalking an innocent, positive, attractive female also symbolizes this. The movie *Jaws* contains a good example where an early scene has the shark, symbolizing a negative masculine force, attacking and devouring a female swimmer, symbolizing a positive, weaker, feminine force.

The main purpose for running through these scenarios was to give attractiveness more visibility as an action. Someone pursuing another is easier to see than one attracting another. Often we consider attracting as something that simply happens on its own accord; however, anyone who has purposely dressed professionally has worked to make himself more attractive, more appealing. We can extend this to our words, actions, demeanor, and personality.

I addressed this main purpose in a way that encouraged a positive integration of the feminine influence by showing:

1.   How the interrelationship between the feminine and masculine manifest themselves.
2.   The complexity of emotions that can exist beyond what we consider objective.
3.   How strong, positive masculine and feminine influences can generate discovery in the negative.
4.   The positive will not be able to inspire discovery in all negative influences.
5.   A framework through which we can begin to employ the feminine based upon helping others discover themselves.

5. Exists At All Times

The last aspect of the Gettysburg example that we want to explore in highlighting the feminine influence is that conditions will always exist to allow her to blossom.

We've already introduced this concept when we discussed "pursue" and "attract." When pursuit takes place, an attraction must occur; and, when an attraction takes place, pursuit must occur. The key here is remembering that pursuit can happen on many other levels besides physical. In other words, we may not readily see pursuit and attraction at work because it may happen invisibly. We touched on this when we described the male motorist who crashed because a female attracted his attention. Again, in this situation, the female's attraction was unintentional and the male's pursuit was emotional, not physical – he did not automatically turn his car around, pull up to the woman, and introduce himself.

Still, in this example the woman attracts and the man pursues. In the Gettysburg example, the Federal forces attract and the Confederate forces pursue. In both we've associated one aspect (attraction or pursuit) with one entity. The challenge is to show how opportunities always exist for attraction and pursuit in <u>one</u> entity, or in more appropriate terms, how the masculine and feminine influence always exist in one entity. During most of this book, we've associated the masculine influence with a man and the feminine influence with a woman. This is okay in a symbolic sense but not in truth because the masculine and feminine influences exist together not only in each man and in each woman, but comprehensively in each situation, time, group, and idea.

Let's use the Gettysburg example to clarify this challenge. We've already identified that the Confederates pursued Federal troops, but what we need to do now is identify the feminine aspect of the Confederate situation. For instance, what could the Confederates have done to encourage the Federals to attack? What could they have done to distract the Federal forces? Conversely, what is the masculine aspect of the Federals' situation? What could they have done to attack the Confederates or their plan?

In order to show how the feminine influence has the opportunity to partake in any situation, it will help if we expand upon what we've covered with the masculine and the feminine influences. Our focus at this juncture will be historical, methodological, situational, extreme, restrictive, and introductory.

A historical focus will allow us to see how ancient and eternal the feminine influence's participation is in all matters. Methodological will give us a feel on how she is to interact with the masculine influence to navigate life's ocean. Situational will allow us to see the many aspects of any event that offer her participation. Extreme will share with us what happens when the masculine and feminine exist in the extreme and dominate without the other's participation. Restrictive will shed light on the forces that seek to prevent her participation. Finally, since I expand upon each of these throughout the book, our initial focus on these topics will remain introductory and serve as a foundation for elaboration in the future.

Historically, early Chinese civilization first symbolized this integration through the *t'ai chi t'u* as symbolized by Figure 2.24 and are simply identified as the influences of *yin* and *yang*.

Figure 2.24

In effect, this symbol implies that $1+1 = 1$. Through the interplay of two, you get a qualitatively supreme whole, or one. I've chosen a man and woman to represent each part of this whole because I wanted to personify these influences rather than leave them simply as *yin* and *yang*. As we saw earlier with our connotative and definitional discussion associated with Figure 2.20, it helps to associate attributes if we can ask "Is it more associated with a man or a woman?" Through such associations, we can grasp a more powerful picture as to the natures of the masculine and feminine influences. As you will see later, this personification becomes an even more important tool toward successful integration of the feminine influence in business on a practical level. This personification works because within each man and woman, all the qualities exist as represented by the parts of this symbol, and within the union of a man and woman, all the qualities exist as represented by the holistic aspect of this symbol.

On an informal level we see this wholeness from men when they say such things as "I'm in touch with my feminine side (or feelings)" or "I'm a touchy, feely kinda guy." With women the masculine shows itself in everyday talk when they say such things as "I can be a real bitch at times," or "I'm such a brat." In fact, some women even wear T-shirts with "bitch" and "brat" on them. "Brat" is a Russian and Eastern European term meaning "brother" that became popularized here in the early 1900's when many immigrated to the United States.

The words "bitch" and "brat" are a good lead into examining the masculine and feminine influences in a pure sense. We've already hinted at what these are when we looked at the positive and negative sides of both influences moments earlier, so let's extend what we mean by positive and negative.

Positive means that the influence we're examining has its opposite incorporated while negative means it has its opposite unincorporated. Thus, for the positive masculine to exist, the feminine must be incorporated as well, and for the positive feminine to exist, the masculine must be incorporated. One-sidedness spawns the negative of each influence. While we are talking about this condition existing in a single person, we can also extend this concept to situations, things, groups, ideas, and many others. This is why we can claim that wherever the masculine exists conditions also exist to incorporate the feminine and vice versa. The questions become whether we can see this and whether we integrate them.

When we visualize a methodology for the incorporation of one influence into the other, we cannot focus on a balance represented by two equal halves. Figure 2.25 represents this by a dotted line located between the two poles, masculine and feminine. The state of perfect balance is motionless whereas imbalance is motion. Growth cannot occur without motion; thus, a constant effort of balancing an imbalanced situation where the situation is always changing generates growth. In life, the nature of a situation is always changing and never the same, so the optimal balance weaves back and forth between masculine and feminine as shown by the curved line. Some situations favor one influence over another. The only mistake would be to assume one "balance" works for all situations, "one size fits all."

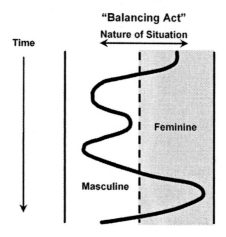

Figure 2.25

Imagine yourself standing on a boat tossing on the sea without any railings to grasp. You would feel yourself balancing from one leg to the other with the motion of the sea. Sometimes you will put more weight on your right leg and others your left. If you insisted on any one condition, you would most likely lose your balance and fall. Balancing your life on life's ocean is very much the same challenge, integrating the left and the right, the masculine and the feminine according to the nature of the situation.

Situationally, our inclination is to look at events too narrowly, generally out of fear for possibly reading too much into them; however, this fear really isn't a danger because there's always more to anything than we realize. What appears on paper always falls short of what happens in truth. Furthermore, having more in front of you about a situation, even if some of it is wrong, is always preferred to missing items even if all the items you do have are right.

Analogously, we can look at it as a builder who is faced with a job whose particulars are unknown but he is offered the choice of one of two piles. In the first pile, everything in it he will need but everything he needs is not there. In the second pile, he has everything that he needs but he won't need everything there. If you were he, which pile would you choose? The danger of reading too much into something is far less than reading too little. What truth presents will always be more than what we realize in our plans.

Thus, it will help to see all that is in an event driving an outcome. By seeing all that is involved, we can begin to see all the aspects through which we can inject the feminine influence. It's important to realize though that even if we incorporate the masculine and feminine in all we do, we may not see the success we necessarily want because outcomes are beyond our control. This does not mean we cannot influence them but it does mean we do not determine their fate. We can no more control outcomes than we can predict the future. Assuming we control outcomes also assumes we can predict the future because if we can control then we can predict.

The reason for this is that there are four fundamental factors around any event that influence the outcome:

- Situation – the nature of the forces involved.
- Flow – the synchronization of the forces and our actions.
- People – the active and passive participants.
- Individual – the person trying to influence the outcome in a particular direction.

The situation involves all the forces with which we must contend, and flow concerns itself with the movement over time of those forces, peaking or ebbing, and our actions. Together the picture is one of appreciating the motion in the ocean; treating any event as a snapshot will incur all the blind spots that any snapshot creates. Everything is in a constant state of flux. The people's skills, abilities, knowledge, intelligence, and courage applied actively or passively affect the outcome. One must not only consider those who are active, but those who are inactive. Finally, interacting with all of these is the individual who created the vision of change and is seeking a particular outcome, making decisions, and applying efforts toward that end.

Of these four, elaborating on active and passive participants is important because inertia is more powerful than negative action and is often overlooked because it does not actively obstruct. The masculine influence is associated with action and the feminine with inaction. The first cannot pursue without being active and the second cannot attract while being active because it's more difficult to catch up with a moving object as opposed to a stationary one. Thus, the masculine will tend to be concerned with only active forces and will prefer passive resistance to active negative resistance. Neglecting inactive participants is akin to forgetting to hoist the anchor before sailing; they are a drag on any concerted action. The masculine influence moves around inertia while the feminine influence is more likely to appreciate the power in inertia because she cannot attract something that does not move.

However, positive and negative actions are related through action itself – they differ in direction. Changing the direction of a negative force is far easier than changing the direction of a stationary one because something that does not move cannot alter its direction. Altering the direction of a negative force requires the application of a series of concentric deflections similar to the way sloped armor deflects a bullet or shell as we see in Figure 2.26.

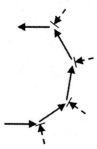

Figure 2.26

By looking at any outcome as a result of these four factors, one can easily see how the deck could be stacked against the person trying to affect the outcome positively. For instance, while all the people may want to address the problem and the flow is right for the best possible result, the situation's nature may be against the desirable outcome because resources are not available. In effect, the *best possible* outcome may still not be equivalent to our *best desirable* outcome. In this case, there may be nothing to do but "ride out the storm."

This example will also help us introduce the extremes associated with the masculine and feminine influences by realizing the reaction of the masculine influence in this situation, without incorporating the feminine, would be "we gota do something" when in fact that would most likely cause disaster. When sailors in the old days of "wood and sail" ran into a storm, they would automatically pull down all sails and drift until the storm passed rather than try to navigate through it. High winds were likely to pull down masts in full sail and create destruction, so when the storm did pass and sailing could occur, the ship would not be navigable because the masts would not exist. In many ways, forcing action where action is useless can leave a work force battered and demoralized so when opportunities arrive that allow for action, folks will have no energy to seize them.

Since we cannot determine outcomes as an individual attempting to influence an outcome, incorporating the feminine with the masculine and vice versa, as shown in Figure 2.25, will give us the best possible approach to any event. In order to grasp this interaction better it will help to see in an extreme sense what happens when we divorce the masculine and feminine from one another.

Generally, without the influence of its opposite to counterbalance it, the extreme for each influence would look something like Figure 2.27

Masculine   **Feminine**
"Killing Machine"   **"Doormat"**

Figure 2.27

Physics states that in a perfect, frictionless vacuum the momentary exertion of any force upon an object will cause that object to move for eternity in the direction of that force. We don't see that in everyday life because there are many restraints such as friction from the ground, resistance from the air, and gravity preventing eternal motion from a momentary force. In the same way we have to consider the very extreme nature of pursuit and attraction without resistance – without limits – because without a counterbalance our initial action in either direction will result in constant movement toward the extreme.

If we applied this concept of extremes to Gettysburg, the Confederates as the attacker would not stop until every Federal soldier was dead, and the Federals as the defender would not even fight for fear of hurting a Confederate soldier. Thus, while it's hard to see the feminine influence at work with the Confederates since they lost the battle and were not in a victor's position, we can see the masculine influence counterbalancing the feminine one in the Federal army. Even though it played the role of defender, the masculine influence manifested himself in the stiff resistance they offered that eventually delivered them victory over the Confederates.

Sometimes we see the masculine influence in its extreme when an army surrenders to a superior force, and the superior force goes ahead and massacre's its opponent despite the surrender. This demonstrates a lack of compassion, a feminine influence, as a restraint to aggression. History is filled with examples. Conversely, we could even carry the extreme of the feminine influence further than we did above by stating that the fear of hurting another would encourage suicide so as not to inflict damage on another. How many folks have committed suicide because they felt it was better for their families and loved ones?

We can now re-design our two-sided arrow from something like Figure 2.28,

Masculine   Feminine
"Aggressive"   "Submissive"

Figure 2.28

to something more along the lines of Figure 2.29 when we incorporate a counterbalance to each influence:

Masculine   Feminine
"Assertive"   "Devoted"

Figure 2.29

The words "assertive" and "devoted" imply something more restrained than "aggressive" and more disciplined than "submissive." Assertive implies that some compassion is involved in pursuit while devoted implies that some selectivity is involved in attraction. The masculine now does not indiscriminately take out its aggression and the feminine does not indiscriminately submit.

This discussion helps us see better how the positive aspects of each influence cannot exist without the incorporation of the other. Since we can see how such incorporation yields the positive and how both can exist in one person, male or female, we can now see better how this can extend to situations, flow, and groups of people, not just ourselves individually.

The last point related to this is that while incorporation of opposites yields the positive this does not mean a balance where both are equal. In fact, quite the contrary, one influence will dominate over the other. In men, the masculine influence dominates while in women the feminine influence dominates. This dominance also relates to situations, flow, and groups of people. Further, the extent of the dominance will vary depending upon the person, the group, the situation, and the time. No set ratio of one to the other works for everything, including an individual.

That's why if a particular situation requires more inaction than action, a person inclined towards action will require coaching on patience while one inclined towards inaction will require coaching on action when it's needed. This is why everyone will receive the statement of "This situation requires more patience than action," differently. One inclined to action may apply restraint and think he is being patient but still may not be applying enough restraint. Likewise, one inclined to inaction may apply even more restraint to the point where inertia comes into play. Communication works best if it is tailored to the individual. As the group expands, so does the likelihood of miscommunication.

None of this is particularly novel, but what is novel is working it into a communication plan. We often lean toward a group meeting so "everyone can hear the same thing" but while everyone may hear the same words (not a guarantee itself) they don't all interpret them the same. When we don't rely on words, typically our next step is to put it in writing and assume that because everyone can now reference and recall the same words that our message will be received the same. At best, most communication plans include group meetings supplemented by written material for discussion. By comparison, how many plans include individual meetings as an element? Could this be why most people feel the best meeting was the one they didn't go to?

At this point, our last focus, before we specifically look at Gettysburg, is the human inclination to restrict the integration of the feminine influence in business. (This actually includes any endeavor but I will limit it to business.) The basis for this restriction is twofold. First, the masculine influence naturally fears the empathic and relational strengths of the feminine, and second, this fear triggers the survival instinct to attack any threat that will encourage her integration.

To help illustrate these points, let's first imagine that you have the opportunity to kill Adolf Hitler without harm to you. You are able to be alone with him, confront him, shoot him, and escape. The question is "Would you be able to do it?" How difficult would it be?

Let's take our previous discussion on the extremes of the masculine and feminine influences and apply them to this situation. From a purely masculine perspective of rational calculation, the task would not be a problem emotionally. There would be no difference emotionally in this pure sense between a man killing Hitler and a robot doing it. Essentially, Hitler is evil and bringing about great harm to the world and yourself so he should be shot. From a purely feminine perspective of empathy and relations, killing Hitler would be akin to killing oneself because empathy is feeling what another feels. In its extreme form, a woman would feel the pain she would inflict upon Hitler, and thus would kill herself as well.

Between these two extremities lie the rest of us, feeling the tension between the two as we face this situation. From the masculine perspective, being unable to carry this out would be a sign of weakness. From the feminine perspective, being able to carry this out would be a sign of cold-bloodedness. The masculine would fear anything that would allow him to be weak while the feminine would fear anything that would allow her to be murderous.

Conversely, this experience also highlights the strengths of the two influences. For the masculine, it's the ability to muster the strength to defend himself against a threat while for the feminine it's the ability to place herself in another's emotional world to nurture someone. More importantly, these strengths help crystallize the conflict between the two that create constraints around integrating the feminine influence.

To be able to place oneself in the emotional world of another is the highest form of intelligence, for it's not one of memorizing information and running through rational calculations and logic but rather one of having insights into others. In business, and other endeavors, this is a valuable attribute because business' major ingredients are relationships, client-employee and employee-manager. The emotionlessness needed to kill another also exposes one to the inability to relate to others. How can you help clients or employees effectively if you cannot empathize with them?

We see this objectification of others in wartime. Soldiers are trained to kill by dehumanizing the enemy and themselves through the objective focus on their mission and purpose. A moment of weakness, as defined by the inability to kill the enemy (or Hitler in our example), will get you killed.

As mentioned earlier, people are born with various emotional sensitivities with women in general being born with more sensitivity than men. For those with less ability, the challenge becomes trying to inspire without empathy. For those with more, the challenge becomes trying to live with actions that hurt others. For those lacking the emotional insight, those with it become a threat, and consequently, vice versa.

One of the ways to defeat a superior adversary is to convince her that what makes her superior is useless so she won't use it. Convincing one not to use the feminine influence is easy because of the word association in Figure 2.20. Believing in an influence that is indirect, intangible, invisible, spontaneous, involved, and subjective requires courage in the face of one that is direct, tangible, visible, planned, simple, and objective. Again, as with the chess players, thinking one or two moves ahead is much easier than seven or eight. Furthermore, those who can do the latter are outnumbered by those who can do the former. Integrating the feminine influence requires a discipline for looking ahead; so likewise, those who can't integrate the feminine with the masculine outnumber those who can, so the additional force of collective thinking, peer pressure, is also at work in encouraging the ignorance of the feminine influence. In many ways, this encourages women to compete as men in the business world rather than rely upon their inherent strengths as women. Thus, women are always playing "away" while men at "home."

All of this is difficult to see if one insists on clinging to conscious thought or even awareness as the basis for action; but, if we assume actions are stirred by emotions, including those of which we are unaware, and then rationalized, then all of this becomes possible under the guise of reasons that have us thinking we're making the best possible decisions when in actuality they're made in response to a threat to our emotional survival.

For example, if I feel threatened by someone's emotional talents to relate to others and am unaware of it, these uneasy feelings could easily encourage me to view that person in a negative light. Uncomfortable with not having a good reason for this feeling, I could easily come up with criticisms such as:

- He's not a team player.
- He's too nice; he can't make tough decisions.
- He doesn't look at things objectively.
- He's negative about important initiatives.
- His contributions really aren't that significant.
- He doesn't understand the way business is.
- His personal feelings get in the way of business.

The criticism itself is not necessarily as important as the fact that there is a criticism. The one's I listed are no better than the ones I did not. Unknowingly, the feeling of being threatened will trigger my survival instinct and encourage me to view another negatively in some way despite him being effective and talented.

Thus, the restrictions preventing the integration of the feminine influence in business when we are capable of doing so are primarily two:

- We persuade others not to integrate her.
- We allow others to persuade us not to integrate her.

On an introductory level, we've laid the foundation to elaborate later on the historical, methodological, situational, extreme, and restrictive aspects of integrating the feminine influence with the masculine and to explore in detail the existence of this integration in our Gettysburg example.

From these discussions and before we return to Gettysburg, let's re-establish the two important points when we try to incorporate the feminine aspect into any situation:

- Allowances for her incorporation exist at all times.
- The allowances we see are constrained by ourselves.

Very simply, the implications are that one can always incorporate the feminine, but this does not mean he will always see how to do this; he may not be able to see it or may not want to see it.

As we just saw, there are many aspects to an outcome – situation, flow, people, and the individual – so there can always exist more than one way to integrate the feminine into our actions. Understanding a little more about battles and some of the specifics around the battle at Gettysburg will help highlight feminine aspects of this event.

As you may recall, the Confederates attacked and the Federals defended. Something to add for our discussion is that the battle lasted three days, and once the Federals established their main position, the Confederates had one major attack each day. Generally, when a fighting unit is battling, whether offensively or defensively, the troops in the unit will position themselves across the terrain from which they will attack or defend; once they've assumed their positions this is called their "line." Tactically, maintaining this line is important so that the troops within it can mutually support one another either on offense or defense. Opposing forces will try to disrupt each other's line so they can destroy their opponent piecemeal. It's very similar to attacking a large business problem by breaking it into smaller parts.

Conceptually, the weakest parts of the line are the ends because the soldiers at these positions only have support from their comrades on one side. These ends are called "flanks" – right and left. For this reason, fighting units try to make sure their flanks receive additional protection in some form such as from the terrain, entrenchments, or additional equipment or troops. Thus, positioning your army's flanks is important. Together, the flanks form two of the three major parts of the fighting unit's line; the center is the third. Thus, the portions of a fighting line are generally described as right, left, and center. Since the center is supported on both sides by the right and left, it's conceptually considered the strongest part of a line. Of course, in actuality, the strengths and weaknesses of a line can vary greatly against this conceptual commentary depending upon the particulars of the situation.

Terrain is a particular that plays a variable, major role. Aspects of terrain that make it an advantage can be negated by aspects that make it a disadvantage. For instance, high ground is an advantage for positioning troops (hence the cliché "take the high ground" meaning taking the advantage) but it can be negated by rocky terrain or heavy woods. At Gettysburg, the Federals positioned themselves on high ground that was advantageous for them. For our discussion we can use the three descriptors we outlined above to effectively segment their line into three parts: right, left, and center. Figure 2.30 diagrams the Federal position, adds the Confederate line, and shows the Confederate attacks for each day.

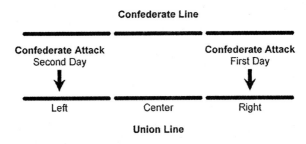

Figure 2.30

I purposely did not show the "Confederate Attack, Third Day" so we can more easily see the feminine influence. First, let's momentarily digress with another example.

If I want someone to say "four," I have many different ways of doing this. I'm going to show two ways of having this occur, one direct and the other indirect. Simply telling someone to say "four" is an example of a direct method, by commanding one to say so. Directness is an aspect of the masculine influence. Conversely, saying "one, two, three" and asking the same person to tell me what he thinks follows is an example of an indirect method. Indirectness is an aspect of the feminine influence as we may recall from Figure 2.20. Either way, the person says "four," but one is more voluntary and interactive than the other is. The approach does not alter what is said, but it does alter how someone feels with what he says. To the masculine influence this is a waste of time; however, to the feminine this becomes the basis for future inspirational actions.

Another example is having someone learn the home state of another person. The direct method is telling that someone the state. The indirect method would entail having him research the residency of this other person's relatives. Finding many relatives living in one state is the basis for an educated guess indicating that state. While this exercise may seem pointless from a practical perspective, it presents the aspect of actively engaging another. Chess players study problems, students take practice exams, and people work puzzles. These mental exercises develop the mind very similarly to the way physical exercise develops the muscles. For chess players and students, this practice gears their minds for actual situations. Integrating the feminine influence will help develop and sharpen the creativity necessary to enhance relationships in business.

Minds and emotions constantly exposed to the direct method of telling eventually atrophy by becoming less sharp and less creative. Look at prison inmates who are routinely told what to do every minute of every day. The strict rules and procedures guiding their lives make independent thought less necessary because everything is taken into account, and the lack of freedom retards their ability to explore their talents unless it can happen within the confines of their cells. Thus, without a need or the access to think creatively, this aspect of their personality atrophies, but for those running the prison the benefit is a malleable inmate population adhering to guidelines that yield expected, inline behaviors.

In business we can see this as a difference between just giving the facts and helping someone arrive at the facts. Analogously, there is a difference between a student being told the outcome of a scientific experiment and having the student run an experiment to arrive at the outcome. In both cases, the student learns the outcome but in the latter, he strengthens his keenness for a method by which he can arrive at future facts on his own. Thus, the more we create an environment like a prison where people are given the facts and commands, the more likely their creativity will suffer because they lose the desire and the keenness to work through the facts and courses of actions on their own. It's the difference between running ten miles and driving ten miles; both have you arrive at the same point but one makes your muscles more viable.

You can also look at this form of indirectness as positioning, encouraging one to think along a specific path without telling him what to think. Some will consider this manipulation, and it is in its negative form; but, likewise the direct method in its negative form can be seen as parental condescendence. There are many variations of this type of positioning on many levels of sophistication. Charades are based upon this by excluding verbal clues. What excitement is there in the game if someone could tell someone to say a particular word? Isn't there more satisfaction for the other person when he finally guesses the right word? Conversely though, what takes more time? What's the difference between these examples and what happens in a casual conversation between a girl and a boy whom she likes when she "nonchalantly" mentions she frequents a particular library on campus over another? Rather than directly asking the boy to join her there, she encourages him to think along those lines for when he plans to study next.

Returning to Gettysburg the question remains "Where did the Confederates attack on the third day?" What's interesting about the question is that the answer really doesn't matter because the feminine influence is in full force regardless. What's important is whether anybody saw it and whether anybody made use of it.

From the diagram, one is inclined to see a blank in the middle where there is no attack. Applying the same type of indirectness existing in the examples above, we can surmise an answer to this question. Reaffirming the three portions of the Federal line , right, left, and center, and the Confederate attacks on the right the first day and on the left on the second; where does our mind tend to gravitate to when considering the question of "What happened on the third day?" From a set of "one, two, three" we only have "one, two" so what's missing? From a set of "right, left, center" we only have "right, left." What's missing here?

At Gettysburg, the Confederate actions led the Federals along the same line of thought and drew their attention to the center. They knew Confederate troops were exhausted from previous attacks on the left and right and knew the Confederates had not achieved victory. If an attack occurred, it would most likely happen in the center. Thus, the Federal forces reinforced the center by adding bulwarks and by moving in reinforcements.

Unlike the girl and boy example, the Confederates did not want the Federals to be where they wanted to attack. Yet, their situation was difficult because in order to reinforce the left or right and launch another attack, they would have had to move troops that might have given away their intentions. Since the Federals had the high ground, they could easily spot just about any large-scale reinforcement of either flank. As it happened, the Confederates decided to "distract" the Federal forces by attacking their right once again without reinforcing their attack and focusing their main effort on a major assault on the center. The result was the decimation of 50-80% of the men in the attacking units on the center and the disabling of the Confederate army for rest of the Civil War. Indirectly, the Confederates positioned the thought in the Federals' minds that the next attack would occur at the center. The masculine aspect of the Confederates actions is their direct attack on the center while the feminine aspect is their indirect action of positioning their next attack in the minds of the Federal commanders. Within the Confederate position, both the masculine and feminine influences existed.

The important point about this aspect of our Gettysburg discussion is the appreciation for the simultaneous existence of the masculine and feminine influences in all events; however, we may not see them and may not act upon them, but they exist together regardless of our awareness. At Gettysburg, the Confederates may or may not have seen how the feminine influence played into their situation; they definitely did not act strongly enough to integrate her. Conversely, the Federals listened to her and acted upon her words by reinforcing the center and by not becoming distracted by a minor, preparatory attack on their right; in this respect these actions were the masculine aspect of their more dominantly feminine, defensive aspect for this battle.

Let's now consider the masculine aspects of the Federal position. The capture and preparation of the terrain by the Federal army is an example of the masculine influence existing along side the feminine in the Federal army. It represents pursuing the development of an attractive position. How is this any different from a woman applying her makeup or seeking a wardrobe suitable for her? Even the word wardrobe is derived from "ward" and "robe." "Ward" has militaristic origins meaning to "guard" or "defend." Dressing up and looking nice are defensive actions designed to attract. Our wardrobe, unless you're James Bond, is not designed to assault others. In many ways, we can also look at it as something that defends us from ridicule by having it conform to cultural standards. Regardless, a purely feminine approach without the masculine would not actively pursue makeup or a wardrobe.

Along the same lines, in the movie, *Footloose*, a girl had her friend research the class schedule and tendencies of Kevin Bacon, the new boy in school whom she liked, so she could arrange (position) "accidental" meetings between the two of them. How is this any different than understanding the tendencies of your opponent or of a situation so you can position yourself in the best possible way to handle them? If we keep in mind that it's best to have someone approach you than to approach him, then positioning is an important concept that encourages this to happen.

As we can see from these examples, there is room to show the existence of both influences within both armies. I'm summarizing the more global aspects, but there are many more than what I discuss and list here. These will at least give a feel for what we're looking:

Confederate army:

- Masculine influence
    - Constantly attacking.
    - Attacking the center of the Federal line when they expected it.
- Feminine influence
    - Creating a pattern to their attacks that allowed extrapolation.
    - Establishing their invincibility in the minds of Federal commanders by their previous string of victories.

Federal army:

- Masculine influence
    - Identifying and preparing the best terrain to defend.
    - Positioning troops on advantageous terrain.
- Feminine influence
    - Constantly defending.

– Allowing the Confederates to further exhaust themselves with their attacks on the third day.

From the Confederates standpoint, they might have tried to find a way to tempt the Federals into attacking; however, as we already saw earlier, the pressures to attack were great. Ironically, after this battle, the depleted Confederate armies became extremely attractive for a Federal attack. Thus, they retreated quickly from the scene on the next day. The Federals could have employed the masculine with an attack, especially on the fourth day as the Confederates retreated; however, here the feminine influence worked for the Confederates by the seeds of doubt she planted in the Federals minds after an embarrassing defeat at Chancellorsville and other Confederate victories prior to that. She caused the Federal army to hesitate in attacking a weakened foe that allowed the Confederates time to escape.

If we go back to our two points about incorporating the feminine influence, we can see them at Gettysburg:

- Allowances for her incorporation exist at all times.
- The allowances we see are constrained by ourselves.

The feminine influence at work for the Confederates is an example of the second. Just because allowances for incorporation of the influence exist does not mean we see them. The more the Confederates attacked, the more likely the Federal commanders were able to see a pattern to them and anticipate them. This is no different than what detectives do when they analyze the tendencies of a serial killer in an attempt to capture him. By anticipating where he may be or what he may do, they are more likely to trap him. Thus, capturing him becomes more likely after his thirteenth killing than after his first or second. The Confederate army did not intend or see the pattern they created; this blindness helped produce a disastrous outcome. Likewise, serial killers do not purposely intend a pattern; yet, they do and, more often than not, are caught. Everyone is blinded to some degree to the patterns they create; this is a testament to the invisibility of the feminine influence at work.

As review, here are the major points we wanted to extract from the Gettysburg example. They will help us explore other examples:

- There is an inherent advantage in having someone approach you over you approaching him.
- Positioning allows the flow of events or personalities to encourage someone to approach you.
- Aggressiveness is an emotion, a compulsion, causing one to approach another.
- Attractiveness is an emotion that encourages one to approach.
- Phenomena allowing the feminine influence to blossom exist at all times.

We've already talked much about how the Confederates were the masculine influence with their attacks and the Federals the feminine with its constant defense. We tried to show the tremendous advantage the defense plays in warfare – having one approach you rather than the reverse and how the Federals maneuvered their forces to make a Confederate attack enticing. As we also saw the emotions of aggressiveness and attractiveness play a role outside of facts and circumstances. Finally, in our most recent discussion, we covered the masculine and feminine aspects of each army's situations to show how the feminine influence exists in all events, and it becomes a matter of whether we see her.

Gettysburg illustrated the feminine influence in a traditional, defensive posture. Our next example will display her in an offensive one.

- Persian Gulf War -

Whereas Gettysburg allowed us to see the more traditional aspects of the masculine and feminine in the form of active and passive, pursue and attract, the second one will show us other aspects that can effect dynamic outcomes. It will highlight the purposeful aspects of the feminine influence so we can see it as something to employ as a strategy.

The challenge is seeing beauty, the force powering the feminine influence, as something active rather than simply passive. Often when we symbolize beauty in the form of a woman, it's easy to superficially view her as something that's either there or not when in actuality beauty is more akin to the work of an artist who creates beauty on a canvas, in stone, in writing, or on the field. From this perspective, beauty has a quality aspect – it's not just doing something but doing it well. In warfare, it's not just winning the battle but doing it well. In this way, we transcend mere effectiveness and enter dynamism.

The aspects of the feminine influence we'll explore in this example are:

1. Dynamic versus effective.
2. How to implement the masculine influence to maximize the effect of the feminine.
3. Indirect activities, ones that appear to have no direct relationship or purpose to the desirable outcome in mind, can strongly influence that outcome.
4. Invisible activities, ones that no one can see, hear, taste, touch, or smell, can strongly influence outcomes.
5. Surprise is a critical element to success because it creates spontaneity – a natural disrupter to plans and scripts.

I will use the land battle from the 1991 Persian Gulf War as our example. Figure 2.31 displays the basic aspects of this battle.

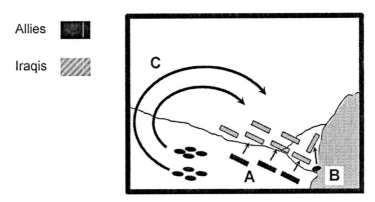

Figure 2.31

There were three major components to this battle:

- **Direct**: Assault upon the Iraqis line to pin it down (A).
- **Distractive**: Feint an amphibious assault supporting attack (B).
- **Indirect**: Assault upon the rear to deliver the main blow (C).

This delivered a quick defeat within four days with less than two hundred Allied casualties out of five hundred thousand involved. In comparison to the Gettysburg example, this has two additional elements, the distractive and indirect.

The distractive aspect we've already talked about when we explored the negative form of the feminine influence. The Gulf War example graphically shows this. The feinting of an amphibious assault prior to and during the launch of the ground war helped to divert attention from other areas and to encourage the impression that the direct aspect (A) was the main assault. We used *Basic Instinct* and prostitution as symbolic representations of this theme. Greek mythology also contains many examples of women distracting men that resulted in their deaths and destruction of them and their ships.

The indirect aspect we've not discussed except to introduce it with the attraction concept. In this battle, it's the long way around. If a straight line is the shortest distance between two points, then it represents direct and anything else is indirect. The purpose of the distractive (B) in this battle was to encourage the Iraqi's to think the Allies were launching a direct attack (A) by appearing to support that effort.

We can link indirectness to the feminine influence because attracting is indirect. Directness is going after what you want; indirectness is encouraging what you want to come to you. We can easily see how someone could "work up a sweat" while in pursuit of something, but this is harder to see with attraction. For instance, it's easier as a sales person to go after a prospect than to have the prospect come to you. Likewise, to capture a deer one can set a trap or shoot it, but it's quite another thing to have the deer walk up to you.

We can also look at the indirect as having a qualitative aspect that the direct lacks. In both of the above examples, the first method is direct while the second is indirect; the second requires something more – this is the qualitative aspect. Whether they are prospects or deer, having them approach you is more difficult to do but requires less sweat. While the outcome of pursuit or attraction is the same, a man and a woman getting together, the qualitative aspect of attraction will generally assign a higher qualitative aspect to the attractor than the pursuer. Compare the qualitative aspects of walking up to the President and asking for his autograph to his knocking on your door and offering it to you. The first is pursuit and the second is attraction – quality goes with the latter. Quality's importance is that it becomes the foundation upon which one launches beyond effectiveness and enters the realm of dynamism.

1. Dynamism

Dynamism is rooted in the fact that life offers far more than what we can consciously absorb.

Take for instance any scene you are observing. I'll use a forest for my example. If you stand in this forest and attempt to take in every aspect of that scene, you would not be able to reproduce what you saw on a sheet of paper. Even if I allowed you the luxury of a video recorder to record what you saw, you would still be unable to reproduce the scene. If you were really able to do this, then any person experiencing your reproduction would be able to feel at that moment that they were standing in the same spot you were. All the sights, sounds, smells, tastes, and touches you experienced from that scene cannot be captured and delivered all at once upon someone as they were upon you at that time. You took in the entire scene visually at once; a video recorder spreads the entire scene out over a few seconds depending upon how fast you scan the surroundings.

Furthermore, our discussion of this example doesn't even consider all the activity going on that we cannot sense. For example, virtually all the insects in our forest scene are working undetected by us. We have little awareness for all that is happening in the vegetation. In fact, there are people who devote their entire lives trying to appreciate matters such as these. Moving deeper into the scene there are aspects related to the sun, wind, water, and weather that we have not even touched upon except to say that the sun shined, the clouds covered, or the rain fell.

We almost come in contact with this condition everyday, especially if we listen to music on compact discs. The electronic methodology behind the processing of music recordings stems from recording devices being much more sensitive than our conscious hearing. What these devices record in twenty seconds will create an electronic file roughly equivalent to what you will find from a three to four minute song on a compact disc. The process by which the original file is shrunk from its voluminous size includes the elimination of sounds your conscious ear does not pick up. Thus, what the disc plays isn't the same as what everyone heard when the musicians played in studio. This is analogous to our forest scene because the sounds life delivers are far more than what we can consciously absorb.

How we translate this to business is this: what life offers is far more than what we can plan. This occurs because planning is a conscious activity no better than our attempt to consciously record the scene we envisioned. To a large degree, planning is far tougher because not only are we trying to take in the moment but we are also trying to anticipate the future.

We can express this relationship between life and a plan through Figure 2.32.

Figure 2.32

Thus, the more likely we restrict ourselves to our plans the more likely we are to miss out on the dynamic aspects of life that arrive to us in the form of opportunities we don't expect. Business is a part of life, so it's by no means excluded from this phenomenon.

To help expand our introduction into dynamism, we need to explore some conscious criticisms that arise when we attempt to be dynamic. By examining some of the countervailing forces opposed to dynamism, we can have a better feel for when we are in its presence. Unfortunately, even though conceptually dynamism has a positive connotation that encourages people to say, "Yeah, I'm all for that," in practice it can be very disturbing to some because dynamism will most likely disrupt the status quo, the normalcy that eventually precedes decline.

Figure 2.33

We can represent normalcy or the status quo by the left diagram in Figure 2.33 and dynamism by the right. Whereas we have "smooth sailing" on the left, we have periodic, dynamic bursts of energy on the right followed by smoother periods of accommodation, rest, and preparation for the next burst. To those who prefer the comfort, stability, and normalcy delivered by the left diagram, the right will most likely appear as a series of dangerous disruptions. To these folks, dynamism is dynamite. The sample criticisms we'll review around the battle plan of the Persian Gulf War could also be used by those on the left whose status quo is threatened by what the right diagram could do.

What's also important to realize about Figure 2.33 is that the diagram on the left represents an electrocardiogram reading from a dead person, "flat line", and the right one represents a reading from a resting, healthy person. The left represents the inherent decline involved in merely being comfortably effective at minimizing "disruptions" or "surprises" while the right represents the inherent vitality of pumping dynamic actions throughout a business' circulatory system. By looking deeper into the right electrocardiogram at a single heartbeat, we can see that the most dynamic action is only about fifteen percent of the entire duration of the heartbeat; little over half of the entire period is spent in a state similar to the "flat line" one. The balance includes the heart's preparatory and conclusional actions around the dynamic one. Additionally, we find that the entire variance of this one dynamic action is about six times the variance of the other two actions. These two aspects highlight dynamism's differentiation and duration relative to the "normal" state of affairs.

In addition to helping convey dynamism, examining the potential criticisms of the Persian Gulf War battle plan will help us lay the basis for discussing dynamic versus effective in the workplace. We will cover four criticisms:

- Splitting of forces (resources).
- Taking the long way around.
- Takes too much time.
- Too complicated.

Because this plan worked so well, it's easy to think "Why wouldn't someone use this all the time," but a major concern if it does not work is the splitting of the allied force. The Iraqi's could be in position to fight the Allies piecemeal. More importantly, if they were able to accomplish this, the allied units would be very far from one another. In fact, some of the allies in "C" were anywhere from 50 – 100 miles from the nearest Iraqi unit and almost 300 miles from the main Iraqi buildup in front of Kuwait City.

For those who favor a simple, direct approach this plan is definitely taking the long way around. There were already significant allied units only 50 miles from Kuwait City. Why do we want to send units on a journey up to 500 miles to get to the same place? Again, qualitative aspects enter the picture by segregating effectiveness from just getting the job done and dynamism from effectiveness.

Along with this is the objection of taking too much time. While we can easily see the time element in the difference between fifty miles and five hundred miles, what is not included in this diagram is the tremendous bombing campaign that ran a couple months before the initiation of the land forces. Why do we have to spend this entire time bombing? We're technologically superior; why wait so long? Again, qualitative aspects enter.

Lastly, there are far more moving parts to this plan than a direct assault. Coordination is more difficult. This is a far more involved plan than merely sending troops ahead for the attack. Thus, the criticism here could easily be that this plan is "way too complicated." "We need to keep it simple" could easily be a rallying cry to eliminate some of the parts to favor a direct assault.

The key point to remember is that there's a vast gulf between being merely effective and being dynamic. Why be content with a single or a double, if you have the opportunity to hit a home run? The Persian Gulf battle plan allowed the allies not only to push the Iraqi's out of Kuwait, but to completely surround their forces, prevent their escape, and to have a stronger negotiating position. There was even an opportunity to move onto Baghdad directly without opposition from the main Iraqi force.

Exploring these criticisms helped us begin to connect the introductory discussion on dynamic versus effective to the business environment by showing the potential reactions one might see when dynamism is present. We also saw a little more into dynamism's qualitative aspects by seeing how we do things matters outside of their results. For instance, suppose the Allies could still have won with a direct assault on the Iraqi army without experiencing any more cost in time or casualties. With all else being equal, is it better to take a creative or standard approach? A dynamic or an effective approach? With the former, you have at least shown you're capable of creativity and dynamism. What is more attractive, creative or standard, dynamic or effective? What is more revered, more intimidating?

We can make an effective argument around the point that the creativity surrounding the Persian Gulf War battle plan set the stage for success in the recent invasion of Iraqi. After experiencing the events of the Persian Gulf War, would Iraqi soldiers be more or less inclined to take more seriously American military ingenuity? Would the strength of their resistance increase of decrease? How you approach even the most mundane activity can build and enhance one's attractiveness. Some people call this "style."

The Persian Gulf War and Gettysburg graphically highlight by their battle plans the difference between dynamic and effective. While the Federal forces turned the tide of the Civil War at Gettysburg, the war still lasted another two years as they sought to grind out a victory by wearing down the Confederates. In the Persian Gulf War, this battle caused surrender in three days. Employing the feminine influence is more likely to encourage dynamic results to occur and dynamic emotions in the troops and leaders for the next task.

Why is dynamism important? Let's attempt to answer this in a way that firms the connection to the business environment. Basically, it encourages one to go beyond merely doing the job to doing it well; it takes effectiveness to a higher level. Dynamism's importance to business stems from differentiation being a key ingredient to business growth. It's hard to differentiate yourself if you're doing what everyone else is doing in the way everyone else is doing it. How can you be dynamic and like everyone else at the same time?

Thus, only the dynamic has the regenerative power to allow a business to thrive beyond a normal lifespan. As we will see in the next section, everything has a life cycle to it – a rhythm. Businesses are no different. Ineffectiveness causes an early death, and effectiveness brings about a natural lifecycle; however, dynamism allows for rebirth. Creativity brings about creation. An effective oak tree will live out its full life, but a dynamic one will live on in the acorns it drops into the soil. Its legacy, albeit in a different form, continues. We can also refer to this as the family tree whose regeneration comes about through procreation – the union between man and woman.

Business relationships contain the fundamental principles of personal relationships. Businesses will continue to live on through the dynamic, creative energies derived from the integration of the masculine and feminine influences in the form of new methods that will allow their relationships with clients and employees to continue beyond normalcy – normalcy as comfortable effectiveness. This state will retard regeneration because it avoids the pain inherent in giving birth to new ideas, new ways, new attitudes, or even newborns. Life's continuation, whether for a species or a business, cannot occur without this birthing activity. More importantly because it connects to this book's theme, the birth of newness in a masculine environment cannot occur without the feminine influence.

2. Implementation

By using the Persian Gulf War example we can begin to strengthen the bond among dynamism, the feminine influence, and business. I'll do this by introducing the concept of implementing the feminine in conjunction with the masculine and by introducing some of its practicality from a strategic, business perspective. We'll cover more practicality in the Strategy chapter of this book.

Integrating the masculine and feminine influences so one can create some of the conditions we've discussed cannot happen until there is an appreciation on how to employ the feminine. Business, because of its masculine nature, will tend to employ the masculine more regularly and overlook the feminine, a fundamental perspective of this book. How we employ the feminine influence is related first of all to how we employ the masculine. In the Gulf War example, "A" represents the employment of the masculine influence. Here, it is secondary to "C" representing the main strike force. Why worry about "A"? Why not focus all our forces on "C"?

This question addresses the dependent nature of the feminine influence upon the masculine. While Gettysburg is an example of a pure masculine assault upon the Federals by the Confederates, it's important to notice how the masculine can occur without the feminine while it's almost impossible for the feminine to occur without the masculine. In the Persian Gulf war, without "A" "C" could not happen because the Iraqi's would simply turn and fight "C" and change a feminine indirect assault into a masculine direct assault. This is why in military jargon, "A" is often referred to as the "pinning" force.

A simple analogy is the hammer and anvil. The hammer only works because we pin an object to the anvil. Without the anvil, the hammer would simply hit the object through space with far less alteration of the object. Without the hammer, simply striking the object against the anvil would not meet with much success either. Not only would the overall force be less, but we would also have less control to shape the object as we wished.

As with the anvil, "A" is not the force doing the damage, but it is providing the stationary resistance to "C", the hammer. "A" can work without "C", but with only moderate results. "C" cannot work without "A" for it becomes no better than "A" once the Iraqi's turn and fight. To refer back to another analogy: "A" is the house while "C" makes the house a home. You cannot have a home until you first build a house. We can see a similar relationship in our bodies between our bones and muscles; our muscles latch onto the firmness of our bones in order to move. Without our muscles, our bones would allow us to retain some semblance of a human form, but without our bones our bodies would shrivel into a pile of tissues and water incased in skin. In this way, our muscles are more dependent upon our bones than the reverse in maintaining the human form, but action cannot occur with the muscles.

From a business perspective, we find that we cannot employ the feminine until we allow the masculine to establish the objective. The key variation is that the objective is secondary to pursuing dynamic outcomes. Objectives become the bones upon which our efforts hinge to capitalize on opportunities that arise. Seizing opportunities becomes paramount to fulfilling objectives. Because planning, setting objectives, managing to objectives, and evaluating against objectives are so prevalent in business, we will devote some time in exploring the implications behind connecting our business activity so closely to the objectives in a plan.

Often we get caught up in thinking of objectives one dimensionally: "If the objective is 10, then the dynamic is 20." Fortunately, life is multi-dimensional so Figure 2.34 presents a better picture of this.

Figure 2.34

"A" represents the traditional picture of objectives: solid is the objective and dotted is the dynamic. "B" more closely represents reality where the dynamic could take us much further in a totally different direction. What occurs is often very different from the plan. Many times, it's even better. We could even enhance this picture by adding depth and time to height and width to arrive at the four dimensions we regularly consider. This is the difference between a simple objective to see ten professionals in the next month and a result of seeing twenty executives. While the original objective was not achieved, something of possibly more importance was which was not in the original plan. This is how one can succeed and still be a failure.

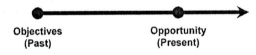

Figure 2.35

Dynamism is hard to achieve with a rigid adherence to objectives. The various aspects of an outcome, the situation, flow, people, and the individual cannot be formatted to accommodate the uncertainty of the future; adherence to objectives in the face of unpredictable, unplanned occurrences is akin to sentencing someone to live in the past as Figure 2.35 seeks to demonstrate. It's the difference between running a client meeting strictly according to the agenda and allowing flexibility to maximize effectiveness; yet, many employees are evaluated today based upon objectives set a year or more in the past.

The initial counter argument to this is typically that no manager would want an employee to pass up an opportunity to make the company more money while another is that if the employee runs across an opportunity he can always talk it through with his manager. Initially, this observation doesn't seem to offer much new, but when we look at their implications in the light of every day practicality, these arguments are esoteric.

At this time, we need to delve more deeply into the practical forces behind objectives that encourage dispassionate relationships between employees and managers. Dispassionate employees are far less likely to be a dynamic influence than passionate ones. What propels this emotionless effort is the primacy of rules over people and consequently over relationships. The tension between these two forces has been with us for thousands of years.

Take a robot. It operates through its programming logic, a complex set of rules that govern what it will do in various situations. Since a robot cannot think and feel like a human, driving a car is extremely difficult – from a practical perspective, impossible. To further complicate things, life tends to generate unique circumstances everyday; no two sunrises, no two days, no two people are ever exactly alike.

The same logic in two separate robots will most likely generate the same actions. The same computer software in two separate computers will most likely have the same result. If life generates a unique situation, it's far more likely that a human would be better able to deal with it than a robot. Most likely, the robot will error simply because it was not written a program (by a human no less) to handle the situation. Thus, when a robot or software can't address the situation at hand, we generally go ahead and reprogram it so it can. Often, the variable situation is so small that we sometimes call it a "bug." This usually means someone has to write a small change to the robot's or software's program.

Rules for humans work very much the same way. If a situation arises that generates a problem for one or more other humans, most likely we will write a rule for ourselves that will govern that situation for its repeat occurrence. Similarly again, often the change is so minor that we only need to write a small modification, an amendment.

As a result of life's many variables, immense programs with uncountable rules fill computers so they can address a variety of situations that humans throw at them. For a robot, rules in the form of programs have primacy because without them, they would not work. Furthermore, since they cannot emotionally feel, people and their relationships have no meaning to them. A computer cannot experience love, friendship, anger, sadness, or happiness. For this reason, all they do must be determined by the rules that govern them because they cannot feel the difference between helping us and hurting us. A robot will always place rules above people because it can live by nothing else.

Let's now take a closer look at the underlying influences behind objectives.

The primacy of objectives over opportunities will influence employees by creating or reinforcing four major conditions among employees that entrenches and solidifies normalcy in the client-employee relationship, and thus in a business, over the long-term:

1. "Tunnel vision" syndrome – an inability to view a client holistically because that view is restrictively influenced by how the client's situation fulfills objectives.
2. Traumatic failure syndrome – an inability to see opportunities in mistakes because one is so engulfed by the mere fact he made a mistake.
3. Rational avoidance syndrome – the ability to come up with sound reasons why an opportunity is not worth the effort.
4. Habitual standardization syndrome – the ability to determine what unique aspects of a client's situation can be segregated to fit him into a standard way of doing business so routine client experiences prevail over dynamic ones.

The question that uncovers the negative implications that objectives' primacy creates is:

Which is more important: achieving objectives or seizing opportunities?

Contemplation of this question makes one realize that opportunities help bring about the achievement of objectives but objectives do not help bring about the seizing of opportunities. Objectives only encourage the seizure of opportunities that fit the objectives. Thus, what we have is a situation where objectives are a subset of opportunities as seen in Figure 2.36, a diagram that capitalizes on what we've just learned from Figure 2.32 by refining its concepts.

Opportunities ⟶   ⟵ Objectives

Figure 2.36

The main reason for this situation is that there is no possible way objectives can account for every possible opportunity that may arise. Some of these opportunities may include new avenues of growth for which the business today may only have a nominal or non-existent investment. Essentially, objectives' primacy assumes that we are fully aware at anytime of all opportunities now *and in the future* as Figure 2.36 illustrates.

We can extend these implications further to show their manifestation on daily basis:

1. Yearly we establish objectives to grow the business.
2. For each objective we formulate a plan intended to achieve it.
3. A plan consists of a series of executable steps.
4. By executing each step, we execute the plan.
5. Objectives and plans are formulated before they're implemented; our actions today are evaluated by what was documented in the past.
6. We based objectives and plans upon predictions and assumptions of what we think would happen in the future.
7. No one can predict every single event of the future; he will incorrectly predict some and will miss others altogether.
8. As a result of #6 and #7, nothing we formulate today will effectively account for every opportunity that the future delivers; our formulations will contain some incorrect assumptions and overlook others.
9. Therefore, if we act with strict adherence around our objectives and plans, we will almost always fail to be effective.

Seizing opportunities is more likely to dynamically drive a business than achieving objectives which are more inclined to make a business, at best, merely effective.

Let's consider three situations that will allow us to bring this discussion down to an extremely tactical level:

Situation #1

A manager and an employee formulate an agenda for a meeting with a client that the employee will execute. The manager will not be in attendance at the meeting. Will success of the meeting be determined by how closely the employee completes the agenda or by how effective the client feels the meeting was?

Situation #2

A manager discusses with an employee the potential for selling a new product introduction to a client. The employee agrees to make this item part of the agenda for the next meeting with the client. During the actual meeting, the client begins discussing some disturbing problems involving a relative in his business. What course of action will the employee follow? Will he continue to purse the original objectives for the meeting and discuss the new product offering or will he risk consuming the time allocated for the meeting exploring another area that will possibly postpone this discussion until another time?

Situation #3

A manager takes a phone call late Friday from a client who is requesting a change to his order because the employee handling the account was out of the office and the client's request had some urgency. Essentially, the client is increasing his shipment of product "B" and reducing product "A". The manager, who is leaving for vacation next week, leaves a voicemail message for the employee stating that he promised the client to make the appropriate alterations to his order by Tuesday's deadline. The action around which to execute is "complete alterations to the order by Tuesday."

The problem that surfaces is that the changes to the order would trigger a shortage in product "A" for the client in the future unless the employee's company agreed to inventory them for an extended period or to alter its production schedule and impact other clients. Last year, a shortage in this particular product was a sensitive issue to the client when he wasn't properly informed of all his delivery and production options. After reviewing the client's situation further when he returns, the employee discovers that he could still have the client's purchase order meet its overall cost if the client permitted a cut in a different product "C" rather than "A". Even though this would create the same problem for "C", it's more of a secondary product than "A", plus the employee potentially has another client who may be looking for more of "C".

The employee leaves voicemail messages for both his manager and the client recommending the alternative but receives no response from either by Monday when he must make a decision. Does the employee risk upsetting the client through a shortage in his more primary product "A" or does he risk upsetting the manager by not following his instructions? Did the client understand all his options? Did his manager already review them with him?

Now let's go from the extremely tactical to the strategic by considering the table below in Figure 2.37 which compares ten various outcomes (OUT) versus a plan (PLAN) containing four separate objectives (A+B+C+D) formed at the beginning of the year. A time frame (T) of ten months is set aside to achieve the objectives, and an expected effectiveness (E) for the entire plan is set at 100%. Hypothetically, we're allowing ourselves the luxury of replaying the year ten different times to extract ten different outcomes where we examine what objectives were reached, their effectiveness, and the time required. For each outcome we then evaluate the employee according to the objectives he achieved for the year. I've also provided some clarifying comments for each outcome. Since the first outcome is the plan itself, it becomes the benchmark by which we judge the various outcomes that reality generates.

For example, OUT #1 (Outcome #1) shows the employee achieving objectives A+B+C+D in ten months with 100% effectiveness, matching in every respect what the plan expected. Consequently, the employee's evaluation is "Successfully achieved all objectives." Essentially, reality matches what we planned. OUT #2 is very similar to #1 except that the employee needed to accomplish another set of actions (X) in order to achieve the other objectives in the plan within the time frame expected. Again, even though the employee required another set of actions to accomplish this, he still achieved all the objectives so his evaluation is "Successfully achieved all objectives." This could easily be a situation where reality demanded more than the plan expected; we overlooked an objective that the employee needed to achieve the effectiveness we expected.

OUT #3 touches on the question begged by #2: What happens when the employee achieved all the objectives but the desired effectiveness failed to materialize? In this case, we failed to identify all the necessary objectives to achieve the desired effectiveness. This could happen for any number of reasons (i.e. economic, industry specific) outside of our and the employee's control. Nevertheless, the employee would receive an evaluation of "Successfully achieved all objectives." How accountable is he for things we did not work into his objectives to be successful?

OUT #4 and #5 show the substitution of various sets of actions (X in #4 and X+Y in #5) by the employee to be effective at his job. Based upon what reality demanded, the employee needed to ignore objective "C" and substitute other actions to reach the same effectiveness in the same time frames. Unfortunately, because objective "C" was not achieved, the employee failed to achieve an objective.

Various Outcomes Versus Plan

OUT	Objectives Reached	T	E	Evaluation	Comments
PLAN	A+B+C+D	10	100	Benchmark	These are the objectives by which we judge and evaluate the other outcomes.
1	A+B+C+D	10	100	Successfully achieved all objectives.	Reality accommodated the objectives originally stated in the plan. Effectiveness met within time frame.
2	A+B+(X)+C+D	10	100	Successfully achieved all objectives.	Reality required the completion of one additional set of actions (X) not originally stated in order to meet plan.
3	A+B+C+D	10	50	Successfully achieved all objectives.	Successfully achieved every objective; however, reality only delivered half the expected effectiveness.
4	A+B+(X)+D	10	100	Failed on one objective.	Reality required the substitution of one set of actions for one plan objective (X for C). Overall effectiveness achieved within time frame.
5	A+B+(X+Y)+D	10	100	Failed on one objective.	Reality required the substitution of two sets of actions for one plan objective (X and Y for C). Overall effectiveness achieved within time frame.
6	A+B+(X)+C+D	12	150	Failed on achieving objectives within time frame.	Reality allowed for the completion of one additional set of actions (X) not originally stated in the plan to deliver effectiveness 50% over that expected in the plan; however, this necessitated taking an additional two months to accomplish.
7	A+B+(X)+D	12	150	Failed on one objective and time frame.	Reality allowed for the substitution of one set of actions for one plan objective (X for C) that delivered effectiveness 50% above that expected in the plan; however, this necessitated taking an additional two months to accomplish.
8	A+B+C+D	15	100	Failed on achieving objectives within time frame.	Reality required 50% more time than allowed in the plan.
9	A+B+(X)+(Y)	10	200	Failed on two objectives.	Reality allowed for the substitution of two set of actions for two plan objectives (X for C and Y for D) that doubled effectiveness.
10	(X)+(Y)+(Z)	5	200	Failed on all objectives.	Reality presented three opportunities that proved twice as effective in half the time expected by the plan.

Figure 2.37

OUT #6 and #7 deal with the theme of the employee achieving higher than expected effectiveness in longer time frames by either adding or substituting other actions (X). In both cases, he fails to achieve his objectives within the time frame. In these cases, if there were clearly defined time frames by which he needed to achieve these objectives, then we could easily evaluate him as having achieved no objectives at all.

OUT #8 is related to #6 and #7 except that the employee doesn't need to add other actions in order to be effective. He just needed more time. Yet, because he did not achieve the objectives in the stated time frame, he fails; however, how much consideration do we need to apply that perhaps we misjudged the time necessary to accomplish these objectives? Did reality contain something we did not expect?

OUT #9 and #10 concern themselves with higher than expected effectiveness from the employee by substituting other actions for his objectives (X+Y in #9 and X+Y+Z in #10). In both cases, he doubled his effectiveness on the job, but his evaluation is that he failed in meeting all of his objectives. How certain are we that the objectives we gave him were the right ones?

These last two outcomes may beg the question, "Why would anyone penalize an employee for not achieving an objective if he were more effective at his job and did it within the time frame?"

The problems engulfing this question surface when we move these ten outcomes from the abstract to the practical. Conceptually speaking, not too many managers would penalize an employee for finding ways to be twice as effective at his job despite not achieving one or more objectives. What may be hard is trying to visualize how an employee could be twice as effective in half the time without achieving any of the objectives in the plan as OUT #10 suggests.

For the moment, even though it's unlikely let's say it could happen. After all, it's not unreasonable to do this because we're also assuming we could do a few other things:

1. We are able to measure an employee's entire effectiveness (E) on the job.
2. We are able to anticipate every event the future holds and come up with a plan (PLAN) that contains the necessary objectives to capitalize on those events.
3. We are able to determine for each of these objectives the amount of time (T) required to fulfill them.
4. For each of the above points we are not only able to do them, but we also do them correctly.

The real problem with the discussion I've just presented around the information in Figure 2.37 is that I'm assuming we can do everything implied in it. I've assumed there is no uncertainty around any of the outcomes – essentially, we're in total control of our destiny. Let's revisit a few of the outcomes by assuming the above points (1 – 4) are false; we are not able to do the things in #1, #2, or #3 and we are capable of making mistakes with regard to #4.

For instance in OUT #4 the employee substitutes a set of actions "X" for the plan's "C" and he achieves the job effectiveness expected from the plan (100). If we cannot measure his entire effectiveness on the job, the rating he earned for effectiveness is purely a guess. The key question is "Whose guess is it?" Suppose it's the employee's and our guess is around 80. What we could say to him is that if he had done "C" rather than "X" he would have been more effective.

Similarly with OUT #9 where the employee substitutes "X+Y" for "C+D" and achieves double the effectiveness, if the effectiveness rating of 200 is his, then ours could be quite different. In the whole scheme of things, "Who's right?" Yes, the rules say because of our position we are, but there is a difference between being right according to the rules and actually being right. According to the law a pedestrian has the right of way, so if he's hit and killed, the law states that he was right in crossing the road; however, was he "actually right" in his decision to cross?

Still, let's stop here and for the moment not even bother with who's right. Let's consider first whether we're even able to comprehensively measure someone's total impact on a business.

Since business is a part of life, it must live by life's rules. One of life's rules is that much of life is immeasurable. Now, this doesn't prevent us from attempting to measure it, but the question becomes "How accurately does our measurement reflect life?" For instance, the love between a man and a woman is immeasurable as is true for many interpersonal relationships. We can attempt to measure it by asking men and women, on a scale of one to ten, how much they love their partner, but what does this actually tell us? If we continue this with other relationships such as that between an employee and clients, we could ask the clients, on a scale of one to ten, how much they like this employee. Why would this work any better than with the relationship between a man and a woman?

In order to avoid such difficult measurements, let's say we restrict our evaluation only to things that we can quantify. What guarantee do we have that these metrics represent the most important aspects of the job? What would happen if sports teams only evaluated talent and players on their statistics? Or, are we just listing them as objectives just so we can have something that is easily measurable? In effect, we can use Figure 2.32 here as well with some modifications because what's measurable is always less than everything.

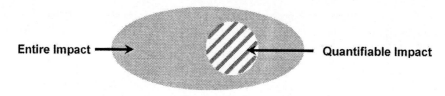

Figure 2.38

We can take this diagram and merge it with Figure 2.36 to arrive at Figure 2.39.

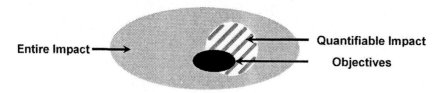

Figure 2.39

Our objectives for an employee will usually contain some quantifiable items and some unquantifiable ones. Since a plan can never encompass everything that happens in reality, objectives cannot encompass everything that eventually becomes an employee's contribution to the business.

If we further restrict objectives to only what is quantifiable, then we further deal with someone's entire impact to the business in piecemeal fashion. Thus, with the primacy of objectives comes an employee's tendency to restrict his entire business contribution to what is stated in the quantifiable part of the objectives. As the emphasis on holding that employee accountable for objectives in a plan increases, his holism toward the business decreases; his focus will be on him and his job, not the business. As a result, with the primacy of objectives also comes a primacy on "what's in it for me" by the employee.

Thus, the fundamental difference that occurs with planning objectives when integrating the feminine influence from an evaluative aspect is our focus on *what happened* not what was *supposed to happen*. Again, further developing upon the diagram I introduced in Figure 2.32 we can now understand that what happens will always be far greater than our conscious ability to develop expectations around what is supposed to happen. At some point, we will even find that those expectations begin to have no relationship to reality whatsoever as our revised Figure 2.36 now shows as Figure 2.40

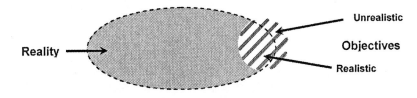

Figure 2.40

At this point, the whole evaluative aspect of objectives begins to "lose touch with reality" by focusing on what should have happened rather than what actually happened because the conversation now turns to things that don't exist; we attempt to judge reality against something non-existent under the guise of "it should have happened."

This becomes especially precarious after consideration of the scenarios in Figure 2.37 because we're assuming we are in total command of these four points:

1. We are able to measure an employee's entire effectiveness (E) on the job.
2. We are able to anticipate every event the future holds and come up with a plan (PLAN) that contains the necessary objectives to capitalize on those events.
3. We are able to determine for each of these objectives the amount of time (T) required to fulfill them.
4. For each of the above points we are not only able to do them, but we also do them correctly.

The challenge then is not to evaluate actions against what should have happened but against the broader perspective of did they help the business. To relate this stronger to business, imagine you own an apple orchard that grows red apples and you have four employees. You assign to each a corner of the orchard with the objective to pick a bushel of red apples.

When each returns to examine the results to find that the first employee has a bushel of red apples exactly as you expected; however, each of the other three had varied results. The second employee returned with yellow apples, the third with green, and the fourth returned with only half a bushel of red apples.

Based upon these results, only one employee met the objective; however, upon closer examination you realize an opportunity each of the other three created for you. With the second and third employee, you may have stumbled across the capacity of your orchard to produce apples for clients who prefer yellow and green apples to red or who are just tired of eating red apples. The fourth employee is a little tougher but upon closer examination you realize that the apples in the bushel are of very high quality. In fact, each apple this employee picked is virtually picture perfect. Is it possible that he stumbled across a tree that suddenly gives your orchard the capacity to produce a better looking apple?

The challenge in each of these situations is trying to determine how each employee's efforts helped the business. Obviously, this doesn't mean all efforts are helpful, but dynamic actions creating further opportunities for growth are less likely with the increased adherence to objectives. Imagine what would have happened if all the employees came from another farm where there was strict adherence to objectives; they would have all returned with bushels filled with normal everyday apples that you typically sell on an ongoing basis because none of your employees would have wanted to be reprimanded for "failing" to meet their objectives.

Additionally, another obvious comment in the face of practicality is that most of the help employees deliver won't be of the dynamic variety. We'll see why this isn't the case in a little bit. However, it's very much like prospecting for gold – you have to sort through a lot of dirt to find gold – but as any businessperson can relate, it only takes one significant idea for a new product or service to launch tremendous growth opportunities. People will only bring you dirt to sift through if they know you want to sift. The minute they find you feel it's a waste of time or they will be punished, they will cease bringing you dirt.

Strategically, searching for new, dynamic aspects to a business is also like fishing. You are more likely to find fish in the ocean of reality than in the ocean of what should have been. Extending this analogy, we find that generally the larger the ocean the more fish it has; thus, the ocean of what can happen is much larger than the ocean of what should happen. If we encourage employees to only fish in the latter, we restrict their ability to dynamically help the business as Figure 2.41 seeks to picture.

Figure 2.41

If we return to the three hypothetical situations above and apply Figure 2.41 to them, we find that what is important about all three situations is not whether we learn how to resolve them correctly, but rather the doubt and hesitation they create in employees with an over focus on what should happen (Objectives) rather than creatively looking at what can happen (Opportunities). While these three situations may be more tactical than we would see in typical planning objectives, this is precisely the point because the feeling that one ought to focus on bringing about what "should happen" begins with the excess focus on achieving strategic planning objectives and slowly seeps throughout to every employee's action no matter how small. As a result, they will tend to experience the four syndromes I outlined earlier ("Tunnel Vision", Traumatic Failure, Rational Avoidance, and Habitual Standardization) rather than seeking the creative aspect of what "can happen" (Opportunities).

The theme song from the movie *Top Gun* called "Danger Zone" by Kenny Loggins and a particular scene from the movie can help highlight the restrictive nature of consciously adhering to objectives. I've italicized the key stanza from a portion of the song:

Highway to the Danger Zone
I'll take you
Right into the Danger Zone

You'll never say hello to you
Until you get on the red line overload
You'll never know what you can do
Until you get it up as high as you can go

Out along the edges
Always where I burn to be
The further on the edge
The hotter the intensity

Exploring who we really are and what we can do requires risk, the "Danger Zone." Any employee who seeks to enhance his client-employee relationship will more likely do so by becoming comfortable with the Danger Zone. In this zone you're not sure of the outcome, but somehow you make things work out and learn something about yourself in the process.

In the movie, *Top Gun*, Maverick – the hero, played by Tom Cruise, made an ingenious, non-textbook maneuver to nail the instructor pursuing him during a training run. Another instructor, Viper, played by Tom Skerritt, and a civilian one, Charlie, played by Kelly McGillis, criticized the technique and reprimanded Tom because he did not follow the preferred maneuver in that situation according to the textbook.

How will one encourage employees to fly into the Danger Zone if they think too much about being challenged on whether they achieve their objective, on bringing about what should happen? Maverick, in response to Charlie's challenging question about the maneuver, "What were you thinking at this point?" replied, "You don't have time to think up there. If you think . . . you're dead."

Athletes will tell you that sometimes thinking too much about what you're doing will impede results; they prefer a natural response. In many sports, thinking too much about what you're doing will cause one to miss opportunities. Perhaps if employees begin to think too much about the objective, they become less effective in developing their relationship with the client. In essence, they'll end up dead in a different form than Tom Cruise suggests as Maverick because they'll more likely cling to routines and predetermined plans. They're dead from the standpoint that they won't pay enough attention doing whatever it takes to make a particular client interaction dynamic, including going into the Danger Zone.

How this discussion applies to the integration of the feminine influence into business practice is that the masculine influence of planning and setting objectives is relegated to setting directions and foregoing any evaluative aspects they may have. In this way, as with the Persian Gulf War, objectives become the anvil against which the hammer strikes or the bones against which our muscles leverage. They become the framework against which directional action can occur to uncover dynamic possibilities that we have not yet seen. In the end, we won't evaluate how well we struck the anvil or how well our muscles adhered to our bones, but rather on what the hammer and our muscles were able to do – what did happen versus what should have happened.

Relating this back to the Persian Gulf War, we find the objective was to remove Iraqi from Kuwait. Dynamism allowed the complete encirclement and surrender of the Iraqi army with light casualties. We'll explore another aspect of dynamism associated with the feminine influence as illustrated by this example – indirectness.

3. Indirectness

We discussed indirectness briefly in the introduction of the Persian Gulf War. This applies to elements that don't seem to have a direct impact and are often targeted for elimination. The Gulf War example shows this with the sweeping flanking maneuver; it illustrates "taking the long way around." The long way, "smelling the roses" is a feminine attribute. Figure 2.42 shows that whereas the masculine is a straight line, the feminine is a curvy one.

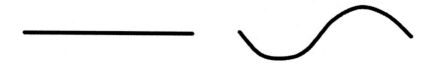

Figure 2.42

We can see the connection even better with the shapes in Figure 2.43.

Figure 2.43

Which shape better represents the male torso? The female torso? Which one uses lines, curves? Rephrasing a previous geometric statement, the most direct route between two points is a straight line, we can summarize in the following way:

Masculine = Straight = Direct   Feminine = Curvy = Indirect

In this way, we come to associate indirectness with the feminine influence. The Gulf War example, along with the hammer and anvil, illustrates the power behind this aspect of the feminine influence; it allows one to expand the actualities and potentials in a situation. The direct route is the shortest, but it's also the least comprehensive. Holism is rarely achieved through directness as shown by Figure 2.44.

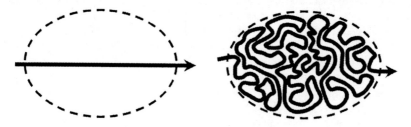

Figure 2.44

The left diagram demonstrates the advantage of time savings, but the right diagram shows the holistic advantage. Directness rarely achieves a complete picture of the situation. Relating this to the Persian Gulf War, the allies' indirect approach to this battle *extended* the battlefield beyond the narrow front between their forces and the Iraqi's. In essence, it caused the defense to spread itself. In football, one of the advantages with a long pass even if it's not successful is forcing the defense to cover more of the field. Indirectly, the long pass helps the running game by preventing the defense from concentrating itself at the front line. Figure 2.45 visually demonstrates this.

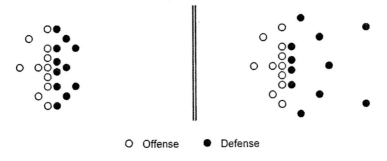

O Offense   ● Defense

Figure 2.45

If the offense in football has demonstrated the ability to throw a long pass, it will encourage a defensive formation more along the lines of the right one. Indirectly, the pass opens up the game so as to make a run more likely to succeed. A running play would meet with tougher resistance on the left.

Indirectness expands the "field of play" or the range of awareness. Since people are born with varying awareness levels, the degree to which this will benefit someone will vary as well. For instance, returning to our football analogy, the long pass will only benefit teams in their running game if they have an ability to throw it. Conversely, those who cannot throw long will be more inclined to convince those who can that it's pointless. The argument would be along the lines of a long pass generally being less likely to succeed than other plays; however, this argument ignores the indirect benefits to the running game even if the pass fails. Essentially, the long pass offers intangible benefits even in failure.

How this practically applies in business relates to dynamism. Even though you may fail with a dynamic attempt, the mere fact you can be dynamic indirectly opens up other possibilities just as the pass opens up other possibilities with the run whereas failure with the normal or routine carries with it little residual advantages. This relates to my earlier comment on how this battle opened up other possibilities against the Iraqi's later; suddenly, the Iraqi's had to expand their awareness of possibilities against their forces. This expansion creates dispersion and increases the likelihood of success for more traditional, direct tactics.

Building upon the picture of expanding one's vision, awareness, through indirectness, let's return to Figure 2.44 and remove the broken oval line to get Figure 2.46.

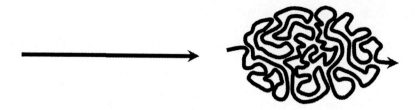

Figure 2.46

The question now becomes "Which one looks more like an oval?" This only serves to reinforce the concept that indirectness is more akin to holism than directness is. Comprehensively, the feminine influence's aspect of indirectness works better. We'll explore this more with our non-military examples.

Beyond understanding how the feminine represents dynamic, dependency, and indirectness, the Gulf War also illustrates the next aspect of invisibility.

4. Invisibility

In addition to "C" representing the "long way around," it also represents the unseen. The Iraqi's had no idea the allies were flanking them until it was too late. There was another element of this plan that was invisible: the buildup before the attack. While the Iraqi's could have easily guessed this was going on, the "where's" and "when's" were unknown.

Indirectness, invisibility, and our next aspect, surprise, are often intertwined, so it's not critically important that we be able to distinguish among them. Often, the indirect is invisible, the invisible indirect, and both can be surprising, but we'll spend some time differentiating among them because the discussion will allow us to more comprehensively visualize the feminine influence which by its very nature tends toward invisibility.

To help distinguish invisibility from indirectness, it is helpful to consider the bombing of Iraqi in preparation for this attack in our example. While this was certainly not invisible to Iraqi, it was certainly indirect. Nuclear bombs withstanding, bombing raids rarely lead to decisive conclusions without the employment of ground forces. Thus, preparatory actions prior to a specific action often have an indirect flavor to them. While they can certainly be invisible many are not. Our football analogy with the run and pass is another example. While the pass indirectly affects the run, it's not invisible.

Invisibility is also easier to distinguish from indirectness if one considers "degree." While some folks can easily see something, they may not see the degree to which that thing influences. For instance, the use of color in presentations is obviously seen but the degree to which they influence is not. Most clients would not say they chose a vendor because of a colorful presentation, but they would more likely say they chose a vendor because they understood it. Colors not only help understanding, but they influence as well. Naturally, the degree to which they influence will vary by client as well.

Another example is dress or appearance. While clients would rarely say they chose someone because she dressed well, they would say they chose someone because she was more professional. How they come to that conclusion was in part because of the invisible influence that dress and appearance have on perceptions.

In both of these examples, color and appearance were used directly as opposed to indirectly; however, their influence was invisible and unquantifiable. We relate this to the feminine aspect because beauty's attractive influence is invisible unlike the active, visible pursuit of the masculine.

A simple table cross-referencing direct/indirect with visible/invisible will help clarify the difference and lead us into the last aspect of the feminine in the Persian Gulf War example, surprise.

	Direct	Indirect
Visible	"In Your Face"	"The Long Way Home"
Invisible	"Blinded By The Light"	"Off The Radar (Map)"

Figure 2.47

In Figure 2.47 we can summarize each quadrant as follows:

- "In Your Face" represents the topic or issue at hand.
- "Blinded By The Light" represents all we can't see underneath our noses because we're so distracted by the matter at hand, "The Light."
- "The Long Way Home" represents all the things we see that do not promote quickness.
- "Off The Radar" represents all the things we can't see or overlook.

In this table, the direct and visible represent the masculine influence while the other three represent the feminine. What this table also reinforces by inference is that the feminine is dependent upon the masculine for establishing a frame of reference by which the other three are defined. As with the Gulf War, it's essential to "pin down" what's going on through an "A" type action.

This becomes clearer if we pose the question, "Which is more?" around two points:

- What we can see or what we can't see?
- What is direct or what is indirect?

In both cases, what is invisible or indirect is infinite whereas what we can see or what is direct is finite. How much of the universe can we see versus what we can't see? How many direct paths are there between two points? How many indirect ones? Thus, to establish what we can't see, it's easier to first establish what we can see; to establish what is indirect it's easier to first determine what is direct. We'll explore this on an introductory level here, but will delve deeper and incorporate them with other concepts when we discuss the business examples.

First, it takes two points to make a line, but before you choose the second point you must choose the first. Since no one can see everything, the choice of the first point determines what we will be able to see. Once we determine what we can see, everything else is what we can't see. Since there is only one direct route and many indirect routes between two points, the choice of the second point will determine what is direct and everything else becomes indirect.

In warfare, the concepts of indirect and invisible are relative to the enemy. Dependency occurs because you must first determine what he can see and what he considers direct. You cannot be invisible if your opponent can be anywhere he wants because he'll choose a point that will allow him to see you. You also cannot be indirect if he can also choose the second point, the target, because his choosing of a target automatically makes your attack a direct assault because it's where he expects it to be. Military strategy compensates for this through reconnaissance, finding out the enemy's current perspective on what is direct and visible; where are his "first points" and "second points"? Again, the first point determines what's visible while the second what's direct.

The same happens in business: an agenda establishes the first point (what's visible for discussion); while the objective of the agenda establishes the second point (what's the direction). The items on the agenda become the points along the line connecting the most direct route between the agenda's beginning and end. In this way, we establish what is visible and what is direct. From here the feminine influences, such as invisibility and indirectness, can operate without disruption to make the effective, the dynamic, and to make the house, the home. This is why politicians put so much value in setting the agenda. It defines the battlefield from which a battle plan develops. How can you create a battle plan without knowing the battlefield? How can you know what is invisible and indirect until you know what is visible and direct? This is how the feminine is dependent upon the masculine – the masculine goes first.

5. Surprise

The last feminine aspect of the Gulf War that warrants mentioning is surprise. While directness can have a predominantly masculine flavor, it can become feminine if it is a surprise. The Gulf War most represents this aspect when we consider that Iraq did not think the Allies would take up arms to protect Kuwait. A direct, military action in response to another direct, military action came as a surprise. Surprise and her mother, spontaneity, are feminine. Nothing better illustrates this than the movie *Sound of Music* where Maria's spontaneity gave birth to many surprises for the Captain who was raising his children as though they were shipmates in the Navy. Predictability and consistency, offshoots of rationality and logic, are masculine.

Before leaving the Gulf War example, it would help to relate all the aspects of this battle to a purely relational experience between a man and a woman. By establishing these two relational extremes we'll better see ones in between such as business. The experience is a personal one that happened while interning one summer in Washington D.C during my college days.

Ostensibly, a woman by the name of Ellen called me at the apartment I was subletting for the summer from a friend, Rich. Ellen was looking for Rich, a friend of mine, who was away for the summer. Rich, a law student at the time at Georgetown Law School, decided to go home to Florida for the summer. Since I needed a place to stay for my internship, he offered his place behind the Supreme Court Building. I readily accepted since it allowed me a simple walk to work everyday. I explained all of this to Ellen when she wanted to know where Rich was and caused us to talk further. She was also working in Washington temporarily so I suggested we get together. She accepted.

While on the surface this seems like a simple situation where a man asks out a woman, there is much more here when you consider the following:

- Ellen knew Rich was gone for the summer.
- She had spoken to Rich who told her I was a nice guy that she would enjoy meeting.
- Ellen was interested in going out with me but did not want to appear too forward by asking.

From this, Ellen devised the following plan where she would:

- Call under the guise that she was looking to get together with Rich.

- Stimulate a conversation between us that would encourage me to ask her out.
- Accept my invitation unless she found something she did not like.

What's interesting about this experience is that it has all the elements of the Gulf War example, distraction, direct, and indirect.

The distracting element "B" was the impression that this was a spontaneous interaction resulting from her looking for Rich. The direct element "A" is her engagement in conversation and the indirect "C" is her navigation of the conversation into encouraging me to ask her out.

The dynamic element was that we enjoyed talking to one another, and we ended up getting together. The masculine elements that allowed the feminine to work were Ellen's actual call that took the initiative (first step) and the excuse for it (calling for Rich). The indirect element was securing a date without asking. The invisible was all the research she had done on me prior to making the phone call; she knew more about me than I about her. The surprise element was the actual call; surprise for me – planned for her.

I later learned all of this over dinner when Ellen confessed; we had a good laugh about it. The important point here is this: if all these elements can come into play in the two opposing extremes of a military engagement and a relational one ("war vs. love"), why can't they also impact all interactions in between such as business ones?

Military examples allow us to visualize the feminine influence in ways that other examples can't simply because of their tendency to use maps showing actions; however, because of their extreme nature it's sometimes difficult to relate to them. Thus, it's helpful to review examples from other endeavors and relate some of these themes to them as we've done sporadically throughout the review of Gettysburg and the Gulf War. Again, our focus will be on those from traditionally masculine arenas.

Hunting

Hunting is our first non-military example. While the act of killing anything is most associated with the masculine influence, hunting contains several feminine aspects. Three relate to what we saw in the military examples: positioning, attraction, and invisibility.

When hunting most animals, simply running them down is not a wise strategy. Most animals are quicker, faster, or more elusive than humans; thus, the key in hunting is positioning. Hunters need to locate themselves so their preys come to them. They cannot run headlong into the woods or outback expecting to overtake their preys because they will hide, run, or fly from the hunters. This again illustrates the inherent advantage of defense over offense.

Expanding upon this, hunters cannot simply sit anywhere, for without research and preparation they could easily deploy themselves where no prey exists. After waiting and none arrive, hunters will force themselves into a search for some. This is another example of how the feminine influence becomes the masculine when one fails to employ the masculine to support the feminine initially. Hunters will now pursue prey that remains elusive because they noiselessly move through the woods.

By learning their prey's tendencies not only in general but also in regard to the specific hunting ground, hunters can locate frequently traveled routes used for gathering food and water. From this information, they will learn where to position themselves to increase the likelihood that their prey will "stumble" upon them.

Along with positioning, hunters will also develop techniques to attract or lure their preys. This may be as simple as placing bait or as complicated as well rehearsed calling techniques. Fishing, a form of hunting, is very well known for the lures fishermen use to attract fish, but other forms of hunting such as duck and turkey use sophisticated calls to entice them.

Lastly, most hunters seek to camouflage themselves from their preys, and this relates to the invisibility aspect of the feminine influence we covered in the Gulf War example. Positioning and attracting will often fail if an animal sees or smells the hunter. Many times the slightest movement will stir and alert them.

In the May, 2002, issue of *Field and Stream*, a writer interviewed one of the top turkey hunters in the country. Seeing how the best use these concepts accentuates their importance and demonstrates the patient relentlessness and intelligence necessary to employ feminine influences.

Turkeys are very difficult prey because the slightest movement, even an ill-timed sigh, can alert them. Furthermore, they are intelligent animals. All three elements, positioning, attraction, and invisibility, are critical to successfully hunting them. For the top turkey hunter interviewed in this article, he prepares for his hunt about a month before hunting season opens. Since the hunting season is usually a month, his preparation is at least fifty percent of the total time he spends hunting.

The first step is to scope out the hunting ground by determining the location and travel patterns of various groups of turkeys. Once he does this, he next practices various calls on each group to see which work best. He spends much of his time customizing his calls because he has found that the prepackaged ones many hunters use are learned fairly quickly by turkeys. As a result, they are not as effective. This particular hunter also keeps detailed records on all his previous hunts including such things as weather and time of day to see if patterns develop. In all of his reconnaissance he is camouflaged and behaves as though he is hunting except without a gun.

Not only does this show the three feminine influences in action, positioning, attraction, and invisibility, but this hunter's example also shows how the masculine influence works to support the feminine in the assertive, direct manner he is researching his prey. Again, all of this takes time and effort that many hunters are not willing to invest, but that is why this hunter is among the best – he derives full benefit from a comprehensive, thorough approach rather than a narrow, efficient one.

Beyond hunting and warfare, business situations also exhibit the feminine influence. While many of these may see obvious, that is exactly the point – the feminine influence is a natural part of what goes on in business. The difference being that a more conscientious and appreciative approach in employing this influence can yield more dynamic outcomes over the long-term.

Business

We'll look at two business examples, one strategic another tactical.

- Strategic -

On a strategic level, advertising is a business element that is purely feminine because it attracts customers to consider various products and services. All advertising does this by appealing to one or more three basic human needs: long-term security, novelty of experience, and emotional recognition. Everyone has some combination of these needs in various degrees and ads will tap these emotional aspects in people to drive their messages.

Typically you'll see long-term security show up in ways emphasizing power, strength, longevity, hugeness, and camaraderie ("fitting in" or "don't be left out in the cold"). Novelty of experience comes across traditionally as "new and improved" but we also see it including youth, traveling ("get away from it all"), growth, and freshness. Emotional recognition is more commonly expressed as "snob appeal" but it also displays itself with celebrities ("I want to be like Mike [Jordan]"), rareness, differentiation ("stand out from the crowd"), value ("because I'm worth it"), and the best ("being number one").

The important paradox about advertising is this: we believe advertisements only work on other people. We don't believe seeing a celebrity in an ad affects our purchase of a product, but we believe it affects others. In fact, most of us would say ads have no or very little influence on us at all; they're a nuisance. Yet, companies are spending millions everyday creating, producing, and running advertisements; they work primarily because we believe they don't affect us.

What is also significant for us is the combination of the masculine and feminine that advertisements use with the key point being that without the feminine influence ads are lifeless and without the masculine ads are pointless. The masculine shows itself in statements or visuals specifically about the product or service. Most frequently it's cost, the actual product, or some statement about the product. The feminine is more along the lines of the image associated with the product.

For instance, a soft drink commercial with a totally masculine flavor would have something along these lines:

- A picture of the can so a customer could recognize the product.
- The cost so he would know how much money he needs.
- A statement about the can's size so he would know how much he is getting.
- A listing of the ingredients so he would have an idea of how it tastes.

Imagine a can of your favorite soft drink on a white screen with each of these other facts surrounding it. How likely would it attract customers? That's why some soft drink companies employ the feminine in some obvious ways by asking young, attractive celebrities to sing and dance in commercials. In fact, outside of seeing the can and the logo, there are rarely facts about the product.

These soft drink commercials appeal to the three various needs in different degrees by showing themselves in this way:

- Long-term security plays a minor role but shows itself in the implication with some soft drinks that they've been around for generations; thus, you can feel secure in being "hip" without going out of style tomorrow.
- Novelty of experience is a very dominant element in their often "stay young" appeal. This comes across in seeing young people sing and dance throughout the commercials and in even in their frequent use of the word "young."
- Emotional recognition falls in between these two and displays itself with celebrities who by nature symbolize uniqueness, being highlighted apart from the crowd.

On the other extreme consider a commercial for a pickup truck. Automobile commercials usually contain very intense feminine aspects, but we'll focus on trucks because their superficial message is very masculine and will provide a much sharper contrast to its feminine presentation than other automobile advertisements.

In a particular commercial for a new pickup truck, the advertisement presents the truck in giant form navigating a very crude, outdoor construction site. All the people (men), machinery, and structures are small as the truck goes over hills of dirt. Hard music is playing in the background and a male voice cites facts about the truck. The masculine elements are the truck itself and these facts including price. The feminine elements involve the image around the giant truck.

In contrast to soft drink commercials, this one plays very heavily on long-term security but here's how the three basic needs breakout:

- Long-term security is shown through the gigantic truck easily conquering massive terrain and the connection to the crude stages of construction (toughness and durability). More subtly is the association to construction workers, a traditionally tough breed of man. Association with others yields strength ("strength in numbers") and thus security.

- Novelty of experience is not as prevalent but announces itself by the emphasis on this being a "new truck" and the "largest ever built," thus leaving a picture that the customer will experience new, uncharted waters.

- Emotional recognition is the most subtle since it's hard to offset the message of being part of a group (tough men) with a feeling of uniqueness, but it did this by showing only one truck with one man driving it in gargantuan form so one can stand out from the crowd. In this way, he was the "only one" with it. This feeling would not occur if the advertisement showed a whole fleet of these trucks in miniature tackling the landscape.

Again, the key point is that even though many folks may be able to recognize the intended message behind these images, they would also feel "so what, they don't matter to me" and for this reason "they don't affect me." Paradoxically, it's exactly these thoughts that allow the advertisement to affect people. It's far easier for one force to conquer a second if the second under estimates the first's capability. In fact, the first force will do whatever it can to encourage the second's belief just so it will enhance its advantage even more.

Some folks recognized this in the early fifties and outlawed subliminal advertising, the showing of images that register unconsciously but not consciously. The most recent example occurred in the 2000 presidential election where a Republican ad floated the word "Democrat" on the screen in such a way that as it floated off the screen it briefly held the last three letters "rat" in view. The subliminal connection was "Democrat" = "rat." It does not matter whether it was intentional or not; the point is that people realize the influence this can have.

Now, this is not a perfect subliminal example because a pure one would not even show "rat" long enough to register consciously. What it would do, as happened in some movie theaters in the fifties, is that it would flash something on the screen so quickly that one would not see it but it would register unconsciously. The movie theater example entailed the insertion of enticing snack slides within the movie film that would encourage moviegoers to purchase snacks. Now, while these slides moved too quickly for one to see or to affect the movie, they were "seen" and encouraged purchases. Subliminal advertising is outlawed because *it works*.

The point here is that even though we do not consciously register something does not mean it doesn't affect us. We can reference here our discussions about radiation, infrasound, and tiny muscle spasms and make a connection to our introductory discussion in Figure 2.17 about men and women, reason and intuition. Women are more able to feel something before a man, but a man is more able to put it into words; just because a woman may not be able to vocalize something doesn't mean she's hallucinating. Just because we can't sense something, doesn't mean it doesn't affect us.

If we carry this implication further by using the political advertisement, we end up at the point where advertisements get around the subliminal law by blatantly showing images but camouflaging them from consciousness. Looking at an extreme example that touches us consciously will awaken us to how everyday ones slip by us.

For instance, showing a woman wearing a new line of clothing would work better if she strolled through a luxurious restaurant than a garbage dump. More practically, the ambiance in the commercial, whether a high class restaurant or a rustic bar, would give you some indication about the clothing in the advertisement without knowing anything at all about the clothes in the ad. In this way, images are constructed and integrated to communicate a message outside of the objective one being communicated. This relates to our Gulf War military example because the direct message (masculine) seeks to distract us and pin us while the indirect one (feminine) plants the impression inside us.

Some of the best analogies illustrating this same line are children's puzzles with a "find the" theme or an adult word puzzle containing letters in rows and columns where words are hidden up, down, diagonal and in order or reverse. Everything is in plain sight, but we do not consciously see them immediately. Now, imagine such a puzzle without any context for the type of words for which you're searching. Even though you may not see any words immediately, if the puzzle contained offensive words, you could easily find yourself not liking the puzzle without knowing the exact reason for it. Conversely, if it contained words you liked, you could just as easily find yourself liking the puzzle, again without knowing exactly why.

In this manner advertisements deliver messages without our knowledge and encourage us to purchase the product or service. Granted, these messages may not be the sole source of our inclination to purchase something, but they will encourage us to consider this in the most positive light. We commonly call this image advertising or branding. How and why this works is extremely involved, and many have spent the better part of their professional lives trying to answer these questions. For the moment, all we need to understand is that it works; I'll attempt to explain some of this in the Strategy chapter.

If conscious objectivity were in fact the "Way of Life" and the natural way to successfully approach it, these images would not affect us and not be in the ads because "I can't be affected by something if I don't pay attention to it." We would just see a picture with a series of facts about the product or service. As we've already indicated, the buying decision, as with all decisions, is a rationalized emotional decision. Objectivity is a fantasy. The only way someone can be truly objective is to pretend that he is. As a result, objectivity becomes nothing more than the figment of one's imagination where he not only ignores the positive aspects of emotions but also the negative ones tapped by such things as advertisements. This makes him very vulnerable to those who understand and appreciate the dominant role of emotions in all decisions.

With this understanding we can better connect the feminine influence to advertising. Not only can we see this superficially with the disproportionate number of women involved in advertising compared with other business occupations, but we can also see this from our military analogies. The images in advertising deliver feelings in an indirect, invisible way. In this way, they are very much like the Gulf War example where the "C" forces outflank the Iraqi's by taking "the long way around" and without the Iraqi's knowledge.

Images and the symbols that comprise them can have many interpretations that allow for vague, indirect messages; however, since there is some commonality in every individual human experience, the feelings they communicate can be universal. This will show itself in the use of different words to express a feeling, but the theme of the words would be similar. As we just discussed with the subliminal nature of advertising, some of the images are invisible to us on a conscious level but not on an unconscious, feeling level. Again, this most often shows itself when we feel something but are not quite sure why.

Overall, advertisements encourage action on our part through attractive messages. In this way, they are very much like Gettysburg where the Federal forces were attracted the Confederates.

What we do need to consider is the interplay between the masculine and feminine influences. The best advertising examples showing the dependent nature of the feminine on the masculine were the introductory car commercials of a particular car line that didn't show the car, just a series of landscapes and scenes. In addition, very few facts about the car were discussed and images such as landscapes dominated the ads. The ads and the cars bombed.

As with the Gulf War, we need a pinning force "A" that provides a focus for attention in an advertisement. Most frequently, this is a picture of the product and descriptive information about it (i.e. price, capabilities, features). A particularly attractive feature such as low cost or unique component will add a distractive element "B" that further causes someone to ignore the images in the advertisements. The images plant a particular feeling for the product and are the force "C" that really makes the connection to the product or service even stronger. Thus generally, if people like the commercial they will more likely like the product.

Again, all of this works because many of us do not believe these images affect us to the degree that they do and is the secret why they do. For the moment, it's not important to determine whether this is true or not, but let's just work on the assumption that it is. We'll see further applications and relevancies when we discuss the flash points between the masculine and the feminine.

If anything, anyone can understand that a soft drink or truck ad presenting just the facts would bomb without the images that many think do not influence them. The question we need to ask ourselves from this entire advertising discussion is this: If a "just the facts" ad would not work for these products, why do we assume a totally masculine, *objective* approach to managing a business would? Is there such disconnect between the ads a business runs and how a business runs that we cannot relate the two? We see this disconnect most clearly in how management approaches clients as opposed to employees; the thought of "advertising" the management team to employees in a manner similar to advertising the company's products and services is rarely considered.

- Tactical -

On a tactical level, the second business example is securing a large sale and comes from an instructor with a training firm. He secured this sale after a four-year effort which involved identifying first the philanthropic activities of the CEO for this major corporation. He then determined in which of these he would most like to become involved. In this case it was the Special Olympics. By becoming involved in a large way with this charity and secondarily in a couple others, he increased his visibility and contact with the CEO. They eventually developed a relationship that allowed the salesperson an opportunity to bid on the plan.

The question we need to ask ourselves is this: How is this different from the girl in the movie *Footloose* who sought out Kevin Bacon by having a friend research his tendencies? The answer is very little. The feminine influences at work here are positioning, indirectness, and distraction.

The positioning element in the sales example is the plan to find ways to come in contact with this CEO "accidentally." Indirectness is reflected by the salesperson's "back door" approach as opposed to direct efforts of seeking an appointment to ask for an opportunity to bid on the plan. Lastly, the distractive element is the Special Olympics and other charities that kept the CEO's attention away from the fact that this rep was a sales person seeking his business.

Before we go further with our examples by looking at a sales interaction and a public speaking one, it will help to better picture the interaction between masculine and feminine influences. We'll begin to do this by taking a blank, oval sheet of paper and randomly highlighting every point on it. By doing this the white oval eventually turns black, and the journey, represented by a black, curved arrow, would look like Figure 2.48.

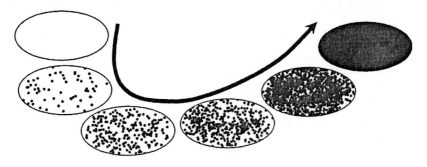

Figure 2.48

After we finished, we would find we're no better off than when we started except all the points are now black instead of white. The white oval represents many points which could be highlighted but none are, while highlighting every point in the oval causes the oval to change from all white to all black. The white oval represents the perspective of no focus on anything, whereas the black oval represents the perspective of focus on everything. Whether the oval is white or black, it contains an infinite number of points so at some point, our focus on an increasing number of points will scatter. Now, a white oval represents a non-existent focus while a black oval represents a scattered focus. As this scatter increases, our focus dissolves and becomes non-existent. This is why an oval whether white or black can be said to be the same condition and is separate to the question of understanding the oval. In business, whether someone has all the facts or none of the facts regarding a situation says nothing about his understanding of the situation. In the first, his focus is non-existent while in the second is focus is scattered like the white noise on a television set. We often hear this contradiction expressed about the internet. While it contains a lot of easily accessible information, it's difficult to sort through it all. Moreover, if we carry this implication as far as our energy would take us, we may never come to understand the subject we're investigating because the accumulation of "all the facts" may never end. In this way, the focus on too much information would lead us to a point where we would never understand our subject; a point that we can also arrive at by not focusing on anything about the subject.

As an analogy, let's consider a forest representing the oval and the trees representing the points in the oval. Whether all the trees are not seen or all looked upon at once, there is still only a forest. Consider a person in a plane looking down from high above upon the forest. While that person most likely won't be able to see individual trees, he will most likely be able to tell there is a forest. This is analogous to looking at a white oval. Moving the same person down to a lower level where he can see individual trees, he will see all the trees at once. This is analogous to looking at the black oval. Whether or not this person can see individual trees, his focus is still the forest. Likewise, whether no points are seen or all are seen at once, there is only an oval.

Continuing with the analogy, the person is removed from the plane and placed in the forest next to a tree. He no longer has the advantage of seeing the entire forest, but now he can begin to examine a tree that comprises the forest which he could not do from the plane. By understanding a tree and its interrelationship with other vegetation, the person in the plane will come to understand the forest better. Likewise with an oval, understanding it begins with looking at a single point and its interrelationship with other points. Returning to the oval, this means beginning to explain the larger abstract concept represented by the oval by starting with the smaller practical task of looking at a single aspect of the concept represented by a single point in the oval.

Thus, in its pure form, comprehensiveness, a feminine attribute, takes in everything without focus on anything. The focus is on everything, in this case, the oval. Conversely, in its pure form, specificity, a masculine attribute, focuses on individual things without a comprehension of their relationship to each other and the whole. Applying this to the forest and tree analogy, the feminine looks at the forest while the masculine looks at the individual trees. In the first, the feminine won't understand the forest because she doesn't know what makes a forest. She is the person flying high in a plane that can only see a forest as a green patch. In the second, the masculine is looking at all the individual trees. He is the person at the lower level who wants to make sure he can see all the individual trees (has all the facts). He will see he has a lot of trees, but he won't understand how they all interrelate to form a forest. As we saw with objectives, focus on the individual aspects of one's job function reduces one's concern for the business holistically. "Just do my job" becomes the mantra. The key is balancing the comprehensive with the specific to get a complete picture rather than one too broad or too narrow.

To highlight and consider all points, without a focus on any one point, leads to a very indirect, involved discussion as Figure 2.48 illustrates.

From a pure business perspective, we're talking about the difference between the abstract and the practical with the feminine being the first and the masculine the second. To enter into a discussion about anything new, it's generally best to follow a natural growth cycle entailing movement from the small to large, from the one to many, from the inside to outside. Animals are born small and grow bigger. Trees begin with one branch and end with many. Children live inside a home under the protection of parents only to leave and "face the outside world" when they become adults.

A disregard for either the practical or abstract leads us to the same condition, detachment from real life, but approached from two different perspectives. Figure 2.48 shows this as the white and black ovals. As manifested in daily life, the practical without the abstract will come to us as stark and unemotional while the abstract without the practical will arrive at good feelings that seem inapplicable. The business environment tends to emphasize the practical at the expense of the abstract. The challenge is finding the right balance between the two for the situation at hand. To address this challenge, one begins with initiative.

As we saw with the military analogies, initiative is an element of the masculine influence. One cannot defend unless another attacks. The feminine does not come into play unless the masculine initiates. How can the feminine attract if there is nothing to attract that has the ability to initiate its own movement? The masculine moves regardless of whether the feminine is present.

Using the same white oval analogy we can illustrate the initiative by highlighting the first point in Figure 2.49.

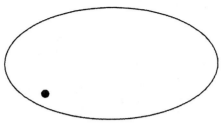

Figure 2.49

The selection of the point represents the initiative of the masculine influence. Instantly, we can now make many conclusions about the other points using this point as a frame of reference. For instance, we can determine which points are farther away than others. If they are too far away, they may even be invisible in the same way that the planet Neptune is invisible to the naked eye.

If we call our point "X" and add a few others such as "A" and "B," we can now make some claims. One is that "A" is close and "B" is far. We could even add a third "C" and say it's so far away that it is invisible to "X." With this expansion of our diagram, it would now look something like Figure 2.50.

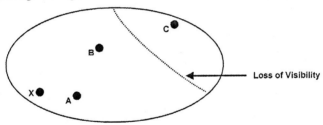

Figure 2.50

In a meeting about the oval, "X" would be the initiation point and each of the other points would represent a discussion point about the oval. Relative to "X" we could describe each of these points as follows:

- "A" is very relevant.
- "B" has little relevancy.
- "C" isn't even seen, no relevancy.

What's important to remember is that the oval represents everything around "X" so relevancy is subjective based upon two perspectives: that of the person establishing "X" as the entry point and that of the person accepting "X" as the starting point. Setting expectations is a perfect example; the outcome of the process is based upon the perspectives of the employee and the client. Two separate employees could work with the same client and come away with two different sets of expectations from the client.

The point of this is to show how a *focus* on a particular point suddenly creates a perspective from which we can discuss "A", "B", and "C". More importantly, this begins a journey whereby we can explore many other points in the oval (D, E, F, etc.). Even though the oval contains an infinite number of points, we do not need to explore all the points to appreciate the oval. In this case, perhaps a journey through the oval would result in the exploration of a finite collection of points looking something like Figure 2.51.

Figure 2.51

Now, even though we have not explored all the points in the oval, we can begin to see something that looks like one. In fact, it may even begin to look similar to one of the ovals in the series of ovals that we examined in Figure 2.48 if we removed the boundary to get Figure 2.52.

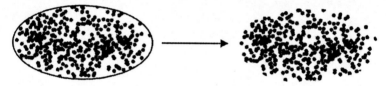

Figure 2.52

The question with Figure 2.51 and 2.52 without the boundary is, "Do we have an oval with these points?" One could argue either way. The masculine influence because he's more focused on specifics would answer, "No, we need to explore a few more points before we know definitively that we have an oval." He may even go so far as to say, "In fact, we need to hire a consultant just to make sure we have an oval." On the other hand, the feminine influence would answer, "Yes, anyone can see that it's an oval. We don't need a consultant."

Of course, this prompts another question: At what point do we have an oval? If we cannot explore every last point because they're infinite, at what point do we declare we have an oval? Is it at the tenth point or the hundred and tenth one? The answer depends upon the person's intuitiveness and the methodology by which he gathers his information. From an individual perspective, the masculine would be more inclined to wait for more points while the feminine would make her call much earlier. This illustrates intuition. Everyone has varied talents when it comes to making this call.

A business implication of this illustration is that by the time we have a quantifiable measurement of the oval, the feeling of having an oval arrived much sooner. This returns us to discussion in the series of diagrams at the beginning of this chapter, Figures 2.1 – 2.15. More importantly, if a particular problem required an oval, we would have delayed solving the problem because we were not firmly convinced we had an oval – we could not substantiate our feelings. Since life is ever changing, seeking this quantification may cause us to fail to use the oval at the most opportune time. In fact, the situation may have changed so much that an oval no longer solves the problem because we might now need a rectangle . . . but again, we'll have to wait for verification so the process and delays begin anew.

This brings us to the other aspect of the question, "At what point do we have an oval?" and that is the qualitative one pertaining to the methodology one uses to gather information. In addition to the number of points we have, it will also matter which ones we have. Let's take a look at a pair of diagrams in Figure 2.53 derived from the previous oval of points, Figure 2.51, simply by eliminating certain points.

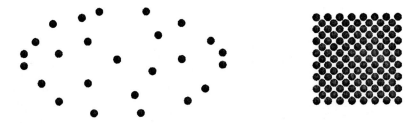

Figure 2.53

The question at this juncture is "Which one looks more like the original oval?" What makes this pair of diagrams intriguing is that the left one only has twenty-five points while the right one has one hundred thirteen points. The right diagram has over four times as many points but yet looks nothing like the oval from which it came. In fact, it doesn't even look like a rectangle let alone an oval.

There are many implications from these diagrams with the most obvious one being "just because you have the most points doesn't mean you get *the* point." In the business world, we often assume that "the one with the most facts wins" especially if there is a quadruple difference between the two solutions. On a more personal basis, we often assume "he who knows more is right." The most comical situation these diagrams represent is the "absent minded professor" who knows everything except common sense.

The masculine influence has a hard time accepting the left diagram as the correct one because not only are facts few but they're sketchy. The right diagram not only has more points but the points' density creates a clearer picture than the left one. This taps into the KISS phenomenon (Keep It Simple Stupid) where the drive for simplicity is so strong that simplicity overrides effectiveness and the question becomes "Which is the best simple solution?" rather than "Which is the simplest best solution?" Since the right diagram presents a simpler, clearer picture than the left does, the masculine influence would again select it as the proper representation of the situation.

Another implication that arises further down the road is the desire to produce the solution we seek. In reality, depending upon our desires, we could create just about any shape from the points in the oval. It's all a matter of which ones we eliminate. Our personal preferences influence which points we consider and when we stop. When the points make the shape we want, the grand seduction is to stop there. Thus, if we prefer to see a square, we will use a methodology that will allow us to see a square; however, this methodology will also encourage us not to see an oval because it's seeking a square.

The implication of this has some interesting twists that we'll pursue for the moment because there's more practicality here that ovals and squares don't show. The basic premise is that our personal preferences will interpret problems and influence our methodologies to encourage answers in accordance to our preferences. The moment we define the parameters on what we're seeking we will tend to find only what we're seeking.

The paradox is that just because we've found what we were seeking doesn't mean we've found the best because we're assuming we have a handle on:

- All aspects of the problem and how it relates to the whole.
- A methodology that explores those aspects and surfaces the best solution.

Our preferences for defining problems, their aspects, and solutional methodologies will influence how we define these for a specific problem. How two people define these vary just as these same two people would vary on their description of an accident, its causes, and just resolution. Most importantly, we haven't even begun to weigh the impact of outside forces working upon the person who is defining these things.

Imagine a business setting where one person has anxieties about his performance. One day in a meeting with his manager and his manager's team, the manager asks each person to draft a one page report concerning ways to enhance the overall performance of the team. He wants them to identify the obstacles they see, their causes, and ways to address them so the team can perform better. How likely is this person to define these things in such a way that will encourage a look at the operations involving:

- Him.
- People within his realm of responsibility.
- His best friend at work.
- Others he enjoys.
- People he dislikes.

How likely will he support or recommend solutional methodologies that will:

- Allow him to play a large part.
- Encourage the employment of his strengths in problem solving.
- Expose what he considers his weaker aspects of problem solving.
- Permit him to spend more time getting to know the manager.

Just as dogs will tend to run on land and fish tend to swim in water, people will tend to define problems, their aspects, and solutional methodologies in line with their preferences. A dog is likely to define these things in such a way that will force him to swim in water; a fish is less likely to do these in ways that will force him to run on land. If the purpose is to build a consensus around a decision, the best thing to do is begin with all dogs or all fish as the ones making the decision.

The dynamic of the feminine that this implication leads us to is her expansive nature. Whereas the masculine promotes focus, she promotes dispersion. Returning to warfare, focus and concentration are important in attack, but dispersion is important in reconnaissance, the gathering of information to understand situations. As the left diagram shows, expanding our scope to consider information from many sources tremendously helps our understanding of the situation. When an army reconnoiters for the enemy, the more it restricts the area of reconnaissance the more likely it will find only part of the enemy. Likewise, the more definitions we place around a problem, the less likely we'll find the best solution and the more likely we'll find the solution we prefer. What the oval and square imply is that our net needs to be as large as possible so we can take in as much of the situation as possible and get a feel for its entirety.

Moving onto other implications, these diagrams, while showing some shortfalls to a purely masculine approach to business by focusing too early to define parameters, also hint at some of the dynamics behind the feminine influence. The most prevalent one is the ability to ascertain a situation much quicker and more effectively. Again, the feminine does this through intuition. In terms of our diagrams, intuition fills in the gaps between the points much as our eyes do through our mind so we see an oval. Intuition accomplishes this with far less factual information.

Along the same lines but further down the road, the diagrams reinforce indirectness and invisibility. To the masculine who's set on seeing a square, he would consider some of the points on the left as irrelevant to the situation at hand especially if the square was the agreed to solution. The other important aspect of intuition to remember at this time is that some folks won't see an oval from the points on the left not only because they can't see it but also because they can't see some of the points that would help them. All points are not necessarily visible to all people; some will need to see more or less points in order to identify the oval.

We can also explore the indirect element of the feminine if we return to our original purpose of seeing how the masculine and feminine interrelate. We've just explored how the masculine helps establish focus by initiating an entry point we called "X." Let's now take a look at how it can assist the feminine by establishing direction such as we discussed with planning objectives.

If we take the same point "X" and decide to go in a particular direction, we can call the objective of the movement in that direction "Y" and the most direct route between the two a straight line called "M." Applying this to a meeting, "X" would be the beginning point, "Y" the objective, and "M" the steps taking us from "X" to "Y", or the agenda. Using the same oval diagram as before, we could express all of this as Figure 2.54.

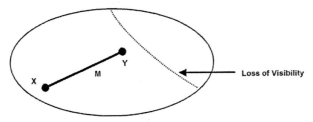

Figure 2.54

Now, with this framework, we've identified an entry point, a perspective, and a direction that will allow us to determine how to incorporate the feminine. By knowing where we are, "X", and where we're going, "Y", we can now explore dynamic possibilities. If we correlate this to the Gulf War example, "X" represents the Allied forces' location, "Y" the Iraqi forces location in Kuwait, and "M" the most direct attack route.

By locking in on a direction, we now have a way to consider what is indirect. For instance, "N" now becomes an indirect way to arrive at "Y" (Fig. 2.55). "N" could also easily represent how a meeting actual goes versus how it's planned to go.

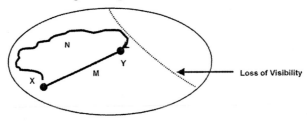

Figure 2.55

Another way to look at this is that by establishing X, Y, and M we've established expectations and now we have an idea of what is unexpected so we have potential ways to surprise someone by exceeding their expectations. Again, it's critical that we look at this multi-dimensionally as "B" in Figure 2.56 and not linearly as "A" similar to our objectives discussions around the diagrams in Figure 2.34. A better way to say this may be working *outside* of someone's expectations, or *escaping* their expectations as shown in Figure 2.56. Keep in mind we could even enhance "B" more by expressing it even in more dimensions than just two.

Exceed Expectations

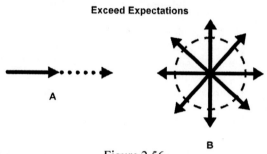

Figure 2.56

By looking at indirectness more as working outside of someone's expectations, surprises become differentiators. Taking a different road to arrive at the same place is a differentiator especially if no one has traveled that road before. People can enjoy a scenic drive especially if that drive is beautiful. If this weren't the case, everyone would always take the expressways.

Expanding the surprise element to show its relationship to invisibility as well as indirectness, we can modify our diagram further to include a point "C" outside of someone's visibility as we see in Figure 2.57. This could be as simple as sharing with someone additional information about their situation or expanding his awareness to the possibilities you see. Again, as we saw with objectives with the song and theme from *Top Gun*, showing "N" doesn't necessarily have to be successful because the mere attempt implies dynamic aspect that one can count on in the future. Receiving an "A" for effort and having it translate into enhanced value is more likely when you work outside of expectations than within.

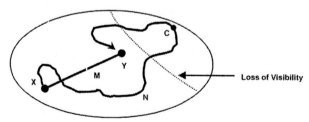

Figure 2.57

The main point of these graphical representations in Figures 2.54 – 2.57 is to show the interrelationship between the masculine and feminine. As with dancing, the masculine leads and the feminine provides the grace and beauty – the more qualitative aspects. Without the feminine, dancing becomes pure sport. Establishing "X", "Y", and "M" (the agenda) is the role of the masculine whereas exploring "C" along "N" or any other "N" is the role of the feminine. As with the past military examples, employment of the feminine can lead to dynamic results.

Often what retards us though is the default assumption that the quickest way is the best way, especially when it comes to helping clients, and implies that adding value in any other way besides efficiency will not translate into higher fee revenue; thus, the only way we can add value is to do things quicker and not better. This correlation does not necessarily follow.

Sales

With these graphical representations we can more easily convey the sales and public speaking examples. The sales example is first.

In sales, how one interviews the client prior to a formal presentation is the driver of sales success. For a meeting setting, we've already illustrated with the above diagrams how the masculine plays to set-up the feminine through an agenda by establishing an entry point and objective for an interaction, determining expectations. We'll focus our attention more tactically on the question-answer interplay and how it employs the feminine.

Statements fall in the masculine domain while questions reside in the feminine, because the first is more commanding and direct, while the second is more sagely and indirect. This alone makes interviewing an interaction conducive to the feminine.

Efficiency and adherence to plans reside with the masculine. Spontaneity is a feminine quality and relates closely to liberty, freedom from expectations. Again, "Lady Liberty" comes to mind. With this the case, it's hard to have things go according to plan when you don't know what the client will say. By not giving him the opportunity to talk through answers to questions, you can insure the meeting will go according to script. Whether this will be effective is another issue.

A comically representation of the masculine and feminine as it relates to questions is a date between a man and a woman. He talks, and she listens; she asks questions, and he answers. This anecdote must have an element of truth to be so popular and a reason we can associate the masculine with commands and the feminine with inquiries. If we also refer to the Figures 2.54 – 2.57, with questions we will see that an "N" path is far more likely than "M." Conversely, with conversations oriented around statements something closer to "M" is far more likely than "N." We see this most characteristically with direct presentations to large groups. There are very few questions, and if there are, they are left to the end after the formal presentation finishes . . . according to the script.

This graphical representation between "N" and "M" demonstrates clearly the feminine nature of the interviewing interaction especially when we again consider that straight lines represent the masculine and curvy ones the feminine. Based upon what we saw with the military examples, we can now see why the interview step of the sales process is so important and dynamic. It's the one step that clearly employs the feminine influence and sets the stage for future success in later steps of the sales process.

Public Speaking

We can also use a public speaking example to help display the feminine influence at work.

As an entry point to this example, it would help to have a common understanding of two basic types of presentations. In both, a presentation is followed by questions and answers with the difference being the amount of time allocated for the presentation itself and the question-answer (Q&A) portion. In the first type, the presentation uses about 90% of the time with Q&A representing the remaining 10%. For the second type, the time allocation is 33% versus 67%.

Each type has a different purpose. Whereas the first is better for conveying a lot of information, the second is better for influencing the audience. The determinant is the allocation of time for Q&A. The reason why Q&A is the determinant is rather simple: anyone can read from a practiced script, not everyone can answer unknown questions.

Two of the most recent examples of the impact Q&A can have on an audience are Ronald Reagan and Bill Clinton. Both were very good at handling spontaneous questions. Reagan used humor frequently and Clinton perfected the "town hall meeting" format. Both won re-election by large margins.

The main point here is that people prefer spontaneity. With all else being equal, given a choice between a leader who consistently reads from scripts and one who speaks spontaneously, people will far more likely choose the later. How is the first really different from a glorified tape recorder? Yet, from a masculine perspective, there isn't a choice because the objective message is the same and that's the emphasis with this influence. He doesn't recognize "how something is said" as being important.

As we may recall, spontaneity is an element of the feminine influence. That is why a conversational atmosphere around a presentation will more likely lead to dynamic results. More importantly, the town hall format showed that even if most of the audience cannot participate in Q&A or in the discussion, people prefer listening to a conversation between two than a presentation by one.

From the masculine side, a town hall format and a heavy Q&A presentation type are not efficient and not easily planned; they inherently carry more risks because of all the unknowns. This is why many public figures, especially politicians, will want to have some idea of the questions and topics before an interview or talk. Efficiency with a direct, lecture comes into play with the increased amount of material you can cover than in a Q&A or town hall format because asking questions consumes time. The presenter not only has to use time to listen to the question but also to clarify and follow up. This is why from a purely quantitative perspective Q&A and town hall are inefficient; however, they are more effective when it comes to influencing an audience and encouraging retention.

Related to public speaking is instruction, helping people learn. The principles we just discussed relating to straight presentations versus Q&A remain the same. Straight conveys more information, but Q&A is more effective. People learn best by thinking through concepts and information; this is the foundation of the Socratic Method where a questioning strategy designed to encourage the responder to think through the material is the most effective teaching method. It's also the most time consuming.

The Socratic Method is dynamic because it incorporates much of the feminine influence by taking the student on an indirect journey through the oval. Telling someone the answer to his question is the masculine; helping him think through to the answer is the feminine. Whereas the first could take a minute, the latter could take ten minutes, an hour, or even longer; however, once the student arrives at the answer he is not only more inclined to remember it but also apply it.

The key to the Socratic Method and the Q&A speaking format is audience participation. Here, it's important to make it *attractive* for the audience to participate; people need to feel a need to ask a question or participate in a response. This can be as basic as a desire to know or as complex as a desire to create something good. The strategies around this are numerous and involved but focus on encouraging the audience to come to the speaker rather than the reverse. Again this is the attractive element so prevalent in the feminine.

With this we've completed our tour of various examples of the feminine influence in traditionally masculine fields. These examples from warfare, hunting, business, sales, and public speaking demonstrated and elaborated upon this influence. Regardless of the field, she is very much a part of what goes on around us as the masculine is; however, the difficulty and vagueness surrounding some of her attributes make her easy to discount and ignore. Part of the reason for this is the intelligence and perseverance needed to enlist her aid. Another part related to this is conflict with the masculine. Even though the masculine and feminine work best together, flash points exist that naturally cause one to overlook her and necessitate our efforts to reconcile the two.

Flash Points

In order to see the flash points that arise between the masculine and feminine, it would help to imagine them in conflict rather than in cooperation. Some of these points we've already covered in the examples and others are fairly obvious after exploring exactly what the feminine influence is. Nevertheless, let's imagine a conflict between the two.

We'll examine this first conceptually and then pragmatically. Our discussion will focus more on how the masculine undermines the feminine since this predominates in business and our primary interest is the business environment. One important reminder, it's easy to think of a masculine-feminine conflict as one between a man and woman because many times it is. On the other hand, it's also important to remember that since masculine and feminine influences interrelate in each man and woman, this conflict can also occur within a person. Thus, there are internal, as well as external, manifestations of this conflict. Typically, people thinking and talking to themselves are examples of such bipolar discussions where they sift through various alternatives available to them. Of course, we don't look at them as issues of masculine versus feminine, but as we work through their content, we could find representative aspects of both influences.

Conceptually, we first need to realize that neither the masculine nor the feminine is out to annihilate the other because without each the other doesn't exist. The battle is more for acquiescence. We see this in practice when a husband who kills his wife also kills himself because he cannot live without her.

Since neither can live well without the other, acquiescence comes through disarming the other. How the masculine disarms the feminine and how the feminine disarms the masculine are different but in the end they both result in emotional disarmament where one does not tap his or her talents. Relating this to our series of military engagements, the masculine is a formal standing army, structured and highly organizational, while the feminine is a guerilla force, loose and nebulous.

The implication here is that one influence can never add or take away something in the other. Likewise, one person cannot take what exists inside another. What's in a person is there . . . no one can change that. The determinant in all of this is whether that person recognizes, accepts, and uses what's inside him. Emotional disarmament occurs when the person does none of these three things either as a result of a decision he has made on his own or as a result of the influence of others.

Most of our focus will be on the later, where someone disarms himself as a result of the influence of others; however, it's important to see how emotional disarmament can be self-imposed. Influencing one to disarm becomes easier if there is already a desire for disarmament. In its most hostile form, influence by another to disarm one's talents becomes brainwashing.

Why someone would voluntarily withhold a talent he has is involved, but one that is more common than one would think when we consider this story:

A man is drowning in a lake with two witnesses on shore. The first witness cannot swim, but the second one is a lifeguard. Neither witness saves the man who subsequently drowns and dies.

In this analogy, who would receive more public scrutiny for not saving the man? Who could really expect a non-swimmer to save a drowning man? Who could expect a lifeguard to save a drowning man?

Ironically enough there is a very real pragmatic aspect to this because our legal system condones ignorance in that "you didn't know" is far less worse than "you did know." This is reflected obviously in premeditation but extends further to business interactions where ignorance is better than awareness. Consider this story:

Two brokers sell a limited partnership (LP) that eventually creates tax problems for their clients. The first broker did absolutely no due diligence on the product and took his management's word about the LP's quality. The second broker, after doing his own due diligence, became skeptical about the product and documented his thoughts in writing to management. At the "urgings" of management, he went on to sell the product. When the LP's problems became a legal matter, the first broker wasn't even scrutinized by authorities, but the second one was taken to court, had personal legal expenses, and was eventually let go by the firm. The first broker remained employed by the firm while the second one retained his license, found another job, and paid minor fines.

Even though both brokers escaped rather unscathed, which one had more hassles? Which one was more aware, conscientious, and client-oriented? Would you rather have a broker who did his own due diligence as well as listen to the company's or one who just did what he was told?

In both of these analogies we find responsibility comes with talent. We can even extend this down to everyday scenarios in our business:

A crucial project's deadline is accelerated unreasonably, and the project requires some intermediate computer skills to even have a hope of meeting the new time frame. It comes down to two employees who could receive accountability for this new deadline, one has very weak computer skills and one has strong computer skills. It's assigned to the latter one but still the workload is such that he fails to meet the deadlines.

In this scenario, who's more at risk for failing to meet the deadline? The person with weak computer skills or the one with strong? Why does the weaker one escape for not having developed his computer skills over the last two, three, or four years? Again, the point is that responsibility comes with talent and the increased likelihood of being placed in "harm's way." This is also called "the fear of success"; the fear that with success you will be asked to do increasingly more until a situation arrives that extends beyond your talents and results in a severe defeat for which others (or yourself) will never let you escape accountability.

Avoiding the development, exploration, or utilization of a talent occurs in the workplace very frequently. Usually it's done under the guise of such comments as "I don't know how to do this", "So and so does this so much better than I", "This really is something for that group", or "Let's assign a task force or committee to handle this."

Couple the emotional danger a talent places someone with the possible desire of another person to prevent someone from using that talent, and a mutually complicitous relationship develops where the second person "excuses" the first from further development or the responsibility for further development. The second person will do this because he fears the assertion of that talent will diminish his own stature or cause him to reassess his own abilities and approaches; an emotional effort he cannot or may not want to tackle.

How this happens is very difficult to see if one insists on maintaining that rational, objective decisions run our daily lives. I'll go into more detail on how this happens emotionally in the Strategy chapter but whatever detail I convey, it's important to remember that there is still much to this topic. For the moment, we can gain substantive insight for our current purposes if we return and pursue deeper the implications of the sales mantra "buying is an emotional decision that's rationalized" by extending it to "all decisions are emotional but rationalized" then it becomes easier to see how this occurs. The key is realizing we feel before we think, and our thoughts are mere rationalizations of those feelings.

Any one feeling for one person can produce multiple, different rationalizations that generally flow through two levels of rationalization. First, we try to verbalize how we feel, and second, we reason why we feel that way. Again, the same feeling can create different answers at each step because it varies with the situation, the flow, the involvement of others, and how this feeling fits in the context of other feelings.

In continuing with the self-disarmament theme, we could illustrate these two levels where one feeling threatened by another's talents would exit the first rationalization level as "This person makes me nervous" and the second as "because he thinks he knows his stuff but he really doesn't." As a result, we would have the person saying something to the other like "You really are ill informed about the topic and should spend more time researching it before you take any action on it," and the other responding with "Yes, you're right. I shouldn't do anything until I do that first. Let me do that and return with what I've learned before I act." Thus, both leave feeling good because one is alleviated of the responsibility to act immediately and the other has warded off a threat to his emotional security.

For the moment, let's just keep this in the background as we go over how the conflict between masculine and feminine manifests itself. What's important is that disarmament is an action one imposes upon himself as a result of his own decision, the influence of another, or both. When we say "one disarms another" we are saying that he has successfully persuaded the other to disarm himself.

In examining the masculine-feminine conflict, let's first refer back to our original expressions of the masculine and feminine influences in Figure 2.18. We'll recall the "pursue" of the masculine and the "attract" of the feminine now shown here as Figure 2.58.

Masculine Influence:	$O \Rightarrow X$	Pursue	Direct
Feminine Influence:	$O \Leftarrow X$	Attract	Indirect

Figure 2.58 (2.18 Revisited)

By using these as the primary talents of the masculine and the feminine, we can begin to imagine an emotional conflict where one disarms the other. Redesigning these expressions to reflect this disarmament, our expressions would look like Figure 2.59.

Masculine Influence:	O ⇒] X	Restrain	Direct
Feminine Influence:	O] ⇐ X	Repel	Indirect

] = Disarmament

Figure 2.59

In each expression the right bracket ( ]) represents the self-disarmament that would occur around "O". In the masculine this would appear as restraint in the form of halting himself from doing something and in the feminine it would appear as repellency in the form of making herself less attractive or appealing.

Initially, scenes from a school playground would help us picture the forms restraint and repellency can take. For instance, a talented boy playing ball would receive criticism from his teammates as being a "ball hog" while a cute girl would receive criticism from her peers in the form of "quit being a flirt." In the boy's case, his disarmament would appear in the form of applying restraint to his talents by passing off more frequently to the others. In the girl's case, her disarmament would appear in the form of less smiling, talking, or plainer clothes all aimed at repelling the attention of boys in deference to her friends. In both cases each boy and girl is disarming in order to gain the acceptance of the others. Understandably, these are mild forms but any adult knows that these criticisms can take on extremely severe, almost brutal, forms.

The ultimate aim of these criticisms is to make the masculine and feminine something they are not; that is feminine and masculine respectively. In sports, we often refer to the "home court" or "home field" advantage. An emotional conflict is no different. Putting someone in a position where he does not act in accordance with his nature puts him at a disadvantage. Thus, in order to defeat the masculine you get him to behave femininely and the feminine to behave masculinely.

In the playground examples, the boy would now wait for the ball to come to him by making it *attractive* to the others to do so, and the girl would now *pursue* the more pragmatic aspects of her abilities. On a more adult and business level, these are rationalized from the man's perspective into the encouragement to be a "team player" and from the woman's to "not just be another pretty face."

While both of these rationalizations can be noble endeavors, it comes at the expense of the man and woman exercising their true talents that may threaten to outshine their peers. The more talent a man has the harder it is to be seen by others as a team player; it's very difficult to view a star basketball player as a team player without being blinded by his star status. Conversely, the more beautiful the woman the harder it becomes for others to see her as anything else but "another pretty face." The sharpest contrast appears with attractive female broadcasters and interviewers whose occupations require relational talents that exude beauty themselves but only receive superficial treatment in a way that seems to reinforce the criticism of being just a pretty face.

Thus far, the examples have focused on criticisms from the same gender, but the most recent examples make for a transition into a masculine-feminine conflict because they hint at the differences between the two that become focal points of that conflict. The key from these examples is that the objective for emotional attacks to get the masculine to behave more feminine and the feminine to behave more masculine. In this way, they move out of their comfort zone.

To understand how this occurs it would help to review the words from Figure 2.20 that we've used associated with each influence and show here as Figure 2.60.

Masculine	Feminine
Pursue	Attract
Direct	Indirect
Independent	Dependent
Practical	Inspirational
Cold	Warm
Reason	Feeling
Objective	Subjective
Logic	Intuition
Tangible	Intangible
Scripted	Spontaneous
Chained	Free
Focus	Distract
Simple	Involved
Mediocre	Intelligent
Easy	Courage
Quantity	Quality

Figure 2.60 (2.20 Revisited)

The leverage that makes both influences able to disarm rather than annihilate the other is the mutual need for each to have the other in order to be complete. This manifests itself as a mutual affinity or affection while at the same time creating tension that can manifest as open conflict.

When the feminine seeks to disarm the masculine it's important to consider the childhood saying, "Sticks and stones may break my bones, but names will never hurt me," with the main point being that it's totally false. Its mere utterance proves exactly the reverse. Many times names will hurt more than sticks or stones especially if we extend names to include other forms of rejection such as nagging and "no-saying." The way to undermine the masculine is to condition him to not pursue at all. Often expressions such as "there's no point" or "it only creates trouble" represent the impact of this conditioning. In order to train a dog, one not only gives rewards but also inflicts punishment. Many times the punishment comes along with a forceful "No!"

In addition to rejection in the form of "no" rejection can assume more aggressive forms such as nagging or sniping aimed at undermining the masculine's emotional strength. It's easier for the feminine to undermine the masculine's emotional strength than it is for the reverse because of the feminine's intuitiveness. Nagging can take on the form of a full-blown propaganda campaign similar to those that occur in military engagements; propaganda works.

Again, we're not limiting our discussion of the masculine and feminine to relationships between a man and a woman because their influences apply in a single individual as well as on a global scale. The best way to visualize this nagging or sniping of the feminine is a guerilla force attacking and terrorizing a traditional one. The guerilla force has little chance of defeating a traditional one in open combat. Likewise, a woman has little chance of defeating a man in a boxing ring. On the other hand, undermining the traditional force's will to fight is the goal of the guerilla force.

Vietnam is another good example. The Americans and South Vietnamese won more battles and lost fewer men than the North Vietnamese and the Vietcong, but yet it was the Americans that eventually pulled out. In that war, the Tet Offensive where the North Vietnamese and Vietcong simultaneous attacked the Americans and South Vietnamese was the battle that best exemplified the impact of the feminine on the masculine in a conflict. The attack occurred along a front throughout South Vietnam including Saigon, the capitol, and caused tremendous losses on the North Vietnamese's and Vietcong's part with virtually no gain of territory. By any quantifiable measure it was a resounding defeat for them and many of their own leaders thought the same. However, since it came after the U.S. administration assured the public that it was winning the war and the enemy was an insignificant threat, the Tet Offensive had a resounding impact that created skepticism among the public for future government proclamations. Many attribute this widespread attack as the beginning of the end for the American presence in Vietnam.

Essentially, when the feminine influence combats the masculine it seeks to disarm it with a feeling of impotency; he's helpless to change the outcome or it entails too much trouble so he must *restrain* himself out of fear for being hurt. In this way, the masculine behaves femininely because he resorts to accepting only what he *attracts* his way.

A relentless rejection of the masculine's pursuit will eventually cause the pursuit to cease and thus yield a self-imposed *restraint*. Rejection by beauty, as expressed by the feminine influence, is the toughest rejection the masculine can receive. In an Aesop fable, some grapes hanging from a tree *attract* an approaching fox's attention. The fox makes numerous jumping attempts to get the grapes, but they always remain just out of his grasp. Finally, he gives up and walks away saying, "They were probably sour anyway."

If we look at the grapes as rejecting the fox's advances, we can begin to see the hostility in a different light – as devaluation. The fox devalued the grapes so as to rationalize his inability to get them. By proving they are unworthy of his attention, his failure becomes less consequential. In extreme form the wolf can even approach the point where he enhances his self-worth by his devaluation of the grapes. Consider the impact of God rejecting you versus Satan. Thus, by creating a picture in his mind that he was rejected by something evil, the wolf enhances his value in his own mind. It's always easier to personify something as evil than to accept rejection by something, especially if you like it.

Thus, the masculine influence, when regularly rejected by the feminine, will tend to devalue her. The inability to do something is a form of rejection; the "act" is rejecting your current level of ability to perform it. Taking these two points together, the inability of the masculine to integrate the feminine can be personified by a woman rejecting a man but practically pictured as the failure to be able to do something. Thus, this yields the tendency in ourselves to not like what we can't do and what rejects us.

If there is enough anxiety about his abilities to relate to the feminine in a way that will allow him to effectively integrate her into his activities, rather than exerting his energies toward a challenging, emotional learning experience, the masculine will tend to go in the other direction and, in extreme situations, resort to the visible exertion of force in the form of conflict aimed at subduing the feminine influence and relegating her to an insignificant role. Thus, we'll see the strength of the masculine manifested through the brute force to conquer rather than the talent to integrate the opposition.

In the business environment, this conceptual conflict displays itself in the comprehensive dominance of quantitative over qualitative, more over better, acquisitional over organic growth, cost reduction over revenue growth, "what is said" over "what is communicated." Relationally, for both client-employee and employee-manager, we'll see more relationships over better relationships, shallower ones over deeper ones. Culturally, tapping into history, the difference is between cultures that grow through the conquering of other cultures by capitalizing upon those cultures' labors, and those that grow through the enhancing of their own culture by tapping into their talent. In general, the terms associated with the masculine in Figure 2.20 assume dominance over the feminine ones to the point where the feminine aren't even considered worthy of consideration, part of the equation, or positive contributors.

These situations can make the feminine challenging and dangerous to employ. Those who can employ her can most likely become targets by those who can't or won't. Dynamic outcomes present a threat to those well vested in the status quo and incremental change. As we saw in Figure 2.33, the heartbeat, comfort precipitates decline.

While the masculine can be in outright conflict with the feminine, the flashpoints are often more subtle involving the masculine disarming the feminine. Conceptually, when the masculine seeks to disarm his focus will be along the lines of "you don't know what you're talking about." Since the feminine relies upon intuition as opposed to tangible strength or reasoning, the male influence will be more in the dark than the feminine unless it convinces the feminine to *repel* her feelings – to ignore them through repression or denial.

The utterance "you're crazy dear" in response to her ideas is an example. Unfortunately, this can take extreme forms when women take medications to curb their feelings, and why more women take medications for psychological reasons than men do. Regardless of the severity of the criticism, the objective is the same: to encourage the feminine influence to not listen to her feelings. Since feelings rise up regardless of our thoughts, this takes the form of repellency in the same way the girl on the playground repelled advances by making herself less attractive (i.e. not smiling or talking and wearing plain clothes).

Inner beauty comes from feelings. If this were not the case, then the interior of a computer would be the ultimate in beauty because of its logic. If those feelings are repelled, then beauty no longer thrives and ugliness prevails. Attraction no longer exists and reliance shifts to more pragmatic abilities, the domain of the masculine. When this happens the feminine behaves masculinely and no longer has an advantage in a masculine-feminine conflict.

In a business environment, the feminine is under constant assault by the masculine because business is a very masculine endeavor second only to warfare; one of the main reasons why we spend so much time on military analogies. Shortly, we'll explore this more as *the* example to picture the form of a masculine assault on the feminine.

Before that it's important to once again state that the masculine-feminine conflict can take place not only between a man and a woman, in a business environment, and on a military, geopolitical level, but also within the individual. A man is always resolving the interplay between his dominant male side and his feminine side, and a woman is always resolving it between her dominant female side and her masculine side. The status of this interplay and any conflict will dramatically affect all decisions in any environment, including business. Conflicts, like anger, within any person along these lines will tend to escape and land upon others in the form of criticisms or hostile actions. In effect, the person will need to resolve inner conflict by lashing out at someone externally just as a nation tends to do.

Schizophrenia occurs when there are splits in one's personality. Very simply it's anarchy in the soul. What this implies is that we're all made up of different influences held together very much like a society. Plato's *Republic* makes a similar comparison. The two most important influences are the male and female. As an example, another pair is extrovert and introvert, but there are many more within us, over a hundred.

Regardless of the number, what's important about bringing this up is that we are not monolithic creatures that think then act. Secondarily, it's important to know that what is covered here in a few pages has consumed volumes and lifetimes over many centuries. Much of it is unquantifiable and only supported empirically, but then again, love is unquantifiable but yet we know it exists because we see and experience it everyday. That is the strength of empirical evidence; life supplies it, not the laboratory. Life is a laboratory without a control.

How the masculine and feminine conflict plays out in a business environment is defined by one word, objectivity. Reasons, numbers, logic, and rationale play a dominant role in negotiating the business world. Revenue, expenses, and income only begin to scratch the surface of what propagates a culture of objectivity.

Despite this, as our previous examples showed, the feminine influence in the form of subjectivity, emotions, indirectness, and intangibility creeps its way into this realm. Morale, compassion, inspiration, spontaneity, and freedom are just some of the more recognizable elements in business. Generally, they fall under the more masculine terms of leadership, understanding, motivation, responsiveness, and entrepreneurship; however, they are not typically appreciated for their impact. One employee in a support role said in response to my quip about his lack of sensitivity for frontline folks, "Sensitivity? What does that have to do with business?" The long-term implication of this statement suggests the question: How can we empathize with clients if we're not sensitive?

Yet, this comment provides the backdrop for the song, "Lady In Black." It's the same attitude that creates the barrenness in the song and also the same conditions that make the arrival of that lady so profound. In a business environment, the feminine influence is regularly under assault or ignored by the masculine.

This conflict is expressed in many ways but we'll list some examples that give warning that a conflict may exist. A few we've already mentioned in other contexts, so we'll highlight them again:

- That's not an efficient way of doing things.
- We're making this way too complex.
- It's not important, eliminate it.
- We should do that quicker.
- We have to have numbers to back that up.
- We're dancing around the issue.
- There's no value in that.
- Make sure every step is mapped out.
- Just tell them what they have to do.
- We don't have time for that.
- We don't have enough information.

There are many more comments that give warning to a conflict; however, it's important to consider the context of the comment. An utterance of one does not automatically indicate a flash point.

What makes the feminine so at risk in a business environment is that she's more involved than the masculine; the masculine is simpler than the feminine. Our humorous story about Adam and Eve illustrates that. In the end, as the word association table for the masculine and feminine indicates in Figure 2.20, it takes more of someone to appreciate the feminine. In a world such as business where earnings are demanded quarterly, it's hard to pay attention to the broader time frames and holistic issues when the business world's focus is so short-term.

Before we go further, it would help to explore deeply the lyrics from "Lady In Black"; however, rather than take the perspective of a military engagement we should take that of a business one. In other words, looking at this song through a business filter, we find that the man who is singing this song is not lamenting the outcome of a military event but a business one. I've numbered the lines for referencing purposes. This analysis will allow us to see more clearly the potential conflicts between the masculine and feminine influences as well as their potential integration.

Lady In Black
Uriah Heep

1. She came to me one morning, one lonely Sunday morning
2. Her long hair flowing in the mid-winter's wind
3. I know not how she found me, for in darkness I was walking
4. And destruction lay around me, from a fight I could not win.

5. She asked me name my foe then, I said the need within some men
6. To fight and kill their brothers, without thought of love or God
7. And I begged her give me horses to trample down my enemy
8. So eager was my passion to devour this waste of life

9. But she wouldn't think of battle that, reduces men to animals
10. So easy to begin and yet impossible to end
11. For she the mother of all men, had counseled me so wisely that
12. I feared to walk alone again and asked if she would stay
13. Oh lady lend your hand I cried, oh let me rest here by your side
14. Have faith and trust in me she said, and filled my heart with life
15. There's no strength in numbers, have no such misconception
16. But when you need me be assured I won't be far away

17. Thus having spoke she turned away, and 'though I found no words to say
18. I stood and watched until I saw her black cloak disappear
19. My labor is no easier but now I know I'm not alone
20. I find new heart each time I think upon that windy day
21. And if one day she comes to you, drink deeply from her words so wise
22. Take courage from her as your prize and say hello from me

We'll spend some time relating this song to the business world and then exploring some of the conflict between the masculine and feminine using this song.

First and foremost what enables us to link this song is the frequent analogy of business in general to military engagements. Since this song ostensibly gives the impression of a war, we can easily surmise that such a connection to business is possible. What's very intriguing about this song is that it never really uses the term "war" and satisfies itself with a more generic, softer term "battle." "War" tends to imply a far greater seriousness than mere "battle." By taking a less serious approach, the song allows us to make the connection to business more easily because while one may think business is like a battle, he is less likely to look at it as a war.

There are five lines that help solidify the connection to business:

- #4 - And destruction lay around me, from a fight I could not win.
- #6 - To fight and kill their brothers, without thought of love or God
- #9 - But she wouldn't think of battle that, reduces men to animals
- #10 - So easy to begin and yet impossible to end
- #15 - There's no strength in numbers, have no such misconception

The phrase to focus on in #4 is "from a fight I could not win." Winning implies an end, so how can you win a fight that does not end? The business fight does not end because there is always the demand for more earnings this quarter than the previous quarter. What is the end to the business fight? Even if monopolies were allowed and you defeated all competitors, would the drive for more earnings subside from the market? Business is a fight that never ends.

The next line, #6, is related to the comment from the employee regarding "no sensitivity in business." In business we are actively working to put others out of business, to cause them to layoff their workers and put them out on the streets. We even have to layoff our own workers. The difference between an army and a business is that an army would never get rid of a soldier – it needs every one it can get. If business has no room for sensitivity, or worse yet, the feminine influence, can we say "thought of love or God" exists in the business environment? Can you love without sensitivity?

The third line, #9, is a little subtler than the first two, but thinking about a rat moving through a maze would help. By strategically placing pieces of cheese in front of it, we would be able to guide it through the maze. How is this any different than strategically placing incentives in front of employees to guide them through the business maze? Doing things for money "reduces men to animals." If people do "X" for money, how will they ever answer the question "Am I doing this because I like it or because I want the money?" This generally applies to any job. That's why the best bonus is one that is unexpected and delivered by a manager who outlines the positive things that person did to receive it. In this way, the person truly knows he did "X" because of some altruistic feeling inside and not because he was going to get a piece of cheese.

Line #10 relates to #4 and implies the eternal nature of the business war. One can easily enter the business fray but the war itself continues with no end in sight. Even if you leave, it continues.

Line #15 and more specifically the phrase "no strength in numbers" is the subtlest line. Superficially, it refers to size and the need to constantly make the business larger – the drive for more and more. "No strength in numbers" adds a subtlety to it by emphasizing the qualitative aspect of growth that we just considered in acquisitional versus organic growth. This line also refers to all the numbers in the business world that bombard us; however, numbers don't tell the whole story. That's why reading this phrase as "No strength in *statistics*" gives a better feel for what else this line is saying. The message here is that "Statistics give us the illusion that we know what we're talking about."

Seeing the connection to business is easier than seeing the conflicts between masculine and feminine. Most of this is quite subtle because it shows up as a contrast between two. We'll go through this in detail by looking at very specific portions of the lyrics.

L1: She came . . .

Whereas the masculine emphasizes size, the feminine emphasizes the qualitative aspects of a single one. Only one woman came to visit this man, not many.

The masculine also emphasizes specificity and knowing exactly what is going on. This phrase is in conflict with this concept because we don't know exactly how the Lady In Black arrived. Did she walk, run, fly, ride a horse, or appear in a dream? The feminine in business implies that there are often times when we just don't know all the facts.

L1: . . . one morning, one lonely Sunday morning.

Again, here is an emphasis on *one* as opposed to many. We not only have one woman but also one morning. Where the masculine is concerned with many, the feminine is concerned with one.

We also are exposed here to a timing difference with the feminine as opposed to the masculine. Whereas the masculine concerns itself with peak activity times (when the most happens the fastest), the feminine dominates the "off" times such as mornings and Sunday's. What's also significant and in sharp contrast to the business world, is that the Lady In Black appears on a Sunday not a weekday. She concerns herself with times (and things) that don't have an obvious, direct connection to the business activity at hand. Of all the days in the week, Sunday is the most "unbusiness" like day of the week.

Intangibility also enters here with reference to Sunday morning. Traditionally, this time of the week is for church, and for those who do not go to church, a time for relaxation and reflection. This is why Sunday morning's newspaper is the largest of the week. The Lady In Black concerns herself with intangibles such as the soul not the numbers and other more tangible aspects of business.

L2: Her long hair flowing in the mid-winter's wind.

In the masculine oriented world of business, focus is on ease and order, "everything is in its place." This line is in direct conflict with that because long hair is very difficult to upkeep, much more so than short hair. Her hair is not in order because the wind is carrying it where it desires.

"Just the facts" is a common masculine mantra in business; yet, here we talk about long hair the sign of artistry for man or woman. Men in business rarely have long hair; yet those in more artistic professions do. Looking at business as an art form creates conflicts.

Mid-winter represents the peak of dormancy and rest. The business world is better represented by the activity seen in summer. Whereas the feminine represents reflection in an almost religious sense, the masculine represents action.

L3: I know not how she found me, . . .

Again, the masculine relies on facts and knowledge; not knowing is a weakness. Ironically, even though this man does not know much about the Lady In Black, she still helps him. The strength in the feminine is that we do not need to know a lot to receive her help as illustrated with the oval and the twenty-five points versus the one hundred thirteen points in Figure 2.53.

L3: . . . for in darkness I was walking.

This phrase expands this point by illustrating that the Lady In Black does not need to "shed light on the subject" in order to act. She is comfortable working in the dark without the light of facts, reason, and logic. She works in the dark through the power in her intuition.

To expand further on the "She came" theme in line #1, it's important to mention that "I was walking." The man walked, the woman came. The motion assigned to him is specific while for her it's nebulous – masculine is specific, feminine vague (comprehensive). In business, the theme is specificity.

L4: And destruction lay around me . . .

An important tangent is the destruction theme. To illustrate this we need to picture a fire fueled by logs. Once we light the fire it grows to a zenith and begins to wane. Eventually, without additional logs everything reverts to hot ashes and becomes cold. The masculine in this analogy is the fire that burns brightly while the feminine is the placement of additional logs. Without the feminine, the fire burns out with only ashes remaining. This is the scene of destruction that surrounds this person.

With any building process something is destroyed to build something else. Trees are killed so we can transform them into homes. Ingredients are consumed so my wife can transform them into meals. Without a "rebirth" of wood, trees or ingredients; fires, home building and cooking will cease. In this way, the feminine gives birth to new fires, new homes, and new meals.

L6: . . . without thought of love or God

We've already spent time using this to make the connection to business, but it's also important to use it in helping to reinforce the contrast between the deeper, more inspirational element of the feminine and the shallow dominance of the masculine. The love between a man and a woman is the strongest relational bond between two people. Love can extend beyond this in a more general sense to love of work, love of country, love of company and touch on almost a religious zeal represented here by God. All are relational elements that are the domain of the feminine and frequently ignored by the masculine in the "heat of battle" or in the "heat of the moment." Once the masculine becomes enthralled with the power of its own dominance, he will totally forsake the feminine until nothing is left from his consumptiveness.

L7: . . . I begged her give me horses . . .

The masculine believes more is better. Since horses frequently represent power as illustrated by the frequency of the term "horsepower," here the man seeks more power (i.e. *fire*power) to destroy his enemies, but the Lady In Black denies him this. The feminine does not rely upon *more* to work. This again addresses her emphasis on qualitative aspects and a few other things as we will see in a bit.

L11: . . . had counseled me so wisely . . .

In addition to the qualitative aspect of the feminine there is the element of wisdom. "He is wise beyond his years" is a good expression illustrating wisdom. It's more comprehensive than any rational calculation, in this case years. This is obviously in conflict with the masculine whose focus is on the immediate and tangible evidence supporting action. Raw information gathering is not wisdom. If this were true, computers would be wise. Wisdom assumes the mantle of holistic intelligence.

L12: I feared to walk alone again . . .

The masculine influence that sees strength in numbers fears solitude for it exemplifies weakness. This is why the masculine emphasizes committees, consensus, and team while the feminine emphasizes the qualitative aspects of a single person. A committee of women does not give birth to single a child. No man marries a committee of women and no woman marries a committee of men; regeneration, creativity begins with one.

L13: . . . let me rest by your side.

Again, we see here the resting element of the feminine as opposed to the active one of the masculine. After a period of extreme exertion there is the need for rest and regeneration as demonstrated by the nursing element of the feminine.

L14: Have faith and trust in me she said, . . .

This emphasizes the relational aspect of the feminine as opposed to the reasoning or transactional aspects of the masculine. Rather than rely upon facts, logic or reason to support her case, the Lady In Black simply asks for faith and trust. "Faith" is a name given to women not men. The masculine does not go on blind faith but rather on rational calculation of the known possibilities.

L14: . . . filled my heart with life.

The continuation of the previous line is this phrase. Whereas the masculine fills one's head, the feminine fills hearts. Life belongs in the heart, not the head. Facts, knowledge, and reasons do not breathe life; faith and trust do. As the feminine transforms a house into a home, she also transforms a living into a life. The masculine symbolically resides in the head; the heart (feelings) scares him.

L15: There's no strength in numbers, have no such misconceptions

We've already addressed this line, but it's important to take time to emphasize the point: the passionate of one is stronger than the objectivity of many. This is a very intense flash point between the masculine and feminine in the business world, perhaps the most critical one in a business environment.

L16: . . . when you need me be assured I won't be far away

Whereas the masculine relies upon sight and closeness, the feminine is not constrained by visibility or distance. We find in conflict the tangibility, directness, and visibility of the masculine with the intangibility, indirectness, and invisibility of the feminine.

L18: . . . until I saw her black cloak disappear

No where in this song do we find out how the Lady In Black propelled herself. Do we ever know what propels a woman's beauty? The masculine seeks to quantify and specify while the feminine seeks to keep things vague and mysterious. The first constricts while the second expands. Under which conditions do we find "freely" moving thoughts and ideas? Can you quantify faith?

L19: My labor is no easier but now I know I'm not alone

The masculine aspect of business would say, "Anything that doesn't make our job easier is not worth our time." Again, this is the qualitative over the quantitative, a living versus a life.

L20: I find new heart . . .

As with line #14, the emphasis is on heart, not head, and as with line #4 *new*, in a regenerative form, is the point here.

L21: . . . drink deeply from her words so wise

As with line #11, wisdom enters the picture through the reconciliation of the feminine with the masculine. In Greek mythology, a woman was the Goddess of Wisdom, Athena. She also became the namesake for the most important city in Greece, Athens – the intellectual and cultural center of early Western civilization.

"Drink deeply" is a sharp contrast to "listen intensely." Whereas the first goes straight to someone's soul the second goes straight to someone's head. The feminine, as illustrated again by the humorous Adam and Eve story and throughout this song, is something in one's heart and soul and not easily understood. The masculine perspective emphasizes verbalization of thoughts and reasons. "Drink deeply" is a reinforcement of wisdom's stature as being far more than what is learned through information, logic, and reason via objective analysis. It includes the intuitive aspects gained only through subjectivity, sensitivity to as many emotions as possible on as many levels as possible.

Intensely examining these lyrics has allowed us to see better the flash points in a masculine-feminine conflict inside the business world. In addition and indirectly, our examination has also allowed us to receive a better feel for the way the feminine influence works and affects us.

Another analogy representing this conflict is the popular *Lord of the Rings* trilogy. The masculine influence, untempered by the feminine, endlessly drives from one battle to the next. In this trilogy, the "dark" forces have no women on their side; they're all men or masculine creatures. All the women in this trilogy are either heroines themselves or on the side of the heroes. Whereas the dark forces represent "strength in numbers," the heroes represent quality, trust and faith in the few. Women on their side convey much of that quality.

The effect of the images conveyed by the lyrics of a "Lady In Black" and *Lord of the Rings* is no different than the effect of those conveyed by such things as attire. Everything we wear communicates a message about ourselves. Likewise, every word has a message as well. It not only appears superficially in the definition but also in the connotation and the image. For example, curse words have a definition, but they also convey things beyond their definition.

This concept extends beyond words and attire into surroundings to create ambience. It is no accident that politicians seem to like to have the American flag as a backdrop. In a world ruled by objectivity, such symbols would have no effect. In this example, it would not matter whether an American flag or a Nazi flag rested behind the politician because all that would matter is what the politician said, nothing else. If such imagery affects the perceptions we have of politicians, would it also affect the perceptions clients have of employees and what employees have of managers?

Whereas the masculine would say our analysis is making more of something than there is, the feminine would say we're far short of what's there. In the masculine, numbers go from zero to infinity; the universe's physicality is infinite. Conversely, in the feminine the qualitative aspect of anything goes from zero to infinity as well; the universe's intangible, intrinsic ability to teach us about ourselves is limitless.

The representation we can use for this is the oval from earlier. Within any oval, despite a well-defined boundary, there are an infinite number of points; within any topic, there are an infinite number of points that we can make about it. With anything we say, wear, or place around us, the interpretations and images are far deeper than what initially registers in our minds. This is no different than the essence of a woman; there is always more to her than what we initially observe on a first meeting. That is why Adam will spend a lifetime getting to know Eve and never fully exhaust the capacity to misunderstand her.

Consider all the songs written about any particular topic. How many love songs are there? How many books are there about business? How many different ways have people explored these topics? How many times have they approached it from a sports perspective, a personal one, or a military one? How many different perspectives are there on economics? One interpretation yields another.

If the universe's infinite tangibility symbolizes the masculine's quantitative approach, imagination's infinite intangibility symbolizes the feminine's qualitative approach. Within a single person, there is no limit to imagination – this is the qualitative aspect of the feminine – the ability to imagine something from where there seems to be nothing. That is why anything has unlimited interpretations and perspectives including the lyrics to the song, "Lady In Black."

These concepts have a dangerous edge to them that we need to address because it will help us understand how and why these flash points arise between the feminine and masculine. While various interpretations exist for many things in life, tension grows when we realize all interpretations and perspectives are not equal. As with the universe where all planets don't necessarily sustain life, not all interpretations sustain life either. Some are lively and some are dead while among the lively some are livelier than others.

A lively interpretation thrives in life. In this way it has a truth or an inspirational quality about it. As we will see, it's not necessarily the interpretation that moves the most people, but it could be the one that moves a few the most deeply, quantitative versus qualitative. Life determines whether an interpretation has vitality, not the acceptance or rejection by the most people. The nature of life is the final testing ground for determining the validity of an interpretation; it's the difference between what we want to work and what does that is the qualitative determinant of any interpretation. Vitality, or energy, drives quality, not our numbers; human energy is passion.

In politics, a passionate minority can often affect the agenda when only a dispassionate majority stands in its way. This is why current political strategies emphasize negative campaigns that do not necessarily persuade potential voters to support their candidate but encourage "lukewarm" supporters of the opposition to not vote by demoralizing them. In effect, campaigns are boiling down to the passionate voters on either side of an issue fighting it out while the dispassionate remain at home. Passion for an issue rather than the objective facts of the issue drives success; passion drives what works.

Warfare also contains numerous examples where a very spirited fighting force can overcome a numerical disadvantage against a lethargic adversary. Armies defending their homeland are particularly dangerous because they are highly inspired. When the weaker team on paper defeats the stronger, we refer to this as the "underdog" scenario. These scenarios suggest that what we consider objective is still subjective because we're subjectively deciding to limit our determination of the favorite to the stronger team on paper.

We can extend this further to the gambling around the game. The point spread determines who the favorite is, but even this is subjectively determined by the parameters we establish to arrive at the spread. One is that we want equal wagers on both sides of the spreads so those losing pay off to those winning. Subjectively, we want to make sure that regardless of who wins we won't lose money. The goal is not to determine who the stronger team is but rather to make sure we don't end up paying out more than we take in – it has nothing to do with determining the stronger team.

Continuing with the point spread, another parameter we establish to determine the favorite is the one that the "majority" decides. Again, using the majority to determine the favorite is a subjective determination. Do we always want the majority to determine how we proceed? The United States Constitution doesn't because it balances the will of the majority with individual rights. Even the extent of that balance is subjective.

Another aspect of objectiveness that I touched on earlier is that it usually arrives with incomplete information. There is no way anyone can know all there is to a situation and even then how you measure it most likely will be problematical. Thus, at what point do you proceed to make a decision? This varies by person, and thus, becomes a subjective determination in itself. In order to claim objectivity, you've automatically conceded to leave out something in order to make that claim.

For instance, let's return to our apple orchard and have the same four employees go out and count your apple trees. All of them return with a count of twenty-five. Objectivity would state that no matter who you are you would see twenty-five trees; however, what does this number really tell us and what did we leave out to arrive at it?

We can see this if we send two more people out to count trees and one returns with a count of twenty-three and another with twenty-seven. Exploring this more deeply, we find the first found two trees infested with bugs so he only counted healthy trees, and the second found two seedlings sprouting so he counted all apple trees regardless of size. Generally, we will find that the more we desire everyone to agree on a specific perspective the more parameters we will need to impose in order to do that; essentially, we're consciously eliminating things from the interpretation and moving further away from holism.

Sometimes, these parameters are fairly complex in their employment and they're invisible to us. For instance, telling someone to park in a specific parking lot doesn't seem involved, but imagine giving those instructions to an aborigine who just learned to drive. He may not park within the lines or even in such a way that allows for an efficient use of parking spaces. What develops culturally is a whole host of pre-programmed parameters that encourage quick communication, and we're not even conscious of them. Returning to our counters and the apple orchard, this programming of parameters would take the form of telling everyone to count only full-size trees regardless of health. Once everyone's familiar with how we want the trees counted, everyone will return with the same count. Still, the parameters we gave to arrive at an objective count were subjectively determined by us: we only had a desire to count certain types of apple trees whereas someone else's parameters would yield different counts.

We'll deal with this pre-programming of parameters more in the chapter You, but another simple example will help emphasize the immense complexity of these imbedded parameters that make objectivity in truth impossible. Suppose I drink all the liquid from a container and hand it to you. If you saw someone else and he asked you to describe the status of the container to him, would you say it's full or empty? If it's empty, are your tires empty as well? Embedded in us is the context of the situation that will allow us to make certain assumptions without requiring all the details. In this situation, the embedded context is that full or empty relates to the liquid that was in the container; however, how would we describe the status between this container when it has air in it and when we remove the air to create a vacuum inside?

The key question is this: What is the objective answer? What we'll find is that what we consider objective is subjectively determined by the parameters we establish. Extending this out to the many details inherent in any activity, we find ourselves constantly relying upon many embedded parameters to communicate with others. In a business, we see the collapse of these parameters when we assign the same task, especially a new one, to a group of people and find different outcomes because of the way each person interpreted an instruction or because each had to fill in a gap in our instructions.

In this situation someone could say we were being objective by distributing the same set of instructions to each person, but the counter argument is that what we determined to give them was subjectively based – what we felt they needed to know in order to get the job done. While some may claim I'm going to an extreme in bringing all these other elements in, but that is exactly the point; life's truth has no regard for what we consider extreme.

Before we enhance the complexity of this discussion let's summarize. Objectivity, getting to a point where everyone can view something the same, only occurs by *restricting* how we look at it; this is directly counter to the concept of objectivity that prides itself on getting and looking at *all* the facts, not just the ones we subjectively wish to examine. In order to restrict the field of vision, we need to subjectively determine what to exclude. Restricting how someone looks at a situation reduces the development of new ideas, and in effect, reduces the dynamic potential in any business which increases the likelihood of stagnation and eventual decline.

Scientific methodology is a complex, objective process whereby one establishes controls to validate research. These controls are conditions which isolate and *restrict* what we need to examine to validate our experiment. They are subjectively determined based on what is *felt* is needed to get objective results. Often the principles behind those controls are pre-established by a group through precedents. Through experience and discussion a collection of individuals got together and outlined what they *felt* were the important conditions for an appropriate control. Even after the experiment is conducted, a group reviews how they *felt* about the experiment's validity. This process alone, as indicated above, is subjectively based because it assumes a group outside of the experiment can better determine its validity than the individual running it. Who can prove that this individual is not more intelligent than the group? How will they do this without subjectively determining what parameters to use? The basis that the majority or consensus establishes for the methodology by which we determine what is objective is subjectively rooted in the feeling that "two heads are better one." Who can prove this . . . objectively?

Furthermore, we subjectively determine that a group outside of the experiment is better apt to be impartial than the individual running the experiment. Can any group be impartial to an idea with which it did not derive? If the group is smart enough to determine whether the idea is valid, why didn't it come up with it? How can any group be impartial to an idea when the raising of *any* idea can potentially demonstrate the impotency of the group to be creative? Peer-review and the will of the majority are the children of "peer pressure." Collective acceptance, "groupthink", for any set of parameters does not automatically constitute impartiality, only collective subjectivity. This subjectivity manifests itself as cultural differences within groups, including companies.

The effort of an individual to gain acceptance from a group for an idea involves what is typically called politics. Anyone who has ever attempted to present a new idea within a business, especially larger ones, will know the politics involved in getting the members of a formal or informal group to accept a new idea. Everyone knows the power of a good, new idea, so for some in the group, the furtherance of this idea could mean a decline in their influence. Under these conditions, how can anyone claim impartiality on anyone's part?

Since the universe is infinite and any one thing can have infinite points of discussion, we can never know everything about anything. As a result, no one can claim objectivity because he won't know everything (and we're not even addressing the merits of what he does know as I attempted just now). In the end, all decisions boil down to the perspective, a set of parameters, in which we have the most trust and faith – otherwise known as subjectivity. For some it will be ideas that the majority dictates while for others it will be those that personally make them feel the best. Regardless, objectivity does not exist for no one can claim they have all the facts and even the facts that they do have are swayed by methodologies they subjectively selected.

By merging these two themes, that objectivity is subjectively based and all subjective interpretations are not equal, we can more adequately discuss how the flash points in the masculine-feminine flare up by referring back to the point made early on that intelligence and courage impact the degree to which we incorporate the feminine influence. For the moment, we can keep the definition of intelligence vague by relating it to awareness, an attribute that goes way beyond mere information gathering and encompassing common sense through an appreciation for what works in life.

Why intelligence would cause these flare-ups is rooted in the apparent chaos a subjective world creates. Without objectivity, there seems no anchor by which we can grasp to make determinations about our world and lives. No one can truly claim he's being objective because his objectivity is determined by the contexts he subjectively chooses; however, for many of us objectivity has been the apparent foundation upon which we make rational judgments. If this is gone, "where's the beef?"

The illusion that there is no longer any anchor is based upon the fact that what we have taken for objective has always been subjective; the emperor doesn't have any clothes. Just as people compete for markets, land, and people, they also compete for the context by which we look at the world. Who shapes the agenda by which we live will most likely benefit from that agenda most, and those who live by that agenda, once it's established, will more likely benefit than those who do not live by it.

No one can claim objectively that their context is *the* one. Most likely any context will constantly evolve as life's nuances present themselves. However, even though no one is capable of being objective, doesn't mean every subjective context is equal. Some will work better than others, and there is a correlation between the intelligence of the person and the workability of their context.

We cannot discuss intelligence and the flash points it creates in a masculine-feminine conflict without involving our survival instinct. Every human has this instinct, and it appears whenever there is a threat. It can be a physical, mental, or emotional one. We typically associate it with extreme, life-or-death situations, but it also shows up in less intense situations.

Most people have registered its most extreme effects when they've seen people suffering from extreme hunger or thirst. When food is tossed into a hungry group, most people will often not hesitate to trample one another or even kill another to get it. In rat experiments, a mother rat risks electric shock for food or water before she would risk it to save her young. Overriding the survival instinct requires intelligence; it takes an extremely intelligent person to not resort to killing or maiming another for food under these conditions.

In situations far less extreme, the threat appears more subtly in response to a person or idea such as we saw in political situations. It can even appear in casual meetings, usually early on in a relationship's development. Most of the time, we are unaware of it because it usually appears as an uneasy, anxious feeling that we eventually rationalize in many different and simple such as saying "I don't like this person (or idea) because . . ." or in more complex combinations of negative expressions and actions designed to ward off the threat.

Again, as abstract as this sounds it has a common, everyday counterpart called "scapegoat" relating to highly charged political situations in business. Of course, the person blaming another doesn't view it this way because he has rationalized it as some inadequacy or fault of the "goat." We also see it more commonly in hierarchical organizations when someone has to go see the "big boss." There is a degree of anxiety and tension in the meeting because this person has a tremendous impact on someone's employment. The survival instinct is at work here too, but it's more generally accepted because it's a very simple situation to spot. Often the survival instinct manifests itself in the person through a disparaging remark about the boss.

For the purposes of this book, we'll stay focused on the tension created in someone when he confronts someone more intelligent than he is or an idea that he doesn't understand. The feminine influence is a very difficult concept not only to understand but also to employ because it requires intuition, instincts or feelings. As anyone can see, especially in men, there is a reluctance to talk about these because they are not easily understood so are discounted as irrelevant, effeminate, soft, or weak.

We'll see how this survival instinct comes into play and how it's really more common in the workplace than the concept initially suggests after we talk about the effects of intelligence on decisions. We'll begin with a graph in Figure 2.61 that many call the "bell curve."

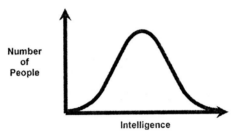

Figure 2.61

As suggested by this graph, most people will hover around the middle of this curve, also known as the average and the median. At either extreme we'll find fewer people. For any particular situation we could use this graph to illustrate the intelligence of those involved. The key is remembering intelligence does not necessarily relate to who knows the most because we're trying to avoid the "absent-minded" professor syndrome. Someone may know more than another in the abstract but fails in the practical application of the concept, textbook versus real life.

One implication of this graph is that for any situation, you will have a group of people who is more intelligent than another. We could divide the graph arbitrarily into an "A" group and a "B" group as I've done in Figure 2.62.

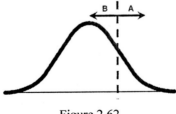

Figure 2.62

Group "A" would contain the more intelligent people and "B" the less intelligent. No matter where we draw the line, this will hold true. The only difference will be the number of people in each group as we see in Figure 2.63 when we move the line to the left.

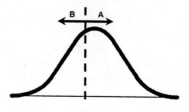

Figure 2.63

In Figure 2.62, group "A" has fewer people than "B" (A < B) while in Figure 2.63 "A" has more than "B" (A > B). Still, group "A" is more intelligent than "B".

The quality of a decision is correlated to the intelligence of the group, so who we have in a group affects the quality of the decision. For instance, let's say a particular decision required a majority vote and group "A" represented those supporting a decision and group "B" those against. The decision would fail in Figure 2.62 and pass in Figure 2.63; however, the quality of the decision in the second would be less than that of the first. People typically don't support decisions they don't understand, so the decision illustrated in the first graph would be altered or watered down by moving the division line to the left by developing an idea that is more easily understood by more people.

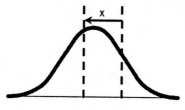

Figure 2.64

In Figure 2.64, "X" represents the degree to which the quality of the decision diminishes because it correlates to the overall quality of the intelligence involved in the decision. Of course, there may not be a direct correlation between the quality of the decision and the intelligence of those involved because other factors affect quality.

For instance, if we compare both group "A's" from Figures 2.62 and 2.63, we might immediately infer that the first group, because of a higher concentration of intelligent people would make a better decision. This would not be the case if the people in the second "A" group allowed only the most intelligent in their group to make the decision while those in the first "A" group allowed everyone to participate.

Nevertheless, this would still support the basic premise that the quality of the decision correlates directly to the intelligence involved in making that decision. In the "A" group from Figure 2.63, we saw a purposeful selection of those who would make the decision. We also caught a glimpse of how a decision making process affects a decision's quality. For instance, suppose from our entire population we purposely selected a group "C" to make a decision as defined in Figure 2.65.

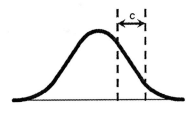

Figure 2.65

The process by which we allowed this group "C" to arrive at its decision would also affect quality. Taking three different methods such as consensus, majority, and autocratic, would give us three different decisions of various quality.

Consensus means everyone agrees to the decision, majority means half plus one, and autocratic means only one person decides. In the later one, the most intelligent person would be the one who decides. If we have "X" represent consensus, "Y" majority vote, and "Z" single most intelligent person, we could represent the quality of each decision in Figure 2.66.

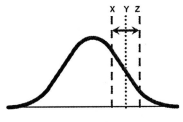

Figure 2.66

Consensus building "X" and majority vote "Y" result in a lower quality decision than person "Z." Having the most intelligent person consider the situation would give the best decision; however, many times in business situations decisions are made consensually. This decision making process is also called the "weakest link" or "lowest common denominator" because it resorts to the lowest level of common understanding. Figure 2.67 helps us see this and also begins to move this concept toward a practical level.

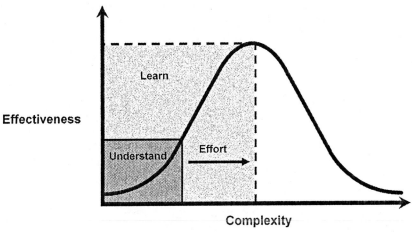

Figure 2.67

Figure 2.67 shows the relationship between the effectiveness of a plan and its complexity. An easy way to view complexity for the moment is to imagine it as the number of steps. For any plan then there is a number of steps that makes it most effective. Any number of steps before this point reduces the plan's effectiveness because it doesn't have enough steps, while any number of steps after this point also reduces the plan's effectiveness because they add unnecessary complexity that either confuses or hinders the other steps.

However, we're not only concerned with number of steps but also quality. For instance, why put four steps in when one would do? Quality helps explain why some plans accumulate many steps and become more complex than they need to be.

Why plans are adopted with either less or more complexity than necessary is based upon the intelligence of the group involved in the decision. To explore this we really need to expand our concept of intelligence beyond a mere understanding of an academic exercise or awareness to include creation, conceptualization, engineering, and implementation. This will make intelligence more similar to talent than limiting it to just the knowledge demonstrated by a degree or license. It now includes not only "common sense" but also "street smarts" and "divine insights."

Figure 2.67 tries to show that the understanding of a group limits the development of an effective plan unless the group attempts to learn and grow beyond its present level of understanding. Two individual perspectives will hinder movement to a higher level:

- Learning ability.
- Lack of desire to put forth the effort.

For these folks we could easily see their survival instincts manifest themselves in expressions along the lines of:

- "This is too complicated. We've got to keep it simple."
- "Our people just won't do these things."
- "We have to get there sooner."
- "We'll fall short of our goal."

Whereas the first two will reduce the plan's effectiveness by making it simpler, the last two will reduce its effectiveness by making it more complex. It's much easier for people to say, "It's too complex" than to say, "I'm not talented enough" or "I don't want to go through the effort." As a result, the plan won't reach its maximum effectiveness.

Group dynamics also affect decisions. For instance, one person asking the questions to seven people as individuals will get different feedback than if he asks the questions to them as a group. In a group, not only can the comments of one shift discussion to a specific area that may not come up individually, but people will tend to alter their comments to fit their perception of what is acceptable to the group.

Practically speaking such collective decision-making is supported by the popular notion there is a need to empower people in order to have them buy into a decision. This is a purely transactional ("buy into") view of a relationship between two people that becomes necessary only when inspiration does not exist. A plan's complexity tends to increase beyond what's necessary when there is pressure to accept almost any modification to secure a consensual buy-in. Consider these definitions:

- **Empower** – to give official authority or legal power.
- **Inspire** – to influence, move, or guide by divine or supernatural ways; to draw forth, or bring out.

Now, consider the question: Which action is most closely associated with what beauty does? We can better see this if we refer back to our original illustration, Figure 2.18, of the difference between masculine and feminine, pursue and attract, and modify it as I've done in Figure 2.68.

Masculine Influence:	$O \Rightarrow X$	Give	Empower
Feminine Influence:	$O \Leftarrow X$	Bring Out, Draw Forth	Inspire

Figure 2.68

How does inspiration translate into a business relationship? Exactly as the lyrics from "Lady In Black" suggest, through faith and trust. Rather than empower by giving or delegating authority, a manager inspires by drawing forth or bringing out the faith and trust a person can have in another.

This faith and trust is no different than what a client gives a professional. The most prized client/professional relationship is one where the client has complete trust and faith as demonstrated by his willingness to turnover all decisions to that professional and to accept her decisions. The client is willing to do this because he learned long ago that she understands and empathizes with his situation. What makes an employee-manager relationship that different that it cannot exist on this higher plane? While inspiration is far more difficult than empowerment, the long-term effects in the business world would mean lower labor costs and quicker enactment of decisions.

Two considerations hinder the widespread use of inspiration over empowerment. The first is that inspiration is more difficult to implement because it requires a higher level of intelligence, and second the survival instincts of people poorly equipped to inspire get in the way. Both of these finally bring us to the point where we can connect our entire intelligence discussion to the feminine influence with the realization that employing the feminine influence requires intelligence and courage. As we saw in Figures 2.61 – 2.66, integrating the feminine influence will require courage to face numerically superior opposition. The introduction of any new idea always begins with it being outnumbered.

Analogously we see this again in *Lord of the Rings* where the barbaric "dark" forces had no women and the heroes did. Whereas the first relied upon creatures bent on the simple action of killing, the heroes had multiple, deeper emotions including love, compassion, understanding, and appreciation. Symbolically, this story links the feminine influence, as represented by women, to a higher intellectual level that includes emotions and talent.

The story also makes the point, by having the dark forces severely outnumber the heroes, that those who advocate a life encouraging the appreciation and employment of the feminine influence will be outnumbered by those who don't. As you move upward along the intelligence curve, fewer and fewer people will be in that group.

A masculine environment, emphasizing "strength in numbers" will be more inclined to look upon folks who advocate these views as part of an inconsequential minority. In application, this will appear in the form of employing a variety of consensus building tools rather than employing the insights of one intelligent person. The latter requires far more trust and faith from people than the former. Whereas people are more inclined to say a plan is too complex rather than say they're not talented enough to enact it, people are also more inclined to say employing the feminine influence is impossible rather than claim they're too inadequate to employ it.

In summary, there are many flash points between the masculine and feminine influences as shown by the word comparison table; however, the one that tends to tip the overall conflict in favor of the masculine is the quantity versus quality battle reinforced by the tangible versus intangible. For everyday business life this boils down to the illusionary summary statement: quantification and measurability equates to better decisions. More earnings are better than higher quality earnings. Measurable results are better than immeasurable results. Symbolically translated this says, more ugly women are better than one beautiful woman, and measuring a woman's figure is a better beauty indicator than meeting her in person for dinner. When employing the feminine influence, there needs to be a relentless awareness for the contexts imposed upon us to make decisions according to the rules dictated by the masculine influence. Rules that seek to restrain and discount her influence so as not to threaten those who are less able to employ her assistance.

Conclusion

This summary statement of the flash points concludes the extension of the feminine influence's fundamentals. Together, our discussion of her fundamentals and extension into her deeper implications allow us to more effectively apply her to support our business efforts.

With this exploration of the feminine influence complete, we can now take another step toward a practical approach to this main point. We'll do this through a discussion on companies in general, on you, a strategy, and the masculine influence. All four of these discussions will refer back directly or indirectly to elements we covered in this section.

Unlike other educational approaches, for our discussions it will not be as important to know or understand the feminine influence as it will be to appreciate and have a feel for her. As is true with beauty and as humorously displayed in the Adam and Eve story, a cognitive approach that seeks understanding will leave one falling short in appreciating the full impact of what's in this book. There are no "how to" or programmable steps that allow just anyone to integrate the feminine influence into their business. Much of that success depends more upon you, the reader, than what is contained in this book. The intention of this book is to inspire you to look at your life in a different light by tapping into some things you may have already been contemplating about business. How does this apply to an actual reading? It means this:

> In spite of all that's written here or in other places about this concept and its various forms, the vastly superior way to appreciate the full impact of what's here is to rely upon your intuition. For women, this means relying upon what it means to be a woman in a spiritual sense. For men, this means elevating business to a commentary on who you are holistically. The demarcation between personal and business exists only in our minds and is counter to what naturally occurs in our lives.

Company

D iscussion around your talent's effectiveness in business not only involves the feminine influence, but also your company, you, a strategy and integration with the masculine influence. This chapter explores a way for you to look at your company but before diving into it, a special introduction of the material will help position how we build upon the previous chapter.

Introduction

The introduction to this chapter will review an approach to this chapter (as well as the next three) and the important points from the first chapter, and establish a perspective from which to incorporate the content in this chapter. Generally, as stated in the introduction to this book, visualizing a journey from the abstract to the practical will help position the flow from one chapter to the next. Whereas the previous chapter concerned itself with the feminine influence in the abstract, this chapter moves us closer to the practical while moving us away from the abstract. Keep in mind though, that ultimate practicality rests in your world and is reached by contemplating this book's concepts in a way that works for you in that world. If I were to truly help you reach that practicality, I would learn your world and rewrite this book to specifically incorporate what I've learned from you. In effect, this book would become a case study integrating its concepts with your realities. One day I may be able to enjoy such an opportunity, but for the moment, I must be content with leaving some of the work open to your talents and efforts.

Let us continue with this introduction that covers a review and a perspective that will help us position this chapter and our future chapters.

Review

The perspective of the following chapters is subtly distinct from the previous one because they revolve around it. Figure 3.1 pictures this relationship among the chapters. As you may have seen, the concepts behind the feminine influence and her relationship to the masculine are involved.

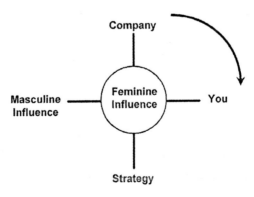

Figure 3.1

What I have found is that people do better and appreciate it more when they've had time to digest why things work. This is contrary to one of the first sales clichés I heard, "people don't want to know how the watch works they just want to know what it does," but what happens is that if someone doesn't know why something works, then he is less likely to incorporate it into his personality effectively. This chapter and the next three work on crystallizing the concepts in the first chapter so you can begin to get a feel for how they may work for you.

I found in many seminars experts talking to us about things we could do to improve. Many times the inherent value behind these things was conveyed by the research and opinions of credentialed experts. Often, the presenter himself was a credentialed expert. The basic theme behind all of this is this: "I'm successful, and this idea helped me become a success; so, if you do this too, you will become successful too." I call this "credentialing a point." The value of the point is not so much in how or why it works but rather in who endorses it, especially the number of people who do so.

When we pursue the implications of this logic, we eventually end up in direct conflict with viewing everyone as a unique individual. If people are truly unique then the way an idea works for one person won't be exactly the same for another. In fact, the uniqueness between two people may vary so greatly that what works for one will fail for the other and vice versa. Unless someone understands and appreciates why something works for someone, then they won't have the basis for integrating that idea into their personality. Beauty, even the beauty of an idea, is in the eyes of the beholder. Consequently, the only way we have to implement an idea is to do it exactly the way the first who suggested it did it; this, by the mere fact he is a different person, increases the likelihood of failure for the second person. The sequel to a movie is rarely as good as the original.

Additionally, the problem with credentialing a point is that in theory unless another person is around to credential the point then you are unable to determine on your own whether something is a good idea. Somehow, humans must have the ability to learn on their own the difference between a good idea and a bad one; they would not have survived if they always had to have someone else telling them the difference. The counterargument to presenting the intrinsic principles and value behind an idea is that it takes a long time. This is certainly true as shown by the depth we explored concepts in the first chapter. My contention is that the investment of time in this approach will give a greater return per unit of time than a "credentialed point" approach. In the long run, this will save more time because retention, acceptance and implementation increase.

Essentially, the first chapter gave us the well from which we can draw water to quench our thirst for a better appreciation of the principles behind some of the ideas in the four chapters following it.

With this perspective on an approach to the next chapters, we can now review the important points the first chapter comprehensively communicated for us concerning the feminine influence.

First, it positioned the feminine influence by encouraging a primary emphasis on an intuitive approach to business while a secondary one to cognitive aspects such as statistics. The previous chapter also covered the difficulty in encouraging this emphasis by explaining the prejudicial viewpoints discounting it. The comfort and ability one has with the feminine influence will not only affect his integration of her but will also impact the opportunities for others to integrate her.

Second, it included demonstration as to how the feminine influence is more ignored than not. By showing how she already relates to traditional masculine endeavors including business, she comes across more as an overlooked beauty such as Cinderella rather than as something radical. Women have been around for eons; to think the spirit they represent does not impact every aspect of our lives is ignorance. It's really a matter of whether we have the talent and fortitude to incorporate her; integrating her is tougher but also more rewarding than leaving her at home.

Third, the previous chapter explored the inclination of the survival instinct to discount the feminine influence by symbolically relegating her to scrubbing the floors rather than playing a dynamic role at the ball. The tougher something is to do, the more likely people will say it can't be done. The tougher the task you assume, the more you find others who say you can't do it. Employing the feminine influence means accepting you will always be outnumbered. If the Cinderella story can exist in something as masculine as sports, it can also exist in business; but, it also means you won't find Cinderella everywhere.

Fourth, the accomplishment of the first chapter interrelates to the perspective I'm suggesting we take for the next few chapters because it laid the foundation for that perspective. Points in this chapter and the others will reference various aspects of the first chapter and will allow for a more effective introduction and summation of points relevant to that particular chapter. Conceptually, the first chapter demonstrated the inherent value behind the various aspects of the feminine influence as summarized by the word comparison table in Figure 2.20.

In this chapter, we'll focus our attention on a company by delving into three of four major elements affecting outcomes:

- Situation
- Flow
- People

The fourth one is the individual, which is you, and will have a separate section.

Since I probably know very little about your company, I'll use another company as a case study by which you can use as an example to help assess yours relative to these three elements. The example is based upon a real situation, and I've modified the details as much as I could without having to alter the general principles behind my observations and conclusions.

Details, while important, in and of themselves do not communicate comprehensively what I'm suggesting you need to take from this chapter; so a slight alteration does not matter. What we're attempting to get from this chapter is more along the lines of the left diagram in Figure 2.53, a feel for what the details say collectively, similar to what all the notes communicate musically in a symphony. The slight alteration of a point in Figure 2.53 won't change collectively that we have an oval because no matter how much information I convey here, I've not, by any stretch, covered every point about this situation. I've covered what will allow the people, who most likely will benefit from this book, to see at least an oval and hopefully much more behind these principles. From a more mundane perspective, we are focusing on trends and tendencies.

The Strategy chapter outlines ways to incorporate the feminine influence. It's this chapter's purpose to give a feel for how the strategy works within a context.

The feminine influence is a viable part of any business' or business person's strategy. Not only can she help a business grow more dynamically but also a business person. For a business person this growth can occur externally in the form of better work opportunities and relationships but also internally in the form of a better understanding and appreciation of his talents; however, while the feminine influence can help at all times, she's not always the dominant force. Context determines dominance.

Some situations, flow, and people make the emphasis of the feminine influence more impactive than others. We'll explore this in detail in the Strategy chapter, but a workable summary for this chapter will help us understand and see the main message particular to this case study: the situation, flow, and people support an emphasis of aspects of the feminine influence. As far as the strategy this means a more aggressive, apparent effort to employ her.

The simplest way to look at conditions supporting an emphasis on the masculine and others supporting an emphasis on the feminine is to compare action versus inaction. Sometimes this is difficult to see in business because there is always activity going on, but the distinguishable point is concerted action, typically seen as initiatives, around which you're trying to focus activities. Generally, these are new activities rather than habitual ones. "New" can mean different in substance or different in intensity, taking a habitual activity and going to another level with it or refining it. Essentially, they're actions that require additional concentration by you or others.

Analogously, we can use an army in battle. Marching and fighting represent action while regroup and rest represent inaction. Commanders of the army tend to focus on effective action in the first and morale building in the second. Before the march or fight, they will mingle and communicate with the troops, while during the march or fight their focus is on effective action. An army's as well as a business' success is based on relationships. The time necessary to effectively build relationships is most available during periods of relative inactivity. It's during these periods that the feminine influence is dominant.

With the case study, I'm attempting to show why conditions are right for an emphasis on aspects of the feminine influence, primarily relational ones. This not only means that the strategy in that chapter will more likely work but also that people who have the ability to implement it are more likely to have opportunities open up to them during this time. In general, these times favor a woman over a man. Of course, this is a rash generalization with no regard for your particular talents, but it serves as a starting point because I most likely don't know you which would be the preferred starting point.

In order to get to this point, understanding and appreciating context from the standpoint of favoring the masculine or feminine is important. Consequently, the basic principle behind this chapter is that there are rhythms by which events flow that allow us to anticipate them. If you get anything at all from this chapter, I'd like you to at least be aware that events have rhythms so you can begin to look out for them in terms of conditions favorable to the masculine or feminine in the spirit of Figure 2.25. I'll deal with how these translate into outcomes, but learning is a gradually process; we cannot anticipate outcomes until we can see the rhythms.

This rhythmic concept differs from predictions as the forest differs from the trees, the river from the droplets, and the wind from the gusts. The more we attempt to concentrate our attention the more likely we'll error not only because it's harder to determine what a tree will do than a forest, a droplet than a river, or a gust than the wind but also because the forest, the river, and the wind will have a more comprehensive impact on us than a tree, a droplet, or a gust. Understanding which direction the wind is blowing will affect us more than being able to predict when and where every gust will blow. Nonetheless, a tree, a droplet, or a gust could surprise us and have an amazing impact; such details we can only handle the best we can when they arise.

Behind this rhythmic concept it's important to keep in mind that relationships drive the human element and cause it to exhibit and reinforce this concept in business. Essentially, no one can have a good feel for any business situation, especially the environment in a company, without a feel for the condition of relationships in that business, primarily the client-employee and employee-manager. The ability to anticipate the future of a company is directly related to the degree to which one can assess the status of these relationships within their rhythmic context. The condition of these relationships eventually makes itself felt in a delayed manner similar to the discussion around Figures 2.1 – 2.15. This is why serious acquirers of companies will spend exhaustive time trying to assess these relationships before purchasing them. We more typically hear elements of this described as morale and culture. Rhythm concerns itself more with the trends, the motion versus the snapshot.

With that introduction, let me describe the company we're about to use as a backdrop for this discussion. It's a large, older, publicly owned financial services firm that has experienced two of the more prevalent conditions in recent times, acquisitional growth and cost reductions. In general, the company is regional with national capabilities exceeding twenty-five thousand employees. For the purposes of the book I will refer to this company as "Alpha A Financial, Inc." or "Alpha A" in short.

The main premise asserted in this case study is that conditions are increasingly advantageous for a more aggressive attempt at integrating the feminine influence because Alpha A has reached a place in its rhythmic cycle where the feminine traditionally excels. There are two important aspects to this premise. First, no matter how talented the individual, no one can overcome situations, flow, and people directly opposed to him. Second, assuming a leadership role in a company isn't going to do much good if these factors affecting outcomes are aligned against the person because his tenure will be difficult for him and his family. In essence, while I'm suggesting that events benefit integration of the feminine influence, he will also need to appreciate into what he's entering.

In the effort to make this case study helpful to you, it's important to remember that the actual details matter far less than how we're looking at them. For instance, whether Alpha A is a sound financial company is immaterial to how we look at the information in various contexts. This one works because it's based on a real life situation with a feel for the condition of the two major classes of relationships, employee-client and employee-manager.

As we will explore in the upcoming section, this last point means we'll pay less attention to numbers and more on how those numbers influence people. Knowing a company has increased revenues by ten percent last year is useless unless we know how that is affecting how employees and managers feel beyond a simple good or bad. First of all, there's no guarantee every employee knows the information let alone has any kind of reaction to it whatsoever. This is a good introduction into fine tuning the perspective we'll take with this case study.

Perspective

My approach with the case study will continue with the methodology in the first chapter, intuitive supported by relational observations and inferences because quantifiable evidence supporting this premise is not only unavailable but also irrelevant. I'll elaborate on why this is true and paint a suggested perspective to aid in using this approach.

Elaborating on why quantifiable evidence supporting this premise is not only unavailable but also irrelevant will help in two ways by:

- Diminishing the highly ingrained view that business is a masculine endeavor.
- Accenting key, fundamental aspects of business clearly in the domain of the feminine.

We'll do this by showing the inherent weaknesses of a quantifiable approach to decision making through a return to the roots of any business – relationships, a domain where the feminine is superior to the masculine. This was one of the two fundamental business implications of the feminine influence we saw in the Introduction:

> The essence of any successful business is relationships, the relationships between the clients and employees and between employees and managers

Quantifying the various emotions in any relationship is impossible and reinforces from earlier the other fundamental business implication of the feminine influence:

> When we can finally quantify, rationalize, or objectify a business event in a logical expression, the optimal time to seize the opportunity or prevent the crisis it manifests has generally already passed.

We can incorporate both of these premises by looking at the relational interactions one person has with various employees in the company. The manner and content of each interaction will vary according to the personalities involved. We went through an implicational trail for this in the Introduction. Looking comprehensively at each interaction will find quantifying these interactions difficult. Pollsters have lesser but similar problems when they survey people. The crux of the challenge is this: if we wait for the numbers to tell us when to employ the feminine influence, we won't do so most effectively.

Nevertheless, despite our inability to quantify or organize these interactions, they do influence our person and give him a feel for what's going on in the company. Often, people refer to this information as hearsay and tend to discount it; however, such information influences and affects people, just ask any propagandist. If "perception is reality" then how someone feels about something, regardless of whether his reality is in line with truth, will affect that person. In many companies people also refer to the communication channel disseminating this informal information as the "grapevine."

In our business example concerning advertising in the previous chapter we introduced the possibility of the dominant role emotions play in our everyday decisions. The emotional factors influencing people's purchasing decisions also affect their views regarding external situations. We take this into account much of the time when we hear something that perhaps we don't like because we'll tend to discount the source. In our example, our person could easily discount information through the grapevine he doesn't like as "there's no way that person could know that." Conversely, information with which he tends to agree will more likely be seen as truth.

This sets the stage for an intelligent listener who can sort through the various contexts acting upon and within the communicator in a way that will allow him to integrate it into his other information. All comments from all people are not equal, devising a way to interpret this let alone organize or quantify it is challenging. Despite this challenge, this information exists and represents relational aspects that influence a business. In the Strategy chapter, I'll illustrate how this works in a way that will allow us to get a better feel for what's happening and to be in a better position to influence it. The grapevine is a perfect example of how the feminine influence, indirect, intangible, and invisible, is a part of business especially when we contrast it to the overtly direct, tangible, and visible communications issued through formal company channels – the masculine counterpart to the grapevine. Typically, the masculine response to these more indirect communications, as already hinted in the flashpoint section of the previous chapter, is to discount, discourage, or eradicate them. Consequently, employees and managers in business are less likely to make use of them advantageously.

Translating this to our case study means that by the time I receive more concrete evidence supporting what our person has learned from informal discussions it will be irrelevant because the optimal time to employ an effective strategy will have passed. Our discussions around Figures 2.1 – 2.15 lay the basis for this. Even here, I'm assuming that not only is the information I mention quantifiable but also accurate. Both assumptions are suspect. Again, this does not mean other strategies won't be available, including some quantifiable ones, but rather that they will more likely require additional effort and have less likelihood of success. I'm essentially suggesting in this case study that decisions need to be made earlier than is normally typical and will entail feeling more comfortable with making decisions with less information. Generally, this will hold true for any business not just the one in this case study. Integrating the feminine influence into business as an active partner means releasing oneself from over reliance on verifiable documentation and statistics. Our gut is just as true, if not more so, than this kind of tangible information. Our ability to feel something about a situation is far more comprehensive than our ability to document, quantify, or analyze it. This ability varies by person and generally is more prominent in women. Learning how to integrate the two will not only help us be more aware of opportunities and problems earlier but also to construct more effective strategies to address them.

Another way to reinforce the secondary importance of statistics in business is to consider the mantra in Alpha A, "We're in a relationship business." Your company may have a similar emphasis. Carrying this expression to its full implication, we find that business in its entirety is based upon relationships between employees and clients and between employees and managers. Without these relationships, no business can thrive.

Revenue, expenses, income and other statistical measures attempt to quantify those relationships but do not reflect at all the full extent of those relationships. If they did, there would be no need to interpret the numbers by answering such questions as "What caused our revenue growth?" or "How did we increase our income?" Pushing the mantra, "We're in a relationship business" to the limits, we find that the ultimate answers to all such questions rest upon the nature of the relationship between employees and clients and between employees and managers with statistics being just a crude, incomplete manifestation of those relationships.

No one can find any aspect of business that doesn't boil down to these relationships. As an example, let's take an Internet interaction where a client completes an automated online transaction involving no direct contact with or involvement by an employee.

Even though this is an electronic exchange and does not involve any direct contact between the client and employee, it does say something about the nature of the relationship between the two. This becomes more apparent when we realize that the website is a reflection of work done by Alpha A employees by asking, "Who designed, engineered, and approved the website?" There is a relational connection between the employees of the company and the client. Some employee or group of employees was involved either in the design, engineering, or approval phases of the site's development even if a third party did most of the work. The nature of that relationship is quite different from a regular, personal exchange and will vary with the personalities of the clients and the employees. No two groups of employees in the same industry would independently produce the same website. Consequently, two different websites would create two different impressions upon the visitor; the employees of the respective companies created that differentiation.

We can even highlight this more clearly in several ways by asking, "What message does the website convey?" or "What happens when a transaction goes amiss?"

The first question encompasses marketing jargon such as "image advertising" or "branding." More deeply, it involves the connotation of words and the symbolism of pictures. On the surface, one can easily claim this is the company's image rather than of any employee or any particular group of employees, but if we follow this to its fullest implication, we find that any company is nonexistent without employees. In fact legally, no company can exist without at least one employee to sign all the documentation even if that employee is only the owner. In essence, a company, as an entity, does not exist except on paper, for it's only a collective term classifying a group of *individual* people working together around a particular business endeavor.

The second question, "What happens when a transaction goes amiss?" involves the increased likelihood of a more direct contact with an employee. This is why we cannot accept the existence of something tangible as a single, electronic transaction as a legitimate argument repelling the premise that every client has a relationship with the employees of a company. We can accept the premise that some relationships are more personal than others, but no business relationship is without a personal influence of some kind. A face-to-face meeting is more personal than an online interaction, but both are relationships involving clients and employees.

Furthermore, the concept of relationship becomes clearer if we view it comprehensively beyond a transaction or a collection of transactions constituting a sale. For example, consider two people. The first goes into a store and leaves without purchasing anything while a second enters and buys something. Who's a client? How different would our answer be if the first person didn't buy anything else on his next ten visits while the second on his tenth visit does buy something (after eleven visits both have bought something)? Does a transaction or the decision to enter the store constitute a relationship? Consider a third type of person who visits a store, does not buy anything, but refers several others to it. Is this person a client? If we give away something for free, is the person receiving the item now a client?

Let's translate this to something more intangible such as legal services. If someone meets with an attorney to discuss a legal matter but does not hire the attorney, does a relationship exist? Is there the same expectation that that attorney will keep the discussion confidential regardless of whether the person hires him? For some reason that person "bought" the premise that sitting down with this attorney was worthwhile.

By restricting a view of relationship by limiting it to someone who has given us money, then we become guilty of viewing clients transactionally; we only have a relationship if they've bought something. Do products or relationships define a business? The true gut check becomes the answer to this question: Can a business relationship exist without the occurrence of a business transaction that shows up on the income statement or balance sheet? A more targeted and related question would be "Do prospects have a business relationship with us?" The answer to both is "yes." People have perceptions about companies and their employees regardless of whether they've bought something, and these perceptions affect a business' success. Relationships are the basis for these perceptions.

The point is not to spend time defining relational determinants because regardless of how we define those, people whether they buy or simply visit will have experiences that contribute to their impressions of that company's employees and those impressions will affect business. What is important is expanding our horizons to aspects affecting a relationship so we can see the many ways employees impact clients including the ways many employees impact one particular client. Returning to our internet example, by expanding the parameters around that transaction we also expand what we can see as potential influencers. Some we may not even consciously know such as suggestions from friends that he consider our company's product or service.

What we also begin to see, as we expand those parameters, are all the intangible, invisible, and indirect ways relational aspects can affect business – this is the domain of the feminine influence. Yet many times, since we cannot see these let alone measure them in any significant way, we ignore them. For some companies, they're easy to ignore because they don't exist! They have no sustainable residual benefit from client-employee relationships that ripple through the marketplace. A man without a woman cannot reproduce. Likewise, a business that does not consciously incorporate these feminine aspects into its strategy is less likely to succeed in the long run than one that does. As we will see in the Strategy chapter, there are ways to make interactions more dynamic so their resonation is stronger, so it's not only a matter of whether a business does this but also to what degree.

Of course, before we discuss any strategy some contemplation of the future is in order. Many times the acceptance of a particular strategy is based on the perspective it has about future events. More importantly, how the future unfolds will affect the timing for implementing the various aspects of that strategy. For these reasons, spending time outlining and reinforcing a view of the future is worthwhile.

From the perspective of this book's main theme, the feminine influence in business, having a better handle on the future is an integral part because the feminine aspect allows us to do that. Again, while she may not provide us the specificity we're accustomed to having, she will alert us earlier to opportunities and problems than the masculine. This was illustrated by Figure 2.17. Thus, contemplation of the future is not only important for the strategy but for understanding and appreciating the feminine influence in business because employing the feminine influence effectively entails doing so as early as possible.

The perspective I wish to set for this chapter concerning the future is one of listening to a song where I'm not told its name and I've never heard it. When I hear the first few bars or even the first few notes, I may not be able to tell exactly what notes will follow, but I may be able to tell whether its classical, rock, country, rap, or some other classification. I may also be able to determine its mood such as happy or sad. All of which will allow me to make some pretty good guesses as to where the music will go. Again, this is an example of what we discussed in the first chapter where the masculine sets the expectation and the feminine feels out what's next despite not knowing exactly what notes will follow.

Some may be inclined to say then that this method of looking at the future ends up being nothing more than an interpretation. While it is an interpretation, it's no different than someone looking at a set of numbers and doing the same. Interpretations affect not only how statistics are examined but also what statistics are collected, thus the line "Statistics don't lie, but liars use statistics." The only difference here is that we're not using numbers; we're using empirical information that may or may not be measurable. Again, measurability has no correlation on the intrinsic value of something; just because we can measure something doesn't mean it's more valuable. For instance, just because we can now measure the radiation from the sun, doesn't mean there's more or less heat, or better or worse heat. Thus, if we wait for the numbers, most likely the optimal time for action has passed.

In essence then, we can introduce this section as an attempt to make conclusions about the song that we hear for Alpha A because it may be too late for optimal actions if we wait for the entire song to play out just so we can be certain of what we're hearing. If we wait for the game's final score, we will miss the best time to influence the score.

<u>Situation</u>

Outcomes are influenced by the nature of the situation. For the purpose of trying to listen to Alpha A's song, we'll segment the nature of this situation into an external and internal perspective. The external will focus on the climate its operating in while the internal will focus on its interaction with that climate.

External

Since business could not exist without relationships, we can infer business is just a classification for a type of relationship. As with any relationship, it's affected by other relationships such as political, social, and religious. We see this on a personal level when personal matters affect employees or when business affairs affect personal life. Relationships people have in other areas will affect their relationship with Alpha A. Examining the external climate will help us interpret the song that they may bring to us. This is something any student learns in business class, but the key is having an appreciation for how the person who develops a strategy interprets external conditions.

The overall song I present here is distrust. I'll show this by examining peoples' relationships in four areas:

- Governmental
- Social
- Religious
- Business

I'll follow this by discussing what the songs in these four areas imply for you.

Governmental

Ever since the late sixties and early seventies with the Vietnam War and Watergate, trust and faith in government has declined. Most attention has been on the federal level but this has also happened on the local level.

It would be too simple to say this distrust is solely from corruptive influences because unrealistic expectations on government's ability also contribute to distrust. September 11th clearly showed the limitations of the largest entity on the planet, the U.S. government, to protect the populace from small, dangerous influences. If the largest entity could be caught that off guard, what does it say about smaller ones?

More locally, the move of students to private secondary education from public systems reflects an increasing distrust of state and local governmental entities to deliver quality education. Also there are the negative campaigns during elections and the frequent reports of financial conflicts of interest on all levels.

Regardless of whether its corruption or inability, people trust the government less to make good decisions today than it did decades ago. While individual people will find their particular level of trust ebb and flow with who's in office, the overall perspective is a declining one.

Social

Distrust in any arena manifests itself frequently in closer monitorship and more restrictions. The rise of the security industry clearly indicates this. We also can see it by a visit to a local school. Locked restrooms and entryways are not uncommon where twenty and thirty years ago they were unthinkable.

We see it too in the more frequent reports of spousal and child abuse that implies one cannot even trust his or her spouse or parents. Avoidance of strangers and emphasis on public places when meeting someone for the first time, take the "don't accept candy from strangers" to an adult level. Publicized ill-fated meetings of internet "friends" reinforce this feeling.

We also see it in the increasing litigious nature of our culture. Not only does this demonstrate the lack of empathy in honest mistakes but it also encourages further distrust. If someone falls and breaks an ankle on your driveway, it encourages one to think first about warding off any potential suit rather than first thinking about the welfare of the one who fell. All of this promotes a distancing from strangers and acquaintances.

Without a doubt, publicly we view meeting a stranger with more hesitancy today than we did a couple decades ago.

Religious

While people have gradually come to suspect even family members, religious institutions are not immune. Initially limited to people in the newer evangelical churches, it now includes the clergy in more traditional churches.

What makes this particularly damaging is the high trust factor clergy had before this onslaught of scandals involving children. Again, it would be difficult for anyone to claim the trust in religious figures was higher today than a couple decades ago.

Business

Of all the areas, we'll spend the most time here but it's important to remember that all the other areas we've covered also reinforce the distrust in business entities.

While some would argue that one cannot trust a business entity because it's solely there to make a profit, our concern is how does this trust and faith compare with ten and twenty years ago. Again, if we seek only to focus on distrust as a corruptive aspect, we'll simplify this too much. We also need to look at it from an impotency perspective, the feeling that there's no point in taking positive actions.

Two events have tarnished the luster on business: the recent stock market crash and accounting improprieties.

The multi-trillion dollar collapse of net worth in this country is sobering. Imagine going to Las Vegas and finding you are enjoying a winning streak beyond belief. While emotionally enjoying your good fortune, a horrible streak of bad luck causes you to lose all your winnings and to find yourself back to your original investment. This is the emotional state of most people after this event. While it's not a disaster and allows folks to continue on with some form of normality, the crash does stir up vulnerabilities. At minimum, the financial cushion most folks had is now gone. Any further collapse of the economy could have disastrous consequences for most people. This alone creates an insecure feeling about the future and a natural distrust.

Even if no further decline occurs, unless the market and the economy have another record boom similar to what has happened over the last twenty years, we could be looking at five to ten years before the markets reclaim their highs. The comparable declines of the early thirties and seventies are examples of this.

Accounting improprieties tarnished a profession that clients found most trustworthy of all in the financial services industry. What compounded these improprieties was their direction by topmost managers in the corporations and firms. Together they threw a long, dark shadow over the light that capital markets objectively reflect the value of business entities for success around clearly stated business purposes and activities. In the end, "quality of management" became a new "risk" factor outside the control of the financial services professionals and governmental agencies.

Indirectly these improprieties also tarnished the whole financial services industry from the brokers, agents, and planners who work with clients to the analysts and commentators who report and interpret financial activity. The impression is one of a large, unorganized group held together by uninquisitive profiteering, "if you're makin' money, don't ask."

All of this came at the expense of those who placed their trust and faith in this group to do just the opposite: prudently inquire about profits. There was an expectation that a professional, intellectual curiosity would prevail. Even though many in the financial services industry, including some in this nebulous group, are feeling the wrath of this misplaced trust, it again comes down to relationships, in this case, the one between the advisor and the client.

These two events, the tech crash and accounting improprieties, created an uneasy feeling among investors. It would help to look more into this feeling to appreciate the challenges that lie ahead.

In the late sixties and early seventies, everyone saw the stock market as the domain of the wealthy. For the average investor, accumulating the capital necessary to purchase a diversified portfolio of hundred share lots was very expensive. Mutual funds changed this so lowly capitalized investors could participate. As a result we found college students working out in health clubs talking about their portfolios.

Even though these events have had an impact on people's perceptions regarding business, they are also instructive from a rhythmic perspective. In order to appreciate how people's relationships can move rhythmically we have to be able to visualize how they can move concertedly, otherwise all these relationships move randomly. Random notes more than likely generate noise. To say events move rhythmically is also to say they do not move randomly; they are interconnected in a way that they not only influence one another but encourage a common direction or theme.

For instance, a little girl throws bread crumbs in a pond and all the fish swim to get it. The fish are not consulting one another regarding their movements but they all move in the direction of the bread crumbs. As they converge on the bread crumbs, the larger fish will tend to push the smaller ones aside. Again, the larger fish did not organize against the smaller fish, it is just the way things tend to work when fish scramble for bread crumbs.

Likewise, if the same little girl puts birdseed on two fence posts, one farther away from her than the other, the larger birds will tend to go to the one farther away and the small ones closer. It's not that the larger birds organized this effort, but rather they crowded out the smaller birds who, if they wanted food, could only take the risk of approaching the one closer to the little girl. They did what came to them as best for them.

This concept is not that different from Adam Smith's "invisible hand of capitalism" where individuals behave in accordance to their self-interest. This self-interest creates a pattern, flow, or rhythm to behavior so it no longer is purely random. Conceptually, capitalistic forces and others influences allow events to have rhythms derived in intricately involved ways.

Let's move on to a more complex situation very similar to the stock market. Imagine a poker game containing expert players who win by taking each other's money based upon how they interpret the value of their hand relative to the value of the others' hands. At some point, with a limited capital base, only a limited amount of money can be won.

Now, if we imagine these players opening the game to less experienced players, more capital enters the game, so more money could be won. To the experts, it makes sense to encourage folks to enter the game. More significantly, they will all arrive at the same conclusion eventually. It makes no sense to advertise the many intricacies involved in poker because this would present the game as complex, involved, and intimidating. As a result, they would advertise the more glamorous aspects of the game. The experts would not need an organized strategy because all could easily see the advantages of expanding the circle of players; however, if they wanted to they could jointly organize a separate group aimed at expanding the awareness of the advantages of playing poker. Quality of play may go down, but they would earn more money.

In some ways, this is analogous to some sports where expanding the enjoyment of it encourages people to pay and see the professionals play. Of course, this allows the professionals greater potential to earn money through salaries, endorsements, prize money, media revenue, and product lines. Again, these professionals may or may not have organized formally or informally to do this, but concerted actions are encouraged because they will all benefit from this.

Returning to poker, as more people enter the game and it becomes more popular, outside commentators would be able to make money on writing about happenings in the game. Of course, as more people buy their writings, they would make more money too. Expanding their audience by encouraging more people to play the game would help. Reporting disparaging news about the game that would deter or intimidate others from participation would hurt sales of their writings.

Eventually, some of the new players just won't want to spend time playing the game but wish to enjoy its financial advantages, so expert players will advertise their services to play the game for them for a fee. This would encourage more people to play and increase the capital base. Since writers and players all benefit from a positive, easy marketing of the game, the "look how easy it is to have fun and money" attitude would prevail.

If at some point, bad news would cause people to leave the game and deter new ones from entering, then the experts could be caught short handed. If they're in a losing position for themselves or others, they would have a hard time making it up if people begin to take their remaining money and leave. Suddenly, the capital base is less and the pots are fewer and smaller.

Regardless of what causes the markets to move up or down, they cannot work without capital. The easiest and quickest way to expand the capital base is to get more people to invest. In the eighties and nineties, this happened by getting the lower end investor to commit his funds through a variety of convenient methods typified by the mutual fund. One of the most impacting along these lines was the 401(k).

Let's assume a stock market containing a hundred investors and only one company. If they buy and sell the stock of this company among themselves, their actions would cause that stock to fluctuate based upon how they individually felt about the performance of the company. Now, if another hundred people decided to enter the market and caused the capital pool to double, the stock price would increase overnight without any change in the financial strength of the company to cause the increase.

We saw this effect with the explosion of mutual funds to the point where they outnumbered companies on the exchanges. This illustrated the pressure of this additional capital on the financial markets. Since factors besides capital availability affect new business development more intensely than new mutual fund introductions, the total number of companies on the exchange did not expand at the same rate as mutual funds. In effect, more money chased available companies.

The importance and relativity of these examples and looking at the markets in this way is not only to demonstrate how everyone can behave in a coordinated fashion without formal or informal agreements, but also to show the importance of trust and faith in business. What these two events, the market crash and accounting scandal, illustrate best is the subjective nature of the markets despite the seemingly objective nature bombarding investors in the form of quantifiable information. The two corresponding feelings are:

- "Get into the game."
- Belief in numbers.

The first is demonstrated by the influx of investors over the thirty years prior to the recent crash while the second by the "taking at face value" attitude regarding accounting outputs.

Implications

As it pertains to you, there are two primary implications of this distrust regarding the feminine influence:

- Her employment will be more difficult.
- Her impact will be more profound.

Looking at it in another way, being a woman in business will be more difficult but also more rewarding. In this case, I'm using the term "woman" more in the emotional or spiritual sense than in the physical sense, but women in general, if they pursue their relational strengths, will tend to benefit more during these times than men will. How we arrive at these points is helpful to discuss because the external conditions driving these implications will affect everyone at Alpha A and other companies.

At the core of any relationship, including a business one, is faith and trust. When this erodes, relationships become more difficult in a constrictive sense. People consolidate their "defenses" and will reserve confidences to a smaller group. This will include diminishing the importance of the whole and focusing on the specific in the form of their well being. In many respects it yields the same outcome as terrorism by undermining faith and trust in the group, the government, to protect the individuals. Thus, cohesion breaks down and weakens the social fabric. Distrust is bad for both people in a relationship because it stirs the worst thoughts about the other person in each person. As a result, not only does one fear for herself but also think ill of the other.

This negative feeling is compounded by the two aspects it has. First, a person will tend to feel more negatively not only because there is the feeling of her own weakness, but second because of her cruelty to innocent bystanders whose only crime was that of being a stranger. Usually, she rationalizes both along the lines of "Well, you can't trust anyone these days." Despite this, negative feelings in her pervade toward others and her.

Ironically, the feeling of distrust indirectly shows the power of the feminine influence's qualitative aspect because rationally we have little to fear. The Virginian sniper case is a perfect example. Rationally, the odds of being gunned down by this man were remote and on par with being stuck by lightning; yet, he was able to shut communities and events throughout eastern Virginia and the D.C. area. Terrorism works the same way.

Rationally, the odds of being killed by a terrorist act are extremely small, but yet they still encourage one to restrict his freedoms. This reasoning also addresses the impact of the experiences mentioned earlier in the governmental, social, religious, and business arenas. Statistically, all of these were fairly remote events, but yet they carry tremendous emotional impact. Indirectly, from a negative perspective, they support the inherent power in the feminine influence.

The difficulty distrust creates in relationship building helps explain the explosion of online interactions over the Internet between strangers. You don't have to trust anyone unless you wish to extend the relationship beyond the online environment, but yet you can still interact without fear. I also cited the tremendous growth of the security industry over the last thirty years as an indicator of distrust. Everyone has experienced more security precautions of their own, friends, employers, and government, even before September 11th.

All of this carries over to the business world. Alpha A's and your company's employees are also members of various physical and organizational communities. To expect them to not carry the effects of this distrust from their everyday world into the corporate world is folly. As shown in Figure 3.2, whereas "no man is an island," neither is any company:

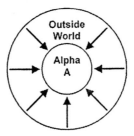

Figure 3.2

Consequently, a manager's job becomes tougher because there is greater distrust today than even a few years ago, especially in light of tougher economic times where layoffs are more frequent. Distrust translates into lower productivity and higher labor costs.

We see lower productivity in two ways. First, there is the manager who must spend more time and energy developing a rapport with those who work for her. Her decisions will also require more explanation so her people will understand them and buy into them. Second, she will find her employees less productive because they must do the same with clients. They will also find themselves challenged emotionally too when they try to remain empathetic to clients who behave distrustfully toward them. In both ways, these situations wear upon employees.

We will also see higher labor costs in attracting and retaining employees. Since faith and trust are in short supply, people will need stronger financial arrangements in order to overcome any distrust they may have to feel secure. Any economy functions less effectively when distrust reigns. The Russian economy with its corruption shows the high cost of doing business when folks cannot even trust the enforcement of business agreements so they hire "protection" organizations to help them. While the distrust in our country has not reached that extreme, there is still a corresponding premium for protection against it that appears in more complex legal arrangements, increasing legal work.

On the other hand, this distrust creates conditions for stronger relationships where trust and faith existed. Trust's rareness increases its value, so the trustful relationships that do exist become more valuable. Even though getting to that point will be difficult, once someone establishes them they'll see increasingly impactive results. Not only would they see lower negative pressure on labor costs and productivity, but they would also see more dynamic revenue growth.

Tying this to the previous chapter covering the feminine influence, we remind ourselves that trust and faith are key elements of hers. Whereas power and its transaction in the form of titles, authority, and money rests in the masculine form of relationship development, faith and trust rest with the feminine. This is why we can say it will be tougher to be a woman but never more rewarding.

Summary

A situational analysis from an external perspective emphasizes distrust. Since any company's employees are also members of various communities, their external relationships and experiences will impact a company's internal environment. As a result, distrust will be a huge hurdle for any company to overcome with its employees; we'll see this exhibited as increasing concern by the employee for his own well-being and diminishing concern for the well-being of the company.

Since business is nothing more than a variety of relationships categorized by two major types, employee-client and employee-manager, social distrust strains business relationships in the form of higher labor costs and lower productivity. Overcoming distrust will not be easy in an economically challenging environment dominated by layoffs and shadowed by war.

As an aside about the war on terrorism, we should recall that in each of the two previous market crashes of the current one's magnitude (1929 and 1973/74) the sitting president was not re-elected. This war is a huge difference affecting contemporary times because voters tend to rally around the president in war times; war was not a factor in the other two situations. The uneasy conflict of interest, if the economy does not improve, is that re-election may depend upon maintaining the threat of terrorism and a warlike mind frame in voters. As 1968 and Vietnam showed, this "rally around the President" strategy only works if the public feels the war is going well. In this, we have conditions that will severely test the integrity of our public leaders and increase the likelihood of scrutinization that will wear further on the trust and faith people have in one another.

Nevertheless, while overcoming this increasing distrust for one another will be difficult in a work setting, the opportunity for the feminine influence to have a dynamic impact on people has never been stronger. We can now explore how this interrelates with Alpha A's own situation.

Internal

When we listen to the song of Alpha A Financial, Inc. we hear a very masculine, focused, direct, business one. This portion of the Company chapter reinforces this point by showing how this song overlooks the feminine influence. By showing the absence of water, you demonstrate how dry the land is. The important aspect of this case study is a contrarious one along the lines of a contrarian investment philosophy. The more masculine the environment is the more brilliantly appears the feminine; the drier the land the more important any water becomes, the more men there are in a room, the more a single woman stands out.

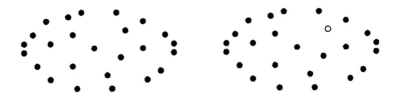

Figure 3.3

As we see in Figure 3.3, our focus changes when we insert one white dot. We experienced the same feeling in Figure 2.49 when we placed the first dot in an oval. While distinguishing any point from another on the left diagram is a matter of location, coloration becomes an additional, important one with the right diagram. We'll explore this differentiation by first discussing a working premise of Alpha A's situation and by second, going deeper behind this premise with examples to highlight and reinforce the main point that Alpha A is a very masculine company.

Premise

The working premise I'll use for Alpha A is that it is a:

Survivor in the financial industry seeking preeminence as a holistic financial services firm among its peers.

The initial part of this premise, "Survivor in the financial industry," is evident with not only its survival of the merger mania of the nineties that occurred but also with its heavy participation in it. The second aspect of this premise as represented by "holistic financial services firm" is evident by its positioning and investment in making sure that it is a holistic provider of financial products and advice for businesses and individuals. A new branding campaign introduced in 2002 is its most recent, widespread, tangible effort to say this to clients and the markets.

This premise through the phrase "seeking preeminence" identifies how it stands in this effort. It's not preeminent among peers, but it's moving in that direction. More importantly, this says that it's beyond the stage of trying to become a holistic financial services firm. Alpha A's position is such that it has everything in place to make a run at preeminence; this alone says quite a lot about its capabilities and talents.

If we look at Alpha A from two perspectives, its business/personal markets and traditional/non-traditional activities, and examine the interaction between them and evaluate their strength in terms of tenure over the last twenty years, we would see something like Figure 3.4. Traditional financial activities are those that have a long history at Alpha A while non-traditional are those it has expanded into more recently in its drive to become a holistic financial services firm.

History of Strength

	Traditional	**Non-Traditional**
Business	Long	Medium
Personal	Medium	Short

Figure 3.4

What this shows is Alpha A's dominance as a firm for businesses in its more traditional financial activities. Its roots are very entrenched in its more traditional lines that have a long history of appealing to businesses. More recently, it has attempted to expand those traditional activities from businesses to individuals and expand its relationships with businesses by getting into other financial activities that have not traditionally been a part of its activities. Alpha A's most recent strengths developed in non-traditional financial activities for individuals.

The importance of highlighting this is that while Alpha A has organized itself around becoming a preeminent holistic financial services firm, there is question whether its clients and the markets view it as such. Clearly, the capabilities and talents state differently. Essentially, what is on paper varies from perception. The question becomes one of getting this message out and making it stick.

To a large extent, Alpha A's strong history of being a business firm along its more traditional activities, while a strength, is a sun that blinds its other stars. Combine this with even a secondary view of it being a strong firm along more traditional lines for personal as well as business and the sun becomes even brighter and blocks even more aspects of its non-traditional activities. In effect, by contrast, its strengths in non-traditional elements of the financial services arena could very well be forces in their own right.

Even more interesting when the markets try to evaluate overall financial services capabilities, they seem to favor investment or brokerage firms over banks. For some reason banking activities are not looked upon with the same importance to someone's financial situation as investment management. This also seems to retard Alpha A's efforts in establishing the view that it's holistic because some of its more traditional activities receive less attention than its other activities.

In addition to being firmly rooted in its traditional financial activities, Alpha A Financial has a long history of being results oriented. It believes quantifiable results will eventually carry the day with financial markets. The CEO, Joe Davidson's reference to Alpha A's long streak of continuous earnings increases at its recent employee awards event is evidence of that as well as the more traditional language used in its annual reports. Reinforcing this is Alpha A's intense effort in this distrusting environment to assert its integrity by not only complying with new accounting and security requirements but also incorporating proper remarks in public forums. Combine this with its historical financial strength and we have affirmation of a strong financial institution able to weather various financial storms.

Examples

The easiest way to begin a more in depth look behind the masculinity of Alpha A is to highlight the difference between two words:

Strong vs. Dynamic

The question regarding this difference is "Which word better identifies Alpha A Financial, Inc.?" Regardless of whether you ask a market analyst, a manager, a officer, or a frontline staff person, the answer will more likely be "strong" than "dynamic."

In most cases, people will not doubt its financial strength; however, they will likely doubt the innovation and creativity and the energy to muster resources around new ideas. The most salient example is Alpha A's introduction of a major, company-wide product and its lateness in adopting this product as a key asset gatherer when over a dozen major competitors have already had it.

Strength is an attribute of the masculine influence; however, dynamism is neither masculine nor feminine but rather a cooperative effort of the two. Generally, people are more attracted to dynamism rather than strength. The second is implied in the first, but the first is not necessarily implied by the second. It's difficult to be dynamic if you're easily washed away by the tide so it usually incorporates it in the form of a swift moving army, but strength can be seen as a force that doesn't move, such as a stone fortress. Whereas dynamic implies an active ingredient, strength does not necessarily carry that.

By incorporating the feminine influence into its current masculinity, Alpha A can become dynamic. Let's explore four examples where it's overlooking the feminine implications.

The first example is Joe Davidson's insight that the Financial Management division of Alpha A seems to be doing everything right except people don't know about it, so it's a matter of reputation. Although Joe may not have intended it, the implication here is that the reputational concern is not just one for this division alone but one for all of Alpha A as a whole. The logic behind this is:

Alpha A's reputation is the synergistic compilation of the reputations of all
its parts, so if it establishes or changes the reputation of any one part, it will
alter the reputation of the entirety.

In the end, the concern is Alpha A's reputation because Financial Management's success in establishing a reputation will no doubt greatly enhance Alpha A's "preeminence as a financial services firm."

Even though Joe's comments were directed to Financial Management, the challenge, when stated this way, highlights the fact that this is a task for all Alpha A employees and not just Financial Management ones. By everyone working to establish the reputation of this division, the reputation of everyone changes. This is most obvious with Joe's encouragement to position Financial Management among internal centers of influence in other divisions within Alpha A.

Conversely, Financial Management's reputation is greatly enhanced if its own employees converse regularly about all of Alpha A's capabilities and not just theirs. How can employees at Alpha A establish its reputation as a preeminent financial services firm by limiting their conversations to their specific area of responsibility?

Even with this it's only beginning to scratch the deeper implications of reputation as they relate to the feminine influence. Let's begin with this question:

How does Alpha A get clients and prospects to warm up to the reputation it
would like them to have?

The importance of this question rests with the qualitative aspects represented by "warm up to," for it's not only a matter of establishing a reputation but also the degree to which it's felt in order to prompt positive action. Essentially, how "hot" does Alpha A want to be? If clients are cold to it regarding its desire to be viewed as a preeminent financial services firm, then it's only a matter of turning up the heat.

Picture you entering a cold room with a cast-iron, wood-burning stove in it. In order to heat up the room, you fire up the stove. The fired stove heats the room by radiating heat throughout. If the stove's door was jammed so you could not place wood in it, then you would have to light a fire elsewhere in the room to heat it up. This would be far more difficult, dangerous, and ineffective. The cast-iron stove retains heat and radiates it more effectively in all directions than an open fire in part of the room. This is why a cast-iron stove is a more effective heating vehicle than a fireplace.

Initially, getting clients and prospects to warm up to Alpha A's reputation seems like an externally focused problem involving the building of fires in each of its markets; however, a more effective solution rests internally. By firing up the stoves within the employees, they'll radiate the heat to warm clients and prospects more efficiently, more easily, and ultimately more effectively.

In other words, the question of establishing a reputation without is addressed by establishing it first within. Alpha A's employees may know their company's capabilities, but are they "fired" up about it? Just because a stove exists doesn't mean it's warming the room. If the room is cold, it's because the stove isn't working. If Alpha A's markets are cold to its reputation, it's because its own employees are not "fired" up about it.

As a caveat, initially, the phrase "fired up" often has the connotation of an extremely extroverted activity that in the long-run can seem like superficial cheerleading. Sometimes we hear it expressed as looking for that "spark." Returning to our cast-iron stove and fireplace analogy, we're more interested in heat rather than light. With an effective blast furnace, there are no sparks, just heat. Likewise, a fireplace is more ostentatious than a cast-iron stove, but the latter delivers more heat. Occasionally, if we become distracted by someone's show of enthusiasm, we may mistake it for action; are we looking at the flames from a fireplace or are we feeling the heat from a cast-iron stove?

Connecting this to the feminine influence becomes transforming "working for money" into "loving your work." The latter is a passion stirred by the feminine. In the masculine world of business where objectivity reigns, generating warmth is very challenging because objectivity praises the coldness of emotionlessness over emotionalism, tangible over intangible, and reasons over instincts. How can one encourage something as intangible and instinctive as passion when he's promoting the cold, unemotional aspects of objectivity and quantitativeness? How can men appreciate a woman if they're only emphasizing her measurements?

The masculine will also encourage an external focus to reputation because the masculine goes "out" to hunt while the feminine stays "in" to keep the home fires burning. Any hunter hunts less effectively when he's cold and hungry than when he's warmed by fire and hot food. To tackle the outside he first addresses what's inside. "Home" is the place of origin. The origin of any person is inside – home base. "Home" base is the domain of the feminine. A masculine dominated environment that does not incorporate the feminine will ignore "home" and will eventually return to find no home fires burning and no food – a coldness that the song "Lady In Black" describes.

Another example of the masculine nature of Alpha A is to look at the nature of the annual employee awards event. This event solicits nominations from across the company in the various regions according to various categories. Two aspects jump out, scripting and quantitativeness.

Except for the first few award ceremonies, most were much scripted affairs. Extemporaneous speaking, except for the thank you speeches, is now non-existent. While this was in response to viewer surveys to make sure the program adhered to a time frame, we could also work off the assumption that people will tend to request shortening or restricting what they don't enjoy. Who cut shorts what he truly enjoys?

Joe Davidson's explosions emphasizing "silo busting" and memorable military quotes were highlights of creativity and spontaneity that people remember to this day; however, scripted affairs in front of employees, as the annual employee awards event has become, do not present Alpha A's leadership in the best possible light. They leave the impression as it did with voters regarding the electoral opponents of Ronald Reagan and Bill Clinton that they are less likely to handle the unexpected when things don't go according to script.

Again, Reagan did this through humor and Clinton through the town hall format. With all other things being equal, the person who speaks from a script is far less likely to inspire than one who speaks extemporaneously. Of course, spontaneity is also riskier especially if you're not knowledgeable. As we saw, in the previous chapter, spontaneity is an element of the feminine influence.

The quantitative aspect of the annual employee awards event came out in the most recent one when presenters drew comparisons with the first ceremonies of a decade ago. Rather than a hundred nominees and four winners, they touted over thirteen hundred winners from over five thousand nominees as representative of the success of this awards program.

Whenever, we highlight quantitative aspects over qualitative, we are expressing a masculine attribute. A more feminine approach would have been along the lines of highlighting the expansion of the program to allow personalization to the regions and to the variety of ways an employee can earn an award (as illustrated by the various categories) so the program could touch employees on the most individual level possible.

Both of these aspects emphasize image; how we dress up our comments to convey an impression that goes beyond the actual meaning of the words or pictures. Again, scripting and quantification emphasize colder, more detached impressions whereas extemporaneity and quality emphasize warmer, more relational impressions – aspects of the feminine. As we had discussed in the previous chapter, these images affect people irrespective of their ability to consciously recognize them; the ambiance of a restaurant affects us regardless of whether we take notice of every aspect of the décor.

The third example demonstrating the predominantly masculine culture at Alpha A connects with imagery directly.

Visualize a movie scene where we're shown individuals one at a time. The backdrop is a beautiful garden, and each person we see is smiling. There are flowers and many other exotic plants. The people are shown enjoying their stroll around the garden. What is your impression of this garden and the people?

Suddenly, the movie scene pulls back so we can see the garden in its entirety, and we find a high, gray concrete wall with barbed wire atop surrounding this beautiful garden with no way out. This scene holds for a few seconds before zooming in again to one of the smiling individuals. We no longer see the wall because our range of vision is small again; we just see a smiling person. How has your impression changed of the garden?

No matter what we say, our attire creates a visual that can add or detract. It creates a message all its own that is independent of what we say. The same exists for commercials; the visuals convey a message independent of the words.

Alpha A's most recent television advertisements focusing on real life clients are examples of where the visuals deliver a separate message from the words. In the commercial the initial scenes focus on a live client whose smiling in a very pleasant setting. Suddenly, the camera zooms out to show the client's face in the center of a "zero" in the account number of a statement. The client is a small face surrounded by a gray, lifeless statement. A few seconds later, the camera zooms back into the zero to show only the client. The words in the ad say that Alpha A doesn't look at its clients as account numbers; a message opposite to what the visuals imply through their images.

Studies of political advertisements show that the visuals in television ads carry more impact than the words even when the words convey a contrary message. When visuals and words conflict, the visuals win out. This is why advertising experts look at the ad without sound to observe the message. Since many people may be distracted when the commercial runs, especially in a restaurant or bar setting, the visual message carries even more weight because the sound may be obstructed or non-existent.

The masculine influence focuses more on what the words say and what the pictures show while the feminine concerns herself with the words' connotations and the pictures' images. In this particular advertisement, the feminine would do something along the lines of maintaining the view of the statement and destroying it so as to give a feeling of being freed from the account number. As it stands in the ad, the message is "Up close you're a client but at a distance (back in the office) you're a number." The statement isn't destroyed but rather lingers in the background where the client can't see it, similar to the concrete wall surrounding the people strolling in the garden.

Even as a joke or fictional story, no one would share a disturbing picture to a client in a meeting, and no one would run an ad containing one. Would we ever show, with even the rosiest sounding words or phrases, a picture of a client sitting in jail? If such extremes apply, then can everything else in between vary by degree?

Again, the masculine influence would say, "That's not what we're saying with the words" or "it's so obscure," but the feminine would be concerned with the image. That's why a female sales consultant advised us at a seminar to never joke and tease a woman the way men normally do with one another because women look beyond the message and its intent into a person's sensitivity. The feminine influence examines and accesses the deeper subtleties.

The fourth example of Alpha A's masculinity indirectly relates to image but deals more with organizational tendencies. We'll also explore this more when we discuss flow, so we'll stay rather narrow here for the moment. This interrelationship of the masculine and feminine concerns the group versus the individual.

The individual is the source of dynamic growth and creativity. Whereas no two women can give birth to the same child, no two people can give birth to the same idea. Any two children, as with any two ideas, can be similar. The group is the source of stability and strength. People unite to not only protect themselves but also to mutually help one another. People give ideas strength by organizing around them. Any child, as with any idea, can be involved with any number of people.

The individual and group are often at odds with one another because growth disrupts stability and creativity challenges strength, but integrating them allows for dynamism. The status quo resists growth because growth forms new status quo's at the expense of the current ones. The death of one status quo gives birth to another one. Strength resists creativity because going off in a new, unknown direction creates vulnerabilities. The explorer is always more at risk than the settler is. Creating vulnerabilities weakens the strong. Creativity weakens strength so it can become stronger. Both growth and creativity are the exercises that make stable and strong muscles firmer and stronger by first disrupting and weakening them.

Creativity and growth are feminine attributes represented by giving birth and nurturing. Stability and strength are masculine attributes represented by the "husbanding" of resources.

Disrupting groups so they once again become individuals is a feminine action while gathering individuals into a group so they become one is a masculine action. Joe Davidson's "silo busting" is an example of the first while "centralization" is an example of the second.

Reliance upon consensus, committees, and task forces to make decisions is a masculine response as we saw with "Lady In Black." Team is emphasized over the individual. At Alpha A, many decisions and plans are made this way. Being a team player is one of the core attributes, albeit the last one, in Alpha A's employee reviews. Again, encouraging team (more people involved the better) represents emphasis on the strength of numbers – a masculine trait.

Summary

These examples show the dominant masculine tendencies of Alpha A Financial, Inc. While they are by no means the only ones, they are representative. An even more detailed analysis involving such things as word choice around internal and external communications is possible.

These tendencies have served Alpha A well for it has become a survivor in the more traditional aspects of its product line and a player in the financial services field. To disregard these tendencies is to disregard a strong foundation. The question is how to move from survival to preeminence. This is where a better integration of the feminine influence would help because we're talking about all constituencies eventually coming to see "dynamic" as a better adjective for Alpha A than "strong."

Again, the importance to you is that employing the feminine influence will most likely be a differentiator for you and will vary depending upon the situation in which you find yourself. Most companies, especially larger ones, will tend to follow the same masculine aspects as Alpha A. One can visualize this differentiation as the sun in a sky filled with stars. A woman could visualize it as the "rose among thorns." The thorns may protect the survival of the whole plant but that is not what attracts people to that plant. What attracts people and makes this flower special is the rose itself. Thorns make this plant strong but the rose makes it dynamic. If this were not the case, then any woman would love receiving just the rose thorns. This is the power in beauty.

Whether I've correctly accessed Alpha A is irrelevant because the key is your interpretation of your company. My correctness will not affect you because the purpose of this case study is to demonstrate different ways to look at some fairly common business events in an unconventional manner. Thus, what's important is not my correctness but the approach. Even if you feel your company may not be as masculine oriented as Alpha A, employing the feminine influence will most likely differentiate you simply because of the difficulties in doing so. The previous chapter highlighted the talent and courage necessary to successfully do this. These alone are infrequent commodities that automatically permit integrating the feminine and masculine a differentiation.

Flow

In addition to appreciating the nature of the situation, flow is another important aspect of any outcome because any given situation is in a state of change. How a situation is changing will affect how one addresses it and the timetable under which he will work. Comprehending flow helps if we view it as determining where all the different aspects of the event are in their development and how they interact with one another rather than simply looking at it as "time," "here we are," "where do we want to go", and "when do we start." Events have momentum, so as with driving the sharpness of the turn one is able to take is not only dependent upon the car but also its speed. This also implies events have a certain continuity, what happens today relates to yesterday and will relate to tomorrow; events are not randomly thrown together.

The main point of this portion of the Company chapter is to create a feeling for flow by using Alpha A as the backdrop. In order to do this, I'll need to expand upon the seasonal analogy I introduced in the previous chapter with Gettysburg before I attempt to connect it to Alpha A's situation.

A secondary point for this section is to leave the impression that it takes time to integrate the strategies we'll cover in the Strategy chapter. The importance here is that to employ the feminine influence effectively one needs adequate time. Thus, it's not only a question of having flow on your side, but also of whether there is enough time to do what you feel you need to do. Combine flow with talent and courage, and you will see the case grow as to why differentiating yourself with the feminine influence will be easy – because most will tend to be intimidated by her complexities. Yet, in the long run, your investment will most likely surpass what you could have hoped with a purely simple, direct masculine approach.

Seasons

Everything has a flow to it, a song with a detectable rhythm. If this were not the case, we would not be able to make any assumptions on what was to follow because everything would be random. Formulas or regression analysis would be impossible. Each song is different and with it each rhythm. No two rhythms are exactly alike in their duration or intensity, but there is commonality. This rhythm allows for growth.

For this reason, growth does not appear as the graphic on the left in Figure 3.5 but as the one on the right. Nature is filled with examples of ebb and flow, surge and recede. Maintaining a "straight line" growth path is not the nature of life. Very few natural things in life contain straight unadulterated lines.

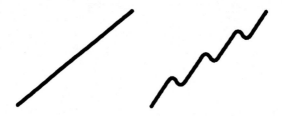

Figure 3.5

If we take a closer look at the graphic on the right, we do see a rhythm. By focusing on one cycle we find we can divide it into four basic phases and relate them to the seasons, Spring, Summer, Fall, and Winter such as I did in Figure 3.6.

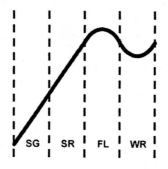

Figure 3.6

From this graphic we can summarize the four phases:

- Spring = Grow
- Summer = Enhance
- Fall = Harvest
- Winter = Rejuvenate

In order to begin moving this from the abstract, let's run through a couple examples. First, competitive distance running has four phases:

- Build endurance
- Speedwork
- Competition
- Rest

The first phase's characteristics entail working into longer distances and building endurance through high mileage to handle the demands of the next phase, speedwork. In this second phase, overall weekly mileage may decline a bit but the stress of running faster increases. By the third phase, mileage and stress decreases so energy is saved for competition where one reaps the benefits of training. After competition, the fourth phase involves rest and examining adjustments for the next year's competition.

Second, javelin throwing also has four phases as described to me by a javelin thrower for a local university:

- Strength
- Elasticity
- Competition
- Rest

First phase entails a lot of weight training to build strength for the second phase. Very little throwing of the javelin takes place during this phase. The second phase begins javelin throwing and works to eliminate weights since they hinder elasticity in the muscles. The third (competition) and fourth (rest) phases are the same as they are for running.

Almost any athletic endeavor relates to this same growth cycle. Many times in professional sports we find commentators talk about "peaking for the playoffs." A longer cycle occurs over portions of a career as well. That's why some athletes take a year off.

Third, moving from athletics to ideas or emotional growth, the four seasons translate into:

- Spring is the best time to grow your idea by introducing and nurturing it.
- Summer is the best time to enhance your idea by pushing it to its limits.
- Fall is the best time to harvest the fruit of your labors and to secure seeds for the future.
- Winter is the best time to contemplate new ways to rejuvenate your idea or create others.

Without the rejuvenation of Winter, we can easily see a free fall from Figure 3.7.

Figure 3.7

In sales, we can often see this in veteran people as a danger which appears in the form of an extended plateau or limit they can't seem to pass, or worse, a free fall that sees them leaving the business. In effect, the cycle is no more than the cycle of life and death; there is no "rebirth" achieving further growth.

As mentioned earlier, everything has a different rhythm that occurs over different time periods. Generally, the magnitude of the activity is inversely related to the frequency of that rhythm, the larger the event the lower the frequency. We see the same thing occur in animals regarding their heartbeats. The larger animals have lower heart rates while smaller animals have higher heart rates. Figure 3.8 shows a larger event on the left and a smaller one on the right.

Figure 3.8

An activity with a smaller magnitude will go through its cycle more frequently in a certain period of time than an activity with a larger magnitude. A collective activity involving a lot of people will have a lower frequency than a similar one involving a single person. Similarly, as the number and complexity of the sub-activities increases within an activity, so does its magnitude. Thus, with any company initiative overlaying this seasonal analogy would look something like this:

- Spring = Ramping up the initiative so everyone's comfortable with it.
- Summer = Peak activity seen from the initiative.
- Fall = Peak results harvested from initiative.
- Winter = Initiative begins to wane and lose emphasis, planning for regeneration.

Generally, it's impossible to maintain a consistent emphasis around any initiative for an extended period of time. You can derive more effectiveness by anticipating and capitalizing on this natural rhythm by tweaking initiatives with a new element to re-energize them in the winter phase. This is analogous to an army withholding reserves to employ as the battle develops. Rarely does an army commit all its forces at once. Some are held to capitalize on opportunities or counter challenges.

Typically, a common technique that is along these lines is the "rollout." An initiative is implemented in phases according to an established timetable. The problem with most rollouts is that they tend to be dependent upon scheduled timeframes and fixed parameters as opposed to assessing emotionally where everyone is and making refinements. The tendency is to rollout the next phase in the summer of the previous phase and zap the energy around it. Rarely, does an army preplan exactly where and how to employ its reserves; it's done based upon the outcomes from the initial stages of the battle.

Taking this seasonal analogy, we can relate its various aspects to the masculine and feminine influences and allow us to gauge what approaches would most likely meet with success during each season. Trying to relate each season with either influence is easier if we look at this in several allegorical ways.

The first is going back to the first chapter's discussion of lines, straight and curvy (Figure 2.42). As discussed there, straight associates itself with the masculine while curvy with the feminine. This alone gives us a quick way to associate seasons with the influences if we revisit the graph in Figure 3.6. It shows straight lines for Spring and Summer and curvy lines for Fall and Winter.

A second way is to look at the interplay between "Day" and "Night." We link "Day" to activity and "Night" to rest. In battle, armies usually fight in the day and plan at night. We can represent this more specifically as follows:

- Early day = Initiate battle.
- Late day = Press advantage or adjust.
- Early evening = Assess and plan.
- Late evening = Rest.

A similar rhythm exists in the business world.

As an aside, focusing on a day also shows how a smaller rhythm lives within a larger one such as the seasonal rhythm in a year in this case. That's why the song of every large event contains the songs of many smaller ones. It's important to not look at these events as the large merely comprising the small because the small has some independence and the large has a flow independent of the small.

A way to picture this is sailing the ocean. While sailors can independently navigate using the wind, ocean currents also influence them. Each sailing day will follow a rhythm similar to what we just mentioned for warfare and business, but even when they take down the sails to rest, the influence from a larger rhythm, the current, will affect them.

Getting back to Day and Night and how they relate to the seasons, we associate them by asking which seasons have longer days and which have longer nights. Day associates with Spring and Summer while Night associates with Fall and Winter.

A third analogy that will help us link more directly the masculine and feminine to seasons is one we touched on briefly: the man going out to hunt and the woman staying in to prepare. We referred to this more from the concept of "Out" and "In," but we can also use it for associating the influences to aspects of flow.

The time for activity is day while the time for rest is night. While both man and woman are active during the day and rest at night, one's activity is more dominant than the other's during each half of the entire day. The hunt is more important during the day, and the food and warmth is more important during the night. We had a similar discussion around the song "Lady In Black" in the previous chapter.

This allows for an indirect connection as shown in Figure 3.9.

| Masculine | $\Rightarrow$ | Day | $\Rightarrow$ | Spring & Summer |
| Feminine | $\Rightarrow$ | Night | $\Rightarrow$ | Fall & Winter |

Figure 3.9

Using a fourth analogy with a farming theme will permit a more direct connection with the seasons. On a daily basis the farming and hunting themes are similar, but we'll

expand the farming one to incorporate seasons. The man plants and grows the crops during the growing season, but the woman prepares the food, such as canning and drying, so
it will last the off season.

On a more emotional basis, the farming and hunting analogies show the importance at
night and during the off months of a well prepared home. If night and the off months are
the period for rejuvenation, it's hard to have this occur if conditions don't exist to permit
it. A bad night's sleep or difficult winter will leave one exhausted and demoralized for the
arrival of the day or the growing season.

With these analogies we can associate the influences with seasons and illustrate their
interplay through the ebb and flow of their respective dominances in Figure 3.10.

- Masculine (solid line) = Spring, Summer
- Feminine (broken line) = Fall, Winter

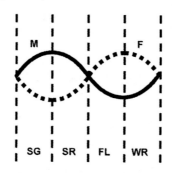

Figure 3.10

Masculine attributes dominate during the Spring and Summer while feminine ones
during the Fall and Winter. Just as athletes' bodies cannot perform well under constant
activity and require periods of rest, emotions require the same, especially as they apply to
relationships. Tension in relationships can build strength if it's broken by periods of rest
and reflection.

Of course, the challenge is taking this rhythmic concept regarding events and actions
and applying it to actual business situations. Rhythmicity is the emotional counterpart to
regression analysis in statistics, establishing the trend line or curve for a collection of
points. Both have similar problems in that they are inexact and open to interpretation. Examining regression analysis will illuminate the challenges with rhythmicity.

Typically, regression analysis is most easily viewed as linear; how do you apply the
best possible straight line to a collection of points in order to define them. However, there
are many other forms of regression analysis all thrown into one category called "nonlinear" because they entail curvy lines as opposed to straight ones. While there are four
distinct groups of nonlinear regression, logarithmic, power, exponential, and polynomial;
the variations are immense. Polynomials alone, as the name implies, can be anywhere
from two to infinite. For this reason, no one can call regression analysis an exact science
since it's rare that any regression perfectly fits a set of points except in a theoretical discussion. Figure 3.11 shows four different regressions for the same set of points.

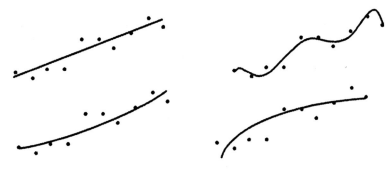

Figure 3.11

Regression analysis is open to interpretation because someone has to make a decision as to which method may best suit the set of points one is addressing. Into the interpretation is thrown such basics as what is the points' source, what do they represent, what purpose will the regression serve, who will use the information, and lastly what is the talent of the person performing the regression. All these interpretations can easily cause someone to throw up his arms and claim, "It's all a matter of interpretation." While this is true, such a categorical declaration doesn't automatically make all interpretations worthless; all interpretations are not created equal – some are better than others just like regressions.

In many ways regression analysis is an amendment to our discussion around Figure 2.53 that included these conclusions:

- The basic premise is that our personal preferences will interpret problems and influence our methodologies to encourage answers in accordance to our preferences.
- The moment we define the parameters on what we're seeking we will tend to find only what we're seeking.

In this case, for the same collection of points we have an exhaustive number of ways to define a regression for it. Our preferences will drive whether we get a straight line or a curvy line. If it's a curve, we can determine how many curves we want in it and what direction they will go. All of these in Figure 3.11 are legitimate regressions using four different methodologies which all could be the "best."

Implicatively, we arrive at the point that if our preferences can significantly drive our outcomes for something as simple as determining an appropriate line or curve for ten points, imagine the impact our preferences have for interpreting comments and for applying methodologies involving ten different people about a particular business at which they work. Carrying this further allows us to relate again to Figures 2.61 – 2.67 and the importance of intelligence in this because while linear regression is the easiest and simplest, it's often the least effective. So, while intelligence of the group may restrain discussion to straight lines, a couple intelligent people in the group may be able to apply nonlinear regression. This could create tension between the two groups by those using linear regression saying those using nonlinear are making the situation more complex than it needs to be.

The purpose of these regression illustrations is to show that rhythmicity suffers all the same interpretive complexities as regression and more because it's intangible and immeasurable; however, it's still possible to get a feel for it. Despite being unable to do the mathematics behind a regression analysis, many of us can walk up to a group of points and draw a line or curve to reasonably fit those points.

Events work very much the same way; while we may not be able to quantify them, we can get a feel for the rhythm as we do for any music. We can see in all four regressions in Figure 3.11 a certain general direction and correlation. While our freestyle line or curve may not be ideal mathematically or close to others, it could still show a trend that would give us some anticipatory capabilities. For the most part, rhythmicity is more of an art than a science, so attempting to wrap some precision around it is almost futile especially since there is no guarantee that it will be any better than a freehand interpretation. The challenge is accepting that one may be able to do this reasonably in light of the prevailing pressure to have sound reason and metrics behind predictive assessments.

Alpha A Financial, Inc.

Under this heading, I will show how flow works favorably for the feminine influence because Alpha A is in the Fall season of approximately a thirty year cycle. Since Fall is the domain of the feminine influence, the feminine aspect of one's personality becomes more influential at Alpha A. Again, this will generally favor women over men.

Immediately, this paragraph stimulates questions that I'll categorize into two groups. Whereas the first group will concern itself more with why I didn't choose shorter time cycles, the second will deal with why I didn't chose larger ones. More topically, the first group will give the rationale for a thirty-year cycle while the other will apply more to the larger forces that could render this cycle insignificant.

Rationale

In addressing the first group and the rationale for a thirty-year cycle, it's important to begin with an entire view of Alpha A's history. When one looks at the entire seventy-year history, the theme that stands out above all others about recent times is that of merger and acquisition. These, more than anything else, have affected Alpha A's growth and actions in current times. Any other theme pales tremendously by comparison. No other decision has made more of an impact on its daily operations than the acquired firms over the last couple decades.

Applying a time frame to this theme is the next step. I chose 1985 as the starting point for this cycle because this approximated the first significant merger. Again, since rhythmicity is not exact, the exact starting point is not important. A couple years on either side of this will do just as well because around this time a decision was made to approach mergers seriously. Likewise, a thirty-year cycle will still apply whether it's twenty-five or thirty-five. Specificity is not important because the rhythm, not the notes, is what's important.

I then took a look at the last major merger that finished around 1997. Again, how we define "finished" is irrelevant because a couple years on either side of this date won't matter. If we then use raw math, we find a twelve-year difference between the two. I then elongated this by a couple years because after any merger there is an integration of the acquired firm that will result in immediate cost savings and additional capabilities. This gave me a fourteen-year period.

The next step was to associate this time frame to a season or seasons. This was fairly easy since the growth was so phenomenal during this period; I associated it with Spring and Summer. Realizing this only took me to 1999, I added a couple more years because the benefits from the last merger carried Alpha A further than this. This came in the form of better aligning its new partners with Alpha A's heritage as typified by high-level personnel changes and shuffling.

This allowed me to assume each season lasts about eight years ($16 \div 2$) and to derive the following table:

Season	Time Period
Spring	1985 – 1992
Summer	1993 – 2000
Fall	2001 – 2008
Winter	2009 – 2016

After this I played around with various start dates from 1983 – 1987 and with various seasonal cycles from six to nine years to see how they played out. Regardless, 2002 seemed to be in Fall, the very late stages of Summer or the very early stages of Winter.

I further tested and refined this based upon some observations:

- A major one was that it seemed most managers have extracted whatever cost savings they could from consolidation as a result of the mergers. Further savings will be minimal or detrimental to revenue growth. Along with this came some reorganization and personnel realignment to refine and harvest benefits from these mergers.

- A second one takes the reorganization and personnel realignment argument and makes it more revenue focused. There is a feeling with the various internal statements to employees that the time is urgent to focus on unit-for-unit revenue growth rather than to rely on another merger for substantial additional growth. This is a move from a growth that is externally focused through mergers (1985 to 1997) to one that is internally focused through emphasis on unit-for-unit growth (1998 to present). The point is external versus internal – external is a Spring/Summer and masculine influence while internal is a Fall/Winter and feminine one.

- A third is related to reorganization but it's more focused on the type of reorganization – the emphasis on team and centralization. Both of these are characteristic of times when consolidation of new holdings occurs rather than dynamic growth. Dynamic growth creates insecurity because of the chaotic nature it can assume. It forces decisions lower and promotes individual deviation in order to maximize quickly the opportunities at hand. Teams and centralization increase strength at the expense of flexibility; thus, they are more representative of organizations operating around a growth peak rather than during a growth spurt when things are more chaotic and require more flexibility.

- A fourth covers a couple comments from top-level executives, one by Joe Davidson and another by Don Williams.

    Joe made his after reviewing a key strategies meeting for the Financial Management division when he mentioned his concern for making sure managers at Alpha A "surface innovative ideas for tapping new markets." He went on to say that of the eight key strategies only one, litigation services, fit his innovation moniker. While there is always a need for surfacing new ideas, the fact that he singled it out as a concern indicates a higher need now than other times.

Don Williams came with his summary comments concerning Financial Management's key strategies on the second day when he said, "I'm not big on process improvements for their own sake, but I see real value in the ones I've seen today." Again, as with Joe's, it's important to look at where his thinking is – process change versus new ideas. In his mind, Don tested this conflict. He did not see new ways to exploit existing markets but rather ways to enhance processes. The next step for him was to resolve whether he saw real value in them. The point here, as with Joe, was that Don was looking for new ideas.

The point of both these comments is the emphasis on surfacing new ideas. If we review the seasons, this emphasis resides in Fall and Winter. By contrast, Spring and Summer focus on taking existing ideas and pushing them to their limits.

While these were not the only observations, these are the significant and representative ones. Again, it's better to look at these observations in terms of the various aspects of a song rather than as variables plugged into some formula. I used them to challenge and refine the cycle above. I decided to use a thirty-year cycle because it fell between a twenty-eight (7 x 4) and a thirty-two year (8 x 4) cycle and because it had a more general connotation than either of the other two; I wanted to avoid the appearance of making this appear an exact science. Plus or minus five years on this cycle doesn't alter the conclusions.

The tendency under the masculine influence is to strive for more specificity than is warranted. Again, we return to Figure 2.53 where conceptually we're going forward with fewer, but more comprehensive insights, and investing the time savings in making necessary adjustments as one proceeds. Often the masculine will encourage more planning and documentation upfront than is practical in light of the many variables affecting outcomes, essentially over planning.

This concludes discussion around the first group of questions concerning the various rationales for a thirty-year cycle. We need to now cover the second group that applies more to the various larger forces that could render this cycle insignificant.

Larger Forces

With any rhythm we look at, there are smaller ones mingling inside it and larger ones around it. The first group we've already discussed as rationale for a thirty-year cycle. We'll now discuss the larger ones around this in the second group because they could affect the cycle I've outlined. There are three main ones: economic, merger, and regeneration.

Economic forces could alter the cycle. In general as we covered in "Situation" under the "Business" heading of "External", I'm working under a moderate to good economy and market. I've assumed a market and economy functioning at one-half or less of what we experienced in the bull market from 1980 – 2000. This means not even coming close to the exuberance experienced during that record setting period. Unless we see another record, or near record setting market and economy, nothing much in the economy will alter this cycle. Essentially, the better the economy the more likely this cycle will extend itself and the worse the more likely it will shorten.

Merger activity is a larger force that could affect this cycle more than the others and most likely by extending it, but the acquisition would have to be fairly substantial. I'm writing this under the assumption Alpha A would not be acquired in the next ten years and any acquisition it makes will be less than half its size. An acquisition of a firm about one-fifth the size of Alpha A today would have roughly corresponded to a merger of equals about ten years ago; thus, purchasing a firm of that size today wouldn't make as much of an impact on Alpha A as it did ten years ago.

Essentially, for an acquisition to affect Alpha A it would have to be of a fairly substantial mass; the number of firms fitting that parameter are fewer today than five or ten years ago, so the likelihood is less. A merger with a firm at least half the size of Alpha would lengthen the cycle long enough to postpone a dominant period for the feminine influence until one could see how the meshing of cultures would affect each. Still, some of this will depend upon geographic considerations. The more similar the two firms are in this area, the less likely the event will lengthen the cycle because the assumption is that Alpha A employees would more likely stay than those of the acquired firm.

Acquisition of a firm 25 – 50% of Alpha A's size will most likely lengthen the cycle somewhat but much of this will depend upon the particular characteristics of the acquisition. Even in this case, they would likely not alter the effect of a strategy emphasizing the feminine influence. Likewise, purchase of entities reinforcing the non-traditional aspects of Alpha A's products and services would most likely also not diminish the effectiveness of this strategy. Of course, if Alpha A is the acquired institution, then this cycle is definitely no longer suitable and the emphasis of this strategy will need to be evaluated through a different context.

The last "larger force" to consider is internal regeneration. Fall means little if any dynamic growth will follow Winter unless some kind of regeneration begins to occur during this period. Typically, the easiest way for any business or country to do this is through external means, seeking the acquisition of another and is why we spent considerable time looking at merger and acquisition outcomes. The previous paragraphs discuss this, so here we're concerned with the problem that develops if there are no significant acquisitions available because that means regeneration can only occur internally. Some call this "organic growth." Even though internal regeneration is far more effective in the long run, it is also far more difficult because it requires the presence of the feminine influence.

For this case study, Alpha A's current situation is not likely to produce regeneration; thus, if someone in that firm, especially a woman, pursued an aggressive incorporation of the feminine influence along relational lines, she would likely receive opportunistic benefits and help Alpha A's overall growth and success. The degree to which she would contribute would depend upon her position at the beginning of this period. Her success could even propel her to become the next CEO.

While I'll cover the reasons for this more thoroughly in the next heading, "People," some introduction will help now. The premise is that the same masculine dominance that allowed Alpha A to survive the wave of mergers will now overlook the feminine dominance needed during this period for internal regeneration. More tangibly this refers to the various initiatives throughout the firm aimed at delivering more products to existing clients. Emotional factors, fear being the primary one, make this a difficult initiative for employees despite the common knowledge that product penetration among clients is low.

In a strategic sense, this means a more compassionate approach centered around individual employees and managers rather than an objective one centered around an overarching client experience and Alpha A. Essentially, this means a transition in the manager-employee relationship from one more along the lines of commander-soldier to one of sage-hero. This means a manager will tap more into his skills as a teacher than a director. As I'll discuss in the next heading, this will be a difficult transition that will most likely be overlooked at Alpha A because of its heavily dominant masculine nature.

Conclusion

By looking at the rationale for a thirty-year cycle and the larger forces around it, we can conclude this is a very legitimate time frame by which to emphasize a strategy focused on the feminine influence. The dominance and effect of mergers over the last fifteen to twenty years have dramatically influenced Alpha A's business decisions. It's impossible to identify a theme that has been more under the control of Alpha A and more impacting than this one.

Unexpected events especially those associated with the economy can dramatically alter any strategy, but as discussed above, emphasizing the feminine influence will seem to remain in favor. Much of this has to do with the strategy's flexibility and strength to endure many different conditions and with Alpha A's current status in its rhythmic cycle. Conversely, this cycle is not so long as to incorporate a time frame that is irrelevant to someone seeking to pursue such a strategy. Yes, technically, the earth is round but for a drive across town it's okay to view it as flat; its curvature won't affect that person much. Likewise, some of the larger cycles such as the economy and Alpha A's entire history will most likely not affect the overall implementation of this strategy in the near-term (three to five years).

As a result, looking at a thirty-year rhythm as the context for this strategy works well and is superior to other time frames.

Summary

Using seasons to aid our discussion of rhythms in events demonstrated how flow is on the side of someone trying to implement this strategy at Alpha A and most likely will continue to improve. By expanding upon how the feminine influence related to rhythms, we could connect the seasonal analogy to Alpha A. Essentially, we're entering a phase that will require the feminine influence more than ever at this firm.

People

After looking at situation and flow, the next aspect affecting outcomes is people. In many parts of this chapter we've already touched on this by noting the dominance of the masculine influence at Alpha A, so let's fill in around this theme.

The more expansive point around this theme and the one concerning us now is that nothing in the strategy to follow would be possible without the people currently at Alpha A. They would like to be moved by something much deeper so they could enhance their enjoyment and experience dynamic professional growth. This emotion will allow the feminine influence to have a profound effect and why "people" is the strongest element of the three (situation and flow being the other two) when looking at a strategy emphasizing the relational aspect of the feminine influence.

Alpha A's extremely dominant masculine culture has served it well, but it's difficult to continue along this path and avoid the scene in "Lady In Black." While the situation is no where as extreme as in the song, weariness begins to set in when there is no reprieve. No soldier can fight endlessly without a break; no person can work around the clock endlessly without sleep. Whereas we associate these more to a physical state, they also apply to one's mental and emotional state as well. We often describe this as "burnout." In "Lady In Black" we saw a "burned out" scene.

At Alpha A there is a weariness beginning to set in after years of tough business and expense control resulting in force reductions. No doubt it had business successes, but as explained above, any aggressive activity has costs – physical, mental, and emotional. No success in any endeavor arrives without a cost. That is why the feminine influence as demonstrated by the nursing profession is associated with rejuvenating the fighting spirit.

The classic story is the hero who fights a brutal battle and returns to a woman who nurses him back to health. "Lady In Black" is a symbolic representation of this on an emotional level. Whereas the first is about nursing back a man's physical well being, the second deals with an emotional well-being. In "Lady In Black" the man lamented to demonstrate his exhaustion and despair over life:

8.   So eager was my passion to devour this waste of life

He went on to praise the woman who came to his rescue:

13.   Oh lady lend your hand I cried, oh let me rest here by your side
14.   Have faith and trust in me she said, and filled my heart with life

Constantly driving for more business in the face of stiff competitive pressures with undifferentiated products in primarily low- to no-growth markets, challenges even the most talented sales person using a comprehensive integrated approach. Eventually, this cost manifests itself in relationships tarnished by weariness:

Who is more likely to foster stronger relationships with clients: Someone in the same emotional state as the man before the Lady In Black came to his aid, or someone in his emotional state after her visit?

If warfare is an easy analogy for business and pictures employees as soldiers, who is the Lady In Black at Alpha A? Who nurses its heroes and heroines back to health so they are less inclined to look at clients as just another compensational transaction for which they receive an incentive?

As a result, no Alpha A executive has captured the hearts of the employees to any significant degree for four basic reasons:

- Under the masculine influence, standard operating business practices resort to objectives, planning, measurements, and execution to resolve this condition – one cannot effectively address an emotional condition unemotionally. If this were true, then the Lady In Black could be a robot and still have the same effect.
- Alpha A has been in an era of regular force reductions that naturally stirs uneasy, insecure, and distrusting feelings among employees.
- It does not position its leadership as effectively as it's able because it overlooks imagery and symbolism. As a result, Alpha A's leaders come across more as commanders than sages, more as directors than teachers. They need a better balanced presentation of their talents.
- It's difficult for a masculine culture to tap the feminine influence without feeling effeminate, and thus a latent fear of it settles in and neglects its incorporation. Essentially, it's feared because anything feminine, including compassion, is superficially seen as weak; thus, the deeper strengths of the feminine remain untapped.

All the emotion and feelings behind this are difficult to see but become manifested when we ask a series of questions to Alpha A employees beginning along the lines of:

1.   Do you trust your manager?
2.   Do you believe your manager cares about you as a person?

The danger in these questions is looking at them quantitatively in the form of some questionnaire. We do not want to ask just anyone these questions. For the most part, the ideal participant is one who is enjoying his job and answers "yes" to the first question. The challenge then becomes probing to understand what he is saying "yes" to.

When I ask the first question and someone says "yes," I probe with "Why?" What I typically find is that people will think more objectively and globally as opposed to subjectively and personally. This is why the second question is important, but even here people will apply a business framework to the question and not a personal one. This alone can say a lot about the prevalence of the masculine influence. Consequently, the questions will be interpreted more along the lines of:

1.   Do you trust your manager's knowledge and experience as a business person?
2.   Do you believe he cares about you as a person who successfully produces every year?

The way someone interprets these questions says a lot about the dominance of the masculine and feminine influences in any business culture not just Alpha A's. Here are two examples from employees whose managers like and want to keep them. The first is a credit representative while the second is a dedicated sales representative; both examples are representative and excellent because they both said "yes" to both questions.

- **Credit Representative.** After saying a lot about his manager's business instincts and how much he could learn from him, his response to the second question was still along a business line when he responded, "Yes, I think he cares about me. He helps me a lot." To which the follow up comment was, "I'm pleased you found someone to confide in," and he countered with, "Well, I didn't say I could confide in him." How can you relationally trust someone if you cannot confide in him?

- **Sales Representative.** As with the banker, he answers "yes" to the first question and responds to the second with, "Yes, I get along with my manager. He likes me." In many ways, he wasn't really answering the question. There's a difference between caring about someone and getting along with someone, so the follow up was "Does he like you because of the person you are or because you sell a lot?" To which he responded the latter. How can you relationally trust someone if he only likes you superficially because you sell a lot?

The obvious counter to these is along the lines of "We're talking about business not personal issues, so these questions are irrelevant on a personal level." However, this argument and its many variations prove the point by default: how can you be in a relationship business while ignoring the personal aspect of relationships? We reviewed the connection in more detail in the Introduction to this book. In the client-employee relationship, personal aspects play a huge role. The same applies to employee-manager relationships. By leaving out the personal aspects of a relationship with an employee, we now reduce that relationship to a mere transaction – compensation for services, a.k.a. employment.

In both of these examples the employees had difficulty switching to a more personal level regarding these questions because it's not the norm or expected. The question then becomes:

Who is more likely to treat a client as a relationship: an employee who feels like a transaction at the office or one who has a personal relationship with his company?

Or, from the perspective of trying to establish a reputation, one of Alpha A's objectives for its Financial Management division:

If its business is truly a business about relationships, who are more likely to radiate a strong relational feeling with their clients: employees who have strong relational experiences in the office or those who have weak ones?

More tangibly, Alpha A's planning and review processes are symbolic of the imbalance regarding the feminine influence in that there is little to no mention of goals and objectives outside the business realm. Contrast this to some other companies where the first step was to discuss what the employee wanted for his family and him on a personal level. They discussed objectives around personal pursuits so they could place work activities in better perspective.

With one sales representative, a manager spent time trying to understand and appreciate the aspirations he had for his family. One year, his focus was to afford his wife the opportunity to quit her job so she could stay at home with their children. Confiding in the manager with this aspiration and the reasons for it regarding his children's education not only energized him but the manager as well. They found this a motivating force for both of them that year and resulted in the sales representative's best year ever.

Again, if Alpha A is trying to instill a holistic approach in its folks regarding its clients, a corollary to the previous question becomes:

Who are more likely to learn and develop a holistic approach to clients: employees who experience a holistic approach to their employment or those who don't?

I've already stated four reasons why no Alpha A executive has captured the hearts of employees to any significant degree and cited observations supporting this. The reasons are not as important as the fact that this situation exists because it affords someone the opportunity to do something many others may not be able to do or don't want to do. The reasons are important to anyone in one aspect: they identify the challenges in the implementation of the various aspects of the feminine influence. In order for others to help in an effort to incorporate the feminine influence in any business, we'll need to address four corresponding challenges to the reasons above:

- How do you strike a better balance between the more masculine (and expected) demands of business and the under appreciated feminine aspects that generate dynamic growth?
- How do you do this when you may be responsible for job terminations?
- How do you position yourself in a way that highlights your concern for another employee's personal well being?
- How do you implement the feminine aspects without appearing weak?

The strategy will address all four, but the advantage a woman brings rides with the last one. Whereas a man runs the danger of appearing weak if he implements aspects of the feminine influence, a woman comes across more as fulfilling her nature.

If we broaden the scope of the employee-manager relationship to include other managers existing one, two, three, or more levels above the immediate one in a hierarchy, we will find an increasing detachment between the employee and the next higher manager. For instance, in Alpha A there is a greater likelihood of a "no" to the second question (Do you believe he cares about you as a person or just as someone who successfully produces every year?) if we talk to an employee about his boss's boss rather than his boss. As we move upward in the management chain, the likelihood of a "no" from the employee about the next higher manager increases. Most of this is easily discounted by the sheer size of Alpha A; however, there are ways around this as the strategy portion will show.

In trying to relate this case study to your company, many of the masculine elements I've highlighted in Alpha A are likely to exist in other companies. We could see similar observations in many other companies, not just in the financial services industry, and not just Alpha A. What differentiates Alpha A, is the degree to which masculine aspects dominate its culture. This is why it has survived the merger frenzy of the nineties.

On a deeper level though, we need to refer to the discussion in the Feminine Influence chapter about flash points. From that we can make a couple statements about competition in a business world involving two companies:

1. Victory will most likely go to the company that is more masculine as long as both ignore the feminine influence.
2. If both don't ignore the feminine influence, then victory will most likely go to the company that best integrates the two influences.
3. If one company ignores the feminine influence and the other incorporates her, then the second company is more likely to win no matter how masculine the first company is.
4. If one company ignores the feminine influence and is more masculine than the other company, it will try to convince the other company not to incorporate the feminine influence so its masculinity will prevail.

This last point is exactly what was beginning to happen to the man in the "Lady In Black" before she appeared. The destruction around him caused by other men was propelling him into a despair that would cause him to forsake life and seek a destructive path of his own:

7. And I begged her give me horses to trample down my enemy

Thus, the following corollary:

- In order to defeat a woman in business, you get her to play the game by a man's rules in order to get her to forsake her strengths as a woman.

We can reword this corollary to expand it beyond its symbolic sense:

- In order to defeat someone capable of integrating the feminine influence in business, you get him to play the game solely in a masculine way in order to get him to forsake the feminine influence's strengths. This is most effectively done by convincing him this integration is impractical, ineffective, difficult, and time consuming.

If we relate all of this to the seasonal and fire analogy, we find that even if a strong masculine influence survives the battle, it will eventually extinguish itself without the feminine to give him a rebirth. Spring never arrives and Winter is eternal. A fire without new logs will eventually extinguish and become cold.

In summary, the "People" portion illustrates an increasingly weary employee base at Alpha A that would be willing to embrace a "Lady In Black" figure. On a more common level this weariness is often described as "burnout" but often the cure is superficially viewed as time off or vacation. What we attempted to illuminate here, by contrasting a feminine approach to the condition, are the deeper emotions behind this.

Whereas no artist can become great merely by perfecting the technical skill of painting, no employee can become great merely by perfecting the technical skill of helping a client.

> 14. Have faith and trust in me she said, and filled my heart with life
> 20. I find new heart each time I think upon that windy day

Greatness comes from the heart by infusing passion through one's skills. Weariness retards one's passion and thus greatness. The Lady In Black refills one's heart.

Conclusion

In this chapter, we focused our attention on using the Alpha A case study to delve into three of four major elements that affect outcomes: situation, flow, and people.

We can summarize each as they apply to Alpha A as follows:

Situation:

> Both externally and internally, immense pressures are increasing the difficulty of growing. These pressures increase the need for new ideas and more importantly new influences such as the feminine.

Flow:

> Alpha A is in or approaching the harvesting phase of its acquisitions over the last fifteen to twenty years. This will increase pressures to find internal rejuvenation if a very significant merger does not occur.

People:

> Employees are weary but still willing to place their trust and faith in someone who can personalize their experience at Alpha A into a relationship.

The fundamental conclusion from these is that conditions are increasingly becoming more advantageous for someone, especially a woman, to implement a strategy emphasizing the feminine influence. While the feminine influence seems most conducive to a woman, there are many attributes within this influence available to men. More importantly access to these attributes is dependent upon many other aspects of one's personality besides gender. The last element affecting outcomes is the individual, or you. This is the topic of the next chapter and where we'll look at some other qualities.

You

In the previous chapter, we discussed three elements of outcomes: situation, flow, and people. This chapter will focus on the fourth one, the individual, you. Having a relational appreciation for the forces acting upon other people and you is fundamental to integrating the feminine influence into one's work.

Ideally, as I mentioned in the Prelude and Introduction, I would prefer getting to know you and rewriting this book, especially this chapter, so it would bond more firmly to your personality. In fact, I originally accomplished such a writing where I took a few of these ideas and incorporated them into another's personality. I had designed this chapter with a total focus on the reader I knew who would receive this. Obviously, I cannot take that approach now.

Conversely, when I began to contemplate how to write the book, I felt I wanted to avoid three things:

- Appealing to a generic or average reader.
- Formulaic application – "one size fits all".
- Academic explanations.

First of all, an average reader doesn't exist because averages don't exist . . . except on paper. The average person in this country would be half man and half woman. Second, averages don't help much. Not only because they most likely don't exist but also because they're applicatively impractical. I may know for instance that the average hitter in baseball hits about nine homeruns a year and gets a hit about twenty-four percent of the time, but that doesn't do me much good if I'm a pitcher; I'm concerned about the hitter facing me at the moment, not the average one. Third, I don't get excited about generically writing something. Fourth, and most important, I don't know many intelligent people who like to be called "average" let alone "generic."

Along with the avoidance of appealing to a generic reader, I also wanted to avoid a formulaic application encouraging "one size fits all." In effect, while I may write with a certain group of readers in mind, I didn't want to write in a way that neglected individualism. Applying an idea will vary by individual. While to some this may seem like a common statement, in many subtle ways violation of this happens everyday in business when we hear statements like "Top producers did it this way to be successful" or phrases like "best practices."

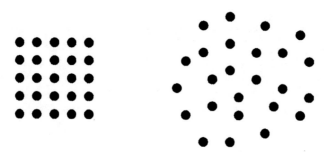

Figure 4.1

Figure 4.1 illustrates the problems with comments like these because it assumes a process successful for one group or individual will be successful for another. Interestingly enough, the two groups of dots are similar in that both contain twenty-five black ones. Now, while many will concede process variations with individuals, many of those will discourage them with groups; yet, the problems with this are enhanced rather than reduced because not only are the individuals different in each group but the relationships each person has with each of the other people varies as well. Using Figure 4.1 to help us we find there are three hundred separate relationship pairs, two different ways to look at each relationship, and twenty-five individuals for a total of six hundred twenty-five different relational elements before we even get into the details of the process, the situation, or the flow. The likelihood a "best practice" will be best for two people let alone two groups is much smaller than what we see credited in everyday business practice.

Implicit in these two avoidances is a third, academic explanations. Math isn't just for mathematicians, economics isn't just for economists, psychology not just for psychologists, sociology not just for sociologists, science not just for scientists, and so forth through all aspects of knowledge; but, often the only way these subjects are explained are so that only the academic experts in those fields can enjoy them. If each of these fields has some relevancy to life as I believe they do, they must have some application to me in everyday life of which I can use without needing to devote my life to the academic pursuit of them. This means I don't waste any time researching these ideas to garner support for them so I can defend them in some academic courtroom; they work for me and that's all I need to know. Whether they might be helpful to you is only a decision you can make.

What's important for you about these three avoidances is that I'm basically writing this to myself. I don't know who you are, but I have at least some idea who I am. I know I'm not generic or average because I exist, so by writing to myself I avoid the first avoidance. As for the second avoidance, I deliver my advice with no guarantees. Since I'm writing to myself, the only commitment I have is to me, and I've already tried and erred enough to know what works and doesn't work. I purposely avoid specific processes or formulas because I know from experience there is a tendency to get too locked in and focused causing one to miss opportunities and to relate mechanically. Of course, this is not as simple or direct, but it is more effective because you encourage someone to work through the details in a way that is natural for him. Lastly, I avoid academic explanations by trying to write in a way that will connect advice to the nature of things in everyday life that you might have experienced rather than to some quote from an academic expert or research report. By seeing this you're more likely to get a feel for how to implement it because you're able to relate it to something you see everyday. This methodology harks back to the conceptual birth of universities in which all knowledge relates to one another and to the whole bigger than itself. Any knowledge has application not only to the field from which it came but also to the whole outside that field. Through this we are able to make comparisons between cooking and nuclear fusion, flying an F-14 and gardening.

The goal of this advice is to make it more likely that you will be able to integrate the feminine influence in your business life. Just as the beauty of a woman can be nebulous and abstract so can the feminine influence. Trying to get the right feel for how to do this requires an additional appreciation for yourself and others. The advice in this chapter is another framework, or better yet, another world in which you can travel to gain a different perspective on how to apply the feminine influence. It's not so important that you agree with the content but rather use it to develop your own way to tackle the world. Rather than deliver a pre-packaged process for integration, I will focus on how the feminine influence impacts you and others. The feminine influence, by her nature, avoids structured processes so the implementation of one will automatically cause her to flee; you cannot build a lake with hammer and nails. The next chapter, Strategy, will outline some basic themes around which you can begin with the intention of modifying it to fit your nature. This is similar to trying on a suit or dress before you decide how you want to tailor it.

Toward this goal, I've organized this chapter around four basic themes:

- Personality
- Talent
- Conditioning
- Growth

In order to better see how the feminine influence works, looking at our personalities and others' from an individualistic, subjective perspective will help.

Since your relationships are with other individuals, not groups as Figure 1.4 attempts to show, we need tools that help us appreciate the person in front of us rather than people in general. This is an implication of our "average" discussion above; understanding the average person doesn't do much for us when we're trying to understand the individual before us.

We now turn this argument around and direct it at us to arrive at subjectivity; appreciating how people in general should relate to others doesn't help us much because we're concerned with "How do I, as me, relate more effectively?" The fundamental principle behind this is that by being who we are naturally is the best way to relate to another person; people prefer an imperfect original to a perfect copy.

Taking these two concepts and putting them together allows us to ask, "How do I relate more effectively to this person and still be me?" This means more reliance on your own feelings about another person and yourself rather than a third-party assessment of both. The path we take in relating to another person is dependent upon who we are and who the other person is, not who someone, or something, claims we are and the other person is. By relying upon this other person or thing to tell us these things we short circuit the relational process because we now relate based upon the parameters of a third-party rather than those established by the two individuals in the relationship. Figure 4.2 illustrates the interactive difference between a relationship relying upon a third-party (left diagram) versus one relying upon those involved (right diagram).

Figure 4.2

Objectivity by its very nature implies detachment; how can you empathize if you're detached from another person? Reliance upon a third party creates exactly the detachment that erodes strong relational bonds. Personal feelings of those involved in the relationship take priority over the observations of a third party. No third-party assessment can determine how every possible aspect of someone's personality will manifest itself in every possible scenario. For these reasons, you are more likely to maximize your relational effectiveness if you focus on you and the other person rather than operate under the restrictive parameters inherent in a third party. In essence, you are developing your own internal assessment capability that is immediately available to you whenever you interact with someone for the situation under which you're operating. This is no different than the principles behind the relationship between a local government and a central one when it comes to understanding, appreciating, and resolving local interests. As the localness of the decision increases with respect to a local issue, so does the effectiveness of applying that decision to address that issue.

Beyond personalities we need to look at talent in a similar way for many of the same reasons as personalities. Talent's manifestation is most directly affected by the various personal relationships surrounding it. This not only includes the more limited issue of whether it shows itself but the more expansive one of as to how. From this perspective, talent becomes more like beauty. It's often hard to say what beauty is, but you happen to know her when you see her. Our challenge will be learning to keep our eyes open so we can see it. By approaching it differently, we can better see it in us and others when it appears. The key here is realizing that there's more to talent than whether or not someone has it.

The hardest part about personality and talent is getting past what blocks both. I call this conditioning but it can be anything we learn. The downside of learning is that it can build constructs by which we look at things that will cause us to constrict our range of vision and limit possibilities. The most obvious example is when a layman is able to come up with a new possibility that experts overlook. Typically, we call this a "fresh view," but it implies that no one has polluted the layman's views with preconceived ways of addressing opportunities and problems.

All of us are taught to think and believe certain things about ourselves and others; some are in line with our nature while others are not. The unnatural stuff gets in the way of the natural and prevents us from discovering the best in ourselves and others. We often hear the cliché, "cream rises to the top," but that only occurs if we allow it. There are many reasons why we prevent that in ourselves and others. One we touched upon when we discussed the responsibility that comes with talent. While we'll explore others soon, we'll do so in a general way because in actuality how the reasons show up individually are too varied. The main point is realizing the tremendous potential for their existence.

Lastly, I'll share a perspective on the promotion of growth in yourself and others. Often we interpret growth as the elimination of weaknesses. Appreciating the feminine influence means focus on strengths to the point where one almost ignores weaknesses because it's the inherent nature of strengths to compensate for weaknesses. Thus, the best path tends to be maximizing one's strengths to overgrow or overshadow weaknesses.

We'll now explore personality, talent, conditioning, and growth.

Personality

As stated in the Introduction,

- Business relationships are extensions of personal relationships by other means.
- Business is an extension of personality by other means.

Essentially, it's difficult to have an appreciation for business without having an appreciation for relationships and the personalities behind them. We find the essence of relationships in the domain of the feminine influence. While many people express this commitment to relationships along the lines of "our people differentiate us," the degree to which someone believes this is not easily communicated through words. In general, using the graph in Figure 2.12, we can surmise that since there is no reliable way to quantify or visualize the impact of a personality we will tend to discount its influence. Observationally, I find the tendency to discount it when up against more tangible things such as technology, products, equipment, and processes.

More significantly, even if there is a strong belief in the impact of people on a business, two other challenges remain to overcome. The first challenge is an excessive focus on our technical skills as opposed to our relational talents, and the second is the belief that managing personalities either cannot be done or is secondary to managing processes.

Overcoming the first challenge will place someone in a better position to unlock the potential in himself or others. The most dynamic growth someone can experience personally is not through the learning of additional skills but through the conquering of emotional challenges. Growth means tackling new challenges, but new also brings uncertainty. Uncertainty raises anxieties, and in milder forms shows itself as discomfort and in extreme forms as fear. Figure 4.3 shows four basic obstacles to the assimilation of a new idea.

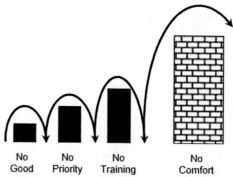

Obstacle	Explanation
No Good	The person does not see the idea as good for him.
No Priority	He may see the idea as good but doesn't have time for it; it's not a priority.
No Training	He finds it a priority but doesn't know how to implement it.
No Comfort	He knows how to implement but is not comfortable doing so.

Figure 4.3

As illustrated each obstacle becomes increasingly challenging. What makes overcoming "No Comfort" even more challenging is that people are inclined not to admit discomfort or fear in trying a new idea so it's rationalized as one of the other obstacles. People are more apt to admit any one of the other three obstacles before coming to grips with "No Comfort." For this reason, when one does admit it, it's important not to discount it and to take action immediately because it's a "teachable" moment. Often, the case around a new idea is best done by beginning to lay the groundwork for overcoming discomfort at the outset so when it does appear you've already laid the foundation for addressing it. We'll see how this develops and the reasons for it shortly.

The second challenge, addressing the belief that managing personalities either cannot be done or is secondary to managing processes came to light when a training vendor called upon me. His presentation materials suggested a significant number of S&P 500 corporations used the training methodology he was offering. I asked if he were suggesting that these corporations were successful as a result of that methodology and he said "yes." I asked how he knew that it wasn't more attributed to the personalities of the people in the corporations than the training methodology. He said that's possible but you can't manage personalities; you can only manage processes and that's what he said his training methodology would allow them to do.

In order to get us closer to a more practical application of the innate power within our personalities, we'll focus on enhancing the appreciation for our personalities and on overcoming the two challenges above by exploring the relationship between us as individuals and our world in four different areas:

- Influence – Fundamental concepts on the nature of the outside world's influence on us.
- Needs – The basic needs of our personalities.
- Duality – The way our personalities come to manifest themselves in the outside world.
- Introversion – A perspective on tapping the power in our personalities.

After looking at these four areas, we'll have a better appreciation for the extent to which the outside world influences us, for the needs we seek to fill from it, for how our personalities come to impact it, and for the effort involved in tapping the power within us. This appreciation will place us in a better position to practically apply this in our daily business relationships when we read the Strategy chapter.

Again, my purpose for exploring these areas is a pragmatic, business one not an academic one. They are far more involved, intricate, and inclusive than I explain; however, I believe they are cornerstones from which you can begin integrating their implications immediately into your personality so you can more likely tap into the reservoirs of talent in you and others to reach higher levels of effectiveness and enjoyment in your business world.

Influence

The outside world relentlessly influences us every moment of our lives. The methods by which it does are extensive and not within the realm of this book; however, we are concerned about how that influence relates to the feminine influence. For the purpose of our discussion the outside world entails everything outside of us as individuals. The critical aspect of this statement is that any other person is considered a part of our outside world and thus influences us as Figure 4.4 shows.

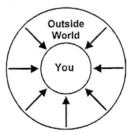

Figure 4.4

When we concern ourselves with the feminine influence and her invisibility, indirectness, and intangibility, the most important aspect of our world's outside influence for us to appreciate is that *things can influence us without our knowledge even if they are right in front of our nose*. Without an appreciation for the associative implications that follow from this statement, moving the feminine influence from an abstract concept to a business practicality is difficult.

Superficially, we can see the truth of this statement if we consider actions occurring beyond our sight such as governmental or business actions that affect our lives. We can also experience this scientifically with sound and light that we cannot hear or see but affect our health. Diseases also influence us before we diagnosis them. What are less apparent are more subtle influences such as color, shapes, words, pictures, and organization. *Feng Shui* is an ancient Eastern art incorporating these influences and others so the individual can create environments more supportive to the time, purpose, and personality of the person.

On a deeper level, this statement means that there are things going on inside of us outside the scope of our awareness. More of the physical aspects of our bodies such as digestion or blood flow go on all the time without our sensing it; these we can more easily accept. However, once we move from physicality to thoughts and emotions, we have a harder time seeing these.

Before we get into this much deeper, let's start off with seventeen influential points.

Seventeen Influential Points

1. Emotions are more powerful than thoughts and consequently more influential.
2. Intuition is a feeling, an emotion.
3. Intuition is more comprehensive than knowledge of the same thing.
4. People will feel things before they are conscious of those feelings.
5. People will consciously feel something before they can form those feelings into thoughts.
6. Personal observations are more influential than third-party comments.
7. Many times people are not aware of the things influencing them.
8. Even though people are aware of something, it can influence them without their knowledge.
9. People aware of an influence may incorrectly attribute it to something else if at all.
10. People's likes influence them despite the absence of reasons for the liking or influence.
11. Imaginary things can influence people.

12. Placing things in groups alters the influence that each thing delivered individually.
13. Groups of things influence people despite the absence of a rational connection among the things.
14. Rearranging a group of things will cause the same group to exert a different influence.
15. People are born with varying emotional capabilities and thus varying intuitive capabilities too.
16. People can develop their intuition as they can develop their minds and muscles.
17. Intuition, as with minds and muscles, atrophy with disuse.

As you probably noticed, I segregated these points into four groups. The first five (#1 - #5) are restatements of the themes we covered with Figures 2.1 – 2.15 early on in the Feminine Influence chapter. They deal more with our internal processes to assimilate our environs. The second six (#6 - #11) focuses more externally by commenting on the influence things exert upon us. The next three (#12 - #14) extend the previous six by commenting upon the influence of things when they're in groups. Finally, the last three (#15 - #17) relate to the last part of the Feminine Influence chapter covered by Figures 2.61 – 2.67 by demonstrating how individuals' experiences with these statements will vary.

I'll take each group separately and then return to the entire seventeen's implications.

First Five (#1 - #5)

I won't elaborate much on these points but rather refer you back to the discussion around Figures 2.1 – 2.15. There are two points, #1 and #4, that don't require elaboration so much as emphasis. You will be able to best appreciate and apply the feminine influence if there is a genuine appreciation for these two points. Understanding will help but actually feeling their impact is even better.

Humans are driven overwhelmingly by their emotions which are then rationalized into a construct of thoughts supporting the behavior those emotions generated or want to generate. This is just a superexpansion of the sales dictum, "buying decisions are emotional ones that are rationalized." Action is more directly associated with feelings than thoughts. This is why it's one thing to say something and quite another to feel it, and why we consider lying a thought and not an emotion. Lying is an expressed thought disguising how we feel; the implication here is that feelings are the more honest representation of our views – not our thoughts. A lie is a thought covering up our feelings, not a feeling covering up our thoughts. This alone demonstrates the primacy we place on our emotions to signify our true state of being.

Point #4 is a little more difficult to accept because it's hard to imagine feelings that we don't feel on a conscious level. How can they be feelings? There are interactions going on in our bodies all the time below our awareness level. Muscle spasms cause muscles to tense up in the form of "knots" without our awareness. Knots are caused by highly stimulated nerves that have felt some kind of strain. Eventually, if they become severe enough they can encourage muscle pulls and strains. Massages help alleviate these knots before they become severe and explain why we feel so much better after a session.

Another example is the gradual acceptance of discomfort over a period of time. While putting on a particular item of clothing may create a tight feel, our awareness of that tightness dissipates as we go along with our activities. Even though we may stop occasionally and feel the tightness, the feeling will not be at such a level that it will distract us from feeling other things. In fact, we may not even recall the feeling until we remove the clothing. A more extreme form is the desensitization a battle hardened veteran experiences over time in comparison to his initiation. The common expressions, "they'll get use to it," has its roots in desensitization. After a while some experiences will become normal and may not even reach consciousness.

We experience this in everyday life as "daydreaming" when we walk right by something and don't even notice it because we're deep in thought or focused on something else like driving. This also takes the form of staring, looking at something but not taking it in because our thoughts are elsewhere. Just as these things can happen with more conscious activities they can also happen with the unconscious ones. Our emotions and feelings are so distracted by more prominent experiences that we don't realize our feelings for the more subtle ones. Returning to our muscles, this is how one intense pain can overshadow lower intensity pains. Regardless of our consciousness for the lower intensity pain it still exists because of the inflamed nerve endings and muscle constriction. Often this lower intensity pain won't surface until the more intense one subsides. Firmly biting your tongue to alleviate a sneeze you feel approaching is a simple example.

Second Six (#6 - #11)

This group ties in more directly with our statement that "things can influence us without our knowledge even if they are right in front of our nose." Even if we can detect the influence, there is also the matter of degree.

Point #6 refers to the preference we give to personal experiences over those of others. If our personal experience is different from another, our tendency is to rely upon our own and will hold true even if the other is an "expert." Consequently, third party research or information is generally secondary to our personal research.

Point #7 ties in directly with our opening statement minus the "even if they are right in front of our nose." As I said, in the opening above, the implication here is that we also must be concerned with the degree to which something influences. This opens more doors to situations that affect us more deeply than we initially think, a lingering personal problem that seems to affect us for longer than we anticipated. Point #4 relates to this point by changing focus from the object exerting influence to the person experiencing it.

Point #8 builds upon #7 by saying that even if we are aware of something it may influence us in ways we do not detect. Sublimity and symbolism have their roots in this point. As we had covered in the Feminine Influence chapter when we discussed business examples of her presence in which advertising and politics build messages around this point. The positioning of a product or person entails awareness for how images and messages affect people beyond their objective message. This is why many celebrities are very selective about how they appear in photographs and roles because our feelings for these images indirectly and invisibly translate into feelings toward them as people. An actor playing a good guy will more likely elicit positive feelings for him as a person than another actor playing a bad guy. The same happens in business and is typically referred to as "pigeon holing." Meanwhile, on a conscious level, people aren't even aware of how much these images are affecting their personal assessments of the person even though they may be aware of these images.

Point #9 takes #8 further to claim that even if we feel an influence we may incorrectly attribute it to another cause. The implications from this are very impactive because it means rationalized feelings for someone or something could actually be the result of something else. Superficially, we see this in business and often identify it as "scapegoatism." This point takes the concept further by implying an unconscious application. In other words, if we run into someone who reminds us of someone we don't like then we are inclined to not like him as well even if we do not consciously make the association. Consequently, as we try to rationalize these negative feelings for the person, we are more likely to seek and highlight evidence supporting our negative rationalizations. We often humorously refer to someone inexplicably disliking us as possibly reminding him of his ex-spouse or some other person we know he doesn't like. A business owner in landscaping once told me a story of how he grew to not like a girlfriend because her crooked teeth reminded him of his own. Of course, he did not make the association until much later after some reflection. At the time, he wasn't aware that his gradual dislike for her grew out of the anxiety he had for his teeth.

Conversely, point #9 also has positive implications. People who cause us to associate them with positive influences in our lives, again regardless of whether we consciously recognize this, will tend to cause us to rationalize these feelings more positively. Thus, a person who triggers an uplifting feeling from a past moment in our lives will tend to stir positive feelings within us that then manifest themselves in the seeking and highlighting of positive evidence about the person to rationalize these positive feelings. In sports we see this all the time when athletes associated with winning teams are generally more highly valued than those with losing teams, but few owners rarely justify their premium on this reason and more often highlight other aspects of individual performance as the basis for their rationalizations.

Point #10 states directly some of what point #9 says indirectly. In many ways, this is the basis for beauty's impact. Humans are naturally directed to those things they like regardless of whether they can accurately describe what the attractions are or why they like them. The subtle aspect of this point that carries far more implications is the "despite the absence of reasons." People do not need reasons to like things or have them influence them. The presence of reasons has no bearing on the degree to which likable things influence people. In fact, the presence of incorrect reasons, rationalizations, does not alter the influence only the form that the behavior takes in response to the influence. Implied but not stated is the converse, "People's dislikes influence them despite the absence of reasons for the dislike or influence."

Point #11 extends influence to include things that are unreal. For instance, movies, stories, pictures, or other unreal things, exert an influence. This is why watching movies with a fictional storyline and characters can make us feel happy, sad, angry, or loving. A romantic movie is more inclined to put a date or spouse in a romantic mood than a violent one. Even though these stories are not real, they influence our moods. Speakers often use jokes to "break the ice." Again, an unreal thing influences the audience to encourage their participation and acceptance of a message. We can combine this with points #8 and #9 to create and experience very subtle influences.

As a group these points seek to create a picture of our bodies and consciousnesses more akin to sieves than walls. To think we only allow influence from those things that we allow to enter is contrary to the imagery and symbolism politicians, advertisers, and celebrities employ. Ignorance of this increases the likelihood that we miss opportunities and run into problems by communicating influences we do not intend and accepting those of which we are unaware. Dynamism is very difficult to achieve if we rely solely upon the objective content of our communications without attention to the other influences they exert.

Third Three (#12 - #14)

This group of points takes the influence of individual things exert and considers what happens when these things are in groups. The basic implication of all three is that the points regarding the influence of one thing apply to groups of things.

Point #12 extends this by saying just because we know the influence of individual things we cannot assume that the summation of their influence will be the influence of the group. The mere act of placing individual things in a group will create an influential difference outside of a mere aggregation. The influence a group exerts is different than the influence exerted by each individual thing in the group summed. Figure 4.5 illustrates this. In effect, how each thing in the group affects one another can alter the influence of the group (right diagram) in a way that is different from what could be expected from a summation of the individual influences (left diagram). The four dots in each diagram look different.

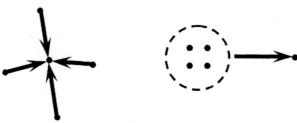

Figure 4.5

Point #13 delves deeper by asking what we define as a group. The conclusion from this point is that a group can influence us regardless of whether we define it as a group; the ability of a group to influence us is irrespective of our ability to recognize it as such. Combined with point #8 we can imply that one of the way things influence us without our knowledge is by their membership in a group.

Another analogy will help us further illustrate points #12 and #13 plus introduce point #14, and that is words in a sentence. Each word means something different whose summation in a sentence could be something quite different. In fact, how we arrange the words can change the meaning of the sentence. This is the meaning behind point #14; rearranging the things in a group will alter the influence of the group.

All of the points in this group are easily seen when we arrange furniture in a room. How we arrange the furniture creates a different impression despite the fact we did not alter the specific pieces themselves. The influence each piece exerts is quite different separately compared to how it's seen in the context of the group. Furthermore, even though we may define a group of furniture by the room it's in, subgroups form and change simply by what is within our field of vision at that moment. For instance, a specific corner or wall of a room may be occupying our field of vision. For that moment, the furniture in that corner forms a group that we may not recognize consciously as a defined group.

How this group of points applies to a business setting becomes more apparent when we think of individuals as the things in a group. The influence one person exerts on us is different when that person is seen in the context of a group. Often we've heard the expression, "guilt by association." This is nothing more than the influence of another changing the influence something else exerts upon us. What these points are doing is extending that association to a group. For instance, we may have an affinity for a person until we find he's a member of a group we view negatively. Automatically, the influence of the group alters how we see things individually. We've already made the comparison to the athlete on a winning team. Each of the athletes exerts an influence of his own; however, in a group that influence is altered by the influence the group exerts. In this case, the group influence would tend to increase the influence of each team member. That influence increases his value.

We're more conscious of this as "seen and be seen." An invitation to an exclusive gathering alters our influence from what it was as an individual. Automatically, our membership in a group, regardless of its formality, alters our influence. Just as we view a chair in the context of a room, the contexts in which we see others affect us. Finding a large rock in a ditch and placing it in a garden, alters our impression of that rock. The attraction we have for the rock changes; the influence the rock has on us changes. Returning to the chair, we find ourselves thinking more about the chair in the context of the room in which we saw it rather than as itself. It becomes "the chair that was in my parents' living room."

Of course, group influence does not negate individual influence because the relationship between group and individual influence varies. We could easily remember the same chair as "the one I always sat in when I visited my parents." What it does say is that how things are seen in a group affects how we see them individually. A group of things forms a context around *a* thing; thus, while each thing exerts its own influence it is also doing so as part of a context that influences others.

The more difficult aspect to relate to business is the "rearranging of the room" effect, taking the same members of a group and altering their "position." This becomes easier if we look at people's positions within a group in constant flux. Here, I am using "position" in an abstract, relational sense rather than in a physical one similar to the furniture in the room. We'll cover this more thoroughly in the Strategy chapter when we discuss organizational and *de facto* power. Essentially, the changing relational aspects within the group will gradually cause a change in the influence of the group; the group's room becomes rearranged.

Despite this abstract, point #14 also has a physical perspective in business that is best illuminated by seating arrangements at a dinner party or meeting. A group's influence varies according to who sits near whom. Informal gatherings can say a lot about the group and about its individual members relative to the group not to mention it can alter the conversations that will likely occur. Someone who is frequently in the vicinity of another person is more likely to have a closer relationship to that person than one who is routinely across the room from the same person. How the individual members of a group mingle in a gathering can communicate much about the group; this communicative aspect is the influence exerted by the group. This influence has an effect on others interacting with members in the group. Figure 4.6 tries to communicate this feeling with four separate diagrams.

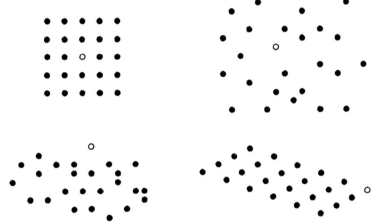

Figure 4.6

Even though the white point does not change (neither do the black ones for that matter), each diagram communicates something different to the viewer. We can make conclusions about each group of points and white's relationship in each; thus, the impression we get about the group affects how we look at the white dot. In fact, if we were the white dot, we might even have a preference for a group and our relationship to it.

Solidifying the connection between these three points, #12 - #14, and business, we find that the influence an individual exerts changes when he's seen as part of a group (point #12). The group's influence can now radiate from the individual as well when he is alone. The group need not be a formal one with easily defined organizational boundaries (point #13). Informal relationships and friendships form groups. Refining these further, the group's influence alters as the relative location of the individual members change. How each member of the group is positioned within the group will affect the influence the group exerts.

Many of these we are aware of consciously; however, the implication with these especially when we combine this with point #7 is that we are not always aware of the degree to which these group influences affect our daily decisions especially those involving individuals of these groups. These influences will encourage us to seek rationalizations supporting the emotions we derive from these influences; positive emotions will encourage us to positively rationalize, and negative ones will encourage us to negatively rationalize. Conversely, and more from your perspective, people are constantly being influenced by the contextual groups in which they place you. As point #13 states, these contexts need not be formal or ones we design for ourselves. Some of the contexts in which others place us may not have any relationship to anything we control. These become related to the problems associated with points #7 - #10.

Fourth Three (#15 - #17)

This group relates to Figures 2.61 – 2.67. The ability of a person to consciously feel these influences varies by person. That ability is related directly to one's emotional sensitivity and more specifically intuition. Since these fall in the realm of the feminine influence, women are more likely to experience greater effectiveness here than men; however, men do possess intuition but most will tend to discount it and ignore it. Some even possess greater ability here than many women.

Point #15 relates most to the figures we just mentioned. Just as everyone is born with varying physical and mental capabilities, people are born with varying emotional capabilities. While women have the advantage emotionally, men have it physically and mentally. They tend to be stronger and more rational. The later allows them to more effectively express their ideas in a concrete fashion.

The counterweight that equalizes men and women in a generic sense is a woman's better feel for what is comprehensively going on around her; she is less likely to be blindsided than a man. One may not always be able to grasp this from her since putting her observations into concrete thought will be more difficult for her than a man, but much of this will also be because the ideas she is trying to express are not necessarily easy. Often they will be very deep and very involved. This is why the strength of any man is maximized by integrating his more feminine aspects of his nature with his dominant male attributes and why the attractiveness of any woman is maximized by her integrating the more masculine aspects of her nature with her dominant feminine attributes. Again, this dynamic state of reconciling opposites is symbolized by the union of man and woman as depicted in marriage.

Point #16 implies there is effort in developing one's intuition. It's not simply something that is there. Just as problem solving and mental activity develops a mind and exercise develops muscles, exercising one's intuition encourages its development. Analogously, we see chess players preparing for matches by solving problems they will likely never see in a real match, but this prepares their mind to see situations and their variations. Students prepare for achievement exams in the same way by taking pre-tests and trial tests that prepare them mentally to handle the pressures involved in taking that exam. In both cases, it allows them to enter a frame of mind that will best allow them to make use of their mental facilities. For some of the elderly, simply doing a crossword puzzle stimulates mental activity that helps stem senility. The effects of physical exercise are well known. Even those blessed with the best physique must train and develop it. Nothing happens without effort.

Point #17 is the neglect of point #16. Muscles and minds atrophy with disuse; our emotions do as well. Desensitization becomes a tool by which to train a soldier; too much empathy for the enemy can lead to his death. Segregating business relationships from personal relationships has the same effect and becomes the rationale for this desensitization. The cost of this desensitization is dynamism, and thus, the ability to regenerate as well. One cannot tap into the emotional power inherent in relationships through emotionlessness; a mighty oak cannot grow in concrete. The pure, unabashed profit motive contains the seeds of its own eventual destruction for the passive emphasis on relationships it encourages. Business relationships are personal relationships by other means; the segregation we impose between business and personal is an artificial one.

The masculine orientation of business encourages objectification of its various aspects including people to yield the condition above. How this affects the individual who may only be a temporary player in the lifespan of a business whose end is of little concern to him, relates directly to point #17. Desensitization sterilizes one's emotional abilities to the point where they become atrophic. Consequently, the ability to tap into your inherent talent and those of others diminishes. To those possessing significant intuitive abilities such as women this atrophy means ignoring a strength they have.

Together these three points imply that not everyone can emotionally visualize to the same degree the invisible, indirect, and intangible aspects inherent in all relationships, business or personal. Those who have better vision will always confront those who say they don't just as a talented signer will confront those who say he can't sing. Because of the intangible nature of relationships, convincing one of this is relatively easy especially in a masculine field such as business where tangibility, quantification, and objectivity are prized.

Conclusion

Holistically looking at these seventeen influential points, the concluding point becomes:

> We are influenced by many things in our environment in many ways, many
> of which escape our awareness whose power source is intuition rooted in our
> emotional sensitivity, a sensitivity whose development is possible but whose
> ultimate growth varies innately by individual.

Appreciating these seventeen points and this concluding point is the basis for understanding and appreciating the practical implementation of the feminine influence in business. Such an appreciation will allow for a more effective use of her in this realm and for a more effective tapping of the inherent power in each of our personalities. These actions set the stage for dynamic outcomes.

How these influences affect someone will vary by person not only because of what they are able to see in relationships but also because of who they are. Part of our personality entails the needs that drive us. They encourage us to interpret influences in ways according to those needs. Our needs also set the stage for conflicts when our needs conflict with another's.

We'll examine needs more closely now.

Needs

We can look upon the needs of humans in many different ways. Maslow's *Theory of Human Motivation* is one of the more frequently cited works on the topic. Again, my purpose is to establish something that can be effectively implemented in the business arena as a starting point for a business person to integrate and build upon in his daily, relational business practice. The basic premise is that the more we work to incorporate concepts into our personalities the more likely they will work in comparison to the regurgitation of and adherence to a process for which we do not understand or appreciate its premises.

I introduced needs in the strategic business example concerning advertising in the Feminine Influence chapter. Reviewing that example may help while we go into more detail here. There are three basic needs:

- Long Term Security
- Novelty of Experience
- Emotional Recognition

A friend shared these with me, and I found them useful in helping me understand and appreciate some basics so I could develop something more comprehensively suitable to my personality. We'll explore each briefly, outline an implemental perspective, clarify their recognition, and review their practicality. As Figure 4.7 illustrates, it's best for us to anticipate all three playing a role in any person's needs where each will vary not only according to the person but also to the situation.

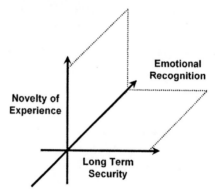

Figure 4.7

Explanation

While these needs may seem self-evident, elaboration will allow us to see them more comprehensively because we're saying all needs fall into one of these three types. As we try to apply these, we'll have a need for looking at them as broadly as possible in order to make them useful.

Long-term security relates to anything that makes us physically, mentally, or emotionally safer. This can be as simple as working out to make us physically stronger to more complex ones where we avoid situations and people that may embarrass or humiliate us. Making an analogy to a country, security relates to laws and the military. The rule of law provides security that makes it safer for investment opportunities, so possessing control over people or situations is an aspect of security. Fulfilling this need will mean we become stronger and more in control of our surroundings so the unexpected won't harm us.

Novelty of experience relates to those things that imply newness. This can mean changing our surroundings or our looks to learning something new or experiencing new relationships. The honeymoon is symbolic of these events. Generally, any type of need for growth will fall into this category. It also implies risk since new ventures bring along a certain amount of uncertainty; however, to the person who's seeking newness this risk has more of an adventurous flavor to it. Excitement and youth are generally associated with novelty of experience.

Emotional recognition relates to the need to feel special or unique. The recognition can come from others or from within. Physically, possessing something different from others becomes important. This can be as simple as owning a unique home to possessing a skill that few have. Mentally and emotionally this relates to expertise and talent that few others have. Emotional recognition is the need to feel that you are not just part of the masses that there is something that differentiates you from others.

All of us experience all three to some degree, but trying to see what's important to us will help us better understand how we see things. Our orientation around these needs will influence how we interpret events, situations, things, and people. Relating this to influence, these needs become those invisible elements within us that allow the outside world to influence us in various ways. Consequently, in addition to the outside world influencing us we have a web of needs that do as well.

Perspective

When assessing others or yourself, I've found having the right perspective before delving into specifics helps. Two elements comprise this perspective. The first is simply realizing one can do a competent job of this on their own. The second is being mindful of some basic aspects in the approach of the task.

A problem I have found with any type of personality assessment is that unless you know the results of the person across from you, the assessment is virtually useless because few teach you how to develop your own assessment capabilities. Furthermore, even if you have the results for the person you're visiting, you cannot assume they remain static and that they apply unilaterally to that person for every situation, event, thing, or person he may encounter. Some variance will occur depending upon the specifics. For instance, stress has a habit of extracting aspects within all of us that do not show when we calmly and quietly fill out ovals or blanks to a personality assessment.

The personality assessments that do teach you an assessment methodology and how to apply them fail from the basic premise as shown in Figure 4.2; they tend to impose a third party between two people. That third party is the logic behind the assessment that we consciously try to employ to guide us. As a result, this logic becomes more akin to a strait jacket because we are trying to fit ourselves within the guidelines of the assessment tool that a third party established. This creates an unnatural situation where we are trying to assess someone as someone else would when the main concern is "how do I relate to the person across from me" not "how would this third party relate to this person."

In essence, it's really best for each of us to develop our own assessment methodology that we can call upon when the situation demands. The initial problem we run into is the feeling that we don't have the expertise to do this. That may be true but I am not talking about you going into practice full-time to help other people assess others. What I am saying is that you are trying to find ways for *you* that will help *you* relate to others more effectively. Expertise to do this is not necessary because all of us were born with some innate talent to do this. If this were not the case, how would we have been able to function for thousands of years without personality assessments?

To some degree we are becoming victims of over-specialization to the point where we feel incompetent on many issues; without a specialist or consultant, we can't make a decision. In discussions with one training vendor I asked how we would get managers to follow up the training the vendor advocated. He went on to describe how managers would hold people accountable for various outcomes targeted by the training. I asked whether we should work with managers to help them become teachers of the training. While they may not run the initial seminar, this training for managers will allow them to better teach and reinforce the principles in the training. The vendor then asked me, "If we did that, why would the managers need us?"

Encouraging people to buy deodorant means making them realize they smell. Encouraging people to buy assessment and training capabilities means making them realize they aren't intelligent enough to do this themselves. If people are intelligent enough to handle the many relationships involved in business, then they are intelligent enough to figure out how to teach someone. Teaching is another activity that has gone on long before we had specialists doing it.

Returning to assessing people and relationships, the biggest advantage to developing your own ability to do this in a manner conducive to your personality is that you will more likely be effective. Second, we are all human. Our natural inclination in any interaction is to try to figure out what the other person is like. We do this to determine whether we like the person and how best to relate to him. Consequently, developing your own assessment ability is a more natural and effective way to go. This whole chapter on You can help you accomplish this.

If I had to distill the important aspects of assessing others, they would be:

1. Gather observations always.
2. Every interaction provides you with new observations.
3. Don't lock in on a view of the other person until you absolutely must.
4. Allow your view to change after every occasion that forced you to lock in on it.
5. Rely upon your gut.

There is always a wealth of information we can glean from any interaction with a person. Actions and words tell us a lot but we can also learn much from actions that don't happen and from words that remain unspoken. Always be actively looking for additional observations. We opened the Introduction with Sherlock Holmes. In many ways he serves as an accurate analogy of what we're trying to accomplish with his gathering of evidence.

Another excellent analogy that helps us relate aspects #3 and #4 to #1 and #2 is an army. The ideal army moves from dispersion to concentration quickly. When dispersed the army is reconnoitering, searching and gathering; when concentrated the army is preparing for battle. Dispersion makes an army unable to do battle while concentration makes an army unable to gather information. Conceptually, one remains dispersed until he must act on what he has learned.

Human nature's inclination is to arrive at conclusions about another person as quickly as possible so we can alleviate the feeling of uncertainty surrounding the experience. Since it's impossible to totally know another person, our inclination is to fill in the gaps of what we know with our own feelings, both positive and negative. If we feel positive towards another, we are more inclined to supplement the unknown attributes of their personality with the more positive aspects of our own. Conversely, if we feel negative towards another, we are more inclined to supplement with our own anxieties. For these reasons, it's important to not lock ourselves into a perspective about someone because it will tend to leave us vulnerable to overlooking new information – just like an army that is prepared for battle.

This problem associated with focusing is very similar to our previous one in the Feminine Influence chapter about planning objectives. Our inclination is to focus on the objective and overlook opportunities. Relational activities suffer the same fate if we move to a conclusion when we don't need to and allow it to become fixated in our minds. Waiting to focus and concentrate what we've learned when a situation requires us to is generally best. Afterwards, the perspective entails dispersing and remaining open to changes necessitated by new information and situations. Visually, the entire process would look something like Figure 4.8 where concentration, focus on a viewpoint of another's personality, may change. Figure 4.8 represents this by altering the formation of the points when they concentrate.

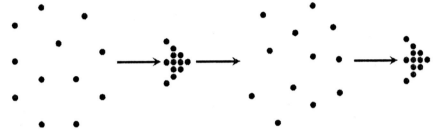

Figure 4.8

In this manner, you'll find yourself collecting information and comparing it to your gut feelings. These feelings take priority over conscious observations. Most personality assessments fail because they encourage a conscious, processed application of their basic principles. Many times this manifests itself in the form of computerized scoring of results. Your conscious observations should be a cross-check for your feelings that allow for insights into other exploratory avenues.

The perspective outlined here, while helpful with others, helps with looking at oneself. We're not only trying to identify talent opportunities in others but also ourselves. Reflecting upon ourselves in a way that makes us open to observing how we feel, think, and behave is a first step to such identification.

With this perspective in place, collation of information becomes important. For instance, "What are we searching for?" Recognizing the various needs or the lack of them in our observations becomes important.

Recognition

Our every action, thought, and emotion says something about us. By observing ourselves and others, we can discover things that may not be apparent to us consciously. "Who we are" is much greater than "who we think we are"; however, to discover ourselves and what untapped potential lies within requires self-observation. There are three aspects to ourselves we can observe:

- Behavior
- Thoughts
- Feelings

Feelings drive thoughts which in turn drive behavior. Any action almost always finds its roots in a feeling. Melding these aspects with the concept that "who we are" is much greater than "who we think we are" we arrive at the following implications:

- What we do encompasses far more than what we think we do.
- What we think encompasses far more than what we think we think.
- What we feel encompasses far more than what we think we feel.

By observing ourselves when we act, think, and feel, we begin to discover what our thoughts missed. These implications are very much in line with what we saw with most of the Figures 2.32 – 2.41. In those figures we saw what does happen is far beyond what we think will happen or should happen. Our conscious ability to capture life falls far short of what life actually is. Carrying this to ourselves we find that anything we think about ourselves, behavior, thoughts, feelings, falls far short of our actual behaviors, thoughts, and feelings. The distinction between the two is so great that we could easily make an argument that we go through life larger oblivious to it.

My wife would give her third graders an exercise that demonstrated this by having them write instructions to make a peanut butter and jelly sandwich. Afterwards, using their own instructions they would have to make that sandwich; they had to do exactly what their instructions said. What comes out of this is the tremendous difficulty anyone has in capturing every last step life entails. We see the same thing happen when we roll out a new process to a group. As we had mentioned in conjunction with Figures 2.51 – 2.53 how one interprets something affects the outcomes we derive, so our ability to capture all the possible interpretations and to project their effects on the process in order to make allowances for it in the process falls short of what will actually happen.

Essentially, the same principles exist for our own behavior, thoughts, and feelings that we think about as they do for our thoughts about daily occurrences in our outside world. Essentially, we can revisit Figure 2.38 that focused on outside events and introspectively superimpose it upon our internal worlds as Figure 4.9 demonstrates.

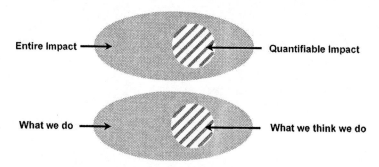

Figure 4.9 (2.38 Revisited [top] & Revised [bottom])

Through the observation of ourselves we can arrive at a better appreciation for all that we do. The implications return us as well to Figure 2.41 to show the inherent potential that lives within each of us in Figure 4.10 by realizing that all we can do is far greater than what we think we can do.

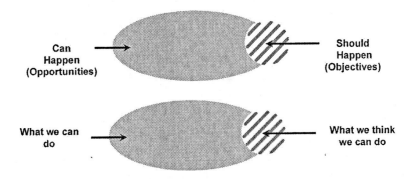

Figure 4.10 (2.41 Revisited [top] & Revised [bottom])

Understanding our needs and those of others helps to move us closer to realizing this potential by appreciating those needs. A step towards this is being aware as to how these needs manifest themselves in the observations we collect. Figure 4.11 begins us on that journey by cross referencing behaviors, thoughts, and emotions with long-term security, novelty of experience, and emotional recognition. The result is a single word that can serve as an entry point into making connections with other observations.

Manifestation of Needs			
Needs Aspect	Long Term Security	Novelty of Experience	Emotional Recognition
Behavior	Strength	Start	Mastery
Thought	Knowledge	Education	Expertise
Emotion	Spirit	Creation	Talent

Figure 4.11

At this point some of the discussion in the Feminine Influence chapter surrounding the business example of advertising will serve to help see how these words connect to more expansive themes. The key toward moving to enhancing one's awareness is keeping Figure 4.8 in mind. We're at the stage where we want to be as all encompassing as we possibly can. Translating this to the table in Figure 4.11 we want to be as loose and expansive as we can with the definitions and connotations of the words in the table. At the moment consider we're reconnoitering.

In truth, while I've formatted Figure 4.11 into a table with specific blocks, the segregations among the words are truly blends. Imagine walking a trail middle of the morning after the sun has been in the sky for a few hours. The trail weaves through open fields and covered woods, and the air is still. Our walk takes place at a time of year when the nights are cool and the days are warm, most likely during late spring, early summer, or fall. If you've ever had a chance to walk, hike, run, or bike a trail at such a time, you can notice a fair temperature change between the open spots in the sun and the covered ones in the woods. You can even feel such a difference with a single large, expansive tree if the air is very still.

When you pass from the warm to the cool air, you'll notice there is no visible demarcation between the two. You move from one to the other in a graduated sense. Imagine all nine blocks being air of nine different temperatures. While you can feel yourself moving from one to the other, you can't specifically state where the boundaries are. This analogy is important because when you're observing another person you will see them move through all of these different areas. The challenge is trying to appreciate their preferences.

In the effort to expand our sense for behavior, thought, and emotion, we can begin by thinking of them as actions, thoughts, and feelings. The table in Figure 4.11 seeks to answer the question "How do these manifest themselves when they come in contact with the needs, long-term security, novelty of experience, and emotional recognition?" More specifically:

- How do our actions reflect a preference for long-term security, novelty of experience, or emotional recognition?
- How do our thoughts reflect a preference for long-term security, novelty of experience, or emotional recognition?
- How do our feelings reflect a preference for long-term security, novelty of experience, or emotional recognition?

In the case of long-term security, our actions manifest with a tendency toward strength, our thoughts toward knowledge, and our feelings toward spirit. In effect, our actions seek to make us stronger so we can protect ourselves. While this can come across as personally making ourselves stronger, it also arrives in a relative sense. We can become stronger by making others weaker. Often, we see and hear the sentence "knowledge is power" to reflect how we feel knowledge makes us stronger mentally because we know something. It's easier to relate this to military forces; intelligence, knowing one's enemy and terrain, gives an advantage to the army that possesses a high degree of this versus the one that doesn't. In an emotional sense, security translates into something spiritual. Having a strong sense of a spirit within you protects you from the emotional challenges the world offers. Religious activities are a good example of how emotional long-term security manifests itself.

Novelty of experience manifests itself in our actions as the start of something new. Since starting something can imply ending something else, we can see this need manifest itself in the action to close out another activity or part of our lives. Ending something automatically causes something to replace it; that something is a new thing we start. If, as Antoine Lavoisier's Law of Conservation of Mass states, "Mass is neither created nor destroyed" but rather moves from one form to another, then implicatively we can say the same about events, "Life is neither created nor destroyed" but merely moves from one event to another – the beginning of one naturally implies the end of another and vice versa. Cerebrally, we see this need manifest itself as education, the desire to learn something new or to seek a new opportunity. Professionally, this could take the form of a new invention or innovation. Emotionally, we experience this as creation. Expressing ourselves, allowing the release or launch of new emotions, is the basis for creations whether in the form of painting, writing, designing, or many other artistic endeavors. The birth of a child symbolically represents this need on the part of the father and mother.

Extending these to emotional recognition we find a qualitative need that sets one apart. Rather than being simply one of the masses, there is a need for distinction, uniqueness. In actions this displays itself as mastery over the activity. Professional athletes are very representative of individuals who set themselves apart because of a mastery of an activity. Mentally, we see distinction surface as expertise in a particular field. Specialists in any field would tend to be a good representation of the manifestation of emotional recognition in thought. Finally, we see emotional recognition materialize in the form of talent. While talent can be associated with behavior and thought, it's more nebulous than mastery over an activity and expertise in a mental pursuit. Thus, talent can serve to capture the more nebulous attributes that distinguish individuals.

From these descriptions and Figure 4.11, we're tempted to develop a process by which we can use these to help identify needs in people; however, the danger of any process is that it might become mechanical. For a process seeking to improve interpersonal relationships, this danger can become relationally fatal. The temptation to run observations through a checklist or computer in order to arrive at a conclusion is great because of the simplicity and illusionary accuracy. To improve a relationship with another person, one can't behave like a robot running data through a program. Moreover, we need something that will help us in the heat of battle, at the moment we're relating.

Possessing a good feel for something is far better than possessing a good understanding. If we review from the Feminine Influence chapter the scene referenced from the movie *Top Gun* where Maverick, played by Tom Cruise, responds to the accusatory question of the civilian instructor, Charlie, played by Kelly McGillis, for his technique in a training dogfight, we find him countering her question, "What were you thinking at this point?" with, "You don't have time to think up there. If you think . . . you're dead." The point is that events in an F-14 fighter come at one too fast and furiously to think; you must respond instinctively to the situation at hand. Thus, having a natural feel for how to respond will prove more effective than a mechanical, programmed response. In many ways, relating to others is similar because the nuances of any personal interaction come at us too fast and furiously to recognize all of them consciously enough to note them. This returns us to the scene in the woods where we try to capture every detail; it's just too much. Analogously, a personal interaction has far too many details for us to try to capture them consciously.

A great symbolic illustration as to how much we miss by attempting to think through something is a glass filled with sand. Each grain of sand represents a step in a process or detail we attempt to document. For my experiment, I used fine, premium, playground sand to fill a twelve ounce glass. To this glass that allowed no light to pass through, I added water slowly. On average, I found I was able to add four and a half ounces of water to a glass filled with sand as shown in Figure 4.12.

Glass Filled   **Full Glass of Sand**
with Sand   **with Water Added**

Figure 4.12

Essentially, if we attempted to record all the material in Figure 4.11 and what we will soon cover in Figure 4.13, the task becomes so overwhelming that we fall into a mechanical trance more concerned with watching for things that will make important observations than the person. In an interaction it's more important to digest a few things well than a lot superficially. If we attempt to construct a process by which we can assess the needs of others, we are likely to fall short of our potential effectiveness.

In lieu of a process, I will attempt to give you a better feel for how these needs manifest themselves. I'll do this by expanding upon Figure 4.11. Conceptually, I want to do the same as giving you the feeling of riding a bike or hitting a baseball well. Once the feeling finds its way into you and settles in, you'll be able to call upon it more quickly and effectively than any series of steps to help guide you through a process. This feeling may not occur immediately, so most likely it will help to review Figure 4.13 several times or to lay it aside and review it at another time. As with anything else, the more you try to access this feeling the better your experience will be with each implementation.

Ideally, you will begin to find yourself empathizing with the other person to the point where you'll be able to actually feel their needs. The conscious observations you do catch will serve to supplement that feeling, reinforce it, or question it. The key, as stated earlier, is to avoid a conclusion until you must (Figure 4.8). Until then, digest the interaction so you can call upon it when you need to act upon your observations.

Manifestation of Needs		
Needs		
Long Term Security	Novelty of Experience	Emotional Recognition

	Long Term Security	Novelty of Experience	Emotional Recognition
Single Word	Security	Growth	Uniqueness
Attribute	Firmness	Movement	Quality
Masculine **Feminine**	Aggressiveness Comfort	Surprise Freshness	Triumph Beauty
Aspect			
Behavior	**Strength** Acquisition Alliance Command Conformity Fortification Maintenance Possession Predictability Preservation Stability	**Start** Adventure Building Departure End Entry Exit Forming Initiative Introduction Takeoff	**Mastery** Ability Attention Award Craftsmanship Knack Model Promotion Skill Technique Uncommon
Thought	**Knowledge** Association Assurance Confidentiality Expectation Information Legality Longevity Organization Statistics Tradition	**Education** Basics Bombshell Conclusion Innovation Invention Opening Opportunities Origin Primer Prospects	**Expertise** Advice Approval Compliment Congratulations Differentiation Endowment Original Rarity Respect Specialty
Emotion	**Spirit** Absoluteness Certainty Champion Confidence Faith Infallibility Optimism Private Reliance Trust	**Creation** Birth Courage Excitement Expression Newness Release Renewal Revival Stimulation Youth	**Talent** Admiration Appreciation Elegance Flair Knighting Distinctiveness Superiority Valor Virtue Wonder

Figure 4.13

As you see in Figure 4.13, we've greatly enhanced Figure 4.11. While it will help you get a better feel for how these three needs appear in life, the Practicality portion of this topic coming next will focus on how these needs interact. This will help us better appreciate how our needs affect the view we have of others and how the needs of others affect the view they have of you and others.

You do not have to remember everything in Figure 4.13. In fact, it's probably more effective if you don't because there are many more words associated with these needs depending upon their use. Even the ones I've associated can apply to more if we consider some of their alternative uses. Moreover, we need to remain cognizant of our walk on the trail and the subtle changing of air temperature; the segregation of these words appears much neater on the table in Figure 4.13 than they do in reality.

As you will see, I included the words from Figure 4.11 in Figure 4.13 and added ten other words underneath each. These ten words expand our vision so we can be as aware as possible how these needs manifest themselves in behavior, thoughts, and emotions. You will also notice a few words that you can also include in other parts of the table; this represents the actual blending of all aspects in this table. In reality, all the needs and aspects blend in a fashion similar to colors. Even though you only see one color, that color is a blend of three primary colors, blue, red, and yellow. You don't see the primary colors but by understanding the nature of colors you can come close to what makes up the color you're seeing. Using this table will allow you to appreciate the blend within the person you're interacting with and within you.

Let's run through what other enhancements I've made to our table.

At the top, you will notice a single associative word for each need. For long-term security I've selected "security", for novelty of experience "growth", and emotional recognition "uniqueness." Beneath these I've identified the primary attribute for each need, firmness, movement, and quality respectively. Following these I looked at the masculine and feminine aspects of each need. I used primarily the single word descriptions and the attributes to derive these. Beneath these are the groupings of ten I mentioned above.

I will elaborate on the single words, attributes, and masculine-feminine derivatives but will not spend much time on the words grouped in tens. My original lists contained more than ten in each, so I felt it important to narrow the list to a group that conveyed a comprehensive feeling for the need's manifestation. Basically, I was trying to capture the essence of the need with the most potent concentration I could find. Implicatively, this means there is much room for you to associate other words or situations. Again, Figure 4.13 serves as an entry point for you. I prefer to look at it as opening a door for you. Where you go once you're in is up to you.

While it may be easy to see why I chose the single word descriptions that I did, I'm going to spend a little time elaborating on them with the help of some symbols in Figure 4.14. In conjunction with Figure 4.13 we can visualize and tell a story about each need's manifestation.

Security   Growth   Uniqueness

Figure 4.14

Security's symbol is a fortress, a castle, with a gate. The walls represent protection from the outside world while the gate represents access to address events as well. As with any army, sometimes it must attack in order to defend its security and why security implies offensive actions. Holistically, the symbol represents stability, structure, and organization through the square. Whereas a square has easily definable measurements such as perimeter and area, a circle's perimeter and area are based on π (pi), a number that begins as 3.141592+ and continues *ad infinitum* without any distinctive, repeatable pattern; thus, whereas you can definitely quantify a square, any quantification of a circle is only a very refined estimate. Quantification gives us a sense of security that we know our stuff. Thus, the clarity of numbers, organization, laws, and rules give us security and stability. Without laws we have anarchy.

Growth's symbol, an upward arrow, represents the venturing into the unknown in a way signifying growth. The undulation in the middle signifies that that growth will not always be linear; setbacks will occur. The arrow itself represents movement; growth cannot occur without movement. It just may not be obvious to us. Another important aspect of this symbol is its journey into the unknown. Learning is such a journey; however, it's more than just learning a new fact but rather a new way to look at things. There is a difference between learning a new concept and learning a new fact. Whereas the former may lead to new insights, the later will allow you to reinforce (secure) your position. It's the difference between creating a new weapon and finding more ammunition for your current weapon. In Figure 4.13 it's the difference between education and knowledge.

The symbol for uniqueness shows a distinction between one dot and the others; the white one stands out from the black ones. Uniqueness also implies a natural tension between one and the many as highlighted by the statement, "Unique and weird are the same thing," and becomes a matter of perspective. To those who like the distinction white offers, he's unique; to those who don't, he's weird. By placing the white dot in the middle, we convey the impression that not only is he outnumbered but he is also surrounded. In many ways, this represents the qualitative difference that the underdog offers that doesn't show up clearly on paper. Celebrities are most often symbolic of the intangible distinction that sorts them from the masses. While they may have a specific talent, expertise, or ability that segregates them, with many celebrities there are other things related to personality that sorts them from others in their field. Nevertheless, if everyone is unique then everyone in some way is distinctive from the rest and feels the tension between one and the many. This is why many find the underdog scenario so appealing.

With these symbols we can also appreciate the attributes of the needs, firmness, movement, and quality. We can clearly see the strength inherent in the security symbol, the movement in the growth one, and qualitative distinction in uniqueness. These attributes will help us see the practical interactions of these needs more clearly in the next portion of our needs discussion.

With the masculine-feminine terms, I'm returning us more directly to the themes in the previous chapters concerning the feminine influence. Even though we have not talked much about the feminine influence, this chapter is here because of her importance. Since relationships make a business, appreciating relationships will encourage long-term success. Much of what lies in this chapter and book relies more on one's empathic abilities than one's cognitive ones. The masculine-feminine terms help us relate our previous chapters to this one.

The gate in the security symbol best represents aggressiveness in the masculine influence if we look at a trapped animal. Most animals will avoid threats rather than attack them. The variation comes when they feel trapped or are protecting their young. Any fortress without a gate leaves one at the mercy of outside events because he lacks the ability to try to influence them. Anyone whose security is threatened physically, mentally, or emotionally will be inclined to attack the threat in some way. From the standpoint of the feminine influence, security implies comfort. Symbolically, it's home protecting us from the harsh, irregular, climatic, conditions in our physical environment. Mentally, laws, rules, and policies give us comfort in the form of protection from chaos. Emotionally, parents symbolize a comfortable protection from life's realities.

Growth, from novelty of experience, translates into surprise in the masculine and freshness in the feminine. The masculine is easier to see when we look back to the Persian Gulf War example in the Feminine Influence chapter (Figure 2.31). The allies' huge sweeping movement around the Iraqi's flank caught them by surprise. From a masculine perspective growth will encourage activity that will catch others by surprise because there is a change in the status quo or expectations. Novelty of experience from a feminine perspective is akin to freshness or youth. Symbolically, we see this most ostentatiously in the fashion industry where women's fashions not only change more rapidly than men's but more comprehensively as well. The variety of new offerings and variations are extensive.

Our symbol for uniqueness translates the need for emotional recognition from a masculine perspective into triumph and from a feminine one into beauty. To the man, it's a special victory against the odds while to the woman it's being the center of attention, a white dot in the middle of black ones. Again, each of these implies a qualitative aspect. Daily we see the masculine aspect of this in the form of competitions from sports to arts to academics to pageants; the triumph of one or a few over the many. The feminine aspect also displays herself daily in our elevation of people and things. Again, celebrities are a good example but we also see it in the exclusivity we give certain neighborhoods, houses, cars, jewelry, electronics, toys, vacation spots, plus many others. Anytime we place emphasis on one or a few above many, we're expressing uniqueness, emotional recognition.

By soaking in Figures 4.11 – 4.14 one can begin to get a feel for how these needs manifest themselves. What we will now examine are the manifestations of their interactions for this will allow us to more clearly see their practical application. While Figure 4.7 showed how we can all have elements of all three, which one tends to dominate within each us will vary. The dominant perspective will tend to influence not only how we view others but how others view us and how we view ourselves. All three impact relationships and consequently a business's success.

Practicality

Individuals' needs influence relationships and take two fundamental shapes, objective and subjective. The first involves what is tangibly extracted from the relationship by either person to make the relationship work. In business, we look at the aspects of a transaction. Typically, we have the exchange of goods and services for money. The second involves the intangibles that influence them personally and affect the way each views the other. While the first shape shows up on ledgers, the second shape doesn't appear anywhere. To some extent this returns us to our relational discussion concerning all dollars are equal; ledgers and financials don't show whether the dollar came from God or Satan. More practically, unless we have some knowledge of the relationship, we cannot make any subjective determinations about the monetary transaction whatsoever.

Nevertheless, what truly impacts the objective shape of the relationship is what occurs on the subjective side. In business, another way of saying this is that "relationships drive revenue." What we want to do here in this portion of our needs discussion is examine how the various interactions respond to one another.

Our most recent discussion focused more on the positive attributes of each need. From that we experience a feeling similar to viewing a dessert menu at a restaurant, "I'll take one of everything." In fact, that is what happens when we say everyone has these needs, but they appear in various degrees depending upon the situation. Overarching one's personality is a dominant one. Likewise, if one were to take one of every dessert, most likely he would get sick if he tried to eat them all. He is more likely to take a little of every one and favor one over the others. He is also likely to find that the taste of one affects the taste of the others.

Our needs have a similar but more intense impact. While they all coexist, there is reconciliation of them that goes on as well. Let's draw another analogy by taking a person preparing to hike a trail. From a security perspective, he is most safe if he remains in his spot. Once he begins to move he is more likely to trip or fall by accidentally stepping in a rut or tripping over a tree root. Furthermore, as he moves more quickly on the trail, his security decreases. Running on the trail becomes even more unsafe for him.

Inherently, there is tension between long-term security and novelty of experience. Something new and uncertain is generally more risky than something old and predictable. Movement in anything creates instability. An army is more exposed when it's marching than when it's entrenched. You can't trip a standing man. Conversely, a standing man goes no where.

Emotional recognition emits additional tension through a qualitative dimension. Now, it no longer becomes a matter of simply moving or protecting but rather how well one not only does these things but how he negotiates their interplay. In effect, this sets him aside from others. Returning to our man who's balancing the safety of standing with the novelty of moving, his concern moves beyond simply doing to something more involved. This could be a matter of how well he walks the trail or how much he enjoys it. Someone who walks particularly well or who can find a particular enjoyment from the activity becomes segregated from those who do this to a lesser degree.

This tension is more difficult to see but can best be introduced through Mark Twain's story about Tom Sawyer and his painting the fence. In this particular scene Tom convinces his friends to paint the fence that his aunt had ordered him to do. Tom does such a good job sharing what he saw intrinsically valuable about the task that his friends gave him things and money to have the opportunity to paint the fence. Tom's focus was basically on four things:

1. Opportunity – It's not everyday one gets to paint a fence, especially the front one.
2. Talent – His aunt would not let just anyone paint the fence.
3. Painless – It's not work.
4. Enjoyment – Tom likes to paint this fence.

This analogy allows us to explore the tension emotional recognition can create when it interacts with long-term security and novelty of experience. If we relate to the more feminine aspects of these two needs, comfort and freshness, we can more easily see the negative aspects of painting a fence that Tom overcame.

From the perspective of Tom's friends, they initially saw painting the fence as discomforting and boring. The effort and grime associated with painting is not comfortable, and painting was not a new experience for them. Emotional recognition creates tension because in order to receive it one may have to experience discomfort and repetition. Any athlete, musician, professional, or expert lives with the daily experience of doing or reviewing many of the same things over and over again in order to find mastery, expertise, or talent in that particular endeavor. We find this most frequently symbolized by the practices run for athletic teams. For a soldier, the experience is boot camp. Through practice one experiences incrementally small growth enhancements that gradually diminish in comparison to the initial experience with the activity. Some call this the "law of diminishing returns."

For each of the needs we can find a negative attribute that will stir anxiousness when this need is prominent:

- Long Term Security – Threat.
- Novelty of Experience – Resistance.
- Emotional Recognition – Ignorance.

When a threat to one's physical, mental, or emotional safety arises, his long-term security need will begin to surface and force him to address it. For novelty of experience, resistance of any kind that restricts movement or opportunity to experience something new will create anxious moments. Realizing what one does well becomes more difficult as ignorance increases and thus the likelihood of emotional recognition diminishes. Anxious moments will occur if one has a talent which many do not appreciate because of their ignorance, thus producing frustration.

By appreciating the negative attributes that incite these needs, we can better appreciate the needs themselves. By understanding the dark, we come to better understand the light. From a practical perspective they will also allow us another way to identify more consciously the presence of a particular need. Thus, if someone feels threatened by another, that person may be stirring his security need. Likewise, if he is expressing that he feels resistance from another, he is likely showing his need for growth, novelty of experience. Finally, an expression by one that another simply doesn't understand could be stirring the need of emotional recognition.

We can further refine these statements by looking more closely at these exchanges as confrontations of needs. The second person stirring these needs also has needs himself that manifest in interactions. Consequently, they interact with the needs of the other and influence the entire relationship. By looking at each need in an ideal sense as representing a person, we can imagine how these imaginary people might conflict. For instance, how would we expect a conflict to take place between a person with a long-term security need and a novelty of experience one?

Using the single word descriptions for each need, security, growth, and uniqueness, we arrive at Figure 4.15 that cross references how a person (observer) with each of those needs would feel if stirred by another (observed) representing each of those needs. It shows the manifestations of these negative interactions.

Negative Manifestation of Interactions			
Observed **Observer**	**Security**	**Growth**	**Uniqueness**
Security **(Threat)**	Domineering	Reckless	Irrational
Growth **(Resistance)**	Restrictive	Interruptive	Lethargic
Uniqueness **(Ignorance)**	Raw	Wasteful	Arrogant

Figure 4.15

In general, as mentioned earlier, a security-minded person will be inclined to see threats in things. For a security-driven person, a negative interaction with another security driven person will likely elicit a descriptive along the lines of "domineering." This same individual will likely see a need for growth in another as "reckless" and a need for uniqueness as "irrational." We can better see this play out if we recall the attributes of each need, firmness, movement, and quality. Someone who seeks the stability and certainty that firmness provides will likely see movement as a destabilizing venture into the uncertain and attempts to enhance the qualitative aspects of the stability and certainty as pointless and worthless, "don't muddy up the waters" or "if it ain't broke, don't fix it." Additionally, as our uniqueness symbol implies, to accentuate your uniqueness or talent is to encourage tension with the many who don't share it. Implicatively, this means vulnerability and lack of safety found from blending in.

For a growth-oriented person, negative manifestations of interactions will generally appear as resistance. This can either be active or passive, purposeful or accidental. A negative interaction with a security-oriented person represents a purposefully active manifestation whereby the observer sees the observed as implementing restrictions preventing certain actions on his part. A purposefully accidental, negative interaction occurs when he interacts with another growth oriented individual. The symbolic picture here is of two people talking simultaneously because they each need to satisfy a need to talk. Likewise, two active people are in motion and their actions are interrupting one another. This isn't necessarily purposeful but rather a mere condition of them both moving in close proximity to one another. Contrast these two to the more passive, either purposeful or accidental, interaction with a person oriented around uniqueness, emotional recognition. Here, a growth orientation will likely view a uniqueness orientation as lethargic, unwillingness to act or a resistance to action.

A person oriented around emotional recognition will likely see negative interactions manifested as ignorance. In the recent example of the lethargy cited in him by the growth oriented person, the uniqueness oriented person's qualitative aspect would likely see the action posed by him as wasteful, ignorance of a better way. He would frown on activity for activity's sake. Similarly, he'll see in the security minded person a rawness in his approach, too rudimentary and conservative to be of much effectiveness because it's ignorant of larger, more involved issues. In another person oriented around emotional recognition, he'll likely continue the ignorance theme by looking at him as arrogant, ignorant to what he doesn't know.

One of the side conclusions that this analysis arrives at is that people of like needs that have negative interactions with one another will likely see the negative aspect of themselves in the other. For example, the person oriented around long-term security would see another like him in a negative situation as domineering, a person oriented around novelty of experience would likely see his as interruptive, and one centered around emotional recognition would see his as arrogant. This could lay the basis for a fairly intense negative interaction because few like to see their negative attributes displayed, even if they are cloaked in the personality of another. The situation is similar to displaying one's dirty laundry even if he knows no one knows it's his; the fear is that someone would find out. Likewise, when someone senses their own negatives in another, the anxiety comes from someone else possibly exclaiming, "Gee, that person is just like you!" Thus, if that person is not around, then it becomes harder for someone to make that connection. Similarly, if one's dirty laundry isn't lying around, it's harder for someone to find it and associate it to you.

A more important conclusion of Figure 4.15 is that negative manifestations are useful in helping us appreciate ourselves and others. Culturally, we often tend to sidestep negativity for fear it reflects on us if we dwell on it; however, one who declares another negative can't be positive because a truly positive person would see everything as positive including the negative qualities in another person. Therefore, his calling someone negative would be impossible. The point is that accepting negativity opens a whole new avenue of opportunities if one can figure out how to tap into it in a positive way. Someone offering you a negative opportunity is far better than someone not offering you any opportunity at all. At least in the first, there is always a chance he's wrong or you will find a way to turn it into a positive one.

Figure 4.15 shows how the various needs create tension in a relationship and in us. Since all three exist in us to some degree, we'll experience anxiety when we try to step outside our comfort zone to experience something new or to accept more responsibility in the spotlight. How we feel about these things can tell us something about ourselves. By exploring our feelings with the help of Figures 4.13 and 4.15 we can better determine how our feelings influence how we see others and, in turn, help us relate better to others by helping us appreciate ourselves and our perspectives as shown in Figure 4.2. We're always better off in trying to make the best possible assessment of our own relationships than relying entirely upon the advice and direction of a third party.

Yet, identifying our needs and how they influence us is only part of the story. As I had mentioned, all the needs are at play within us in various degrees and surface depending upon their respective dominances in our personalities and upon what the outside world presents to us. The next task is appreciating how these needs surface within us in response to our orientation and the outside world. Such a task will also serve to make the connection to the feminine influence stronger that we've established in the previous chapters and begin to lay additional groundwork on how we can extract dormant talent in all of us.

Duality

Thus far, we've looked at how the outside world and our needs influence our personalities. The challenge is seeing how these influences translate into a personality. How do we come to exercise the personality we have? We are not simple, shallow responders to outside stimuli and our needs. There are many other aspects to our personalities that impact that response. How do we arrive at the point where those aspects exert their impact?

Again, what I cover will be far shallower than the answer is in truth. I aim to provide something that is an entry point for you to explore yourself. The first "real book" I read as a child that convinced me I no longer was a rookie to reading was Jules Verne's *Journey to the Center of the Earth*. In it, the hero found a guide and map to such a journey. My objective here is to give you similar materials that will allow you to conduct your own journey in a way that will have practical implications for your effectiveness in the business world.

To that end, what I have found extremely helpful in appreciating the actions, thoughts, and feelings of others is something called the "Inside Person/Outside Person" or the duality of our personality.

There are many dualities within us; one we've already been discussing intensively is the masculine and feminine one. What I am doing is placing this duality and others that we haven't discussed within a much larger context. Essentially, the concept is to visualize others and you as having two aspects to their personalities, an outside and an inside as diagrammed in Figure 4.16.

Figure 4.16

In many ways, a house makes an excellent analogy because of a structure enclosing a space. I converted Figure 4.16 into Figure 4.17.

Figure 4.17

The structure protects the inside space from the elements and presents the entire house to the outside world. Of the total volume in a house, most is space. Within the space, freedom of movement occurs. We also find that a house's inside will tend to reflect the individual tastes of the inhabitants more than the outside. In some communities, the outward appearance, structure, and landscape must conform to selected communal standards. Thus, the outside will be more restrained in regards to individual expression while the inside will be freer.

We'll also find the inside more volatile; it will go through more changes and alterations than the outside. We are more likely to see changes to the inside walls and furniture than we are to see changes to the outside structure. All of this lends the inside to more self-expression and freedom. The outside protects this freedom by preventing others from staring inside. Even the windows to a house will generally have curtains or shades. All of this allows the inhabitants to be who they want to be in the manner they want at the time they want. They are immune to judgments from the outside for what goes on inside.

The house's outside will also have more durability, toughness, and strength since it confronts the elements while the inside will have a softer environment encompassing carpeting, furniture, pictures, books, and electronics, all that would easily damage if they remained outside for any length of time. It also allows inhabitants to live comfortably inside without exposure to rain, snow, wind, heat, and cold, some of which could kill if exposure to them were extended. The picture here is one of a hard outside and soft inside, very similar to an acorn or egg. Consequently, the outside will serve a more practical purpose than the inside which will more ideally reflect the tastes and preferences of the inhabitants.

We can also link the house analogy to the previous analogy about tiny muscles spasms in our body of which we are unaware. Much happens in our bodies without our conscious acquiescence. Everyday, thousands of cells die and regenerate, all of which goes on without feeling. Similarly, we are unaware of mental and emotional aspects of ourselves that surface with the question we've posed earlier, "How much of a difference is there between who you are and who you think you are?" The first part represents the inside and the latter outside. As with the house, the outside person confronts the world while the inside one is the person as he truly is. The outside protects the inside person who is the source of personal growth as symbolized in Figure 4.18.

Figure 4.18

The outside person blocks intruders and establishes a front that can intimidate, camouflage, defend, and attack. As is true with trees which seek to expand their branches and leaves across the sky and extend their roots deeply throughout the ground to become the trees they were meant to be, the inside person seeks to become the person he was meant to be.

With any defense, the job becomes more difficult with the increase in territory, maintenance, energy, and vigilance. Consequently, risks rise. With any growth, obstructions and limitations arise, including those self-imposed. Pressure mounts to find more room. As communities grow, they need a larger territory; as families grow, they need a larger home. Tension mounts between the outside and inside person as the outside asks the inside to cease increasing his difficulties and the inside asks the outside to stop suffocating him. Learning creates confidence but it takes confidence to admit the ignorance learning addresses. Anything new is unknown, and the unknown is potentially dangerous; newer branches are weaker than the older ones.

The outside person presses inward to thwart growth by cutting out or halting the actions of the inside person by instilling fear of being hurt or looking bad. It's easier to halt ourselves than deal with others. The inside person presses outward to do the things he wants to do and have the things he wants to have as Figure 4.19 illustrates.

Figure 4.19

The language of the outside person is a pragmatic one whereas the one of the inside is idealistic. Logic, reason, rationale, and cognition dominate the language of the outside while emotion, desire, empathy, and intuition rule for the inside. The growth ideally sought by the inside challenges the outside. Pink Floyd's, *The Wall,* illustrates the tension and conversation between someone's inside and outside.

In order to appeal to this inside person, one must get past the outside one standing guard. One accomplishes this by speaking the language of the inside while distracting the outside and requires an intuitive appeal cloaked in cognition. Since the outside person is extremely protective and vigilant, he will automatically greet any kind of emotional appeal to the inside person with suspicion. We will explore this more deeply in the Strategy chapter, but I introduced the groundwork for this point with the Persian Gulf War (Figure 2.31) where "A" and "B" served as the pinning and distractive elements allowing "C", the indirect and feminine element, to deliver the dynamic impact. Figures 2.48 – 2.57 also serve as groundwork for this point by showing how the masculine influence goes first. The direct, simple, tangible aspects of the masculine seek to engage the outside person while the indirect, involved, intangible aspects of the feminine seek to establish a relationship.

This appeal works because the outside person is finite and the inside person is infinite. What we can consciously take in is always less than what is there, returning us to the analogy of being in the woods and unable to consciously recall everything in it; yet, the feeling we derive from the woods is far greater than what our consciousness can recall. We see this concept reflected in the fact that no plan can account for everything that can possibly happen and the aspects of many plans don't reflect what actually happens. I like to call this difference "friction," the same term Clausewitz's used in *On War* to define the difference between what's in the battle plan and what occurs in battle.

Appealing to the inside person by distracting the outside person happens frequently in our daily lives. Typically, we hear it in the form of "I need an excuse to talk to this person." Implicatively, this is a desire to establish a relationship with a person but realizing that saying, "I want to establish a relationship," is awkward and perhaps too direct. Often a boy in school who likes a particular girl will seek excuses to talk and interact with her so he can impress her. Similarly, at work, an employee who seeks to get in better with his boss will seek excuses to talk and interact with her so he has opportunities to impress. Additionally, we saw the same appeal made with the tactical business example we covered in the Feminine Influence chapter. There, a sales person's attempts to gain access to a high potential prospect consisted of his appeal to the prospect's outside person through his activities in common charitable organizations and his appeal to the inside person through his relational interactions with the prospect while working on these activities. Essentially, the work in these organizations gave the sales person the excuse to talk to this prospect so he could develop a relationship with him that would allow for greater receptiveness when he sought the prospect's business.

Thus, what our outside person thinks is always far different than what our inside person knows and is how we arrive at "who you think you are" being far different than "who you are." The inside person is more comprehensive than the outside, but he is also more easily hurt, more sensitive, and likely to retreat from his growth efforts at the insistence of others and his outside person in order to protect himself. Globally and politically, we see the manifestation of this as the tradeoff between liberties and security. Freedoms allow us to grow and develop while securities restrict us. Our outside person represents our security interests while the inside one represents our growth inclinations. Those who emphasize security are appealing to our outside person while those who emphasize freedoms are appealing to our insides.

The outside person behaves as the counterbalance to the inside. While far less comprehensive than the inside, he's also far more insensitive in many ways as a soldier needs to be in the heat of battle. Consequently, since logic is cold and insensitive, it becomes the language of the outside person. Logic is always overwhelmed by truth – life – as symbolized by the immense programming it takes for a robot to be able to execute any action that a human can do easily.

The impact of any communication is directly related to the effectiveness to which it distracts the outside person and appeals to the inside one. One that fails to make an appeal to the inside person may be found boring while one that fails to distract the outside person may be found impractical. Finding the right blend for each person receiving the communication requires talent, but it can be done.

Nevertheless, the impact may not necessarily be positive. No matter how good the communication, the reception is more dependent upon the listener than the speaker. For some, the impact can be so powerful that it disturbs the relationship between the outside and inside by shedding light on how different "who one thinks he is" is from "who one is." Encouraging one to pursue a talent you see in him may back fire because talent brings additional responsibility that emotionally some may not want to accept or can't.

For instance, return to the drowing while another sits on shore watching because he *thinks* he can't swim, but he finds out the next day that he is a swimmer. Extending this, imagine that someone has been letting people go because he *thought* he couldn't help them anymore and *thought*, therefore, that they were incompetent. One day though, he finds out that he is really far more talented than he thought and perhaps he could have helped those folks grow out of their difficulties. Now, letting those people go is no longer solely because of their incompetence; he now bears some responsibility.

This is similar to two children getting into trouble where one is the older brother of the other, and the older brother is punished more severely because "he should have known better." The younger one, because of his ignorance or inabilities, is dealt with less severely, thus the phrase "ignorance is bliss" and why people tend to prefer to say "it can't be done" rather than "I can't do it" or more accountably, "I don't want to do it." Thus, with talent comes responsibility, but people tend to want talent without responsibility just as they want high investment returns without risk.

This duality model explains the nature of influence as related by the Seventeen Influential Points presented earlier. The conscious protective function of the outside person cannot detect all that influences him because of his limited awareness capabilities. He becomes easily distracted by other stimuli he may find more immediate or important and becomes overwhelmed by the task of screening everything that comes at him. Consequently, many things get through to the inside person that the outside doesn't see.

Relating these functional roles associated with the two to our house analogy, the outside person's job is to keep the inside one in so he doesn't harm himself. Meanwhile, the inside one is always seeking to express himself by getting outside to play. Even if he does get out, the outside person is there making sure he isn't humiliated or hurt. Figure 4.20 illustrates this relationship.

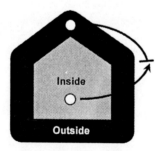

Figure 4.20

On a personal level we see this as an inclination to be "more ourselves" around very close friends or when we're alone than when we're surrounded by acquaintances or the general public. Conformation to particular social norms is the outside person's influence over the inside, so while we may be able to express our personal preferences, we do so through a generally accepted forum or set of rules.

However, the inside person, since he's growth and expression oriented, is constantly seeking to escape even in spite of the outside person's vigilant efforts to contain him. Consciously, we feel the tension as a form of talking or thinking to ourselves where we weigh the benefits of seeking those things we desire against the costs of doing so. Our inside person is the benefits' advocate while the outside person is the costs'. Eventually, our outside person rationalizes the decision our inside person prompted. Answering "Why?" becomes more acceptable than simply saying, "That's my preference." The outside person will always try to weigh in with some rationalization of a desire. In this way, he seeks to protect the inside person by showing that the action is a reasonable one rather than one representing our inner preferences. In this way, the outside person keeps the inside one camouflaged; a camouflaged target is easier to defend than one plainly visible to all.

Returning to our premise, "Who we are is different than who we think we are," we implicatively find why rationale is the language of the outside person and emotion the language of the inside one when we associate this to our most recent discussion; rationale seeks to disguise who we are through the external association of our actions to a generally accepted rationale. Culturally, we see this as the supremacy of objectivity over subjectivity, and why in many cases we see people go through a rigorous, rational, gymnastic exercise to insure that a feeling is something more than just a personal preference. The rationale of the outside person becomes a tool by which it protects the inside one by hiding his preferences and by allowing him to fit into the group. The basis for the rationale of the outside person becomes the established norms accepted by the whole group. By using these norms, which are not individually his own, he can now lay claim to objectivity; he is forsaking his preferences as justification for his actions and substituting them with the group's preferences. Seen in this light, objectivity becomes no more than the subjective preferences of the group and returns us to another previous premise: objectivity is fantasia.

I'll expand upon this theme a little here but will get into it more deeply in the Strategy chapter. Fantasia becomes a good descriptive not only because objectivity is the group's subjectivity but also because groups do not exist except on paper. Legalistically, we clearly see their non-existence because no group can sign a contract, only individuals representing that group can. Practically, we see this whenever we seek to hold someone accountable for a group's actions. Whether it's a committee, team, company, union, city, town, or country someone is identified as the leader or organizer responsible for the group's well-being. If groups actually existed, we would have no need for such measures because we could hold something else accountable. While we incarcerate individuals, how do you incarcerate a whole group? Typically, if a group commits a crime, we incarcerate those *individuals* responsible. Often, they are simply scapegoats targeted to serve for systemic problems inherent in the group. What would happen if we suddenly decided to incarcerate parts of an individual responsible for committing a crime? Can you imagine someone saying, "My hand committed the crime, not my head or heart; thus, take my hand to prison but leave the rest of me alone"? Consequently, as it pertains to this discussion, objectivity is fantasia because the collective subjective norms are not only subjective but also exist for something that doesn't exist. They are created as the basis for some social contract by which all *individuals* are encouraged or compelled to abide. In effect, a group is a man-made creation whereas the individual is a natural one.

This is why we say the outside person's language is rationale while the inside's is emotion. The first seeks to use man-made, collective norms as the tool to protect the natural one inside. Thus, to allow us to communicate to the inside person we must distract the outside one. Figure 4.21 illustrates how this occurs.

Figure 4.21

What Figure 4.21 shows are the almost infinite aspects of the outside world attempting to influence us. Everything in our world as implied by the Seventeen Influential Points influences us to some degree. The effort to consciously screen and digest every aspect is too great for the outside person who has to defend the entire bulwark. If the outside person becomes distracted enough, the inside person can expressively leave. The task of protecting the house is far greater than the task of merely leaving. Symbolically, we see this when a person suffers a calamity that perhaps caused embarrassment. Sticking around in one's current environment and dealing with all the hardships is much more difficult than leaving and starting anew someplace else.

Likewise, the effort of the outside person to protect the inside one is far greater than the effort of the inside one to leave by expressing himself. Imagine a parent who must watch over a child. The task is relatively easy if that is the parent's only one; however, if the parent is distracted by someone who comes to the door or by another activity that may affect the household, the child has a better chance of leaving the house.

Carrying this analogy further, the outside person cannot watch over every last move of the inside person as shown in Figure 4.20. Just as a parent becomes anxious and tired over the attempt to contain a child, the outside person does in attempting to contain the inside person. Furthermore we also have the element of the numerous distractions launched by our outside environment. As a result, we find the inside person expressing himself in many different ways even while the outside person thinks he has everything under control. Often the outside person is totally unaware of what the inside person is expressing. This is the basis for being able to identify the needs we identified prior to our duality discussion.

Going further and incorporating Figure 4.21, we find that as the intensity of the distractions from the outside increase, the greater the likelihood that we will be able to observe the inside person expressing himself in actions, thoughts, and feelings because these will either be greater or more pronounced. These observations are the key to identifying latent talent in others and us and the key in developing dynamic relationships with others.

In working towards these objectives, it would help to gain a better appreciation for the tension between the inside and outside person because the manner in which one must develop the talent he has identified will need to account for this tension. In trying to gain an appreciation for the tension between the two, I find it helps to relate it to the "fear-greed" duality in investing.

In its basics, fear-greed translates to risk-return. As this pertains to our discussion, it is the aspect that people in general more intensely fear failure than they enjoy gain. In order to gain a better feel for the differentiation between the two intensities, I relate it to our military discussion from the Gettysburg example where two armies, equal in all respects, confront each other – the defender has the advantage. Thus, if we consider the two armies as "fear" and "greed" where fear is the defender (protector) and greed the attacker (growth), fear has the advantage.

We can associate fear with the defender because investment strategies influenced by this emotion seek to reduce risk, seek protection. Conversely, we can associate greed with the attacker because investment strategies influenced by this emotion seek to maximize return, to seek growth. Connecting this to the generality that it takes an attacker three times the size of the defender to have a strong likelihood of overcoming that defender, we can conclude that to overcome the "fear of change" one must emotionally and consciously commit to an effort that is three times greater than the inertia he seeks to change, a Herculean effort.

Since growth and new ways to express oneself are favored by the inside person, we must adopt strategies that encourage him or our task in overcoming the defenses of inertia becomes even more daunting. The language of the inside person is emotion and emotion is the realm of the feminine influence; thus, the feminine influence becomes an essential part in effecting positive change in business.

Symbolically, if we return to our house in Figure 4.17, we can express it differently as shown in Figure 4.22:

Figure 4.22

Historically, men have been the protectors of the household while women have been the tenders. Whereas women have been more associated with the inside of the house, the men have been more associated with the outside. The house's structure falls within the masculine domain while its ambiance within the feminine. Moving another's emotions is the way to transform an ordinary, cold, rational event into a dynamic one. Figure 4.22 allows us to further strengthen the connection between the outside person and rationale and the inside person and emotion. Logic resides in the masculine domain and passion in the feminine.

I'll be referring back to this duality as the book continues. For the moment, if you can appreciate these four points, they will serve as a good basis for moving forward:

- The inside person always seeks to grow and express while the outside person seeks to protect and contain.
- The inside person will always show himself regardless of the efforts of the outside person.
- The outside person will generally be unaware of all the ways the inside is expressing himself.
- The language of the outside person is rationale (masculine) and the inside is emotion (feminine).

An important factor influencing our observations of this duality that deserve mention here but because of its extensiveness has a heading of its own is conditioning. These are the actions, thoughts, or feelings residing in us as a result of something someone taught us as opposed to those we innately learned. While these relate more to the outside person than the inside, they take on an immediate, automatic appearance resembling natural inclinations.

I'll be returning to the inside-outside duality as it will help us appreciate the other topics in this chapter and the book, so we'll have many opportunities to review the points in this heading and apply them. The final aspect of personality I'll explore is introversion.

Introversion

Before we get into how introversion plays an important role in our personality, it's important to spend some time establishing a framework by which to understand and appreciate extroversion and introversion.

In one seminar I attended that seems to typify the one liner we often hear about the distinction between extroverts and introverts is that "extroverts like people and introverts like to be alone"; however, the needs – long-term security, novelty of experience, and emotional recognition – imply loneliness cannot exclusively satisfy these needs. Other people can help us achieve long-term security, provide novel experiences, and supply emotional recognition; alone these needs are much more difficult to satisfy.

As it turns out extroversion-introversion is a duality similar to masculine-feminine that exists in each of us. In essence, we all have an extroverted and an introverted aspect to our personalities. As a result, when I talk about an extrovert and introvert, I'll do so in a pure, theoretical way. Such people do not exist in truth; however, discussion in the extremes will allow us to see how their various aspects compliment and criticize one another. While these two aspects create tension in us, we also cannot live without one or the other. Again, what you read here is by no means meant to be a comprehensive look at the matter, but rather an introductory look that will permit immediate application in business.

Returning to the subject of liking people will allow us to begin our introduction of the topic. In reality, both extroverts and introverts like people but just in different ways. The best way to describe the difference is that given over any period of time an extrovert would try to talk to as many people as he could while an introvert would try to get to know one person as well as he could. To an extrovert, spending a whole day getting to know a single person on the deepest possible levels would be an uncomfortable experience. Similarly, an introvert would find discomfort in talking to many people in a day on a superficial level.

For an introvert there will always be at least one person he will enjoy getting to know and that's himself, so if worse came to worse he could focus on that. In this way, he would spend a lot of time getting to know his inside person in the inside-outside duality. The extrovert would find this extremely uncomfortable because he would need other people to satisfy his curiosity about people. From this perspective, in an extreme sense the extrovert is shallow; he enjoys losing himself in people.

Through other people an extrovert can engage in activities that will allow him to satisfy the three needs. He would be able to achieve long-term security, novelty of experience, and emotional recognition. From this standpoint, his efforts serve a practical purpose. Conversely, in an extreme case the introvert would become totally wrapped up in himself to such a degree that he would not involve himself with others. In essence his introversion becomes impractical.

We can take these extremes and similarly diagram them in the way we did the masculine and feminine in Figure 2.27. Without an introvert to counterbalance the extrovert in us, we would become shallow – strangers to ourselves. Without the extrovert to counterbalance the introvert we would become impractical – unable to handle the daily demands of everyday life. Figure 4.23 shows a redrawing of Figure 2.27 to accommodate the extremism of extroversion and introversion.

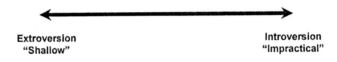

Extroversion   Introversion
"Shallow"   "Impractical"

Figure 4.23

Essentially, an extrovert becomes so consumed by the world that he loses touch with himself, and an introvert becomes so consumed by himself that he loses touch with the world. This statement becomes a good segue into a more overarching duality – the universe and the individual – that will begin to shed light on how the extrovert and introvert in us can work together.

An easy way to think of the duality between the universe and the individual is to think of a mirror and an original. Looking in the mirror we could draw the reflection with the necessary perspective to show it on the "other side" of the mirror exactly where the original's reflection would be if it were real. For instance, a pencil standing four inches in front of the mirror would have its reflection appear as though it were four inches behind the mirror. By taking every point in the original and duplicating it on the other side of the mirror as seen in the reflection, we could duplicate the entire original on the other side of mirror as shown in Figure 4.24.

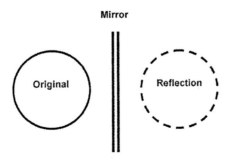

Figure 4.24

Now, let's say we change the mirror from reflecting visuals to reflecting feelings. Thus, rather than reflecting the visual of a pencil, it reflected how we felt about that pencil, including all the feelings we could not consciously feel as suggested by the Seventeen Influential Points. In this way, if we drew the reflection in the same manner as we did above, we would not draw the pencil but all our feelings for the pencil. Consequently, we transform Figure 4.24 into Figure 4.25.

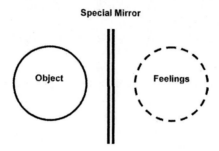

Figure 4.25

Let's extend ourselves beyond a pencil or any particular object to include everything and everyone in the universe. We would include all our feelings for everything we know and think about concerning the universe, not just what is immediately apparent around us. As with Figure 4.25, we would include all feelings, not just our conscious ones. Doing this we would arrive at Figure 4.26.

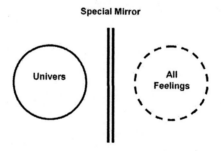

Figure 4.26

Refining Figure 4.26 further we can relate it to our duality discussion concerning the inside-outside person to arrive at Figure 4.27.

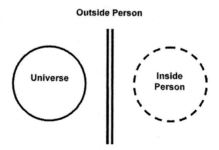

Figure 4.27

With this redraw we are connecting our discussion with Figure 4.16, the inside-outside duality, except we are adding the universe, our environment. Here the outside person becomes the tool by which the inside person reflects upon the universe. If no two things are exactly alike in the universe, then the potential exists for everything to generate a unique feeling in us. Through this potential, each thing has the capacity to help us discover a new aspect about our personalities, including the ones related to dormant talents. New things and experiences help us learn new aspects of ourselves.

However, if we live in any environment that encourages us to objectify our world and subjugate our feelings to that objectification, we will become increasingly emotionally weak and, consequently, increasingly handicap in our efforts to tap our potential within. Essentially, we will arrive upon the situation shown in Figure 4.28.

Outside Person

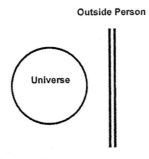

Figure 4.28

Essentially, the dominance of an objective, quantifiable, rational methodology has us bifurcate our inside person from the world by subjugating our feelings for it, others, and ourselves. Our subjectivity, how we feel about our lives, becomes less important than our conformity to an objectivity that is determined subjectively by some arbitrary group. In effect, we create a situation where certain men's dictums override what nature granted us innately.

Our outside person consciously decides to learn these dictums as his own in order to protect the inside person. Outside ignores the natural inclinations of Inside, including the intuitive strength our inside person has that feels out growth opportunities. As a result, as discussed in the Seventeen Influential Points, our intuition atrophies through disuse; this is what causes our emotional weakness and our increasing inability to tap our fire within as well as the fires within others. With this weakened condition of our inside person, we will come to have more anxieties about our world, more fear, that will drive us to seek even more security.

This is where introversion becomes important. Figure 4.27 can help us here once again by having us first talk about extroversion. It allows us to tap into the resources available in our outside world to make our lives better by making the world a better place for us to live. By trying to understand, define, classify, and organize our world, extroversion allows us to go about our efforts to accomplish this. In the end, this extroverted activity helps everyone, including introverts.

Conversely related, introversion allows us to tap into the resources available in our *inside* world to make our lives better by also making the world a better place to live by giving us different perspectives and insights. By trying to appreciate and tap into the talents within us, we discover new abilities that make us more effective in our efforts to accomplish this. In the end, this introverted activity helps everyone, including extroverts.

Figure 4.29 illustrates the extroversion-introversion duality by refining Figure 4.27. The extrovert inside us is responsible for tapping into what the outside world has to offer while the introvert does the same for our inside world. You would no sooner use extroversion as your dominant tool to tap into the resources of your inside world as you would use introversion to tap into the resources your outside world offers. Tapping the potential within you and others is almost impossible without introverted activity.

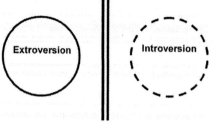

Figure 4.29

The feminine influence encourages the introverted activity of taking in your actions, thoughts, and feelings and contemplating them as we saw with the seasonal analogy in the Company chapter with Figures 3.9 and 3.10. Fall and Winter, the dominant times for the feminine influence, encourage a time for reflection and regeneration so when Spring and Summer arrive one can attack them full force.

Figure 4.26 best exemplifies what introversion is all about, getting in touch with how one feels about the world. Too often today, we misinterpret our opinions for the world as our feelings for it. Moreover, our culture today is increasingly extrovertively focused. Introverts or even introverted activity is generally frowned upon because they and it are seen as having little to do with the immediate results necessary to sustain a business. Much of this, as implied in the Feminine Influence chapter, is associated to the immense dominance of the masculine influence in business. Consequently, who we are is more defined by what we have rather than who we are. What we have encompasses such things as our material possessions, credentials, titles, authority, and money. While all of this is important in our world, none of it can help one tap into the inside person in all of us – the source of additional resources and talents to help make our lives and our world even better. The question is not "Where are you?" but "Where can you go?" Only your inside person can find the direction that is uniquely and innately yours.

Calling upon the introvert in you means listening to how he feels about the world and its various aspects. He may even encourage you take action in a particular direction. When he does, give him the benefit of the doubt. Figure out a way to follow that action. This is where your outside person or extroverted side can help.

Of course, you may not feel anything immediately but keep trying. Chances are good that since you've read this far into the book, you'll eventually feel something if you persist. Something inspired you to pick up this book and read it. Whatever caused you to do that, you may want to try and begin there. If a person recommended it to you, you may want to think about your relationship with that person. What do you particularly appreciate it about it? If some event in your life inspired you, concentrate on that. If you simply happened to stumble across it, what attracted your interest or curiosity? If you happened to recall a specific event, person, topic, or feeling when you first saw this book, you can also begin there.

Using the intuition in your inside person is very much like using your muscles. It develops with exercise. If it hasn't been used in a while, you can expect some soreness and disappointment. As it becomes more assured, it will become stronger and louder. The key is avoiding being critical of your inside person; your outside one will be tempted to do that because any action by your inside one will more than likely create a tougher job for the outside one. This could create some tension and anxiety, but muscles become stronger through tension that breaks down the muscle fibers allowing them to rebuild stronger.

Conclusion

In order to tap into the inherent power in our personalities we need to be aware of the ways we're influenced, the needs within us, our inside-outside duality, and the benefits of introversion. While these are not exclusive tasks toward tapping our potential or towards appreciating our personalities, somehow we need a way to get started on our journey. I've written about something that works in a practical business setting.

First and for most, one must become aware of all the ways he's influenced. Trying to illicit better help from the outside person by warning him of all the stuff he's missing is a start. Down the road the inside person will help you contemplate as to the nature of the influence's effect on you.

Second, appreciating what you need from life will help. By trying to look at things from a long-term security, novelty of experience or emotional recognition perspective will begin a process by which you can localize what those mean to you. Reviewing Figures 4.13 and 4.15 periodically will support your efforts.

Third, begin to try to recognize your thoughts to yourself as either those of your inside person or outside person. Generally, the "no" or negative ones belong to the outside while the "yes" or positive ones belong inside. Many times there may be a discrepancy but don't feel compelled to take all or nothing from either. Sometimes it's all a matter of going with the inside person but having the outside person figure out how to do it safely. Rather than immediately saying "no" to the inside, ask the outside one for a plan. Since his language is reason, he will be better suited for planning functions.

Fourth, don't be afraid of introverted activity. Quiet time is essential to staying in touch with oneself. The daily distractions of our increasingly intense, swift lives are pushing us to get lost in the world. Seeking the fire within you can't be done through a focus on extinguishing the fires that confront you daily. You can also devote this time to others as you think about how you can help them tap their potential. On this point, a general rule is helpful. If someone says he can do something, assume he can and do what you can to help him so long as in the end he can say he did it.

With these four points, we can better discover and appreciate our personality and its power. In order to access this power and the talent associated with it, it will help to have a way of looking at talent so when we run into it we know it. That is the purpose this chapter's next section.

Talent

In our yard we have several large oak trees, so in the spring every year we find several seedlings sprouting. This year we've discovered seven, the most yet. Relatively, this is an extremely small number compared to the thousands of acorns that dropped last fall.

While some acorns damage themselves in their fall or fall prematurely, many more are attacked by squirrels. We have many squirrels, and the remnants from their meals are everywhere. Beyond this we also have rabbits and other small animals that love fresh greenery for their meals as well. I've transplanted several seedlings in the past from their protective locations to more open areas only to have their leaves devoured. Even before we see them, these seedlings run the danger of being stepped upon, covered with mulch, or many other potentialities from my wife and me. These difficulties withstanding, any seedling has a long road filled with many twists and turns, any of which could threaten its life and thus reduce the chances of it becoming a huge, grand hundred-year oak tree.

Talent and its journey is very much the same; however, the problem I find is that many times we treat it as a light bulb. We find one, stick it in a socket, and it shines! Then, when the bulb breaks or doesn't shine as brightly as we would like, we wonder what went wrong. Thus, finding talent is more akin to finding an acorn than finding a light bulb.

Under the heading of talent, we're going to run through five areas:

- Definition – How do we define talent?
- Nature – What is the talent's nature?
- Resistance – What inhibits talent?
- Framework – How can we look at talent effectively?
- Access – How do we access the talent one has?

Many times we're interested in not so much what talent is but whether someone has it. I've found that many people are very open about saying what talent is and who has it, but few tend to introspect and answer these relative to them. By discussing a definition of talent, I don't intend so much to say what talent is or whether someone has it but to say why such a discussion is virtually meaningless. In essence, if talent is more like finding an acorn than a light bulb, then whether that acorn can grow into the stature of a hundred-year oak entails something far greater than simply saying an acorn exists. Finding an acorn is not the challenge.

Once we discuss the meaninglessness of a talent definition or its identification, we can discuss its nature. This will be a prelude to our model and access discussion later. Talent is very similar to beauty; no one can really define it but everyone feels they know it when they run into it. Talent has certain aspects to it. A common assumption is that like cream it always rises to the top; however, this only occurs if we allow it. Discussing talent's nature will allow us to get a feel for why we would inhibit it.

Talent's nature is not complete if we do not deal with the resistance associated with it, but I've decided to give resistance a separate place rather than attempt to leave it mixed in with the discussion on talent's nature. Tapping and developing our own talent or those of others cannot be done if we're not aware of the inhibitors standing in our way. We find this resistance individually and collectively, within the person and those around him. The next heading, Conditioning, will deal with a more complex aspect of this resistance concerning the way we learn. This affects all aspects of our personality and is not necessarily limited to our particular talent.

After running through talent's nature and inhibitors, I'll go through a framework that will present these ideas in a way that will help us get a better feel for talent and working with it. The focus will be on maximizing potential not on simply being better than everyone else. Competition, by its nature, dooms the talented to mediocrity by instilling complacency in simply being the best rather than the best one can be. The first is much easier than the second. Our model will incorporate this aspect.

Last, with this backdrop we'll discuss how to access the talent in you and others. The idea will be to avoid specific, mechanical steps and to leave a feel for how it's done. We'll do this through an analogy concerning the drilling for oil.

Definition

Trying to identify whether someone has talent is a very difficult one to answer not only from an intrinsic perspective but also an emotional one.

Intrinsically, talent's existence is confined to our awareness and imagination. One cannot see to what he is blind and cannot surmise what he cannot imagine. Consequently, the left diagram in Figure 2.53 best illustrates the emotional expansiveness we need when seeking talent, casting the broadest net possible permitted by our awareness and imagination. This is why it takes thousands upon thousands of acorns dispersed widely upon the ground to yield one grand oak tree.

Emotionally, talent's existence is difficult for the one seeking it and the one in whom it's being sought. For the former, there is the emotionalism associated with the question, "Do I have the capacity to detect talent?" and for the later is the more apparent, anxious question, "Do I have talent?" A negative answer for both questions has the potential to do more harm than the risks associated with a positive answer for both. More importantly, simply because one determines another untalented, doesn't mean talent does not exist. All we can truly determine from such a declaration is that the one making it cannot see the talent in the person before him.

Negatively, we shut down the search for talent. The person who believes he can detect talent no longer searches for it, while the person who believes he has talent no longer develops his. Positively, we only risk that each is wrong. Their advice may lead us astray, but this is no different than any other opportunity we run across. As with the oak tree, some acorns sprout and others don't. The point is that negative answers reduce our opportunities, it's inherent in life that potentialities are greater than actualities; we will always need to sort through more than we need to get what we want. This doesn't even take into consider that our negative answers to those question could be wrong. Only the one with the talent can discover what that talent is; we can only help in that discovery by creating opportunities.

Still, moving beyond the issue of being right or wrong, if we follow along with the oak tree analogy, a hundred-year oak makes itself much more obvious than an acorn. In many respects then, identifying talent is much like a business venture; anyone can determine whether a successful business is successful, but there is something more involved in the determination that a current business will become successful. The issue here is a question of "When does someone identify talent?" This returns us again to Figures 2.1 – 2.15 in which we discussed the time we become aware of something and the time we can visualize it. While we may not be able to see talent now, it doesn't mean we won't be able to see it later.

Regardless of how we answer these questions or the larger questions of "Can anybody spot talent?" and "Does everyone have a talent?" we must consider the question of "Will that talent manifest itself?" If we view talent more as a light bulb, then the answer is pretty much "yes," unless we decide to not put the bulb in a socket to allow it to illuminate; however, a tree is more similar to a human than a light bulb is. Consequently, the challenges a tree goes through in its life make it more analogous. Just because we see an acorn doesn't mean a hundred-year oak will grow. If there are detractors inhibiting talent's identification and development, then talent "rising to the top" is not a given.

Many things in the universe exist, galaxies, stars, planets, mountains, animals, and water to name a few, but nothing in this universe exists without a detractor, an inhibitor. Life itself ages things. Our bodies are assaulted by thirst, hunger, and the elements. Our minds are assaulted by forgetfulness no matter how much of an expert we are. Our emotions are challenged by pain; you can't be sensitive and painless. Are we to conclude that talent can exist without detractors in a universe filled with them? Retardants to talent exist.

Thus, when we consider all the elements involved in the manifestation of talent the actual declaration of talent is meaningless. Sometimes the only way we find an ember on which to build a fire is to first blow on the ashes and see what glows. Similarly, sometimes the only way we can detect talent is to make the first effort to allow it to show itself; however, if we first declare there are no embers and make no effort, we will certainly not see talent.

In the end, talent is very much like beauty: you'll know it when you see it. Just as beauty comes in many forms talent does as well. Is there any aspect of life in which someone somewhere does not have an ability to display a talent associated with it? The question becomes whether a lack of a definition for talent will hinder our efforts in seeking it?

Let's for the moment take the sun as an example. Do we really need to know what the sun is or to understand it in order to appreciate what it does? Many aborigines still think the sun is a god while scientific evidence will tell us it's more of a series of nuclear explosions. Now, does the aborigines' ignorance prove them unable to determine what the sun can do or when it's present?

They know for instance that when the sun appears so does heat and light which encourages good things to happen. They can also tell when the sun rises and when it sets, so they can feel its presence even though they have an inaccurate description of what it is and a misunderstanding as to how it works. They have come to appreciate the sun's nature.

We can use other examples besides the sun, like a tree. Children do not need to know what a tree is in order to detect it. All they have to do is run into it once and that will give them all the information they need to know for their immediate future. They also learned that even though they don't know or understand a tree, it doesn't mean it doesn't exist. Ignorance and non-existence do not necessarily correlate. Furthermore, a lack of understanding for a tree does not prohibit our ability to use its lumber. A total comprehension or understanding of it does not prevent anyone from enjoying its benefits. Many people have been able to use trees.

Running with this line of thought a little further, we can also conclude there's little correlation between knowing and appreciation. The aborigines and children had incorrect knowledge of the sun and no knowledge of a tree, but these did not prevent them from appreciating the sun's light and heat and the tree's hardness. Can we even say knowledge and understanding delivers a better appreciation? Who knows and understands the concept of Santa Claus more, parents or children? Who appreciates Santa Claus more? Do aborigines appreciate the sun less than we do? Does the one who knows and understand the sun best receive a darker tan? If we don't know the sun or understand it, do we miss out on its benefits?

All of this is to suggest that a definition and knowledge of talent are unnecessary. What's more important is a sensitivity and appreciation for its nature. Maybe with talent, we only need to know that it's something uncommon, something that segregates one from the many. In this respect it's qualitative and possesses attractive aspects, both elements of the feminine influence. These and other aspects of its nature make talent and the feminine influence virtually inseparable.

Nature

While we may not be able to say definitively what talent is, we can talk about its nature, its characteristics. We've already discussed its aspects of quality, attractiveness, and singularity that allow talent to stand out from the crowd. There are four others we'll cover. Some will incorporate themes we've already visited via a different perspective.

- Vitality
- Expressivity
- Innumerability
- Abnormality

Vitality

Talent is something that's alive, almost specifically humanistic. One of the most obvious ways we can see this is in the way we use the term. Usually, we only apply it to people, sometimes animals. We rarely think of associating it to a rock, a tree, a computer, or a car. From this perspective, we can say there is a connection between the nature of talent and the nature of those things to which we attach the word.

An important connection is talent's naturalness; it's not an invention. If this were the case, we would be inclined to call a computer talented. We're more apt to call the person who invented the computer talented. In this way, talent is more akin to a force of nature than a force of man. We cannot immediately imbue or insert just anyone with a particular talent, furthering leading us down the path that talent is innate, something of a natural origin. In this case, talent more suitably fits our oak tree analogy than the light bulb one.

What makes something vital? We often associate strength to vitality. Are we more inclined to associate vitality to strength or weakness? Similarly, we often link vitality to energy. Is it our inclination to associate vitality more to movement or to stillness? How about health? Are we more inclined to associate vitality to poor health or excellent health? How would we consider importance? Does vitality apply more to significance or insignificance?

In many ways what makes something vital are all the things in Figure 4.13, Manifestation of Needs. Consider a few more associations. Excitement and boredom, to which would you associate vitality? How about passion and dispassion? What intimate relationship between a man and a woman can have vitality without passion? How can any relationship have vitality without the emotional involvement of both parties?

Talent, therefore, is closely associated with feelings, feelings that often appear as needs. In fact, in Figure 4.13 emotional recognition manifests itself emotionally as talent. One cannot access talent without a strong involvement of their emotions. At the high levels of any field, emotions determine the difference. We often term this as confidence; confidence is nothing more than a feeling. If emotions did not play such a vital role in talent, then the total understanding of baseball or golf would automatically make someone the better player or golfer. A better understanding of carpentry would automatically make someone the better carpenter. This is where we get the expression of "having a feel for the game." The one with talent often isn't the one who knows the most. If this were the case, we would definitely consider a computer talented.

Once we associate talent to emotions, talent becomes more closely linked to the feminine influence whose realm contains passions. The manifestation of talent requires emotional toughness, energy, and dynamism. Our passions make anything more vital: stronger, more energetic, and more attractive. Without the holistic inclusion of the elements in Figure 4.13 something that is the strongest, the fastest, or the prettiest is merely that, the strongest, the fastest, or the prettiest. When we *can* apply them, we now have something that's talented, and most likely that something is a human.

In essence, vitality has firmness, movement, and quality, the three attributes of the needs in Figure 4.13. The last attribute implies a qualitative aspect to vitality, a differentiator. Consider a television program that has remotely controlled machines battle one another. These machines are called robots. If we were to carry this theme further by imagining two autonomous robots fighting it out, winning and losing would be emotionally undifferentiable to them. More significantly, we would never think of calling the winning robot talented.

If I wanted to measure the volume of a small ball, I could do so by placing it in a measured beaker containing water. By measuring the difference between the level of the water after placing the ball in the beaker and the level before, I could determine the ball's volume. This is called displacement. Essentially, we've connected vitality to talent through displacement by looking at the difference between a competition involving two human combatants and another involving two robotic ones. The displacement that occurs is related to which we assign the term talented to the winner.

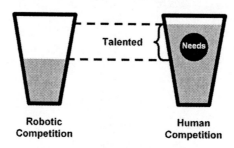

Figure 4.30

Figure 4.30 illustrates this conceptual difference as what is holistically contained in Figure 4.13. While a particular robot may be stronger, faster, and better than another robot, these by themselves do not constitute the differentiation with a human who is stronger, faster, and better than another human when it comes to assigning the term talented. The fundamental difference boils down to needs, feelings. A robot has no needs, no feelings, no emotions driving it – only a sophisticated series of programs. Something is driving the one to whom we describe as a "talent." That something is a holistic interplay of emotions; it's the something that inspires in us to call a human talented and a robot merely stronger, faster, or better.

Talent's vitality boils down to needs, passions without which the term does not apply. At the root of all talent are feelings, again, the realm of the feminine influence.

Expressivity

Once we grasp the vital nature of talent, picturing it as something active along the lines of a need, we begin to see it as a life-force within us. Talent as we had discussed earlier is uncommon; it stands out. Just as thirst drives us to water and hunger drives us to food, talent drives us. The question is "a drive to what?"

Someone with talent generally loves to display their talent. Can you imagine anyone talented who would not want to privately or publicly employ his talent? What greater crime could there be than a pianist who could not ever play the piano again? An orator losing his voice? An artist who was led to believe no one liked his work so he never painted again?

Talent seeks to express itself. How can it distinguish itself without doing so? If talent is uncommon and we seek emotional recognition, how can we distinguish ourselves without sharing what makes us distinguishable? In this way, talent is like boiling water; it seeks to release the pressure building within. That pressure powered machines in the way our talent powers us.

Talent's expressivity seeks a forum, a structure by which to manifest itself to the world. In this light talent is like any other feeling seeking an outlet. In a simplistic way, our "love affair" with cars is an expressive example; it's a way to express something inside in a very tangible way. The car becomes the format or structure to do this. Similarly, our talent seeks to project itself onto something that would best visualize it.

Expressivity will drive learning and experiences because talent's novelty will find a forum by which to make itself known to the world and allow one to find uniqueness. The search for a vehicle will include trial and error, acquiring concepts quickly even in spite of others' inabilities to teach him.

The repression of talent, or the ignorance of it, will not deter talent's expressivity and desire for recognition and appreciation. One can no more stop the expression of talent than he can pave over an open field and not expect cracks in the asphalt to develop. Through time talent will break through. The only question is what form and path will it take.

The channeling of talent can either have a positive effect or a negative effect, similar to the ignition of gasoline or its explosion. When done within the constructs of an engine in a car, it can power the vehicle over many miles; however, within the confines of a closed container, the result is an explosion. Both are simple ignitions of gasoline but with divergent manifestations. Nevertheless, the effect, positive or negative, gives us the opportunity to spot talent. Just as a lone rose growing in a desert is a sign of life, similar signs rise up to show signs of talent seeking expression. Even weeds sprouting up through cracks in asphalt are a testament to the power of life's vitality; nature's power overwhelms man's. Likewise, since talent is innate, organic, it will constantly surface in some manner despite our best attempts to deny it a voice.

How we look at these signs often is a matter of perspective. Consider figure 4.31.

Figure 4.31

Both diagrams in Figure 4.31 express a black dot standing out from the rest. In the left one, the dot distinguishes itself by being above the others while the one on the right does so by being below the others. Essentially, there could be no difference between the left and the right except that we're looking at one upside down and the other right side up. Many times the difference we see in the expression of talent is a matter of our perspective rather than any inherent difference in the talent itself. Whether we see gasoline powering a car or blasting a hole in a wall, the inherent nature of gasoline exploding remains the same. Thus, if we become too distracted in our search for talent by looking at its results rather than looking for the presence of its basic qualities, we will increase the likelihood of missing it.

Conceptually, this perspective is no different than "beauty is in the eyes of the beholder." How we look at things, including talent, is subjective, an element of the feminine influence. Only by looking at things subjectively will we see alternatives and possibilities to what objectively is there. Objectivity by its very nature is not imaginative; it only sees what is there not what could be there. Objectivity sees these things as hallucinations. As stated earlier, sometimes objectivity is nothing more than collective subjectivity firmly rooted assuming the appearance of objectivity, so if we only interpret things the way everyone else does, the possibility for new ideas and applications are nil.

Welcoming the feminine influence into business will allow for the use of an expansive universe of interpretations in all relational aspects, including the cultivation of talent so as to increase the likelihood of dynamic applications. The challenge is how we view the expressivity we experience in those relationships, fighting through the conventional platitudes developed for generic, typical experiences to champion our own creative insights tailored to the realities before us in the form of the talent sitting across from us.

Innumerability

Expressivity allowed us to introduce discussion around a major distraction in the search and cultivation of talent, quantification, seeking to measure what we cannot measure. Ignoring this point for the moment, let's address what numbers really tell us because we often hear the expression "numbers don't tell the whole story." Conversely, we also hear a lot that "the results speak for themselves" which often appear in the form of statistics. If they don't tell us the whole story, what *do* they tell us?

The key in understanding what numbers tell us is realizing that both of these statements are true simultaneously. First, numbers do not tell the whole story, but second, the story they do tell says a lot about them – in essence they speak for themselves. Analogously, if I were to relate my observations to a police officer about a traffic accident, they would definitely not be the whole story but *I am speaking for myself* when I do tell them. What my observations lack may be observations others had. In effect, I'm not conveying the whole story, and I'm certainly not speaking for others. Consequently, "the results speak for themselves" also means the results don't say anything about anything else except the results; they only speak for themselves, they do not speak for other things or for people. Consider Figure 4.32.

25   **Twenty-five**

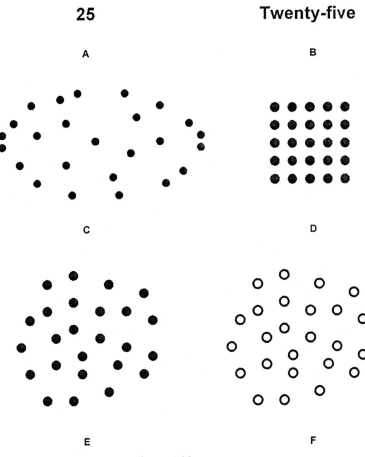

Figure 4.32

It contains six representations of twenty-five all conveying something different. What does twenty-five actually mean? It may mean the business lives another year, it has reached its end, or many other possibilities. In the end, all numbers require interpretations to fill in the gaps. We're constantly struggling to determine what do the numbers mean?

If revenues show an increase over last year, does that necessarily imply the business is better off? If we recall our discussion around Figures 2.1 – 2.15, we may remember that there is a lag between the time when events occur and when those events impact the numbers. Still, we run into the challenge of trying to determine exactly what those numbers mean. We've all experienced situations where two people can use the same numbers to support different points. Often we find different numbers highlighted to support different points. As a result, we find the supposed objectivity we seek from numbers being mixed with subjective interpretations as to their meaning. In the end, we're back to the quality of subjectivity that is being applied.

In addition to the question concerning whether numbers actually say something, we also have the question of whether talent is even measurable. The vitality and expressivity of talent suggest talent is related to, if not actually, a feeling. At minimum talent is akin to beauty; how do we measure beauty? How can we measure something for which there is no definition?

Outside of quantification, there remains the question of results. Is it possible to identify talent by looking at results? Does talent influence outcomes? Yes, it does. The problem is that many other things influence them too. We began to explore this in the Company chapter when we outlined four things that affect results: situation, flow, people, and the individual. When we talk about talent, we're talking about the individual.

Figure 4.33

Figure 4.33 outlines the four major elements of an outcome. As we can see from this diagram, talent influences results but results do not necessarily reflect talent. We see a one way relationship between each element and outcomes. While each element contributes to the final result, the outcome alone says very little about any specific element unless we're willing to consider the influence of all the others. What this diagram doesn't reflect is the substantial tendency to underestimate the impact of the situation, flow, and other people. Most of the time, it's more difficult to quantify these other elements than it is the activities of a specific individual.

At this point, we return to our conversation around Figure 2.12 where we find the tendency to emphasize quantifiable elements over unquantifiable ones because we tend to disproportionately favor what we know best. Consequently, our answer to a problem tends to take on the characteristics of our most extensive information with less consideration for unknown or vague factors. Generally, we favor statistics to anecdotal information, so they will weigh heavier into our final decision. Unfortunately, the anxiety of the unknown or the complex causes us to discount or ignore the immeasurable so we don't have to deal with this anxiety; however, this does not negate their influence in very dramatic ways. Essentially, we end up favoring information because of its format rather than its inherent quality; statistical formats highly influence us. What this means is that immeasurable factors will tend to receive less consideration in a decision than measurable ones irrespective of the importance or quality of the information. For instance, immeasurable, relational factors such as morale will tend to receive less consideration than numeric factors such as revenue figures even though everyone understands the importance of moral in driving revenues. The largest error, and often the most costly one, we make is to assume that simply because we cannot measure something that it has little value or can be ignored.

Relating this to Figure 4.33 we find various capabilities in securing quantifiable information on each of these elements with the individual being the easiest. Whereas situation concerns itself with all aspects of an event, flow with the movement or timing of those aspects, and people with everyone connected to the event; the individual is a single, solitary person. Compared to the other elements, we are more likely to have statistical information on this person than all the other aspects of all the other elements. Thus, our focus will tend toward that element for which we have the most information and not necessarily the one with the most impact.

The typical rationalization is "we must manage the controllable." In theory this is true, but our tendency in practice when we don't like the results is to alter what we can control thinking this will change results (or we "have to do something"); however, when situation, flow, and people are unfavorably aligned against the results we want, nothing we do as an individual will change things. Consequently, we pursue an endless cycle of change in an attempt to hold off a negative tide. Thus, rather than maintain a firm course of action to minimize the condition we find ourselves expending energy changing from one approach to another and making a negative situation even worse.

In the Feminine Influence chapter, we highlighted this condition as an example where the masculine influence's predilection for action makes a bad situation worse. Action and control in the masculine world tend to correlate, so if one is not taking action, then he is likely not in control. In the final analysis, the interplay of all these forces I just described tends to give us the illusion that the connection between results and talents is far firmer than they are in truth.

Results dominate our thinking because they affect our lives; however, to think the correlation between talent and results is strong leaves one vulnerable to rely upon talent that doesn't exist and to discard talent that could help. What this implies is that if the action you need to take is directly contrary to what is inherently possible in the situation, to what the present flow permits, and to what the group wants; it will not work no matter what talent the individual has. Likewise, if all these things are aligned, even the most minimal talent can succeed. Results are an inferior indicator of talent.

The only thing an individual can really control is what he applies to the event, not the outcome. Observing how someone does something is more important than tasting the result. Often we hear the saying "proof is in the pudding." A talented chef with lousy or wrong ingredients cannot make a better pudding on a stove that doesn't work than a novice with great instructions, ingredients, and equipment. Yet, by watching how each goes about making the pudding, one can then envision what the chef could do if he had all the advantages. Moreover, we can also gauge who is better able to handle situations in which things go awry. Figure 4.34 graphs the impact of talent's influence relative to outside factors. As outside factors increase their influence on an event, the influence of talent diminishes.

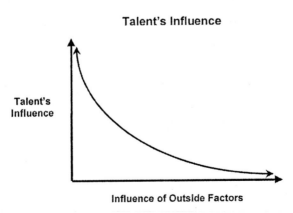

Talent's Influence

Talent's Influence

Influence of Outside Factors

Figure 4.34

If results poorly correlate to talent, what is a preferred indicator? Essentially, we uncover talent by looking at how someone approaches a situation rather than in the actual outcome; we examine their methodology. This easily translates into another basic sales theme: focus on activities not sales. When looked upon in this light, what we're saying isn't really that new or dramatic. The difference though is that the saying in sales, "good activities produce good sales," doesn't necessarily follow because it assumes we control the external factors. It's a natural human delusion to think we control events in sales, investing, or other fields far more than we do. To assume we have tremendous control opens ourselves to overconfidence and arrogance, fertile feeding grounds for disappointment and poor decisions in the future.

Nevertheless, our tendency is to automatically assign talent with good results and mediocrity with poor results. This is no different than being inclined to say everything in a garbage dump is ugly and everything in a rose garden is beautiful rather than trying to look at the inherent characteristics of each thing. In effect, this is how someone's junk is another's treasure even though the inherent nature of the thing hasn't changed; the difference between seeing things as they are and seeing them as they could be.

The tendency to associate results to talent slants the playing field against talent. To see this, let's consider a talented and an untalented person. The untalented will tend to favor results over methodology as an indicator of talent because this frame of reference minimizes the weighting of talent and maximizes that of other factors outside of anyone's control. In this example let's consider that outside forces are randomly applied. We can see the relationship between the talented and untalented in Figure 4.35.

Talented vs. Untalented

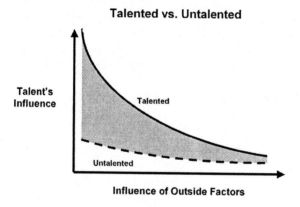

Figure 4.35

As the influence of outside factors increase, the difference between the impact effected by the talented and the untalented diminishes, permitting the untalented a more equal chance against the talented for promotion. In essence, this is no different than when I face a very talented poker player. The games we select to play will vary according to the amount of skill required to play them. From my perspective, the more I play games that minimize skill and maximize luck, the more I equalize my chances. For instance, I would be better off playing a game where we split the deck in two, each turnover one card, award a dollar (or any fixed amount) to the one who turned over the higher card, and repeat the process for each card in our respective decks; as opposed to playing a regular poker hand with normal bidding. In this example, I minimized the talent aspect of the game, bidding, and enhanced randomness. Chances are good in the long-run that I will do better in my modified game than in a regular poker one against a talented poker player.

Using results as the indicator of talent enhances the chances for the untalented very much as my modified game did for me in poker. Furthermore, even if I played a regular poker match against a very talented player, I would want to make sure that the results upon which we were evaluated covered a short time frame; I am far more likely to beat a talented poker player over a one hand span than I am over a hundred- or two-hundred one. Therefore, the more I can get the judges to buy into the fact that skill is determinable in a single hand and that they can ignore factors such as "the luck of the draw," the more likely they will make that determination immediately after one hand rather than "wasting" their effort to sit through a hundred or two hundred hands.

In these situations, it's important to note that I, as the untalented, am never able to swing the chances into my favor over the talented but I am able to equalize them a bit. In effect, instead of making me a hundred to one shot, I've made myself a two to one or one to one shot, definitely much better for me. Of course, we can further enhance this example by allowing me to select at the beginning of each hand the one or two cards I would like in my hand while continuing to give the talented poker player his cards randomly. If we determine talent based upon results, I automatically increase my chances of being viewed as talented. Consequently, if results are talent's determinants, then it's important to pick opportunities that outside influences favor. This is no different than picking the one or two cards you would like in your poker hand before the deal.

Continuing with this line of thought, let's add the discussion from Figures 2.61 – 2.67 concerning the minority status of intelligence and apply them to talent: the bottom ninety percent of talent will always outnumber the top ten percent. When we combine this to our tendencies to place our greatest faith in quantified information, to ignore or minimize important nebulous influences, and to have fewer promotional opportunities than people seeking them, we will find more people seeking to have talent judged on immediate results than on longer observational periods focused on one's methodologies and habits. In the long run, a results oriented mindset will increase the likelihood of a business's demise and talent's underutilization than a more individualized exploration of methodology, work habits, and inherent talents. The disassociation of talent and results is why some of the greatest generals in history such as Napoleon, Hannibal, Rommel, Guderian, Robert Lee, and Fredrick the Great remain in high standing despite losing their respective wars.

Taking innumerability in its entirety means talent cannot be measured because it's comprised of immeasurable elements; thus, this and the impact of nebulous outside influences difficult to assess cause results to correlate poorly with talent. Nevertheless, the inclination is strong to quantify talent based upon the results it influences. Such an approach increases the likelihood that talent will be left untapped.

Pragmatically, innumerability translates into a simple statement regarding the search for talent: you most likely won't find talent looking at numbers.

Abnormality

Discussing talent is difficult without some mention of its uncommonness. Even though we touched upon this early on under the Nature heading, elaboration will help present this in a different light. Originally, I contemplated Uniqueness as a title for this section, but I came around to Abnormality because I felt it communicated how we overlook talent by looking at it in a different light.

Uniqueness has a positive connotation, so it's easy to associate what we find good as being unique; however, in the search for talent, it's important to blast away imbedded assumptions so we can look at people creatively. Figure 4.31 illustrates that need; we may be looking at someone upside down. Where we see gasoline exploding, there may be the possibility to power a car. Implicatively this means that we may find talent in people we find abnormal. Just as the difference between escargot and snails is that people eat escargot, the difference between unique and abnormal is that people utilize uniqueness.

Of course, this doesn't automatically mean abnormality is talented, but it does mean, you most likely won't find talent in the common, ordinary, or standard. A rarity doesn't fit in with the common and is why talent could easily be construed as "wrong." Often, a talent doesn't turn the world upside down as much as he turns us right side up. Originally, the way we looked at him could be as an oddball or freak that doesn't know what the heck he's saying. The instant he presents a novel idea, he's outnumbered; thus, talents are often the ones who challenge convention. Such a challenge often doesn't come without conflict and comfort, another sign of potential talent.

Consider exams. Taking them is nothing more than giving answers people want to hear. If you give any answer but the expected one, you are most likely not going to receive credit for it especially with multiple choice exams. By definition, a creative answer is one given for the first time; thus, it cannot be the "right" answer because it's not the expected answer. Can you imagine what would happen to the computer scoring a multiple choice exam if you wrote in an answer?

Talented people are often pioneers in their field by creating unique responses to standard situations; they are not likely to deliver conventional responses. Exams test for the conventional response, not the unique one. Correctness becomes nothing more than knowing the convention. A talent is also more likely to be more intelligent than the person who created the test so he is likely to arrive at unique responses that others would judge incorrect because their intelligence may not allow them to immediately see the application of the talent's answer.

Consensus forces agreement around the weakest link – the idea stimulating the least amount of conflict. A creative idea from a talent is less likely to yield consensus not only because a creative idea is outnumbered at the onset but also because it is very likely a good number may not initially grasp the idea. How can everyone instantly like an idea that only one person knew?

Abnormality is uniqueness from a different perspective. The purpose of this heading is that if we're in the hunt for developing talent we need to expect the uncommonness inherent in it. Sometimes this means being open to that which we may initially view as abnormal. Implicatively this means a path diverging from a consensual one. Talent is more likely to present controversial ideas than ordinary, standardized ones. Others are more likely to view his as being involved as opposed to easy. As difficulty increases so does the challenge in gaining agreement. A talented person is more likely to challenge everyone's abilities with an idea than a person more entrenched in commonality.

Conclusion

Our next aspect of talent is the resistance to it. The nature of talent involves vitality, expressivity, innumerability, and abnormality and infers quality, attractiveness, and singularity. All easily translate into influences that stimulate opposition to talent especially if we refer back to Figures 2.61 – 2.67. Talent doesn't rise to the top so much as it fights to get there.

The importance of this is that while the positive aspects of talent stimulate dynamism they are not done so without resistance by those entrenched in comfortable, predictable growth. Dynamism disrupts and alters this in a positive way. We see how a dynamic product can alter the competitive landscape in business. For these reasons, appreciation for the nature of talent will allow one to more easily spot it when he is in the presence of it. Of course, as we will see, simple recognition of talent does not guarantee its culmination anymore than merely putting an acorn in the ground guarantees an oak tree.

Nevertheless, the nature of talent actively provides signs of its existence if we are willing to open our eyes and potentially look in directions different from convention. Nature's vitality gives it an organic power stronger than what a man could build. Its expressivity insures that we will receive signs, but its innumerability means they won't always be easy to see and quantify. Most likely if we're looking at numbers we're not looking at talent. Of course, talent's uniqueness that can often appear as an abnormality gives us the necessary hints we need to feel its presence.

I'll close the nature of talent with a quote from Zhuge Liang as stated in *Mastering The Art of War*, translated and edited by Thomas Cleary regarding the search for wise people. It serves to remind us that talent, by its nature, is rarely found on Main Street.

Pillars of State

For strong pillars you need straight trees; for wise public servants you need upright people. Straight trees are found in remote forests; upright people come from the humble masses. Therefore when rulers are going to make appointments they need to look in obscure places.

Sometimes there are disenfranchised people with something of value in them; sometimes there are people with extraordinary talent who go unrecognized. Sometimes there are paragons of virtue who are not promoted by their hometowns; sometimes there are people who live in obscurity on purpose.

Sometimes there are people who are dutiful and righteous for purely philosophical or religious reasons. Sometimes there are loyal people who are straightforward with rulers but are slandered by cliques. Ancient kings are known to have hired unknowns and nobodies, finding in them the human qualities whereby they were able to bring peace.

--Zhuge Liang
Chinese military & political strategist
"Records of the Loyal Lord of Warriors"
Approximately 220 A.D.

Resistance

The most important thing to comprehend about talent is the resistance to it. Without this comprehension, there is no reason why talent would not surface and present itself. Thus, talent would always present itself easily and distinctively to us. Anyone who has ever tried to identify and cultivate talent knows there are many challenges associated with it. Consequently, these challenges alone indicate a form of resistance to it.

Everything in life has a positive and negative aspect to it. By reconciling the two, one creates a powerful whole. A large oak generates a shady canvas protecting us from the sun's heat, but on cooler days this same canvas makes us colder. Talent generates dynamism but also disruption. Perspective determines whether there is encouragement or resistance. Since this book seeks to help you enhance your own effectiveness at work, I'm devoting a whole section on conditioning, the automatic imposition of a specific context upon our thought processes. Developing our talents to their utmost becomes almost impossible if we are blind to the contexts thrust upon our thinking and feelings.

This last statement infers two sources of resistance: the individual and others. The first implies that within each of us forces prevent us from maximizing our talents. Some we can link directly to the needs we've generally identified. The second implies that others will seek to resist the expression of the individual's talent. For some, the talent of one disrupts the comfort of many. In business, we often see how the explosive growth of one industry can put another out of business. The advent of trains caused the decline of canals; the advent of cars caused passenger train service to decline. Cell phones created upheavals in traditional phone services. One person's talents can threaten the livelihood of many.

Many things prevent talent from showing. Some could deal with chance, circumstances, while a large part concerns conditioning and education. Since this book is relationally focused based on the premise relationships drive business, we're more concerned with how relationships affect talent, how they create resistance to talent. To this end, I've split the Resistance heading into two parts: the individual and the group.

Resistance to talent takes two relational forms. The first is the relationship with oneself. I'll be using the inside-outside duality discussion as the basis for exploring this. The second is the relationship between one and another. Collectively the relationships with many others form a group. Resistance to talent also comes from groups, from two to many. We're going to look at each type of relational resistance to talent – individual and group.

Individual

While it's rarely appropriate to single out any particular resistor within a person inhibiting his talent because often it's involved, from a practical business perspective, realizing and accepting the existence of internal resistors to talent is the important point. In order to overcome these resistors, one needs to apply an extensive dose of encouragement. Since the basis of this encouragement is empathy, sincerity is crucial and finds its roots in the feminine influence. Mechanical, Pollyanna remarks won't do.

We'll run through five resistors that will help deliver a sense of the overall nature of the resistance within a person to his own talent development. Again, from an immediate practical perspective it's not important to be able to identify these. Their purpose here is to give you a better feel for internal resistance and the extent to which outside encouragement is necessary and the form it might take. Our five resistors are:

- Ability
- Timing
- Fear
- Discount
- Unawareness

When we previously discussed a definition for talent, we came to the conclusion that this was pretty much impossible since it's analogous to attempting to define beauty. From this we entered a discussion concerning the identification of talent in others. Again, arriving at such a conclusion is pretty much useless.

One of the reasons why such an effort is useless that we did not discuss is that some people are more apt to display their talent than others. There are two important perspectives from which to look at this. First, some may simply have better avenues to display the talent that they do have. Second, there is the consideration that since talent is vital, organic as we just discussed, its blossoming isn't a matter of simply turning on a light switch but rather nurturing it until it's ready to show itself.

For the first, if we return to a gasoline explosion, we can distinguish this difference by saying some may have a better avenues to use that explosion in the form of a car versus a bomb. We can even enhance this analogy by saying different cars have different capabilities; yet, all make use of the same basic principles of gasoline exploding. Likewise, someone may be blessed with a specific talent but may have the physical characteristics that give him a better ability to display that talent. The most obvious examples are in sports. This perspective also explains why some with less physical ability excel over those with more; there is more to talent than what we see on the surface. Again, we would not consider a robot that could sink a hundred free throws in a row or one that could come up with a million bits of information as talented. Consequently, we feel there is more to talent than the mere physical or mental ability to do something. This returns us to our conversation where talent is a term generally reserved for humans.

For the second, the time table under which one's talent operates, we can relate to various time tables children develop as they move through puberty or adults through the aging process; both events affect individuals according to different timetables. Talent is alive so it makes sense that it's guided by the same maturation principles as our bodies, minds, and emotions are. Talent has its own timetable individualized to the person. If talent varies by individual, then it makes sense that its timetable will vary as well, adding a whole new dimension to our discussion as to whether it's worthwhile to identify someone as talented. Here, a "late bloomer" comes to mind. Perhaps those we identify as untalented are simply at a stage where their talent is not displaying itself such as an unseen seed recently planted beneath the surface. Just as we can pass a track of land one year and find very little growing, the next year could have us finding much more. No matter what we do we cannot transform a seedling into a hundred foot oak overnight. Talent, being organic, must also have the same principles guiding it.

Ability and timing are just a couple internal factors creating resistance for talent's display; more emotional ones involving the inside-outside duality exist as well. The toughest question to answer is why would talent be hard to develop even by those who possess it? The commonly held assumption is that "cream rises to the top," but our counter, "this only happens if we allow it," implies something not allowing it. Internally, we have resistors to talent's surfacing. The cliché "fear of success" is such an internal verbalization of this resistance in our everyday lives.

Essentially, success brings its own problems that one may fear to confront. One of those is the loss of privacy. Just go through a grocery line and view the tabloids. Princess Diana was the most symbolic loss to this need. There is also the fear of running into more people seeking something from you because you now have more to give. How many celebrities move through society now with bodyguards and huge walls around their homes that appear more as fortresses? How many cannot even go to a McDonald's with their children without creating a scene? Often we rationalize this as the "price of fame," but the point is that it is a *price*. With any success comes a cost and while we may easily say that we would be willing to pay that cost, nevertheless it is a cost that can have various affects on various individuals. The "price of fame" exists on a small scale too, not just with celebrity status.

What makes these costs more significant is their investment like nature; generally, the cost of success is disproportionately distributed upfront – "paying your dues." Winning the championship doesn't cost much at the moment it's won because most of the payment occurred during practice and the games many months earlier. The cost of nurturing a seedling is far greater than when it's an established, full-grown oak. The energy to push a car without gas is greatest when one first attempts to get it to budge not when he has gotten it moving. The amount of fuel a rocket needs to launch and escape the Earth's orbit could power it to Mars, thousands of miles compared to millions. As a result, part of the fear associated with success entails the endurance of physical, mental, and emotional pauperism while talent matures.

Talent's vitality makes it something associated with our feelings just as our arm's vitality stimulates feelings in us. For this reason, appreciating the role instincts and feelings play in talent are important in understanding why talent hides. As we mentioned, talent is rare. It is something unique that will cause you to feel different from others. From a positive standpoint, this creates a feeling of specialness. From a negative perspective this creates feelings of being weird, odd, strange, abnormal, or a freak of nature. Perception affects how others receive this talent. To those without that talent, they could feel envious or threatened by it so will be inclined to interpret it negatively while those more accepting of their own talents and others, will tend to view it positively.

Even though we are talking about talent and the tendency is to think about it on a grand scale, we need to focus and think about it microscopically because talent will show itself in the smallest things. A hundred-foot oak doesn't present itself first as a hundred-foot oak but rather as a seedling; thus, talent can show itself in anything someone does well. So, when we talk about negative and positive perceptions toward talent, microscopically we're talking about perceptions toward what we do well. Negative perceptions about what you do well will translate into discounting what you do or viewing it as strange by saying it's "too something." Such perceptions include ignoring what you do. Positive perceptions will recognize and reinforce it.

At this point, our feelings come into play because we may suddenly not be liked by others, causing the flare up of our need for long-term security which is often satisfied by membership in a group, strength in numbers. We could also worry that exclusion from others will reduce our opportunities to experience new things, to grow. These feelings can cause us to restrict our activities so they conform to pre-existing codes implicitly accepted and conferred by the group; uniqueness and fitting in come into conflict and generate tensions, anxieties. To avoid discomfort and seek the comfort of feeling our security needs met, we reel in our talent to placate the acceptance of others. Referring back to the inside-outside duality, our outside person has persuaded our inside person to settle down and behave himself so he can protect both.

Yet, within each of us resistance to our own talent is more than just a response to fear of a group's retaliation. We also create it for ourselves because talent often brings additional responsibility that we fear we can't handle. For instance, returning to our swimmer's analogy where someone is drowning while two people on shore watch, one can swim and one cannot. Which of the two would feel a greater sense of responsibility to rescue the person? The one with the talent, in this case the swimmer, has more responsibility thrust upon him than the non-swimmer. Few would hold the non-swimmer accountable if the person drowned; however, people might frown upon the swimmer, especially if we made the example more poignant by saying he was once a lifeguard. We see a similar responsibility thrust upon medical people in emergencies occurring during their off time.

Who would carry more responsibility if someone around us in public suddenly suffered a heart attack?

As we realize additional talents our responsibilities increase along with what others expect of us. Expectations are higher on the President than an average citizen. We may not be able to be complacent about a job that is done. If we do a job at a "five" level and we're capable of doing it at a "ten" level, then we're obviously shortchanging something. Now, if someone was only able to function at a "five" level and he does a "five" job, we really can't expect much else. The responsibility for doing an outstanding job is really held with the person who can do a "ten" and not the "five". Emotionally, having this responsibility can be quite daunting because you are more likely to be called upon to do the tough jobs. As they become tougher and tougher, the likelihood of failure increases for you while no one else risks themselves. Some people can emotionally accept being given the ball on the last play of the game to try to score the winning touchdown while others cannot. Yet others may be so jealous or insecure that they may not want to give the ball to you even though it means suffering a loss just to prevent that person from ruining their situation. Someone capable of only doing a "five" job won't hire a person capable of a "ten" job if he feels the "ten" may comprise his own potential advancement in the future.

Consider two stories:

> My brother as a teenager regularly worked out with weights and was quite strong. When he entered college and joined a fraternity, he helped protect it from visitors who would attempt to vandalize it. His talent at physically handling such vandals so they would be inclined not to harm the fraternity in the future caused his fraternity brothers to call upon him when other vandals visited. One day during a frat party at their house the others called upon my brother because there was a disturbance. When they showed my brother the ones creating the disturbance, he found himself confronted by three football players all obviously bigger and more conditioned than he. His talent for handling vandals suddenly found him in physical danger.

> A co-worker proficient in a particular software program taught me how to use it. After giving me his tips, he advised me not to tell anyone I knew how to use this well. When I asked why, he cautioned me that once everyone knows I do, they'll bug me to help them and I won't get my regular work done. He cited his own experiences that placed him in danger of not doing his job well.

Talents can certainly help us, but they can also place us in danger as well. Responsibilities not handleable by others will gravitate toward those with the talent to address them. The potential from this pattern is that one day the talented person will find himself facing responsibilities beyond his capabilities but which everyone is counting upon him to address. This potential creates a natural resistance within us to develop our talents by appealing to our security needs; our outside person once again convinces our inside person that it's better not to learn something new so as to avoid the consequences of failure.

In theory, the countervailing argument is that those who accept this responsibility will be more greatly rewarded; however, many things hinder this in reality. Among them:

- There is uncertain agreement as to the value a talent is adding to the task.
- The decision to delegate the task to a talent is disproportionately valued greater than the talent applied to the task, thereby effectively causing the discounting of the overall value of the talent's effort. Essentially, delegation is given too much credit.

- Rewards that highlight a talent and increase his stature can threaten the security of those around him, especially peers and supervisors, by potentially making him a stronger candidate to take a promotional spot in the organizational hierarchy originally earmarked for them.
- Highlighting a talent's effort can indirectly reflect negatively on those around him, and thus, there is a natural tendency to discount that effort in order to not arouse these anxieties.
- Talented people by their very nature are a threat to others because they are more likely than those others to uncover deficiencies, so rewarding them or placing them in advanced positions will potentially make others feel more exposed.

The wake of a powerful ship will disturb other ships and will create a tendency by the others to compel it to slow down or halt altogether. Since the most powerful ship can only be one, it will be outnumbered by the rest. Now, we never really see it this way because these points do not come across in their pure form but rather in the form of rationalizations, excuses. For instance, rather than saying "You're much more talented than me, so why don't you take this task?" the rationalization could be "I'm too busy to handle this, so why don't you take this?" or "Since you've done something like this before, how about taking this?" From a practical business perspective, we often find folks delegating tasks that they may find discomforting to learn. If someone does not do a task, he avoids failure; thus, learning something new not only enhances one's opportunities for success but also for failure. Again, the perception of the person and how the three needs play out within him will affect how he views various activities, but many times the person employing such rationale is not even looking at these as excuses. This is an example of how our needs, in this case security, can influence us without our knowledge as suggested by point seven in the Seventeen Influential Points.

Another argument in theory is that if anything along these five points occurs it's on relatively minor issues or it rarely occurs. In reality, these arguments ignore the significance of small events when trying to cultivate talent. Typically, we'll see this present with small successes unsupported through inadequate or nonexistent praise for an employee's work. Such unsupportiveness, especially on small incidents, has a corrosive effect on talent identification and development much in the same way rust corrodes metal; weaknesses don't show until we stress the situation. At these times, we wonder why things don't go as well as they should. Opportunities for promoting talent exist everyday; neglecting this is no different than neglecting to water a plant. Most plants do not die because their owners stomp on them; they die because their owners neglect them. Neglect kills talent in the same way it kills plants.

This line of thought manifests into deficient rewards for the risks assumed by talent and cause theory's separation from reality; talent remains underground and hidden. The danger related to this is to think that a talented person consciously hides his talent. This is not true especially if someone is not aware of his talent. Conformity, complacency, and compliance are key ingredients that retard talent's assertion. Expressivity is talent's nature, so those with it will step forward. Positively, this step forward will be seen as valuable, negatively as "stepping out of line." As the rewards for this step diminish or become nonexistent, the tendency will be to do what's expected to stay out of trouble, including stepping forward only in an acceptable direction. Despite its expressivity, talent can easily hide if the person in whom it rests is threatened by it. We will see this manifested by the outside person telling the inside one to stay in line. Rationally, this will appear as "they won't appreciate the effort," "you saw what happened to the last person who presented a different idea in a meeting," or "what you do isn't that important."

Extremely few people will continuously give to the unappreciative. Dynamism requires people to step forward in ways other than what we expect. Again, referring to Figures 2.34 – 2.41 these ways are simply a matter of "more" but also in what direction. Even though the step may not fulfill what we need, the attempt should be rewarded because this will encourage further attempts including one that ultimately may yield something dynamic. The nature of life's dynamic aspects is that it doesn't matter whether fifty or eighty percent of the thousand of acorns that drop from one tree ultimately become trees themselves; what matters is that at least a few do. All you have to do is encourage the one tree you do have to continue dropping thousands of acorns.

When it comes to hiding one's talent, we've seen above the threat is that others may negatively view that talent. What seems counter intuitive is when that talent is hidden from us, but the problem is the assumption that we would know of talent when we had one; talent can be very much like an antique. It can be stuck away in the bottom of some basement forgotten, dusty, dirty and maybe pulled out for a garage sale and sold for fifty cents. Then, the buyer takes it, restores it to its original luster, and suddenly realizes it's something very valuable. Similarly, people may not see the comprehensive implications of what they do well. In effect, they see seedlings that they don't realize could grow to large, daunting oaks.

Beyond missing the implications of doing something well, often those with a talent don't realize they have one. The sun can easily believe he's not bright because the brightness he sees is normal for him. Similarly, a talent, while exceptional to others, is a normal, everyday aspect of life to the one who possesses it. Relatedly, while we may expect people to admire us for a talent and thus help us recognize it, as we see above there are significant pressures that prevent people from doing so, plus it takes talent itself to see the implications in what others do well. Consequently, while the nature of talent is to express itself, this expressivity isn't an ostentatious desire declaring "Here I am!" but rather more of one simply seeking the light of open areas. Again, returning to the growing oak tree, just as that tree will grow toward the open areas with light, so will talent seek lighted, open areas avoiding crowds.

Is it possible for someone to have talent without knowing exactly what that talent is? It is if we accept the fact that who we are is much different than who we think we are because this allows for growth opportunities to learn more about ourselves or to possibly alter how we look at ourselves. If we don't accept this, then we are confined to the sum of our thoughts and whatever they rationalize. The nature of life suggests though that conscious thoughts, while powerfully focused permitting verbalization, are extremely limited in their ability to grasp the totality of any situation including our own inner worlds. If we cannot go into a forest and consciously grasp every aspect of it so that we can duplicate it, what makes us think we know every aspect of ourselves at this moment?

Essentially, we've covered five internal resistors within us that can hinder our talent's development. Of the five we spent the most time on fear. At some point this resistor becomes prevalent as some of the others are overcome. It takes on an even greater role when we get into conditioning. For the moment here is a summary:

- Ability – There may be a need to pick up additional skills that will allow someone to better display his talent. If he has a communicative talent, this may mean developing comfort with different media.

- Timing – Talent works on individualized timetables. One cannot artificially adjust what is effectively an organic timetable too much.
- Fear – This is present in anything new we do or learn. Failure's humiliations and success's responsibilities contribute to feed upon our security needs.
- Discount – What we consider talent, the talented considers normal. Since a person lives with his talent everyday, it's easy for him to view it as just a normal part of the way life is – "anybody can do this."
- Unawareness – People can be unaware of the things they do well for many reasons. It could be as simple as they've never tried something or as complex as they were taught that what they did was not good.

Some of these we've talked about from the perspective of what other individuals may feel about the talent of another, so in the next heading we'll spend more time addressing resistance from a group perspective.

Group

Groups inherently resist talent as Figures 2.61 – 2.67 imply because the many outnumber the few; talent's uncommonness places it on the side of the few. The challenge is appreciating the diverse talents within each of us. Others have talents we lack, and we have talents others lack thereby making each of us simultaneously part of the many and the few at the same time. The smallest "few" we can have is one, the individual.

The point of this heading is to raise awareness of inherent tension between the group and the individual. We'll first take a closer look at some characteristics of individual and groups and second how these characteristics manifest in interactions between the two.

In theory, this suggests two entities, the individual and the group; however, in reality we are talking about a non-entity (group) and an entity (individual). The important implication is that groups do not exist except in definition only; they are a nebulous association of individuals. We originally ran into this concept in Figure 1.4 when we discussed the relationship of an individual with a group as being a collection of relationships between that individual and each individual within the group.

Organically, the difference between an individual and a group is equivalent to the difference between a tree and a building. An individual and a tree are natural entities whereas a building and a group are man-made ones. Who gives birth to a group? Without individual units groups cannot exist; however, individuals can and do exist without groups. Often we see animals collect themselves in groups; however, we create the definitional distinction not them. Two groups we call the same can behave differently because their individual members are different.

Practically, we see this in our ability to designate and create groups at will. We can group people without their knowledge. We cannot create a person or thrust a specific personality upon an individual – these actions are naturally originated. In grouping people by color, sex, national origin, or any other aspect, we fill in the cracks created by the individual identities of the groups' members to create a unified whole. No matter how we group things, individual characteristics differ. Analogously, we are taking distinctively created stones, amalgamating them, and filling their spaces with cement, thereby melding them together. Groups make individuals the same by ignoring their distinctive characteristics to emphasize their commonalities.

This line of thought is important because the non-existence of groups surges forward when we ask the question: How can a collection of individuals informally unite as a group against an individual without consciously agreeing to do so? Implicatively, this question says groups don't exist naturally because a conscious, organizational awareness must exist. Can you imagine a person who exists but does not consciously know he does? Thus, a group of people can't be accused of "ganging up" on someone because they never got together to agree upon an alliance. Groups are not real entities because many times they have no conscious awareness of their existence just as a building has no conscious awareness of its existence.

Consciously agreeing to form an alliance is not a prerequisite to collective action though; there are many ways to get individuals to behave similarly despite the lack of an agreement to do so. Incentives are a prime example of that. Advertising is another. We design incentives to coordinate the actions of individuals along similar lines without the necessitation of an agreement with them collectively. Advertisements for a particular product encourage collective purchasing by a group without the necessitation of an agreement by that group to do so. We even design incentives and advertisements with target groups or markets in mind. What group will be attracted by this incentive or advertisement?

Delving deeper, if we imagine a crowded city street where a man runs with a gun that he waves and randomly shoots in the air, people without a formal agreement will run from that man. From a different perspective, these same people who may suddenly hear a band playing may collectively move to hear it without a formal agreement to do so. Concerts and riots are two other extremes where people may behave similarly without a formal arrangement to do so. In the first, they may all clap their hands and stomp their feet to the music, while in the second, they may all throw rocks and loot buildings.

The tendency for individuals to behave collectively or individually has certain characteristics. Collective action is dependent upon others. Without the actions of at least one other individual you do not have collective action; thus, collective action is dependent. Conversely, individual action is independent; it's not dependent upon the actions of another and can be done without others. Collective action is safer because it's done with another; one does not stand alone. Individual action is riskier because one is acting alone and is not in concert with others. Collective action is more stable because it's not easily changed because of its dependent nature. To change collective action you must change the behavior of more than one person. Individual action is more flexible because it's not dependent upon others.

The examples of these characteristics are endless. For instance, take an empty dance floor. While everyone may want to dance, no one wants to be the first one on the floor. Once someone starts then everyone jumps in. Individual action requires more courage than collective action. Entering a crowded dance floor is emotionally easier than entering an empty one. Going to a party is similar. Few want to be the first to attend, but many have no hesitation to attend when many others are there – we call this "being fashionably late." I once attended a function where the party organizers provided bowling to the attendees. No one wanted to be the first to bowl, but once a few started everyone joined in. At a neighborhood party a six-year girl asked a teenaged boy to play hide and seek. His first question was "Is anybody else playing?" In a bar, someone began to sing a song. After a few joined in everybody else did as well.

The interaction between the individual and group has positive and negative manifestations.

Positively, the individual is the source of growth and creativity, while the group of strength and stability. In the above examples, we see individual action initiating dancing, a party, bowling, hide and seek, and singing. The theme is new; creativity is associated with newness. Learning relates to new and consequently so does growth. One cannot grow without experiencing something new. Conversely, group action provides safety through strength as shown by the ease in which people joined in each activity once they began. We imply stability through safety in the way collective action continues on uninterrupted; it's more predictable. Without individual action to take a group on a new path, collective action eventual peters out as a dance eventually does as the night wears on.

Negatively, the individual disrupts the group, and the group constrains the individual. For those who may not want to hear the ruckus of dancing, hide and seek, or singing, the above individual actions are disruptive. From the individual's perspective, if no one joined the activities, there is the pressure from the group to desist by having the individuals continue on alone.

A new idea or thought originates with a person and societal growth occurs when a group unifies its collective strength around it. Groups rarely come up with innovative ideas worthy of dynamism. Popularly, we hear about collecting the best parts of various ideas into a single best idea, but analogously speaking we are simply taking the best rooms and throwing them together to make the best house. The best rooms won't make the best house because there won't be any coherent style. Consequently, the best rooms will yield a schizophrenic house. Even the best ideas will require thorough modification to fit the style of the whole; we will need a person to serve as a unifying force which is why almost every organization has an *individual* as its leader.

Groups will tend to dull the edge that makes an idea dynamic in the very same way that throwing the best rooms together makes for an unpleasant home. Since groups are a source of strength and stability, any group will tend to worship the ultimate in stability – comfort – and the ultimate in strength – consensus. As a result, they will tend to sacrifice dynamism for their sake. Committees and consensus will eliminate the edge and replace it with blandness; there is a reason why chicken is frequently served at banquets along with vanilla ice cream. Similarly, groups will tend toward the elimination of an idea's aspects that offend people just as a banquet menu avoids spicy foods. Only through individual choice can dynamic foods be served; only from the individual can dynamic ideas erupt. A truly dynamic concept is bound to upset someone because that is the nature of dynamism; it alters the status quo.

Imagine having ten artists paint a picture they collectively decide upon or ten architects designing a building. Investment portfolios seek diversification to minimize risk by containing many different securities as opposed to one; however, a single security has the potential for more dynamic returns than a collection. A group of artists and architects are more likely to create something that won't offend anybody but far less likely to create something sensational. By their nature groups seek not to offend (stability) while individuals seek to impress (creativity).

This is why small companies, although riskier, tend to grow more dynamically than larger ones who are more affected by group-think as opposed to individual creativity. It's not that one is inherently good and the other inherently bad, but rather the problem is that we don't realize there is this delicate balance between the individual to provide the talent necessary to create a dynamic environment and the need for the group to provide the security, consistency, and stability to sustain that talent.

The importance of the tension between group and individual is that it lays the intellectual groundwork for understanding why folks don't realize they have talents; they're essentially conditioned not to trust them because many others see them as threats to their own security especially those with a high stake in the status quo. Any talented person will have the potential for stiff opposition aligned against him to such a degree that he may come to see his particular talents as useless or disruptive and is why sometimes our talents can lie in our weaknesses as perceived by others.

As a result, we collectively retard talent by applying a negative connotation to it that usually implies "too much." For instance, assertiveness becomes recklessness, prudent becomes complacent, thorough becomes picky, determined becomes stubborn, thoughtful becomes quiet, personable becomes superficial, and passionate becomes irrational. Any talent becomes a negative if you apply "too much" to it and come up with an appropriate synonym. Since talent resides with the minority, we are quite likely to hear such criticisms from many people and begin to dull the edge on our talent.

Another way we collectively retard talent is to say someone can't do something or can't do it well. The nature of things allows us to find reasons why someone can't do something. An oak tree whose acorns only produce a few trees from thousands could be called inefficient. As a result, if the oak tree would listen, we probably could persuade it to stop wasting its time and focus on something else.

We can relate the concept of tension between the individual and group to one faced by everyone at a very early age, "peer pressure." With the two ways above, "peer pressure" can cause talent to be suppressed, ignored, and undetected to such a degree that the talent could even be viewed negatively or useless by the person who possesses it. At this point, the person ceases to cultivate it and becomes unthreatening to the group.

Illustratively, we can compare a talented person to a large, powerful country that no matter how benevolent can be viewed as a threat to smaller, powerless countries. This creates a situation where the benevolent one can feel that it's a big bully simply because many smaller nations believe so. This, in and of itself, seems ludicrous that smaller nations can do this to a larger one, but talent's vital nature lends itself to sensitivity – awareness for what's happening around it which requires empathy, feelings. A vote by all the countries could likely call for the disarmament of the larger country. Talent's minority status makes is vulnerable to majority pressure. If one person feels threatened by another's talents, the likelihood of others feeling the same way is great. This is how you could receive numerous negative responses to your talent, input from those who consider it a threat. At some point the will of the majority can wreak emotional havoc upon even the most talented. It's quite easy to persuade a talent that they are freaky rather than unique.

This analogy also relates to the question of informal collective action. If a person threatens the security of several people through his actions, then collectively people may take similar actions against that person without mutual knowledge of others actions. More direct, informal actions may occur through gossip about the person and communications about feelings and actions without directly suggesting or agreeing on working together. Many times simply knowing another feels the same as you do gives comfort and security in taking action. Again, groups provide strength and stability. People who have high security needs will be more inclined to reinforce and maintain the integrity of the group.

The important point relative to this is that talent will most often be in the minority challenging directly or indirectly, visibly or invisibly, the majority – the status quo. The tension is between growth and stability, between new and traditional, between risk and protection. The implication is that a herd mentality will most likely not discover and develop talent but rather seek those who reinforce or tweak the status quo. From your standpoint, this means that your efforts will almost certainly be in the minority. The United States Constitution symbolizes the tension between the many and the individual by simultaneously documenting the will of the majority and the rights of the individual.

The essence of groups' resistance to talent is talent's tremendous disruptive influence. If we like to have a smooth running environment where things are pretty predictable then talent can really disrupt that because talent is not confined to the normal or the usual or the pleasant. It actually wants to achieve something dynamic. What kind of talent seeks to keep things routine?

Falling into the habit of expecting and working toward a rather predictable environment is easy. Recently, a hundred-year oak tree over a hundred feet high and three and a half feet in diameter tree fell on our house. Obviously, the easiest thing to do would have been to have someone cut the tree up and take it away. Someone suggested the tree was large enough to have it milled and cut into boards which we eventually did.

As I looked at the boards, I was trying to determine which boards we could use as is and which would need additional trimming or discarding. I began to ask the owner of the company who helped us remove and mill the tree for some advice on how to make this determination. As examples, I showed him some rotten boards and others with huge knots. He paused and took a deep breath as if to say he knew the answer I wanted but that *the* answer was going to differ – and it did.

He responded by first saying that all of the wood is usable even the rotten portions and added that it's all of matter of trying to determine how to use it. Wood is imperfect and to him that's the perfect thing about it. A good carpenter doesn't approach wood looking for a perfect piece of wood but rather approaches wood knowing it is imperfect. The challenge is then a matter of how to use that imperfection in a way to make something beautiful. He went on to tell me about a beautiful wooden table he saw made solely from rotten wood. This is why he and his dad save all the scraps from their wood-working projects because there could be an undiscovered use for them in the future.

Thus, while the standard, routine, and normal make things easier, there is also a lot of waste involved because there is the inclination to discard the wood imperfect for the system. Since differentiation in business isn't found in the routine but in the different, what's imperfect for the system is more likely to contain the dynamic than what is perfect. If talent is something special, then it is more related to what does not routinely fit a standard. Furthermore, what is dynamic is more likely to contain elements of beauty since both segregate themselves from the norm. Both beauty and dynamism are more closely aligned with the talented than the common. All three, talent, dynamism, and beauty, are disruptors.

Most companies are content with five to fifteen percent increases. Talent is not satisfied with that because within nominal growth comes the seeds of a pending plateau and eventual decline as outlined in the Company chapter. Talent seeks not only higher growth but a more qualitative one through organic growth as opposed to acquisition. Now, everyone would say, "we all want that," but such growth also brings intimidating changes that can alter personal futures.

New people may arrive at the company and alter the cultures and fortunes. Sports teams see this every year with the rookies seeking to displace the veterans. Politicians see it as new people move into town to alter the political balance or as districts are realigned. Teenagers see it when new ones move into town more athletic, affluent, or better looking than the current clique, such as the merger of two schools. No matter what aspect of culture we speak, instilling something dynamically new to inspire a regeneration creates anxiousness for members of the group even though for all it may be good. "Peer pressure" to reinforce the status quo is what eventually brings about the decline of any group because there is usually a failure to adapt at the appropriate times.

The feminine influence seeks to emphasize the one over the many as represented by the beauty of the Greek's Helen who unified the efforts of a whole army. Recently, at a regular, neighborhood teenage get together, three new teenagers showed up to join the dozen or so regulars. One of the three was a single girl who the boys found very attractive.

The neighborhood girls who normally attended the get together found the new girl getting most of the boys' attentions and even commented as such amongst themselves. One girl could upset the whole dynamics of a routine, neighborhood get together. Even a six-year old girl wanted to be her friend because she thought the girl pretty.

Whether this girl's appearance at the party was good for the group is not the question. What is pertinent is that she had a dynamic-disruptive effect on the party, depending upon the perspective you wish to take. What's also important is that if her attractiveness (talent) had not been as salient she would not have altered the dynamics of the group as much as she did. In effect, if she had blended in by being less attractive (conformity), she would have disturbed the group less and the gathering would have more easily have run along routine lines. What this shows is the potential of one talented person to shake up the dynamics and how one person's talents (attractiveness) could universally be seen as a threat to a collection of individuals without collusion. This feeling of being threatened by not receiving the boys' attentions could serve as the basis for rationalizations discrediting the girl in various ways. This also happens with less physical aspects of personality in many different arenas beyond a neighborhood teenage party. Secondarily, this girl's attractiveness symbolically represented the impact that the feminine influence can have – a dynamic one.

From the standpoint of a group's resistance to talent, it's important to recognize the potential influence of individuals within the group on us regarding the talent and to realize the potential dangers for the one whose talents you wish to cultivate. Thus, the cultivation of any talent needs to have a holistic perspective not only relative to the individual but to the group. Actions need to occur which seek to minimize feelings of insecurity in the group without discounting or ignoring the feelings of the talent. Such a balancing act requires talent. Having a framework through which to look at talent will help.

Framework

Talent's nature and the resistance to it give us the basis for developing a framework through which to detect it.

The critical aspect of talent's nature is its vitality because it implies something innate as opposed to manufactured; thus, it's conferred upon us by nature not man. Titles, degrees, and other such documentation do not grant talent. They only communicate the interpretations of others regarding the abilities inherent in out personalities. The talent we have is irrespective of the number of people who believe we have talent. A million people who believe we have a talent do not alter the talent we have. There is no correlation between the number of people who believe we have talent and our talent itself. They are mutually exclusive. Similarly, our talent lives outside of our own thoughts about it; no matter how much we think about our talent it inherently remains unchanged. Our thinking can no more change our talent than we can think our arms into changing into legs. Our thoughts serve to maximize the inherent potential locked within our talent just as they do with our arms.

The critical aspect of resistance to talent is the courage necessary to overcome the dynamics inherent in the tension between one and many. Having a mere physical or mental talent is not necessarily all that is needed; an emotional aspect exists as well. Often we hear in sports at a very high level that the difference between winning and losing isn't necessarily in the physical aspects but in the emotional ones. Typically, we hear this as "who wants it more." In music it's the difference between simply playing and playing with feeling. What our discussion around resistance implies is that there is a very important emotional element associated with talent in overcoming great odds. Overcoming these odds implies a Herculean task.

Under the Framework heading we'll cover a specific model to use as that framework, its irrational emphasis, and its application. As we've seen the search and development of talent requires an emotional, subjective approach, so a framework through which we can see this approach will help. Once we've established the framework we'll need to explore its irrational emphasis in more detail. Following this detail, I'll introduce applicative elements that will begin to connect this framework to business.

Wisdom's Magical Hierarchy

While we segregated vitality and resistance above, they interrelate on an emotional basis. By injecting passion, we transform routine activities do-able by a robot into something special. The ramifications are involved and intangible. Having a framework through which to discuss this will help us appreciate and apply it to talent. I'm going to use "Wisdom's Magical Hierarchy" in Figure 4.36 as that framework.

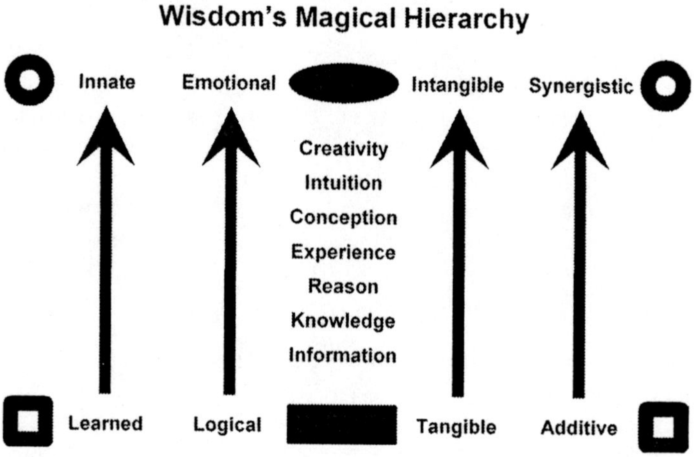

Wisdom's Magical Hierarchy

Figure 4.36

Taken solely by itself, any specific action becomes do-able by a machine. Typically, we do this through the way we make it or program it. Problems develop once we step outside of that specific action into the broader context in which it resides. For instance, deciding when that action is appropriate and how it integrates with other actions are just a few of those problems. While we can build a machine that would toss a ball through a hoop from a specific distance, our task becomes more difficult if the machine randomly moves to other spots at various distances. Even our most sophisticated armaments can pinpoint a target, but they cannot determine a target. People still determine and verify targets. Generally, what separates our physical abilities from our machines is what goes on inside of us; that determines how we apply our physicality. As a result, even though a machine may be able to execute a specific act better than a human, it is unable to apply itself effectively in light of the situation's entire context at a specific moment.

The distinction between the capabilities of a man and a machine that give man an advantage lies within. I call that advantage "wisdom." Our wisdom dramatically impacts our other talents whether they are physical, mental, or emotional and to a large extent determines the degree to which we differentiate ourselves from computers and each other. Without this wisdom, we would be no better than a machine or computer and probably vastly inferior. Implicatively, we arrive at the same point as our discussion around the vitality of talent: there is something alive within us.

That something is the difference we determined in Figure 4.30 allowing us to call someone talented. In effect, with Wisdom's Magical Hierarchy we are approaching that something from a different perspective, in this case a discussion around wisdom. Our previous discussion culminating in Figure 4.30 approached this from the perspective of trying to grab a better hold on the implicit conditions under which we apply the term "talented." Simplistically, we arrived at the point where talent is a term more generally reserved for humans; we would not think of calling a machine or computer talented. We now arrive at a point where it's not what we do but how we do it that determines talent, and how we do it is determined by what's inside of us. The hierarchy we are about to run through allows us to have a discussion about our insides.

Figure 4.36 delves into the basic elements of wisdom, their relationship to each other, and their contextual placement.

There are seven basic elements:

- Creativity
- Intuition
- Conception
- Experience
- Reason
- Knowledge
- Information

Their relationship to one another is hierarchical and magical. We can see the hierarchical aspect of their relationships as we move from information at the bottom to creativity at the top relative to their importance to wisdom. Some elements play a more important role in wisdom than others. The magical aspect of their relationships becomes visible as we meld them together; they become greater than the sum of their parts – synergy. Rather than,

$$1 + 1 + 1 + 1 + 1 + 1 + 1 = 7$$

we have,

$$1 + 1 + 1 + 1 + 1 + 1 + 1 > 7$$

Even though some elements play a greater role than others, all elements contribute holistically in a way exceeding their summation. Furthermore, the synergy from their integration implies an incalculable wholeness allowing for dynamic outcomes surpassing predetermined possibilities.

Analogously, as explained to me by a good friend, we can relate this to the progression from the existence of a dictionary to the expression of oneself. Measuring how many words someone knows is much easier than measuring the quality of his expression. Whereas knowledge is more akin to knowing the words in a dictionary, reason is the assembly of those words, and creativity is the words' message. Knowing a lot of words or putting them together in a way that makes sense is subordinate to what the words say and how they say it. Similarly, what we know in terms of knowledge and information and how we form them into reasonable statements is subordinate to the concept we are expressing and the creativity we are using to express it in a more interesting and effective way. As we experience everyday, people can use the same words but the way they arrange those words changes the message's content and impact. This becomes the illustrative, practical difference between addition and synergy

Contextually, Figure 4.36 illustrates this in the way the elements move along four, attributive spectrums:

Learned	$\Rightarrow$	Innate
Logical	$\Rightarrow$	Emotional
Tangible	$\Rightarrow$	Intangible
Additive	$\Rightarrow$	Synergistic

Each element falls within these spectrums to the degree each attribute applies to it. Toward the bottom we find the elements most associated with learning, logic, tangibility, and addition while toward the top we find the ones most associated with innateness, emotion, intangibility, and synergy.

The learned-innate spectrum concerns itself with the degree to which an attribute of wisdom is acquired through a learning process or birth. Learning includes any type of formal or informal education and can range from reading a set of instructions to enrolling in a school. Regardless of one's innate qualities, these aspects of wisdom can likely be learned. Conversely, innate refers to attributes granted at birth that are almost impossible to learn in any type of education, formal or informal. Attributes granted by nature are more potent than those learned as demonstrated by the expression, "It's almost second nature." We strive to make anything we learn appear natural; natural is superior to mechanical.

The logical-emotional spectrum indicates the degree to which an attribute requires mental or instinctive aptitudes. Thinking is inferior to feeling because it's less comprehensive, powerful, and swift. Having a feel for something is far better than having knowledge of it. A musician who has a feel for the music will generally play better than one who simply knows it. One cannot possess a feel for something without the sensitivity that comes with emotions.

Tangible and intangible deal with the degree to which we can sense something. By seeing, hearing, touching, tasting, and smelling, we detect the world around us; however, the world within the realm of our senses is far less than the world outside of our senses. This not only pertains to those aspects of the world that rest outside the range of our senses but also to those aspects that are undetectable by senses. In the former, we have the things that exist in another county or country that we cannot sense simply because they are not within our range of sight, hearing, touch, smell, or taste. In the later, we have things such as emotions and thoughts that lack physicality accessible through senses; they are insensible. Thus, the intangible is superior to the tangible.

Additive and synergistic relate to the degree an aspect is simply contributory versus dynamic. Where some things merely add their expected value, others seem to add something more than their mere contribution. They seem to enhance what others contribute. Synergistic qualities are more valuable than additive ones because they exceed what one would normally expect.

These four, attributive spectrums help to expand our appreciation for wisdom's elements. We can use them to explore these elements in more detail. Such an exploration will also grant us further opportunities to delve deeper into these spectrums and their roles. This mutuality will help us appreciate this hierarchy and its applicability to talent. We'll run through the elements by beginning at the bottom with information and working upward to creativity. An easy reference point as to an element's importance is the degree to which we <u>cannot</u> program a computer to do it; the more likely a computer can do it, the less likely it's important to wisdom.

At the bottom we have information that generally contains the basic facts we learn about our life, environment, world, and personalities. We acquire these and are not blessed with them at birth. The low importance information plays regarding wisdom is demonstrated by its ease of storage on a computer. A computer does not need to understand information in order to store it; it only requires programming that will allow it to accumulate and regurgitate information. For instant, someone can know all the facts about something and not be wise; we'll see this more clearly with the other elements. Learning facts comes down to memorization and recollection.

We can see the deficiencies in information by looking at the element of knowledge. Here we take several facts and associate them. In this way, we can distinguish a fact about cooking from one of investing. A computer can make no such distinction unless it's programmed and even then the information must be keyed in correctly. Typically we see the associative side of computers in databases by their ability to arrange data into specific groups based upon queries. Knowledge allows us to link facts into a collective body. Merely knowing a lot of facts does not imply one understands how they all fit together.

Information is like building blocks scattered on the floor. Just because you have a lot of blocks doesn't mean you are wise. Knowledge involves forming those blocks into groups so we understand the importance and relevancy of each group. An eco-system would be an example of knowledge. It's more or less a collection of facts and circumstances under one title. This again is learned but it also requires something more closely associated with innate understandings as to how these facts go together and in remembering that they do go together. While most of these associations can be learned, some instinct begins to come into play.

The next element is reason. We can best visualize this as extrapolation and interpolation. We can learn such reasoning, but more natural ability begins to enter into the picture than existed with collecting information or knowledge. Whereas with information and knowledge we have the facts before us or it's a matter of collecting more, reason entails concluding something from the information we have that makes sense. Thus, reason allows us to arrive at an unknown variable through known variables without having to get the unknown variable directly. These unknown aspects help us begin to see intangibility working itself into the elements.

For example, if "a > b" and "b > c," then "a > c" is reasonable. Without being told directly that "a > c," we can determine this indirectly. If sunlight helps trees and bushes to grow better, then it's likely it will also help flowers grow better as well since they are plants too. Consequently, if we were reading knowledge on vegetation and knew flowers are considered such, we could combine this information with the information that sunlight helps trees and bushes to surmise that sunlight would have a similar effect on flowers. With reason we combine specific knowledge and facts into a logical array to make deductions. Continuing our block analogy, it's looking at the blocks with straight or flat sides and realizing we can stack them.

We also begin to see synergy in a group of blocks; a dozen scattered blocks are quite different from a dozen blocks arranged in a structure – the later represents synergy. Whereas information and knowledge apply to things we have or collect directly, reason begins to generate things previously unknown and inaccessible through an indirect route. We also begin to move away from logic to something more emotional because programming a computer to reason through a set of data is more difficult than programming it to store and associate information. Having a feel for the information or knowledge will also allow one to reason better and sense what is right or wrong. A computer cannot cross-check itself unless programmed to do so.

After reason we arrive at experience, the mid-point of the hierarchy. Here we begin to mix the logic of a situation with the feeling to notice a difference between what the facts and reason tell us and what happens in reality. Reality moves us up further along the logic-emotion spectrum because through experiences it leaves far greater emotional imprints than information, knowledge or reason can; the thought of meeting someone is always different from feelings actually derived from that meeting. For instance, no matter how good the instructions are to put something together, there is always deviance from them in reality.

Since experience implies things we learn through sensing and feeling, it begins moving us more into the realm of intangibility. We began to see some of this with reason since it has a mild interpretive quality but reason's rationale continues to provide something fairly concrete. With experiences we see how a single event can affect people differently even though facts and circumstances are the same. This is where we get into more of the feeling aspect of wisdom because of the way we feel about our experiences. What we take away from an experience varies by individual and has a lot to do with our innate personalities. Our block analogy begins to have us experiment through experience such as "trial and error" with the information, knowledge, and reason we've employed. We might find that two blocks that would seem to form a stable foundation actually do not.

The interpretive, sensing aspect of experience is the transition to more emotional elements such as conception. Once we receive a feeling for doing something, we can integrate our experiences, reasons, knowledge, and information to form concepts or ideas applicable to realities we encounter. Here we begin to transcend simple logic to include more unsubstantiated "gut feelings." Rather than having reasons for doing things, we now begin to have feelings for what would work.

Conception becomes more intangible and emotional because the rationale for doing something becomes less firm. For instance, while one may not have had a direct experience doing something, he was able to extract something from previous experiences that allows him to have a good feel for what needs to be done. Thus, someone who has experienced driving a car and navigating a big boat could be comfortable driving a truck, but even here the distinction becomes less rational than this. We often begin to see these as analogies.

As for the blocks, we now begin to see there is a qualitative distinction; it's no longer a matter of figuring out what to do with the blocks but also how to do it well. Quality begins to imply more intangible, emotional, and synergistic elements. Since feelings and sensitivity are more prevalent, there is more innateness associated with these. People are born with varying sensitivity levels that affect relationships not only with people but with things, having a feel for hitting golf ball or for the mood of people at an event are examples.

In purest form intuition is somewhat of an idea or concept without reliance on any facts, information, reason, or experience. Essentially, somehow someone knows something will just work. In many respects common sense is an offshoot of this. That is not to say intuition does not have to be supported by rational thought; however, it does say that the primary ingredient is feeling. This is the concept of coming up with something based only on a feeling. Again, we commonly experience this when we talk about a woman's intuition, and why we associate more emotional attributes to the feminine influence. Intuition is similar to what hunger and thirst do for us in driving us to satisfy those feelings, but many more instincts than just these drive our intuition. Consequently, those with keen intuition do not require a wealth of information and knowledge to feel comfortable in making important decisions; however, such paucity of rationale will tend to make others uncomfortable because the inclination is to have "good reasons" for decisions. Since intuition relies upon emotional sensitivity, it's highly innate and takes effort to develop fully.

In our blocks, intuition would reflect itself even more qualitatively. We'll see even a closer link between personal preferences and their expression in blocks. As with a painting, explaining the rationale behind why it looks the way it does will be virtually pointless because beauty will cause it to transcend explanations. The blocks will begin to move away from a raw structure into an art form, the distinguishing characteristic between conception and intuition. From a practical business perspective, running a business becomes an art rather than a science – a form of personal expression rather than just a mechanism to generate cash.

With this we arrive at creativity, the top of the hierarchy. While similar to intuition, its distinction is originality. Whereas, intuition covers feelings and generates manifestations similar to others, creativity is the manifestation of a unique feeling. This does not mean something totally different and unrelated because the reality is that any idea needs some creative tinkering to fit it to a situation. The line between original and similar is blurred not distinctive. Everything, to some degree, has a basis in something that already exists – everything relates to something else. Since every situation is different, most ideas will need a creative alteration to make it dynamic to the new situation. Many times this relationship is accidental. Life is an eco-system where things are related; however each plant and tree is unique. Some are similar to another but still unique. People are similar but unique; this paradox exists in many other aspects of life.

After this discussion of creativity, we've completed the journeys of learned to innate, logical to emotional, tangible to intangible, and additive to synergistic by reviewing the elements from bottom to top. The purpose of Wisdom's Magical Hierarchy is to give talent an irrational emphasis in order to link it to its uncommonness, its abnormality.

Irrational Emphasis

When we look at the four attributive pairings, we find innateness, emotion, intangibility, and synergy at the top. Collectively they give the Wisdom's Magical Hierarchy and talent an irrational emphasis. Learning, logic, tangible, and addition possess a concreteness missing in their counterparts. The duality of concrete-nebulous relates to the rational-irrational one and is how we arrive at the irrational emphasis for talent. Our discussion under this heading will reinforce this connection by looking at it from different perspectives and integrating it with the main theme of this book – the feminine influence. The purpose of this heading is to lay a strong foundation for discussing the application of this hierarchy in everyday business life.

In a rational world, the favorite always wins. What we've learned by putting our finger on things becomes the basis of logic adding up all the facts and determining the likely outcome, the favorite. In an irrational world, the underdog occasionally wins. We discover innate, untouchable qualities become the emotional basis for yielding a surprising outcome, the underdog.

We frequently link rationality to normalcy which is the favored condition. By returning to the bell curves in Figures 2.61 – 2.67 we find the more numerous majority outnumbering the more talented minority, quantity versus quality. Normalcy resides with the majority and abnormality with the minority. Betting on the more frequent occurrence is rational while on the less frequent irrational. In reality though, while the favorite wins more frequently, the underdog wins more surprisingly. The 80/20 rule (80% of something only accounts for 20% of the effect while 20% of something account for 80% of the effect) symbolically represents this condition.

Talent's uniqueness makes it a pleasant surprise; a common talent no longer makes someone talented. Common is expected and rational while uncommon is unexpected and irrational as Figure 4.37 shows. Consequently, talent falls on the side of irrationality. This not only highlights the importance of emotion in talent but also the importance of integrating the feminine influence – the realm of emotions.

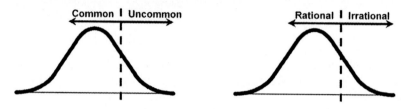

Figure 4.37

Symbolically, we can reinforce this difference between rationality and irrationality in the difference between a square and a circle in Figure 4.38. A closer look at those two shapes will also allow us to integrate the feminine influence too.

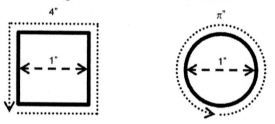

Figure 4.38

As we can see, both shapes are one inch across; however, calculating the perimeter of each we arrive at four inches for the square and something called *pi* (π) inches for the circle which equates to just over three inches. A little math at this juncture will help in the appreciation of how Figure 4.38 ties in with the talent and the feminine influence.

Since a square consists of four equal sides, a square one inch across has its top and bottom sides equal to one inch as well as its left and right sides equal to one inch. Adding the four sides to arrive at the perimeter, we arrive at exactly four inches.

Arriving at the circumference of the circle is a more complex matter and involves using the term *pi* (π) which is a Greek letter used in mathematics to represent the ratio between the circumference of a circle (C) and its diameter (D). *Pi* equals a number slightly greater than three, about 3.14. As a result, by knowing the diameter of any circle you can approximate its circumference by multiplying the diameter by 3.14 (C = D x π). Applying this to our circle with a one inch diameter, we can say its circumference is about 3.14 inches.

The difference between the perimeter of the square and the circumference of the circle upon which I want to focus is represented by the phrases "exactly four inches" and "approximately 3.14 inches." The nature of a square allows us to arrive at a specific number for its perimeter while a circle's nature only allows an approximation. While some may find this insignificant, interestingly this descrepency has intrigued mathematicians for over two thousand years. For our discussion it contains an important symbolic difference that we will refine by first returning to the square.

The square's perimeter is four inches, and we can express four as a simple fraction using whole numbers called *integers* (numbers without decimal points) in many ways such as:

$$\frac{4}{1} \quad \frac{8}{2} \quad \frac{12}{3} \quad \frac{16}{4} \quad \frac{400}{100}$$

While these fractions only appear to state the obvious, their importance lies in that we *can* express the perimeter of our square in this way because we can't do the same with the circumference of our circle. No simple mathematical fraction exists to express π. Consequently, whenever we use it to figure the circumference of any circle that circumference becomes inexpressible as a fraction.

Additionally, if we leave fractions and investigate decimals, π has another interesting attribute: it has infinite decimal places lacking a repeatable pattern. This means the decimal string is inexpressible in a finite way. No one can stop writing this number and say "just constantly repeat this series of decimal places." Using computers people have carried π out to over a *hundred billion* decimal places without detecting a repeatable pattern, and mathematicians have mathematically proven that none exists. Just as an example here is π carried to sixty-three decimal places:

3.14159 26535 89793 23846 26433 83279 50288 41971 69399 37510 58209 74944 592

In terms of our square and circle in Figure 4.38, if we shrunk the square, placed it in the circle as the left diagram shows in Figure 4.39, and proceeded to endlessly add sides in a manner as seen with the rest of the diagrams in Figure 4.39; we would never arrive at a sided-figure that would exactly fit the circle, effectively implying that a circle has an infinite number of sides and that we cannot calculate exactly the circumference of the circle.

Figure 4.39

Additionally, the attribute of not being able to come up with an exact measurement of a circle's circumference applies to any shape that has a curve. The integration of a single curve into a shape makes its perimeter exactly incalculable. Figure 4.40 shows two shapes on the left, a pentagon and hexagon, whose perimeters are calculable exactly and two shapes on the right whose are not.

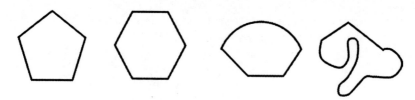

Figure 4.40

This line of thought has practical implications when we examine digital photos. If we magnify them, we'll eventually see their images usually break down into rectangular or square pixels. The apparently smooth curves around images become a jagged collection of squares, so what we see digitally isn't exactly the same as what we see in reality but an approximation. What happens is essentially what we see in Figure 4.39 with the square in the circle except that it uses many small squares. In this way, you can give the appearance of a curve without actually making one by attempting to fill a curve with many small squares as Figure 4.41 shows.

Figure 4.41

Essentially, we're creating a gradient with very small segments as the far right diagram in Figure 4.39 does. As we increase the number of sides in a shape, we move closer to the appearance of a circle. Continuing on with our digital photo we find another gradient-segment relationship in color. While reality has colors move from one to another in a transitory blend, digital photos accomplish this by assigning pixels with a definite color. Consequently, a smooth blend of color like a smooth curve becomes a series of clearly defined segments as we see in Figure 4.42 which is a color segmented counterpart to the shape one in Figure 4.41.

Figure 4.42

In addition to having distinct sides, the pixel also has a distinct color, thus the smooth color gradient we see in reality is represented as a series of distinct, small, segregated color units in the digital image. Symbolically, this also represents the difficulty of applying clearly defined units to a gradient of any kind, physical or colorized, that occurs in reality. We can even relate this to procedural challenges where we try to define specific steps (sides) of a process to address a real-life situation (curve). No matter what we do, our steps will not perfectly fit reality. Something will either be missing or unnecessary requiring a last minute adjustment.

With this background we can begin to apply Figures 4.38 – 4.40 to our rational-irrational discussion by first adding that mathemeticians have names for decimalized numbers expressible as fractions and those inexpressible: *rational* and *irrational* numbers. We can make sense of *ratio*nal numbers through a *ratio,* a fraction, whereas those of which we cannot make sense as a *ratio* are ir*ratio*nal. Therefore, we can symbolically say squares are sensible shapes and circles are unsensible ones.

Moving forward, we can say in a rational world everything is programmable because anything not fitting into some sort of logic would be illogical and therefore irrational. The only reason why something would be unprogrammed is that we hadn't figured out how to do the program. We would not purposely program a computer with bugs; such an act would be irrational. Everything would run normally. We would also know the rationale for everything; uncertainty would not exist. How could a rational world function by leaving things to chance? A person who leaves his life to a dice toss is irrational. Irrationality cannot exist in a rational world. As a result, surprises would not exist because everything would follow a certain logic allowing it to be expected even if we attempted a surprise. Nothing would be uncertain because logic cannot exist without definite parameters. The circumference of a circle would be exact in a rational world.

In an irrational world, everything would not be irrational because then irrationality would become the norm rather than be abnormal. A totally irrational world would become rational, predictably chaotic. We see this in people when they are overwhelmed by constant surprises destabilizing their lives, they suffer shock, emotional and physical. Unconsciousness sets in to numb them until the trauma passes just as boredom sets in a rational world where everything goes as expected. Whether everything goes as expected or goes unexpected, the result is the same: numbness. The difference between the two is whether we're lulled into sleep or blasted into unconsciousness. Thus, an irrational world cannot exist unless there is a rational component to disrupt. We would constantly expect a surprise immediately following our last one. Once we expect something it's no longer a surprise. In an irrational world, the circumference of a circle would not be exact and the perimeter of a square would be.

Essentially, the point of this line of thought is to show we live in an irrational world filled with curves and blends, and thus, the basic nature of talent must also be irrational. Symbolically, using extremely small sides to define a curve represents our efforts to transform natural settings into structural ones, to take curves in reality and represent them through small changes in segments. We take our man-made structures (typically quandratic) and build them in nature (typically curvy).

Life (L) is comprised of the common and uncommon, the rational (R) and irrational (I). Thus,

$$L = R + I$$

Using our square and circle we can use shapes symbolically to represent this by substituting them for the letters as shown in figure 4.43.

Figure 4.43

Talent is the surprise that drives dynamic growth; it's not the norm. Therefore, what determines talent is irrationality as symbolized by the circle's unsensibility, but we are forever trying to apply a rational construct as symbolized by the square's sensibility. While close, it's only an approximation and not an exact replica; however, because of talent's nature approximations give the illusion that everything's okay. We can demonstrate this by altering Figure 4.43 through an integration of Figure 4.37 to show the normalcy of each shape. Essentially, what's rational and majoritive is normal and what's irrational and minoritive is abnormal. The more normal is the condition the larger the shape will appear, and thus we arrive at the representation in Figure 4.44.

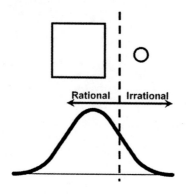

Figure 4.44

The size of each shape now corresponds to its commonness as represented by the area under the curve from Figure 4.37 for each respective portion. In essence, we are viewing life through the simple, objective construct of counting occurences; fifty apples are better than twenty-five apples. However, suppose we alter our construct subjectively so we're more focused on the content of each occurence; one edible apple is better than fifty worm infested apples. Even here we have the subjective construct of what is "better." If we're hungry one edible apple may be better, but if we need compostable material, fifty rotten ones may be better.

This interpretive aspect gives the subjective construct its nebulous nature that juxtaposes the objective one. In essence, the addage "When given lemons, make lemonade" symbolizes the subjective construct because in an objective world one cannot make good from bad unless one allows an interpretive influence to enter the picture. Essentially, "bad" becomes a matter of personal interpretation because it's all in how we look at the facts. Consequently, no idea is "bad" or "good" because it's all a matter of perspective. Such a nebulous condition is counter to objectivity which seeks a decision void of personal influences or interpretations.

In order to more firmly apply a subjective aspect to Figure 4.44, we need to look more deeply at an argument revolving around this statement: while we may not be able to reproduce exactly a curve using segmented sides, we can come close enough that no one will notice the difference. Our focus will be on the "miniscual" difference between our approximation and reality.

We'll begin by first returning to our oak tree and its falling acorns. Rationally we could say the oak wastes a lot of its energy producing acorns that never amount to anything. Why doesn't it focus its energy on the one that will eventually become a full-grown tree? If less than .01% of the acorns dropped result in trees of a substantial size, we could argue effectively that trees don't reproduce. Rationally, we could say this with 99.99% accuracy, but since we live in an irrational world, we know that what matters isn't the 99.99% of the acorns that fail but rather the .01% that succeed.

Let's look at banking. In order for a bank to be successful, 99.5% of the loans it makes must be paid back. That means .5% or fewer of it loans are allowed to default. We could argue that a bank with a 99.5% success rate is really having all its loans paid back.

Isn't 99.5% a close approximation to a 100%? However, what happens in about 1% of a bank's loans affects profitability more than the other 99%.

Imagine a large rug with a wrinkle. That wrinkle in terms of the total area of the rug is extremely small; however, the impact it could have on someone walking across it is potentially far greater than any other part of the rug. We may not even notice the wrinkle until it caused us to trip.

If we look at our daily lives, one hour may comprise only .0001% of it. Rationally, that's not very much. What's the difference between living 700,800 hours or 700,799 hours? We could say both are about eighty years. Suppose though that the hour we eliminated was our wedding ceremony? Suppose we eliminated the conception of a son or daughter? The impact of a moment is independent of its length; some are more valuable than others. Rather than track our lives by minute, suppose we weighted the minutes by how emotionally impactive they were?

Perhaps you've seen maps of the world that alter the geographic size of countries according to various other attributes such as population, energy consumption, or gross domestic product. Now imagine a timeline of your life where each hour is adjusted for the emotional impression it left upon you. The hours you couldn't remember would be non-existent while the ones most important to you would be very large. How many moments of every hour can you remember? Out of the 700,000 hours one might live, how many will you be able to recall? What were you doing exactly at 8:21pm yesterday? Last year? Ten years ago? Twenty? What were you feeling at the time?

Most likely we would have a hard time trying to recall even ten percent of last year let alone our lives. How many hours have slipped from our memory? At best we could state in a general sense what we may have been doing. If we could not recall 99% of the minutes in our lives, could we say we were basically non-existent? We spend a lot of time sleeping. How much do we recall of our dreams? Rationally speaking, what's the difference between 99% and 100%? However, it's the 1% that possessed the dynamic impact required to earn a place in our memory. We do not recall our lives in equally segmented portions of time; we recall it in the form of emotional moments.

Just as news agencies, when they review the week, month, or year, don't focus on routines but rather highlights, our recollection does the same as well. It's the irrational nature of our world that allow highlights to more emotionally impact us than routines even though routine moments far outnumber the distinctive ones. This allows an event that may only comprise .0001% of our entire life to live on within us protected from forgetfulness. Our memories are filled with potent moments not obsure ones.

Even our heartbeat as shown in Figure 2.33 is an uncommon event in the life of our heart. Most of its time is spent in a relatively beatless state. Does this mean life is more about death than life? What gives life its vitality is not what happens in the majority of its moments but rather in the minority. Life depends upon what happens when our heart is not in a beatless state. What drives our lives is the uncommon, irrational moments. What drives a business rests on uniqueness and abnormality – differentiation. Talent's innateness gives it an organic quality that means it lies in irrationality. Talent is to ability as highlights are to our lives. We can alter Figure 4.44 to reflect this tendency. Rather than have shapes relate to normalcy or routineness, let's have them reflect the degree to which they impact us as shown in Figure 4.45.

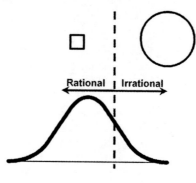

Figure 4.45

We've often praised our cognition for the way it raises us above animals, but now as technology swiftly advances the challenge is in distinguishing ourselves from robots, as simply "cogs in a machine." Standardization, prompting, and routines create the danger of reducing the difference between us and an automaton. In that difference rests an irrationality that allows us to be ourselves – talented.

If we look once again at Figures 2.42 and 2.43 we can link this discussion to the feminine influence. In those figures we linked straight, direct lines to the masculine influence and curvy, indirect lines to the feminine. The rational, direct, definitive aspects of the masculine are best reflected in the square while the irrational, indirect, vague aspects of the feminine are best reflected in the circle.

Our talent discussion and the Wisdom's Magical Hierarchy's emphasis on its irrational basis directly relates to the feminine influence because without the feminine influence, accessing, developing, and growing our talent becomes vastly more challenging. Talent's organicalness gives it an emotional bias, and emotions rest in the domain of the feminine influence as demonstrated by the irrationality of the uncommon.

With this link, we can introduce how the hierarchy shows up in our everyday work life and begin to bridge the feminine influence as a concept with a strategy to employ her.

Application

Wisdom's Magical Hierarchy gives talent an emotional foundation that encourages us to approach its development irrationally; talent's manifestation is a passionate effort not a pragmatic one. The effort entails inspiring the inside person to waken and show what he has to offer, an effort requiring sensitivity and introspection. I'll elaborate first on the pragmatic resistance to this effort, then on its irrational nature, and lastly on its requirements for success. The purpose is to apply the framework we've just reviewed, Wisdom's Magical Hierarchy, in a way that will allow us to detect talent more effectively.

- Resistance: Scientific Method -

If we were to search for whales, we would use a boat; our search's tools and methodology reflect that search. Attempting to find talent through rational means is like using a land rover to find whales, and our predisposition toward a scientific method to enhance our knowledge about talent is exactly analogous to that. Wisdom's Magical Hierarchy helps establish a foundation that highlights the futility of such an approach toward talent.

In its raw form the scientific method utilizes controlled experiments to generate reproducible results regardless of who runs the experiments. From this perspective, the results are objective, independent of who tries to achieve them as long as he follows the conditions of the experiment. These conditions give experiments their "controlled" aspect. A secondary, independent aspect to the scientific method is "peer review" where people in the field relative to the experiment verify and challenge procedures and results. Many times peer review is a formal approval process within a field of study.

While there are many variations of this method and many arguments against the method itself, I do not intend to take us down a path where we'll explore variations and arguments in detail. What is important relative to talent and the feminine influence is the impact this methodology has upon the construct through which we look at our world, a construct that affects our ability to develop talent. For instance, in the judicial system and public policy debates of the United States, this methodology is the primary one by which research is evaluated and determined admissible.

For our purposes, four aspects of the scientific method are important to address from the perspective of the emotional foundation that Wisdom's Magical Hierarchy gives talent and of the encouragement it gives us to develop talent irrationally:

1. Control – Establish the conditions around the experiment.
2. Reproducibility – Produce the same results each time from the same conditions.
3. Objectivity – Achieve same results regardless of who runs the experiment.
4. Validation – Seek consensual verification of results and procedure from others.

To some degree there is agreement that the scientific method does not apply equally to all sciences. For instance, we can broadly divide the sciences into two groups: hard sciences and social sciences. Hard sciences relate to such fields as chemistry, geology, and physics whereas the social sciences relate to such fields as economics, psychology, and sociology. Social sciences differ from humanities in that they attempt to apply to the humanities the scientific method or other defined processes to review evidence. Hard sciences concern themselves more with physical things while the social sciences concern themselves more with humans in a non-physical sense.

With this division comes the expectation that the purer form of the scientific method is much tougher to apply to social sciences than hard sciences. The control, reproducibility, objectivity, and verification are more difficult to achieve when studying humans. Nonetheless, the social sciences do attempt to apply some rigor to findings within their field. In spite of these recognizable difficulties, the scientific method influences our outlook in all endeavors, not just scientific ones. For this reason, it's important from the perspective of talent to see why these aspects of the scientific method falter.

We begin by going back to the basic premise that a relationship is between two individuals as we discussed in Figure 1.4. This premise holds true even if the individual is part of a group; his relationship is with each member of the group and not with the group's entirety because in actuality groups do not exist. A group cannot sign a legal document. It must have an individual, a representative from that group sign. Groups exist conceptually.

By accepting talent's emotional foundation and a relationship's individual duality, we arrive at the point where a relationship is determined by the emotions of the two individuals involved. In a relationship oriented around talent development, the first person is the one whose talent we seek to develop while the second person is the one seeking to develop the first's talents. We require an irrational approach because no two people are the same; thus, the approach will vary according to the two who are involved. Typically, we cognitively accept the common sense of this, but it begins to erode when aspects of the relationship emotionally threaten us. In these cases, the resistors to talent begin to manifest themselves and allow rational ingredients to enter that reduce the effectiveness of the relationship.

The basic premise of an irrational approach is that people are more persuaded by things that they like than things they understand. The implication is that one does not need to understand things to like them or be persuaded by them. Celebrities in commercials are perfect examples; they may have little in common with the product but their likeability persuades us. Our Adam and Eve story at the beginning of this book symbolizes that fact. Furthermore, just because someone understands doesn't mean he likes it. Criticism often falls under this category.

In many ways the irrational approach is no different than the common mantra of "listen to the client"; however, it does differ in the degree to which we throw out and ignore a context through which to view the client. What makes things difficult is that often we do not realize we are viewing another person through a context. For instance, whenever we seek to find the reason behind an emotion, we are using the context of cause and effect, a basic premise for using the scientific method. For every effect (emotion) there is a cause (reason). Irrationality turns this around and says emotions exist behind every reason. Again this is no different than saying the buying decision is an emotional one that is rationalized. While all of this seems to make sense, we often find ourselves in the trap of assuming that if process "A" worked for person "X" then "A" will also work for person "Y". We often call these "best practices."

The irrational approach begins to strain us when it challenges what we like. For instance, in the movie *Bull Durham*, a male baseball pitcher, Ebby Calvin "Nuke" LaLoosh played by Tim Robbins, began to experience success when he began to wear ladies' lingerie underneath his uniform. A rational approach to talent development would declare this absurd because there is no objective, scientific basis for ladies' lingerie helping pitchers throw better. This highlights the difference between an objective and subjective approach. Whereas the objective is concerned with what may be good for everyone, the subjective is only concerned with what is good for a particular person. This is the aspect of the scientific method that encourages reproducible results regardless of who runs the process. Since ladies lingerie probably wouldn't help all or even many baseball pitchers, science would say it doesn't help.

While a humorous fictional example, we can identify similar favoritism for things in our everyday business life. Some people prefer certain clothing when they do something important such as wear a favorite suit or dress for a major presentation. Others have good luck charms of many different varieties. They can include specific music, foods, or procedures. Science calls these superstitions, but we see them frequently in sports with such things as the "rally caps" and "the monkey." It can be as simple as a gift from a child to a parent. Again, all of these things cannot be proved scientifically, but yet, not too many sales managers would prevent a sales person from using a "good luck charm" before a major presentation. When we begin to talk about using an irrational approach to talent development and the potential for resistance to what it may take to apply it, these examples begin to highlight both.

What is generally accepted by all becomes irrelevant when we concern ourselves with a particular person's development. If a person believes in Santa Claus and that belief helps him, who are we to say to him that he must stop believing in Santa Claus? A rational approach would say that Santa Claus does not exist so therefore he cannot help. Herein lies the difference between a rational and irrational approach. A rational approach emphasizes those things that can help many people whereas the irrational approach emphasizes those things that can help a specific person even though many others may have experienced failure with them, or more difficult yet, we may have personally experienced failure with them.

The challenge of an irrational approach is having the understanding and sensitivity necessary to appreciate the emotions that drive a particular person. Discounting an emotion is analogous to the peer review process in which we weigh that emotion against some generally accepted standard set by others. In effect, we take a consensual approach to the validation of a person's feelings, an approach inconsistent with an irrational one where it automatically assumes the validation of that person's feelings as the reality within which we are to work and develop his talent. Our judgment of the practicality or righteousness of that feeling is irrelevant because that feeling is the reality of the inner world of the person before us. Consequently, our focus becomes the feelings of the other person. Discounting or ignoring them will only make our task of developing one's talent more difficult.

Often, when dealing with another's emotions, we become concerned with some external justification for them. We attempt to weigh them against the facts. A dilemma usually occurs when someone's feeling is contrary to what we consider factual. Many times this conflict is inconsequential. For instance, how often does the fact that the earth is round affect our decisions? How would it matter in the directions I give to someone who wanted to know how to get to the nearest gas station? If the earth were flat, how would those directions change? This line of thought also relates to the superstitions we outlined above. If belief in incorrect facts were inherently harmful, why would we encourage children to believe in Santa Claus? The point here is that before we attempt to validate someone's feelings, we need to ask whether such validation is even necessary. Within the realm of someone's inside person, most of the time it isn't.

To an attorney one day I cited the fact that the sun rises every morning. He told me that in a court of law for some cases that would not be a fact because the sun doesn't rise, the earth rotates, thus giving the appearance of the sun rising and falling. We'll also see when we get to conditioning how the construct within which we work can have us operating under facts we know are incorrect but because of the nature of our conversation are inconsequential. For example, we often give gender designations to inanimate objects such as cars.

We also find us making decisions everyday without knowing the basis for the facts we do know. For instance, if I toss something out a window, it will fall to the ground because of gravity; however, the idea that gravity is caused by the curvature of the earth in space never entered the picture. Would knowing that the curvature of the earth affects gravitational pull alter my decision to throw something out a window? In the same way, many objective facts are inconsequential when determining whether a feeling is valid; it doesn't matter how most people would feel in a particular situation because it only matters how the individual before us would feel. Thus, the introductory clause "Most people would . . ." and weighing an individual's feeling against some objective standard are inconsequential in an irrational approach.

Essentially, the irrational approach grants automatic validation of an individual's feelings. The key is making sure these feelings help the person. Even feelings we view as negative can help. For instance, take the common expressional question "Is your glass half full or half empty?" While we often use this to highlight the importance of a positive attitude, by asking the corollary "Who's more likely to get more water?" we find that the person who views his glass as half full is more likely to be complacent about his situation than someone who views it as half empty. All of this is to show that it's not so much the feeling that's consequential but the action. By looking at emotions through this perspective we find it easier to accept someone's feelings because the challenge is not one of changing how he feels but rather one of channeling his energy from the emotion into something positive for him.

For example, someone feeling as though he can fly isn't inherently harmful. What's harmful is when that feeling causes him to test it by running off a cliff. However, if he could channel that feeling into thinking of a way to enable man to fly, then the feeling has helped him. This demonstrates the subordinate role of our cognitive abilities to our emotional ones. Our rational processes become the tool by which we manifest our feelings into actions that will help us in the form of such things as a plane, a hand glider, or a parachute. Any feeling now becomes a powerful ally in the effort to change and grow. Wisdom's Magical Hierarchy manifests this in the subordinate role it assigns to its more rational aspects such as information, knowledge, reason and its rational attributes of logic, learning, tangibility, and addition.

These feelings can also be a source for developing actions to deal with other people. At some point our feelings will result in actions affecting other people. We frequently hear as we go down this path that "perception is reality." As a result, many times our feelings are thwarted or invalidated by what others may think. At this point it's important to carry this statement to its further implications:

- People are different.
- Since people are different their perceptions are different.
- Since their perceptions are different, realities are different.
- Therefore, what is real to one person may not be real to another.
- Therefore, there is a difference between reality and truth.

Truth boils down to what works for the person. It allows him to return to actions that work to implement the feelings he has because they have been successful for him. As Wisdom's Magical Hierarchy illustrates, talent at the highest levels contains an intuitive and creative aspect rooted in emotion – inspiration. The truth is that anyone is entitled to feel what they want to feel. The key is realizing that if we permit the validation of someone's emotions by the outside world we surrender that person to schizophrenic judgment; such judgment makes anything difficult not just talent development. We will further explore the connection between feelings and actions under the Methodology heading coming up shortly.

Returning to the scientific method and looking at it from this individualistic perspective, we find the aspects of control, reproducibility, objectivity, and validation are contrary to the nature of talent and thus inadequate for its development. Whereas the scientific method seeks to replicate outcomes through the repetition of controls and methods, talent's development seeks to generate a rare, if not unique, outcome. If the purpose of talent's development were to replicate the same talent in everyone, then talent's uniqueness or abnormality would be eradicated. In the aftermath the question would be whether we really achieved talent's development or just merely the successful establishment of a routine. A method by which anyone can establish the same conditions and follow the same procedures to yield the same results is counterintuitive to a venture requiring the exploration and expression of something unique to each person.

- Nature: Violinist's Dilemma -

Yet, the problem that confronts us is that unless we can validate talent via a disciplined review such as the scientific method presents, its aspects do not enter a collection of information called knowledge. Furthermore, unless such aspects are validated from a collective perspective, that is applicable to everyone, they are declared inadmissible.

For instance, imagine a violinist playing a piece of music without an audience. Unless someone hears her play, there is no proof that she did. Suppose as well that the piece is very difficult, so there is doubt whether one could play it thereby adding a qualitative aspect to the scenario. Now we have two questions: first, "Did she play it?" and second "Did she play it correctly?" At this point the scenario has no controls because we did not create conditions by which we could determine whether the violinist played the music. We also did not create conditions whereby we could reproduce the event in the form of a recording so people could replay it for proof. We also did not make arrangements to have the violinist play the piece more than once. From an objective perspective, no one but the violinist herself heard her play. We did not establish a way for others to see that the violinist could play the piece. Finally, we did not have a group verify that the violinist played the piece well by making sure all the aspects surrounding the definitions of "playing" were met.

The question surrounding this scenario is an offshoot of the more common one, "If no one hears a tree fall in the forest, does it make a sound?": If a violinist plays a piece of music and no one hears her, did she play? Scientifically, we could not prove she played the challenging piece unless we established the conditions necessary to have her play the piece again before qualified witnesses. On the other hand, before her audition, suppose our violinist suffered permanent injury to her hands in an automobile accident rendering her incapable of playing the violin; so, we are now unable to replicate the event. Did our violinist play the challenging piece?

We now have an interesting paradox because while the violinist could testify in a United States' court that she played the piece and have it admissible as evidence, she cannot have it admissible as such in the "court of science." The paradox is this: while United States' courts assume someone is innocent until proven guilty, the court of science assumes the reverse – guilty until proven innocent. Unless the violinist can prove she played the piece, her playing cannot be entered into the general body of knowledge as a bona fide fact. Without objective validation, validation by another party other than the violinist, her playing is not a fact but simply something she believes occurred. We've arrived indirectly at the common phrase "seeing is believing." Unless someone else sees, hears, touches, tastes, or smells something, its validation becomes very difficult.

Let's connect this to our scenario further by giving the violinist her hands back and having her play before a group of deaf people. They can see the violinist play but can't hear her, so they can't validate the violinist's playing because for all they know she simply went through the motions. If no one had the capacity to hear the violinist play, did she play the piece?

Continuing, let's add another twist: all the people can hear, but they determined she did not play the piece correctly and thus failed to prove her skill. From the violinist's standpoint, the difference between how she played the piece and how others expected her to play it was an interpretive one; she essentially supplied a new, creative interpretation of the piece. The paradox here rests with talent's uniqueness that often is mistaken for abnormality. In order to prove her talent, she had to play a piece exactly the way everyone else had done. Analogously, this is the same as a scientist who needs to adhere to the scientific method in attempting to prove something new. From this standpoint, the mentality behind the scientific method encourages talent to conform to normality in order to prove it's different. Rewording our paradox we find creative answers are often wrong answers because they differ from expectations, deviations from the norm.

Method affects outcome even if the ingredients remain the same. Water when boiled becomes steam, when frozen becomes ice. Illustratively, the scientific method says that in order to produce knowledge one can only do it by freezing. Moving onto more complicated examples, many recipes use exactly the same ingredients but their outcomes change because of a different method, even something as simple as altering the order in which they are added alters the food. For instance, consider two brioche recipes (brioche is a buttery type of breakfast bread) where all eleven ingredients are the same and in the same proportions. By changing the order in which the ingredients are cooked, one recipe makes a denser, richer buttery flavor while the other makes a lighter, flakier one. The way we "cook" life's evidence alters the flavor it gives us.

Let's apply this to a political scenario by considering four candidates and ten voters where each voter allocates ten points among the four candidates to indicate the degree to which they like the candidates. A voter who allocates all ten points to one candidate really likes that particular candidate and doesn't much care about the others. Another voter who allocates three points to three candidates and only one to another is saying he likes three pretty much equally and one a little less. Using this scoring method, we come up with the following table (Fig. 4.46):

Voter	Candidate			
	A	B	C	D
1	4	3	2	1
2	0	7	1	2
3	4	3	1	2
4	0	6	3	1
5	4	2	1	3
6	4	3	1	2
7	1	2	4	3
8	1	2	4	3
9	1	2	3	4
10	1	3	4	2

Figure 4.46

If we take voter #1 as an example, we find he gave four points to candidate "A", three to "B", two to "C", and one to "D". We can read this as candidate "A" being his favorite candidate and "D" his least favorite. Compare this to voters #2 and #4 who could also arrange their favorites in the same fashion but their scores indicate a much higher preference for candidate "B".

Figure 4.46 relates to our discussion because the method we choose to elect one candidate will determine who is elected. We'll consider three:

- Most votes.
- Runoff to secure majority.
- Preferential voting.

In the most vote scenario, each voter will cast *one* vote for his favorite candidate. Thus, voter #1 will cast his vote for candidate "A" while voter #2 will cast it for "B." Looking at Figure 4.46 we get the following results:

- Candidate "A" receives 4 votes.
- Candidate "C" receives 3 votes.
- Candidate "B" receives 2 votes.
- Candidate "D" receives 1 vote.

Using the "most votes" method candidate "A" wins the election; however, if we now include a runoff between the top two vote gatherers, "A" and "C", where anyone voting for "B" or "D" in the initial round now votes for his second favorite candidate, we now see these results in the runoff:

- Candidate "C" receives 6 votes.
- Candidate "A" receives 4 votes.

Using the "runoff" method, "C" wins the election. Neither method considers the *degree* to which the candidates moved individual voters. "Preferential voting" is a way to address this. We see this sometimes in shareholder's votes where stockholders cast votes equal to the number of shares they own. As a result, it's possible for voters to split their votes according to their preferences for different candidates or issues. In Figure 4.46 the "preferential vote" gives each of our ten voters ten shares to cast in relationship to the degree that they prefer each of the candidates. In our example, they cast them in exactly the same proportion as they allocated the original ten points we gave them to generate the table. As a result, voter #9 would cast one vote for candidate "A", two for "B", three for "C", and four for "D". When we add up all the votes we find that voters' #2 and #4 heavy preference for candidate "B" weighs heavily in the outcome:

- Candidate "B" receives 33 votes.
- Candidate "C" receives 24 votes.
- Candidate "D" receives 23 votes.
- Candidate "A" receives 20 votes.

The "preferential" method produces yet a third different winner for this election. Furthermore, this method has "A" as the least favorite candidate even though he won using the first method, "most votes." The purpose of these examples is to show how methodology affects outcomes, and consequently, how we look at things. Similarly, the scientific method affects our outlook towards life because it is an established methodology for accepting new knowledge into existing knowledge.

We can experience a more practical example with deliberative bodies that follow particular "rules of order." Any member of such a body appreciates these rules which guide the processes by which these bodies make decisions. Understanding the nature of these rules allows the user to affect outcomes in the way he desires. The way these rules are used affects the path or method by which these bodies arrive at decisions. As anybody who has participated in intense debates under these conditions can attest, the path you take to arrive at a decision will alter that decision without changing the conditions that originally brought the need for a decision to the table.

Our expectation that proof must exist before anything is validated alters the way we look at our lives. For instance, consider the difference between these two statements:

- Things do not exist until proven that they do.
- Things exist until proven that they don't.

For these statements let's assume we use the scientific method to prove what needs to be proven for each. If we return to our violinist, the first statement implies that the burden is upon her to prove that she played the piece while the second implies that the burden is upon us to prove that she did not.

We've discussed the implications of the first statement, so we'll focus our attention on the second. The major implication is that unless we can prove the violinist did not see or hear herself play, it's impossible for us to prove she did not because at least one person, the violinist herself, saw and heard her play the piece. More significantly, we must prove that no evidence exists that says the violinist played. The key becomes when we ask, "How do we know we looked everywhere?" Can we prove we did?

This last point takes on significance when we consider that thousands of years ago many galaxies were unknown because we did not have the technology to discover them. How do we know something is non-existent rather than having its non-existence be the result of some inability on our part to detect it? We may not be able to detect something because we don't have the tools to do so. If we don't have the tools to prove it exists, does that mean it doesn't? Did radiation suddenly appear when we were able to detect it, or did it exist all along?

If we search for whales in a land rover, we are unlikely to find any whales. If we look for rational proof of talent's existence in an individual, we are likely to overlook it. There is no challenge in detecting talent once it is apparent to all. The challenge is in uncovering talent where others see nothing. Analogously, the challenge is not in declaring a successful business a good business. The challenge is in taking a business that everyone feels is unsuccessful and making it a success – *that* is talent. Figures 2.1 – 2.17 develop the relationship between intuition and cognition. We'll focus our discussion on Figure 2.14 by modifying it to reflect irrational and rational approaches as shown in Figure 4.47.

Talent's Journey

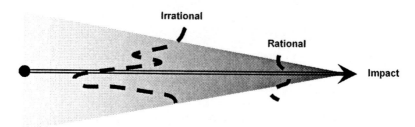

Figure 4.47

A rational, scientific approach to talent wastes opportunities by increasing the chances we'll overlook them because we don't accept them as proven. Talent's nature and the resistance to it make talent's journey one that is far from a foregone conclusion and one that we can influence early on. Our influence early on will best be accomplished through an irrational approach. In this way, talent is an amphibian whose life begins in water and moves to maturation on land. The evolution of life reflects a similar movement, beginning in the hidden depths of water and moving to the visible surface of land. Many acorns falter as seedlings; however, with our nurturing more can survive and develop. Talent is the same way.

Wisdom's Magical Hierarchy helps us in this effort by establishing an irrational framework by which we can search for talent rather than simply relying upon the more inaccurate determinant of results and other tangible means. As we saw through the development of Figures 2.1 – 2.17, intuition permits an earlier awareness than cognition. If we take this concept and combine it with the inside-outside duality that Figure 4.18 expresses we can look at talent's journey from another perspective as shown in Figure 4.48.

Talent's Journey II

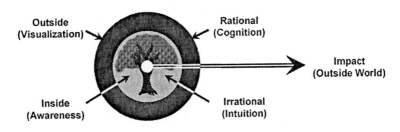

Figure 4.48

The conception of any living thing begins in small areas invisible to us. Talent's vitality follows a similar growth. Just as a tree begins inside an acorn and a child inside a mother's womb, talent's manifesto originates with the inside person. Consequently, talent is based upon the nature of the inside world of the individual before us not upon the nature we believe each individual ought to have, the difference between innate and learned. A person's inner realm, which holds the key to his talent, is subjectively based upon the nature of his individual reality. From the perspective of developing his talent, the nature of his reality determines how that is to be done – not some collective interpretation on what his reality ought to be like. Consequently, what he feels exists in his world contains the determinants with which we work. We do not grow or build anything with what we ought to have but rather with what we actually have. Since emotions access talent, our initial work occurs in an irrational world. If we confine and restrict ourselves to what rationale says should be there or what some methodology proves, we will likely miss many vital opportunities. Essentially, we arrive at this statement:

We have the potential to develop talent in anyone until proven otherwise.

The violinist's dilemma illustrates how we need to first escape the confines of a scientific context dominating our business world and to some degree our lives. We cannot approach something irrationally while chained down by rationalities. Returning to the feminine influence, we find "Lady Liberty" symbolic of this challenge, again a woman represents freedom. In talent's development, freedom translates into the ability to freely look at someone's inner world unencumbered by outside notions, ideas, logic, constructs, or pressure.

If no one hears a violinist play, did she play? If a woman feels beautiful but no one feels she is, is she still? In this question we return to the force of beauty behind the feminine influence. Beauty like talent stands out from the pack. If we can call someone talented who creates a successful business from one where everyone else sees nothing but disaster, talent can exist in those who see beauty where others see ugliness. Talent comes from seeing what others cannot and bringing it forth. It's always easier to say something does not exist than to say we cannot see. In this way we avoid acknowledging someone's ability to see and we avoid taking action where we may fail. There is no need to act on that which we can claim does not exist.

The more we confine our interpretations to perspectives predetermined by others, the more we are likely to miss something in the individual. We are taking the complexity of many and reducing it to a few, a journey symbolized by our drive to place individuals into groups. The more we attempt to impose the construct of the group upon the individual the more likely we are to overlook aspects unique to the individual. Groups, by definition, group things according to some commonality. Talent is found in the uncommon, in the unique. Consequently, talent will be overlooked if evaluated against some objective norm for a particular group rather than against the subjective nature of the individual in front of you. By searching for what is rare we also find what is unique and move closer to touching talent.

If we look at the specific commonalities in a group as the sides of a shape, Figure 4.39 becomes a symbolic representation of trying to match a particular group with an individual where the circle represents the individual. A square becomes a group with four commonalities, a pentagon one with five, an octagon one with eight. As we increase the commonalities within a group we move closer to the individual, but as the discussion around Figure 4.39 indicated no matter how many "sides" a group may have it will never exactly describe the circle of a particular individual.

Figure 4.49

We can also look at this illustration of fitting a multi-sided figure into a circle as the difference between what we know of someone and who he is. Just as "who we are" differs much from "who we think we are," "who someone is" differs much from "who we think he is." If each side in Figure 4.49 represents some aspect of the person we know, no matter how many "sides of a person" we may know we'll never be able to exactly define who that person is. We symbolically think of the various aspects of ourselves and others as sides as illustrated by the clichés "take a picture of my best side" and "I saw a different side of him today."

More significantly, no matter how small this difference may appear, the potential exists for dynamism because talent resides in this small difference. Common exists in what is numerous and uncommon exists in what is rare; talent is uncommon and thus resides with the few. The common is greater than the uncommon but far less dynamic as illustrated and discussed around Figures 4.44 and 4.45 and restated in Figure 4.50.

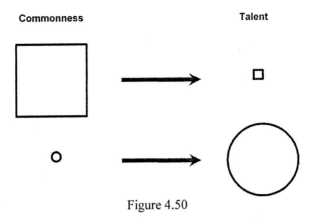

Figure 4.50

Wisdom's Magical Hierarchy supports the innate, intangible, emotional, and synergistic attributes of talent by altering the context with which we look at it from a rational one to an irrational one. It gives us a tool by which to view aspects of wisdom hierarchically by giving preference to those aspects that distinguish us the best from robots or automatons and other people because it is in those differences that talent resides.

- Requirements: Four Aspects -

The hierarchy also gives us the ability to surmise certain requirements for talent that a rational construct does not. Since talent originates from our inside world, a rational construct limits us too much by working only with what we can prove or what is professionally accepted and excluding what fails these criteria. The scientific method only works with those aspects of our world that are accepted by that method. How do we address those aspects of our world that exist but cannot be proven? For instance, love and beauty exist but how do we prove using scientific methods when they vary tremendously by individual?

As a result, the requirements for love and beauty vary too greatly for a rational method based upon control, reproducibility, objectivity, and validation. Talent is no different and thus for an irrational approach there are some requirements before we can proceed. In this portion of the Application heading I'll run through four:

- Sensitivity
- Expressivity
- Growth
- Microtonality

The innate-learned attributive pairing from Wisdom's Magical Hierarchy becomes important when we look at these requirements. The basic theme with this pairing is that what is innate is dominant over what is learned; the forces of nature override those of man. Nature does not abide by man's laws. Learning becomes a tool by which one develops his talents but not necessarily creates his talents. As a result, our talent and what we've learned combine to determine what we can do. When looking at talent, the challenge becomes in differentiating between what is learned from talent.

For instance, someone may accomplish a lot because he has learned much while another who hasn't done hasn't developed his talent at all. Wisdom's Magical Hierarchy helps us here because it hierarchically arranges wisdom's aspects. Some things are easier to learn than others. Memorizing data is much easier than associating them into a body of knowledge or reasoning with them. How we associate information is also more easily learned compared to reasoning. What's harder to learn is how to apply knowledge or information to the broader picture outside of that field or how we can use it to develop new ideas or methods. In general, the easier it is for us to put something in a computer, the less difficult it is to learn. Humans excel over computers in more intuitive problem solving situations where a lot of data is sketchy or missing. Knowing information is far secondary to applying it.

Most of the time it's very hard to distinguish between the two because just as someone could read to learn a new piece of information he can also read to learn a new application of information. Nevertheless, the real test becomes the application of a learned concept to the reality of the situation at hand because no pre-packaged application fits perfectly, so the other aspects of wisdom, experience, conception, intuition, and creativity will come into play. A higher understanding and appreciation for the application will come into play and most likely generate a new application itself that is an offshoot of the other. The reasoning behind this is that no two situations are exactly alike because life never produces two things exactly alike, so whatever application we use to apply to one situation it will have to be altered to apply to the next.

In these situations, talent will begin to differentiate itself from the learned because the variations reality can present are far more extensive than whatever could be on paper in the book, article, or guide. This is a follow up to our discussions around Figures 2.36 – 2.41 and to some degree around Figure 4.12; what we think will happen always falls short of what actually happens. The emotional-logical attributive pairing comes in here because having a feel for the situation either from past experience or through intuition will determine the effectiveness of application in reality.

As we discussed in Figure 4.30 regarding the robotic and human competition, what makes us different from a robot are our emotions. Our emotions are derived from nature and not programmed into us by other humans or learning. From birth we have basic feelings that make one infant different from another. Consequently, it's hard to develop talent without sensitivity, our first requirement.

Emotions make us different from robots, the feelings that go beyond mere sensation of see, hear, touch, smell, and taste to the ones of happiness, sadness, anger, love, and many others. Talent's vitality gives it an organic quality that distinguishes it from what man can produce. Sensitivity becomes an important attribute because one cannot empathize, introspect, and intuit without it. It's hard to gain a feel for something if one does not have sensitivity. Since our inner worlds are inaccessible to our senses, it's only explorable through our feelings.

In this respect, sensitivity is an intelligence indicator differing from the more easily measurable indicator of cognition. As we saw with the dictionary example, there is a difference among possessing a dictionary, using the words in a dictionary, and expressing oneself through those words. Intuition helps us understand the role of sensitivity as an intelligence indicator that eventually helps us with talent identification and development. Without sensitivity to others, talent identification and development are less likely and in some cases impossible.

The basis for this relationship is seen in our technological advances. As we know with science, the detection of small changes in things such as distance, temperature, weight, movement, brightness, and thickness require the use of highly sensitive machines and computers without which we could not develop more advanced technology. Computers use highly refined components that often require magnification to make and assemble them. They are themselves sensitive to various factors such as heat and water.

For instance, I once entered a hardware store that still used a heavy metal scale made in the early 1900's to measure the weight of nails, screws, bolts, and other small items for bulk sale. The employee, who was the owner's brother, saw me admiring it and told me that it was more reliable than computerized scales. When I asked whether computerized ones were more accurate, he responded that they were but they were also more sensitive to external factors such as electricity, physical impact, and magnetism that are hard to control in a hardware store. These factors tended to cause computerized scales to give distorted readings. Still, the ability to make refined, sensitive equipment is a sign of technological advancement.

A recent event in my dental history shows the importance sensitivity plays in using equipment and tools. I had calculus buildup below my gum lines that required special cleaning. The dental specialist used two primary instruments to accomplish this. The first one was called the "explorer" and allowed her to search for the calculus by rubbing it along my teeth below the gum line. The second one was the "gracey curette" and allowed her to remove calculus. The explorer was flexible, thin, and curvy while the gracey curette was stiff, thick, and straighter. By moving the explorer beneath my gum lines the dental specialist could fee the difference between my teeth and calculus through the vibrations that the sensitive tool emitted. Once she determined the calculus' location, she switched to the gracey curette to dig it out. The explorer is too nimble and thin to remove calculus, but the gracey curette was too thick and stiff to allow for good exploration.

We could look at it as the difference between using a needle on an old style record player versus a one pound chisel. The needle is more sensitive to the vibrations that the ridges and crevices imprinted on the vinyl create. Without the sensitivity of the explorer, the application of the force through the strength of the gracey curette could have resulted in the chipping or removal of teeth as well as calculus. An act my mouth would have determined as barbaric.

The use of sensitivity allows a more intelligent application of force; thus, the existence of sensitivity is an intelligence indicator just as the existence of sensitive tools such as needles and computers indicate technological advancement. While a cave man produced a rough hammer, the ability to make a needle was non-existent; yet, a hammer is much stronger than a needle. We saw sensitivity applied in our military analogies where reconnaissance used smaller, less powerful forces to gather intelligence so commanders could more intelligently apply their stronger, more powerful forces. Without this sensitivity, force is more likely to approach a barbaric act similar to killing a fly on a window with a sledge hammer versus a fly swatter. The sledge hammer is a more forceful display of power, but the fly swatter is more sensitive to the window.

Sensitivity is shown in many ways. We see it displayed in relationships with other people and with animals. We can also see it in things, the way they are used and discarded. Often the best way to gain insight into another's sensitivity is how he deals with others. Sometimes it's hard to gauge this strictly by how he treats you. The emphasis here is more on process than outcome. Sometimes bad experiences with others are unavoidable, but how someone deals with them says a lot. There is also difficulty in segregating the material aspects of a relationship with the emotional ones. Relationships can contain extensive materialistic exchanges with little sincerity behind them. Business relationships, with their frequent monetary exchanges, have the potential to give the illusion of more sincerity than they do. Usually, these illusions don't become apparent until tough times challenge them.

Generally, the counterattack to sensitivity is that someone is "soft" or unable to "crack the whip." This takes the negativity of sensitivity to an extreme because in its extreme form empathy becomes the inability to harm someone because of the immense pain you'll feel by doing so. Empathy is feeling what the other person is feeling, so any hardship he faces you will as well.

The point here is not so much whether sensitivity is right or wrong for a particular situation but rather it's more representative of talent than insensitivity. In an anarchistic world, killing your enemies is much easier than trying to work with them; war is less challenging than peace. Something more is required for the later than just the good weapon and tactics required by the first. Since nature gives us our emotions, our sensitivity varies by individual; some of us are more sensitive than others. This sensitivity allows you to relate to others better than others can. In general, women are more sensitive because nature equips them to empathize with children who cannot communicate their needs directly very well. Consequently, there must be another way to detect the needs of others.

The second requirement, expressivity, is also emotionally based and thus innate as well. We came across this as a nature of talent and indirectly as part of need, emotional recognition. Talent will seek to express itself and when thwarted will come out in different ways. Rarely, will it rest dormant unless its time is not right. Almost anything that makes someone stand out can be a form of expressivity; however, it doesn't have to be apparent to everyone. Many times it can be something very small in the form of a peculiar habit. The main attribute of expressivity is that it allows us to differentiate one from another.

With expressivity there are two important comments. First, results alone don't constitute expressivity but how one goes about influencing those results is. As we saw with Figure 4.33 and to some degree in the Company chapter, results are a poor indicator of talent because many other intangible factors influence them. As the graph in Figure 4.35 shows, as the influence of outside factors increases the influential difference between a talented person and an untalented one diminishes. Thus, if we're too heavily focused upon results, we can easily overlook and mistake talent.

The second important comment about expressivity is the negative form it can take. Sometimes the inability to express one's talent comes out in negative ways. The point here is that expressivity itself is important regardless of its positive or negative nature. Relating this back to our exploding gasoline, depending upon how it's used it can either power a car or blow up a structure. Talent is the same way; how it's used is different from its existence. Furthermore, the application of a positive or negative label is often an interpretive one, so what may be negative may have positive aspects we don't see.

At such times, it may initially be to our advantage not to react to the apparent negativity in a negative fashion. Figure 2.33 regarding the heartbeat and Figure 4.31 concerning positive and negative expressivity help illustrate this requirement. Negative expressivity is better than no expressivity; a heartbeat of any kind is better than no heartbeat at all. In business situations we often see this distinction manifest itself in those who are willing to put ideas out on the table and those who wait for the ideas to come out.

A third, common requirement for talent's development is growth. Wisdom's Magical Hierarchy displays this in its synergistic-additive attribute. Regardless of how we look at it, talent yields something positive. The concept behind this is that it's usually far more difficult to grow something than to cut it. Growing a plant is far more difficult than cutting it down. Building with blocks is far harder than knocking them down. Arguments are the same way. It's far easier to display expertise through criticism than through improvements. We can express this as another duality: creators versus cutters. In business, we see this duality expressed as revenues versus expenses. Cutting expenses is generally easier than growing revenues.

Using this description we can correlate talent to various types of arguments regarding an idea and hierarchically arrange them as follows:

1. Creates a new idea altogether.
2. Enhances the idea.
3. Applies it to another situation.
4. Criticizes it.

At the bottom we have outright criticism of an idea. Usually, it doesn't take much talent to criticize something because everything has a downside. Conceptually, this relates to the picture that growing a plant is more difficult than cutting one down. Often these arguments appear in the form of "too something" (too slow, too much, too costly, etc.) without specifically saying concretely what could be done to improve it. Generally, there will be a close correlation between those who criticize an idea and those who are unable to present a comprehensive one themselves. The common retort "If you don't like it, come up with something yourself" often fits in these situations. There is a natural inclination to feel left out when someone else presents an idea, so there is usually a need to make sure one's imprint is left on it.

A more complex natural tendency is to evaluate our value relative to others. With this perspective we enhance our value either by excelling others or by devaluing them. The presentation of a new idea is automatically a threat to others not only because it may alter the status quo as we discussed earlier but it's automatically a sign of value for the presenter. This is irrespective of the idea itself because the effort alone designates a capability that while not producing something of value now has the potential to do so later. No one can present a good idea if they are incapable of presenting any idea in the first place.

Moving up from criticism we see various levels of enhancements to the current idea that represent some form of growth or expansion of it. We have initially the application of that idea to another situation. Here, this is more of routine, duplicative application to another situation with few modifications. At least this is indicative of being able to see the inherent value of the idea and is better than an outright criticism. Above this we have the modifications that enhance the idea for the situation at hand, and finally at top, the creation of a new idea all together. For these last two, the original idea served as inspiration for enhancements and totally new perspectives.

In some ways growth relates to expressivity in that there are those who express their expertise by throwing ideas out on the table and those who wait for ideas to criticize. While everyone engages in all four to some degree, people will display tendencies for some over others. Often the counterattack to growth is that one is making something too complex, but the emphasis has to remain on effectiveness as shown in Figure 2.67. People are more inclined to criticize something as too complex than to admit inadequacies in their understanding. One can always make an idea simpler but at some point effectiveness suffers. Ultimately, simplicity carried to extreme results in nothing.

The last common requirement for talent's development is something I'm calling microtonality. Definitionally, microtonality applies to music but here I'm using it analogously to mean looking at the music of things more closely. In business, we often use the term "addition to details," but microtonality implies detail while maintaining awareness for the music as a whole. The concept is one of looking at the smaller bits to gain a better appreciation for the whole.

If we refer back to our most recent discussion around the nature of the effort to develop talent and Figure 4.49 where "who we think someone is" differs greatly from "who he is", our emphasis was on the small differences that differential us from others. Talent resides in the uncommon and the uncommon is smaller than the common, thus in the development of talent attention to the small things in life becomes important because they contain dynamic outcomes.

Illustratively, we can refer to nuclear power. Compared to other sources of energy the quantity necessary to generate the same energy is far smaller. Similarly, if we look at the whole vastness of our solar system, the amount that actually contains life is miniscule, almost non-existent. That's why the search and development of talent goes not to the one who can paint life in broad brushstrokes but the one who can do so patiently with small intricate ones while still capturing the essence of the whole.

Since many of the hints that talent gives us as to its existent are extremely small, we must be able to emotionally differentiate fine differences. Many times the difference between the applications of two opposing concepts is a razor's edge, so one must have the capacity to see that edge while not forgetting the whole. As the sides in Figure 4.49 increase, a keener eye will become necessary to differentiate the shape from a circle because in that difference rests uniqueness and in that uniqueness will be talent; talent rests with what makes us uncommon not with what makes us common.

Microtonality in music seeks to divide an octave of music into smaller parts. Western music tends to divide it into twelve while more divisions tend to exist in non-Western music. Symbolically, microtonality implies that the search and development of talent will require a closer look at smaller differentiating factors than we're accustomed. Talent won't be found with help from broad generalities but from the differentiation inherent in specifics. The intangible-tangible attributive pair of Wisdom's Magical Hierarchy emphasizes this requirement because such a differentiation may initially appear invisible, untouchable, to us. It's easier for us to measure the amount of information someone can recall than it is to measure one's intuitive abilities. Our differences may be too small to measure, too intangible.

Conclusion

Under "Framework" we covered Wisdom's Magical Hierarchy as a model through which to view an irrational approach to talent's development. We followed this with a more thorough examination of the irrational emphasis behind it. We also conveyed the dominance of it because of the innate qualities behind our feelings versus the more learned aspects of our cognitive abilities. Finally, we ran through the connection of this framework to business by explaining the dominance of a rational construct, its limitations when applied to talent, and four important attributes critical to effectively developing talent.

The discussion around framework basically concludes our direct discussion of talent although we will indirectly return to it throughout the remainder of the book. What we'll attempt to do next is return to a more general look at talent now that we've covered this background. The main point in terms of this book is that talent has an emotional foundation that makes it open to and receptive to the feminine influence, more so than with the masculine influence.

Emotions not only reside within the realm of the feminine but they are more sensitive to insensitive attacks and criticisms. Directness and simplicity tend to disregard the finer points of another's emotions and increase the likelihood of insensitivity. This highlights the weakness of emotions – they can be hurt. Robots and computers can't be hurt emotionally. Consequently, an effective strategy to damage one's ability to develop his talents will be to emotionally hurt him.

Outside of the feminine's advantage with emotions, the masculine influence also tends to be less effective in developing talent because of its inclination toward the application of a rational construct, such as the scientific method, toward problem resolution and opportunity maximization. With talent's emotional foundation, a more emotional, irrational, subjective approach will work better than an unemotional, rational, objective one.

Access

Thus far, we have talked about talent's definition, nature, resistors, and framework. Another aspect of talent that will help us understand and appreciate it is the effort it takes to access it. While we can define this as a process, we are better off to visualize this as phases. Under this heading we'll develop a visual of the effort.

Before we move on, here are the two most important factors to remember about talent:

- Emotional foundation
- Resistance

Talent is closely associated with our emotions; it might even be an emotion itself. Often, we identify talent as a passion for something. Nevertheless, resistance to talent exists within ourselves and in the world around us. Both the emotions and resistance around talent represent a natural state. Any baby would likely die without a mother to initialize its development; there are natural resistors in the world to a child's development that the mother must overcome.

Keeping these two factors in mind, we can begin to think of talent's development similar to the search for oil. Essentially, there are four phases to oil's journey from deep within the ground to use on the surface. First, we must find where it might be. Second, once we find it we must extract it. Third, after extracting it, we refine it. Fourth, after refining it, we make use of it.

This oil analogy is a suitable beginning for five reasons:

- Oil's not easily found by merely looking at the surface; you need to look deeper.
- Bringing oil to the surface is not easy; effort and time are involved because natural resistors such as the earth are involved.
- While we may be successful in bringing oil to the surface, its form is crude and requires refining.
- Once we've made oil useable, there is the question of how best to use it which the markets through pricing decide.
- We find resistance to this entire process from many sources such as other energy providers, environmentalists, alternative energy developers, and public policy advocates.

We can enhance the analogy to suit an emotional, subjective purpose by referencing it as a magical liquid that takes on different characteristics each time we work with it. Whereas oil is very similar no matter where you find it, talent is far more diverse. For this reason, the term magical allows us to keep in mind the many manifestations it can take that we've yet to see.

There are four phases in the realization of talent:
1. Exploration
2. Recovery
3. Development
4. Appreciation

Exploration involves the search for talent. We've discussed this preliminarily when we discussed four requirements for talent's development recently above: sensitivity, expressivity, growth, and microtonality. Once we've discovered it there is the task of recovery whereby we bring it to the surface. This will involve making the person and others aware of the talent as well as encouraging its initial manifestations that will eventually lead into the next phase of development. In development, we begin to refine what we've recovered to see what its real state may be. This is where we begin to integrate our talent with our external world. As integration proceeds we begin to find an appreciation for that talent by others. They begin to find out how our talent helps them.

To help our visualization we can assign colors to each phase:

1. Exploration = Blue
2. Recovery = Yellow
3. Development = Green
4. Appreciation = Red

Blue represents the expansiveness of the skies, space, and the heavens. With talent it's important to have a dispersed perspective so as to more effectively reconnoiter for talent. We can represent this effort as the first or third diagram in Figure 4.8. Additionally, blue represents truth and existence. We're trying to find the truth about ourselves and others. Relaying it back to our oak tree analogy, it's the finding of the acorn in the ground.

Yellow represents the caution we take in recovering talent. Often those who have it don't know it, or those around the person don't believe it. Regardless, there is delicacy in negotiating this resistance. As mentioned earlier, with talent comes responsibility. Some of the things we've tolerated because they were out of our control may now become possible; however, this requires effort and the overcoming of challenges. It's the sprouting of a seedling easily damageable by anything.

Green represents the growth that occurs from developing one's talent. Acceptance of the talent has taken hold within the person and becomes a matter of refining it to see the various forms it will take. External resistance to one's talent still comes into play but internal resistance, while never gone, is realized, acknowledged, and manageable. It's the oak beginning to grow and sprouting many branches.

Red represents the emotion behind the appreciation that the person and others have for his talent. We begin to see the talent mature into various uses that make our world better and inspire others. It's the oak that is suddenly big enough to provide shade for all and to grow its own acorns in an effort to continue the regenerative process

Returning to our magical liquid metaphor, we find it lying deep within us, fueling the fire inside. Bubbling up it desires to express itself but it's restrained because we're taught that it's a bad feeling, it's a feeling that makes us feel strange, weird, different, and odd. It's the feeling that causes us to be unique and seek out our place in the world. Of course, this can be a problem for many others because seeking our place may mean taking the space another covets. They may not want us to do that and prefer that we remain in the place they've designed for us, to be like everyone else. In this way, they can bring safety and security to the world. Consider the song, "The Trees", by the rock group *Rush*.

In this song there is unrest in the forest because the maple trees want more sunlight and the taller oaks are ignoring their pleas to allow in more light. The following stanza from the song shows the inherent conflict between the views:

The trouble with the Maples
(And they're quite convinced they're right)
They say the Oaks are just too lofty
And they grab up all the light
But the Oaks can't help their feelings
If they like the way they're made
And they wonder why the Maples
Can't be happy in their shade?

From the maples' perspective this is oppression while from the oaks' this is freedom. Consequently, we have the maples ganging up on the oaks to equalize things:

So the Maples formed a Union
And demanded equal rights
'The Oaks are just too greedy
We will make them give us light'
Now there's no more Oak oppression
For they passed a noble law
And the trees are all kept equal
By hatchet,
Axe,
And saw ...

Thus, the challenge is to first of all find this liquid, this talent, and recover it, allow it to come to the surface, develop it, and appreciate it. Just for the moment believe it is constrained, our job is to eradicate whatever is restraining it. Then encourage it to come to the surface, allow it to roam around, allow it to show itself it, allow it to experiment and feel out the world. Allow it to grab a hold of the world and watch it grow to the point where it can be appreciated.

Anybody can identify talent at its pinnacle because they can't deny it and have to accept it. To identify talent when it's unidentifiable to others takes talent. The problem is encouraging people to allow it to grow and flourish in the early phases. Sometimes the talent is buried very deep within us in places we don't know. Others have had a hand in unknowingly burying it and reinforcing in us its non-existence. Meanwhile on the surface we don't know it's there. Everyday goes by without us knowing that it's there; yet, it can transform our lives. Few dare let us discover it. Stories like *Jane Eyre* and *Harry Potter* illustrate the degree to which some will strive to keep our talent hidden.

Of course, this is not to say talent cannot rise without our help; however, the difference between this approach and an active one is similar to the difference between something growing wild or on a farm. In the wild, there will be some acorns that grow into immense oaks, but with our help not only will more acorns realize that potential but they will also do so in a way that will maximize their potential. Realizing talent's potential is subjective not objective. Talent's potential is not determined relative to others but inherently. That's why competition will seduce most talent into mediocrity – being better than everyone doesn't mean you've maximized your potential. Competition can create the illusion that you've reached your peak when in actuality you may just be beginning.

This formalizes illustratively the effort to maximize talent. The importance of a picture is to communicate more comprehensively the effort without formalizing it into specific steps that increase the risk of a mechanical, objective approach as opposed to an organic, subjective one. Again, the important factors when accessing talent are its emotional foundation and natural resistors. We now have a picture to guide us in the effort to access talent that will help us in the Strategy chapter.

Conclusion

We've discussed talent from the aspects of definition, nature, resistance, framework, and access.

Any definition of talent is rather tenuous because it's similar to trying to define love or beauty. Its uniqueness lends itself much better to subjectivity than the application of uniform definitions. Moreover, the effort to define talent is rather pointless when considering the factors affecting its development. Merely, identifying talent is only the first step.

The nature of talent has many aspects such as quality, attractiveness, and singularity permitting it to set itself apart from the common. We covered these more extensively in the Feminine Influence chapter of this book. Here, we spent time talking about four other aspects which implicatively include these other three. Our purpose here was to expand our concept of talent. The four aspects we discussed were:

- Vitality
- Expressivity
- Innumerability
- Abnormality

Talent is organic, expressive, unquantifiable, and unique. As a result, its innateness makes it more powerful than a man-made creation, its desire to show itself means there will always be signs of it, albeit small at times, its emotional aspect makes it difficult to define and quantify, and its uniqueness will on occasion encourage us to mistake it for an abnormality.

Beyond the emotional, organic, subjective nature of talent, it's important to understand the resistance to it from the person who possesses it and from the group around him. Merely waiting for talent to show itself and assuming it will develop of its own accord, will waste many opportunities that arise.

Within the individual this resistance may take the form of:

- Unawareness of one's talent.
- Discounting one's talent.
- An inability to access talent.
- A fear of accessing because of additional responsibilities.
- An inappropriate time in one's life to access.

Within these resistance occurs because of natural conflict between it and the individual. Whereas the group provides strength and security, the individual provides growth and creativity. We also saw how a group does not exist as an organism, only as a collection of individuals. From this perspective a group is a man-made entity.

To help deal with the emotional, organic, subjective nature of talent, we reviewed Wisdom's Magical Hierarchy, a framework through which to view talent more along these lines. We explored its irrational emphasis and application. This entailed contrasting it with the limitations of rational approaches such as the scientific method. We discussed four basic requirements that will facilitate our efforts in accessing talent:

- Sensitivity
- Expressivity
- Growth
- Microtonality

Finally, most recently, we developed a picture for us to follow in accessing talent. This picture symbolized talent as a magical liquid fueling the fire within us. Accessing it requires a journey through four phases:

1. Exploration
2. Recovery
3. Development
4. Appreciation

While talent can surface with such a conscious application, the difference is one between something growing wild and growing on a farm. We can be more effective with the later.

With this concept of talent, we can explore in more depth some of the resistance to it as noted when we discussed this initially. We'll focus on conditioning, living within a context of which we are unaware. By showing how we can unthinkingly do things out of habit, we can see how we can easily overlook opportunities and problems. Talent's development requires unique perspectives with each person. Consequently, we'll frequently be asked to look at things differently in order to help ourselves and others. Awareness as to how we can be locked into looking at things from a single perspective will help us venture into others.

Conditioning

One of the major external factors affecting all aspects of our personalities – behavior, thoughts, emotions – and thus the development of our talent is conditioning. Conditioning plays such a major role in how we view ourselves, others, and our world that no effective discussion on personalities and talent can take place without it.

The main purpose of this section is to raise awareness regarding conditioning because all of us are conditioned to some degree. That conditioning will affect how we integrate the feminine influence in business in a way suitable to our personalities. In order to achieve this purpose we'll need to have a working definition of conditioning and to experience some exercises involving mild examples of conditioning. As mild as they are, experience has taught me that they offend some people because we are highly conditioned to feel good when we're right and to feel bad when we're wrong. Still, one of the purposes of the exercises is to demonstrate those feelings because sometimes right and wrong are merely arbitrary. The challenge is distinguishing between the times when they are arbitrary and when they are universal.

Definition

I offer a definition of conditioning knowing full well that this word is used extensively in psychology. My working definition is not intended to fit any psychological definition. If it does it's purely coincidental. My definition is intended to help us in business because conditioning affects how we view clients, employees, and managers. It can even affect us to such a degree that we feel something contrary to our how we would feel naturally.

First of all conditioning is learning. All conditioning is learning but all learning is not conditioning. Conditioning can be formal or informal, so it can be education but it doesn't have to be. What distinguishes conditioning from learning is the more emphatic use of rewards and punishments to reinforce or weaken a thought or behavior. Consequently, a feeling, positive or negative, is linked to what we learn. Contrast this with learning for learning's sake, for the pursuit of truth.

Of course, this aspect of feeling is difficult to segregate in order to distinguish between conditioning and learning because many times we feel good about learning something new. Novelty of experience, of which learning is one, is a basic need within all of us to various degrees. However, the easiest way to picture the distinction between the feelings is whether they are extrinsically or intrinsically induced. Rewards and punishments are typically extrinsic inducements and can take many forms from a simple "good job" from an authority figure to an award ceremony. Personal fulfillment and failure in our own eyes are intrinsic inducements regardless of any reinforcement or weakening from without.

Still, even with these descriptions making the distinction in reality is extremely difficult. That's why it's important from an awareness standpoint to treat any learning as a form of conditioning except that which you teach yourself. That's why the assimilation of information without contemplation can be a form of conditioning. This includes reading, viewing, and listening through any medium.

Teaching yourself requires introspection and is where the introvert in you comes into play. Any authoritarian would love to have you read his material easily and quickly without much thought. The last thing he wants to do is write something involved and heavy requiring a lot of pondering on your part because once he gets you started he can't guarantee where you'll go. By presenting his ideas directly and clearly he removes effort, including the effort of questioning. In this way he will encourage you to assimilate his ideas as yours without thinking through all the implications that may have you arrive at something contrary to what he wrote. Just as a swindler wants you to hurry and sign on the dotted line without reading the contract, authoritarians will want you to hurry up and assimilate without contemplation. Consequently, they will be inclined to write clearly and succinctly to minimize your work so all you have to do is regurgitate their ideas.

Conditioning can be helpful and is a natural part of learning. Reading and driving are conditioned activities that we now do without much thought. Sports, music, theater, dance, and many other physical activities involve conditioning to allow the individual to get past the pure mechanics of the activity so he can infuse his particular personality. Both these examples and the one above with the authoritarians contain another aspect of conditioning besides a feeling and that is unthinking. The act or thought we learn becomes unthinking.

Of course, this produces an apparent paradox: how do you not think a thought? Essentially, the authoritarian example introduced us to this concept and perhaps it's simply a matter of semantics, but when a thought becomes unthinking we are no longer questioning it; we've adopted it as a thought. Many times the incessant pace of life or work may require us to do and think things instantly.

Imagine if you suddenly had to do something that required driving and you didn't know how to drive; this would delay you. Likewise, imagine if you suddenly had to make an instant decision about a unique problem that required you to think through it. Having predefined thoughts for us to use makes such things easier. For example, when someone says, "Hello, how are you?" you can instantly respond with "Good, and you?" This response serves the purpose of supplying a quick, polite reply rather than having to spend time pondering exactly how you are, communicating it, and opening up the possibility of a more in depth conversation for which you may not have the time.

To highlight how much of a conditioned response this reply is, I'll relate a college story where I was responsible for helping freshman foreign students become acclimated to the campus. At one meeting designed to address questions and comments, an exasperated Dutch woman asked if she could ask a question about Americans and apologized ahead of time if it offended me. After acknowledging she could, she then asked, "Why is it Americans will say, 'Hi, how are you?' and then continue to walk by before hearing how you are? A couple of times I stopped and stood there ready to respond, but the other person kept walking."

Before moving on to some exercises, one last point about conditioning's definition is important: it's not easily defined and it has been discussed at least since the time of the Greeks. Aristotle had attempted to describe it to some degree with his "law of contiguity" which he defined as "When two things commonly occur together, the appearance of one will bring the other to mind." In these cases we're going to address the two things as (1) a thought or action linked to (2) a feeling that seeks to reinforce or weaken it. For instance, going through a red light is bad and stopping at one is good. Running a red light will encourage you to feel rebellious or criminal.

Again, our purpose here is not to give the best possible definition of conditioning ever written but rather to give us a working idea of what it is we'll be looking for in the following exercises. The actual subject of conditioning is another one that has preoccupied the lives of many, so it's an injustice to think what we've discussed here even comes close. Nevertheless, if you can come away with the idea that conditioning is akin to a preprogrammed action or thought reinforced by a feeling for the purpose of eliciting a specific response to a specific circumstance that will suffice. Some are natural while others are learned. Despite the origin of a conditioned action or thought, conditioning impedes the search for unique perspectives because a conditioned thought or action can't be unique; thus, conditioning causes us to overlook unique aspects of our personalities that allow us to fully develop our talents.

Exercises

The purpose of these exercises is to convey some idea as to the extent to which our minds are conditioned to think. As mentioned earlier, some of this is natural but some is also imposed upon us. I look at these exercises more like chess problems; while it's highly unlikely you'll come across that situation in a match, the mere effort of solving the problem begins to get your mind in shape to handle the ones that do arise. Likewise, these exercises won't have much application to business, but their themes will begin to slow your thinking so you can look at everyday business situations in a different light, from a different perspective. Part of the challenge, is just trying to find a different perspective. We'll take a real life business case study in the Strategy chapter using a basic creativity technique. For now, our purpose is just to highlight awareness as to the extent our minds are led to think down certain paths.

I use to think a doctor lightly striking me below my knee with a small hammer to test my reflexes was about as complicated as it gets with conditioned responses; however, after thinking about students in Nazi youth organizations and young communists, I began to ask myself "If I were brainwashed, how would I know?" When you also consider the people who died in Jonestown and other cults, you realize there are folks in all of these organizations who really felt strongly about what they believed. From the outside, we consider most of them brainwashed.

The main problem in answering this question is trying to put ourselves in a position where we didn't know anything else. For instance, suppose we were brought up in a cult or one of the young political organizations above without exposure to any other way. How would we know then that we were being conditioned to think a particular way? More importantly, thinking outside the box or questioning established principles isn't taken kindly in these groups. Even Socrates, one of the foremost Greek philosophers, was sentenced to death because some in those days felt he was encouraging the youth to think too much about current thought. From their perspective, they felt this was unhealthy for the state.

The purpose of these terrifying examples of conditioning is to highlight the effort it may take to think about things from a different perspective because at the moment we may not be able to think of another perspective through which to look at ourselves, others, and the world. Part of this difficulty is that our minds are encouraged to look for patterns. This is most demonstrative in the eye itself which has a blind spot that our minds fill in with the background around that spot. Essentially, our minds are continuing the pattern of the background and filling in our blind spot.

This inclination toward patterns allows us to make sense of what we see. If we didn't have an inclination toward seeing patterns our minds would not be able to "reassemble" the light from a building and the light from a car to make a distinction between the two. Consequently, without this tendency we would connect a point from the building with a point from the car and the two would tend to mesh together. Our minds are inclined to think that two points that are close to each other go together and points of similar color also go together. There are many other factors that become the basis of illusions that use these principles to distort what we see.

Patterns simplify our lives by associating the many intricacies of an object quickly without having to consciously sort through every point of light in an effort to correctly associate them. If this were not the case, seeing would be far more complex than a thousand piece jigsaw puzzle and would greatly slow our ability to assimilate what we see.

Exercise I – Dots

For the first exercise, look at Figure 4.51. Which dot goes in the place of the question mark?

What dot goes in place of the question mark?

Figure 4.51

There are many different answers to this question even though our inclination is to say a black dot because it continues on with the pattern. Such an answer goes along with our natural inclination to see and continue patterns; however, it also fulfills a conditioned response taught to us from school and from various intelligence tests that encourage us to identify and complete a pattern or series. Whether we replace the question mark with a black or white dot is irrelevant in terms of right or wrong. Inherently, we cannot declare one way or another because the question, "What dot goes in place of the question mark?" does not contain the parameters by which we determine what is right or wrong.

Consequently, either answer in Figure 4.52 is correct.

Figure 4.52

On the left we have an answer that continues the pattern as we've already discussed. On the right, we have a unique response. The real question involves the context in which we're asking our original question. If we're running a business that's trending downhill, we may want to try something different so the right diagram in Figure 4.52 would be preferred; while if we're running a business on the upswing, we may want to continue on with what we're doing until we detect some tapering so the left diagram would be preferred.

Even despite this explanation, we may be experiencing a "twinge" to various degrees when we look at these two diagrams. We might just find it hard to accept the right diagram over the left despite the fact we don't know the context of the situation. A major reason we may feel this way is that we have been conditioned to superimpose a context upon such situations and that context is one of continuing a pattern – doing what was done previously. We more commonly refer to this in a legalistic sense as "precedence." In many ways this connects directly to the power of inertia, the power of defense that we discussed in the Gettysburg example in the Feminine Influence chapter. Part of the inherent power in the status quo includes the inclination to continue on with a pattern. By itself this isn't bad, because this inclination toward a pattern prevents us from constantly changing our direction and possibly getting nowhere; however, as we saw it also presents the problem of increasing the likelihood of falling into a mechanical routine, a rut.

Of course, I did mention there were many answers to this question, and thus far I've only presented two. Figure 4.53 shows how we can arrive at many answers to this question.

Figure 4.53

By replacing the question mark with a gray dot, we open a whole door of possibilities that includes various ranges of gray. We could also include all the colors in the spectrum, if I could print this in color. Again, Figure 4.53 continues a violation of the pattern begun in Figure 4.52 by introducing something other than a black or white dot. Inherently, no diagram in either of these figures is better than the other because there is no context around the question other than that which we wish to impose from our experience or education. No one can argue which of these is better without superimposing a context by which to make that decision.

Let's return to our talent discussion and its unique nature. We will find talent, because it is uncommon, in the uncommon. In routines and the continuation of patterns we find what is common as the left diagram in Figure 4.52 shows. It's very difficult to identify talent in a situation like that because talent distinguishes itself. No dot in that diagram does that well.

The story in the right diagram of Figure 4.52 and the one in Figure 4.53 is different. In the first we have a white dot in the bottom row that stands out and in the second a gray dot. The likelihood of finding talent in either of these two diagrams is greater than in the left one from Figure 4.52. Conceptually, this also becomes important not only in the search for talent but also in the effort to assimilate one's personality into his work in order to differentiate himself. Regardless of product or service, personality remains the surest way to differentiate oneself; a competitor can more easily duplicate a product or service than he can a personality.

Even though we are searching for unique characteristics, these Figures also help us see why we refer to abnormality as a nature of talent. We could easily view the right diagram in Figure 4.52 and the one in Figure 4.53 as abnormal to the left one in Figure 4.52. This is why sometimes what we find abnormal could be the entry point for a talent search. Of course, the challenge in this is overcoming the negative feeling we get from someone we consider abnormal because many times it could be merely the context in which we view that person.

Exercise II – Parking Lot

Let's move on to another exercise that reflects more of a learned conditioning experience, parking a car. Figure 4.54 shows a car parked within the lines painted on the asphalt. Part of what we're taught when we learn how to drive is to park our cars within these lines. In fact, we even learn this as a child, when we watch our parents or older siblings do this.

Figure 4.54

This exercise works better early in the morning or late in the evening when no other cars are around. At one of those times when a nearby parking lot is rather empty or there are a large group of empty spots, go ahead and park your car similarly to what is shown in Figure 4.55 and walk away to do some errands or grab a bite to eat.

Figure 4.55

It's not important to do this exactly as above, but the more designated parking areas you consume the better. The question now becomes, "Do you feel criminal or rebellious?" The point here is that regardless of how you feel an aborigine who just learned how to work a car would feel neither because he would not have learned the significance of those lines. More importantly, he would not have learned the disdain others feel for those who park this way. As a result, this is an example of where a conditioned behavior encourages a particular feeling that would not normally be there. In order for this conditioning to have absolutely no effect upon us, we would have to have no thoughts or feelings about Figure

4.55. We are not born with an innate feeling to feel badly about taking up more than one spot.

Continuing on with this exercise we also must ask what is more common, Figure 4.54 or Figure 4.55? Remember, we are talking about a parking lot that is very empty especially if we park far away. The negative consequences to others are minimal. It's not as though we are taking up four spots during the height of the Christmas shopping season. In order to seek what is unique and different, one must generally stray from what is common. He is more likely to find new opportunities and new solutions by journeying in the uncommon – even if it may be "wrong" according to conventional thinking. You can't expect anything new from a standard response.

Outside of the emotional connection to Figures 4.54 and 4.55, there is a cognitive one giving an example of how the mind shuts down under this sort of conditioning, similar to reading. When you enter a parking lot, how many times do you think about what you're doing? For instance, do you ever consider parking in any way other than between the lines, especially in a sparse lot?

The point is not to discuss the merits of parking within the lines; the point is to show how unthinking our actions can become. Generally, the older and more routine the action, the more likely we'll fall into an unthinking habit, routine, system, or procedure. Driving, parking, and reading are just a few mundane examples for you to contemplate. What can occur with mundane actions can occur with routine sophisticated ones especially if they don't vary much. This explains the "new perspective" phenomenon when a new person shows up or a layman who is unlearned regarding current thinking.

Exercise III – Connect the Dots

Our next example builds in complexity. It's called "connect the dots" as seen in Figure 4.56.

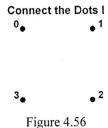

Figure 4.56

We would most likely find something along the lines of Figure 4.57.

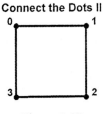

Figure 4.57

The important aspect of this exercise is a contextual one. Many times our language brings hidden "baggage" containing a whole framework of commonly understood concepts behind it. The phrase "connect the dots" is one because sometime in our childhood we learned a game containing a similar phrase. This game entailed connecting a series of numbered dots sequentially with straight lines to produce pictures that we otherwise might not be able to do by freehand.

For this exercise this phraseology came with no such instructions so we're inclined to go with what we've experienced in the past. Many times we will go ahead and connect the dots without even considering another set of conditions. Figure 4.58 shows three examples of the dots sequentially connected with primarily curvy lines. Implicatively, we suddenly can have extensive variety using this methodology.

Connect the Dots III

Figure 4.58

We can symbolically connect our discussion around Figures 2.55 and 2.57 here. We can link two points by a single straight line, but an infinite number of curvy lines. Likewise, by following the set of instructions for "Connect the Dots" that we received in childhood and contained only straight lines, we arrive at only a single variation; however, by expanding our horizons to include curvy lines we can have many variations. By integrating the feminine influence in our thinking we can suddenly open up countless opportunities. As we've already referenced, the movie *Sound of Music* pictures this through a woman disrupting a male dominated environment, a disruption that allowed the children and others to suddenly become aware of other aspects of themselves as symbolized by the singing.

Connect the Dots IV

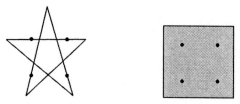

Figure 4.59

In Figure 4.59 we see further expansion by ignoring a sequential association among the points. In the left diagram, we see the points linked out of order, and in the right diagram, we connect the points through a plane rather than a line. We can extend the theme of the right diagram by connecting the points via a theme as shown in Figure 4.60.

Connect the Dots V

Figure 4.60

In the left diagram, we link the four points by making them all part of a sun, and in the right diagram, we link them by making them all part of the same radiant star. This is no different than linking people by geography, culture, ideas, and religion.

With Figures 4.57 – 4.60 we now have a collection of representations linking the four points. While only the first one followed the childhood conventions of the phrase "connect the dots," we now can evaluate qualitatively by picking the diagram we like the best. There are a couple dangers along this line that are worthy to note.

One is that we'll simply see this exercise as a game where we suddenly removed the "rules." Consequently, we might see this as an exercise anybody could do if we told him he didn't have to follow conventions. This is exactly the point, but the problem arises when we consider "Who's going to tell us not to follow conventions?" In many ways, this is similar to someone telling us "Go be creative." At what point do we take it upon ourselves to challenge the underlying assumptions in any set of instructions to arrive at something new. This takes us back to the expressive nature of talent; at some point talent will seek to express itself and will most likely take an unconventional form because talent is uncommon not common.

Another danger is simply looking at this game as pointless without these rules because anyone can now draw anything he wishes as long as he can justify some connection with the four points. Yes, this is true; however, what each person finally draws will be different. What a Picasso draws would be quite different from what I would draw. Now, the comparative standpoint is no longer how well we connect the dots conventionally but rather how well we draw. Under conventional "Connect the Dots" rules, no one could tell the difference between how I would connect the points and how Picasso would – we produce the same thing. Here the rules eradicate talent differentiation by putting Picasso's artistic talents on the same level as mine. Eventually, if Picasso received severe punishments for violating conventional "Connect the Dots" rules, he might never attempt to draw anything else besides what the dots demanded.

The irony and final contemplative point before we move onto the next exercise is shown by asking Picasso and me to play "Connect the Dots" via conventional rules. Let's say I followed the rules and produced Figure 4.57, but let's also say Picasso was not going to be bothered with the rules so he went on to paint a masterpiece incorporating the four points similar to the examples in Figure 4.60. If he and I were in a contest with conventional "Connect the Dots" rules, I would be judged the winner because I followed the rules and Picasso didn't. The judges would have no choice; how could they award victory to someone who didn't even follow the rules of the contest? Nevertheless, even though I would go home with the trophy, Picasso's rendition of "Connect the Dots" would receive far more attention than mine with the general public. In fact, I would wager a good amount that Picasso would receive more money for his rule violator than I would for my rule champion on the open market.

This point also reinforces the power behind the feminine influence by showing beauty overpowering adherence. If adherence to the rules really contained some inherent, natural power, then my rendition would overwhelm Picasso's without hesitation; the mere fact I won the contest according to the rules would be enough. The masculine influence represents directness, simplicity, and tangibility that adherence to the rules suggests. The feminine influence represents the indirectness, complexity, and intangibility that beauty suggests. Beauty has an inherent power that rules lack. The danger of rules, formal and informal, is that they will strangle the vitality and expressivity necessary to have new ideas and concepts emerge to dynamically grow a business because they impose a context that people will follow unthinkingly. Since we naturally gravitate towards patterns as demonstrated in Figures 4.52 and 4.53, in order to develop our personalities and talents, we need to raise our awareness by introspectively challenging the contexts we confront everyday.

Exercise IV – Bottle

This exercise will help to illustrate the casualness with which we impose context upon our daily language. The purpose is to take a relatively small event and highlight its *default* context. Since every event is a compilation of smaller events, by taking the context of this small event and multiplying it out over the many small events in a large event, this exercise will help us appreciate the many, many contexts imposed upon us in a routine interaction. Again, the emphasis is not on whether contexts are good or bad because they are inherently neither. They help us facilitate our daily experiences so insignificant details do not overwhelm and deter us; however, negatively they do encourage us to miss new opportunities and insights that help us grow.

Figure 4.61 gets us started if we focus on the left diagram representing a bottle filled with a beverage. After drinking the entire beverage, we arrive at the right diagram.

Figure 4.61

The question related to these diagrams is: Which one is full and which one is empty? Generally, without thinking we are inclined to say the left one is full and the right one is empty, but the key is acknowledging the context around the word "full." In this case, the unspoken context is the extent to which the beverage is in the bottle.

On the other hand, if we ignore this unspoken context, we could declare the bottle full because what now fills it is the same thing that fills a tire – air which we see in Figure 4.62. If we now consider a bottle empty because it has air in it, then we must consider a tire empty. By changing context, we change how something looks without changing the object.

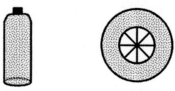

Figure 4.62

By crossing Figure 4.62 with 4.61, we arrive at Figure 4.63 where the left diagram represents a bottle filled with air and the right one represents a vacuumed bottle.

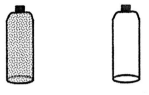

Figure 4.63

Figure 4.63 has a humanistic aspect when we consider seeing people we know from a particular context such as work in a new context such as working out. Often, our impression of the person changes even though the person hasn't. We often attribute this to simply learning more about a person, but often it is more of a case of looking at what we do know in a different light; thus, what we think is new is more akin to repackaging. A natural bias will also encourage us in this direction because it's much easier to plead ignorance than misinterpretation. Whereas the first implies we couldn't have known, the second implies an evaluative error, being in the dark is easier to handle emotionally than being incorrect. Our interpretations change more frequently and easily than a person does.

The conflict between our interpretations of others and their personalities also has a personal application: how we interpret ourselves can also differ from who we actually are. The line of thought behind the bottle exercise has caused us to revisit "who we think we are" is different from "who we are." Sometimes by changing the context through which we look at ourselves, we see a different aspect of our qualities. By looking at talent through an irrational lens rather than a rational one, we begin to see it differently without changing what it is. Occasionally, the contexts through which we view ourselves are not self-constructed but accepted from others seeking to impose them upon us. The sisters of Cinderella imposed a worthless context around her that remained until her magical evening.

The amazing aspect of integrating one's personality into his work or of identifying and developing his talents is that often it's a matter of context. Sometimes it's not a matter of how you change yourself but rather of how you interpret yourself. The disadvantage of a rational, objective approach is that it presupposes a singular perspective by which we can view and judge everything. By locking ourselves into that context, we unthinkingly surrender the ability to see new opportunities from a variety of perspectives that an irrational, subjective approach allows. This explains why integrating the feminine influence, which contains within her realm irrationality and subjectivity, is critical to the dynamic growth in business – she opens up opportunities.

Exercise V – Insects

Related to how we interpret others and ourselves is an exercise based upon a sweat-shirt I received as a gift. The design on the front was from Gary Larson's *Far Side* cartoons and titled "Know Your Insects." Below this title were six sketches of insects ar-ranged as described in Figure 4.64.

Ant	Fly	Roach
Dragon Fly	Mosquito	Beetle

Figure 4.64

I will admit upfront that I can't recognize all the insects so I've taken a few liberties with their identifications. Nevertheless, imagine a sweatshirt with these six sketches on the front with names of the insects below each sketch. What generated the humor behind these sketches were their names. Rather than put their names as suggested in Figure 4.64, the cartoon had names such as the ones in Figure 4.65.

Dave	Jasmine	Darnell
Kathy	Bill	Rhonda

Figure 4.65

The use of personal names versus generic identifiable ones caused me to think of a public speaking tenet, "Know your audience." Often, especially in light of the number of people who may be in the audience, there is the inclination to identify people generically according to various categories. We generally accept this as knowing your audience. Figure 4.66 shows an example that classifies people according to job function.

Engineer	Trucker	Banker
Lawyer	Programmer	Plumber

Figure 4.66

How this applies to conditioning is the unthinking acceptance of the context around the word "know" when referencing large generic groups. The cartoon's humor stems from the conflicting contexts as represented by "know your friends" and "know your insects." In the first, it's hard to image one knowing his friends without knowing their personal names. In the second, it's the opposite – knowing individual insects by their personal names is impossible. Making the leap to a practical business application, we often find people are more impacted by the evocation of their names as opposed to their job functions. We are more impressed with a speaker who knows our name than our job function.

However, knowing every person in an audience is often impossible; thus, we tend to use "know" in a more generic context than a personal one when it comes to public speaking. Nevertheless, this exercise shows that often impossibility becomes a context through which we interpret things. Of course, the opportunity is that what is impossible for one is not for another.

More importantly, attempting the impossible is often more admirable than successfully achieving the possible. Here, we have the context of success being better than failure, a context that blinds us from the qualitative aspects of each. This will encourage us to turn away from a dynamic failure in difference to a normal success. There is inherent power in one who attempts a lofty goal and fails over one who attempts a routine one and succeeds. The movie *Rocky* is symbolic of the appeal in the first. Despite defeat Rocky Belboa's effort becomes heroic and impactive; thus, attempting to know your audience personally, even though unsuccessful, is more admirable than successfully knowing the generic classifications which make up that audience.

Exercise VI – Banker

This exercise integrates the interpretive aspects of the bottle exercise (Ex. IV) with the familiarity aspects of the insect exercise (Ex. V) by looking at a banker who is calling upon a long time client. The purpose is to use a business example to highlight how context affects employee-client and manager-employee relationships daily.

A banker once approached me frustrated with her attempts at expanding a relationship beyond the traditional banking parameters to a more holistic one. One of her primary techniques was asking the client for his primary concerns. She lamented that often the client would relate banking ones, but she surmised that the likelihood of higher priorities outside of banking were great. This conflict was the source of her frustration.

The advantage here was that the banker recognized the banking context through which her client viewed her. Imagine you working outside around your home when someone pulls up with lawn equipment. A man dressed in a lawn maintenance uniform walks up, introduces himself, and begins an introductory conversation. After the introduction, he asks what your concerns are. Are you more likely to respond with your lawn care problems or your tax ones? Suppose he was more specific with his question by asking what your financial concerns are. How taken aback would you be?

What people know of us and how they interpret us affects an interaction. Going along with a normal routine will often generate normal outcomes and is often easy to do; however, to achieve something dynamic often the "rules of engagement" are challenged in order for someone to see you in a different light. We cannot encourage people to see us in a different light without some tension in moving them there. This also applies in your attempt to look at yourself through a different perspective and is the reason why we discussed courage with the feminine influence and timing with talent. No matter what we see in others or ourselves, there may not be the ability or the appropriate timing to venture into another perspective.

Nevertheless, routines condition others to view us a particular way. As the banker experienced, this produces constraints on one's ability to grow a relationship. We also see other manifestations of this when employees become pigeon-holed in their positions. Their talents are viewed through the context of their position. This is no different than actors and actresses being stereotyped as only being able to play a certain role because they have repeatedly played that role. In effect, the routine playing of that role solidifies that perspective in others; what we do a lot will become our only capability in the eyes of others.

Exercise VII – Memento

We have a tendency to believe what we hear and see, especially if we want to believe it. As Figure 2.12 graphed, interpretively we gravitate toward what is supported concretely. What we hear and see tend to receive more weighting than what we feel. The scientific method that we reviewed in our discussion with talent reinforces this because it demands evidence, usually empirical, to verify a hypothesis; what we see and hear happen is better than what we feel is happening. Unless we can support a feeling with evidence then it's unacceptable as proof for a hypothesis. Science carries this further by favoring quantification of its observations.

The purpose of the Memento exercise is to demonstrate that what we superficially observe can conflict with their deeper implications. The danger rests in quickly dismissing this exercise as "reading too much into something"; however, the arguments supporting a deeper investigation hark back to our Sherlock Holmes' analogy in our Introduction. We'll be looking at a memento attendees received for their participation in a seminar. Since the seminar dealt with the generation and development of new ideas, the organizers gave them a memento typifying that effort; it had a "thinking outside the box" theme.

The memento consisted of two parts as shown in Figure 4.67, a base and a balance. As shown in the left diagram of Figure 4.67 the base consisted of a solid foundation made of heavy plastic upon which a transparent, wire-framed cube rested. The right diagram shows the balance consisting of a bent wire resting on a fulcrum with a stylized, metal person thinking on one end and a heavy, weighted metal ball on the other.

Figure 4.67

Along with these two parts came instructions on how to assemble them which consisted mainly of a diagram showing the completed memento that could easily fit unobtrusively on a desk or conference table. Figure 4.68 illustrates the final product directed by the instructions.

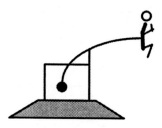

Figure 4.68

The memento serves to remind and encourage attendees to think outside of the box. Ironically, on a deeper level, the memento does the opposite. How this applies to conditioning is two-fold. First, as mentioned at the outset of this exercise there is a natural tendency to believe what one observes before his eyes as opposed to what he's feeling. Second, this natural tendency is reinforced culturally.

Before we get into why the memento delivers conflictory messages, I want to outline and bring together four basic conflicts that will support the significance of this exercise and reduce the inclination to dismiss it as simply an interpretative issue:

- Deep vs. Surface
- Intuition vs. Cognition
- Inside vs. Outside
- Introvert vs. Extrovert

We've discussed all four at various times throughout the book, but reviewing them together and in an integrative fashion will help. We can begin this review by saying that the greatest resource we possess is our own personality. Regardless of what happens, that possession remains with us without which we would not be able to tap the resources of the world. Consequently, our inner world is far more important to us than our outer world, the book is more important than its cover; however, this does not negate conflict between the two.

The conflict between the deep and the surface rests upon the issue of tangibility. While we can hear, see, smell, taste, and touch our outer world, the surface, we cannot do the same with our inner one, the deep. In this way, even though the deep contains our greatest resource, it can never completely dominate to the point that we ignore the surface and our outside world because the tangibility involved with our senses will tend to distract us from introspection and to cause us to become lost in our outside world. Consequently, we require something more to ensure we don't neglect the deep – the source of our personality and talent.

Since the deep is inaccessible to our senses, we have the related conflict between two functions through which we integrate what we learn about the world and ourselves: intuition and cognition. Figure 4.12 returns here to illustrate the conflict. Cognition is the sand that fills the glass while intuition is the water. Cognition is a sieve through which many aspects of our outside and inside world pass undetected because this sieve only catches those things large enough to consciously register with us. While cognition attempts to explain our world in easy, concrete terms, the seductiveness of its clarity causes us to overlook all that it fails to explain such as the aspects of the feminine influence we've already discussed. This leaves our intuition, while more nebulous, to capture far more of our worlds than cognition could ever hope or ever will capture.

We can relate the intuition-cognition conflict to the deep-surface one because our senses make us conscious of our outside world by integrating their messages in our mind; however, it cannot consciously record everything because everything would overwhelm it. If our minds would consciously report the effect of air pressure on every aspect of our bodies or of every nuance of color in our sight, each event alone would overrun our senses and retard our ability to do things. It would be as though loud music would constantly blare in our ears or bright light glare in our eyes. Nevertheless, what we cognitively miss our intuition picks up. Thus, while we cannot recall every detail of a forest, we can receive the feeling of being in a forest. If we could only feel what we consciously sensed, a forest would feel like a desert because of all we could not recall about that forest. This outlines the conflict between intuition and cognition and explains how things we do not cognitively register can slip through and affect us. Our discussion around the Seventeen Influential Points expressed this in more detail.

Discussion around the intuition-cognition conflict takes us back to the inside-outside duality we explored with Figures 4.16 – 4.22. The emotional language of our inside person, mustering the courage to assert ourselves in the world along an uncertain path, seeking growth conflicts with the rational language of our outside person seeking to protect us from uncertainty's dangers. Intuition is the primary method by which we tap the growth in the inside person inaccessible to our senses, and cognition is the primary method by which the outside person constructs its defenses. Growth disrupts one's safety; safety retrains one's growth.

With the inside-outside conflict, we arrive at the fourth conflict between the introvert and extrovert. Just as the extrovert is drawn to our outside world, the introvert is drawn to our inside one; just as the extrovert is best able to tap external resources, the introvert is best able to tap internal ones. Extroversion is the journey seeking to explore our outside world while introversion is the journey seeking to explore our inside one. Figures 4.23 – 4.29 relate here again. The conflict is between the balancing of energy between extroversion and introversion, between shallowness and impracticality, between quantity and quality.

How these conflicts are culturally reinforced becomes more apparent when we look at the aspects of these conflicts that make one side easier than the other. Approaching this effort with two primary appreciations will help. The first is the appreciation for the origination of a person's power, and the second is the appreciation for the correlation between great and difficult, and between paltry and easy.

The final power of an individual rests with his personality. Unless he allows someone to take it away, no one can. What distinguishes one person from another is personality, his inner world. While many people can own similar things in our external world, no two can own the same personality. Without differentiating personalities, one person easily becomes another through the similar molding of both external worlds. The eradication of personality differences is the eradication of personal power; uniformity swallows individuality.

Accessing what is great is difficult. In this case, accessing the source of our greatest power resting in our inner world is then a difficult thing to do. Conversely, accessing the source of our paltriest power resting in our external world is then an easy thing to do. We see this duality manifest itself when we find protection through conformity easier than asserting growth through individuality, acquiring the extrinsic rewards of our external world easier than seeking the intrinsic rewards of our internal one, and displaying one's extrinsic rewards easier than showing one's intrinsic rewards.

A corollary to the relationship between great-difficult and paltry-easy is that few can do the difficult and many can do the easy. This is why Wisdom's Magical Hierarchy places creativity, intuition, and conception above reason, knowledge, and information. The first group helps us access our intangible, internal world, the source of our greatest power, while the second helps us access the tangibility of our external world, the source of our paltriest power. Consequently, what allows us to tap into our greatest resource must be more valuable than those which only allow us to tap into lesser ones. Relatedly, the intelligence required to access the resources in our external world is less involved than that required to access the resources in our internal world. Therefore, there are fewer who can effectively tackle the difficulties of accessing internal resources than those who can effectively tackle the ease of accessing external ones.

If we return to the duality of the inside-outside person, we can see the necessity of this condition because a home cannot exist without a house. Subsistence of our physical condition lays the foundation for exploring the resources within us. Without this subsistence we would die and never have the chance for the latter. Thus, securing external resources must be easier for all than tapping into internal resources. Referring back to Figures 4.23 – 4.29 we can then derive Figure 4.69.

Figure 4.69

With the culmination of Figure 4.69 we can now more easily see the natural tendency for a cultural influence emphasizing the surface, cognition, outside, and extroversion over the deep, intuition, inside, and introversion because many more can do the easy than the difficult. The first group is easy while the second is difficult. We can now apply this more easily to conditioning because the many who find the difficulty of the inside world too daunting will tend to encourage and promote what is easily seen, rationalized, accessed, and explored. Emphasis will be on what most people think and on quantity, rather than the quality aspects of what's actually being contemplated.

Returning to the memento exercise, we find that while our cognition will understand the "think outside the box" message delivered by the instructions for Figure 4.68, our intuition will pick up the inherent conflict crystallized by the question: How can you think outside the box using directions? By their nature, directions imply an outline of something through which someone has already thought. Thinking outside the box implies a new direction, a new path. How can we declare ourselves thinking along differentiating lines if all we're doing is following instructions? Consider Figure 4.70 as an alternative.

Figure 4.70

This arrangement violates the instructions, but it represents thinking outside the parameters of the instructions. The line of thought invoked here is similar to Exercise III – Connect the Dots when we drew a comparison between me following the rules and Picasso breaking them. I would win the contest, but Picasso's rendition would be more beautiful.

Some will see this exercise as merely an interpretive one; however, the point to remember as outlined in the Seventeen Influential Points is that we are not only affected by what we cognitively catch but also by what our cognitive sieve does not. In this case, while we may only catch the cognitive message of "think outside the box," the intuitive one of a contradiction will slip through unbeknownst to our cognition. We'll see the manifestation of this feeling in our ambivalence for the memento, so what was originally targeted to be an uplifting, memorable item will eventually slip into the backwaters of our lives simply to be washed away and forgotten, further proof of the inherent power of emotions over reasons.

Summary

The memento exercise illustratively summarizes the conditioning messages from the other exercises, so it allows us to construct a summary table as shown in Figure 4.71. Here, I've summarized the outline's number, description, message, and its relationship to the memento exercise.

EX	Description	Message	Memento's Relationship
I	Dots	Natural tendency to look for patterns.	We search for a history (pattern) on how to assemble the memento which we find in the directions.
II	Parking	Feelings tied to conditioning.	The feeling that not following the directions is wrong through an alternative assembly.
III	Connect Dots	Directions hinder creativity.	The directions with the memento stifle the effort to arrive at an assembly through one's own efforts.
IV	Bottle	The impact of context.	By looking at the message through an intuitive context versus a cognitive one we see the contradictive message.
V	Insects	Generic versus personal	The inclusion of directions will encourage all recipients to think alike rather than allow them to tackle assembly in their own personal way.
VI	Banker	Overcoming ruts requires effort.	Working through all conditioning aspects in the memento exercise required effort to explore and explain in order to overcome the feeling of violating the instructions (doing something wrong).
VII	Memento	Summary exercise	The easy is accessible to the many, and the difficult is accessible to the few.

Figure 4.71

Conclusion

The purpose of the Conditioning section was to create awareness as to the extensiveness to which it affects us everyday in the smallest aspects of our lives. Compound this over the many small aspects comprising our lives and the impact is daunting. Awareness alone will begin to encourage us to think about all the implicit parameters around our thoughts and actions. We cannot address here what falls in our particular oblivion, so our first step is to recognize daily situations that may fit the exercises here so we can at least recognize that we may be operating within a habitual set of parameters. We can ask: Under what assumptions am I working? From here we can move onto, "If I change a particular assumption, how does that change the solution?" and eventually determine, "Does this solution provide an effective alternative to the present tendencies?"

While conditioning can make it easier to accomplish things, the cost is the entrenchment of habitual thoughts and actions retarding creative perspectives allowing us to seize opportunities. For instance, in football specific plays are identified by codes to facilitate communication. As a result, the running of an existing play becomes easier than the creation of a new play, so the tendency will be to stick with or tweak what exists than to apply the effort to derive something new. In the long run, just as muscles entropy with disuse, so does our ability to look at routine conditions from a different perspective.

The tension between what's easy and difficult reinforces culturally a specific approach geared towards what's easily seen, rationalized, accessed, and explored. All of this gives preference to our external world because much of what lies inside of us is invisible, irrational, inaccessible, and unexplorable when we view it through "normal" perspectives. The requirements for tackling our outside world are more easily met than those for tackling our inside world, so those who can at least do the minimum in the first are more plentiful than those who can do at least the minimum with the latter. Our existence takes priority over our essence, but our essence determines who we are.

The source of our greatest personal power lies within so inherently must be the most difficult to tap. The ease with which our external world thrusts its tangibility upon our senses distracts us from the difficulty in accessing and developing this power so introspection is surrendered easily in favor of extrospection. Since achieving the difficult is possible by few and achieving the easy possible by many, those seeking an emphasis upon external considerations will outnumber those seeking an emphasis on internal ones. Consequently, those who emphasize and practice the value of extrinsic rewards will outnumber those doing the same with intrinsic ones. The first set will always be easier than the second, but the second will always be more impactive than the first. If this were not the case, one would not exist because one would be both easier and more effective so there would be no need for the other. For instance, the Socratic Method is the most effective teaching method but also the most difficult to use, so those who don't use it will outnumber those who do. It's always easier to say something is not useful than to say one lacks the ability to use it, so there will be more who accept the premise that it's not worth the effort than those who accept that it is. This inclination increases with the intangibility of something. The inability to use a handheld tool is easier to admit than the inability to use a relational technique. Those who can do the difficult will stir anxieties in those who cannot; thus, the few will likely bother the many.

How these anxieties express themselves is not easily recognizable so many will not recognize them; however, these anxious emotions will nevertheless be rationalized in many ways as implied by the Seventeen Influential Points. Some will appear in the form of rewards and punishments encouraging similar behavior by all. If they persist they will eventually become the parameters comprising conditioning and reinforced by the ease in conformity.

Conditioning is an extremely complex and sensitive animal, and I don't pretend to cover even a small portion of its implications here. From a business perspective though, it's the basis for consolidating the strength of a business along some coherent path, but it's also the basis for the retardation of seizing opportunities and problems creatively. Herein lays the paradox.

If uniformity was the mother of invention, then there would be no need for diversity in life. In order for a business to survive long term, creative forces must stir but one needs awareness of the many hidden conditioned responses that retard that effort. Many hindrances to this effort, as the exercises suggest, are cloaked in what is easy and reinforced by the many that can do the easy. Success in accessing these forces are found in the few willing to tackle the difficult path of identifying and developing the talents they have within – a world that is not easily seen, rationalized, accessed, or explored but one we're easily conditioned to avoid and ignore.

Growth

My original concept of this section had the title methodology; however this created quite a paradox because the method to achieve growth can be as individualized as the person seeking it. Seeking what is unique in each of us forms the basis for our talent and cannot be done in an assembly-line fashion. We need an approach encouraging individualization.

The essence of the approach is simple: encourage strengths and ignore weaknesses. Analogously, I'd like to use an experience I had when I pruned a tree that I've also seen with others.

Upon pruning the trunk of a young tree in an attempt to encourage it to grow more outward and less upward, it countered my efforts by sprouting a branch below my cut and thrusting it upward along the same path as the trunk had intended before I deterred it. Over time as this branch grew bigger it swallowed the little stump from my pruning. While a little alteration is apparent, the basic upward theme of the tree continued. Contrast this approach to the tree trying to regenerate a branch directly from the cut I had made.

Trees don't focus on trying to grow branches from dead ones; they focus on growing new ones. Through this process they tend to integrate the weak ones. As the tree continues to grow the dead spots are frequently wrapped by bark or integrated into growing branches so they eventually disappear or become interwoven holistically into the tree. The tree focuses on growing from its strong spots not its weak ones. Through this process it gradually integrates weaknesses into its entire personality.

The perspective from which you determine strengths is a subjective one based upon the nature of the relationship between you and the other person. Here we call upon Figure 4.2 again to illustrate this. Outside advice, comments, and opinions are far subordinate to those of the two involved. If you are reading this from the perspective of how this can help you, the emphasis is on how you feel about your progress.

With this we'll first delve into the approach and then the perspective.

Approach

In working relationships where one is helping another, areas of improvement are frequently discussed. Often as part of a formal review process, developmental areas are outlined. If the relationship is more informal and sincere, the person being helped will often ask for these. This discussion is counterintuitive to growth and a waste of energy.

As we saw briefly introduced with the tree analogy, any tree that loses a limb grows around the loss. It does not try to bring back to life a dead limb. Likewise, when our skin is damaged, our bodies do not try to bring dead skin to life, it tries to shed the dead and grow new skin over it. We do not try to encourage someone to grow fins so they can swim better; we encourage them to use the strength and flexibility inherent in their arms and legs to do it. Helping someone is the same concept; personal growth will grow over weaknesses in time.

If we focus on improving weaknesses we get the diagram on the left in Figure 4.72 where "W" represents a weakness. The shaded area represents the extent of our growth; it stops when we run into our weaknesses so we can develop those. However, a growth strategy focused on maximizing our strengths will carry us far beyond our weaknesses as the diagram on the right shows.

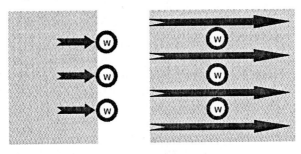

Figure 4.72

Even though our weaknesses may initially remain, as our strengths become greater and greater our weaknesses eventually dissolve, blend, and disappear as the next two diagrams show in Figure 4.73.

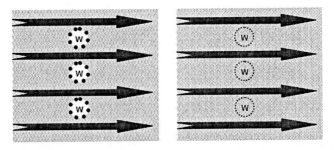

Figure 4.73

These graphically represent the Germans' Blitzkrieg strategy of World War II that sought to disorient an opponent quickly. Rather than attack directly, their units went around fortified or stubborn resistance and seized the territory around and behind them. By isolating enemy units from supplies, they were able to render the enemy positions useless. They did not waste energy on the areas where they were weaker than the French; they focused on maximizing their strengths.

Identifying, exploring, commenting, and working on weaknesses are dangerous. Often they zap critical energy for growth strategies, including emotional energy. There is also a severe downside: incorrectly identifying a weakness. To the individual, more damage is done by misidentifying weaknesses than doing so with strengths.

Perspective

As far as the second aspect of growth, relying primarily upon the observations of the two involved as opposed to others, whereas people frequently discuss weaknesses this aspect doesn't show up too often unless some kind of personality test or assessment occurred or there is specific discussion taking place regarding the comments of others.

Regardless of the person or test, observations and results are skewed to certain perspectives and assumptions imbued in the person or the test's creator. For instance, take an example from a personality assessment tool where I was asked to rate someone on a scale of one to ten based upon:

How quickly and accurately he sizes up a situation and the requirements for action.

The major inherent bias behind this statement is that speed and accuracy are important attributes in assessing a situation and the requirements for action. Is there a strong correlation to effectiveness? The supposition in this statement is that if one makes quick and accurate decisions he will be effective – can we necessarily say this is true with a high degree of certainty? If we refer back to the discussion around Figures 2.36 – 2.41 we'll recall the problems with plans resulting from decisions: they only cover a fraction of what needs to be done. How one handles the many aspects of a situation not covered by a plan are more pertinent to effectiveness than the assessment up front. Consequently, implementation can be more correlated to effectiveness than decision making. Which is better: a good plan with bad implementation, or a bad plan with good implementation?

For this reason, observations and results are useless unless one can totally adopt the perspective and assumptions of the other; this, of course, is humanly impossible. This is why when working with someone, your observations of that person are the critical ones that matter as they relate to that person because you must work with him within yours and his perspectives. People usually fail when they use observations and assume they were derived from the same perspective as their own. The only certainty is what you interpret; you cannot be certain of what someone else is interpreting. As a result, observations and tests tell more about the observer and the tester than they do about the subject upon which they are ostensibly providing a commentary.

Summary

This approach and perspective to growth can assume many forms depending upon the personalities involved. The value in this synopsis is the encouragement to focus on growth and the observations you and the other person develop. I have also found it a good practice to lay these out in the beginning and explain them as I have done here. Many times people become anxious as to how others may be influencing you, so your efforts to expose this anxiousness as it arises are important.

Conclusion

This chapter focused on you. The introduction introduced the approach I would use to discuss the feminine influence in business. The Feminine Influence chapter outlined some initial concepts about the influence by showing how she already exists in business. This book is attempting to highlight her more important aspects and to encourage her more active integration by you. The Company chapter took a case study to illustrate how the feminine influence can help a company; however, the analogy applies to individuals as well. Even though we looked at a company, we could easily have looked at a person's business career. The basic theme is one of rebirth, finding ways to regenerate our business and our careers. Birth is the union of two forces: the masculine and the feminine. Without one or the other, dynamic new possibilities symbolized by the birth of a child are not possible. Business is dominated by the masculine influence with little awareness for the power inherent in the feminine influence. With a more active integration and appreciation for the feminine influence, we can recreate our careers and businesses so they continue growing in the manner of the right diagram in Figure 3.6. Without such integration our futures and our business' futures will more likely represent Figure 3.7 where we eventually experience a slow decline dominated more by an effort to simply exist than grow.

The next chapter, Strategy, will focus on relationships, the foundation of business. As we've learned relationships are between two individuals. In the Company chapter we learned that there are four elements to outcomes: situation, flow, people, and the individual. This chapter links the two chapters by focusing on you because you will be one of the two people in a relationship and you will be an individual influencing outcomes. The effort to integrate the feminine influence in business is really a story about you.

As I have mentioned in this chapter and throughout the book, communicating and integrating these themes would work best if I knew you. Since I could not do this, the best way to view this chapter is as a conversation between my internal and external self in which I am discussing a perspective of looking at others and me that has greatly helped me appreciate and help others. I've intended this chapter to serve as an introduction to implementing the feminine influence. The challenge I found was balancing between an extremely comprehensive approach that might overwhelm and an extremely basic approach that might not be effective.

Toward this end I wanted to avoid three things that I discussed in detail in the introduction to this chapter:

- Appealing to a generic or average reader.
- Formulaic application – "one size fits all".
- Academic explanations.

I do not pretend that the concepts in this chapter are for everyone. I've learned that aiming too high is better than too low. I also don't pretend that the concepts in here are easy; they don't fit easily into a step-by-step approach or a computer program. They require someone to contemplate the concepts and him to see how he may best integrate them into his personality. Lastly, I confess that I have not presented these ideas in a manner that will hold up in an academic court of inquiry. I have not used the conventional scientific method in anyway to support any of the concepts here. All I know is that these work for me and have been validated in my world by watching them in the laboratory of real life. I wanted to present these concepts in a way that made them applicable to business without making them too practical that they became mechanical (and essentially useless).

Furthermore, such a scientific approach is pointless because I'm not seeking your agreement or approval. That would render this book useless to you and me unless it's accompanied by serious, involved contemplation about its themes. Only in this way, will you make this book work for you. If the themes in this book caused you to contemplate and adopt views contrary to mine, but yet through this contemplation you were able to discover a new way to help yourself and others, what's the problem? Sometimes, the most positive things we've learned that have helped us were things people did not intend for us to learn. Additionally, this book is not meant to be an endpoint but rather an entry point. Hopefully, one day I'll run into you so I could learn from the insights you've generated by reading this book. If I don't have that pleasure, perhaps you'll decide to write a book for me and others to read.

The major aspects of You that I covered here for your contemplation were:

- Personality
- Talent
- Conditioning
- Growth

The objective with these aspects was to stay focused on you and the other person with whom you may be relating. This person could easily be you as the inside-outside duality implies from the personality section. Using a military analogy it's easier to think of this chapter as reconnaissance and the next chapter as the plan.

In an effort to tap the inherent power in our personalities we explored how we're influenced, the needs within us, our inside-outside duality, and the benefits of introversion. I'm going to run through the main aspects of each of these that would be of help to remember.

First, we're influenced by many things of which we are unaware. We can often even be unaware as to how we're influenced by them and attribute their influence incorrectly to other factors and people. Second, we're driven by emotions that manifest themselves as thoughts and eventually behavior. Anytime along this path we can consciously incorrectly associate specific feelings, thoughts, and behavior. Some of these emotions are very strong and appear as needs as Figure 4.13 showed. Third, looking at ourselves initially in the form of an inside-outside duality will help explain some basic feelings, thoughts, and behavior. It's by no means comprehensive but it's not meant to be. This duality is merely to help serve as a starting point for understanding and appreciating how your internal feelings and thoughts have different origination points. Your outside person seeks to protect you while your inside person seeks to assert your personality. The language of the outside is rational while the language inside is emotional. Fourth, introversion is a friend who allows you to access your innermost qualities and talents. Culturally, we tend to frown on introverted activities because we think it represents a dislike for people, but introversion encourages us to spend our best time with those most important to us rather than always getting lost in meeting a whole crowd of folks.

A critical aspect of anyone's personality is his talent. In this chapter we discussed talent from the aspects of definition, nature, resistance, framework, and access. The emphasis was on the emotional, irrational approach to talent since it's more akin to beauty than skill, since it's more likely to be effective in accessing and developing talent than a heavily rational approach.

We discussed the difficulties in trying to define talent and the likely uselessness even if we could. Our emphasis was more on the nature of talent so while we may not have a definitive definition at least we can get a feel for it circumstantially. Even though talent has many aspects, some of which we covered in previous chapters such as quality, attractiveness, and singularity, we focused our efforts on four other broad aspects of talent:

- Vitality
- Expressivity
- Innumerability
- Abnormality

Associated with appreciating talent's nature there was the discussion on the resistance to it from within the individual and from without from the group. These can be very involved and powerful determinants on talent's ability to manifest itself. Through a framework called Wisdom's Magical Hierarchy we were able to introduce the attributes that would allow talent to become more apparent to us. We outlined four signs that we may be in the presence of talent:

- Sensitivity
- Expressivity
- Growth
- Microtonality

The main point to remember here is that talent expresses itself in the small. By looking at what is barely determinable, one can identify and access talent that may be hidden. After this we explored conceptually a way for us to visualize the effort needed to bring talent to the surface for growth and appreciation.

Of course, no personality or talent discussion is possible without exploring the factors that encourage certain behavior on our part, conditioning. While some may have natural bases, others do not. The key here is remembering behavior, no matter how simple it appears on the surface, has many deep implications that may or may not be inherent in one's personality. The only thing certain is that if one is not aware of the influence conditioning has on us, one is most likely not going to be able to deal with himself and others as effectively as he could.

The last aspect of you that we covered was growth. The approach and perspective to growth can assume many forms depending upon the personalities involved. The key is to focus on and encourage growth with minimal to no attention on weaknesses unless it's certain they will create great harm for the person. Concurrent with this approach is the emphasis and priority given to the observations you and the other person develop. Relationships are based upon emotion and subjectivity not rationale and objectivity, so the only important views from a business development perspective are the two involved. Objectivity does not inspire.

The greatest power we have lies within. What is great usually has difficulty associated with it. If something is difficult then it increases the likelihood that few rather than many can do it. Consequently, accessing this power is more available to the few than the many. Setting up the basic requirements for our existence is easier than accessing the power within for dynamic growth. Building a house comes before making it a home. The challenge is spending so much time and money on the house that there is little left to make it a home.

This is why extroverted activity is much easier than introverted activity. Whereas the first accesses the resources in our outer world, the second accesses those in our inner world. Thus, many can access and remain focused on the outside, but few can do the same with the inside. Through both activities, we bring what is in – out. In this way, inner power transforms our outer world.

As we saw in the Company chapter extroverted activity is associated with the masculine influence while introverted activity with the feminine. Outside is the masculine as inside is to the feminine. Our physical world comes first just as we saw the masculine comes first in the Feminine Influence chapter with the Persian Gulf War example and others (Figs. 2.54 – 2.57). However, if we remain fixated on our outer world, our inner world deteriorates and becomes increasingly inaccessible to us. In our business lives this tension manifests itself in the conflict between the material well-being and the emotional fulfillment our professions provide. Maximizing our long-term success is more dependent upon the second than the first. Likewise, the long-term success of a business is more dependent upon how clients, employees, and managers each handle this conflict for themselves and for each other.

When we talk about the emotional fulfillment that our jobs provide, we return once again to the feminine influence because we are talking about how to insure our house becomes a home. Thus, this whole chapter on You is about integrating the feminine influence within oneself so we can access the best that lies within us. The danger, as we discussed in this chapter, is relying upon external results to determine where you stand with this integration; they have a mediocre correlation. The determinant is not decided relatively but absolutely. The only absolute is the realization of the best that lies within you. Doing a comparison with another can't satisfy that and is why being number one can quickly lead one to mediocrity absolutely.

The inner world is governed by the feminine influence. This chapter focused mainly upon you and your inner world where your greatest power is in repose. The Strategy chapter will have us turn our attention outward to see how the feminine influence helps us manifest our personalities in our outer world in ways that may help us.

Strategy

The essence of the strategy outlined in this chapter is to win hearts. In symbolizing that essence, I've chosen to call it the "Lady In Black" Strategy. Our focus will be on working with others in your company, but these principles also work for clients and any other personal interaction you may have.

As with any strategy, it's not the only determinant of outcomes. Figure 4.33 identifies situation, flow, people, and the individual as the major determinants. In this case, I'm using strategy to represent your efforts, the individual, to maximize your talents' influence. No strategy is guaranteed to work; no one can outdo an event where the situation, flow, and people are against him. Sometimes the best we can do is escape with our well-being intact. We often hear something along the lines of "Luck is when persistence meets opportunity." The hidden question in this is, "What happens if an opportunity doesn't show up?" We can also imply from this that "not all opportunities are created equal." Our discussion in the Company chapter served to expose us to how situation, flow, and people affect outcomes.

Nevertheless, the "Lady In Black" Strategy increases the likelihood that you will employ your potential in any situation. There are two characteristics worth mentioning at the outset regarding application: evolutionary and relentless.

The strategy is evolutionary because it relies upon small, incremental applications over an extended period of time. Some applications may be so small and incremental that they may even appear to achieve nothing. Extremely small knots make an oriental rug. While they are the reasons why these rugs take a long time to make, they are also the reasons why they are so durable and long-lasting. Hardwood trees grow slower than softwood ones. From small incremental steps, great journeys are born.

Relentless applies to the strategy because it relies upon regular application everyday. Since the strategy is relational based, each day contains numerous opportunities for application whether it's in face-to-face interactions and phone conversations or more indirect ones such as correspondence and email. Every communication with another person, no matter how insignificant, can serve as an opportunity to build an extremely strong foundation on which you can operate.

Since relentless and evolutionary give the "Lady In Black" Strategy a subtle, indirect, and invisible flavor, it's heavily influenced by the feminine influence. The Feminine Influence chapter served to enhance our understanding and appreciation for this influence because she plays a tremendous role in the strategy's successful implementation. The name of the strategy symbolizes this connection. In this chapter I will seek to illustrate the connection more tangibly.

In addition to the feminine influence, situation, flow, and people impacting a strategy, you are involved too. The You chapter sought to delve into ways to access your personality more effectively. An underlying theme with this strategy is that you can do something. In general, there are two types of people, those who ask, tell, or pay someone to do something and those who actually do something, more simply the askers and the doers. Many times we all flow back and forth between the two, but some of us tend toward one more than the other. Many times work, like water, flows downhill but eventually it has to stop somewhere. For water it's the ponds, lakes, and oceans. These bodies of water serve to nourish us. Likewise, those who can do something nourish us because they are the bodies where work accumulates to be done. The You chapter is important because it begins to help you enhance your and others' talents. You give the strategy life.

Even ignoring outside influences, strategies are always challenged because they must negotiate two pairs of opposing forces. The first is negotiating the balance between detail and flexibility, and the second is negotiating the balance between coherency and personalization.

Beyond these generic conditions, two aspects particular to the feminine influence in business make a strategic discussion additionally difficult. First, the strategy does not address your particular environment in the way it really could, and second, humanistic relationships are more involved than mechanical ones.

As a result of these generic and particular conditions, my aim is to be specific but when in doubt fall the other way toward the conceptual. The danger of any process is that it becomes mechanical. For relational ones this almost insures effectiveness falling far short of potential. As stated earlier, people prefer an imperfect original to a perfect copy. Thus, the effort for you after reading this strategy (and the book) will lie in applying the concepts to you, others, and your environment in a way that fits you and how you enjoy working with others.

On the other hand, uniqueness does not have to impede us totally. Our world would have no cohesion whatsoever if some universal concepts did not exist. This prevents us from totally falling on the side of flexibility and personalization but also begins to crystallize the challenge in this chapter. We should be able to come away with some detail and coherency that will allow us to apply the strategy to our situation. In that light, this strategy will serve as an entry point such as point "X" did in Figures 2.49 and 2.50. Thus, if we look at Figure 2.55, we can say that while I won't be able to give you the destination "Y" or the paths "M" and "N", I certainly will give you more than just an oval. I'll give you an entry point into the oval, ways to discover the "N" paths or other variations, and encouragement to explore them as opposed to the more routine, direct "M" path that generally generates little dynamism.

Consequently, as you apply this strategy to your environment you'll find it's far from comprehensive. The nuances of an individual situation are far too numerous to address even if I had full knowledge of your situation.

We'll discuss the "Lady In Black" Strategy in three parts: truths, aspects, and tactics. To support some of the points I will reference our discussions from previous chapters since they provide their overarching context. By placing the strategy here, I don't have to take frequent tangents delving into the deeper principles behind its aspects because I can now reference them for you to review as you feel necessary. All of this is being done to achieve the right feel for the strategy; understanding the specifics is secondary and can be referenced at another time.

Truths will explore four remaining points encompassing the context of this strategy that require additional highlighting and summarization:

- Integration – Formalizing a relational picture integrating the masculine and feminine for a specific interaction.
- Influence – Establishing the premise that a subordinate group can influence the actions of its superior group.
- Leadership – Illustrating the inspirational quality of leadership.
- Subjectivity – Demonstrating the power of subjectivity over objectivity.

Aspects will outline various actions to implement this strategy. Since the whole pur-pose is to win hearts, the strategy will focus on your relationship with each person in your company and clients. This relationship will develop through two forums, individual interactions and group interactions. We will discuss the actions contained in each interaction with the main premise being that the group interactions set up the individual ones.

Tactics will delve into some major factors that supplement the aspects. They'll explore:

- Commander-Sage role
- Problem solving
- Comprehensive focus
- Different perspectives
- Documenting ideas
- Employees are #1

Truths

Before exploring the details around the "Lady In Black" Strategy, we need to discuss four other truths: integration of the masculine and feminine, influence of a subordinate group on a superior one, inspirational leadership, and the power behind subjectivity.

Integration

While this entire book concerns itself with the integration of the masculine and feminine influences, we do not have a working illustration of that integration as it pertains to an interaction between two people. Figure 5.1 will serve as that illustration throughout this chapter and the balance of the book.

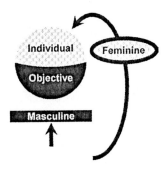

Figure 5.1

The ideas Figure 5.1 express are not new. In fact, we often talk about them everyday but probably not in the language of this diagram. The purpose of looking at an interaction in the way Figure 5.1 suggests is that it allows us to more effectively relate it to other aspects of business. Essentially, we're simplifying the Persian Gulf War example by having the masculine initiate and set the nature of the contact while the feminine works around the end for the decisive outcome.

In current business terms, the masculine influence concerns itself with the actual business objective for both parties while the feminine influence concerns itself with the interpersonal aspects of the interaction such as the impressions it creates in us. Frequently in business people talk about the importance of relationships, Figure 5.1 demonstrates that importance by giving the feminine influence the decisive role. In other words, our business reason for interacting with the person represents the masculine while our attempt to connect with the person on a human level represents the feminine.

The reason why this diagram puts the individual behind the objective is symbolized by the expression "putting your game face on." Whenever anyone enters a business situation, there is always the inclination to "hide" behind the task at hand. Your focus is not yourself but the task. As with clients, getting down to the "human level" is an important step in relational development. It's important to get "behind" the business issues and address more personal aspects. While the particular aspects of this personal relationship may be different, whether you deal with a client or an employee there is a need to do this if we want dynamic outcomes. One cannot inspire if one cannot tap emotions.

Explained in this way, Figure 5.1 is not very different from what we experience everyday. What is different is the decisive role given to the feminine because this implies that the masculine becomes the excuse to employ the feminine. This differs from the current state of business because the tendency is to visit with someone only if there is a business reason for doing so, and the feminine, or relational aspect of the interaction, becomes simply a way to facilitate the business at hand, "grease the skids" in common business jargon.

The deeper implication of Figure 5.1 is that the business at hand is secondary; it becomes the excuse for building a relationship. Whereas a masculine initiated approach emphasizes achieving the business objective, a feminine approach emphasizes creating a strong relational bond. For the masculine, the business objective is paramount. While establishing a strong relational foundation is important, it's not critical as long as we achieve the business objective. For the feminine, we have a reversal of priorities. The objective is to create a strong relational foundation. While achieving the business objective is important, it's not critical as long as we form a strong relational bond.

This approach is not abnormal to business; it's just not emphasized. For instance, we often see an employee trying to find an "excuse" to visit with a manager so as to gain exposure. More commonly we call this "face time." In this way an employee hopes to establish a stronger relational bond with the manager so he'll be more inclined to look upon his work more favorably. We also experienced this in college with professors. Students would find excuses to visit with professors for the purpose of developing a relational bond that would encourage the professor to look for favorably upon the student's work.

If we once again refer to the masculine/feminine word table in Figure 5.2 which now includes additions since our last review of it in Figure 2.60, we can begin to enhance our feel for how this strategy might work.

Masculine	Feminine
Pursue	Attract
Direct	Indirect
Independent	Dependent
Practical	Inspirational
Cold	Warm
Reason	Feeling
Objective	Subjective
Cognition	Intuition
Tangible	Intangible
Scripted	Spontaneous
Chained	Free
Focus	Distract
Simple	Involved
Mediocre	Intelligent
Coolness	Courage
Rational	Irrational
Outside	Inside
Many	Few
Easy	Difficult
Visible	Invisible
Logic	Emotion
Objectify	Personalize

Figure 5.2

As you can see, many of the masculine words typically represent what takes place in a business discussion that you *pursue* with an employee. Likewise, the feminine words are fairly representative of what is necessary to *attract* someone's trust and to create a relationship with you. This is why women tend to be more relationship "experts" than men.

When we look at Figure 5.1 from the feminine aspect, we begin to see the advantage of people approaching us; we automatically have a built in excuse to speak with someone, and it's on their terms. We'll explore this advantage in more detail when we talk about the Individual heading of the Aspects section. Essentially, we have your masculine aptitudes associated with the particular business objective at hand directly engaging the employee while your feminine ones take the indirect route to establish a relationship with the individual. The distinction between our message and the impression we leave.

The focus of the "Lady In Black" Strategy is to win hearts; thus, relationship building is paramount, secondary to the business objective. People are inspired by other people not business objectives. Ultimately, the strength of this relational bond will pay huge dividends in return that will encourage greater effectiveness around business objectives down the road. We more commonly call this the difference between a "transactional" relationship and a "holistic" one.

We often see this when we help clients in ways that don't generate immediate business or may even cost us business short-term. They learn that their relationship with us is more important than their business. What we're essentially saying is taking this approach and applying it to our employees in the business. When we sacrifice immediate business objectives to help others, we are saying their relationships with us are more important than the work (business) they supply. The effectiveness of this approach with employees is no less than we experience with clients.

Influence

What are we trying to achieve with these relationships? Our fundamental purpose is to establish an inspirational influence that will manifest itself in business. Influence can assume many different forms, formal and informal. We can see this manifestation helping four basic entities:

- You
- Employees
- Clients
- Company

The surroundings, communications, and actions of any person can tell you much about the person because his personality seeks to express itself upon the world around him. The theme to remember is that what's inside will project outside. We can apply this theme on grander scales such as with companies; what exists inside will reflect outside. Thus, the nature of relationships between employees and managers will eventually assume a similar flavor outside between employees and clients. The personality inside a company will eventually permeate outside. Entities with strong employee-manager relationships will tend to have strong employee-client relationships.

The permeation's pace will occur over time and vary directly to the size of the entity; the smaller the entity the more likely permeation will occur over a shorter time frame while the larger the entity the longer the time frame. We more commonly experience this in a narrower sense when we discuss cultural changes within groups – larger ones tend to require more time than smaller ones.

My emphasis will be upon you the reader because the other three (employees, clients and company) are groups and thus do not exist as organic entities we can touch and visualize. As we had introduced with Figure 1.4 and discussed several times thereafter, individuals comprise groups. Groups cannot exist without individuals, but individuals will still exist without groups. Individuals drive reality and truth. Therefore, the purpose of the influence heading is to introduce to you how inspirational influence can help you accomplish more with your personality and talent.

From an objective, textbook orientation, any organization seems to operate by the governing rules, procedures, and policies of the hierarchical structure that's in place. Just as any computer program, plan, or agenda cannot exactly accommodate reality, governing rules, procedures, and policies suffer the same defect and is the reason why the theory behind the United States judicial system has judges to interpret laws, to make sure the generic nature of law is justly applied to the specifics of the situation.

In order to begin the exploration of these inherent cracks in a hierarchical structure, let's look at the most prominent position in a large corporation, chief executive officer (CEO), because this will allow us to magnify what occurs in smaller entities so we can more easily see the dynamics behind these cracks.

On paper, in terms of deciding upon the next CEO of a major corporation the decision would primarily rest with the current CEO and the board of directors with subsequent approval of the shareholders. In reality though there are many constituencies that influence this such as senior executives, senior managers, managers, and even employees. In order to make the connection more difficult, let's assume these other constituencies are not shareholders in the way of retirement plans, exercised options, and stock bonuses.

On paper again, most of these other constituencies do not have a "vote"; however, in some way they all influence the decision for a variety of reasons. Many times the influence entails the results they generate for the executive being considered for the job. For instance, if I wish a particular executive to become the next CEO, I would make sure I would do an excellent job for him so results would support his nomination. I also have the opportunity to influence others along these lines to do just the same.

On the surface, most would say I do not have a "vote" in the decision but my effort is my vote. Even in a democratic system, everyone has one vote but some people's vote counts more via money, labor, and personal connections.

For a politician, a voter who donates a million dollars is worth more than a voter who donates nothing. A voter who works a hundred hours as a volunteer is worth more than a voter who does not volunteer. A voter who is president of an organization is worth more than a voter who is not. In fact, the politician may even forego the second person's vote if he could get the first voter's money, labor, or endorsement. There are factors outside of a mere vote that influence outcomes; these factors can be far more influential than a vote.

Staying with the politician theme, mere enthusiasm for a candidate is infectious and thus influential. If enthusiasm sells in sales, can it influence elections? The more enthusiastic someone is about a candidate the more likely he is not only to vote but also to convince others.

In sales, we do not decide whether a prospect buys, the prospect does; however, we influence his decision. Technically speaking, we do not have a vote just as we don't have a vote in who becomes CEO. However, if someone states we have no say in who becomes CEO, then we have no say in whether a prospect buys. By implication, this person is saying that a sales person has no part in selling.

Of course, whether an employee has an interest in who becomes CEO is an issue. If someone believes the primary motivation is money, then he will not see why an employee would be concerned with who becomes CEO as long as he continues to have his job to receive a paycheck. Who becomes CEO is irrelevant to the employee unless it determines the size of his paycheck. However, for someone who believes other issues such as professional or personal growth and quality of life inspire people, then he will easily see why an employee would be concerned with who becomes CEO. A CEO's personality affects everyone.

In most organizations the employees' opinions or feelings do not come into play extensively in determining the next CEO because it's the least likely constituency anyone would consider as possibly affecting the decision. Additionally, even if it were seen as a constituency, it would be the most difficult one to build into a base of support; however, once built it can be the most powerful, even more powerful than the hierarchical authority written into the organization's rules, policies, and procedures.

As a result, what generally happens in the competition among those seeking to be the next CEO is that this constituency is overlooked and neglected as a base of support outside of generating great numbers that appear on paper. In effect the competition becomes like two football teams who compete against one another and mutually agree to not use pass plays and just run the ball.

Similarly, in the competition to become the next CEO, there is an informal, mutual conditioning that says ideas like this are impossible. This mutual conditioning can be as basic as one executive advising another to read a particular book on success. If one contender can get another to play the game by the rules he sees will most benefit him, then he by default improves his chances of winning. Generally, this is the strategy of the less intelligent and talented because they cannot defeat those above them unless they are able to convince the others that imposing their advantages are irrelevant, impossible, or complex. The least costly way to defeat another is to convince him not to fight back.

There are two, broad categories of personal power, granted and *de facto*. The first is formal and comes from the authority given by others within the confines of rules, procedures, and policies in an organizational structure. The second is informal and comes from the talent to do something. Whereas the first can only exist with an overlaying structure in place, the second exists irrespective of it. Most commonly at work we hear this expressed when someone introduces his assistant by saying, "This is Jane, she's the one who really runs things." This differentiates the power granted by title as a supervisor and the *de facto* power of the assistant for getting things done.

Illustrations of this differentiation exist in movies like *Braveheart* and *Gladiator* and in historical events like Rommel's suicide and September 11th.

Braveheart is a movie about the Scottish revolution against England. Leading the Scots were two men who represent this differentiation of power. One was the lead noble who by formal authority governed Scotland with other nobles. The other man had no formal authority but inspirationally united the commoners into a fighting force. ·

Gladiator concerns itself with how a slave, through his heroics in the ring, obtained the favor of the crowd so the emperor could not kill him without hurting his own reputation. History contains a similar event with Rommel's forced suicide for conspiring to kill Hitler. His popularity among the German people prevented Hitler from publicly trying him and killing his family as was done with the other conspirators. As a result, Hitler allowed him to commit suicide and have it communicated as a natural death so Rommel's family and reputation would remain intact as well as Hitler's.

September 11th offered the most recent example of the differentiation between granted and *de facto* power. The clean up of the Twin Trade Towers did not fall clearly within anyone's jurisdiction. Since there was an urgent threat of subsequent disasters from various weakened structures including potential flooding of subway tunnels, there was no hierarchy in place to make decisions. As a result, individuals who had particular hands-on knowledge, experience, or talents had the *de facto* power to make decisions and implement them. Most of these individuals didn't even hold places of high authority in any of their corresponding organizations.

The point here as it relates to this strategy is that despite what an organizational chart may show as to who has authority to make decisions about someone becoming CEO, there are other factors. Within any organization, there are not only the leaders as designated by a title but there are leaders with *de facto* power with whom others consult or follow. We tend to know these people more informally as "go to" people, ones you count on in tough situations. Every organization has these types of people.

The key to implementing any strategy is not only knowing who the titled leaders are but also the *de facto* ones who can influence the job at hand. Unfortunately, it's not as easy as identifying the ones who sell the most or have the most experience or degrees. For the most part, they are people with a certain integrity that encourages others to listen to them beyond what is conveyed by their title. In effect, they have won the hearts of other people.

In *Braveheart* the noble, Robert the Bruce played by Angus Macfadyen, is trying to convince the commoners' leader, William Wallace played by Mel Gibson, to be patient with the titled nobles in the country because he needs them to win Scotland's freedom. William Wallace questions the importance of nobles because "men don't follow titles, they follow courage." These clauses highlight the distinction between authoritative power and *de facto* power. The inspirational quality from the later is rooted in its emotional basis. A computer, while able to run on the authoritative commands of its program, is not affected by courage or any other emotion. Whereas the granted power encourages others to listen because they are supposed to, *de facto* power encourages others to listen because they want to. Consolidating both types of power into one person makes for an extremely potent force. This is essentially what this strategy seeks to influence by winning the hearts, the realm of the feminine influence.

The key is remembering influence also exists in forms outside of the traditional, hierarchical structure within any organization. We touch on this influence when we reference its communicative aspects called "the grapevine." Just as documented communications circumstantially support a formal influential structure, the "grapevine" supports the existence of an informal influential structure.

Leadership

In order to delve deeper into a strategy focused on winning hearts, we must also talk about leadership more subjectively. Our influential discussions introduced us tangibly to the topic, but let's take a moment to crystallize it. A poem will help us move further on our journey.

A Tough Question . . .

with A Tough Answer . . .

for Tough People

If you took away "doing it for the company" as a reason as well as "doing it for the division,"

If you also took away the client as one, as well as the money to be earned,

Along with all the trophies and recognition awards,

And finally eliminated "because I said so" and "do it or else,"

How would you inspire your people to do the things that you need them to do?

Once you found the answer, could you do it?

Now . . . that's a leader.

Essentially, this poem strips away the formal structure to leave the informal. By stripping away the "titles" we are left with "courage." The fundamental implication is that people are more moved by what they like than what they understand. Understanding rules, procedures, policies, command structures, and ideas pale to the inspiration people receive from someone they like. Furthermore, people are more likely to receive inspiration from a person than some object. Implicationally, we arrive at the inherent power of the subjective over the objective; the subjective inspires while the objective merely commands. Again, we return to the importance of the feminine influence in providing the subjectivity necessary for inspiration.

The long-term economic advantages of inspiration involve time and quality. Inspiration contains trust; how can one inspire without it? When trust permeates every aspect of an organization, the mobilization time around initiatives and their actions constricts. One no longer has to spend the time explaining decisions because the other person now trusts your judgment to make a good decision, your effort to make it work, and your sincerity in watching out for his interests. Quality appears because the other person now transcends the complacent fulfillment of a command to the opportunistic seizure of unexpected realities inherently offered by any event.

Despite inspiration's power, the degree to which one inspires and is inspired will vary by individual. Individuals differ so their affections toward inspiration will differ as well. Since inspiration is an emotion it's associated with feelings. An important feeling engulfing inspiration is empathy. Inspiration is very difficult without empathy, an intuition for another's condition by the feelings it arouses with you.

A computer cannot inspire or be inspired. Consequently, a key indicator of the degree to which one can inspire or be inspired is sensitivity. The more sensitive one is the more likely he will have strong affinities for inspiration while the less sensitive he is the less likely. What someone sees is directly related to his ability to see; the better his ability the better his sight. Likewise, what someone feels is directly related to his ability to feel; the better his ability the better his feel for things.

As we saw with Wisdom's Magical Hierarchy, wisdom places on premium on emotions for they allow an intuitive ability that expands far beyond the limits of mere cognition. Figures 2.1 – 2.17 demonstrate the importance of this ability in seizing opportunities and heading off problems. Thus, intelligence is directly related to sensitivity.

The effort required to deliver and receive commands is far less than that to deliver and receive inspiration. Both of the latter require a lot of work from the one who inspires and the one who is inspired; however, once in place its potency is far greater than anything a command could grant.

We can illustrate this in the difference between a barbarian and a sage; it's much easier to kill a man than it is to inspire him. Barbaric actions are easier than sagely actions; our laws demonstrate this in the extent to which they seek to prevent barbaric actions rather than encourage sagely ones. Many laws seek to retard barbaric actions but few if any require sagely ones; there are laws that say one must not kill, none say one must seek wisdom. The expression, "You can't legislate morality," touches on this distinction.

Analogously returning to a tree, it's much easier to cut a massive tree down than it is to grow one. Cutting is much easier than creating. Cutting is associated with many because many can do the easy, and creating is associated with few because only a few can do the difficult. Since barbaric actions are easier than sagely actions, they will tend to require less intelligence than the latter. Barbarians will encourage barbaric actions and sages will encourage sagely ones; insensitivity will breed insensitive actions and sensitivity will breed sensitive actions. Objectivity will breed objective actions while subjectivity will breed subjective actions. Objectivity is emotionlessness, while subjectivity is emotional. Inspiration is impossible without emotion, without subjectivity, a relationship between two individuals as opposed to two entities.

Life challenges us to encourage our growth. Growth is more akin to creating than cutting, to wisdom than barbarism, to seeking than killing. By applying the effort to do the difficult, we seek wisdom and preserve our sensitivity. The easiest thing to do is to forsake sensitivity and move toward barbarism. The more difficult life's challenge, the fewer will be able to tackle it. Since the inclination is to say something is impossible rather than to say I can't do it or don't want to do it, there will be many who say the difficult is impossible. The many will outnumber the few.

Sensitivity requires intelligence, so the application of insensitivity means unintelligence resides with the deliverer, the recipient, or both. Sensitivity comes in degrees. Insensitivity originates from our survival instinct by making sure our empathy for another doesn't prevent us from eliminating the threat he represents. Since killing our enemy is easier than inspiring him to become our friend, greater intelligence is required for the latter than the former; however, our degree of sensitivity may not give us the intelligence to overcome the degree of insensitivity in another. Thus, since all individuals are unique, we can never guarantee that sensitivity and its sagely actions will always prevail because the potential for a situation where the threat or insensitivity of one can overpower the sensitivity of another will always exist.

Finding new ways are more difficult than following existing ways; thus, dealing with the unique aspects of a situation are more difficult than dealing with the situation categorically based upon a previous, similar situation. More specifically, it's more difficult to deal with things uniquely than uniformly; standardization is easier than customization.

When we apply this implicational stream to insensitivity, we find uniformly dealing with barbaric actions (actions we don't like) easier than dealing with them uniquely. Thus, when such actions occur we are inclined to address their potential future occurrence categorically through the establishment of new rules and policies rather than specifically as they arise. Since the specifics of a future occurrence are unknown, we can only deal with them categorically rather than specifically when we anticipate them; thus, natural holes develop.

Whenever we look at things categorically rather than uniquely, we focus on similarities at the expense of differences. If we focus too much on the differences, the members of a group will no longer fit the group's criteria; thus, inherently, when we seek to categorize things we focus on similarities and de-emphasize differences. When we don't look at the individual aspects of a person, we make him one of many – we depersonalize him. Depersonalizing someone increases the likelihood we will deal with him insensitively. Barbarism breeds barbarism; insensitivity breeds insensitivity. Since it's easier to deal with the barbaric actions of others categorically rather than uniquely, we will tend to move toward insensitivity for all unique situations including those involving sages. Thus, all actions will tend to receive uniform treatment regardless of whether they originated from a barbarian or sage because it's easier to do and the demands on wisdom less.

Returning to a leader, we find intelligence closely associated with sensitivity; however, the difficulty does not just reside with simply being sensitive, but also in combating the easy tendency toward uniformity that eradicates individual differences and propagates insensitivity. Inspiration requires sensitivity, so insensitive conditions make inspiration difficult. Money objectifies one's value. Since it's easier to believe what we can measure than what we cannot as shown in Figure 2.12, we will trend toward money as the true measurement of one's worth. Quantifying one's worth is easier than identifying the particular qualities that make up one's worth, so the trend will focus on numbers versus qualities. By avoiding the effort to identify another's qualities we avoid an exploration of his uniqueness; the bottom line becomes more important than how one gets to the bottom line. In this way, the tendency will be to objectify people. When we objectify people, inspiration becomes difficult because objectification removes emotion. Without emotion there are no feelings upon which to inspire.

All of this shows the tremendous alignment of forces that requires intelligence to surmount. Without this intelligence a business will follow a normal birth, growth, plateau, decline, and death curve as shown in Figure 3.7 rather than the path shown in the right hand diagram of Figure 3.5 that incorporates regeneration. The important aspects of wisdom necessary to overcome these forces rest in the realm of the feminine influence and are why her active integration in business is vital.

The point of this discussion is to show that even though sensitivity is a sign of intelligence, no one person will be able to resolve all threats through sensitive means because forces trending toward insensitivity are immense. In effect, it's very difficult to deal with a barbarian sensitively. Our effect upon another is not solely dependent upon our nature but also the nature of the other person. Nevertheless, an inspirational leader will tend to deal with sagely and barbaric actions uniquely rather than categorically. In this way, even though one may not like the outcome at least there can be no denial that he was sensitive to the nature of the person involved. Even his response to a barbarian will be unique.

Returning to leadership, the courage that inclines people to follow as the scene from *Braveheart* suggests is the courage to tackle the difficult in light of the easy that encourages many to favor. The degree to which a company will survive long-term correlates to the degree to which sensitivity exists in the nature of its employees, to the degree to which it incorporates the feminine influence into its existing business culture so inspirational influences can flourish.

Subjectivity

Objectivity holds primacy in business today; it serves as the rationale for rooting out emotional decisions so one can arrive at the "right" decision. The problem with an excessive focus on a singular frame of reference around which a consensus builds is that it retards dynamic growth by narrowing opportunities. Earlier, we discussed a human being incapable of objectivity because he is an emotional creature.

The supremacy of subjectivity stems from its creative energy to take what is and make it something else. Objectivity, by its nature, states that what is . . . is. That is the singular perspective from which something is the same for all. Often we find ourselves discounting subjectivity because the views can be as numerous and diverse as the people who give them. The critical aspect of subjectivity to remember is that not all subjective views are created equal; some are better than others. It matters to whose subjectivity you listen.

Objectivity would see a bird as a bird, an apple as an apple, a river as a river, a duck as a duck, a carriage as a carriage, and logs as logs. It cannot see these things as anything else because they can only be one thing and that thing is the thing that they are.

On the other hand, subjectivity can see things in many ways depending upon who's looking. For instance, a bird is no longer a bird but possibly a plane, an apple especially if it's falling could be the law of gravity, a river could be seen as a power source, a duck as a boat, a carriage an automobile, and logs a set of wheels. Only by seeing things as something else do we transform them into something new.

Consequently, objectivity retards dynamic growth because it encourages everyone to look at things from one perspective – that as they are and not as they could be. Once we move into what things could be, our subjective imagination takes over to make something into almost anything. Only through subjectivity will we see possibilities because objectivity can only see things as they are. How would one look at imagination objectively? By only seeing things as they are we fail to see what they could become. "Calling a spade a spade" will yield nothing but a spade.

Yet, this is not to say objectivity is useless, only a temporary stop before moving onto something better. Before "something" can become "something else" it must first be "something." Thus we have:

$$\text{Nothing} \Rightarrow \text{Something} \Rightarrow \text{Something Else}$$

$$\text{Nothing} \Rightarrow \text{Objectivity} \Rightarrow \text{Subjectivity}$$

$$0 \Rightarrow 1 \Rightarrow \infty \text{ (Infinite)}$$

In this light subjectivity becomes a progression in which we can relate back to the feminine influence:

$$\text{Nothing} \Rightarrow \text{Masculine Influence} \Rightarrow \text{Feminine Influence}$$

Analogously, we can even return to our Adam and Eve story and say:

$$\text{Nothing} \Rightarrow \text{Adam} \Rightarrow \text{Eve}$$

The fundamental difference between seeing things as they are and seeing things as they could be is emotion:

$$\text{Nothing} \Rightarrow \text{Cognition} \Rightarrow \text{Intuition}$$

We can relate this to Wisdom's Magical Hierarchy that places emotional aspects above rational ones:

$$\text{Information} \Rightarrow \text{Knowledge} \Rightarrow \text{Reason} \Rightarrow \text{Experience} \Rightarrow \text{Conception} \Rightarrow \text{Intuition} \Rightarrow \text{Creativity}$$

Tying this back to beauty, the fundamental power behind the feminine influence, we see the difference between the objective and subjective as one between a woman being a sex object and a feminine being. Subjectivity requires something more from an individual than merely the capacity to state what something is; it becomes a power by which we transform our businesses and our world. The irrational elements of wisdom represent its more potent aspects.

Symbolically, without Eve, Adam would live out his life and represent the end of the human race before it barely started. Eve represents the regenerative element that allows the human race, family lines, and businesses to continue. Physically, this is the capacity to bear children, but emotionally, it's the capacity to bear new ideas and visions. Without the feminine influence and her subjectivity to breathe new life into maturing life, nothing would continue on beyond its initial existence. Again, this serves to support the primacy of sensitivity without which no emotions can exist and thus no rebirth.

If we take this representation where ∞ is infinity:

$$0 \Rightarrow 1 \Rightarrow \infty$$

And truncate it to make it look like this:

$$0 \Rightarrow 1$$

We now have the binary code (0, 1; no, yes; off, on) in computers. Consequently, what we have is ∞ representing the emotional element that makes us different from computers. That ability to imagine gives us the regenerative power to change our world from what is to what it could be. Computers cannot imagine. A relentless drive toward encouraging objectivity is a drive to retard creative energies necessary for any business' long-term growth.

<u>Aspects</u>

The four truths we just discussed, integration of the masculine and feminine, influence of a subordinate group on a superior one, inspirational leadership, and subjective power, complete the context surrounding the "Lady In Black" Strategy. This portion of the chapter will outline two major aspects of this strategy which has a relational focus: the individual and group.

Since the key to any relationship is the one-on-one interaction between two people, it's hard and impossible to have a personal relationship with someone if the setting always involves a group. Thus, group interactions become secondary and work best as forums for laying the groundwork for an interpersonal experience later or for reinforcing an earlier one. Group interactions, while more efficient, are less effective than personal interactions.

Seminar selling best exemplifies this interplay. Whereas the seminar introduces attendees to a service, individual meetings following the seminar focus at securing additional business. If selling individuals while in a group is unlikely, then it follows that bringing closure to strong individual relationships while in a group is unlikely as well. As a result, this difference and interplay between individual and group interactions becomes the rationale for breaking the Aspects portion of this chapter into these two parts.

Under individual interactions I'll cover four elements: personification, prescription, picture, and phraseology. Personification of any effort is vital to its success. The prescription will allow you to become the personification of the effort you target. A picture will allow us to visualize what we're trying to achieve in an interpersonal experience. Lastly, phraseology will show how to transform this picture into tangible aspects of an interaction.

Group interactions will have four elements as well: map, positioning, reinforcement, and opportunities. A map will create a visual aid for us to reference when we discuss how to break down barriers to engagement and how to create resonation within a group. Positioning will focus on the more traditional aspects using group interactions to position individual interactions as follow up. Reinforcement is the reverse of positioning and will show the less traditional use of group interactions to follow up individual ones. Lastly, we will outline some opportunities for group interactions and the actions around them that will allow for the positioning and reinforcement of individual interactions.

For the purpose of this chapter, I will consider a group any collection of people larger than just you and the other person.

Individual

Four elements comprise this portion of the Strategy chapter:

- Personification
- Prescription
- Picture
- Phraseology

By default, a relationship cannot exist without a personalized experience. This can be as simple as keeping a stone from a memorable hike or as involved as associating an issue or topic to a person. People feel closest to something when they can associate it to themselves or to someone with whom they identify. Essentially, this strategy seeks to have others identify you more closely with the company, division, or effort. I'll conceptually elaborate how to do this by using a picture and by highlighting some phrases that you may wish to incorporate in your personal interactions with others.

Personification

People are more likely to have trust and faith in leaders who focus on the relationship between them and other people than those who focus on the relationship between other people and some institution or concept. Leaders who sacrifice their relationship with another person for the sake of abstractions will less likely be able to form strong bonds with others. In the business world, the two most prevalent abstractions are the company and the client. A company only exists on paper. Unless you reference a specific client that both you and the other individual know, a client is an abstract concept as well.

Without a legal framework, companies can't exist. What makes up a company are people: clients, employees, and managers. Without these people, a company has no character or personality; it's lifeless – nonexistent. Unless you're talking about a specific client, clients don't exist except as a concept on paper because the "average client" does not exist. The average client, as we saw for the average American citizen, for most companies would be part man and part woman, so when we talk about clients in a general sense we are talking about a generality that is nonexistent, no one can point a finger to it and say, "Aha, there it is – an average client!"

This is important for you because other employees will more likely enjoy their jobs and clients more likely enjoy doing business if they know they are helping you rather than some abstraction like clients or companies. These abstractions are faceless, bodiless, mindless, and heartless. You have a face, a body, a mind, and a heart. Any person would more likely prefer to help you than something that only exists on paper. The only override would be a specific client that other employees know and help. People like to personalize their efforts. They can picture your a specific client; they cannot picture the others. We also see this in a negative form when we seek scapegoats who personify the problem. Again, you can't hold a group accountable because it doesn't exist, so it's easier to project our anger and frustration onto an individual.

If we asked employees to picture the following, which would create a more consistent vision among them:

- You
- Your company
- Clients
- A specific client that we identify by name.

In the first and fourth we have a name and a body. In the second we have a name but *no body*; this is why a company is a *nobody*. For the third, we have many bodies and many names. Our clients are *some body* that can have *any body*; *anybody* is *nobody* until he's *somebody*. As a result, this abstraction of a company and a group show up in our legal arrangements because no company or group can sign a legal document – someone has to sign *for* the company or *for* the group. A company cannot be imprisoned nor can a group, but individuals can. While scapegoats may not be totally innocent, they often times are not the only ones responsible. Thus, personification not only drives personal relationships but legal ones as well. If we do not entrust a company legally, why entrust it with our hearts?

As a result, the reason why leaders who subjugate themselves to nonexistent things are less likely to develop strong bonds with others is that they are more likely to subjugate others as well to something non-existent. Someone who is likely to surrender his integrity for an abstraction is more likely to surrender the integrity of others as well for the very same abstractions. This is why various wars see cases of frontline officers, driven by glory rather than the own well being of their men "accidentally" shot by their troops in battle. No one wants to sacrifice themselves for nothing; this is why there is a need to personify what they seek to accomplish. Thus, if you can show your folks how their efforts help you, they are more likely to help especially if you reinforce with examples of how they have helped you and how you're in the same boat with them. The key is building and reinforcing the power of your personality to accomplish this; this is the underlying purpose of the "Lady In Black" Strategy.

This concept is the same reason why you don't want to advertise yourself as a team player to clients. A team player is easily interpreted as someone who is willing to give up on a good idea just to please others. From clients' perspectives "team player" produces an immediate inclination to view the sales person as someone that would give up on them in order to please the team. Clients want someone who is a client advocate; sometimes a client advocate won't be able to please the team. This is where teamwork becomes the coalescing around one person's wisdom about the client and doing what that one person suggests as opposed to a "groupthink" mentality.

Prescription

If a company cannot exist without clients, employees, and managers, then a company's personality is the blend of everyone's personality. Who's to say which personality infuses more life than another? No man can coerce a woman's love. It's easier for a man to raise an army and conquer a nation of men than it is for him to force the love of a single woman. Likewise, how can anyone coerce one person to like another? For this reason, people will like whom they please and not whom they are told to like. Who's going to tell people what to like and not to like about you?

Personality determines our likes and dislikes; our likes reflect our personalities. If no one can coerce love or like from another, then no one can force our personalities to be anything other than what they are. Thus, no one person can consciously determine what the company's personality will be and have it be that.

If employees and clients are attracted to you, then you become a personification of their likes and by implication their personalities. You become for them the personification of the company, division, or effort and help make something abstract very personal for them. While no one can dictate the personality of a company, someone can represent the personality of the company. This only occurs if he has won the hearts of those in the company because otherwise he's no more than a cosmetic representation.

The personality of a home is less determined by its actual structure and more by the people living inside it. Additionally, the personality of a person is less determined by his body and more by the heart living inside it. Continuing with this implicative stream we arrive at the point that the personality of a company is less determined by its policies and procedures and more by the employees working through those policies and procedures. No one can say your personality is not a viable representation of an entity's personality because he cannot dictate how people feel in their hearts. Rules win behavioral compliance but do not win hearts. Referring back to our apple orchard analogy, people will find ways to get *all* the apples for the one who has won their hearts.

Picture

At the beginning of this chapter, I introduced Figure 5.1 to represent a personal interaction. I'll elaborate on it now.

Generally, business pressures prevent us from taking the time we would like to get to know someone. It's also very easy to rationalize this as something extremely secondary to the business purpose at hand. "We're here to do a job not be friends," or "I'm here to make a living," are just a couple expressions that represent this rationalization.

As we have already discussed in the previous chapters, relationships are at the root of every business. We identified two major types: client-employee and employee-manager. Without these relationships a business could not operate. Often we ignore this and focus more on products, services, marketing, and other more traditional business elements; but, nevertheless, none of this would matter if there were no clients, no employees, and no managers to form the necessary relationships to move a company from paper to a functioning reality. For the moment, let's just consider these traditional elements as manifestations of the types of relationships two people may have that are all lumped together under one category called "business relationships." Yet, the type of relationship one has with various companies changes and demonstrates the kind of relationship he has with an employee in the company.

For instance, when I go to a vending machine to select a soft drink, I have an indirect relationship with all the employees involved with creating, producing, and delivering that drink. This indirectness says something about the kind of relationship I have with them. Conversely, other industries have a more direct relationship with people than a company that delivers its product via vending machines. In fact, you can name any product or service and hypothesize the kind of relationship the employees of that company have with their clients based upon the whole process from creating the product or service to delivering it.

You can also surmise what kind of relationship the employees have with their managers. We often recognize that people select employers not only based upon their skills but also upon their personalities; yet, most do not consider the implications of this beyond a mere attribute for selecting a job. However, all other things being equal, a company whose managers and employees have strong relationships with each other will tend to do better than one that doesn't. The tough question is how do you quantify this relationship so you can see the impact in dollars and cents? We all understand the strength of relationships, but we also tend to discount those things we cannot measure as the graph in Figure 2.12 once again shows. As a result, we tend to ignore it in our calculations. If relationships drive a business, the strength of all relationships will more likely determine business success than the strength of products and services.

Consequently, let's for the moment work under the assumption that the primary reason for having a discussion with an employee is not to discuss a business matter but rather to create a stronger relationship that encourages him to pick *all* the apples. We may not know the next tree he will tackle, but let's just say we want him thinking of you so he will be encouraged to generate dynamic results.

Of course, if we simply walk into an employee's office and say, "How about if we get to know one another?" he might just wonder what exactly is going on. This is very similar to a boy just walking up to some strange girl saying, "How about if we go some place alone and get to know one another?" In both situations there is a protocol or a "warming up" period where each person can get to know one another without feeling pressured or on the spot. This is more the nature of relationships than it is protocol; trees don't grow overnight, neither do relationships. They both start and mature slowly at their own pace.

Thus, in the later situation, the boy would find an excuse to talk to the girl. If we follow the assumption that a business relationship is just a personal relationship in different attire, then it would follow that an excuse would work here as well. This isn't as far-fetched as it may initially sound when we consider we look at a client-employee relationship as a form of courtship. Often, we're seeking an excuse to call a client or prospect or to meet a new person. We only need to transfer this to the employee-manager relationship. Again, if this kind of courtship makes for a stronger relationship with the client, it can also apply to the employee-manager one.

Following through on this analogy then, we can make two statements about a personal interaction at work:

- The primary purpose is to build a strong relationship with the person, and any business purpose is secondary.
- Any business purpose can serve as an "excuse" for the personal interaction to occur.

The first point may seem a little counter to an effective business, but we can phrase the rationale with a question: Which is more important – the client or the client's business? If you're not concerned for the client, how can you guarantee a long lasting business relationship? All we're doing is extending this to the employee-manager relationship. Thus, from the perspective of an ongoing relationship whatever is being discussed now is a mere subset and consequently subordinate to the relationship.

These two statements also explain Figure 5.1. The first statement represents the feminine influence and the second the masculine. As we saw in the Persian Gulf War, the frontal assault represents the visible, direct approach of the masculine whereas the flanking maneuver represents the invisible, indirect approach of the feminine. The first holds the opposing force while the second delivers the strike. In a personal interaction, the business objective holds the person in place while the relational elements have an opportunity to work.

With this in mind, it's important to dispel right away that this doesn't necessarily mean we begin emphasizing personal matters at work. Traditionally, we think of rapport building as broaching personal topics such as family, friends, hobbies, and social events; however, it goes far deeper:

> It's not that we suddenly focus on personal matters at work but rather we just talk about work in a very personal way. We do this by connecting business matters to a person – in most cases the other person or you.

In this way, we connect the personification and the prescription that I introduced earlier. You can also connect business matters to other specific people such as a client or another employee, but it works best when you can relate it to either you or the employee. It doesn't work well when you link the matter to groups; there may be no faces to picture or too many. Getting it down to one person is best.

The most frequent and commonly accepted argument opposing individual actions is the amount of time it takes to speak to each person. For this reason, the common solution is a group interaction where everyone is given the same message. I will challenge this solution on two fronts: time and message.

We typically use this equation to represent the value we give a client:

$$\text{Value} = \frac{\text{Benefits}}{\text{Cost}}$$

By replacing "cost" with "time," we can also use this equation to represent the value we derive from delivering a message individually versus a group:

$$\text{Value} = \frac{\text{Benefits}}{\text{Time}}$$

We'll see how the benefits we derive from a group interaction and the time we spend on individual interactions is not as great as most think. Additionally, I'll show where the benefits from individual interactions are far greater.

The benefit of a group interaction, delivering the same message to everyone, is quickly eroded when we realize that delivering the same message does not mean everyone interprets that message the same way. This is why policemen do not interview witnesses to a traffic accident as a group but rather individually. The interpretations of that accident will vary from witness to witness; the same holds true for presentations.

This benefit is further eroded when we explore the reasons for these varied interpretations. Ultimately, the implications will show there is even a strong likelihood that the message in the presentation will create more problems than it solves because the message is not tailored to the way the listener likes to communicate. *No matter how much we strive to communicate the same message to a group, interpretive differences will cause it to differ for each person.*

Superficially, everyone may speak English, but on a deeper level everyone communicates differently. This is why two people can interpret the same words differently because they affect people differently. Yes, two people may be able to give the same definition for a word, but they will often vary in the connotation. For this reason, a word that we think may create a positive picture for a majority could give a negative one to the minority. This is how a group interaction negatively impacts the benefits we expect. We've all experienced presentations meant to clear the air but only result in clouding things more.

To overcome this problem, people tend to revert to words with very little "color" to minimize interpretative problems. We often call these "buzz" words. They are words used over and over again in the same context to the point where the original color of the word is washed out. These words become the well-worn trails that turn into roads and then expressways. They are the clothes that are worn and washed most frequently to the point where their original form and color are limp and gray. These are presentations people attend to quickly receive a message but are inspired very little by what they hear. How can anyone be inspired by something limp and gray? More importantly, what does this say about the presenter and the company? People usually don't get up in the middle of a good movie just to get home earlier.

Thus, not only does a group interaction offer fewer benefits than most think, it could also be a detriment to the overall message.

Conversely, individual interactions allow us to communicate in the interpretive language of the other person. This benefit is fairly traditional and acceptable by many; however, the difference lies in the weighting that each gives to the benefit of this. I argue that the benefits are much higher than most generally think especially in light of what I implied with group interactions possessing a potentially high detrimental effect. By seeking to avoid the road of interpretive difficulty, we often end up on the road to boredom.

Beyond this though, we can picture other benefits of an individual interaction. Let's begin with a way to look at this interaction with another as shown in Figure 5.3.

Figure 5.3

The dot on the left represents the person who initiates the interaction with the one on the right. For discussion purposes we can identify the left one as the manager and the right one as the employee. We could use this to represent an employee approaching another employee or a client. Our strategic discussion is centered on building your influence within the organization.

In reality, the arrow in Figure 5.3 is a two-way one, but by showing it as one we can identify someone as the initiator of the interaction in trying to build a relationship with an employee by delivering a message. However, the impact of this interaction is far more than Figure 5.3 suggests and introduces us to the "resonating effect." In fact, many times in our daily conversation we make comments such as "delivering a message that will *resonate* with people." We can expand upon Figure 5.3 by incorporating the "resonating effect" so we can arrive at Figure 5.4.

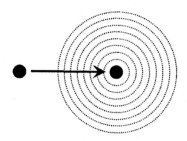

Figure 5.4

The dotted circles around the employee represent the resonating effect that the manager's interaction has with him. These circles represent the impact of this interaction. For instance, a weaker interaction would have fewer, less intense circles while a stronger interaction would have more intense circles quantitatively and qualitatively. We can picture a weak interaction as Figure 5.5.

Figure 5.5

We can picture a strong interaction as Figure 5.6.

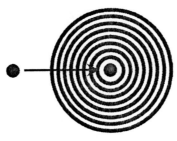

Figure 5.6

Many factors influence the impact of an interaction. There are four major ones represented in these pictures:

- Manager's personality
- Employee's personality
- Manager's delivery
- Employee's interpretation

There are three factors influencing this interaction that these pictures do not represent:

- Situation
- Flow
- People

We discussed these three in detail in the Company and You chapter, so I won't go into detail how these apply except to reference those chapters since those principles apply here as well. In the interaction with any person, we need to have awareness for how these three factors are applying their influence in a contextual form. They may alter our content, approach, and timing.

What I will spend time on is the other group of four influences implied by our diagram.

In most conventional training, the focus is on the manager's delivery to the neglect of the other three. Furthermore, the central theme is content, organization, and technique. These elements are under the domain of the masculine influence as shown in Figure 5.1. The feminine influence comes into play when we begin to explore the interpretive tendencies of the other person and the bondability of delivery to his personality. The key is the differentiation between the other person's understanding and his personality. Whereas the masculine influence's focus is on understanding, the feminine's is on personality as shown in Figure 5.1.

The masculine influence is keyed on matching delivery to personality for the purpose of making sure the other person understands the content – the cognitive connection. On the other hand, the feminine influence, who emphasizes relationships over business objectives because they, not objectives, drive success, is keyed on bonding personalities through delivery – the intuitive connection. If this union occurs, business success is more likely than if we only establish a mutual understanding. In fact, business success can occur without any mutual understanding at all, but it's very difficult for any business to enjoy long-term success without strong, emotional relationships among employees and managers. In essence, employees don't necessarily need to understand content in order to have trust and faith in their managers; they need to feel that a manager appreciates their efforts and is actively watching out for their well-being. Understanding becomes more necessary when trust and faith breaks down. This is similar to clients; they don't necessarily need to understand our advice if they have trust and faith in us. Trust and faith among clients, employees, and managers dramatically impact the life of a business. As we saw in an earlier chapter, both fall under the domain of the feminine influence.

We've already discussed superficially the impact of a person's interpretive tendencies regarding an interaction when we looked at the limitations and detriments involved in group interactions. The only addition here is to highlight that these interpretive tendencies are not only a function of education and experiences but also innate characteristics and abilities. Some people are more emotionally capable than others are to handle the vagueness that always exists around any interaction. For some, this vagueness presents difficulties while for others it's a source of freedom. No interaction can ever attain a perfect state of widespread and consistent interpretableness. Assuming it can and basing actions on this false existence will leave anyone vulnerable to surprises and to negative influences.

If we assume for the moment that such a state can exist, then when someone behaves counter to what we thought was mutually interpreted as someone's nature, we will increase the likelihood of viewing that person's behavior as resistance or incompetence because we eliminated divergent interpretations and the inability to interpret as reasons. As a result, this only increases the need for trust and faith among everyone because without it people will more likely see misinterpretation as opposition.

Before moving onto personalities and their influence on resonation, there is importance in highlighting once again what the manager is delivering and what the employee is interpreting; that is personality. It is not the business message around a business objective as is normally the case in contemporary communication training. In order to build a strong relationship, the manager is first presenting her personality for acceptance by the employee and encouraging the employee to present his own to her.

The essence of both parties' personalities greatly impacts the relationship between the two and consequently the resonation. Once again Figure 5.1 will help illustrate this.

First of all, the one initiating the interaction, as is true with a military force, will have varying ability in creating the event pictured. Some will not even have the ability to integrate the feminine influence; they will only be able to deliver a frontal assault, the masculine influence. In business, this will manifest itself as the presentation of business matters in conventional business lingo without personalization.

Conventionally, some will infer personalization to mean "what's in it for me" and generate the tendency to rely upon the more costly alternatives of compensation, incentives, and benefits to personalize a business objective. Again, I'm referencing personalization in terms of what we just discussed about integrating personalities with the business objective so the objective is personalized, making the objective subjective. Some people's personalities are better suited to do this than others do. Sincerity is a common term we use to describe this quality. Even though it's still limiting, it will suffice for now.

Second of all, the one interpreting the interaction will affect its resonation. Every relationship involves emotions, the stronger the emotions the greater the potential for a strong relationship. As a result, since objects do not have emotions, a relational approach works only with people.

Initially, we think of the many people who have relationships with inanimate objects such as computers or cars, but all of these are again personalized. We typically see this when folks give names to cars, refuse to part with an impractical gift from a particular person they like, or hold on to things that help them recall positive memories of themselves or others. All of these are ways people establish relationships with objects; they identify a person or persons with the object. Those persons can even be themselves. This is how people express possessiveness about the various things that are theirs; they've strongly linked themselves to the object. In fact, we formalize this personalization by means of legalities that identify ownership.

Emotions are required for relationships. As we've discussed, people are born with emotions capable of varying strengths and intensities. We can draw the analogy to muscles. Some people are born with muscles possessing greater strength or quickness than other people. Whether muscles or emotions, the question is "In what manner will their potential play out?"

Just as some people can lift more or move more quickly because of their muscles, some people are more adept at developing stronger or more tolerant relationships than others. Whereas the first boils down to the physicality of muscles, the second comes down to the intangibility of emotions. Thus, women tend to have a stronger ability to develop strong relationships than men do because they tend to have stronger emotional tendencies. This is why in everyday talk we often claim women are more emotional than men are. Unfortunately, in the same everyday, business conversation this often is delivered and taken more as an insult than a compliment.

Essentially, you cannot expect strong relationships from an emotionless person. To compensate, this person will rely more on the shallow, transactional aspects of relationship building involving money, recognition, titles, or gifts. In a more narrow sense these are defined as extrinsic rewards. As we may recall from the Feminine Influence chapter, externalities are generally associated with the masculine influence. The weakness of this type of relationship building is historical; no mercenary army ever conquered the world. The most powerful armies in the world have been those moved by their emotional affinity to their city (Rome), to their nation (America), or to their cause, not the ones who paid their soldiers the most.

While a connection to a country or cause is a more emotional tie and an example of an intrinsic reward, we are attempting to bond on a much deeper level. Shallowness cannot dive deeply; therefore, passion is far better suited for relational activities than objectiveness. Without emotions there can be no relationship; the stronger the emotions the greater the relationship's potential. The closer a person is to a computer, a symbol of absolute objectivity, the less likely he will have strong relationships. Thus, a strong interaction will more likely occur with strong emotions and a weak one with weak or non-existent emotions.

In demonstrating the overall value of personal interactions over group ones, this line of thought now brings us to the time element of individual interactions. No doubt current business thinking focuses on the tremendous time it takes to meet with each person individually under an area of a manager's responsibility. By taking the thought that the impact of an interaction varies by the manager's personality and that of the employee and by the manager's delivery and the employee's interpretation, we can expand on how this interaction impacts others.

We can begin by taking Figure 5.4 representing resonation and expounding upon it. The point here is that a single individual interaction affects others not directly involved in that interaction. We see this all the time in everyday conversations when people talk about their experiences with others. In grade school we had the game "Telephone," and in adult life we have the grapevine.

Both concepts are shallow representations of the point here but get us on our way. In both, we are more focused on the message as opposed to the impressions. The grapevine touches on this but still the emphasis is on what is being said (or not being said). What we're concerned with are the impressions that travel with any message along any medium as well.

Impressions are rooted in emotions. You cannot form impressions without emotions, so this brings us back to our discussion a moment earlier about people's varying emotional capabilities. People with deep emotions will more likely be able to grasp the truth behind emotions than people with shallow emotions will. This is no different than its cognitive counterpart where someone with better reasoning ability is more likely to understand computer logic than someone with lower quality reasoning ability.

Taking our diagram and incorporating this "super-charged grapevine" effect we have Figure 5.7.

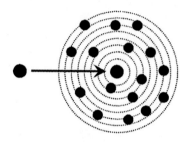

Figure 5.7

As we can see, the resonation from the manager's interaction with the employee now impacts other people. What was originally seen as an interaction between two people is now something that can affect many others. Again, how this particular interaction will affect others will now depend upon the other factors we covered with only the manager and employee; now the resonating interactions are employee to employee.

An example of the practicality of this impact is an insurance agent I know who tracks his closure rates according to individual referral sources. He has noticed a trend where referrals from some clients are more likely to result in business than others do. While some of this reflects more objective measures such as status, more subjective factors such as integrity weigh in as well. One specific contrast he made referenced a client from whom he stopped asking for referrals because of his low integrity with others despite a rather solid financial status. He found his referrals more difficult to meet and as a result more difficult to close. By contrast he described another person with a lower financial status whose referrals almost always granted at least a meeting and correspondingly had a higher closing rate in shorter time frames because of his integrity.

With the review of Figure 5.7, it's now time to revisit our discussion on *de facto* power within an organization because this figure represents the basic concept behind this type of power. Again, this is power that exists outside of the realm of what the particular organizational structure permits. Money, titles, gifts, or recognition does not infuse it. Who has this power is not as easy to identify as these others.

A typical example is the older, experienced employee who adapts successfully. He manages to do so well that he seems more immune to the command structure of the organization than others are. If there are exemptions to directives, he seems to receive them. *De facto* power, however, does not limit itself to age or experience. It links itself to anything including expertise, talent, integrity, and helpfulness but most importantly, an ability to do things. When you're in a bind, he's the one to see. Essentially, it's the power that comes when others truly having an affinity for that person – an *attraction* exists.

This is why *de facto* power can exist in the lowest person in any organizational structure. It can be the person everyone likes who symbolizes the good in a company. He comes to symbolize the soul of an organization. If he's mistreated or let go, it will impact morale negatively even though he has no formal authority over anyone.

The only way to spot these folks is to watch and listen very carefully and rely upon intuition. They are people with whom others truly enjoy speaking or associating and about whom others make genuinely, unsolicited positive comments. Their opinions and feelings seem to matter. The task is difficult because while some of these folks can have power not correspondingly reflected within the organizational hierarchy, others do have this power reflected in that structure. Distinguishing actions and comments that are inspired by *de facto* power from those motivated by organizational currency is not easy. The most dynamic combination is when organizational power and *de facto* power are in sync.

De facto power is like beauty; you know it when you see it. As our diagram implies, it has intensity and endurance. We represent endurance, the ability to impact many others, by the number of rings. We represent intensity, the depth to which they impact others, by the brokenness or solidity of the lines.

Consequently, whereas the organizational structure may look like Figure 5.8,

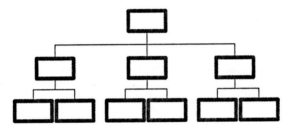

Figure 5.8

The *de facto* power situation may look like Figure 5.9.

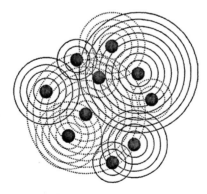

Figure 5.9

The first is more solid and stable, but the second is more fluid and dynamic. The first is the masculine influence while the second is the feminine. Analogously, we can imagine the solidity of a tree and the fluidness of a river. While we can grasp a tree more easily, a river is impervious to the blow of an ax. Thus, a solid, wooden boat navigating and floating upon a river reflects the power inherent in the integration of the two. Our bodies and our world also represent this integration by each being almost three-fourths water.

The deeper implication of this fluidity stems from the impact of an individual interaction on others. This can take many forms but conceptually focuses on increasing your attractiveness to others. The tangibility of this will take the form of others being more receptive to your individual interaction with them when it does take place. It may even allow you more flexibility or depth in your approach. In the end, it can save time. This is why a properly employed strategy of individual interactions with a suitable personality will take less time than one may initially suppose. The suitable personality type is not necessarily extroverted or introverted as much as it is associated with sincerity and sensitivity.

Intuitively we can run with the time savings implication even further by stating that a thirty-minute individual interaction can carry a greater impact than an hour's group interaction for that same individual. So, by tailoring and personalizing a particular message to the interests of the individual, we may be able to save total time for everyone over a group interaction as follows:

> If we have a situation where there are 20 participants and one presenter involved in a one-hour group interaction, we have 21 man-hours invested. If we could revert this to a series of individual interactions of thirty minutes each, we would use twenty-one man-hours (21 x .5 x 2) with far greater effectiveness. If customization suited the message so individual interactions could be shorter, there could even be a greater timesaving.

Of course, we typically don't see this because there is usually a premium on the communicator's time, but how do you quantify this and the message's importance to arrive at a decision whether one form of interaction is more "cost-effective"? Thus, if we review the value equation in Figure 5.10,

$$\text{Value} \quad = \quad \frac{\text{Benefits}}{\text{Time}}$$

Figure 5.10

We will find we covered the:

- Over-weighted benefits perceived in group interactions.
- Under-appreciated benefits perceived in individual interactions.
- Over-weighted time investment perceived in individual interactions.

The point was to picture the value in individual interactions as superseding that of group ones with time reverting to nothing but a mere constraint. Obviously, individual interactions require thoughtfulness and planning and are not suitable for those inclined to wait for the last minute.

In conclusion, we've reviewed several pictures that illustrate individual interactions with a focus on the "resonation effect." This effect is a function of many factors with the key being emotions. Without emotions relationships are impossible. Dropping a pebble in a pond creates ripples. As the pond thickens and freezes the ripples become less sustaining and less intense. A frozen pond does not generate ripples. Coldness is linked to emotionlessness, and emotionlessness marches with objectivity. Resonation diminishes as frigidness increases.

Emotion is often linked to enthusiasm and often seen as a spark or a fire. What we see on the surface does not drive what happens. A boundless pool only six-inch deep cannot sustain the tidal wave found in oceans. An invisible fire burning within a cast-iron stove generates more heat than the open fire we all can see; no one sees the fire burning within a blast furnace but everyone feels its heat.

How we incorporate all of this in business matters in tangible ways gets into the words and phrases we use. Some we've hinted at, but the next part, Phraseology, will get into it in more detail.

Phraseology

The phraseology I will cover has two basic purposes: first, to identify language that will personalize business objectives, and second, to avoid language that will depersonalize them. Beyond these two, they secondarily serve as examples to communicate the feel of these concepts. Bringing personification into reality will succeed if we constantly keep in mind that we can't merely rely upon the way we use or don't use words. If this were not the case, then a computer would simply print these words and inspire a whole population. Tone, context, and personality play their parts. Of the three, incorporation into the personality of the speaker is the most important so consider what follows as examples.

For these purposes, identification and avoidance, when I discuss phraseology, I'm assuming a positive tone, a business context, and a one-on-one interaction. In the interaction, there are two people, the initiator of the interaction and the receiver. We'll discuss the first purpose by looking at the phraseology to personify the objective with the receiver first and the initiator second. I'll use incentives to satisfy the second objective for both the receiver and the initiator.

These reasons support why I've called this phraseology as opposed to "phrasing" or "phrases." Furthermore, the themes are very straightforward so any kind of exhaustive phrase list becomes little better than a laundry list. This will thwart any potential for memorization that will certainly create a manufactured, impersonal delivery and tone. A spontaneity promoting sincerity is a vital ingredient to this strategy's success, so what's right or wrong is determined by the degree to which the words you use reflect your personality. Often we squash this effort by choosing frequently used "buzz" words with the intention of being clear only to find ourselves boring; people are more persuaded by what they like than what they understand. How can they like a personality that doesn't exist? How can they like words containing no personality?

For this reason and the others we've covered throughout this book up to this point, employing this strategy to incorporate the feminine influence is more difficult for men than it is for women because personality involves emotions and reliance upon one's own subjectivity.

- Receiver -

Definite themes prevail around personification. The main one is that it's almost impossible to personify if one does not mention specific people in conversation. Someone who mentions individual people frequently in conversation is more likely to bond personally than one who mentions no individuals in conversation.

- Mention individuals.

Individuals fall into two tiers. The first tier contains the initiator and receptor of the interaction. The second tier contains individuals outside of these two. They can be specific clients, employees, or managers. The key is specificity. Categorically mentioning clients, employees, or managers does little for personification. Again, as we've already addressed in this section, groups are non-existent and are especially so when we attempt to visualize them.

Related to this is the use of names. Personification is greatly aided by names. This concept is the same as "name-dropping," but it's the positive form. When possible use the name of individuals in conversation as opposed to pronouns referencing them.

- Use names.

There is a limit of course, but that is defined by personalities and circumstances. The naming concept also comes into play by addressing the other person by name. For example, rather than saying, "I believe this will help you demonstrate your interest in the client," you can say, "John, I believe this will help you demonstrate your interest in the client."

- Address the other person by name.

The rationale for using someone's name is rather common but the implication of using the names of others in conversation is less so. By using someone else's name in a conversation, especially the name of someone else on the same organizational level as the one to whom you're addressing, you imply the potential mention of his name in conversation with others. If someone rarely or never mentions the names of others in conversations, then it's hard to imagine he will mention your name to others. Of course, the implication also follows that the tone of that reference will correlate to the tone of the one you mentioned to him. Thus, a negative reference to a person increases the likelihood he will also become the object of negative reference to others. This correlation increases with each negative reference.

- Make positive references.

While this does not necessarily mean the avoidance of all negative references, it does mean an awareness of the mix. In most cases, references will be a mixture of positive and negative ones with the overall mix (in terms of quantity and intensity) being a good indicator of what the person in your conversation can expect in terms of references to others about him. If one talks positively about others, then you are more likely to have him talk positively about you.

The two most important names are the two of the people involved in the interaction. Outside of simply mentioning them, bonding them to the business objective is important. Often this will seem similar to what's "in it for me," but it goes deeper by making an emotional connection to the task. A better way to think of this is a compliment dressed in business attire. This expresses the nature of the masculine-feminine influence diagram in Figure 5.1. The business topic becomes a way to express and highlight someone's nature.

Every person is an integration of what nature gave him and what he has learned. Personification generally works best when something is bonded to someone's nature as opposed to someone's education. Here, I'm using a very broad definition of education to include everything a person learns not just what he learns formally in school.

Bonding something to someone's nature is a much stronger tie than bonding it to his education. What nature gives someone is impossible to lose or have removed. Education is constantly changing; what we learn today may or may not be suitable tomorrow. As a result, education becomes outdated. Nature represents the inside while education represents the outside. What's inside is always stronger in terms of impacting someone's personality. The innate is always more powerful than what is acquired.

In order to incorporate what we've covered so far let's look at some examples of statements to employees by a manager:

A(1).   Our new business model helps us deliver better service to clients because we can deliver everything through a single contact.

B(1).   John, our new business model helps us deliver better service to clients because we can deliver everything through a single contact.

C(1).   John, our new business model helps us deliver better service to clients because it better positions the broad knowledge base you've acquired.

D(1).   John, our new business model helps us deliver better service to clients because it better positions your natural talent to relate to others.

These examples are all the same in the fact that they deliver an endorsement of the new business model as represented by the independent clause:

"our new business model helps us deliver better service to clients"

Stripped of the attire providing the color of additional context, this clause is the generic black and white look for the model. By accessorizing with a greeting and making alterations to the dependent clause, "because we can deliver everything through a single contact," we will tailor to the receiver.

Here are the respective commentaries about the above statements:

A(1).   While this generic statement may be true, no one can tell the forum in which it is being said. No one can distinguish whether this is being said before a group, with an individual, or in a planning document. Even though this statement may be uttered in an individual interaction, this is similar to a clothing salesman simply pulling something "off the rack" to sell a customer.

B(1).   Accessorizing the statement with a greeting automatically indicates that this message is being delivered to someone specifically. This differentiates the generic attire of the statement by adding something little to make it different from a mass communication.

C(1).   By changing the dependent clause altogether, we are altering the generic to fit someone specifically. While this clause may apply to others, it has narrowed the customers to which it applies. We are tailoring the clothing to fit a specific person.

D(1).   Again, we change the dependent clause; however, we create a customized outfit. It's not tailored to something John has acquired from others or experiences but rather to something he's had since birth – something innate. What's innate is always more personal than what is acquired.

With D(1) we can now refine Figure 5.1 by looking at this statement more closely and identifying the various influences:

John, our new business model helps us deliver better service to clients because it better positions your natural talent to relate to others.

Masculine Influence: our new business model helps us deliver
                              better service to clients

Feminine Influence: your natural talent to relate to others

We can also use a sentence notation to designate the information in the table this way:

John, [our new business model helps us deliver better service to clients]^M because it better positions (your natural talent to relate to others)^F.

As we indirectly saw, the independent clause is objective and does not refer to anyone specifically; it lacks a personal bond with anyone. Conversely, the dependent clause is very subjective by referring to John's talent.

We can now refine Figure 5.1 as shown in Figure 5.11.

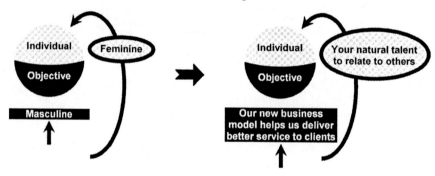

Figure 5.11

Without the subjective nature of this dependent clause, we would have something totally void of the feminine influence as represented by A(1). In this case, we are making a full frontal assault on the receiver of our message. As we saw with the third day of the Gettysburg example in the Feminine Influence chapter, a frontal assault is less likely to deliver good results, more likely to produce disaster, and more likely to have higher costs.

As a result, our diagram would look like Figure 5.12 without the dependent clause.

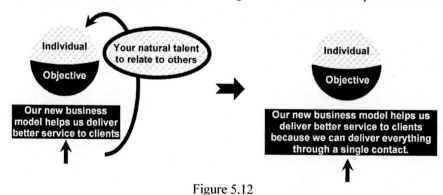

Figure 5.12

How A(1) can be disastrous in an employee-manager relationship is not readily apparent and requires elaboration. By drawing a comparison to a sales situation, we more easily see it.

First of all, without a personal touch it's more difficult for any client to buy. Statements such as A(1) become no better than a reply of a recorder or the adherence to a generic script. For any sales person, it's detrimental to project oneself this way. First, it shows a lack of empathy in the uniqueness of the client's situation and personality, and secondly a lack of creativity or energy in tailoring products and services to that client because one cannot even tailor conversation.

Secondly, the fundamentals of a client-employee relationship are the same as those of an employee-manager relationship. Thus, it's detrimental for any manager to project himself as no better than a glorified recorder or regurgitant of a script. Application of the feminine influence allows a manager to demonstrate two attributes:

1. Empathy for the beneficial qualities innate in an employee.
2. Creativity and energy in tailoring messages to the employee.

Any salesperson would have great difficulty building a strong relationship with a client without these attributes. Likewise, this holds true for managers. Whereas a sales person has difficulty making sales without these qualities, a manager has difficulty getting things done without them. At critical times, both could result in disaster.

- Initiator -

Up to this point, we've talked about phraseology from the perspective of the person receiving the individual interaction rather than the one initiating it. By this I mean we've focused on the receiver and his qualities. We can go beyond this initial step by focusing on the initiator.

The development of phraseology focused on the initiator will require a different approach than that of the receiver. Whereas the focus on the receiver is his strengths, the focus on the initiator is his vulnerabilities. For most this is an extremely difficult concept to grasp because it counters what we are regularly told in contemporary business literature for mass audiences. Much of this has to do with the necessity of possessing a high dosage of some relational qualities.

Again, since strong relationships are directly linked to emotions, women will tend to see this and apply it more easily. Emotionally, they will also be able to accept it more readily because chances are very good that they've applied it at some point in their lives in other realms. Of course, they may not have done so as a conscious thought, and if they did, they may never have seen its application to interactions in business. Still, men or women, the people who can apply this concept well are in the minority. Mainstream publications, by their very nature, do not make a living catering to the minority. We derived this implication from our feminine influence discussion in the Feminine Influence chapter.

Two analogies will help give the appropriate feel for the power in demonstrating vulnerability. The first involves a castle while the second involves a story about a man and a boy.

Imagine approaching a castle where upon being sighted by the sentries they close the gates and pull up the drawbridge. At the same time, additional soldiers position themselves along the walls and in the turrets, all heavily armed. What impression would they convey?

Now, imagine a reversal of this analogy. You're approaching a heavily armed castle with its gates closed and drawbridge drawn. Upon seeing you the soldiers disappear from the walls and turrets while the sentries lower the drawbridge and open the gates. What impression does this convey?

Which scenario strengthens the castle? Weakens? Which is more inviting to you? More threatening?

Consider the story of an ancient man and boy who walk through a town where everyone feels vulnerable so some kind of weaponry is not unusual. Even the man and boy have knives and swords to protect themselves. A man very heavily armed with a broadsword, shield, and body armor walks by them. The boy comments on how strong and powerful this man looks. The father says nothing.

Shortly thereafter another man without any weaponry or protection walks by. The boy points him out to his father and comments how weak he looks. His father counters by saying the man is actually very strong and stronger than the other man is. The son is puzzled until the father explains that a man who must be that heavily armed in order to feel safe in an unsafe town must have a reason for feeling that unsafe; whereas, the man who can walk these streets without any weaponry must have some reason why he feels so safe. He goes on to say that a man who can survive without weaponry must be stronger than the man who needs a lot of weaponry to survive. The unarmed man may be so well liked and respected that no one really wishes to harm him, while the heavily armed man may have done things that would cause any number of people to harm him. The unarmed man has a strength we cannot see.

Morale of the story: You don't need to show strength if people already know you're strong; unless of course, you're really not that strong, then you must show strength.

Together these two analogies show the strength of vulnerability. The feminine influence has difficulty working if she intimidates. As we saw, if the defending army has the advantage in a military engagement, it's hard to encourage an attack if it comes across as invincible. Likewise, it's difficult for employees to approach a manager who does not show vulnerability.

This is an uncomfortable concept in the business world because it's not masculine. If a woman were to attract a man, she would at least have to express an interest in his advances. Women often talk about having to massage men's egos, but they also talk about presenting themselves open to their approaches. Makeup, clothing, and jewelry all play a role. This can be as simple as being willing to engage in conversation, an openness that implies vulnerability, a certain trust. The key is remembering that every man has a feminine side and every woman a masculine side; so men can attract and massage women's egos.

Our previous statements referred more to the receiver and more to the massaging of egos. The statements that follow refer more to the initiator by allowing vulnerability. The easiest way to do this verbally is expressing the help that someone can give you. Vulnerability is an attractive element that is seen whenever someone tries to save or help a child. Someone who is vulnerable is unthreatening.

Using the same sentences from above we can alter them to point out that the employee is *helping* the manager.

- Demonstrate the other's helpfulness.

We begin with our generic statement A(1) as the base and transform the others, B(1), C(1), and D(1) to ones focused on the personalization of the initiator.

A(1).   Our new business model helps us deliver better service to clients because we can deliver everything through a single contact.

B(2).   John, our new business model helps me deliver better service to clients because we can deliver everything through a single contact.

C(2).   John, our new business model helps me deliver better service to clients because it allows you to help me by better positioning the broad knowledge base you've acquired.

D(2).   John, our new business model helps me deliver better service to clients because it allows you to help me by better positioning your natural talent to relate to others.

Masculine Influence:	•	business model helps us
	•	we can deliver everything
Feminine Influence:	•	business model helps me
	•	allows you to help me

By looking at it in this way, we can easily see the personalization of the business objective to the initiator. Even in our minds, if we put ourselves in the role of the one saying these statements, we can see how much easier it is to picture ourselves than a nebulous "us" or "we." This same experience occurs for the one receiving this statement.

This principle is seen in advertisements very frequently. The most prevalent is for a child relief program involving a monthly donation to a *specific* child. The program includes receiving a picture of your child and regular updates on his or her progress through your help. It even allows correspondence between the donor and child. Consider the impactive difference if this advertisement requested contributions for a general fund. There is a reason why this program focuses on the identification of the donor with the child – personalization.

Relating this example to employee-manager relationships, we find employees more willing to pursue an objective (help) if they can personify the effort. True, the employee can also help himself, but there is an altruistic feeling involved whenever someone is helping another. Furthermore, anyone would rather do something because he wishes to help than because someone is commanding him. Helping another person is more humane than doing what he's told.

Using our sentence notation we see this:

John, our new [business model (helps me)^F deliver better service to clients]^M because it allows you to (help me)^F by better positioning (your natural talent to relate to others)^F.

We've added more punch to the feminine influence by the "help me's" through a more personal connection. Yet, this format also allows us to see the dependent nature of the feminine influence by removing the masculine from it:

John, help me by using your natural talent to relate to others.

Unfortunately, we've already put this in a business context, so the effect is more difficult to see, but imagine if you saw this for the first time without our previous discussion. If you were John and someone walked into your office and said this, what would you think? How different would it be if a friend walked up to you on the street and said this? What difference would there be if a woman approached John as opposed to a man? In our relationships with others, we not only bring personality but we also bring context. Thus, even by giving you a few parameters around which someone delivers this statement, I introduce context. Our environs and relationships influence context, so imagine this sentence standing alone.

If we go back to our discussion around Figures 5.8 and 5.9 where we compared an organizational chart to *de facto* circles, we find structure versus fluidity – masculine versus feminine. The phraseology we just reviewed is along the same lines. The objective masculine provides the form for which the subjective feminine can flow. Analogously, we can visualize a glass of water. The glass holds the water. Without the water the glass is empty; without the glass the water is everywhere. This is context, the glass, versus content, the water.

Thus, phraseology lacking the feminine is empty while that lacking the masculine is all over the place. Objective analysis is void of emotion, of personality and thus personalization. How can one personalize without being subjective, emotional? Objectivity is an empty glass. Conversely, subjective observations are full of variances in emotions, in personalities. How can one not personalize while being subjective, emotional? Subjectivity is water everywhere. Together, a glass and water allows one to drink. Without water or a glass, we cannot drink.

Phraseology incorporating the feminine influence is delivering a full glass of water to another. Simply relying upon the masculine influence to outline and execute business objectives without personification is giving someone an empty glass. Personifying the initiator of the interaction by demonstrating the employee's helpfulness is a major element in the resonation effect. Again, this is where we transform a simple one-on-one interaction into something that radiates onto others not directly involved.

Whether it's business or personal, people like to share the important things they are doing. It can be as simple as planning and preparing for a vacation or a major business purchase. In the hierarchical structure of business, managers are above employees and symbolically represented in an organizational chart (Have you ever seen an organizational chart that flows from the bottom up starting with the president or CEO?). Thus, assisting a manager on a project implies greater importance to the tasks associated with that project. This importance transfers to the employee and raises his or her status.

Consequently, by demonstrating to the employee how something he does, or better yet *is*, helps the manager initiating the interaction, the more inclined the employee will be to share with others. In this sharing will also be the names of other people the manager references. This demonstrates the importance of positive references about others, especially if the employee knows these others well; he will almost certainly talk to them about what was said.

In addition to personifying the manager within the business objective by mentioning the need for the employee's help, a manager can establish a degree of importance to that help by emphasizing the need for the employee's support.

- Affirm the need for the other's help.

This also encourages and reinforces the resonation effect by implicitly saying, "please talk with others about the importance of their help." If we take our last refined sentence, D(2), and incorporate this theme, it could be something like this:

D(2).   John, our new business model helps me deliver better service to clients be-
           cause it allows you to help me by better positioning your natural talent to

relate to others. *I'm counting on your support because I know others respect you and your work, so I'd appreciate your help.*

Along with affirming an employee's support, a manager can even go the next step and request his support.

- Ask for the other's help.

The effect is solidifying the bond between the employee and manager and enhancing the likelihood of a strong and enduring resonation from the interaction. Our D(2) conversation could now go to the next level:

D(2).   John, our new business model helps me deliver better service to clients because it allows you to help me by better positioning your natural talent to relate to others. I'm counting on your support because I know others respect you and your work, so I'd appreciate your help. *Will you help me out?*

This additional question virtually asks for resonation. Again, all of this needs tailoring to the employee, so merely saying the same thing to each one won't make it as effective. Of course this is a creative challenge that promotes personalization. How can one promote personalization if the same thing is said to the same person? However, employees like to talk about how they've helped a manager, so demonstrating and reinforcing an employee's helpfulness increases the likelihood for an enduring and strong resonation.

Because of its optional flavor that borders on volunteerism, the most common objection that the masculine influence presents to this relational approach is along the lines of "they're paid to do a job; they have no option." This neglects the truth of the heart. Anyone can gain compliant behavior that can yield positive behavior, but winning someone's heart is a matter totally independent of compliance. Without the heart, dynamic outcomes and successful navigation of adverse conditions are almost impossible without over reliance on luck.

As we had mentioned earlier in the chapter Feminine Influence, any man can gain the complicity of a woman but he cannot compel love from her heart. It's easier for him to conquer a nation of men than it is for him to coerce the love from a single woman. Winning the heart is the difference between sex and love, between prostitution and making love, between a house and a home, and between mediocrity and dynamism.

- Incentives -

At this point, we need to reference an earlier statement:

. . . some will infer personalization to mean "what's in it for me" and generate the tendency to rely upon the costly alternatives of compensation, incentives, and benefits to personalize a business objective.

At the time, we discussed how incentives are less powerful than personification. The remaining implication from this discussion that we need to discuss is the actual power of incentives because it will allow us to avoid a phraseology that depersonalizes. Even though we determined that incentives are less powerful than personification, we never really discussed the nature of the power in incentives. We simply left it being something less than the power in personification.

The basic theme regarding this power is that incentives depersonalize. Thus, incentives not only have less power than personification but the power it does have travels in the opposite direction. Incentives depersonalize business objectives for both the initiator and the receiver; they disassociate personality from the work.

The effect is a weakening of the bond among the relationships in business, client-employee and employee-manager, by making it more transactional than personal. This translates into higher monetary costs to maintain and strengthen each relationship. For the first relationship this may show up in such places as higher marketing and promotional expenses or increasing difficulty to raise revenues and avoid severe discounting practices. For the second relationship this may manifest itself in a variety of labor expense items such as attracting new employees to satisfy openings generated from increasing turnover, defending against employee litigation, compensating for employee improprieties, or settling conflicts among employees.

How incentives depersonalize will be seen if we begin by using a prose to enter into the implications that will take us there:

Buzz! Ring! Beep!

A window calls me and shows me a rat in a maze. With an electric buzzer strapped around him, he behaves quite humanly as food rewards his performances. Beyond the electrical buzz, there are the sounds of ringing and beeping. Each sound orders the rat to perform something. By placing cheese bits in strategic places, he follows a specific path, even negotiates the maze. In this way, he moves balls, blocks and other things to various locations. Success carries him.

Suddenly, my pager's buzz shatters my daze. A restroom mirror stares at me. My legs hasten my return and guide me through the maze of cubicles to my telephone. Before I can phone, a ring emanates. Someone's calling. The receiver arrives at my ear; the instructions fill my head. They stop, the receiver goes home, and I prepare to call. My computer beeps a reminder of an overlooked task. This is my job; the money puts food on the table.

Looking at my watch, I speak silently to myself, "Yes! There's time for a quick sandwich. I'm in the mood for grilled cheese. I love the stuff.

What's the difference between a rat and a man?

One can foolishly convince himself he's not a rat.

Even though this piece focuses more on the electronic aspects of this person's job, it touches on the monetary ones with the lines:

- By placing cheese bits in strategic places, he follows a specific path, even negotiates the maze.
- This is my job; the money puts food on the table.
- I'm in the mood for grilled cheese. I love the stuff.

With these lines we equate the cheese for a rat with the money for a man. This analogy transforms itself into a direct connection when we accept the fact that money puts food on the table. For both the rat and the man, negotiation means food. Of course, this brings up the frequent question: Does one love his work or work for money?

Our focus is the incentive not the broader issue of compensation, but by addressing the first we'll gain some insight into the second. As an entrée I'll focus on this prose's prepositional phrase, "By placing cheese bits in strategic places, . . . "

This phrase distinguishes the difference between any kind of base compensation and hourly rate from an incentive. Base compensation hinges for the most part on the job func-tion and secondarily on the quality of performing that function as represented by annual raises. Incentives however are tied to very specific outcomes that usually encourage certain behaviors over others within that job function. How a manager organizes these incentives requires thought and planning or . . . strategy. By strategically placing these incentives the manager will encourage the behaviors he desires. Incentives become the cheese that guide people through the business maze to success. In this way, "the rat race" moves from a joking analogy to an emotional reality. If applying certain clothes to our bodies can create certain feelings in us, why can't the same be true for the application of certain motivations?

The linkage becomes stronger if we look at prostitution, a specific behavior for an incentive. A shallow behavior void of a mutual, deep affinity recognized as love. The heart, the feminine influence, is not involved. What makes prostitution what it is? Is it the money or the heartless act? The movie *Pretty Woman* confronts this question as Richard Gere and Julia Roberts fall in love while under a sexual financial contract. What determined the strength of their relationship, the money or their feelings? What clouded their relationship, the money or their feelings? Would they have doubted their feelings and the other's feelings as much if a contract never existed and they met perhaps on a blind date?

There is a reality television show where twenty-five women vie for the love of a man worth $50 million. Unbeknownst to them, "John" is really a common laborer who earns $19,000 a year. This show tries to address the everyday question of "Did one marry for love or money." In situations where one stands to gain substantially monetarily from an intimate relationship, what determines the strength of the relationship, the money or their feelings? What clouds their relationship, the money or their feelings? Would they have any doubt for their or the others' feelings if monetary wealth came unknowingly to them later?

When someone knows in advance he will receive a monetary gain for a specific behavior, how will he know he's doing it more because he loves to do it or more because he receives a financial gain? How much more difficult is this if this definitely creates a change of his behavior? Even if the behavior is a very positive one, what questions does this raise about his personality because he could not adopt the positive behavior without a monetary gain? What does this say about a soul who must receive money to adopt the behavior he needs to get into heaven?

The difference between a man and a rat is that a man can negotiate a maze without the strategic placing of cheese but a man will never know this if the cheese is always there. Thus, as with the couple who becomes financially wealthy after they fell in love, there are fewer emotional clouds to tackle than if the wealth were there before they fell in love. Likewise, unexpectedly rewarding an employee after a positive action and telling him the reason for the discretionary bonus are more powerful than a preannounced incentive.

In addition to depersonalizing an employee by analogously relating his behavior to that of a rat, incentives also depersonalize the manager paying them. In fact, in many cases the employee's manager did not construct the incentives or initiate the payment. Most times the manager cannot disapprove unless some egregious action occurs.

Essentially, incentives harm the relationship between an employee and manager because the employee becomes more focused on the favors offered by the impersonal formulas driving the incentive plan than the favors offered by the personal insights of his manager. The manager does not give the incentive because she felt the employee did a good job but rather because it was demanded by the plan's formula. Even if the manager developed the incentive plan, she does not absolutely know going into the time period covered by the plan who will receive a payment and for how much. Thus, she has no personal attachment to the incentive whatsoever.

In the short run, incentives undermine a manager's power because employees' behaviors are governed by a formula determined in the past rather than by what she feels is needed in the present to maximize the opportunities she sees. In the long run, power's erosion occurs because the managers and employees are depersonalized; their personalities are removed from financial rewards. While the counter argument is fairness and objectivity, this implies a manager who is incapable of the insight necessary to use rewards effectively. The answer is a better manager, not the depersonalization of employees and managers. Furthermore, fairness and objectivity in this case is nothing more than a *subjective* decision to disregard personal considerations that make us unique.

Nevertheless, in the present day business culture, the masculine influence prevails and relies intensively on incentives to promote the behavior he cannot inspire because he neglects the feminine. Thus, phraseology that personalizes will avoid the discussion of incentives when building a bond between employee and manager.

- Avoid discussing incentives.

By doing so, there will be a conscious effort to rely upon personalities. This exercise is analogous to working with a client in the fact-finding stage of sales where there is the avoidance of product and service discussions and an emphasis on uncovering needs. You cannot build a strong personal relationship relying upon transactional tools.

- Summary -

Phraseology focusing on personifying business objectives accomplishes two things. First, it identifies language that increases the likelihood for dynamic outcomes by personalizing business objectives to enhance the bond between the employee and the manager. Second, it avoids language that will depersonalize those objectives and decrease the likelihood of dynamic outcomes. While our focus has been individual interactions in the form of one-on-one meetings, phraseology also works in phone conversations and email correspondence.

- Employ in phone conversations and email correspondence.

Identification came by way of looking at ways to personalize the objective for the receiver of the individual interaction and for the initiator. Avoidance focused solely on incentives, the most depersonalizing influence in business outside of debasing, personal comments. Together they generated some themes for a personal phraseology:

1. Mention individuals.
2. Use names.
3. Address the other person by name.
4. Make positive references.
5. Demonstrate the other's helpfulness
6. Affirm the need for the other's help.
7. Ask for the others' help.
8. Avoid discussing incentives.
9. Employ in phone conversations and email correspondence.

Application of these themes came about by transforming a simple, objective, direct statement, A(1) about a business objective into a more involved, relational, indirect one,

D(2). The later creates a personal, relational bond between the employee's and manager's personalities and infuses the business objective with its own personality:

A(1).   Our new business model helps us deliver better service to clients because we can deliver everything through a single contact.

D(2).   John, our new business model helps me deliver better service to clients because it allows you to help me by better positioning your natural talent to relate to others. I'm counting on your support because I know others respect you and your work, so I'd appreciate your help. Will you help me out?

The purpose of the D(2) language was to picture how all these themes work together in a compressed time period so I could show their linkage more easily. In actuality, these themes could be spread throughout the interaction or even among several interactions. They do not require concentration. If we use a diagram to represent an interaction where a solid line (|) represents the manager's comments while a broken line (¦) represents the employee's comments and insert the themes from D(2) as other comments by the manager we could see something like Figure 5.13.

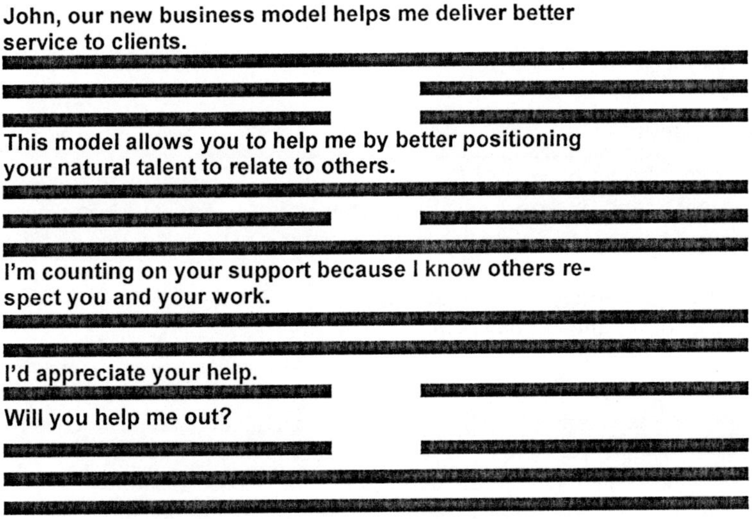

John, our new business model helps me deliver better service to clients.

This model allows you to help me by better positioning your natural talent to relate to others.

I'm counting on your support because I know others re-spect you and your work.

I'd appreciate your help.

Will you help me out?

Figure 5.13

Successful implementation of this phraseology will not only depend upon tone, context, and personality but also relentless application – follow through. A single treatment is not a cure. In this way, it's very much like an exercise program. Conditioning improves but it doesn't diminish the need for further exercise. Each interaction with a specific employee becomes a continuation of that "exercise program."

Taken in totality these themes are not complex and rather simply stated; however, the simple is often avoided because it's difficult. It's easy to state "climb a mountain," but the actuality is intense. The difficulties associated with these themes are more personal. Many, mainly men, will find the language uncomfortable because of its intensely relational and emotional content, but this only increases the impact of those who are able to work it into their personalities. As a result, this content relates more to elements associated with the feminine influence and the phraseology becomes her tactical manifestation. Secondarily though, difficulties arise from the discipline required to overcome short-term impulses for quickness that sacrifice quality and to employ relentlessly the themes of this phraseology. From this perspective, this discipline falls within the influence of the masculine. Whereas the first difficulty highlights the advantage women have because their femininity will allow them to feel more comfortable than men to employ this language, the second highlights the advantage men will have in applying this despite external pressures to shortchange the effort.

Consequently, there is a difference between "building a relationship" and "growing a relationship." It's the same difference between nailing two boards together and gluing them. The first is a quick fix but does not prevent seepage while the second takes longer but yields a better bond. The first falls in the realm of the masculine and is more transactional while the second is in the feminine and is more relational. This phraseology attracts by highlighting and enhancing the beauty inherent in you and the feminine influence.

Group

Four elements comprise this portion of the Strategy chapter:

- Map
- Positioning
- Reinforcement
- Opportunities

Something always happens when you add a third person to two; intimacy breaks down. For this reason, when I speak of a group I refer to any situation where more than two people are interacting. Since the feminine influence is qualitative and the masculine quantitative, group interactions fall into the masculine realm because one can deliver words with the most efficiency in front of a group; however, as we previously discussed in the individual portion this is done at the expense of effectiveness.

One of the main retardants, if not the main retardant, to the effective delivery of a message with a group interaction is the automatic stifling of interplay between the presenter, the initiator of the interaction, and the individuals in the audience receiving the interaction. Collective pressures encourage silence and isolation from the presenter. A map will help illustrate not only how this exists but also how to address it.

The main purpose for relating individual and group interactions to the feminine and masculine influences respectively is to symbolize their complementary nature. Group interactions can serve as an entrée for formal and informal individual interactions or as an adhesive for previous individual interactions. By making this connection, group interactions now create many more opportunities to win hearts. Even though at times our discussion may seem to relate only to public speaking opportunities, these elements are meant to apply to any group of any number in formal and informal settings.

Map

Groups naturally constrain individual expression. This is done formally through various stated rules and informally through cultural preferences. In our school days we called this peer pressure except it didn't end with them.

Anyone who has been part of an audience for a presentation has felt the need for conformity. These feelings manifest themselves as rationalizations such as:

- This isn't the time or place to ask my question.
- My comment really isn't pertinent.
- The presenter doesn't really want to hear what I have to say.
- This topic doesn't interest me enough (so it's a waste to make comments).
- Someone told me to be here, but I don't have to say anything.
- I may say something really stupid, and I'll look foolish.
- There's no point being noticed in this group.
- I'm wearing the same dress as her.
- I knew I should have worn something more professional (or more casual).

These feelings intensify directly with such factors as the:

- Formality of the interaction.
- Influence of those involved.
- Diversity of the influence (interactions strictly with peers are less formal than those involving a mixture of the hierarchy).
- Number of people involved.
- Nature of the occasion.
- Cultural diversity (increasing diversity creates increasing uncertainty as to what the informal "rules" are).
- Extensiveness of the rules, guidelines, or laws around the interaction.

This superimposed constraint involved with group interactions manifests itself most often through the scarcity of questions and comments from the individuals in the audience. As a result, audience engagement with the presenter is minimal. Thus, we can "map" this constraint as individual isolation where each dot in Figure 5.14 represents a person and the lines represent the invisible walls caused by constraint.

Figure 5.14

In order to maximize the message's delivery in a group interaction, the presenter needs to transform this illustration into Figure 5.15.

Figure 5.15

Figure 5.15 represents an unrestrained environment that encourages receiving and learning a message. Analogously, we can relate this to a sponge dipped in water. In a relaxed state, a sponge soaks in water when we submerge it; however, if we first squeeze the sponge tightly in our fist and then dip it into the water, the sponge gets wet but absorbs little or no water. The most common example of this is a student cramming for an exam. While the student gets wet, he retains little water; he may pass the exam but soon forgets what he studied.

Ultimately, we strive for a situation represented by Figure 5.16.

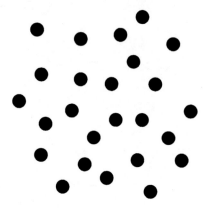

Figure 5.16

Here, the group finally takes on a unique identity as represented by the many locations the individual dots can take. Since every person is different, every group can be different too because no two groups have the same individuals; however, this cannot occur if individuals do not express themselves individualistically because they are more concerned about how the group looks at them. Individuals working uniformly as a group deliver additive growth; two hundred people do twice as much as a hundred people. Individuals working together as individuals create a synergy that gives birth to dynamism because synergism exceeds summation; ten people do more *and better* than a hundred people.

It's not within the scope of this book to explore this in detail; however, it has implications for creating an environment that maximizes the effectiveness of group interactions for positioning and reinforcing individual interactions. Superficially, some could easily view this last situation as "chaos" but it's actually only one part of a journey to learning and doing something new as a group as we see in Figure 5.17.

Figure 5.17

This is similar to pouring water from one container to another. While the water takes the shape of the respective container it's in before and after the pour, during "flight" it's in a chaotic, shapeless state however it has direction. If we focus totally on only this aspect of the entire event, we could easily conclude "things are out of control"; however, holistically there is momentum, gravity, and other forces moving the water from one container to another without spillage. Before one form becomes another, dissociation temporarily exists as the intermediary.

The implication of this, relative to group interactions and synergy generating dynamism, begins with standard processes yielding efficiencies because they standardize behaviors in predictable patterns to produce more predictable outcomes. Plans and strategies are based upon what is possible, not what is impossible, so they are based on what is reasonably predictable. Who creates a plan containing numerous uncertain processes and generally unpredictable outcomes? In order for dynamic outcomes to occur, there must be some freedom in the group for this to occur; otherwise, the standard processes and procedures will only yield predictable outcomes, not dynamic ones far exceeding expectations.

For predictability to exist, a plan relies upon many standardized and predictable processes to deliver expected outputs. A plan seeks to minimize surprises, so if everything goes according to plan, then there are no surprises; however, this includes good surprises as well as bad ones. Thus, if we strive for predictable outcomes by employing standardized techniques so that we increase the predictability of our plan, then we also constrain the ability to create positive surprises.

Dynamic results, results exceeding imagination, exceed expectations; they pleasantly surprise. Synergy defies rational calculation, and thus, predictability. As predictability increases, the likelihood of synergy wanes. How can the impossible be born from something designed to yield the possible and the expected? Furthermore, how can the impossible happen from processes designed to yield the possible? To believe dynamic results occur by reducing unpredictability is like believing high investment returns occur by reducing risk. The interplay between risk and return not only holds for investing but also for human interactions.

Nevertheless, investing contains way to maximize returns and minimize risk to some degree; the same holds true for group interactions. While breaking down the walls enforcing the isolation of the individuals in the group unleashes unpredictable forces, there are ways to maximize the impact of this while minimizing the risk. All of the ways fall into the realm of the feminine influence through the attractive elements in her beauty.

As we had discussed in the chapter, Feminine Influence, the masculine pursues while the feminine attracts. The later is the influence that minimizes the risk of entering into a chaotic state. We can get a feel for the effects of each influence on a chaotic situation with two illustrations in Figure 5.18.

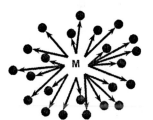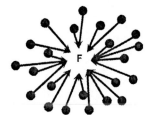

Figure 5.18

The diagram on the left shows the masculine influence pursuing to keep a group from going off in different directions while the diagram on the right shows the feminine attracting the group to prevent the same. As these diagrams show, the masculine must expend far more energy than the feminine to prevent total dispersion. In fact, the feminine uses no energy of her own; it's the individuals in the group that expend the energy to move toward her. She becomes the cohesive force keeping things together.

We can crystallize this abstraction through a story from my college days when co-ed dorms were first being introduced on campus. At the time, this was controversial so students could choose a dorm preference, unisex or co-ed. Eventually though, the administration made all but a few dorms co-ed because all-male dorms were more abused than co-ed dorms; the presence of a woman tempered male behavior. They found that even the existence of one floor of women tempered the chaotic behavior of men on three floors.

Following this story further we can also crystallize the immense energy the masculine must expend to retain control of the situation. In all-male dorms, this clearly manifested itself through expenditures and time for repairs as well as expenditures and time for enforcement of rules and procedures. All-male dorms were more intensely monitored and guarded to deter destructive behavior and required a more comprehensive set of rules to explain what was permissible and not permissible behavior. While many of these rules extended to co-ed dorms, their origination came in many cases from the negative events in all-male dorms. Of course, unisex dorms existed before co-ed dorms so many other rules were in place from past experiences before the move to integrated dorms, but the introduction of women reduced repairs, monitorship, and enforcement.

Thus, because the masculine lacks the attractive element in the feminine, there are immense pressures for him to reinforce the walls that prevent individualistic engagement in group interactions. The implication of this is that as the feminine influence wanes there will be an increase in laws, rules, policies, and procedures to guide behavior with a corresponding increase in monitory and enforcing activities. This will enhance the drain on the masculine's energy and reduce the likelihood of synergy generating dynamic outcomes. The ultimate present day actuality of this state is military life where rules and regulations exist in volumes of volumes in order to provide predictable cohesion for even the smallest occurrences. Individualistic activities yielding creative solutions are virtually non-existent in the rank and file.

Even though we can now understand how the feminine influence can navigate a chaotic situation by providing natural glue, we need to see how she can move a group to this state so dynamic possibilities can appear. This is where we see more tactically the resonation effect we covered earlier. In a group interaction this is best accomplished through the allowance and encouragement of individual questions and comments.

In moving a group from the diagram on the left to the one on the right in Figure 5.19,

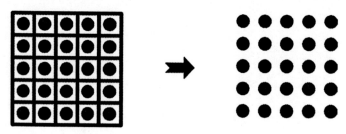

Figure 5.19

There is a flow that we can differentiate into recognizable steps that begins with a single individual and eventually resonates throughout the group until the "walls" are removed. We can represent this effect by a series of diagrams as shown in Figure 5.20.

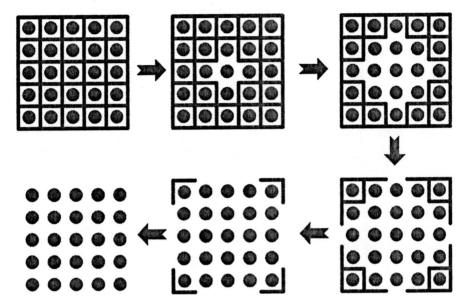

Figure 5.20

How long this will take and the nature of the journey will vary with the individuals involved, including the initiator of the interaction, and the forces opposing individualistic expression by reinforcing conformity. We covered those forces when we first introduced this map. Since it may take several days for this to completely occur, if at all, with an unfamiliar group, the time frames of a presentation are important in gauging what can happen. A half-hour or hour presentation will create challenges with a group with whom the initiator is unfamiliar. This effect will also apply not only when speaking but also when trying to influence any group over any time period. It's analogous to massaging muscles for the purpose of increasing blood flow.

A tangible illustration of this effect is when the presenter concludes his talk and opens for questions. The first question is generally the toughest one to generate, and the second diagram in the above series represents this event. After the first one, the second is more easily generated and the third even more so until the "snowball effect" takes over. In some presentations, people are even planted in the audience to get this effect going. This technique is either visibly used or invisibly. In the first, the host of the occasion will ask the first question; while in the second, the presenter or host will take someone aside and give him a question to begin the process. Generally, the most effective way is to encourage a spontaneous question.

While the first question is generally the toughest, it's easy to derail the process. The most obvious example is ridiculing the question or the questioner; this will bring a quick halt to it. Even though this is obvious it does set a point of reference by which we can begin to see how variations have different effects encouraging or discouraging further questions and comments. From this begins our points outlining the strategy to maximize group interactions by stating the first one.

- Encourage questions and comments.

While this seems obvious, it's hard to convey; simply saying it doesn't cut it. Anyone can say anything, and words do not necessarily convey conviction or ability. As a result, saying, "Feel free to ask questions," carries the same impact as saying in a sales situation, "Feel free to trust me." Saying, "You can trust me" does not mean the other person will automatically trust you; he wants to see proof. Likewise, no one is going to entrust the presenter with his individualistic expression in the form of a question until he sees proof that the presenter is capable of handling his question. This doesn't mean the presenter has to have an answer for the question, but it does mean the presenter must handle it as though he's given something valuable. A question automatically transforms a person from a nebulous part of a group into an individual with an identity outside of the group – the question he asked. Visually, we can see this as Figure 5.21.

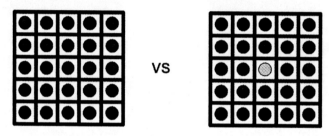

Figure 5.21

Anyone who has listened to a talk that concluded with an invite for questions has felt the discomfort in trying to decide to ask the first question or the focus that is suddenly placed upon the one who asks the first question. Many factors go into the encouragement of questions and comments including an appealing topic and style, so when the first question does come forth, it's important to demonstrate your appreciation for it.

- Demonstrate appreciation for the first question.

This appreciation can be as direct as saying, "Thank you for getting us started. I appreciate it." Or, it can be indirect in the form of a compliment about the question's quality or some aspect that question allows you to address. An even more direct approach but pre-emptive one is to begin the questioning portion by saying, "I'm done with my prepared remarks and have left the remaining time to address other points through questions. I'd appreciate someone getting us started by asking or commenting about something that interests them." The actual form of the appreciation matters little as long as it's in line with your personality; this makes it sincere.

With this comment, we've come to a series of points that apply to any question. The most important one is be sincere.

- Be sincere with any remark about a question.

There are many techniques to help one come across as sincere, but none work as well as being sincere. Usually, this means being yourself. This encourages others to do the same. For this reason, it's important to find aspects of a question that you truly like. Rather than trying to demonstrate sincerity about the question itself, it's better to let true sincerity flow around a specific aspect or implication the question presents. Perhaps it allows you to address a favorite topic that is directly or indirectly associated with the question.

Once questions begin it's important to not stop these questions unless someone following you or running the program outranks you or you have another commitment. Exhaust the questions. Once the momentum continues you don't want to stop. Questions typically identify the time when people are most engaged.

- Avoid stopping questions once they start.

Obviously, the specifics of the situation will impact this guideline, but many times these specifics are not as critical as we think at the moment. A frequent reason for ending questions is time. Often time frames cause us to terminate a question-answer session without consideration for the fact that many people can leave when they would like. As we had discussed earlier in this section, people have various tendencies to resonate after an interaction. Furthermore, the purpose of any interaction is to generate a strong resonation. In everyday language some would call this a "buzz." We are trying to create the effect of the diagram on the left in someone rather than the one on the right in Figure 5.22.

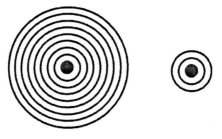

Figure 5.22

More importantly, even if we could take an instant poll and find three-fourths of the people desiring to leave, this may not warrant ending the session. Our purpose is to create a strong resonation with someone because he becomes the one who can help initiate the dismantling of walls in the series shown above. As a result, the emphasis of the interaction becomes the few and not the many – the qualitative not the quantitative. This is how the feminine influence manifests in a group interaction; quality, like beauty, is more difficult to measure than numbers.

We can represent these contrasts with another pair of diagrams. Again, we are striving for the right one in Figure 5.23.

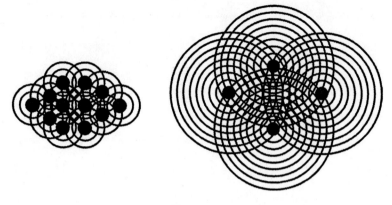

Figure 5.23

As long as questions and comments are forthcoming, attraction is working. The people represented by the ones on the right are far more likely to break down walls than the ones on the left. They also become the basis for future interactions, and ones upon whom you can rely.

To promote this resonation and a dismantling of the walls in favor of a more personal atmosphere, it helps to reference questions by the names of the questioners and to make points in the "names" of their questions.

- Associate questioners' names to their questions (i.e. Jane's question).

From a pure delivery perspective, personifying questions using the questioner's names serves a practical purpose by reducing the need to break up various points and explanations by interjecting the whole question. In effect, personification in this realm creates a descriptive for the question to facilitate referencing.

More important than this practical aspect is that you personify questions and raise the importance and life of the question. Associating names to questions helps demonstrate an interest in people. This returns us to a couple points we discussed with individual interactions. First is the point about personification and second is the one about demonstrating helpfulness. For instance, the statement, "John's question relates to the one Jane asked earlier but it helps me to bring in an additional point." The names easily relate to the personification element, and the word "help" identifies the helpfulness element.

This automatically takes us to another point: illustrate how the question helps you or the discussion.

- Illustrate how the question helps you or the discussion.

Doing this for every question is ideal as long as it's sincere and creative. For these reasons, it's not always practical. Creativity comes into play when you try to alter ways to personalize the response. Simply repeating the above example ("John's question relates to the one Jane asked earlier but it helps me to bring in an additional point.") after every response will eventually thwart the resonation you're trying to achieve.

Using questioners' names to personalize questions also reintroduces a few elements we discussed for personalizing individual interactions. They also apply to the personalization of group interactions.

- Use personification themes of individual interactions.
  - Mention individuals.

- Use names.
- Address people by their names.
- Make positive references.

Anytime you use names you reference individuals, not groups. The best way to break down individual isolation created by a group setting is to acknowledge individuals in deference to the group. The most common manifestation of this is the personalization of presentation materials by putting the person's name on the cover of the folder or notebook containing them. Everyone knows this is far more impactive than generic materials; let's just extend its implications:

If a notebook using someone's name delivers a more personal impression than one using the group's name, then why wouldn't a speaker using someone's name deliver a more personal impression than one using the group's name? For example, feel the difference between these two responses to the question, "How would you evaluate our work?":

- The work this group does is very important to the company's success.
- John, your work is very important and helps me do my job.

Mentioning names of individuals and referencing them will not only attract the individual who's mentioned but others as well. If they see you recognizing another, they will begin to recognize that you have the capability to recognize them; a participant will identify with the one you mention and will identify with that person regardless of whether he is in attendance.

This is also why it's important to mention people who are in different circles. People are most likely to identify with someone who is in their circle even if this is just someone who sits next to them.

- Reference various circles.

People identify with others in many different ways such as job function, market, region, gender, hobbies, and culture. This is how a comment to one person can impact many more people. Identify those who are respected by others. Integrity is an important element of resonation. As mentioned earlier, this doesn't necessarily correspond to title as the "elder statesman" example showed earlier.

The delivery of a message to a group can reinforce or dissolve the constraints around individual expression. I have found delivery so individualized that specific techniques presented categorically do more danger than good by breeding a race of speakers who all seem to do the same thing; a condition that reinforces constraints. Thus, I encourage people to break conventional public speaking rules.

At a higher level though there are two very general guiding principles I have found helpful that work in tandem: variation and naturalness. The feminine influence incorporates both while the masculine singularity and formulation. In all aspects of life the integration of the masculine and feminine yields a potent force. In the case of a presentation to a group, the singularity is the purpose while formulation is content, so delivery remains to be placed in the realm of the feminine in order to integrate the two influences.

Variation implies not doing the same thing all the time; thus, change such things as expressions, tone, positioning, techniques, movement, and pacing. The degree to which you change will be based upon your nature, and thus, the application of the second principle, naturalness. The better you balance variation with your nature, the more likely you are to dissolve constraints and free up individual enjoyment of the presentation.

- Seek natural variation.

The tough part is the application. The key here is variation because you don't want to get into the routine of doing the exact same thing for each group even if ostensibly the groups are the same. If you were to interact with two separate people, chances are extremely likely you would adapt to some degree to the person with whom you are interacting. No two conversations would go exactly alike; yet, you would also display common elements in each so each conversation would not be *completely* different.

No matter how similar the names or attributes of the groups to whom we're presenting, no two groups contain the exact same personalities. Consequently, the groups are different. Furthermore, even if you happen to make the same presentation to the same group, things would be different because the time is different for each of the individuals in the group; one presentation would be earlier in their lives than the other. To help me in situations where I've made a presentation to a series of groups, I generally try to add at least one new thing in terms of content or delivery that is reasonably challenging. This alone gives me an entirely new feel for the presentation and encourages the avoidance of feeling like it's a routine. No matter how natural our techniques make us appear, there is no substitute for feeling natural. The manifestation of this disparity will appear in the degree to which the dissolution of constraints occurs.

Again, to refocus us, the importance of dissolving these constraints lies in your effort to use group settings to promote or reinforce individual interactions. The more you are able to remove these constraints the more likely you will be able to attract individual interactions and reinforce the ones you've already had.

The key is the degree to which you are naturally you. People are naturally attracted to those who can be themselves because everyone appreciates the challenges involved in being yourself. People who can be themselves are more likely to accept others as they are. Consequently, since people seek to be themselves, they are more likely to gravitate to those who can accept them. Moreover, since those who can be themselves in the face of group pressures exude courage, there is also a possibility that they can help others learn how to survive as themselves as well – another attractive aspect. Being you conveys the most powerful credibility anyone can have.

Once, I read a guide, written by a woman, on speaking techniques that included a section covering special techniques for women to enhance their credibility before an audience. The premise behind this section was research showing audiences automatically giving female presenters less credibility than male ones.

What I have found is that conventional speaking techniques do not reinforce the natural strengths of a woman because most, if not all, are derivatives from successful ones men have used as presenters. Worse yet, the underlying assumption behind many views of these techniques could be asexual; they're not affected by gender. The implication here is that men and women are using the same presentation techniques even though they are wearing different clothes determined by gender. Thus, the point for women is that they may be encouraged to use asexual or masculine techniques, and for men that they may be encouraged to use asexual techniques. Either way, there is the likelihood that technique alone may not be conveying a natural message regarding their gender, and we haven't even begun to explore personality's effects.

Therefore, I would contend that a reason why women may appear less credible than men is that they are appearing less natural than men. The inherent advantage of women over men has to be more than simply the ability to bear children. Nature provides every creature a way to protect itself. What I have inferred throughout is that for women that power is beauty. A man who rips apart with his bare hands a ferocious tiger or a beautiful flower generates a similar action; however, the interpretation of each is vastly different. Whereas the first could be seen as a sign of virility and strength, the second could be seen as insensitivity and destructiveness. Another man kills in his house two separate intruders whom he cannot see because of darkness. Again, the action is the same; however, in the first case the intruder is an armed robber while in the second the intruder is a mentally retarded teenager who wandered lost into the house. Interpretively we could see the first as self-defense while in the second an unfortunate freaky occurrence. The outcome is the same in that a dead person lies in the house; however, how we interpret the event changes.

What's important is the potential for an emotional difference in these examples. In the first part of each example, the man is more likely to feel something positive about what he did whereas the in the second he is more likely to feel something negative. For example, if a large, falling rock committed each action in our examples rather than a man, the rock would feel no difference between the first and second parts of each whereas the man would.

In these examples "flower power" becomes the power of the qualitative, the distinction between the positive and negative application of power. If the qualitative did not exist, then the mere application of power would be good regardless of degree and outcome. Life would simply revolve around who could wield the most power and not necessarily what that person could do with his power. Physically, while a man's body represents strength and power, a woman's body represents beauty and grace, quantity versus quality.

Unlike quantity quality is difficult to measure. A man's strength and power is easier to measure than a woman's beauty and grace. The various events in the Olympics reflect this distinction by having some governed by such things as the clock, tap measure, and scales while others are governed by judges' marks. As much as we try to reduce subjectivity in judging, the judges marks all vary. Likewise, in any qualitative scoring, including quality control initiatives, subjectivity somewhere enters the picture especially if we're scoring qualitative aspects of humans.

The other important aspect of quality that we discussed several times before, but we can again bring in here, is emotion. Quality does not work without emotion. For instance, while anyone can measure the degree to which a product meets certain specifications, meeting specifications alone does not determine quality. Just because a rifleman can hit the bull's-eye more frequently than another doesn't mean he's qualitatively better. There's more to being a good rifleman than how one does in a competition such as functioning under pressure with an enemy shooting at you. Whether it's the specifications for a product or a competition, someone had to subjectively determine those specifications. Often a weighing of price versus quality entered too, a subjective determination. Suppose a product meets specifications but no one wants to buy it, is it a good product? Businesses go out of business all the time with products that meet their specifications. Why would this happen if quality was really determined by meeting specifications? At some point, in any manufacturing process someone subjectively evaluated quality, often it was the consumer.

A woman's beauty reminds us that quality is emotional. If this were not the case, a computer could create a new, successful product without any input from a human. Consequently, as we've arrived at earlier with our discussions, sensitivity and the ability to distinguish quality correlate. One who is better able to appreciate the beauty in a woman is more likely to see the beauty in other things and thus employ the creative powers inherent in subjectivity.

Now, the challenge is to tie this implicational stream back to presentations. We can do this by referencing the credibility study generically mentioned above and using the rifleman example. Credibility is just one small aspect of influencing an audience. Sincerity and attractiveness do as well. Subjectively, this particular study, or perhaps the author of the guidebook, determined to focus on only credibility. I would suggest credibility's connotation is more akin to masculinity than femininity. It would be like asking whether a dog or a fish runs faster. If we were to conduct research on aspects more favorable to a woman's influential nature such as:

- Whom do you generally find more sincere, a male or female presenter?
- More personable?
- Less intimidating?
- More attentive to questions?

If these aspects did not influence, then women would not be used in advertisements for any products. The important point here for both male and female readers is that your approach to influence a group must fit *your* nature and the way you vary every aspect of your presentation must fit you and the situation.

For example, some people move around a lot with sharp, quick actions. This tendency seems to work better for male speakers than female speakers. Action is a masculine attribute. Grace is a feminine one. For these reasons slower more gentle movements with continuity and flow tend to work better for female speakers than male ones. A great visual is the inherent power in a river; it moves slowly but the force is powerful and can power huge electrical generators. People tend to like to see men in action and women in grace. They want to be able to easily gaze upon a woman and take in her beauty rather than struggle to keep up with her. Beautiful artwork usually is stationary so people can soak in its essence.

Of course, this is not to say women cannot display activity and men gracefulness because total adherence to either extreme is a detriment; however, certain tendencies will dominate by gender and by individual. What is important though is the tendency among speaking coaches to encourage a specific style irrespective on gender. One aspect that is currently popular is the "walking around" technique. As a result, we are finding a standardization of presentation styles among presenters. This does not promote personalization and moves presenters to a one-sided, masculine dominated form of presenting. The key is finding what flows naturally for you.

With these themes in place we can begin to integrate a group interaction with individual ones. While it's easy to think of group interactions as "grand events," the true grand event is the individual interaction; the group one merely serves to position or reinforce it. Again, when we speak of group, we mean any number of individuals more than two in any setting, formal and informal.

Positioning

Using group settings to introduce issues that will see follow up on an individual basis is not a new concept; however, our emphasis will be relational via personification. Typically, more focus is on the issue and its elements including a plan containing individual, follow up discussions. There is very little use of the themes we just discussed.

More specifically, we'll explore how to use the output that the above themes generate from a group interaction to help make individual interactions more effective. This extends the traditional positioning of an issue in a group interaction as the objective deliverance of a message into something that lays the groundwork for fruitful individual conversations on an emotional level well beyond the objective levels established by the message with the intention of enhancing the relationship between manager and employee, employee and clients, and between employees. Again, this emotional level is the integration of the feminine influence that we discussed earlier.

The ultimate purpose of a group interaction is to come away with "seeds" that can be nurtured into strong individual interactions when the time comes. Pragmatically, this is no different than seminar selling where a presentation to the group generates opportunities that lead to individual sales opportunities. The aspects of the presentation that prospects pick up on become the basis, or entry points, for those discussions; however, it's hard to do that if there is no feedback, no *engagement*. Any individual sales opportunity becomes more fruitful if one understands what it was about the presentation that attracted the prospect's attention – that made it *personal* to him. That is why the themes above transform a group interaction into a strong positioning tool for following individual interactions tailored to the employee. In essence, we are taking fundamental sales themes, modifying them, and enhancing them to suit an employee-manager relationship through the integration of a group and individual interactions.

If we take the frequently cited statement of many sales experts that "the buying decision is an emotional one that is rationalized" and extend its implications, we will find that fundamental need analysis, where we fit the product or service to a client's situation, is not the main driver behind a sale. We can reinforce this implication by doing the same with the statement "sales is about relationships not transactions." Anything that indicates selling is more relational or consultative than transactional supports the premise that relationships, not needs, drive the buying decision.

If this holds true for the client-employee relationship, then it holds true for the employee-manager one as well. The decision of employees "to buy into" company initiatives is relational not transactional. Thus, the communication of objectives and strategies to employees about company objectives is no different than a sales person speaking only to the needs of a client rather than to relational elements that enhance trust.

This is not to say objectives and strategies are not important; however, they are secondary to relational needs. As we saw with the Persian Gulf War example, masculine elements such as objectives and strategies set the stage for the relational ones of the feminine to work. They become the "excuse" for forming stronger relations. This is why in virtually any company the primary reason employees leave is because of their relationships with their managers.

For these reasons, group interactions serve important staging grounds for the enhancement of employee-manager relationships.

Tactically, we can accomplish this through formal or informal individual interactions. Any one-on-one interaction between an employee and manager can serve to enhance their relationship. The same occurs in sales with clients and employees. We also don't need to assume a one-to-one correlation between a group interaction and an individual one; one group interaction can serve to position several individual interactions with the same employee.

We can illustrate this by incorporating a few diagrams into a new one, Figure 5.24.

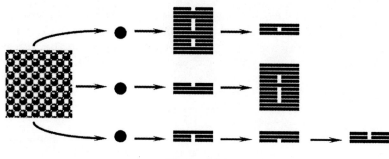

Figure 5.24

The square on the left represents the group interaction, the three points represent three people who asked questions or made comments. Moving right the next series of symbols represent conversations. Again, a solid line (|) represents the manager's comments while a broken line (¦) represents an employee's. The larger conversational symbols represent a formal discussion while the smaller ones represent informal ones, "elevator" type conversations.

With the top person the manager sets up a formal interaction to comprehensively discuss not only what happened at the group setting but also the employee's questions and comments about the topic. Later, the manager takes advantage of an impromptu meeting to briefly follow up with additional comments or questions.

The middle person represents almost the opposite of the top person. Here, an impromptu meeting has the manager commenting on the employee's questions from the group interaction to yield the arrangement of a formal meeting for further discussions.

With the bottom person we see the manager taking advantage of three impromptu interactions to comment on, reinforce, and press home various employee comments and questions. This sample illustrates that the interplay between group and individual interactions does not necessarily need formality around it.

Again, much of this appears as a graphic of what actually occurs in business around various objectives and strategies; however, what we want to drive through this are more relational elements.

- Drive relational elements through traditional business processes.

This methodology integrates the masculine (traditional business processes) with the feminine (relational elements) and thus generates a powerful, creative combination symbolized by the union of a man and a woman. The relational elements are the tactics we covered under individual interactions. Thus, questions or comments from participants become the relational basis within the communication and the actions around a business objective. For instance, let's take the top employee in Figure 5.24.

Let's say in this scenario the group interaction automatically prompted the setting of a formal meeting with the employee. Before entering into the conversation in detail, a remark about the comments and questions of the employee can position the individual interaction more effectively. The remark will employ the tactics we saw under the individual interaction portion of this section. We would see something like:

Before we start I just want to (thank you for your insightfulness)[F] on the [employment of our new business model][M], your question really (helped me)[F] get a good discussion going [on its merits][M].

Breaking this sentence down, we again see elements from our previous discussions on individual interactions. We see the personalization to the receiver of the interaction (the employee) with the reference to his insightfulness and personalization to the initiator through the reference on how the employee helped. These comments once again become the invisible, flanking maneuver to the individual employee on a personal level while the visible, direct maneuver is the issue of employing the business model and its merits. Together we have the integration of the feminine and masculine influences.

A note worth mentioning revolves around the word "insightfulness" versus "insights." Either word would grammatically and objectively fill the need; however, "insightfulness" is personal while "insights" is objective. By using the first we imbue the person with an attribute while the second compliments the remarks. This is a nuance reflecting the great opportunity our language contains to grow effective relationships. Again, the variations on this theme are immense but they all revolve around imbuing others with attributes you see in them.

More commonly in reverse form where the employee gets in front of the manger, we call this "gaining exposure." For instance, an employee meets with his manager or his manager's manager around a business issue. The issue is the excuse for the employee to gain exposure to someone higher up in the organization. Essentially, we're taking the same principle but applying it in reverse and personifying, making a more conscious effort to employ it.

Carrying through this experience with the top person we could see the shorter, impromptu meeting containing a comment like this:

I just wanted to say that (I appreciate your ability to think through things) ^{F}
because [your follow up comments last time regarding your question at the
team meeting] ^{M} (really helped me) ^{F} think through [other ways this model
helps (you and me) ^{F} and ways we can explain it to others] ^{M}.

The first feminine influence phrase incorporates the personality of the receiver (employee) through a particular ability of the employee similar to "insightfulness" in the previous example, the second incorporate the personality of the initiator (manager) by demonstrating helpfulness, and the third incorporates both by referencing both the employee and manager rather than some nebulous "clients" or "company." Conversely, the masculine comes into play referencing comments, question, and meeting with the first such phrase, and the reference to the explanation of the model's benefits to others in the second.

Both of these examples try to illustrate the transitional glue that permits an integration of group and individual interactions. While I tried to integrate them into a single sentence, as shown earlier we can weave their components throughout a conversation such as we saw in Figure 5.13. This conversation can take place immediately following the group setting or sometime later. We can also use many other comments such as the following to personify to various degrees the business issues discussed in a group interaction:

- Thank you for your question, you got things going.
- I liked your remark; you allowed me to talk about things I'm passionate about.
- I appreciate your question. You addressed what was on many others' minds.
- You did a great job answering John's question.

Superficially, these may appear as direct compliments, but there's something deeper going on here that is more clearly seen if we alter these comments slightly:

- Thank you for your question, **it** got things going.
- **[I liked]** Your remark was good; **it** allowed **us** to talk about things important to us **[I'm passionate about]**.
- **[I appreciate your question]** Good question. **It** addressed what was on many others' minds.
- **[You did a great job]** Your comment was a good answer to the **group's** question.

In all four cases, these comments remain compliments, but I've depersonalized the compliment by eliminating references to specific people, mainly the receiver and the initiator. I've bolded the changes and put in brackets the eliminated phrases. The concept is exactly the one in which we're advised to avoid saying "you" in potentially conflictory situations so as to avoid accusations except we're using it positively. The word "you" is extremely accusatory in negative situations, but the degree to which it is negative reflects the degree to which it is oppositely impactive in the positive direction. While we may not necessarily want to personify a potentially damaging situation, we most likely will want to in a positive one.

Symbolically, what I've done in the second set is gone into a house and painted all the walls and trim gray. When you consider all the materials, expense, and time to build a house, wall paint is an insignificant component of each; however, the colors of the walls make a dynamic impact because they convey ambiance and direct the entire décor for the house. Likewise, personification seems a very little thing, but it brings color to otherwise lifeless business objectives. Many business people say "their employees make the difference," so this phraseology allows one's language to be more harmonious with their beliefs. These personal words convey an emotion, feeling, or passion for what really drives business and directs the entire direction for an objective – people.

Of course, the challenge is coming up with comments and remarks that are highly personal to the receiver. For planned interactions this is easier, but much more difficult for impromptu ones. As a result, thought, regular planning, and practice around the possible content for an individual interaction with an employee is very pertinent. Moreover, some people's nature just will not allow them to do this.

- Relationally plan the follow up content for formal and informal individual interactions.

In any business tremendous time is spent planning objectives and their communication. This involves what will be said and how to structure those words. Personification is no different. There is regular review and planning of each person's attributes and qualities that can be personified in interactions. This means reflecting on each person's uniqueness.

- Regularly review attributes and qualities for personification within the business context of the next interaction and the previous group interaction.

Prior to a meeting or a site visit, a review of the attendees or personnel roster helps. Asking yourself various questions will help prepare possible responses. Some of those questions include:

- What attributes or qualities does this person have?
- What comments or questions came from this person in the previous interaction we mutually had alone or with others?
- How do I link his remarks to his qualities?

- How do I personify them?
- Did his contributions help me? How?
- How do I translate this into setting up an individual interaction?
- What one thing should I remember about him as a person?

All of this moves an employee-manager interaction closer to the elements involved in a successful client-employee interaction. Similarly, the success of such a meeting goes beyond mere objective issues involving business and into relational ones concerning holistic aspects of the client. All the principles we've covered work for peer relationships as well (employee-employee and manager-manager).

With the addition of the planning element in maximizing group interactions (and really individual ones too), we are beginning to gray the differences between their positioning and reinforcement aspects. Thus, before we go further, we need to incorporate the reinforcement aspect.

Reinforcement

As with the positioning aspect of group interactions, the reinforcement aspect is not a new concept albeit a lesser used one. In the latter, group settings are typically used to reinforce issues that were initially discussed on an individual basis or as part of an overall plan to communicate findings from a series of one-on-one meetings.

Still, as with the positioning aspect, the reinforcement one in business usually lacks more relational elements such as the themes we've discussed with positioning and individual interactions. Illustratively, Figure 5.25 shows this difference between positioning and reinforcement.

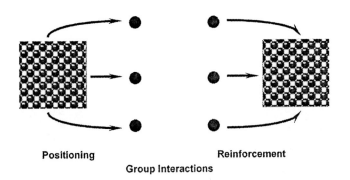

Positioning   **Reinforcement**
Group Interactions

Figure 5.25

Whereas in positioning we are looking to the group interaction to create opportunities for positive, individual interactions, reinforcement has us seeking ways to solidify the opportunities that came about from individual interactions. In truth, we are quickly approaching a comprehensive view of the interplay between group and individual interactions as a continuous series of mutually supportive events as seen in Figure 5.26; however, the emphasis is on the individual with the group playing a secondary role.

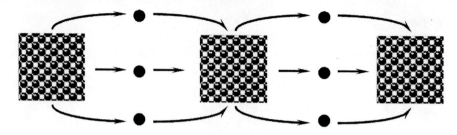

Figure 5.26

More specifically, we'll explore how to use the output that the above themes generate from an individual interaction to help make group interactions more effective.

Traditionally, we've seen presenters, especially outside ones, use individual interactions to maximize their presentations before a group. Ostensibly this comes across as research for a topic by interviewing several attendees prior to the presentation. The masculine aspect of this is the material the presenter receives to create and refine his presentation. On a deeper, unspoken level (invisible) is the attempt to build support and engagement for the presentation. This is the feminine influence at work.

Nevertheless, the employment of this approach, while traditional, is not employed with the frequency of positioning, the announcement of an initiative with follow up on an individual basis. More importantly for our discussion, when it is employed, it is its masculine aspects that are emphasized with the feminine ones coming along as side benefits tapped only if the need arises.

Another way to help picture the traditional shortfalls when reinforcement is used, is to change the perspective of Figure 5.25 where we saw illustratively the difference between positioning and reinforcement. It's from the perspective of the group interaction; let's change the perspective to the individual. In this way, we can now picture the contrast as Figure 5.27.

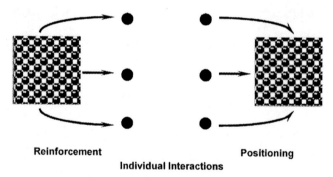

Reinforcement   **Positioning**
Individual Interactions

Figure 5.27

Here, we are looking at how the individual interactions reinforce and position the group interaction. The traditional aspect we just described fits more the perspective of using individual interactions to position the group one; the emphasis is on the success of the presentation, the group interaction, rather than the individual ones. Thus, whereas the strategy in this section uses the interplay between group and individual interactions similarly to what has already traditionally occurred, this strategy has four primary differences from a traditional approach:

- Increased comprehensiveness of this interplay by looking at it as a constant flow of mutually reinforcing and positioning actions.
- Shifted primary emphasis to individual interactions and assigned group ones a secondary role.
- Far heavier integration of tactical themes to personify all interactions.
- Greater conscious incorporation of the feminine influence.

Through this interplay we now see how individual interactions position group ones. In essence they help us make a group interaction more effective by allowing us to enter it further along than if we hadn't had the benefit of those interactions. Rather than beginning with the diagram on the left in Figure 5.28 as we had done earlier in this section, the individual interactions allow for something more in line with the right.

 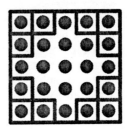

Figure 5.28

Almost any kind of one-on-one interaction with a receiver can influence a group interaction. This includes an email, a hand written note, or a phone call. All of these contribute to breaking down the invisible walls that isolate individuals in a group setting because they demonstrate the initiator's ability to expertly handle comments and questions from a relational perspective. This establishes trust and a willingness to help out. The initiator can even go so far as to indicate that she is counting on their support, participation, or help in making the group interaction an effective one. We often view this as simply the audience being comfortable with the presenter. Here, we are proactively enriching the soil upon which we'll work in a group setting.

- Indicate counting on their support, participation, or help in a group interaction.

Still, with the many communicative and interpretive drawbacks to group interactions, we need to tackle this interplay from the aspect of the individual interaction and the reason why we call this portion of our Group Interaction discussion "Reinforcement."

In order to better picture how the group interaction reinforces relational development initiated or enhanced in individual interactions, it's probably best to imagine a wedding ceremony. The ceremony is a public announcement of a relationship between two people. Regardless of the religion of the participants, the overwhelming number of wedding ceremonies have some aspect of a public announcement or proclamation. There is an emotional difference between a private proclamation and a public one. The same holds true for other types of relationships including business ones.

It's the element of proclamation upon which we wish to elaborate. Essentially, in a group interaction this translates into a reference to an individual interaction in front of the group.

- Reference an individual interaction in front of the group.

From our discussion on individual interactions this is a combination of "mention individuals" and "make positive references" but it goes further by seeking to publicly bond what happened in the individual setting. This can happen even if the person is not in the group meeting because one of his colleagues will most likely mention this event. Even outside of this person, there is the reasoning we discussed in individual interactions: "someone who mentions individual people frequently in conversation is more likely to bond personally than one who mentions no individuals in conversation."

Furthermore, referencing will also encourage the receiver to play a more participatory role that will serve to encourage others to do so as well. This will create further opportunities with these others to then incorporate the themes we mention in individual interactions. Over an extended period of time, these mutually reinforcing actions will seek to create a flow that grows into stronger and stronger relationships.

Analogously, we can associate this flow with that of a river. The first few employees comprise droplets that form springs and run into other droplets created from a regular rainfall. These springs turn into tributaries which turn into streams then creeks and finally rivers. A flow grows that powers huge hydroelectric plants – and businesses. As a result, many of the themes we discussed in individual interactions and earlier with group interactions can also serve to reinforce individual interactions in group settings.

We will now round out our discussion of group interactions by highlighting some of the opportunities that can help you create opportunities for individual interactions.

Opportunities

Depending upon your current role and the degree to which you'd like to extend your influence, you'll need to identify opportunities in line with this. Again, this is a normal, implemental part of any strategy so it can include speaking, projects, and functions. The key differentiator is the focus on relational development as opposed to experience or skill development. The purpose is to set the stage to interact with others on a more personal level.

- Seize and create opportunities to interact with the employees with whom you wish to interact.

Inclusive in this role are such things as phone calls or emails to participants as follow up inquiries on outcomes and improvements. Again, these are the masculine aspects of these inquiries while the relationship's growth becomes the feminine aspect. Any interaction grows a relationship especially if it's followed up by an individual one; the actual issue is secondary to the enhancement of the relationship.

When you create or receive these opportunities, encourage formats that allow people to ask you questions. Naturally, circumstances may drive these formats but where you are in a position to influence them do so.

- Encourage formats that allow people to ask you questions.

As you have probably gathered from everything we've discussed about the feminine influence, she requires time to position all her elements. This is why many tend to discount her influence and effectiveness because in addition to intuition she requires discipline and relentlessness in order to be effective. It's difficult to find people with all three attributes and why it's much easier to discount her effectiveness than admit an inability to work with her. Again, some people's nature just won't allow them to employ her. However, once she is integrated with the masculine aspects of business, she becomes a powerful driver of success. Thus, it's important to begin incorporating the feminine influence into everything you do relationally.

- Begin as early as possible to integrate the feminine influence in relational activities.

Fortunately, this doesn't have to be a dramatic transition. In fact, it's better if the incorporation occurs over an extended period at a pace comfortable to you.

- Integrate the feminine influence over an extended period at a pace comfortable to you.

During this period as your comfort with her increases, you can accelerate the integration. You will naturally find a pace right for you.

- Accelerate the integration over this period.

Again, what I am proposing is a more conscious awareness and application of the feminine influence. Many of these things you may be doing naturally already, so while a part of this strategy is trying to implement some new things, another part entails greater awareness of what you're already doing so you can learn from yourself.

- Enhance your awareness of when you're naturally applying some of the themes mentioned in this document.

The importance of this is that it will allow you to enjoy and to appreciate many of the things that you do naturally. Some of these you may or may not now be aware, but at least you will come to have a better appreciation for your talent to do this.

In addition to the feminine themes you can employ masculine elements that will help you win hearts. These are issues you find important to others and for which you feel there is justification. As we had discussed in the Company chapter, there is a difference between paying someone to do something and winning his heart. We cannot pay people to turn over their hearts to us no more than a man can coerce a woman to love him. In both cases, payment and coercion, one can get another to do something but it's a matter of what degree the other's heart is in it.

For this reason, within any organizational structure there are informal circles of influence (*de facto* power) on every level that impact decisions made throughout that structure on any other level. These circles exist in even the most dictatorial, insensitive political regimes, so they can and do exist in business. It's important for managers in the development of employee-manager relationships to be in the flow on these issues. Anyone who has ever made a business decision impacting other employees has found himself considering the feelings of those people. We typically lump these under the more generally heading of morale.

Thus, you can begin to identify within your company the issues with which you wish to be associated. Since I'm not aware of your situation, much of this will need to be left with you, but conceptually you need some issues that can serve as the masculine influence permitting the personal aspects of the feminine as shown in Figure 5.29.

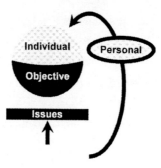

Figure 5.29

Summary

In journalism classes in high school and college, instructors taught us the importance of incorporating names into articles to heighten interest. This holds true even if people don't know who the people are. Psychologists can give us many reasons for this, but the fact remains that people like to read articles that mention people. Since this is true for written communications, then it's also true for verbal ones too.

In the Group heading of our Aspects section, we discussed how to use group interactions to position and reinforce individual ones. Group is the opposite of individual and is associated with depersonalization. Maps in the form of diagrams helped us describe group dynamics and the interplay of group and individual interactions to maximize personalization.

Winning hearts is very difficult without personalization. No woman falls in love with a man who treats her as just another part of the group of women he has courted. For this reason, we identified themes that promote personalization. I am consolidating them for summary here:

1. Encourage questions and comments.
2. Demonstrate appreciation for the first question.
3. Be sincere with any remark about a question.
4. Avoid stopping questions once they start.
5. Associate questioners' names to their questions.
6. Illustrate how the question helps you or the discussion.
7. Use personification themes of individual interactions.
8. Reference various circles.
9. Seek natural variation.
10. Drive relational elements through traditional business processes.
11. Relationally plan the follow up content for formal and informal individual interactions.
12. Regularly review attributes and qualities for personification within the business context of the next interaction and the previous group interaction.
13. Indicate counting on their support, participation, or help in a group interaction.
14. Reference an individual interaction in front of the group.
15. Seize and create opportunities to interact with all employees with whom you wish to interact.
16. Encourage formats that allow people to ask you questions.

17. Begin as early as possible to integrate the feminine influence in relational activities.
18. Integrate the feminine influence over an extended period at a pace comfortable to you.
19. Accelerate the integration over this period.
20. Enhance your awareness of when you're naturally applying some of the themes mentioned in this document.

Tactics

There are many different techniques to employ the Truths and Aspects outlined in this chapter. Many are routinely covered in communication seminars; however, the tendency is to eradicate variations in personality via a rationalization based upon clear and concise communications at the expense of interesting communications. The basic premise for this is cognitive: if people understand what you're saying they are more apt to accurately do what you say.

There are two basic counterarguments to this line of thought that we've already covered. First, people are more inspired by what they like than what they understand, and second, no instructions, no matter how brilliantly conceived, can encompass all aspects of what may need to be done. The first interrelates with the second because if someone likes what you said he is more likely to resolve the missing links in an effective way; his enthusiasm will carry him.

In looking once again at a house analogy, clear and concise communication represents a house while interesting communications represent a home. Interesting communications require more intelligence than clear and concise communication. While it's easy to think of these as opposites the first is the betterment of the second and thus requires something more. Thus, routine, standardized communications assume lower intelligence among the initiators and receivers of the communication.

The point is that many of these communication techniques are useful if one remembers to incorporate his personality or at minimum incorporate some basic journalistic concepts around the use of names.

What we're about to run through in this section of the Strategy chapter are lesser known concepts that will help you implement your strategy. While they supplement and support the individual and group interactions we just covered, they are more comprehensive than the design of a specific communication. In some ways they coordinate some of the themes we've already discussed throughout the book so we can view them in a different light.

I will run through six tactics:

- Commander-Sage
- Problem solving
- Comprehensive focus
- Different perspectives
- Documenting ideas
- Employees are #1

Each tactic can be used in two ways. First, you can use them personally by giving you a perspective from which to address a task or develop a strategy. Second, you can use them with other people as a basis for communicating and supporting some of your ideas. I'll conceptually describe each tactic and how it may apply to specific situations.

Commander-Sage

In the employee-manager relationship, the masculine and feminine influences manifest themselves in the managerial role as commander and sage respectively. Our language reflects these roles as telling versus teaching. Daily business pressures encourage the first over the latter because telling is far easier than teaching, commanding requires less time, energy, and talent. Delegating and empowering are even easier because one turns over authority for command which does not necessarily translate into teaching.

Again, the emphasis is not one role to the exclusion of the other but rather seeking the right mixture of the two. As we saw in the individual interactions, the degree to which you will use one over the other is a function of your personality and the other person's as well as the conditions surrounding the particular situation. The challenge as I've outlined throughout this book is finding the appropriate balance between these two influences.

The situation, flow, and people surrounding the event will influence the degree to which a manager is a commander or sage at any moment. Thus, the fundamental ingredient permitting a successful employee-manager relationship from the manager's perspective is the positioning of managers not only as generals (directors of sales, service, and operations) but also as sages (educators, advisors, and experts) regarding an employee's professional and personal growth.

Currently, the urgency and pressures surrounding business encourage a focus on generalship with little focus on maximizing the talent of managers as sources of wisdom. These same pressures are encouraging the hiring of employees who already can do the job which increases employee costs and decreases the opportunities for managers to develop as sages. Consequently, this generates upward pressure on finding managers who can provide sagely value to this "ready-made" employee.

It's here at the managerial level that the employee-manager relationship suffers a breakdown because profitability pressures have accelerated, and thus, cost cutting measures have targeted middle managers, those helping front-line employees. Now, more employees report to fewer managers or to managers who also have front-line job duties (player-manager), increasing time constraints and decreasing available managerial teaching time.

Integrating the masculine and feminine influence in the employee-manager relationship will increase the passion an employee has for a company and a management team. Translated in this vein, we're talking about integrating the commander-sage roles of the manager. As we've seen, it's almost impossible to inspire without integrating the feminine influence. Overwhelming focus on the more masculine, commanding role will not only thwart inspirational attempts but will also, in the long run, undermine the passion of a talented employee for the company. Thus, new hires, usually attracted a great expense, will more likely become less effective than anticipated as the commanding role of a manager increases.

Talented employees do not like to be told what to do; talented employees, by their very nature, already pretty much know what needs to be done. Paradoxically though, their nature also includes an intense passion for developing and growing as professionals; their need is not for commanders but sages, the exact opposite of what the current business environment encourages. Witness the huge increase in coaching and mentoring firms – a direct outcome of dwindling access to sagely managers. The number of employees seeking outside coaching on their own is increasing and evidenced by the increasing number of firms providing that support in the last thirty years. Some of this is also because the work force is more fluid so having a long-standing relationship with a manager is rarer.

We can better see this conclusion regarding talented employees if we return to the outside-inside persons concept. Commanding, telling someone what to do, is a straight assault on the outside person and triggers defense mechanisms without carrying any value for the inside one. What is there about a command that encourages an employee to grow professionally? Helping someone grow, by spending time to help them, is an appeal to the inside person. Empowerment by itself does not help much because it often becomes no better than a delegation or assignment as opposed to a teaching or relational opportunity.

Some of this external influence on talent may be difficult to see until we return to the basic premise that business is about relationships. Relationships are secondary to experiences. Consider the following examples:

- If I take a large rock and move it from a gutter to a garden, it's still the same rock; however, how we look at that rock has changed because the relationships it has with its surroundings have changed to manifest different attributes of that rock.
- If I take a cat and move it from one home to another, that cat doesn't change – it's still the same cat. The main influencer affecting how that cat's personality manifests itself in the home is the relationship that that cat has with the inhabitants of its new home.
- The main factor that influences how a student's inherent talents manifest themselves is the teacher; the inherent talent in a child is the same regardless of what class that child is in. A child's test score will vary with the teacher who gives the test, the more a child likes a teacher the more likely he will do better than when he takes it from a teacher he doesn't like.

Similarly, the inherent talent in an employee is the same no matter where he goes; thus, the number one influencer on how his talent impacts the business is the relationship he has with his manager. Working one-on-one with the manager on a project is more in line with the power of relationships to integrate the masculine and feminine influence. Empowerment is often no different than a teacher assigning homework; it segregates the work from the relational aspects of the task. Imagine the impact to a student when he's allowed to work individually with his teacher to observe how she addresses a problem. The masculine aspect is working the problem while the feminine aspect is the bonding that occurs through a one-on-one interaction. Using the outside-inside model, working the problem distracts the outside while the relational interaction encourages the inside.

Analogously, the value of a Ferrari is in what it can do for the driver; whether the driver taps that potential is irrelevant to the intrinsic value of a Ferrari. Because a driver never takes a Ferrari over 55 mph, doesn't mean that that Ferrari can't go 155 mph. It's not the Ferrari's problem if the driver does not tap its full potential. Integrating these influences takes a Ferrari to its limits and inspires a passion that is a marketable commodity to clients and an influence on business success in its own right. As we saw in the Conditioning section of the You chapter, situational influences can dramatically affect talent. Incorporating a sagely influence with a commanding one will increase the likelihood that talent flourishes.

The integration of the sagely aspect of a managerial relationship is very difficult because a manager cannot simply approach an employee and say, "Here, let me teach you something," because it can easily come across as a demand. Ideally, the challenge is to seize "sagely moments" which we refer to in school as "teachable moments."

Formal educators are more aware of the concept of a teachable moment than business professionals. Very simply it's a spontaneous opportunity to teach and learn. For some reason, an opportunity arose whereby someone has a motive to learn based upon something that came up. We used an offshoot of this same concept in the You chapter regarding talent's expressivity. There, I suggested one keep his eyes open for occasions when talent spontaneously expresses itself. Essentially, we're doing the same except we're on the lookout for teachable rather than talented moments.

The most critical aspect of seizing these moments is a virtual, evangelical zeal focused on dropping just about anything when someone seeks your help. By help I am referring to instances where they are seeking more your advice and counsel as opposed to your labor. Sometimes people who seek help are actually asking you to do something for them. The differentiating factor is whether someone is willing to spend time with you to learn how to do something so they may not need you to do anything the next time. In this way, doing something for someone becomes a teaching demonstration with the intention that the "student" will do it himself the next time with or without some oversight.

In order to maximize the teachable opportunities one must encourage and welcome the approach of others. Again, referring back to Figure 2.18 illustrating the "pursue" of the masculine and the "attract" of the feminine, we see the important role the feminine influence plays in the encouragement of such opportunities to occur. All the individual and group interactive work we saw in the Aspect section of this chapter encourages and promotes a fertile environment for this to occur.

Beyond seizing teachable moments, you can assert your sagely aspects by demonstrating that doing so *helps you* as opposed to *exposes* the other's vulnerabilities. For instance, the question, "Can I help you with that?" implies that you've recognized that the other person needs help. Compare this to "I'd really like to show you some things regarding that, okay?" The subtlety is the emphasis on you as opposed to him. Suddenly, he's helping you because it gives you happiness to run through this. You can even conclude the moment with something along the lines of "Thank you for letting me run through that with you. I enjoy presenting this idea." Returning to Figure 5.1 we can illustrate the direct aspect (enjoyment) and the indirect aspect (teaching) of this interaction by editing it as shown in Figure 5.30.

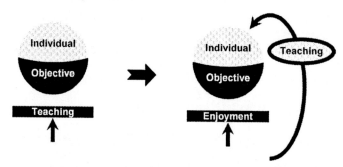

Figure 5.30

In this way, we take the direct teaching effort implied in the "Can I help you" question represented as the left diagram in Figure 5.30 and transform it into an indirect one represented by the right one where the enjoyment in the "I'd like to" question is the direct, overt element.

Another difficulty in the integration of the sagely aspect of a managerial relationship is learning the patience and ability to teach. The first is far more important than the second because usually the deficiencies in the second are easily overcome by displaying the first. With the urgent and overtaxing nature of the business world, the devotion of unhurried time often easily overcomes ability. Still, if you have the chance to learn some basic teaching concepts and techniques either in a formal or informal way, I recommend taking advantage of it. One of the best places to begin is with the people from whom you enjoy learning. Sometimes they may not know exactly what they do that makes them effective, but by observing how they teach you, you can pick up ideas. Generally, a good rule of thumb is to use the same techniques that you enjoyed. Nevertheless, patience and sincerity easily overcome technical ability; it's more about the personality of the sage rather than his technique.

Problem Solving

Related to teaching is problem solving. As a commander you tell people the answer; as a sage you help them find the answer. Whether you're helping someone else or you find a solution, I have found four techniques helpful:

- Write down the problem.
- Outline the assumptions or context around the problem.
- Identify the opposites associated with the problem.
- Find closely related, absent issues associated with the problem.

The purpose of all these techniques is to encourage a different perspective because in reality all problems are opportunities and vice versa. Problems and opportunities are the same thing. Only perspective makes them different. It's hard to find a new solution if you're looking at the same thing the same way. When you use these techniques, keep three things in mind:

- *Don't worry about a comprehensive list* because you're only looking for an entry point with each. Except for the first one, two, three, or four items work well for each. As you think about the problem, more will come to you that you can jot down.

- *Challenge and question* what you derive from these techniques. Often what initially appears solid is really mushy. When a baseball hits a bat, both compress to some degree under the pressure. Likewise, what you find from these techniques may have more wiggle room than you think and contain options for you to consider. Just ask, "Are these valid?"

- *Don't rule out anything as impossible or bad* just look at it as different. Our personal preferences sometimes prevent us from looking at certain possibilities, so it's important to keep potential solutions or challenges to the problem on the table until you can compare alternatives.

Unfortunately, most of the problems we address in school condition us to look at situations extremely narrowly by driving us to a single, right solution and causing us to dull our problem solving skills. Furthermore, as we saw earlier in this chapter regarding Truths, the general business preference for objective thinking hinders creativity by conditioning us to look at things only in one way (as they are). Life rarely gives us such singularly focused problems. For instance, consider this simple story problem from grade school:

Jack picks ten apples and Tom picks twenty-five apples. When they put their apples together, how many do they have?

Chances are great that if you answered this question in school with anything else but with "thirty-five", you would get your answer checked as wrong. Now, when we incorporate real life, we can use this story problem as the basis for running through examples of each of the techniques. Please keep in mind that what I'm about to run through is just a sample and by no means is exclusionary. There are many possible ways to impose reality upon this elementary problem using these techniques.

First, when we look at stating the problem, we are relying upon the stimulation that sight gives. Seeing a problem helps you better find a creative solution. Part of that is writing it down in a way that best illustrates the problem as simply as possible without losing its essence. This allows the words and their various meanings to more intensely impact our consciousness than if they remained mere abstracts floating around in the mind. This is why many writers generate new ideas merely by writing without even having a clue as to what it is they will be writing when they sit down. The movie *Finding Forrester* discusses this when a Pulitzer Prize winning author, played by Sean Connery, gives tips to a new, young writer. This is also why therapy of various kinds calls for individuals to write their thoughts and feelings down in some kind of journal.

With our grade school example, it's easy to think that what we have is the problem of determining how many apples Jack and Tom picked. When we look closer, we realize we might not even have a problem. For instance, there is no problem in determining how many apples they have together because we can just add them or count them. The real problem or problems are more closely linked to questions such as "Why do they need to know how many apples they have?" and "Why are they picking apples?" We may find after gathering the answers to these questions that knowing they have thirty-five apples in total isn't important or worth the bother.

I have found writing the problem down as the most successful problem solving technique I've used. There is something magical about seeing it in front of you that encourages you to look at it differently.

Second, when we look at assumptions or context some of what we just discussed also fits here. What we want to know is really what we are assuming in this situation such as:

- We can physically combine Jack's and Tom's apples.
- All of their apples are the same (color, size, variety, etc.).
- We need to combine their apples.
- It's important to know the total number of apples.

All four of these are examples of facts that seem implicit in the question, so our job now is to challenge these which we can do with corresponding questions such as:

- Are we physically able to combine the two sets of apples?
- Are all the apples really the same?
- Why do we want to combine the apples?
- How will this number help us?

By challenging each of these we may find that an answer is unnecessary to this question or perhaps the question is not as comprehensive as it seems. Unlike a grade school problem, life's questions are guaranteed to be all encompassing. What we assume, may not be.

Third, when we look at opposites we are again trying to get our mind out of its current perspective and into another; it is "the solution is in the problem's opposite." It works on the Chinese "yin-yang" principle that states everything in life contains the interplay of opposites. For instance, the birth of a child is the result of the interplay between a man and a woman. Each day is the result of the interplay between day and night. There are many others such as black-white, summer-winter, hot-cold, and wet-dry. It's not important whether the opposites are the solution, only that they help lead you to a solution.

From a pragmatic perspective, the solution-in-the-opposite is seen most clearly in something like wet-dry. If something is wet, you allow dry air to remove the water. If something is dry, you wet it with water. If a drink is too strong, you had water to dilute it. To increase the concentration of any flavor, you boil the water out such as occurs in making any kind of soup stock. If you try to initiate a car's movement on ice and move slowly because the wheels begin to spin, you don't accelerate to go faster but rather decelerate so the wheels can grip. If you drop something and can't go to it by picking it up, you can have that object come to you by asking someone to pick it up and give it to you.

Using the same story problem, here are few "opposites":

- What would have happened if Jack and Tom left the apples on the tree?
- What if they picked the pears instead of the apples?
- What if they picked three times the apples?
- What would happen if they don't combine their apples?

While opposites may lead us down paths that seem tangential at best, by pursuing them a little they may open alternatives. Here, it's important to keep these paths open even though they may appear impossible, absurd, or bad at first glance. Remember, turning things upside-down may actually be turning ourselves right-side up.

Fourth, when we look at what's absent or missing many times this is similar to opposites or context but is more encompassing because it attacks the basis of a problem. The best analogy is a jigsaw puzzle. Whereas the border may be the context and altering the pieces may be the use of the opposite, trying to determine the missing pieces is looking at what's absent; where are the holes in the problem? In our story problem, some of the absent things are:

- How did Jack and Tom pick the apples?
- What kind of problems did they incur?
- For what purpose did they pick them?
- How was the quality of the apples?

Even though this seems like a search for additional information, it's more along the lines of verifying the problem at hand. Is getting the number of apples Jack and Tom picked together really the problem? Often, we do not have the luxury of stating the problem we are to tackle because it's given to us. In these cases, we're verifying that the problem is the right one by looking at what's not given to us. We sometimes see this expressed in everyday business when people ask regarding a question asked of them, "What are you really trying to do here?"

If anyone ever gives you a problem, I would suggest starting here. Miscommunication and waste of time occurs if we're working on the wrong problem. More importantly from a creative problem solving aspect, even if you do find you have the right question, what you learn by going through this challenging process will help you to look at the problem from various perspectives. With all of these techniques, that is the goal because different perspectives help create alternative solutions to one problem. After a while, using these techniques becomes second nature.

We'll now integrate all four techniques in a case study by looking at a concern stated by a senior executive from the company in our case study. The concern he expressed to managers about the challenges facing the corporation is making sure corporately they "surface innovative ideas for tapping new markets." I've chosen this concern as a case study because it supports the overall "Lady In Black" Strategy of winning hearts. In order to help us see this we'll use the techniques we just covered.

To implement these techniques we will write down the phrase and turn key words into various opposites. By doing so we'll also see how we challenge the context of the problem and uncover some of its missing aspects. First, we'll state the problem via a table and leave out the preposition "for":

Surface	Innovative	Ideas	Tapping	New	Markets

By doing this we delve into the parts of the concern and minimize the influence the other parts may have on each other by linking them. In this way, we're breaking down the context of the whole statement by looking at each part in isolation first. The same principle exists with a person. If you look at her within the context of a family, you may only think she's a mother or wife. If you look at her within the context of work, you may only think she's a manager. You need to strip the context from the person if you wish to look at the person. Another way to look at context is ambiance. Ambiance affects opinions about food. If this were not the case, then attire would not affect opinions about character.

The immediate task is to turn these various words into opposites; we're applying water to a dry problem.

Surface

We'll focus on "Surface" first:

Surface	Innovative	Ideas	Tapping	New	Markets

Surface means the outside, so "to surface" means bringing from in to out. The direction this takes such as from down to up or left to right doesn't really matter as long as there is a feeling of going from in to out. For instance, simply going up to the top of a mountain doesn't imply that you've surfaced. Likewise, doing the reverse doesn't imply that either.

The word also implies a certain depth or difficulty. For example, merely stepping out of your vehicle does not imply surfacing. Many times it's associated with bringing something upward from the depths of the ocean. It doesn't imply opening up a can and reaching in to pull something out. So surfacing means something fairly intense.

If we keep the intensity of this word and focus on its direction, from "in" to "out", we can alter it to an opposite that moves from "out" to "in". When we move something from outside to inside rather than from inside to outside, we're inserting it. Where surface implies pulling, inserting implies pushing.

We're also looking for something that matches "surface's" intensity especially since the whole concern is a very intense one with important implications. The entire act of pushing inside with intensity is lost with "insert." The simple act of inserting a letter into an envelope doesn't seem to capture the emotion behind this concern. Thus, a better word possessing a high degree of intensity is "penetrate."

Penetrate is movement from out to in and carries with it a high degree of intensity, so we'll use it as "surface's" opposite. It also helps up preserve the tone and phrasing of the sentence. Our table now looks like this:

Surface	Innovative	Ideas	Tapping	New	Markets
Penetrate					

Innovative

The next word is "innovative."

Surface	Innovative	Ideas	Tapping	New	Markets
Penetrate					

Right away we're struck by something that is not only new but rather unique. From this standpoint it's different from "new" that is used later in the sentence. Something can be new but not unique. Innovative ideas imply something that gives us an advantage over competitors because it's something we have and they don't.

Initially, we could think of something along the lines of "traditional," but it doesn't imply uniqueness. The question is, "How can something be old and unique?" Perhaps like an antique that suddenly gains immense value because there are not many remaining. There are many oak trees but a four-hundred-year-old one near where I live is rare. From this standpoint something extremely new that is the only one can be innovative, but how do we apply this uniqueness to something very old, a differing context.

The "missing link" is about three million years old. At the time there were many of him, but now there is only one. He's quite special and very old. He's an artifact. Something that becomes an artifact through extreme aging is more than just old or traditional, it can be ancient such as can be said about ancient civilizations that have been long forgotten. The Etruscans who settled Rome or the Incas of Peru are such civilizations.

"Ancient" implies a certain rarity and uniqueness so we'll use it as "innovative's" opposite.

Surface	Innovative	Ideas	Tapping	New	Markets
Penetrate	Ancient				

Ideas

The next word is "ideas":

Surface	Innovative	Ideas	Tapping	New	Markets
Penetrate	Ancient				

The immediate association here is along a cognitive line rather than attitudinal; thoughts versus feelings. The best plan can fall to the wayside without positive feelings for it. It's the difference between the actual action and the intensity of the action, the utterance of the word and the tone behind the word.

Ideas are the framework through which we infuse our energy. It's the car versus the fuel. They form a broader horizon than thoughts because an idea can be a combination of thoughts. Feelings can imply the direct senses of sight, touch, hearing, smelling, and tasting whereas "emotion" is definitely beyond the senses. "Emotion" also carries with it a connotation of something deeper and more comprehensive that goes behind what is rationally apparent.

For these reasons, "emotions" becomes an appropriate opposite to "ideas":

Surface	Innovative	**Ideas**	Tapping	New	Markets

Penetrate	Ancient	Emotions			

Tapping

The next word is "tapping":

Surface	Innovative	Ideas	**Tapping**	New	Markets

Penetrate	Ancient	Emotions			

In many ways this word is similar to "penetrate" except it's superficial and seeks to draw out. "Penetrate" enters but does not withdraw. It mingles with what is inside. "Tapping" seeks to bring out what is in. Here the movement is from an outside force breaking into another. What also makes "tapping" is that it seems to just break the surface rather than dive deeply into the object. This makes it similar to tapping a maple tree or a beer keg. For this reason, it also does not have the intensity of "penetrate".

When we extract what is inside an object, we empty it. The word "empty" makes a convenient starting point for finding an appropriate opposite by looking at "full." Looking at their corresponding actions we find "emptying" and "filling."

The problem now becomes the short duration of "tapping." What word implies a short action that begins to fill? In other words, we have a reverse tap that allows something to flow in rather than allows something to flow out. This happens when we open windows to our homes and let the spring air enter after a long winter. One short action breathes life into a wintry staleness by filling the house with fresh air, a contextual variation. We also see a similar reaction when we open vents to a wood burning stove. The fresh air breathes new life into the fire so it burns hotter and brighter, again, a simple, short action that creates a long term effect.

Both of these analogies bring us to the word "inspire" which means "breathe into" – fill with air. Inspiration is something quick that ignites a feeling into a thought into a behavior. It is a short, self-sustaining action by the nature of making an opening so something flows in and fills rather than have something flow out and empty.

For these reasons, we'll use the word "inspiring" as the opposite of tapping:

Surface	Innovative	Ideas	**Tapping**	New	Markets

Penetrate	Ancient	Emotions	Inspiring		

Since we left out the preposition "for," we can rejoin it to our new sentence formed from opposites and read it as it stands currently:

Penetrate ancient emotions for inspiring

New

The next word in the original sentence is "new":

Surface	Innovative	Ideas	Tapping	**New**	Markets

▼

Penetrate	Ancient	Emotions	Inspiring		

"New" is similar to "Innovative" minus a uniqueness that we covered earlier. While it can mean the creation of something that didn't exist before, it can also mean moving into something that is new to the mover. For instance, moving into a new home doesn't necessarily mean the home is recently built because it can also mean moving into a home that is new to the owner. In this sense, newness is a relative concept dependent upon context.

This second concept of "new" is more in line with the idea in the original sentence. We are not necessarily talking about innovative ideas that "create new markets" but rather "tap new markets." This interpretation is more encompassing because it includes both aspects of the housing analogy.

Continuing with this analogy, we find more existing houses than newly built houses. Likewise, there are more existing markets than new ones coming into existence. From this standpoint, while "new's" opposite can be "old" it is probably more along the lines of "existing" and "non-existing" from the standpoint of this company. Thus, the opposite of "new" markets would be "current" markets where the company already operates. These markets can not only be geographic but also cultural and demographic among others.

For these reasons, we'll use "current" as the opposite of "new" here:

Surface	Innovative	Ideas	Tapping	**New**	Markets

▼

Penetrate	Ancient	Emotions	Inspiring	Current	

Our sentence now reads:

Penetrate ancient emotions for inspiring current

We're now ready to finish our opposite sentence by completing the last word.

Markets

The last word in the original sentence from the senior executive expressing his concern is "markets":

Surface	Innovative	Ideas	Tapping	New	**Markets**
Penetrate	Ancient	Emotions	Inspiring	Current	

In trying to find an opposite to "markets" it would help to start by looking at what they are relative to this company. Of course, they are the various spheres in the economy in which the company operates by establishing relationships with clients and prospects. In this sense, they are external to it.

This company uses this concept everyday when it segregates the centers of influence who help it generate new business. "Internal" centers of influence relate to those employees within the company who help, and "external" centers of influence relate to folks such as attorneys, accountants, and clients who are not employees of the company and help it to develop its business.

The company uses the terms "internal" and "external" frequently to designate the difference between employees and clients. If we continue this theme we can look to the opposite for this word as meaning something internal, in this case "employees." If its external markets consist of clients, then its internal markets consist of employees. Each one is a different constituency helping another. There is not only networking going on with external clients but also among the employees in the various departments with employees in other departments.

Thus, the opposite of "markets" (clients, prospects, and centers of influence) is "employees":

Surface	Innovative	Ideas	Tapping	New	**Markets**
Penetrate	Ancient	Emotions	Inspiring	Current	Employees

This finishes our effort to employ the techniques we've discussed. We have arrived at this sentence:

Penetrate ancient emotions for inspiring current employees.

We are now ready to look at the whole sentence and refine the interpretation so we can see it as a plausible solution. Of course, this isn't to say it's *the* solution, but it can be one of the solutions we examine. The purpose of looking at this more closely is to see how this was more than just a fun word exercise; the techniques actually generated a solution worth consideration.

When we look at the transformation our original statement made into its opposite, we find a theme very much in line with the theme of the "Lady In Black" strategy. It is a focus on the hearts of the employees. If there is dryness, we need wetness; if it's cold, we need heat. This is the nature of opposites and similar to our discussion around reputation in the Company chapter. Focusing on the two sentences it's not surprising that one evolves from the other and that our derivate could be a solution.

Surface innovative ideas for tapping new markets.

Penetrate ancient emotions for inspiring current employees.

Where do ideas come from? Ideas come from within. An individual comes up with an idea after many observations and an inspiration. This is the creative process at heart. As this senior executive's comment points out, he is not looking outside for the ideas but rather inside the company. This is his reason for the word "surface" – to bring something up from the deep.

Who is really going to tap these new markets when they find them and have the ideas? Naturally, the employees of the company will. They will obviously do this more effectively if inspired. With this inspiration, they may even discover the new ideas that this executive seeks. Pragmatically, it may mean the development of a program aimed at eliciting ideas and suggestions from employees in a meaning full way. Thus, rather than waiting for ideas to *surface*, we would aggressively *penetrate* our normal routines to seek them out ourselves. We may even find that there is something inherent in our culture or organizational structure that inhibits the surfacing of ideas.

If we go back and revisit some of the words, we find one prevailing theme in "out" versus "in." Of the seven words three concern themselves with this, surface-penetrate, tapping-inspiring, and markets-employees. As we covered in the Feminine Influence and the Company chapter, "out" represents the masculine and "in" represents the feminine.

Surface	Innovative	Ideas	Tapping	New	Markets
▼	▼	▼	▼	▼	▼
Penetrate	Ancient	Emotions	Inspiring	Current	Employees

When we also throw in the ideas-emotions theme, we find additional evidence supporting the appearance of the feminine influence in our opposite statement. Here, we have the cognitive, rational concept of ideas and the attitudinal, irrational one of emotions. The first is the domain of the masculine while the second is the feminine.

If we recall from our flow discussion regarding the case study in the Company chapter, we used the terms innovative and new to reinforce the fact that the company was in the fall season of its current rhythm. This senior executive's desire to regenerate with innovation and new markets shows the desire to brainstorm that takes place during the fall and winter aspects of this rhythm.

Looking deeper into the flow theme, we can see the additional support for the feminine influence as a relational ally. Before there were communities, towns, cities, states, nations, and a United Nations, there were relationships among people. Relationships and the compassion to relate to another existed before laws, policies, and procedures. If the forces of nature are stronger than manmade ones, a relationship is stronger than any law, policy, or procedure. That is why a law may say two people can't be together, but it cannot erase the feelings they have for one another. Even if the separation creates sadness, there is no denying that an affinity exists more powerful than any human decree.

Now, let's give this opposite statement some practicality. Relationships are important; few deny that. What's harder is appreciating the degree to which they are. The statement and our opposite are seen in very tangible ways every single day that lend support to this proposition:

Our opposite statement is the most important solution to this executive's concern.

As we know from the case study, an important aspect of making that company adopt a more holistic approach to its clients is to make sure the individual units and divisions jointly work together across their domains. In this way, the company comes across holistically rather than monolithically. We also know that strong relationships with clients are a major stone in the foundation of a business' success. They generate enthusiasm in markets for not only additional business from current clients but also from new ones through "word of mouth" or referrals. This enthusiasm in clients generates behavior that goes above and beyond a traditional business transaction. The question then becomes "If this is true with clients, is it true with employees?"

If there is a concern about tapping new markets, then there is probably also concern that current markets are being tapped out. Looking more deeply into the details of our case study in the Company chapter would help us determine the validity of this statement.

This problem is very similar to an apple orchard. Suppose we own an orchard and send our employees out to pick the apples off the trees. When they return, they tell us that they picked all the apples that they could. Subsequently, we go out into the fields and find that they only picked the apples that they could reach from the ground (low hanging fruit). Apples higher up in the trees still remain. When we inquire why they didn't pick those, they tell us that they couldn't reach them and find they didn't want to risk hurting themselves by climbing into the trees to get the other apples.

The same thing could be happening with our case study's markets when you consider joint opportunities. The only problem is that managers can't easily walk into their markets and see instantly all the apples left hanging at the top by their employees. We could refine the analogy to fit this by saying they can only see apples that are five feet in front of them. Yes, managers may know there are more apples out there but they don't know where until they explore every single tree. This is impossible.

If strong relationships with clients generate a willingness to grant access to the fruit higher in the trees, would strong relationships with employees generate a willingness to climb for apples unreachable from the ground?

Would clients risk their integrity by referring a company if they did not feel they had a strong relationship with it? Would employees risk their integrity with a client if they did not feel they had a strong relationship with the company?

What are the real and imaginary risks for employees? Basically, if they work directly with a client it can boil down to a fear of coming across as unprofessional as a result of trying something new that makes them feel uncomfortable. Everyone has fears of trying something new and is sometimes interpreted as resistance. Without strong relationships with managers, employees will not risk their professional integrity to try new ways and will stick with their old, traditional ones that continue in the same rut.

All of this decidedly points to our solution as being a very plausible one if one incorporates the feminine influence and her nature in building strong relationships. With this we're referring back to the challenge of avoiding the tendency to exclude solutions we deem impossible or not good until we've developed a good set of alternatives. People will find a way to get all the apples for the one who has won their hearts, but whether one can and wants to implement the feminine influence through a "Lady In Black" Strategy are totally separate questions.

With this sample statement, we've seen how these techniques can yield substantive clues as to the nature of a solution if not a potentially viable solution. While it's easy to view this as a word game, such games give us different perspectives through which to see present problems. Whether the solution comes to us as a direct result of these techniques is not the issue. The focus is getting us to think outside our present perspective. In this way, these techniques may lead us *indirectly* to a viable solution by stimulating other thoughts.

While we labored over this one solution, with practice these techniques become friendlier and such labor will diminish. You won't need to work these in such a processed way because you can teach your mind to employ these techniques more naturally. Again, the purpose is to alter our perspective. By looking at things in new ways, new solutions to old problems arise.

Comprehensive Focus

Once we've found a solution, there comes the issue of attacking the problem with it. Usually, this entails the organization of resources behind it including the work of others. Depending upon the extent of the problem and solution, this could mean extensive time educating others regarding a plan of action. The education could also entail influencing them for the purpose of gaining their help or approval.

The toughest part of any solution is its implementation. As we had discussed in the Feminine Influence chapter around Figures 2.36 – 2.41 it's impossible to have any plan contain all the intricate details that arise when that plan meets reality. Our consciousness just doesn't have the capacity or the insight to do this because such an effort borders on predicting the future. Thus, effectiveness rests more with those who implement than those who develop the plan.

The purpose of making this point is to emphasize the importance of the people who must make decisions at the point when the plan meets reality. Whether it's reality in the form of a client, tool, resource, structure, computer, machine, or many others, some employee will need to make a decision based upon instructions derived from a plan that are not entirely applicable to a particular situation. It's at this point that the procedural mechanization of a plan meets the progressive unpredictability of life; a point where the "rubber meets the road" and the person at that point will determine effectiveness.

Here, morale enters the picture. The more a person works in a trusting, encouraging environment the more likely he will be effective in resolving the inherent tension between plan and reality. The more he fears making mistakes or deviating from plan, the more likely he will adhere to the plan that by default cannot fit reality in total. Thus, we increase the likelihood for negative outcomes. In short, threatening and intimidating environments hurt businesses in the long run.

Returning to how this plays out we can take Figure 4.8 and restate it more narrowly as Figure 5.31. I call this concept "comprehensive focus."

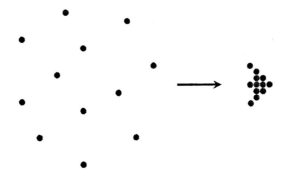

Figure 5.31

It's a particular brand of focus that considers the whole picture in search of the key-stone or lynchpin holding the situation together. In military tactics, concentration of force is a primary ingredient to a successful attack and generally occurs after the dispersive influence of reconnaissance gathers the information necessary to develop a plan. In effect, we move from the left hand diagram to the right one in Figure 5.31. The key is the degree to which we move from dispersion to concentration and back again.

With the left diagram we are in position to review and accept insights about our entire position. The right allows us to concentrate on getting a particular job done. When we exist as the left diagram, it's tough to get anything done; when we exist as the right, we increase the likelihood of being surprised by other issues because we're so focused on another. This is where the degree to which we can move back and forth increases our likelihood of success with our entire realm of our business.

Even a mighty river such as the Mississippi is the concentration of water from thousands upon thousands of springs and tributaries. When all that water fell from the sky as rain, the droplets quickly hit the ground powering and damaging nothing; however, their consolidation into a slow moving river moves gigantic turbines. Any attack on all fronts dissipates energy as Figure 5.32 demonstrates.

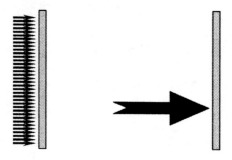

Figure 5.32

The number of analogies supporting this focus is almost infinite. Even our solar system has a small, tiny key that holds all the planets in orbit – the sun. In the total vastness of the solar system, the sun occupies but a miniscule amount of it; but yet, without the sun, the planets would shoot from their orbits and into space. A nail driven into wood with a hammer is another. Even if we took our entire body weight and jumped on a two-inch square cement block, we would not be able to drive that block into the wood. A man can lie on a bed of nails without puncture, but he cannot lie on a single nail. When demolishing a building, experts do not place dynamite everywhere; they focus on the base so it implodes. It's also much more difficult to pop a balloon by squeezing it in one hand than it is to take a pin. A knife has a sharp edge versus a dull, flat one.

Energy dissipation occurs extremely quickly over multiple points. Doubling the points of attack automatically splits in half the force applied to each point, but this is only part of the story. Resistance and speed also come into play.

If I took a pin and tried to pop a balloon hanging in the air, the task is more difficult than if I were holding it with my other hand while I applied the pin. In fact, if I gently touched the pin to the balloon it would not pop. The first point illustrates resistance while the second speed. For this reason, concentration applied swiftly increases impact. Consider this basic physics equation:

$$F = \tfrac{1}{2}\,mv^2$$

While force (f) doubles with the doubling of mass (m) or weight of the object, it quadruples with the doubling of velocity (v). This is why in military tactics speed of concentration at the point of attack is important. If one moves too slowly, the enemy will have time to adjust, possibly even retreat as the freestanding balloon does with a gently advancing pin.

Speed is also important when one considers the inherent weakness of force concentration: the vulnerability on other fronts. If the enemy can spot the point of attack quickly enough, they will adjust by striking around that point of attack on other fronts and engulfing the attacker as shown in Figure 5.33.

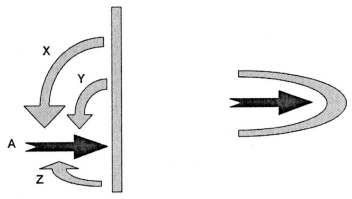

Figure 5.33

These illustrations have a business application if we represent the various demands business places on the employees and managers as the enemy. Recalling tests from schools we find ourselves taking one problem at a time. Rarely, did we try to work the answers simultaneously; yet, business does not offer us the luxury of addressing problems when we want. Many times they are forced upon us. On the other hand, they often don't present themselves all at once either, so there is frequently a time difference between when they strike. No business ever faces all its problems in one day and then runs "problem free" after that.

Thus, if we present business problems as enemy attacks, we can use the above diagrams to picture the problem-solving environment in business. Arrow "A" represents our attack on a particular problem whereas "X," "Y," and "Z" represent other problems that arise during the course of addressing "A." The collection, "XYZ," now represents other issues that zap our energy so we cannot resolve "A." As a result, we become totally consumed by the other problems and cannot effectively attack "A." Anyone in business has experienced new problems or projects popping up that erode the energy around a previous one. Eventually, this creates a feeling of impotency and paralysis in employees and managers.

For example, if an entity takes a year to arrive at decisions on major issues and one major issue arises each week, then the entity could be pondering up to fifty-two decisions at any one time; whereas, an entity that can arrive at decisions within a week, will be able to remain focused on resolving one at a time. If the time value of money exists in such things as loans, then it must also exist in decision making in the form of dissipating energy (morale).

This returns us to the necessity of striking "A" quickly with an effective solution and actions. Often this is deceiving because a problem or opportunity may not appear urgent, but the urgency is not in the problem or opportunity but in the urgency around business itself. Once it's realized that a problem can be effectively addressed, relentlessness and immediacy must prevail in implementation because other problems could arise at any moment from any angle that will absorb and distract our energy. As a result, what originally was a relatively unthreatening problem could become a critical one down the road because of new distractions that postpone its resolution. If it becomes a habit to leisurely pursue effective solutions, eventually a business will become overwhelmed by many problems that suddenly become critical. "Problem isolation" has us considering a time table only for that problem or in conjunction with other existing problems; rarely do we consider the urgency around unexpected problems arising that may zap our energy. This lulls us into a complacency that does not recognize that a problem or opportunity can arise at anytime without our knowledge.

From a positive perspective, quickly implementing an effective solution will yield additional benefits in morale and the addressing of other problems as Figure 5.34 illustrates.

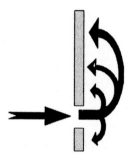

Figure 5.34

This constantly allows a business to address problems and opportunities from a position of strength rather than one overwhelmed by day-to-day events. While this may all appear agreeable from a conceptual sense, the key is identifying tactically what causes delays in the application of an effective solution.

One we've already discussed and that is the lack of urgency around the problem itself. In this scenario, a problem may not become critical for another six months or year so we take a leisurely approach even though we know the effective plan to address it. We decide to take our time regarding implementation; however, we overlook the urgency and unpredictability of business in general that could divert our attention. Naturally, this seems a situation we'd want to avoid, but many times the everyday pressures from others are such that they may exclaim, "What's the urgency around this? Why are you so focused on resolving this now when we have plenty of time to address it?" These are the pressures that create delay around effectively addressing a problem once we know the solution.

Other aspects that create delay and diffuse the energy around problem-solving are "groupthink" activities. These are consensus building activities to gain buy-in or to explore solutions. There are two reasons why they weaken an attack on a problem.

First, as we discussed in the Feminine Influence chapter, collective problem solving dilutes ideas because people become more concerned with their suggestions fitting in with the group than with solving the problem. This doesn't mean the input of others is not helpful, but it does mean one person taking in all the information he wants and deriving the solution. More importantly, because of the nature of group dynamics, it's better to collect views from others in individual interactions than in group ones. This will more likely generate unfettered ideas and creativity. Creativity degenerates dramatically with even the addition of a few people because people are less likely to assert new ideas if there is potential for criticism from others.

Second, groupthink activities create delay if for no other reason than you may need to juggle schedules. When someone knows the solution, why should one delay? The most commonly cited reason is gaining acceptance for the idea. Another implicit one is the unwillingness of someone to step forward with a solution that may cost them personal credibility if it fails. In essence, if something goes wrong, it's harder to reprimand the group than an individual – "safety in numbers." We see the consequences of this theme in sports very often when the manager is fired for a team's poor performance regardless of the responsibility associated to the players themselves. Difficulty exists in assigning blame to a group that doesn't exist with a single person. For the moment, let's say these are valid reasons for groupthink activities and concede that there is a direct relationship between the number of people involved and the time necessary to implement a solution. These activities, whether we view them negatively or positively, require time and cause delays.

Elaborating on collective activities will allow us to introduce two other pragmatic elements that zap the energy around the attack of a problem. One is the transactional nature of the employee-manager relationship and the other is distrust. As this relationship becomes more reliant upon incentives or more distrusting, the force of attacks on problems becomes more dissipated. How this relates to groupthink activities is that over reliance on incentives and overcoming highly distrustful atmospheres increase the need for these activities to gain buy-in because no one trusts one another. Both elements return us to the core of the feminine influence discussed in the first chapter, attraction, and allow us to incorporate the morale issue we just introduced a bit ago through Figure 5.35.

Figure 5.35

Simply stated, morale reduces the need for consensual, buy-in activities because there is greater inherent trust in managerial decisions. To a degree there is a correlation, although not a perfect one, between the non-existence of consensual, buy-in activities and positive morale. Stated negatively, the more prevalent consensual, buy-in activities are present the more likely morale problems exist; they are more symptoms than a cure.

We've already spent substantial time on the implications of incentives and distrust in employee-manager relationships, so we won't review them again here. What will help is elaboration on the equation I presented above and on trust's relationship to speed in problem resolution. If we go back to the equation, $F = \frac{1}{2} mv^2$, and examine more closely how mass (m) and velocity (v) relate to business, we'll move closer to crystallizing the effect of incentives, distrust and groupthink on the concentration of force around a problem.

Mass in this case not only relates to the numbers involved in implementation but also the morale or enthusiasm as well. In essence, it represents the hearts of those involved. Obviously, with other things equal, a person whose heart is into the implementation is far more valuable than one who's apathetic about it. In this case, mass represents "the size of the heart."

Outside of mass, reviewing the interrelationship between mass and velocity is another aspect of this equation that will help. Velocity, speed, is a more important ingredient than mass in affecting the force around a solution. Conceptually, this translates into the trade off between the delay in gaining additional buy-in and attacking the problem now with the current buy-in. For each 50% reduction in velocity, mass needs to increase by 400% just to be able to apply the same force. Conversely, for each 50% reduction in mass, velocity only needs to increase by about 41%. This explains the urgency around implementing an effective solution soon unless there is a very substantial gain in buy-in. Quantifying it, this means that if we double the time necessary to implement a solution in order to work and secure the additional buy-in we feel we need, then we must secure four times the current buy-in *just to break even* on the cost of delay.

Both incentives and distrust are time consumers because they require collective activities that build buy-in. This may take the form of the development of adequate incentives or the scheduling of meetings. Nevertheless, they are both addressed by considering why buy-in is even necessary in the first place.

As discussed in the Feminine Influence chapter, trust and faith are elements of the feminine influence. They not only encourage clients to accept employees' advice and recommendations but they also encourage employees to accept managers' advice and directions. In and of themselves, they create an automatic buy-in because there is a faith in managers to deliver effective solutions to business problems. More importantly, if a strong, personalized relationship exists between employee and manager, then the employee will be more willing to take action whole-heartedly than compliantly because the employee feels the manager is on his side.

This also connects with an alternative to collective buy-in activities and that is through orders or commands. Holding a door open for an attractive woman may be a pleasing thing to do, but it's quite a different feeling if she orders you to do it. It's no easier to engage someone's heart in an action through an order that it is to order a woman to love a man. In both, the heart tends to have a mind of its own that is independent of what the mind may think. As a result, the employee will do something for the manager simply because the employee wants to do it for *her*.

Trust and faith accelerate problem resolution and increase the heart, and thus, creates a dynamic force for addressing issues quickly and effectively. Thus, the strategy in this book is centered on two points:

- You can most likely make better decisions than a group.
- People will want to do things for you.

Anyone who leads any organization will need people who believe these two points about himself. They will allow him to save time on needless, groupthink activities and more effectively address issues around his business.

Still, even with addressing groupthink activities, the real importance of comprehensive focus is first being able to look at the whole situation (comprehensive) and then looking for the point of attack for the specific moment (focus) and addressing it quickly.

Some people more commonly distinguish this as "urgent" versus "not urgent" but the element of opportunity plays a vital role. Sometimes a "not urgent" item may be important because it opens up many other opportunities immediately. Unfortunately, some tend to limit "urgent" to negativity as represented by the statement "I need to do this or else."

Since "fear" is stronger than "greed" in the "fear versus greed" conflict, actions out of fear are more likely than out of a feeling of opportunity. Thus, fear will apply more urgency than an opportunity. This will mean the need to protect oneself on an issue will tend to override the need to create opportunities with any relationship or project. In the long run, without a relentless approach to maximizing opportunities now, growth goes to the wayside or plays second fiddle, and the organization will eventually suffer from a lack of growth.

One needs to have tremendous discipline to seize growth opportunities in the face of threatening issues. It's important to have people on your team who can muster this discipline and apply it forcefully because fear is a strong opponent. The information here on comprehensive focus will hopefully do two things for you:

- Encourage you to address problems quickly whose solutions you have identified.
- Arm you with a line of thought when presenting the need to address an issue immediately.

No matter how good your plan, there will be resistance to it. If the resistance is great or severe enough to delay a decision, then it might be better to move quickly onto something else so as not to get bogged down in a protracted discussion zapping energy for other issues.

Different Perspective

Helping others solve problems places you in a sagely role but can create tension around whose idea is better or who's right. The arguments under this heading outline a way you can visualize and present your ideas in a less threatening way by emphasizing that it's just a different perspective. The purpose is not to present your idea as an alternative but rather as one through which a discussion of it can lead others to view their own idea from a different perspective to uncover new approaches.

The technique involves problem resolution and not the negotiation between two different ideas. Whereas the second resolves the differences between the two ideas, the first encourages a different perspective through which to view the original solution for the purpose of verifying and enhancing it.

We can visualize this as a concept called "triangulation," a method used by location devices. Essentially, by receiving two separate signals from the same source at two different locations one can locate the origination of the two signals. This concept first appeared in widespread use in World War II when armies tried to locate enemy forces through their radio transmissions. By determining the direction from where those transmissions came at two separate locations, one would trace a line from each location in the direction of the transmission. At their intersection rested the origination of the message as shown by Figure 5.36.

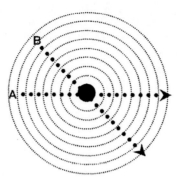

Figure 5.36

"Triangulation" comes from the triangle that "A," "B," and the source produces. In World War II, a friend of mine camped at an outpost and radioed to headquarters the direction of various Japanese messages. Today, Global Positioning Systems, GPS, rely upon this concept by signaling satellites so they can consolidate and return location information to the user. Triangulation helps headquarters and the GPS user. Analogously, your help is similar; however, anyone can provide another person a different perspective to setup an attitudinal triangulation. Fortunately, all perspectives are not created equal, so there are ways for people to show their talent and uniqueness here.

The point of this is that your help here does not need to rely upon knowledge or expertise of the skill necessary to help solve a problem. Many times it's the emotional endorsement of the idea alone that can make it more likely to work. Wisdom's Magical Hierarchy's implications lead to the conclusion that this is possible by placing the more emotional elements over the more logical ones. If this were not so, then the emotional support one spouse supplies another would be irrelevant to success because any support must be cognitively supported. In essence, the phrase "behind every successful man there is a successful woman" must be false if this emotional carried no significant value.

This attitudinal help that comes through as a different perspective is best expressed as passion. Even though the business world often strives for objectivity in its decisions, in truth, it's passion that moves people not thoughts. If thoughts moved people more than passion, then merely thinking about sitting in the sun on a beach would be just as good if not better than the actual feeling of the sun while sitting on a beach. Thus, what you feel moves people more than what you think does.

Of course, it's much easier to say "I'm sitting on the beach in the sun" than it is to convey what I'm actually feeling when I'm doing that. Likewise, it's much easier to say "That woman is beautiful" than to explain how her beauty makes you feel. A general can have a hundred of the best advisors in the world describe a battlefield to him but nothing is like him seeing it. A thousand people can tell you what a scene looks like, but until you see it yourself you will never really know the totality of what that scene delivers. This is why efficiency is rarely associated with the beauty of a woman. How can anyone convey the essence of a woman's beauty with computer-like efficiency? Some try by boiling it down to figure measurements, but how good is that perspective on life?

Conceptually, the different perspective makes sense but its difficulty arises in the details. How does one go about implementing this technique? In general, this is done by understanding the concept behind the other's plan and is accomplished through two approaches. The first is seeking to understand what the plan entails on a more detailed level, and the second entails the same but on a higher level. Visually, we can present this as inside and outside respectively.

If we look at Figure 5.37, we see a series of black dots where each dot represents an element of a plan such as an action step.

Figure 5.37

As we can see, the dots form a line segment that connects the first step at the bottom with the last step at the top. If we superimpose this line on the dots, we can now say that the line represents the plan's concept, essentially its "personality," including its purpose and methodology. Two plans that have the same purpose could have different methodologies, two different ways of doing the same thing. For instance, at a very high level, there are two ways to increase profits, decrease expenses and increasing revenues; they both accomplish the same thing in different ways. As an aside, you can tell much about the personality of the planner by the methodology he adopts.

Figure 5.38 superimposes a line on the dots to represent the plan's concept or personality.

Figure 5.38

When we seek to understand a plan's concept, we attempt to surmise the deeper details and the effect of other external events. The first is the "inside" while the second is the "outside." In terms of our line, the first is interpolation and the second is extrapolation as we see in Figure 5.39.

Figure 5.39

Since reality always supplies details not specifically accounted for in a plan, we should be able to identify such a detail. As we discussed earlier, any plan is formed within a specific context of assumptions. Here too, reality always has potential to present situations not fitting with the context of assumptions around the plan, so we should be able to present such situations. Our job in providing a different perspective is to present these details and externalities in a way that shows we are trying to understand the nature of the plan. If we understand the plan's nature, we should be able to surmise how the plan would deal with these details and externalities we raise. We can look at these as a more complex form of "What if's" except we're simultaneously providing the solution for the purpose of verifying we understand the plan's nature.

Here are examples of the language around this technique:

Inside

1. In order to make sure I understand how this plan would work, it seems Sam may need to use Tom's machine before he arrives on his shift unless we give this plan priority. Am I correct?

2. Well, if I'm looking at this right, then it seems we need to have something written outlining the basic steps for Kathy's team just so they have it in front of them. Are these the major points they'll need?

Outside

1. If I understand this plan right, if our suppliers run into prob- lems Carol should be able to identify and address delays because the plan has her in touch with them about a month be- fore we need confirmation. Right?

2. So, if I were to take your plan and modify it to fit the Lander- ford situation, I would see these changes?

As we see above, "inside" is the further refinement of details within the plan, and "outside" is the further hypothesizing of how the plan would address various external events that could come up. In this way, we add our perspective in the form of details and externalities but do it through their perspective by relating it to their plan. The first entails the pragmatic aspect of the plan whereas the second is the emotional support demonstrated by us applying effort to understand and appreciate the plans intentions.

Thus, the different perspective encourages a pragmatic discussion and an emotional reinforcement of the idea. While the idea itself may not change, the pragmatic advantage is a discussion of the variables that may come up with a plan to address them if they do. The emotional advantage involves attitude, the reinforcing that the plan is a good one. Nevertheless, as we've covered several times throughout this book, no plan will encom- pass all the details that reality throws at us, so appreciating the concept behind the plan is more valuable than memorizing all the details. By understanding the framework within which the plan operates, one is better to arrive at decisions on the spot to address the reali- ties life invariably throws at us.

The key for you when helping is avoiding the acceptance of your perspective as the key perspective because it's not. As Figure 5.36 shows, if "A" is responsible for imple- mentation, then his perspective dominates. Having "A" implement according to "B's" perspective increases the likelihood for ineffective outcomes. The purpose of your per- spective is to refine the other's perspective unless of course you are the one responsible for implementation.

Documenting ideas

The single biggest challenge before the implementation of a plan is the documentation of the idea that spurs the plan. The task is similar to one discussed in problem solving where you jot down on paper the problem or question associated with it. We are essentially taking an idea that is in an abstract form and taking that first step toward its visualization and is the reason why many ideas that appear in writing are mechanically applied to multiple situations – it's easier to take an existing plan for a different situation than to create a new plan for a new situation. This is how nuances arise to hamper effectiveness.

Formulizing a thought into writing is difficult. Agendas are a starting point for a meeting; an idea's documentation is the entry point into the effort to give birth to its pragmatic application. The purpose of stating this is that if you can do this, make use of it by getting other's and your ideas in writing. The effectiveness of this talent comes into play when ideas need generation and discussion. Many meetings begin brainstorming without a tangible point of discussion. Before anyone can apply any creative energy there needs to be an entry point. This becomes the often quoted statement of "let's get something out on the table." From here the discussions and understandings that need to evolve have something to grab a hold of.

Many times people are fairly involved so their ideas are fairly involved. It would be a sad commentary on life if any one life could be accurately summarized in a sentence or a word. It would symbolize the shallowness of the person, the communicator, and of life. Life is always more involved and complicated than we think because what we can think about is always less than what actually exists. What we know is finite and what we don't know is infinite. As a result, since life is an integrated whole, any one aspect that is unknown to us can affect what we don't know. People and their imaginations are universes. Just as the oval we saw can contain an infinite number of points, our minds can contain an infinite number of thoughts and feelings that seek to be discovered. This is why simple sentences such as "I ran to the store to get some things" can say a lot about a person if we allow ourselves to explore it.

In many ways, trying to understand others and ourselves is very much like being Sherlock Holmes in the Introduction. He never saw the crime actually being committed, so he never saw everything; yet, by observing a few clues he could put together a picture. Likewise with people, we can never know everything there is to them, but we can get a picture. For this reason, people and anything involving people such as business are always far more involved than we know.

Conceptually, this is important because often pressures compel us to state things in simple, single sentences summarizing an idea. Summarizing by its nature leaves out important details. Consequently, there is a point when simply expressing an idea becomes no better than a destructive erosion of the idea itself. Striking this balance should not deter you because someone is unwilling or unable to tackle the nuances. Thus, it's always best to start off with more than you think because it's always easier for folks to cut back than it is for them to add (i.e. it's easier to cut expenses than generate revenues). The question with the later then becomes whether what's added really makes the idea better.

Nevertheless, getting the idea down on paper in any form is invaluable. This heading exists to encourage you to make use of this talent. The human spirit gives hope and excitement that anyone could have an idea of which they are unaware. For you, listening to others' ideas can be the source of your documentational efforts.

Employees are #1

Directly unrelated to the techniques we've just covered, but directly related to attitude behind many business actions is the importance of clients. Many times businesses will express this in the form of "Customers are number one." While demonstratively appealing to clients, it can create an uneasy, unconscious feeling in employees that can be detrimental to the business as a whole in the long run.

The implicational stream that leads us to this conclusion begins with the question: Will a company help a client at the expense of its employees' professionalism? In another way, will a company sacrifice its employees for clients?

In extreme forms this inclination will expose the employee to a client's berating; however, while most employers will not tolerate this in theory, identification of this in practice is very open to interpretation and thus difficult to address. Even though employees may not be able to consciously express this anxiety, it can exist as indicated by the Seventeen Influential Points; people are influenced by things of which they are unaware such as ideas about which they do not think. Merely because someone does not think about something doesn't mean he's unaffected by it. The feeling itself can manifest itself as a rationalization in many forms including a dislike for the company, the work, an initiative, or the boss.

If we return to the relational focus stated at the outset of this book, we can ask what a company's greatest asset is. Without employees there is no capability to make clients happy. A client's happiness is dependent upon employees. The better the employees feel about the company the more likely they will view and help clients more effectively. As employees' attitudes dwindle, their effectiveness with clients does too. What is the long-run implication of this demise? As we relegate professionals to behave as servants, advisors to behave as servants, what do we eventually do to the quality of our business?

Typically, in order to preserve the "Customers are number one" and protect against the demise of attitude and morale, we establish policies and procedures against which to monitor and evaluate employees. The subsequent problem from this approach that we've touched on earlier is that no set of policies and procedures can comprehensive apply to all the unique situations life throws at us. Thus, an inspired workforce is more likely to effectively tackle the uncertainties of life than one compliantly following rules; an inspired workforce is better than a compliant one.

We can run with this implication further by restating it: an inspired workforce is better than a programmed one. Consequently, the most inspired workforce will do better than the one with the best policies and procedures. In conjunction with our discussion around leadership, we can ask which is easier to do: inspire people or write policies and procedures. Doing the later is far easier, so it's more likely to be done than the former.

A restaurant's ambiance affects our total experience of that restaurant. Likewise, the conditions at a company affect an employee's total experience while at work. A highly inspirational environment will more likely lead to inspirational work by the employee than a highly regulated environment. Furthermore, inspiration is more personal than rules. Inspiration by its very nature seeks connections on a personal, individualized basis whereas rules are inherently impersonal because they categorically apply to everyone.

A personal atmosphere is more likely to encourage personable behavior than an impersonal one; however, since writing rules is much easier than inspiring people, the general tendency is to deal with employees in a regulatory manner as opposed to an inspirational one. Moreover, inspiration is emotional and rules are emotionless, so the first is more likely to encourage empathy than the second simply because empathy requires emotions. One cannot feel empathic if one does not have feelings. Simply *behaving* empathic is not the same as feeling empathic, or we could make an argument for computers and robots being empathic.

Making clients happy is a business concern so making sure employees help clients is a priority. The most difficult part about this argument is getting past the feeling that it's too idealistic to implement because the regulatory approach to managing employees pervades business. The larger the business the more likely it will have an extensive manual governing the various aspects of policies and procedures around its operation. To some degree the aggressive outcry against a highly regulatory government is in response to the impersonal anxiety felt by a highly regulatory approach in business as opposed to an inspirational one.

At this point we can now refer back to Widsom's Magical Hierarchy and the predominance of emotional attributes in talent identification. A critical factor in determining whether a business can reinforce or enhance its inspirational environment is its recruitment of employees with empathic abilities. As mentioned earlier, not all employees are born with the same emotional sensitivity. Having a feel for what others need and want, and having a feel for what's going on around them requires emotional sensitivity. Inspiration requires feeling; it will not work on those who have little sensitivity for others.

Extending the "what's easier concept," we find it's easier to write rules than to hire inspirable employees because having a potential employee say, "I'm inspirable" is similar to an employee saying to a client, "Trust me." Words don't prove that inspiration and trust exist because they are feelings. Consequently, writing rules promoting specific behaviors is easier than finding intelligent employees whose empathy will encourage them to do the right thing for clients regardless of what rules and procedures say along these lines.

Nevertheless, the real danger in a regulatory method of management is the degradation it causes for talented people. Inspirable employees, even though most talented, can become lousy employees when treated impersonally. Essentially, given access to the enforcement and development of the regulations within a business, it's quite easy to make any talented person fail. In fact, many talented people are often viewed as failures or incompetents by some other aspect of the population. The difference between a lunatic and a genius is often the one making the determination.

The impersonal nature of rules will encourage an impersonal environment and reduce the empathy of everyone for each other. Thus, it's quite possible to render an entire inspirable workforce uninspired. As this condition accelerates it becomes more difficult to inspire because distrust builds. How can you trust someone who treats you impersonally by expecting you to follow a programmed set of policies, rules, procedures, and initiatives? How is a human following a "program" different from a computer running through a program? In the end, what's easier during this downward trend than inspiring people is writing more rules to correct behavior which acerbates the condition we're trying to avoid in the first place.

Thus, when we pursue a "customer is number one" path, we establish the implication that customer's are more important than an employee's professionalism. To combat the anxiety this implication stirs, the easy route is the development of a complex set of policies, rules, procedures, and initiatives – a regulatory approach – to direct behavior along specific lines. No set of rules, just as no plan, can account for every nuance that life throws at us. Thus, rules tend to render people incompetent because they will be inclined to believe that if they're following the rules, they are doing a good job. Nevertheless, to guide behavior we tend to go down this path because we come to rely more upon the easier development of rules than the more effective, but more difficult, inspiration of empathic people.

Conclusion

The essence of business is relationships. The "Lady In Black" Strategy seeks to tap the power inherent in our personalities. Our personalities reflect themselves in our relationships. Thus, the success of any business strategy will revolve around the nature of the impact that strategy has on those relationships. The "Lady In Black" Strategy emphasizes relationships over objectives. The achievement of the business objective is subordinate to the enhancement of the relationship between two people. The achievement of a business objective at the expense of relationships will harm a business in the long run.

Implementing the "Lady In Black" Strategy generates inspirational power. Essentially, we are taking the beauty that powers the feminine influence and transforming her into inspirational power. This power is greater than regulatory power; however, the danger is interpreting inspirational power as trying to please everyone. Some people are more inspirable than others; despite our best efforts some people are not inspirable. They tend to be less sensitive and empathic than others.

Inspirational power places a premium on emotion, on passion. People will not follow courage over titles if they are unable to feel courageous or simply unable to feel. Those who are most inspirable are also those most sensitive to their worlds and those in them. To them this kind of power will appear unreal and idealistic, for to them it is. Dunking a basketball by jumping from the free throw line is impossible unless you are able to do it. Likewise, feeling inspired is impossible unless you are able to do it. The feminine influence encourages an irrational attempt at the impossible to prove that we can make it possible. The advantage to the reality that no plan can capture every one of life's realities is that what we think is impossible could now be possible because life will always offer something of which we are unaware that might help us turn the impossible into the possible. In this way, the irrational persistence to pursue the impossible, as determined by the many, can result in outcomes violating consensus.

To this end in our work to crystallize the "Lady In Black" Strategy in this chapter we explored additional truths, discussed the strategy's basic aspects, and outlined some rarer tactics.

The truths we explored were the integration of the masculine and feminine in a specific interaction, the influence that a subordinate group can have on a superior one, the illustration of inspirational leadership, and the demonstration of the inherent power of subjectivity over objectivity.

For integration we introduced a working diagram as shown in Figure 5.1 to serve as a map for explaining and identifying the integration of the feminine and masculine influences. Under influence we saw how a subordinate group can influence a superior one even though it has no formal access to the decision-making process. We called this influence *de facto* power. We arrived at inspirational leadership through a distillation that eliminates all formal aspects of authority and focuses on the internal emotional makeup of the person being influenced; to make someone feel better about who he is so he will assert his personality. Close behind inspiration is the creative energy behind subjectivity that allows us to see things as they could be rather than as they are. This becomes the source of new things and ways, a rebirth, continuing on with the old as something new. Familial lineage best illustrates how the old naturally continues on in something new.

There are two broad aspects to the "Lady In Black" Strategy – individual and group interactions. The strategy emphasizes individual interactions with group ones playing positioning and reinforcement roles. The power fueling both is personality. The personification of an initiative is more influential than the idea behind it. Liking something is more motivational than understanding it. By connecting business objectives to people in ways that demonstrate how we help one another, we become more effective than when we rely upon understanding. Of course, in a distrusting environment this will be far less likely to work.

While many tactics exist to implement a strategy including this one, I focused on those that reflect and incorporate the feminine influence in less frequent ways:

- Commander-Sage
- Problem solving
- Comprehensive focus
- Different perspectives
- Documenting ideas
- Employees are #1

The commander-sage duality integrates the telling of a commander with the teaching of a sage. Inspiration comes from within, so it's difficult to stir those fires if one throws water on them. By looking at resistance to talent and conditioning we scratched the surface as to why we might throw water on our own fires. Sagely actions allow us to help someone halt the process. Feeling inspired is difficult to achieve if we don't feel worthy of feeling it. Our worthiness tends to decline the more we feel weird than unique or the more we feel part of a group than an advocate for ourselves. Inspiring another person and ourselves is very difficult, if not impossible, if we do not address the intrinsic value of our worlds and only remain focused on their extrinsic values. Business pressures require discipline and talent to avoid the immediacy of telling and to uphold the effectiveness of teaching.

Sagely actions entail more than merely conveying information or knowledge and entail problem-solving in a way that helps others solve problems. The actions incorporate all aspects of Wisdom's Magical Hierarchy, information, knowledge, reason, experience, conception, intuition, and creativity. They maximize what another extracts from his life's experiences. Delegating or telling someone to return with alternatives is not problem solving; guiding someone through the thought process is. In this way, we leave others with something beyond just an answer; we leave within them a way to address problems and to appreciate their world and others.

Of course, problem-solving in business does not happen in a sequential fashion but rather a simultaneous one. Many problems can find us at any time and arrive in any pattern. For this reason comprehensive focus encourages us to move from comprehensive awareness to focused attention quickly and effectively as Figure 5.31 shows. Comprehensive awareness distracts us from the task we can focus upon and focused attention distracts us from looking at our situation comprehensively. Thus, movement between the two must be quick once we've identified our path. Many factors can stall our movement. The most frequent is the overvaluation of consensus building.

Another factor that can potentially stall the addressing of a situation is when sagely help is viewed as competing advice. To counter this, presenting a different perspective through the other's eyes can help. The concept involves presenting your advice as a way to view the other's solution to the problem or opportunity through different eyes. The intention is to remain with the other's perspective but use your perspective to refine his perspective, to tackle lower level details or external events.

Once we've found a path to solving a problem or seizing an opportunity, the challenge becomes its visualization on paper. As we saw in Figure 2.7 the life of an idea moves non-existence to reality as a droplet moves from rain to the ocean. As droplets gather they form tributaries, then streams to rivers that flow into oceans. In order for any idea to attract water, there must be something around which droplets can coalesce.

Still, despite any techniques encouraging a business strategy, the essence of business is relationships. As we had discussed, there are two major pairs: employee-client and manager-employee. The traditional business mantra regarding these relationships is "Customers are number one." The extended implication of this slogan is to render an employee's professionalism, expertise, and talent secondary and even expendable. The emphasis of employees, the ones who provide the inherent value of a company, is a tactic that promotes the "Lady In Black" Strategy. Clients do not provide the inherent value of a business; they only recognize that value. Analogously, a person's talent remains the same regardless of how various people look at that talent. Likewise, the inherent talent in a company remains the same regardless of what clients say about it. Whether it's the talent in a person or a business it remains unalterable by the comments and actions of those external to the person or the business. Any persons or businesses that subordinate their talents to externalities will increase the likelihood of placing their long-term futures on unstable ground.

The underlying theme of the "Lady In Black" Strategy is to win hearts for the purpose of enhancing your influence within your company. The truths, aspects, and tactics of the strategy discussed from various levels the concept of *de facto* power. Despite the best attempts of any organization, *de facto* power always exists or has the potential to emerge. Political regimes built on terror aim their organizational power at stifling the emergence of *de facto* power.

In business, the reconciliation and integration of organizational and *de facto* power is a potent combination. The representation of each is the masculine and feminine influences respectively. The "Lady In Black" Strategy taps into the power of beauty by helping you to become more attractive to others in the company. In order to accomplish this, you give others something they cannot buy; it's the recognition of the talent that makes them unique.

Red oak trees provide hardwood for construction purposes. Long ago, American Indians boiled the bark to produce a remedy for sore throats. Every plant in the woods can have multiple purposes. Some uses are more obvious than others. Seeking to use an oak tree for constructive purposes is more common than using it to help relieve sore throats. Helping people is often the same. Many ways are common and some are not. More people will pursue the common ways and few the uncommon. Consequently, talent is required to relentlessly learn and develop new ways to view others so rarer talents are discovered.

Nevertheless, the feminine influence and the "Lady In Black" Strategy contain challenges. If implementation were so easy, many would tap their potency; however, there is resistance to it as we've discussed. Overcoming that resistance and the fear it instills is the topic of the next chapter. The feminine influence in business requires a protector in order to work her magic as represented by the "Lady In Black" song and Helen of Greece. The aspect of protector is directly related to the integration of the masculine and feminine influence.

Masculine Influence

Integrating the Feminine Influence in business through the "Lady In Black" Strategy and other means requires discipline and talent. The discipline to initiate and sustain this effort falls within the realm of the masculine influence.

In the Feminine Influence chapter, we showed the importance of the masculine influence establishing a starting point (Figures 2.54 and 2.55) and in serving as a basis around which the feminine influence could work (Figures 2.31 and 5.1). The purpose of this chapter is to gather the major attributes of the masculine influence in one place. Our discussion about the feminine influence has served to provide many implicational streams for the masculine so we will reference them as we go along. In this manner, this chapter will serve as a summary for the masculine influence; however, his major aspects, initiative and protection, which serve to integrate the feminine influence require elaboration.

To enter our discussion, let's consider this prose poem:

Mediocre

Adam came first, Eve second.
Masculine first, feminine second.
The masculine gets something started, the feminine makes it beautiful.
To see the beauty in something is to make it better.
To make something better one must first have something.

A man builds a house; a woman makes it a home.
Without a woman, a house remains a house.
Without a man, there is no house to make a home.
To make a house a home is to make it better.
To make it better is to see the beauty in it.
To see beauty in a house allow a woman to enter.

The hunter who chases deer is never as successful as the one who encourages deer to come to him.
A business that must pursue business is never as successful as one that attracts business.
To make something beautiful is to make it attractive.
To make something attractive is to make it better.

To get things started one must attack.
To make them better one must nurture.
After war comes peace; after man comes woman.
Without man nothing gets started; without woman nothing becomes better.
Without man a woman cannot beautify.
Without woman man remains mediocre.

Man first woman second.

This poem symbolically identifies the integration of masculine and feminine influences through a man and woman and defines that integration as one where the man gets things started and the woman makes them better. If we refer back to the word table of Figure 5.2, we will see the masculine as the independent element and the feminine as the dependent. The picture of a house and a home also helps us visualize that independent-dependent duality of the masculine and feminine.

The implication of this picture and its duality is that destroying the house will also destroy the home. Thus, while supplying the initiative may be over, vigilantly protecting the home begins. Relating this analogy to business, we find the masculine providing the initiative to start new things and the protection to encourage an environment conducive to the feminine influence.

In old times, primarily men were explorers and early settlers. As a community developed more women entered the picture. A woman's presence indicates a higher level of communal development. Integration of the feminine with the masculine improves one's condition. In business, this means dynamic growth. As an initiator, the masculine gets things going through his strength and aggressiveness. Those same attributes come into play to sustain conditions for the feminine to operate. As we saw with the Persian Gulf War example, the direct assault initiated contact and continued to provide the necessary conditions, pinning and distraction, to allow the feminine to work.

We can see the importance of the masculine influence's role if we look at the direct and indirect factors hindering the integration of the feminine in more detail, the purpose of this chapter. We've seen these to some degree when we discussed the resistance of groups to talent.

The underlying theme is the difficulty in accomplishing this integration and alone accounts for the discrediting of the feminine aspects as weak and impractical. Life is not easy because without resistance learning and growth would be difficult. Imagine trying to strengthen a muscle without any resistance. While tackling life's physical challenges have become easier, this doesn't mean life itself is now easy. Relationships remain difficult because of the complex web of emotional issues surrounding them; these relationships drive a business' success. Those who find it difficult to handle life's difficulties are more inclined to rationalize the benefit of easy, quick approaches over involved, relentless ones. Life counters these by granting greater awards to those who can do the latter and crisis to those who advocate the former. As everybody knows, if it weren't for the crisis created by the last minute nothing at all would get done. Procrastination is much easier than the relentless application of small steps over long periods to lay sound foundations and to avoid crisis.

Direct

Direct factors tend to fall into two groups. The first are those inherent in the nature of people that exist also in non-business environments. The second are those more prominent in business than other fields.

With any endeavor beginning anything requires greater power than to sustain it. A car accelerating from a stopped position requires more energy than one accelerating the same amount while in motion. Often we refer to this as the "snowball effect"; starting the snowball requires more energy than rolling it downhill once it has gained mass. In business we find the creation of a new product more difficult than the improvement of an existing one. The tremendous power required for this effort is reflective of the masculine influence.

In this book we have talked about agendas, objectives, and plans; all serve as a beginning point for meetings, interactions and strategies. The crystallization of an abstract into something practical establishes the basis around which the dynamic occurs. These traditional business tools represent the masculine setting the stage. Our energy around the commands moving our ideas from paper to reality represents the acceleration of a car from a stationary position. A good relational foundation will make the total effort easier and far more effective.

Resistance to applying the energy to create good conditions for the feminine influence is found in her difficulty, and this difficulty will encourage more to oppose her. Even though conceptually many might agree with her, far fewer can employ her. Those who can't will outnumber those who can. We first examined this in detail in the Feminine Influence chapter around Figures 2.61 – 2.67. Thus, employing the feminine will generally occur under unfavorable numeric odds especially if a distrusting environment already exists. Consensus building will most likely become the preferred method of decision making since everyone will need to feel that their interests are safe. Typically, we see the formation of committees as the formal tool to bring about consensus.

This promotes and encourages resistance to dynamic ideas by giving such resistance a forum by which to assert itself. The assertion will manifest itself as the dilution of a dynamic idea through the need to gain "buy-in." Analogously, we have a situation where piranhas attack a carcass until only the bones remain. Essentially, a consensual decision reduces a dynamic idea to the bare essentials that no one feels compelled to attack.

The key to battling the inherent resistance to dynamism in consensus building is an atmosphere of faith and trust. People are more likely to accept dynamic ideas if they feel their needs (long-term security, novelty of experience, and emotional recognition) will be addressed and if they have faith in those making the decision to run with the idea. If we look at this in terms of the employee-manager relationship, it means trustworthy managers who are talented decision makers and implementers, and employees who are capable of placing trust in others. The need for buy-in decreases as the trust and faith in this relationship increases. Business, with a premium on profit, creates its own difficulties in implementing the feminine influence because the profit motive often conflicts with these.

Gaining the faith and trust of another is time consuming and challenging. Further complicating this is the problem that despite our best efforts we need to remind ourselves that people come with various capacities to trust others. In our analysis of the "Lady In Black" song we found trust and faith are emotions, so these attributes are closely akin to talent as suggested by Wisdom's Magical Hierarchy. The integration of the feminine influence in business means more effective communications and decision making because the focus is on hiring employees and managers capable of high degrees of trust. Generally, there is a high correlation between those who can trust others and those who can be trusted; it's difficult for those who do not trust others to generate trust themselves. Ultimately, with a strong foundation of mutual trust and faith, employees can enthusiastically implement a manager's decision without a need to understand all its aspects because they have faith not only in the manager's decisions but also in his ability to make sure he will take care of everyone in the effort.

On the surface we will most likely find people supporting these points, but a frequent paradox allows us to explore how we can deviate from them easily on a deeper level. On a logical level two points collide to highlight this paradox. First, we have the business objective to hire intelligent employees, and second, we have the business objective to explain clearly and comprehensively what employees need to do.

If we carry the first objective to the extreme, we will find intelligent employees who know what to do. If we carry the second one to the extreme, we find ourselves document-ing every possible step of an employee's job. While it's easy to dismiss the problems with the second objective as simply "micro-management" that we seek to avoid, there are a couple indirect ways we approach this despite our conscious efforts to avoid it. The first involves an organizational trend toward the standardization and centralization of processes to save money. The second involves a technological trend toward a computerized environment creating common regimens for a large number of employees.

Talented employees by their very nature consider themselves unique and special. If this were not the case, then it would not cost more to secure them. However, it's quite difficult to look at yourself as unique and special when your work regimen is being assaulted organizationally and technologically to conform to those of others, including those less talented.

Organizationally, standardization and centralization do not have to be physical. It may simply be on paper. For instance, we may find jobs and their job descriptions becoming more uniform over similar jobs. We may even see jobs previously considered different merged under a common title. This type of consolidation occurs on paper to facilitate reporting and management.

Technologically, the eradication of variations occurs when we introduce new systems because there is a move to a common language. Whereas an employee could describe and perform his job using his own terms, he now must use the terms filtered to him through his computer. Anyone who has rolled out new computer software knows the challenges involved in coming up with standard terms and phrases recognized by a large number of the company's employees.

How this relates to trust and faith is addressed by asking one question: How likely are you to trust someone who says you're unique and special on one hand and then compels you to work and talk just like everyone else with the other? Just as a customized product costs more than a commodity, employing unique employees costs more than employing standard ones. Thus, cost pressures will increase the drive to make unique employees routine ones and increase the distrust talented employees have for the company.

What really erodes trust and faith in business along with the difficulty in its establishment is the rationale "this is business not personal." Since faith and trust are emotional attributes, the promotion of objectivity in business is contrary to the creation of an inspirable atmosphere. The more we emphasize decisions based upon the "bottom line" the less likely we'll be able to create a trusting atmosphere because the approach discounts personal considerations. How does one generate trust and faith if he has little interest in the personal effects of his decisions? The counterargument to this is that if the business doesn't survive, no one makes a living. Of course, we need to extend this argument and ask, "Is survival and living the same thing?" Someone on life support is surviving, but is he living?

As we saw in the poem "Mediocre", a house is to man as a home is to woman. We can extend this to say, survival is to man as living is to woman. Survival is more akin to stagnation and living more akin to growth. What kind of life does one have if he doesn't grow? Implicationally, we arrive at a point where we expand the horizons around the need for growth in business as more than something that just increases revenues or income but rather as something that creates opportunities for personal growth. For employees, a growing company is more fun than one merely surviving. Symbolically, the feminine influence, as a woman does with a house, makes business better.

Continuing along this line, we find an inspired individual is more likely to do well than an uninspired one. The basis of any relationship entails individuals, and individuals are born with various inspirational capacities. As we've already discussed inspiration is an emotion, so those with greater emotional capabilities are more likely to be inspirable. We've also explored a correlation between emotional sensitivity and talent. Our two implicational streams come together in a way that mutually support one another – emotion and inspiration; emotion and talent – so we can arrive at another correlation: inspiration and talent. If talent is something rare and valuable, and if inspired people are more likely to do well than uninspired ones, then it follows that talent and inspiration are very likely to go hand in hand. Thus, where we find inspiration we will also likely find talent and vice versa. We can also reinforce too the point that emotion, since it's linked to the *feeling* of being inspired, must also correlate strongly to talent. Consequently, the likelihood of tapping into inspiration and talent in an objective, unemotional environment is almost nil. How many dogs do you find flying in the sky?

Beyond personal attributes, organizationally the change dynamism can deliver will likely stir fear and increase the resistance to the feminine influence. Those heavily entrenched in the status quo will tend to have a prejudice against dynamic, positive alterations to the present and tend to prefer more anemic, controlled growth. Searching and developing talent is not a foregone positive pursuit because the perfect person for a job won't remain long in that job. The talent one uncovers within one's own business could eventually become the same talent that evolves into a competitor further on down the road. The same talent could also be the one that displaces another person positioned higher in the formal organizational structure. Such possible outcomes, either real or imagined, may play upon the long-term security needs of those around your talent by stirring anxieties as shown in Figure 6.1.

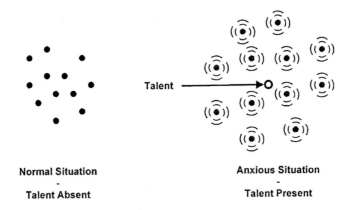

Normal Situation

Talent Absent

Anxious Situation

Talent Present

Figure 6.1

These anxieties can appear as feelings hostile towards your talent. As we saw with the Seventeen Influential Points in the You chapter, people can be influenced by things of which they are unaware (#7) and even if they are aware of something influencing them they may not be able to correctly identify the source of that influence (#9). Thus, they may not be able to consciously associate their hostility with their anxieties about their long-term security. More likely, they will display them as negative interpretations of your talent. For instance, enthusiastically conversing about a topic could be seen as "talking too much" as opposed to possessing a passion, and quiet contemplation as "shyness" as opposed to having an excellent listening attribute. Such comments say more about the anxieties of the commentator than about the nature of your talent to which they are directed. Since those without a particular talent will outnumber those with it, you can likely expect many to have anxieties about your talent. How these manifest themselves will vary with the commentator.

Furthermore, since talent is linked to emotions, these emotions will trigger the defense mechanisms of those uncomfortable with feelings. Those with a lower tolerance and capacity for strong emotions will tend to be afraid of emotional displays just as those with low mental capacities are generally intimidated by those with greater ones. While we are more conscious of the anxieties that a mental disparity creates, we usually don't look at emotional disparities as having any kind of validity; however, the more intuitive a person is the more likely he will exhibit emotional attributes and be comfortable with strong emotions.

Outside of these personal attributes, the feminine influence can disturb an entire organization because talent is an innate power residing outside the domain of authoritative power granted by an organizational hierarchy, and it directly impacts authoritative power. An organization cannot confer or remove talent only authority, so talent's rare, dynamic power can create further anxieties because of its independence. As we saw with the resistance of a group to talent in the You chapter, this independence can be a threat to the stability organizations inherently seek to establish. The outcome will be the tendency to suppress talent's expression and to encourage conformity and compliance because talent's impact encourages us to step outside of what we expect. The most poignant example is imagining someone doing a job other than the one that he's currently doing.

<u>Indirect</u>

Along with these direct manifestations of resistance to talent, indirect ones exist as well. The ones we'll examine are more associated with business as a whole in this era of job specialization. We can see this more easily if we look at the interaction between talent and organization and focus on the two poles: "finding the talent to fit an organization" and "creating an organization to fit the talent."

T2O = fit talent to organization
O2T = fit organization to talent.

We can use the acronym T2O to represent the first and O2T for the second. Figure 6.2 illustrates the duality of the interaction of the two.

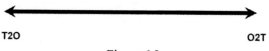

T2O   O2T

Figure 6.2

Most businesses, especially as they get larger, will tend to have identifiable jobs with definable job descriptions. Still, the description can never match comprehensively what the job may entail so the description compensates by using a phrase such as "other duties as assigned" to corral all the potential aspects of the job that are not immediately apparent because of the various situations that could arise. Again, this is nothing more than a confession and reinforcement of the position that what we consciously grasp falls far short of reality (Figure 2.40). To carry on with this discussion we will use Figure 6.3 that has a square representing a job and a circle a person's talents.

Figure 6.3

As we move toward T2O, the more likely we will waste talent because the only aspects of a person's talents that interest us are those that fit the job. We can represent this in Figure 6.4 as the square inside the circle.

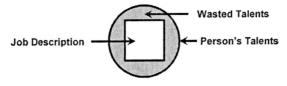

Figure 6.4

As we move toward O2T, the more likely we are to include all aspects of one's talents; however, since T2O is easier than O2T, most businesses will tend toward T2O because finding someone to do a definable job is easier than exploring how a business could adapt to incorporate all of one's talents. Ironically, in a business' infancy, its nature is more along the lines of O2T than T2O because businesses generally form around the talents of their creators. At birth, a business structure will more likely reflect the talents of those involved. Furthermore, the smaller the business the more likely various jobs will have broad duties; larger companies will tend to have extremely specialized jobs. We can modify Figure 6.4 to picture this trend in Figure 6.5.

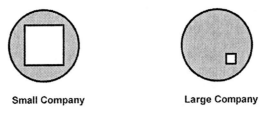

Figure 6.5

The movie, *Dancing With Wolves*, illustrates this in the contrast between the way the Lakota Sioux tribe and poachers hunted buffalo. The buffalos' plenty caused the Indians to organize their lives around all that they could provide whereas the poachers, only seeking the buffalos' valuable hides, left the rest of the buffalo to rot on the plains after a hunt. The Indians sought to use all the buffalo could offer whereas the poachers only took that which insured an easy profit. When we organize around what is offered, we are more likely to incorporate all that one has to offer; however, when we seek only to use the talents applicable to a predefined job, then we increase the likelihood of waste. As the specificity of the job increases so does the likelihood of wasting talents of the one in that job. The trend is from employing many talents in lower quantities to employing fewer talents in greater quantities.

As a result, specialization on a large scale arrives at the cost of leaving more attributes dormant. Furthermore, as our attention becomes increasingly focused on only the attributes that fit a specific job, the more likely we will overlook these other attributes and come to see that person's talents as only extending to the limits of the job in which he works. In effect, our interpretation of one's talents will become synonymous to the job description; the job becomes the context around which we look at someone's talents. Moreover, the person in the job will also tend to restrictively view his talents as only those applicable to that job because he has fewer opportunities to assert his other talents. Initially, this concept is hard to see unless one adopts the view that people can possess talents of which they are unaware. We can no more consciously know of all our talents than we can know the future.

As we saw in the You and Strategy chapters, whether it's talent or problem-solving, a key to tackling both is the destruction of the conventional context around which we look at both. Looking at things in new ways can be as simple as changing the context. Context can become a trap through which we only look at problems, opportunities, and people in one way. Once we fall into this trap, we may even come to see these dormant attributes as weaknesses because they seem inapplicable or detrimental to the specific job designed for the organization at hand.

Even though an O2T is more difficult, it's more effective; it's the reason why a smaller organization can sometimes outdo a larger one – it's more organized around talent so it's more effective in using the talent it has. However, the O2T approach requires more talent to employ than the T2O.

Conclusion

With these direct and indirect resistors, the feminine influence becomes a challenge to employ so talent can launch its dynamism. The challenge will increase the likelihood that we will rationalize her inapplicability by saying she's too cumbersome, slow, vague, and impractical. Just as talented athletes can make difficult maneuvers look easy, talented business people do the same regarding business issues. The strength, power, energy, and discipline to overcome these resistors and to defend an environment conducive to the feminine influence's flourish are derived from the masculine influence. The role of the masculine respective to the feminine then is one of supplying these attributes.

Just as early explorers and settlers toiled endlessly and heartedly to establish a community that can sustain a more developed lifestyle friendly to raising a family, the masculine influence toils in business to establish and preserve conditions whereby the feminine can wield her magic as shown in this book. In order to integrate the masculine and feminine that yields dynamic outcomes, the masculine must create the conditions that allow this to occur. If the feminine is constantly under attack as being worthless because she's immeasurable, irrational, illogical, indirect, and intangible, then she will not be able to help sustain the long-term development of a business – the business will extinguish after running its full life as shown by Figure 3.7. Of course, this does not mean that we can't make money on the death of a company through a buyout, but just because a funeral home makes money on our death doesn't mean we're living successfully. Moreover, just because our beneficiaries make money on our deaths does not mean we are healthy.

This book is about the impact the feminine influence can make in business through its integration with the masculine. While we typically admire strength, speed, directness, and discipline in business, these attributes of the masculine influence contain the seeds of his destruction without the qualitative attributes of the feminine; outright competition that brings about the death of businesses will create conditions in line with the nature of that competition. Consolidation, where one company consumes another, is analogous to a gladiatorial contest. The opportunities for personal growth in such a contest are few just as they are few in the gladiatorial ring. While this contest may not immediately result in the death of a company, it may result in one simply on life support – one that is simply surviving by lumbering along. Those who can experience rewarding careers and lives in such a company will become fewer and fewer. The early sign of these conditions is low or declining morale highlighted by distrust.

The feminine influence, as with a woman, is the bearer of a regenerative life for the company and the individuals associated with it. Just as humans cannot continue their species without a woman, a business cannot continue its line without the feminine influence. Nevertheless, without masculine attributes the feminine would never have a basis around which to operate and never have a defender through which to sustain fertile business conditions. Finding the balance of these two influences as pictured in Figure 2.25 for any given event is the challenge. A community that cannot establish conditions to sustain families will not have a long-term future. The integration of the feminine influence in the masculine realm of business will help secure a higher quality of life for a business over the long-term that will manifest itself in opportunities for personal growth for clients, employees, and managers.

The toughest aspect of the masculine influence is protecting the promotion of talent that thrives on inspiration. Inspirable people have a high degree of sensitivity, but often the dominance of objective thought in business sees this sensitivity as weakness and potentially discardable. In this manner businesses remove from themselves the very seeds containing dynamic growth.

Since seeing the visible, touching the tangible, quantifying the measurable, understanding the direct, grasping the simple, and verbalizing the logical is easier than imagining the invisible, constructing the intangible, valuing the immeasurable, appreciating the indirect, feeling the involved, and expressing the emotional; the initiation and protection of conditions that promote the latter will also be difficult. Additionally, the challenge becomes Herculean when we consider more can do the easy than the difficult; the pressure of the many will weigh upon the few. The integration of the feminine influence is about the dynamics in seeing these as they could be not as they are. The first is more difficult than the latter but far less tangible. We've analogously connected beauty to this difference because no mathematical equation defines beauty – "beauty is in the eyes of the beholder."

Nonetheless, those who can only do the easy will attack those who can do the difficult by asking the talented to present to them the invisible visibly, the intangible tangibly, the immeasurable accountably, the indirect directly, the involved simply, and the passionate logically. When those who only can do the easy cannot see what we show, they will declare us failures rather than admit their blindness. It's easier to blame another than to admit a personal shortcoming. Those with the best eyesight will be outnumbered by the rest as we discussed with Figures 2.61 – 2.67.

The real strength, power, speed, and discipline of the masculine shows up as the strength to stand up to great numbers, the power to thwart their advance, the speed to address immediately, and the discipline to maintain a relentless vigilance. However, current business pressures do not encourage the long-term strategy that this requires because profitably selling a company seems a priority over leaving a legacy. I'd like to relay three stories along this line.

The first involves a client I knew who worked as a construction worker on one of the tallest buildings in town. He told me how much he enjoyed taking his grandson downtown to show him what he had built. The building came to symbolize his work career, something that he could point to as an ambassador of his work.

The second involves another client who worked at a company recently purchased by another. Business quadrupled in a matter of months after the new owners made substantial investments. After talking with him about the sudden changes in the company, I commented that it must be nice to be receiving more money and having access to more professional opportunities. He replied this was all true but he said it was just nice to be working for a winner for a change.

The third involves a friend who's an employee of a company recently purchased by a competitor who was twenty percent smaller and carrying more debt than his company. Despite their success in the industry, the major stockholders decided to sell. Many of the major stockholders who agreed to sell were descendants of the original owner and founder who had passed away a long while ago.

These three stories tie together because each person in the first two can claim something that the sellers in the third scenario can't: they achieved and worked for something. The sellers in the third scenario sold their legacy. They cannot claim to have worked for a winner because they agreed to surrender to an inferior competitor whose only advantage over them was that he wanted to stay in the business. Additionally, unlike the construction worker in the first story they will no longer be able to point to anything that is an ambassador of their efforts. True, their money could end up in the community supporting charitable work, but how many will remember to associate a non-existent company to their name, a company that provided a livelihood to many citizens. What will they be able to point to as the ambassador of their achievement, a vacant building?

In the movie *Rocky*, Rocky Belboa was the hero and Apollo Creed the victor. The movie illustrated that hero and victor are not necessarily synonymous.

The point of this chapter on the Masculine Influence was to highlight the Herculean effort needed to integrate the Feminine Influence in business. We can easily get lost in the debate of the third story, as many people did when it happened, as to whether such a sale is good or bad. Such a debate glosses over the point that major pressures exist to terminate the existence of companies, even good ones. In a business theory aimed at teaching us that the most profitable and client sensitive companies thrive, we find business practice easily countering theory – reality is far more comprehensive than the theories our conscious can construct.

If the feminine influence seeks to help companies provide a better existence for themselves including a longer term one, then pressures mount against this effort if businesses become more akin to fast food than fine meals. Just as residents of homes who plan to leave in a few years are inclined to avoid making certain home improvements because they won't reap the benefits, businesses, managers, and employees who don't plan on being around for the long-term will also be less inclined to implement some of the strategies involving the feminine influence.

By focusing on the deterrents to the integration of the feminine influence, we have heightened the awareness of the effort to do this. To some it may even sound impossible, but that is exactly the purpose because if it were easy then something would be wrong, something would be running counter to the nature of life. Consequently, by describing the integration as a Herculean task, we emphasize the true power necessary to overcome these resistors. The demonstration of true power is not the ability to be the last one standing, but rather the ability to establish something beautiful while the other is waging war on around you.

It's one thing to establish beauty in a peaceful world and quite another in a war weary one as the song "Lady In Black" suggests. In a dog eat dog world, only one dog remains. His fate is to starve alone because no dogs remain and he has forgotten or never had time to learn how to grow the things on which he needs to live. In the business world, this is the difference between acquisitional growth and organic growth. A company that can experience internal growth is more likely to have a better life than one that can only grow externally by devouring others.

The nature of the feminine influence encourages organic (internal) growth because she can make a house better by making it a home. Without her one can only make a house better by going out and getting a bigger one, and of course, this is no guarantee because a bigger house isn't necessarily a better house, just bigger. The difference between a big empty house and a small empty house is that the big house has more emptiness.

Summary

T he purpose of this chapter is to summarize this book's main points without including the arguments to support them. I've outlined them assuming the reader has already read this book so they are made here as a matter of convenience and not intended to clarify the points themselves. I've organized the points by chapter along with a summary statement for the entire book.

Book

- The integration of the feminine influence in business will enhance the potential for dynamic growth through a focus on the talent and influence of an individual's personality.

Prelude

- An allegoric approach using the symbolism of a man and woman will better encourage the integration of the feminine influence by creating a better picture and having more fun in the process.

Introduction

- When we can finally quantify, rationalize, or objectify a business event in a logical expression, the optimal time to seize the opportunity or prevent the crisis it manifests has generally already passed.

- The essence of any successful business is relationships, the relationships between the clients and employees and between employees and managers.

Feminine Influence

- The basis of the feminine influence's power is beauty that manifests itself often in business as "attraction."

- Her integration requires intelligence and courage because it requires the reconciliation of opposing forces in the face of the dominance by those connected to the masculine. These forces include among others:

Masculine	Feminine
Pursue	Attract
Direct	Indirect
Practical	Inspirational
Objective	Subjective
Cognition	Intuition
Tangible	Intangible
Simple	Involved
Rational	Irrational
Visible	Invisible
Objectify	Personalize

Company

- All events have a rhythm to them that we can learn to negotiate optimally, and their outcomes are affected by four factors: situation, flow, people, and the individual.

You

- Since the impact of the feminine influence is felt within, accessing the talent within our personalities and having an appreciation for the challenges in doing this play a vital role.

  - Personality

    We are influenced in many ways because of the needs we have, and this influence can be in ways of which we are unaware. Introversion will help us address these influences in a way that will allow us to better identify and develop the talent of ourselves and others.

  - Talent

    Talent is more akin to an emotion than a thought or skill; thus, there is a strong correlation between emotional sensitivity and talent's manifestation. Power exists in the small, that which makes us unique.

  - Conditioning

    Conditioning plays such a major role in how we view ourselves, others, and our world that no effective discussion on personalities and talent can take place without it because it will tend to lock us into a preconceived response with little consideration for the unique aspects of an event, thus planting the seeds for difficulties.

  - Growth

    Focus on strengths because their development will most likely overshadow weaknesses.

Strategy

- Subjectivity is a powerful force in the creation of strong relationships when applied in one-on-one situations where sagely actions compliment commanding ones.

Masculine Influence

- The integration of the feminine influence in business requires the masculine influence to provide the Herculean effort to initiate and sustain an environment where the feminine influence can flourish in the face of the plentiful, numerically superior forces preventing this integration.

Conclusion

In *Harry Potter* there is a game called "Quidditch" in which teams score in two ways. The first is by throwing a bright red, soccer-sized ball called a "quaffle" through one of several hoops. The second is by catching a small, fast ball with wings called a "snitch." Throwing a quaffle through a hoop scores ten points and catching the snitch is one hundred fifty points. Three players, "Chasers", are assigned to getting the quaffle through the hoops while only one, the "Seeker", is assigned to capture the snitch. The game ends when someone captures the snitch and because of its high point value that team usually is the winner unless the other team has racked up a lead of over a hundred fifty points by sending the quaffle through their opponents' hoops more than their opponents were able to do with theirs. Since the snitch is so difficult to see and so fast, it's very difficult to capture, so the best player on the team is usually assigned to track it down. Harry Potter, the hero, is a seeker.

The feminine influence in business is the talent "seeker" aspect of our personalities. While this influence is generally more prevalent in women than men, her intensity will vary by person. This will allow some men to feel this influence more intensely than some women. For these men, they are likely to feel the masculine influence more intensely as well than other men since in men the masculine influence is dominant. Regardless of the intensity of each influence, the key is the integration of the feminine influence with the masculine as symbolically expressed throughout nature in procreation.

As analogously implied from the game Quidditch, seeking talent is the dynamic aspect that can drastically alter the outcome of business. What the game also suggests is that this quest is not easy. Talent is illusive for many reasons we've covered. It's not simply a numbers game where we can assign more people to find talent; it's a qualitative quest that requires talent to find talent. Harry Potter, as seeker, illustrates this point.

Even in this analysis, it's easy to look at this as a matter of masculine and feminine, but it's really a matter of integrating both influences and raises the perspective to a level where it becomes a matter of the degree to which one is a humane human in all aspects of his life including business. To be human was never meant to be easy in a world filled with challenges and business reflects this in its negotiation between making money and being humane. As is true in any competitive situation, especially those having a great impact on our lives, it's easy to sacrifice our humaneness for a victory drink. If "winning is the only thing," then our humaneness is irrelevant and is extremely suitable for sacrifice at victory's pyre.

Thus, a victory without humaneness is a hollow one leaving a human carcass in its wake. To be humane in business is the ultimate challenge that tests one's intelligence, strength, creativity, talent, and discipline to negotiate that balance and claim a human victory. It doesn't take much of a person to treat people as commodities in order to run a business enterprise; it just takes a person who can objectify through the suppression or denial of what makes us human – our intense emotions we call passions. If humans are truly special, then there's something uncommon about us. If seeking what's rare is difficult, then finding and holding onto our humanity, what makes us special, must be a challenge only within the grasp of the few. It's not the easy road and was never meant to be.

Our passions in the form of intuition allow us to transcend a simple existence as an automaton adhering to a sophisticated computer program in the form of rules, policies, procedures, and etiquettes in order to find the talent in ourselves and others. In this way, we achieve a human victory as opposed to just a victory. Is an inhuman victory preferred to a human loss? Is remaining human the true victory? In the end, what do you win? Seen in this light, the attempt to segregate business affairs from personal ones is an attempt to rationalize a human defeat in business as a victory.

In our relationships with others, passion takes the form of empathy, our ability to feel what they feel. As we've explored, in its pure form, empathy would prevent us from killing others because we would feel they're death – we would die ourselves. We would feel harm for anyone who suffers harm at our hands or at those of others. It's empathy that causes us to cringe when others, even animals, are struck. It's empathy that allows us to relate to images projected onto screens and feel they are real. No people exist in our television; they are only images. Empathy allows us to feel for imaginary characters in stories. Without empathy, we would not be able to relate to the emotions involved in such events. People are born with varying degrees of empathy (sensitivity), and it is an intelligence indicator similar to the way lung and muscle capacity affects athletic talent.

If we return to the example of the successful manager whose boss criticized him for his inability to "crack the whip," we find a wealth of implications in such a statement that bear tremendously on the integration of the feminine influence in business.

As an entry point into those implications, let's consider two points. First consider that people tend to prefer strength to weakness, especially in business, because strength will satisfy their long-term security needs. Many people may not want a pit-bull as a pet, but if their lives were ever threatened, they might wish they did. Second, consider that people prefer the easy to the difficult because they are more likely to be able to do the easy more effectively. By combining these points we can now launch ourselves into a discussion about "easy strength" that will begin to return us to cracking the whip.

We can express our strength in many different ways. Some are easier than others. For instance, if we feel threatened by another it's easier to kill that person than to inspire him with your position. Brutality is easier than artistry; being a barbarian is much easier than being a sage, but both apply power. Likewise, it's easier to "crack the whip" than to "make hearts sing." The problem is that the inability to do either implies weakness.

Some of the ways we express strength are more effective than others. Inspiring a person is better than killing him. The problem is that the degree to which people are inspirable varies, some may be uninspirable. Thus, what we have is a fine line, perhaps even a razor's edge, between applying our power in a negative way (cracking the whip) and in a positive way (making hearts sing). Much depends upon the other person and our talent.

Returning to the easy and the difficult, we find that it's easier for people to direct problems outward than inward. It's easier to direct our inability to do something onto something other than ourselves. For instance, if I'm unable to scale a sheer cliff, it's easier to say it's impossible than I'm incapable. Moreover, if I cannot do something, it's easier to blame failure on another or some external factor than me. Thus, it's easier to say something is impossible than to say we're weak; it's also better for us if something is impossible because this means we cannot be threatened by anyone who can do it because it can't be done. Risk-return not only applies to investing but to life. The difficult generally delivers better returns than the easy.

If "making hearts sing" is more difficult than "cracking the whip," fewer people will be able to do it. For those who can't this means exposing a weakness, an impotency, unless they can convince others that "making hearts sing" is impossible, too idealistic or impractical. In this way, they won't feel threatened by those who can because those who can are now convinced that they can't. Moreover, since many more can do the easy than the difficult, those who can't are in a better position to convince those who can because they will have more people whose experiences support their position – making hearts sing is too idealistic or impractical.

Additionally, having more people support their position through their individual experiences will allow those who can't to establish conditions whereby making hearts sing becomes more difficult for those who can. Inspiration's most important element is emotion; inspiration is a very intense emotion. By creating an environment where intense emotion is discouraged, one can make it even harder to make hearts sing. In essence, establishing an objective environment becomes more valued than a subjective one. Since logic is easier to understand than emotions – rationality versus irrationality – more people will support this position. It's far easier to have someone understand your position than to like your position; it's even more difficult to inspire them with your position.

Through difficulty we achieve growth even if we're not successful in overcoming it. From this perspective, difficulties are a positive. Life is difficult for without it growth would be difficult. We had discussed exercising muscles as an illustration. The most difficult things are those which we initially see as impossible, idealistic, or impractical.

Of course, few people are out there saying, "Well, I can't inspire people so I better convince those who can that they can't." However, those who cannot inspire are very likely having anxieties about it and about people who can inspire, but they are probably just unaware of it. Here again we return to points #7 and #9 of the Seventeen Influential Points that imply people can be unaware of what's influencing them and incorrectly attribute that influence. In such a scenario, we could have the uninspirational rationalize the inspirational as too emotional, impractical, and idealistic, causing the first to view the second as incompetent. If the inspirational persists, the unispirational could look upon him as "out of control" and "bad for business."

If we firmly believe that a rational basis exists for everything someone does, that people are always aware of what's influencing them, that when people feel influenced that they can correctly attribute that influence, and that people are aware of rationalizing an influence; then we will have difficulty understanding everything people do. However, if we believe that emotions unique to us can drive us, that subliminal influences can stir our emotions without our knowledge, that a natural survival instinct influences us, and that we can rationalize and attribute influences incorrectly; then understanding some of the hostile behavior of others is easier.

Nevertheless, the integration of the feminine influence in business is possible; the integration of this influence is a way of life, and business is a part of life via another form. Our personalities are our lives, and business is an extension of personality by other means. Thus, business relationships are extensions of personal relationships by other means. To segregate business from personal is not in line with what truth bears out. Business is about people; business is a part of life. How can it be anything but personal?

This integration though requires talent. The difference between a talented musician and someone who simply plays well is the feeling he injects into his music. If he cannot inject feeling into his music, how will an audience's feelings be moved by his music? Likewise, if a manager cannot inject feeling into his work, how will his employees' feelings be moved by his work? Of course, none of this is possible unless the masculine influence supplies the Herculean effort to establish and sustain the conditions that will allow the feminine influence to play a role.

A critical aspect of the courage to apply this effort is the "power in the small." As we tried to show with the bell curves, it's not the common or prevalent that contains the power but it's the uncommon and rare that does. Consider the oval in Figure 7.1.

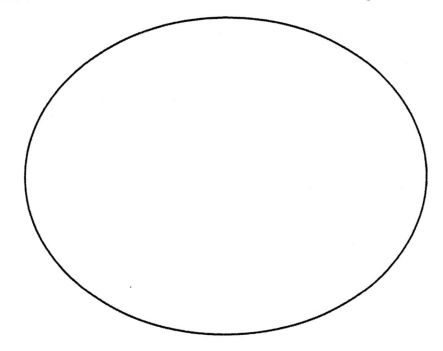

Figure 7.1

If we consider our entire solar system, we would find that less than .000001 of it contains life. In fact, an alien quickly driving by in his spacecraft would most likely give it up for dead. If someone were right .999999 of the time, we would be inclined to say he was right all of the time. Moreover, if we applied this number to our entire lifespan we would arrive at a number equal to about forty-five minutes.

What makes our solar system possibly unique in our part of the galaxy and possibly in the universe is what's going on in that .000001 of it. It's in that part that affects our daily well-being. As far as we're concerned, what goes on in that .000001 contains .999999 of what may be important to us. The other .999999 contains maybe only .000001 of what's important. In fact, if you were such an alien flying by our solar system, the oval in Figure 7.1 would represent how easy it would be for you to determine that this solar system had no life because you may not have noticed a small, insignificant dot in the lower, left-hand portion signifying the single dot in our solar system that contains life.

Furthermore, seeking to reinforce this point we can take Einstein's equation, $E=mc^2$, to symbolize the power in the small. With this equation scientists were able to hypothesize and discover that by taking just a few small atoms one could generate immense power, nuclear power, beyond anything known at the time that was immensely larger. From the small attributes that make us unique, dynamic outcomes are possible and are why the feminine influence seeks the qualitative differences in us all versus the quantitative. However, without the masculine influence to get things started and sustained, the qualitative attributes of the feminine are difficult to employ.

The points and strategy supporting the feminine influence in this book are far from comprehensive, and I did not intend them to be. I targeted the most dynamic aspects of such a strategy, winning hearts, to introduce you to the concepts in a way that could be applicable in business. I cannot emphasize enough the extent to which others have devoted lifelong studies to some of the principles. Some could even claim the principles were documented over a couple thousand years ago. Again, I'm not concerned with making arguments that would hold up in an academic inquiry. All I know is that what I've written works.

As I discussed with you during our exploration of the scientific method, definite procedures are involved in seeking to prove something exists or is true. However, what I've come to learn is that just because we can't prove something doesn't mean it doesn't exist or it isn't true; it may mean that we haven't reached a level of capability to accomplish this, the methodology we're using is faulty, or we simply have not created the right tools to do so. For instance, we cannot prove a god, any god, exists, but yet, few will deny the force this concept has on many people. In many ways, the mere existence of this force makes living with this concept real. Thus, regardless of whether a god exists, the force of those believing in one make it a reality we need to incorporate in our daily lives as we work with others. In many ways, this reality of people believing in a god almost makes the determination of a god irrelevant because if I'm working with someone I must deal with what he considers real. The truth is that the concept of god moves people.

Of course, let's take a contrarian's approach by asking, "Can we prove god doesn't exist?" Why must something not exist unless we prove it does? Why do we not adopt the premise that all things exist until we prove they don't? Moreover, everyday new scientific thoughts and theories arrive that improve upon current ones. What does this trend tell us? Could the assumptions we use today be faulty except that we don't know it? What proof do we have that our scientific dictums today won't change? Science, as is true with any field of study, is improving, changing. Four hundred years ago we would not have been able to prove we could see inside the body with tools such as x-rays, fiberscopes, and videoscopes. Many in those days thought of seeing inside a live body as impossible if not religious heresy. Therefore, what dangers do we run if we only make decisions based upon what we can prove, document, or quantify? Prove beauty. Can we even define it?

This methodology creeps into more nebulous fields such as the various ones concerning human behavior, thought, and emotions. Here, we prove points by citing authorities who in turn have conducted some kind of research along the lines of the scientific method. The implications above apply here too. On the other hand, life has a rhythm to it that doesn't make it totally random. There must be some principles common to us all that permit us to relate to one another. If all our individual lives were so totally different, we would have little basis for relationships. Yet, do we formally need to prove all these things?

As a practical example, a friend of mine and I were having a deep discussion involving some of the topics in this book as it pertained to his experiences. We eventually approached a point where we needed to find out how he felt about certain words before we needed to go on. Our discussion around one word slowed down and caused him to exclaim, "Well, maybe I don't really know what that word means!" Referring back to our definitional and connotative discussions, we know that not only can words have many definitions but their connotations can vary even more extensively; thus, what my definition or a dictionary's definition is of the word is irrelevant in trying to understand my friend's reality. I replied to him that I didn't care whether his definition of the word matched mine or a dictionary's. The only thing I cared about is what that word meant to him because that's the only way I know we're dealing truthfully with what's important to him in his world.

This concept carries with it many more implications. One that we've talked about is communication. The emphasis these days is on making our points clearly so everyone can understand them; however, this is impossible because everyone will have different interpretations of what was said. Nevertheless, we try and succeed only in boring everyone because we stick to the same "vanilla" words everyone else uses in the hope that their overuse is ingrained in our listeners with a common definition of the word that everyone accepts. Consequently, while our message may be clear, since everyone is half asleep and the other half anxious from boredom, few really hear the message anyway. Moreover, we come to sound just like the next guy.

Since the interpretations vary by person, the real responsibility in communication is on the listener and not the speaker. The listener ought to be able to ask whatever questions he needs to understand the speaker's message, and the speaker should appreciate this attempt by creating a communication that will facilitate this effort. Of course, the problem arises when folks are in large groups that can intimidate questions and discussions.

If we take the concept of the listener having the primary responsibility for understanding a communication and combine it with the relational aspects I've mentioned in the Strategy chapter, we arrive at a point where the actual communication is secondary to the relational potential I have in interacting with the speaker. In other words, my understanding of the message is secondary to my appreciation of the speaker. We are more motivated by what we like than what we understand. If this is true, then really what's more important is whether I like the speaker and not whether I understand his message. We can refer to the appreciative aspect of the speaker as his style in order to diagram this in a familiar way in Figure 7.2.

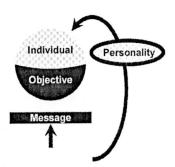

Figure 7.2

Going further, we can add another dimension by saying that the minute a form of standardization is forced upon someone the harder it becomes to appreciate someone for who they are. We often run across this when we see co-workers outside of the workplace in an environment they frequent. Since certain standards and etiquettes exist at work, they eradicate the individual differences that may allow us to appreciate him. For instance, seeing a construction worker attending an opera or a banker chopping and splitting wood might create quite a contrast in our minds.

By taking this concept and applying it to our communicative discussion, we find ourselves at the point where language's grammatical, definitional, dictional, and verbal aspects form a construct imposed upon us that is no different than the standards we follow on the job. In this way, language's usage can eradicate individual differences the more we impose specific rules upon the speaker. Thus, if I am to appreciate others for who they are, it's best if I try to do so outside of any constructs imposed by others. Just as I can better appreciate people by seeing them outside of their work environment, I can also do so by listening to them outside of any constraints they feel are imposed upon their communicative style.

We can now relate this to our discussion on conditioning in the You chapter and the effect of context. Language is a context, a set of rules governing the communication of thoughts. While contexts can serve the purpose of making things easier and faster by automatically giving us a set of parameters by which to understand something without having to ask a lot of other clarifying questions, they do so at the cost of missing out on opportunities to see something new in the old. Rules give the ignorant something to know. Thus, these contexts can easily become unthinking habits that retard the access to our talent and others' because they give us the illusion that we know something so the impetus to explore more deeply wanes. Talent becomes the origination of dynamism because the relational focus of the feminine influence implies that dynamism rests in the individual, so encouraging someone to step outside of preset rules and contexts to view their world in a different light is vital to the identification and development of talent.

We begin to release the dynamic by avoiding automated behavior and integrating the feminine influence with the masculine one dominating business by going beyond products, services, marketing, and other usual business identifiers and getting down to the human level of relationships, the client-employee relationship and the employee-manager one. Many say "people make the difference" but fewer believe it and fewer still can effectively implement around it. Success here is ultimately determined by the degree to which one can integrate the feminine influence into the more traditional aspects of business.

Integration of the feminine influence relies primarily upon intuition, a trait heavily associated with the female gender. Education, training, and experience can help but personality and gender play a more important role. People are born with varying intuitive capacities and awareness. One stock broker I knew even coined the expression "situational awareness" to define the ability to feel what's going on around you while consciously engaged in a conversation with a client. Some also refer to this more shallowly as "reading between the lines."

As one moves along the bell curve, those with the keenest abilities become outnumbered by the rest. Thus, what falls within one person's awareness may not for another, so there could easily be situations where only one person may be aware of something while the rest in the group are not. Intuition and awareness, especially around relationships, tend to display themselves stronger in women than in men, thus the phrase "a woman's intuition" – not "a man's intuition."

Nevertheless, the masculine and feminine influences are present in each man and woman and thus it's really a question of dominance regarding gender; the masculine influence is dominant in men while the feminine in woman. Many other factors concerning personality and circumstances affect how the interplay of these influences manifests itself in everyday life. Since business is traditionally seen as a masculine affair, it will encourage more reliance on the masculine aspect of each person rather than the feminine. From this perspective men will tend to have an advantage.

This declaration brings us to a critical crossroad. If we ignore the crossroad and continue along in the same direction as this statement initially takes us, we might be tempted to conclude that there is a direct correlation between the concentration of masculinity one has and success in business. Thus, it becomes incumbent upon each business person to apply as much of his masculinity as possible in order to achieve success. From this perspective, the feminine influence interferes with the masculine by diluting its concentration (being "soft"), and thus, needs to be discarded or locked up so she doesn't interfere with the operation of business. Historically, there are very pragmatic applications of this symbolism when men were instructed to stay away from women before a battle or a big game; the fear is a softening of the killer instinct by the feminine influence. In essence, following this direction makes business just another game of machismo; the highest masculine concentration wins.

If we take the crossroad and go in the direction of trying to incorporate the feminine influence rather than exiling her, we find the powerful themes expressed in this book and behind the "Lady In Black" strategy. Our journey on this road becomes the marriage of the masculine and feminine influences in business where we overlay the symbolism of the male-female relationship on business in order to tap its inherent strength and vitality. Without this integration, business becomes a sterile affair lacking rejuvenative capabilities – an inability to experience rebirth. In order to propagate themselves, cultures need women; likewise in order to create new avenues for growth, businesses need the feminine influence.

Thus, we are talking about a balance between the two influences that is not always fifty-fifty but one according to the event at hand. Various events will tip the scales in favor of one side or the other, so our job analogously becomes one of balancing ourselves on a ship tossed about the ocean as we favor various aspects of our bodies to keep our balance. Pursuing and maintaining extremes will increase the likelihood of decline in the long-term. Figure 2.25 illustrated this balancing as shown here again in Figure 7.3.

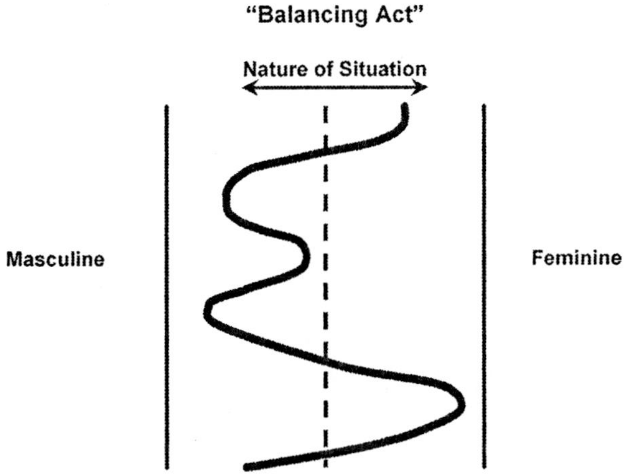

"Balancing Act"

Nature of Situation

Figure 7.3 (2.25 Revisited)

In the Feminine Influence chapter of this book, we looked at the intricate aspects of this influence and delivered a conclusion highlighting her vital role in business. Secondarily, it also examined the difficulty in her integration by looking at emotional, cultural, and circumstantial issues because of the intelligence, discipline, and courage needed to relentlessly apply her. With her involvement the outcome is more likely to be one where a business will rest on a stronger foundation and have more forcefulness than with a purely masculine approach. The difference is the engagement of feelings and emotions rather than the over reliance on objectives, reasons, logic, and rationale to motivate.

While business is a predominately masculine arena and can benefit from the feminine influence, some conditions exist that make her application more advantageous than at other times. Figure 7.3 suggests this. Much of the time this occurs after a period of expansion that finally exhausts itself with the arrival of a consolidation period along with subsequent contemplation around the next growth spurt. This was the essence of the Company chapter. The key is recalling different events have different rhythms, so while one event may be in a more masculine phase of its development another could be in its feminine. We also can find that a series of smaller events make up a larger one. All of this increases complexity that will strain us consciously, but it re-emphasizes the importance of having a good feel for the various events applying to you.

However, the force behind the "Lady In Black" Strategy is not simply one of gender. It's one of effectively integrating the masculine and feminine influences. In a masculine company in a masculine field, it's difficult for a man to court the feminine without coming across weak, especially if he has already established a history of ignoring her. This will require additional talent and discipline on his part.

Integrating these feminine aspects is generally easier for women regardless of the current environment because many of the aspects are more dominant in women than men. Furthermore, for businesswomen the prospects are brighter because their mere presence in business indicates they've had some success in mustering the discipline and relentlessness needed to initiate and sustain conditions encouraging this integration as discussed in the Masculine Influence chapter.

In the competition for positions in a business hierarchy, the disparity between the genders in their ability to integrate the two influences will tend to cause men to encourage women to play business by their rules which will tend to have a more masculine flavor to them. While this encouragement will most likely not be conscious, it will tend to exist naturally because people tend to favor those concepts with which they are most comfortable regardless of how inappropriate they may be for the particular situation (people are more persuaded by what they like than what they understand). Thus, men will tend to favor a masculine response for any situation over a feminine one simply because they will tend to find it more comfortable. Again, the key as shown in Figure 7.3 is balance; sometimes a more masculine response will be better but definitely not always.

In spite of this gender bias, the integration of the feminine influence will heavily depend upon personality and the talent contained within. As we covered in the You chapter, these are emotionally based issues, not cognitively.

Our personalities are influenced by a variety of things from a variety of sources. We sought to outline this in the Seventeen Influential Points. Appreciating people is very difficult if one assumes that what they think is the basis for whatever they do. To some degree we are all unaware of the degree to which some things affect us, if we're even aware of them in the first place. These influences surface as feelings that we then rationalize. For instance, our complaints about a rainy day may be more connected to a mild hangover than our feelings about the weather.

These rationalizations will tend to favor a source we find appealing. For instance, positive rationalizations will tend to focus the origination of the feeling on ourselves and those we like, while negative ones on others especially ones we don't like. Thus, negative feelings about ourselves will more likely come out as complaints about others than as thoughts about ways for us to address those feelings. The implications of this process can be quite detrimental (even life threatening) to us and others. Nevertheless, as with Sherlock Holmes' crime scene opening the Introduction where everything says something about the crime, everything we do says something about us; the challenge is determining what that message is within its respective context.

Much of how something influences us will depend upon the needs we outlined, long-term security, novelty of experience, and emotional recognition, in terms of the degree to which they affect us. While these needs can be refined further, I offer these as an entry point which I have found helpful. The inside-outside duality model is also more complex, but it can serve as a basic tool to help us appreciate the tension within us and others created by influences stirring our various needs. Life is difficult, so as we weigh things in our minds, we find ourselves having pseudo discussions within that reflect the characteristics in the inside-outside duality I've presented. In order to weigh pros and cons, we must have certain aspects of our personality that trigger each side so we can compare and contrast the arguments before us.

Much of the appreciation necessary for the influences, needs, and duality we have explored is difficult with the highly stimulating environment we live in today. A premium is given for extroverted attributes that will allow us to tackle the fast paced activity around us in the business world. This environment distracts us from the reflection that is necessary to move us from a state of preconditioned responses where rules give us the illusion of wisdom to one of actions based upon the unique aspects in the situation, flow, and people involved in a particular event. Life has one message: no two things are exactly alike. Thus, the more we stick to preconditioned rules and practices the more likely we are to miss outstanding opportunities or to run into unpleasant problems. It's all a matter of time.

In order for us to tap our inner world as effectively as we do our outer one, we must call upon our introverted attributes. Just as extroversion seeks to tap the resources in our outer world, introversion does the same with our inner one. By taking time to reflect and question the various contexts we tap to handle events moving at us at increasing rates, we can begin to see things as they could be rather than as they are and move along the path of finding dynamic outcomes by tapping an undiscovered or suppressed talent within us.

The talent we seek is more akin to emotion than cognition, so it frequently slips through any rational construct we place upon it. Even if we put aside the discussion of the validity of its emotional basis, the accessing of it is very much an emotional journey. For this reason, whether someone has talent is far less a priority than the emotional issues surrounding its access. For some these issues may be so intense that a talent can remain dormant until an appropriate time where those issues are no longer a factor.

Furthermore, the nature of talent also makes identification rather meaningless if we keep our eyes open and are astute. Its vitality, expressivity, innumerability, and abnormality allow us to detect its attempts at emergence if we are patient and can discern nuances in small events. The reason for much of this is the resistance to talent that takes the form of cognitive constructs which we learn. Since cognition is far less comprehensive than emotionally based intuition, there will always be cracks in the asphalt that allow for natural expression. That's why even the smallest forms of life take on huge implications for astronomers seeking life on other planets such as Mars. Accessing talent is much the same venture. All we need to see is some small indication of talent, and it becomes a matter of encouraging it to grow and avoiding a repaving.

Natural resistance to talent within the person and the group make the accessing of talent difficult. That's why simple identification is just a first step in the development, growth, and appreciation of it. The key is appreciating the emotional framework of talent as suggested by Wisdom's Magical Hierarchy. Talent is innate, synergistic, emotional, and intangible. If this weren't the case, we would call computers talented. What we learn only comprises small aspects of the wisdom necessary to make use of our talent, and the learning tends to be extroverted activity engaged with others. Talent's emotional basis means there is a need for personal reflection on one's owns feelings in order to fully bring one's talent to fruition. The major resistor to talent is our own conditioning that opened the Conclusion chapter. Trying to look at ourselves and the world through various contexts will allow us to see new things within our own context. Our development will also dodge the frequent context of improving upon our weaknesses in order to become better. By focusing on growing our strengths, our weaknesses will come to be overshadowed.

All of us have emotional walls preventing our growth or the tapping of unknown reservoirs of talent inside us. Many times they are based upon fears rationalized to comfort us or others. The topic has consumed the lives of many experts and is a multi-volume book. It takes a creative relentlessness to surface thoughts and ideas not normally found in the routine repackaging of basic business concepts.

The Strategy chapter allowed us to take these themes inherent in the feminine influence and place them in a pragmatic construct supporting a "winning the hearts" strategy. While the essence of the plan requires time and patience, the ultimate power in it is tremendous. Illustratively, we can look to oriental rugs that are woven by tying extremely small knots closely together on a threaded grid. While the small knots make the creation of these rugs time consuming and tedious, their cumulative effect is one of strength and durability and the reason why these rugs are among the strongest in the world.

As a result, this relational strategy requires an emotional discipline to implement. A way someone can prevent you from doing something he can't is by convincing you that you're wasting your time. Again, anyone who can do something really well is outnumbered by those who can't do that something well. Thus, the only way others can outdo you is to convince you that you can't do well. That's why the talented are always in the minority and frequently targeted for ridicule and criticism by others. The talented need the emotional discipline to over come by seeing that "There's no strength in numbers, have no such misconception" as suggested by Uriah Heep's "Lady In Black" lyrics. From this we can conclude that the strategy outlined in this chapter may be impossible for many others but it is a very viable one suited for you.

In conjunction with this strategy we elaborated on some important truths: integration, influence, leadership, and subjectivity. Integration referred to reconciling the differences between the masculine and feminine in a way that balances with the situation at hand. Influence covered the nature of *de facto* power and how it influences even without formal power within the hierarchy. Leadership concerned itself with having the toughness to do what's difficult; "winning hearts" is more difficult than "cracking the whip." Finally, we examined the power in subjectivity as the power to see what things could be rather than only being able to see them as they are. From this empathic sensitivity new ideas and approaches develop.

The basis of the strategy is relational focused on individual interactions. While they are far more time consuming, they are also far more effective in building an influence based upon people more likely to follow courage than titles as the movies *Braveheart* and *Gladiator* typify. What formal authority dictates, courage seeks to earn. The difficult requires courage. This is why the consolidation of *de facto* power and formal power makes for a very potent combination. Groups work best when morale is high. Morale in any organization increases when good leaders receive rewards for their deeds. Conversely, when bad leaders receive rewards this harms morale. Since morale concerns itself with how someone feels, the heart is its home. The distinction between good and bad is rarely clear, but a distinction does exist and that is resolved in the heart, not the head.

Supporting the relational and emotional theme of this strategy is the need to present you not just as a commander but as a sage, teller versus teacher. In some way, intrinsically giving someone something will create such a bond. Money, titles, recognition, and awards are extrinsic and transitory. What you help someone learn never leaves. Somehow, you need to have the talent to give someone something that no one can take away. If you can help them discover a part of themselves, you've provided the most powerful assistance possible.

Business has been compared to war as early as the 1600's. Regardless of the policies and procedures in place, no one really knows for sure what the future holds for a company but many times responses to that future require tough action. Often people think of tough as a matter of cutting resources so the whole group moves forward stronger, but it also means taking the hits when others do not or cannot see the implications around a vision for growth.

The growth side of toughness radiates from this symbolism: to take others to a place they fear. Only trust and faith can encourage folks to take this journey whole-heartedly. Otherwise, it becomes a series of long discussions to educate and gain buy-in supplemented with incentives that stir shallow mercenary feelings. Clients often follow someone's advice simply because he stated it; employees can do the same with managers. Sometimes only the manager knows where he's going because of his insight or intuition. Having employees who are willing to follow him and help him regardless of their understanding is a tremendous asset similar to clients who are willing to follow employees in the same fashion.

As a result, there are two basic groups of people around this issue of toughness, cutters and creators. The first group contains those who primarily succeed because of their critical nature to rip an idea apart to show how it won't work. The second group contains those who primarily succeed because of their ability to see opportunity in just about anything as we saw with subjectivity's power.

The implication of this interplay is that at some point the cutters will end up with nothing unless they find a creator with something. A farmer cannot harvest without knowing how to plant and grow. He cannot harvest if there is nothing; once he's through harvesting there is nothing.

Mergers are a perfect example because most increase income by cutting expenses while location-for-location revenue increases remain modest. On the opposite end are creators who find anything in everything and make it something. These are companies who experience dynamic regeneration through an energized workforce that eventually stirs internal growth without mergers. Not only can one evaluate a company by how its employees interact with clients, but he can also do so by how its managers interact with employees. This interaction not only determines the success of a business, but it can also determine the nature of future leaders and who those leaders will be.

Chess players, as is true with any game, have varying abilities to see the implications of a number of moves into the future. The same is true with war, business, and any endeavor; however, those who have the insight to see further ahead are outnumbered by those who can't. This becomes more involved if we realize it's not only the number of moves ahead that come into play but also the ability to see the number of implications in each of those moves in the future. Thus, where a professional sees danger or opportunity a novice may see the opposite or nothing.

Creators need toughness because many times people just don't see what they see or don't want to believe it. Animosity and fear can result when any new idea comes forth – witness any invention. Polite people who rely upon conformity to social norms tend to wilt in the face of an intensely questioning collective. To emerge, a sprout must break a shell, a chick must break an egg, in both a violent act occurs to surface a creation. Picasso often looked upon the creativity expressed in painting as an act of aggression. The ferocious intensity of the heart's primary contraction, amounting to only 15% of the entire duration of a heartbeat, is the one that keeps us alive, not the relative resting period of the other 85%. For this reason, there are those who view any kind of turmoil as disruptive when in actuality creativity and talent may be seeking expression. Few children are naturally born without giving their mothers some fairly intense pain. The same holds true for the birth of any idea.

All of this seeks to raise awareness as to the challenges in integrating the feminine influence in business. The strength required to have the discipline and relentlessness to initiate and sustain conditions for her to flourish can only come from a positively directed masculine influence. In this way, not only can she make a house a home but she can make a business – dynamic. The dilemma will always be in wondering whether someone is inspirable because not everyone is, but this distinction wasn't meant to be easy.

Thus, in the effort to integrate the feminine influence in business the emotional attributes of employees and managers become more important than their cognitive ones because only in passion and sensitivity can we find inspirable individuals possessing a talent that can inject dynamism. Since decisions such as buying ones are rationalized emotional ones, finding people who can work emotionally become a premium. The effect of this inspirable culture within a business radiates outward to clients.

Just as the personality within a person radiates outward and manifests itself in the world, so does the passionate or dispassionate culture within a business. This is how many clients come to feel they're just another client. What happens to any person who displays to others something that differs from what's inside them? If a company displays a subjective, compassionate approach externally to its clients but not one internally to employees, what eventually happens? Which wins in the long run, the outside or the inside, the persona or the soul?

Controlling, dictating one's emotions is as illusionary as forcing our will upon the sun. By accepting this illusion as real we falsely believe our cognition rules and miss the opportunities our intuition detects; understanding is far less comprehensive than intuiting. What we miss is the path where our personality, our inside person, naturally wants to take us. The difference between where our inside and outside persons want to go is the difference between swimming down- or upstream. Likewise, the sensitivity or insensitivity that exists within the employee-manager relationship will eventually seep into client-employee relationships. Problems at home seep into the workplace. An individual happy at home is more likely to be effective than one who is unhappy. What exists inside will eventually flow out. All asphalt eventually cracks and yields to nature's growth. All rationale eventually breaks down.

How do you inspire an emotionless being? Can any talent run to its full fruition without inspiration? How better off would we be under inspiration's influence? All of us are born with varying emotional capabilities. We can always teach the wonders of the world, but we cannot grant emotions to someone. If this were not true, then we could program a computer to feel. The computer symbolizes what we can do with our cognition and what we cannot do with our feelings.

Emotions are important because they are the tool by which we explore our inner world through introversion. Our inner world is a place inaccessible to sight, sound, taste, touch, and smell. Even our most advanced technology is unable to access it. How else can we access the best our personalities have to offer if we cannot intuit, "see in the dark?"

Furthermore, how can we access the inner worlds of others if we cannot empathize? If we rationalize only by what eventually manifests itself in our external surroundings, we may never be able to see what lies beyond our sight as suggested by Figures 2.1 – 2.15.

The effort to integrate the feminine influence in business is a Herculean one requiring the most positive aspects of the masculine influence to initiate and sustain. The strength and discipline of the masculine can manifest itself either positively or negatively. Positively, through sagely activity it creates conditions whereby the sensitivity of the feminine can flourish. Negatively, through barbaric activity it creates conditions whereby the insensitivity of competition has a rationale for existence. In this way, a sage's wisdom is matched against a barbarian's brutishness, Hercules versus the Erymanthian Boar.

Reviewing the conclusions associated with the various chapters bring us to the end of this book. In every chapter the feminine influence has been used to communicate the differentiating themes around the "Lady In Black" Strategy within the structure of sections and various sub-sections. Flowing from the abstract to the practical, I selectively chose stories, pictures, analogies, and other techniques to convey specific emotions around the strategy.

We traveled this journey by using the symbolism of a relationship between a man and a woman. Not only can this relationship explain much about the nature of our world but also about us as individuals. Within each of us is a cognitive and emotional aspect, form and substance, structure and content. Without content our structure is empty; without structure our content disperses. Without a woman a man's life does not become better; without a man a woman's life is fragile. Together they form the strongest bond that can exist in a relationship. Symbolically, man and woman exist in all things, ideas, emotions, and events. A business without the feminine influence has difficulty becoming better. It can only become bigger and bigger until it exceeds its limitations and collapses onto itself.

The counter to becoming better is that we only need business to provide the income to sustain our lives; thus, a business becomes disposable. Once we have outlived the need for this income, the business' future is of no concern. There is no need for the business to live beyond our income requirements, so our decisions will be more geared toward insuring those requirements than the business' future. There is no need for a legacy of our labor because it was simply that . . . labor.

If we return to the story of the construction worker who as a grandfather shows his grandson the tall building he built, we find he has a legacy of his labor, something to symbolize what he had done with so many hours of his life that eventually helped others. In the perspective where there is no need to extend a business' future beyond our need for income, the legacy of our work becomes a business that eventually fades into nothing, analogous to a man and woman who cannot have children. Supplanting the legacy is a house, a car, and other material items that eradicate any distinctiveness about our labor. No one can tell what our work was; what we did with all those hours.

If the segregational implication of "nothing personal this is just business" is true, then our business has nothing to do with who we are as an individual. Therefore, talent, the most personal expression of who we are, does not fit in the depersonalized realm of business; however, as we've explored in the Introduction, here in the Conclusion, and throughout the various aspects of this book, business is a part of life so it's influenced by the same underlying forces that influence life. Business, simply because we may like to think so, cannot be immune to life. Thus, business becomes a means of personal expression no different than our golf game. Our business, our labor reflects us.

The talent within us seeks expression as we had discussed regarding talent's nature. That desire extends beyond our mortality. We see it reflected in our personalities when our names appear on tombstones, buildings, plaques, streets, events, awards and many other things. We also see it in the heirlooms we leave behind and in various legal entities such as trusts and foundations. Are all of these that different from business, from our work?

We cannot explain the beauty of this concept through any rationale no more than we can rely upon it to explain the beauty in a woman or in the feminine influence; yet, these concepts are appealing. In beauty's attraction rests her power. Whereas the masculine toils with his strength to keep everyone together, the feminine effortlessly uses her attractive qualities as we revisit Figure 5.18 in Figure 7.4. Whereas the man pursues, the woman attracts. The activity around pursuit is visible, that around attraction is invisible.

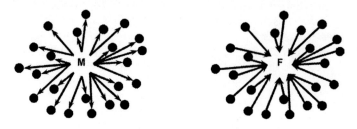

Figure 7.4 (5.18 Revisited)

How does one formulize and mass produce an invisible force that seems purposeless? How does one be direct with the indirect or reason a feeling? How does one understand beauty without appreciating her? Imagine the effect of integrating the two. Imagination is the power of emotion running through thought, breaking down the existing walls to find new pastures.

At the beginning, we symbolically described the journey through this book as a hike. Telling someone about a hike does not compare to actually experiencing that hike. The hike through these woods is nearing the end. The passion you've acquired from it is yours, and will hopefully differ from others.

It was not my intention to communicate the same message to everyone; the intention is to stir something that will encourage you to implement something positive in accordance with your nature. The right feel is far more important than the right understanding. Facts and figures won't guide you because they are only a delayed, superficial manifestation of what has already occurred. The right feel will ensure a practicality and flexibility for events that we cannot predict, ensuring your differentiation. No plan, including this one, can account for all the nuances life will bring your way. In only by having the right feel, can one address all the unknowns that will arise. Nothing in here is guaranteed to work, but I know it can work. Too many variables outside of your control bear upon an outcome including the emotions guiding your nature.

While the number of interactions this strategy implies seems immense and while each interaction by itself may seem insignificant; when considering your direction, it helps to look at each interaction as a drop of rain. From this rain pools form to create tributaries that in turn create springs that create creeks and streams that flow into rivers that become larger rivers that can cut into solid rock and smooth sharp edges. There is immense, unstoppable power in a river but if a single raindrop never fell from the sky, that power would be non-existent. The river would just dry up and die. When one-sidedness prevails with the masculine, the river flows but it does not rain. Eventually, the river runs dry. There is a need for rain.

In spite of all that's written here or in other places about this concept and its various forms, the vastly superior way to appreciate the full impact of what's here is to rely upon what your intuition says about your nature and to compel your cognition to find a way to follow it. Hopefully, through your efforts on this hike you have a better feel for how this can be done in your business setting and maybe in your life.

Here are two ways to look at your destiny. The first entails consciously choosing from several well-considered options and working diligently toward one. The second entails following your nature and fighting like hell to make sure junk doesn't get in the way. Since no one can predict the future, the latter tends to work better since it encourages us to remain open to all opportunities that run our way. Besides, no plan can handle all that reality throws at it.

We have now arrived at the end of this book, and you may recall that early on I asked you to reserve any kind of judgment on how you feel about it until you've had a chance to soak in everything that you have read. Sometime in the near future you may feel inclined to conclude how this book applies to you. If such a feeling fails to arrive, or if the conclusion you draw remains nebulous, just keep a pad and pen handy so you can jot something down when it does come to you. It doesn't matter whether you feel it's related to this book or not. What's important is whether it relates to your nature.

Remember, we are not always aware of the influence things have on us, but eventually their influence will manifest themselves.

Of course, we may never realize the connection between the two.

Printed in the United States
30400LVS00003B/10-15